GLEANINGS
in
EXODUS

GLEANINGS

in

EXODUS

By

ARTHUR W. PINK

MOODY PRESS • CHICAGO

ISBN: 0-8024-2975-0

Eleventh Printing, 1972

Twelfth Printing, 1973

Thirteenth Printing, 1974

Printed in the United States of America

CONTENTS

5

CHAPTER 1

INTRODUCTION

In commencing the *study* of any book in the Bible it is well to remind ourselves that each separate book has some prominent and dominant theme which, as such, is peculiar to itself, around which everything is made to center, and of which all the details are but the amplification. What that leading subject may be, we should make it our business to prayerfully and diligently ascertain. This can best be discovered by reading and re-reading the book under review. If other students before us have published the results of their labors, it is our duty to carefully examine their findings in the light of God's Word, and either verify or disprove. Yet, concerning this there are two extremes to guard against, two dangers to avoid. The first, and perhaps the one which ensnares the most, is the assumption that other students have done their work so well, it is needless for *us* to go over the same ground. But that is laziness and unbelief: God may be pleased to reveal to you something which He did not to them; remember that there are depths in His Word which no human sounding-line has fathomed. The second danger is the craze for orginality and the egotistical belief that *we* shall search more diligently than they who went before, and that therefore the results of *our* labors will be an improvement over all who have preceded us. This is unwarrantable conceit, from which may Divine grace deliver us all. With some books of the Bible we can more readily discover the central theme than in others. This is noticeably the case with the first few books in the Old Testament. It is as though God had made it easier at the beginning so as to encourage us and prepare the way for some of the more complex books that follow—complex so far as their leading subjects are concerned. Historically considered, the book of Genesis is the book of *beginnings;* but viewed doctrinally, it is seen to be the book which treats of *election:*—God choosing Shem from the three sons of Noah to be the channel from which should issue, ultimately, the Saviour; God singling out Abraham to be the father of the chosen Nation; God passing by Ishmael and choosing Isaac; God passing by Esau and choosing Jacob; God appointing Joseph from all the twelve sons of his father to be the honored instrument for making provision against the famine, and being raised to the second place in all Egypt; finally, in the passing by of the elder of Joseph's sons and the bestowal of the firstborn's portion on Ephraim (48:13-20) we behold another illustration of the same principle. Yes, *election* is clearly the characteristic doctrine of Genesis. And this is exactly what we might expect. "God hath *from the beginning* chosen you unto salvation" (2 Thess. 2:13), hence this truth is illustrated again and again in this book which *begins* the Scriptures. Just as surely may we anticipate—in the light of the New Testament—the dominant theme of Exodus.

Historically, the book of Exodus treats of the deliverance of Israel from Egypt; but viewed doctrinally, it deals with *redemption.* Just as the first book of the Bible teaches that God elects unto salvation, so the second instructs us *how* God saves, namely, by redemption. Redemption, then, is the dominant subject of Exodus. Following this, we are shown what we are redeemed for—*worship,* and this characterizes Leviticus, where we learn of the holy requirements of God and the gracious provisions He has made to meet these. In Numbers we have *the walk and warfare of the wilderness,* where we have a typical representation of our experiences as we pass through this scene of sin and trial—our repeated and excuseless failures, and God's long-sufferance and faithfulness. And so we might continue.

But to return to Exodus. This we have pointed out (as others before us have done) treats of redemption. To the writer it appears that its contents fall into five divisions, which we may summarize as follows:— First, we see the *need* for redemption—pictured by a people enslaved: chapters 1 to 6. Second, we are shown the *might* of the Redeemer—displayed in the plagues on Egypt: chapters 7 to 11. Third, we behold the *character* of redemption—purchased by blood, emancipated by power: chapters 12 to 18. Fourth, we are taught the *duty* of the redeemed—obedience to the Lord: chapters 19 to 24. Fifth, we have revealed the *provisions made* for the failures of the redeemed—seen in the tabernacle and its services: chapters 25 to 40. In proof of what we have just said we would refer the reader to Ex. 15:13, which we regard as the key verse to the book, "Thou in Thy mercy hast led forth the people which Thou hast redeemed: Thou hast guided them in Thy strength unto Thy holy habitation". Note that here we have the *need* for redemption implied—God's "mercy"; the *power* of the Redeemer is referred to—His "'strength"; the *character* of redemption is described—"led forth the people"; the *responsibilities* of the redeemed and their *privileges* are signified in a reference to the tabernacle—"unto Thy holy habitation".

Another thing which is a great help in the study of Exodus is to note its numerical position in the Sacred Canon. Exodus is the *second* book of the Bible, and it will be found that the character of its contents fully accords with this. The number two, in its scriptural significations, treats of *difference* or *division*. Proof of this is found in its first occurrence in the Bible: the *second* day of Gen. 1 was when God *divided* the waters. Hence, two is the number of *witness*, for if the testimony of two *different* men agree, the truth is established. Two is therefore the number of *opposition*. One is the number of unity, but two brings in another, who is either in accord with the first or opposed to him. Hence, two is also the number of *contrast*, consequently, whenever we find two men coupled together in Scripture it, is, with rare exceptions, for the purpose of bring-

ing out the *difference* there is between them: for example, Cain and Abel, Jacob and Esau, Moses and Aaron, David and Solomon, etc.

Let us now see how these slightly varied meanings of the number two are traceable in the character and contents of this second book of Scripture. Two is the number of *division*. In the first chapter of Exodus we find Pharaoh ordering a division to be made among the babies of the Israelites: if a son was born he should be killed, if a daughter she should be spared. In the plagues, the Lord made a division between His people and the Egyptians: "And I will *sever* in that day the land of Goshen, in which My people dwell, that no swarms of flies shall be there; to the end thou mayest know that I am the Lord in the midst of the earth. And I will put *a division* between My people and thy people; tomorrow shall this sign be" (Ex. 8:22, 23). So, too, He divided between their cattle: "And the Lord shall *sever* between the cattle of Israel and the cattle of Egypt: and there shall nothing die of all that is the children's of Israel" (Ex. 9:4). When Israel came to the Red Sea we are told, "And Moses stretched out his hand over the sea; and the Lord caused the Sea to go back by a strong east wind all that night, and made the sea dry land, and the waters were *divided*" (14:21). Again; it is only in Exodus (26:33) that we read of the veil which was to "*divide*" between the holy place and the most holy".

Two is also the number of *witness*, and mark how this note is sounded throughout the book. The sufferings and groanings of the Hebrews witnessed to their need of deliverance. The plagues bore witness to the power and wrath of God, and it is noteworthy that God employed *two* witnesses, Moses and Aaron, in announcing these to Pharaoh. The Passover-night witnessed to the value and sufficiency of the blood. The wilderness experiences of Israel witnessed to the faithfulness and tender love of God. The giving of the law witnessed to the righteousness government of Jehovah. The tabernacle bore typical witness to the manifold perfections of Christ.

Again; two is the number of *opposition*. This is something which is prominently marked in Exodus. The antagonism of the Enemy is very manifest throughout. First, we behold it in the determined and cruel effort made to prevent the increase of the Hebrews. Then we see the children of Israel oppressed by merciless taskmasters. Next, when Moses goes in and performs his miraculous signs before the king, Pharaoh's magicians "withstood" him: and it is striking to observe that only *two* of their names have been preserved in Holy Writ (2 Tim. 3:8). In connection with Israel's exodus from Egypt, Pharaoh opposed every step of the way. Even after Israel left Egypt and crossed the Red Sea, we see the Amalakites opposing them in the wilderness (17:8)—note it was not the Israelites who attacked the Amalakites, but the enemy who came to fight against the people of God.

Finally, two is the number of *contrast*. Even a casual reading will reveal the marked differences between the first two books of Scripture: let us note a few of them. In the book of Genesis we have the history of a family, in Exodus the history of a nation. In Genesis the descendants of Abraham are seen few in number, in Exodus they are to be numbered by the million. In the former we see the Hebrews welcomed and honored in Egypt, in the latter they are viewed as feared and hated. In the former there is a Pharaoh who says to Joseph, "God hath showed thee all this" (41:39); in the latter there is a Pharaoh who says to Moses, "I know not the Lord" (5:2). In Genesis there is a "lamb" promised (22:8); in Exodus the "lamb" is slain (chap. 12). In the one we see the entry of Israel into Egypt; in the other we behold their exodus. In the one we see the patriarchs in the land "which flowed with milk and honey"; in the other we behold their descendants in the wilderness. Genesis ends with Joseph in a coffin; while Exodus closes with the glory of the Lord filling the tabernacle. A series of more vivid contrasts could scarcely be imagined.

The central doctrine of the book of Exodus is redemption, but this is not formally expounded, rather is it strikingly illustrated. In earliest times, God, it would seem, did not communicate to His people an explicit and systematic form of doctrine; instead, He instructed them, mainly, through His providential dealings and by means of types and symbols. Once this is clearly grasped by us it gives new interest to the Old Testament scriptures. The opening books of the Bible contain

very much more than an inspired history of events that happened thousands of years ago: they are filled with adumbrations and illustrations of the great doctrines of our faith which are set forth categorically in the New Testament epistles. Thus "whatsoever things were written aforetime were written for our learning" (Rom. 15:4), and we lose much if we neglect to study the historical portions of the Old Testament with this fact before us.

The deliverance of Israel from Egypt furnishes a remarkably full and accurate typification of our redemption by Christ. The details of this will come before us, God willing, in our later studies. Here, we can only call attention to the broad outlines of the picture. Israel in Egypt illustrates the place we were in before Divine grace saved us. Egypt symbolizes the world, according to the course of which we all walked in time past. Pharaoh, who knew not the Lord, who defied Him, who was the inveterate enemy of God's people, but who at the end was overthrown by God, shadows forth the great adversary, the Devil. The cruel bondage of the enslaved Hebrews pictures the tyrannical dominion of sin over its captives. The groaning of the Israelites under their burdens speaks of the painful exercises of conscience and heart when convicted of our lost condition. The deliverer raised up by God in the person of Moses, points to the greater Deliverer, even our Lord Jesus Christ. The passover-night tells of the security of the believer beneath the sheltering blood of God's Lamb. The exodus from Egypt announces our deliverance from the yoke of bondage and our judicial separation from the world. The crossing of the Red Sea depicts our union with Christ in His death and resurrection. The journey through the wilderness—its trials and testings, with God's provision to meet every need—represent the experiences of our pilgrim course. The giving of the law to Israel teaches us the obedient submission which we owe to our new Master. The tabernacle with its beautiful fittings and furnishings, shows us the varied excellencies and glories of Christ. Thus it will be found that almost everything in this second book of the Bible has a spiritual message and application to us

It is also to be remarked that there is much in the book of Exodus that looks forward to and anticipates the future. The

historical portions of this second book of
Scripture have a dispensational as well as
doctrinal value, a prophetic as well as a
moral and spiritual signification. There
is not a little in it that will minister instruction and comfort to the people of
God in a coming day, as well as to us
now. History repeats itself, and what is
recorded in Exodus will be found to foreshadow a later chapter in the vicissitudes
of Abraham's descendants. The lot of
Israel in the Tribulation period will be
even worse than it was in the days of
Moses. A greater tyrant than Pharaoh
will yet be "raised up" by God to chastise
them. A more determined effort than that
of old will be made to cut them off from
being a nation. Groanings and cryings
more intense and piteous will yet ascend
to heaven. Plagues even more fearful than
those sent upon the land of Pharaoh will
yet be poured out upon the world from the
vials of God's wrath. God shall again
send forth two witnesses, empowered by
Him to show forth mighty signs and wonders, but their testimony shall be rejected
as was that of Moses and Aaron of old.
Emissaries of Satan, supernaturally endowed, will perform greater prodigies
than did the magicians of Egypt. A remnant of Israel shall again be found in
the wilderness, there to be sustained by
God. And at the end shall come forth
the great Deliverer, who will vanquish
the enemies of His people by a sorer judgment than that which overtook the Egyptians at the Red Sea. Finally, there shall
yet be an even greater exodus than that
from Egypt, when the Lord shall gather
to Palestine the outcasts of Israel from
"the uttermost part of the earth to the
uttermost part of heaven".

In addition to the illustrations of the
various parts and aspects of the doctrine
of redemption and the prophetic forecast
of Israel's lot in the day to come, there
are in the book of Exodus quite a number
of precious types of the person and work
of our Lord Jesus Christ. In many re-

spects there is a remarkable correspondency between Moses and Christ, and if the
Lord permits us to complete this series
of articles, we shall, at the close, system-
atize these correspondencies, and show
them to be as numerous and striking as
those which engaged our attention when
Joseph was before us. In addition to the
personal type of Moses we shall consider how the burning bush, the passover
lamb, the crossing of the Red Sea, the
manna, the smitten rock, the tabernacle
as a whole, and everything in it, looked
at separately, each and all tell forth in
symbolic but unmistakeable language the
manifold glories of Christ. A rich feast
is before us; may God the Holy Spirit
sharpen our appetites so that we may feed
upon them in faith, and be so nourished
thereby that we shall grow in grace and in
the knowledge of our Lord and Saviour
Jesus Christ.

As the title of these papers intimates,
we shall not attempt a complete verse
by verse exposition of the book of Exodus,
rather shall we continue the course followed by us in our articles on Genesis.
Our endeavor will be to stimulate the
people of God to a more careful and
systematic study of the Old Testament
scriptures, by calling attention to some of
the hidden wonders which escape the
notice of the careless reader, but which
cause the reverent student to say with one
of old, "I rejoice at Thy word as one that
findeth great spoil" (Psa. 119:162). While
we shall not ignore the practical application of the message to our own lives, and
shall seek to profit from the many salutary
lessons to be found for us in Exodus, nevertheless, our chief concern will be the
study of those typical pictures which meet
us at every turn. The next article will be
devoted to Ex. 1, and in the meantime we
would urge the interested reader to make
a careful study of its contents. May the
God of all grace anoint our eyes, and may
the Spirit of Truth constantly guide our
thoughts as we pass from chapter to chapter.

CHAPTER 2

ISRAEL IN BONDAGE

EXODUS 1

The opening verse of Exodus carries us back to what is recorded in the closing chapters of Genesis, where we read of Jacob and his family settling in the land of the Pharaohs. On their entry they were accorded a hearty welcome, for Goshen, which was "the best of the land" of Egypt, (Gen. 47:6), was allotted to their use. But not for long were they suffered to dwell there in peace and comfort. It would seem that about thirty years after their entrance into Egypt a spirit of enmity began to be manifested toward them, engendered at first, perhaps, from the fact that they were shepherds (see Gen. 46:34); and which terminated in their being subjected to hard bondage in the days of the new king which "knew not Joseph". That their peace was disturbed thirty years after their settlement in Goshen seems clear from a comparison of Acts 7:6 and Ex. 12:40: in the former we are told they were "evilly entreated four hundred years", in the latter we are informed that "the sojourning of the children of Israel, who dwelt in Egypt" was "four hundred and thirty years".

Several questions naturally suggest themselves at this point. What was God's reason for allowing Israel to spend so long a time in Egypt? Why did He suffer them to be so cruelly treated? The purpose of God was that the descendants of Abraham should occupy the land of Canaan, which He had given to their father. But why should an interval of more than four hundred years elapse before this purpose was realized? To this I think a twofold answer may be returned. First, to prepare Israel for their inheritance. The rough schooling they had in Egypt served to develop their muscles and toughen their sinews. Also, their bitter lot in Egypt and their trials in the wilderness were calcu-lated to make the land that flowed with milk and honey the more appreciated when it became theirs. Moreover, the land of Canaan was too large for a single family or tribe, and the lengthy sojourn in Egypt gave time for them to develop into a na-tion that must have numbered fully two millions.

The second answer is suggested by Gen. 15:16: "But in the fourth generation they shall come hither again: for the iniquity of the Amorites is not yet full." God had told Abraham that his seed should so-journ in a strange land for four hundred years, but in the fourth generation they should return to Canaan, and then the iniquity of the Amorites would be filled up. The time for God to deal in judgment with the Amorites was not fully ripe in the days of Abraham: their iniquities had not reached the bound God had appointed. Thus God ordered it that by the time the iniquities of the Amorites were "filled up" (cf Matt. 23:32 and 1 Thess. 2:16) Israel was ready, as a nation, to be His instru-ment to destroy them. "Whatever the act-ings of men in wickedness and high-handed rebellion, they are made subservient to the establishment of the Divine counsels of grace and love.... Even the wrath of man is yoked to the chariot wheel of God's decrees" (Ed. Dennett).

But why did God allow the descendants of Abraham to suffer such indignities and trials at the hands of the Egyptians? Ah, does not the book of Genesis again supply the answer! Was the wicked treatment of Joseph by his brethren to pass unpunished? No, that could not be. They, like all oth-ers, must reap what they had sown; reap the bitter harvest not only themselves but in their offspring too, for the sins of the fathers are visited upon the children unto the third and fourth generation. So it

proved here, for it was the *"fourth* generation" (Gen. 13:15) which came out of
Egypt. Four generations, then, reaped the
harvest, and reaped precisely "whatsoever"
had been sown; for just as Joseph was
sold into *slavery,* and carried down into
Egypt, so *in Egyptian slavery* his brethren
and their children suffered!! And what a
foreshadowing was this of the bitter experiences of Israel during these nineteen
centuries past, for their wicked treatment
of that blessed One whom Joseph so
strikingly typified! They, too, have reaped
what they sowed. Israel delivered up
Christ into the hands of the Gentiles, and
so into *their* hands they also have been
delivered. Christ was shamefully treated
by the Romans, and the *same* people were
employed by God to punish the Jews.
Christ was "cut off" out of the land of
the living, and from A. D. 70 Israel, too,
has been "cut off" from the land of their
fathers. Thus we see again how inexorable is the outworking of this law of sowing and reaping.

In our last article we intimated that the
deliverance of Israel from Egyptian bondage foreshadowed the redemption of sinners by Christ. The land occupied by the
enslaved Hebrews fitly portrays the place
where the unregenerate are. Egypt symbolizes the world, the world as a system,
away from God and opposed to Him. Concerning this we cannot do better than quote
from the excellent comments of the late
Mr. F. W. Grant:

"The land of Egypt is a remarkable land
in this way, that it is a little strip of country along the great river which makes it
what it is, and which is in perpetual conflict with the desert as to it. This desert
runs on both sides, and a little strip through
which the river flows alone is Egypt. The
desert on each side hems it in, blowing in
its sands in all directions, and the river
is as constantly overflowing its banks and
leaving its mud upon the sand, and renewing the soil. The Scripture name is indeed
not Egypt but Mizraim; and Mizraim
means 'double straitness'. This doubtless
refers to the two strips, one on each side
of the river.

"The land is a very remarkable one,
looking at it as the scene of perpetual conflict between life and death. The mercy
of God, feeding that land by the rain of a
far country, no rain coming down there.
It is another remarkable feature that rain
seldom falls in Egypt. The rain falls far
off. The people know nothing about it.
It comes rolling down in the shape of a
mighty river, and that perpetual stream
ministers unfailing plenty to the land.
They are, so to speak, independent of
heaven. Of course, I do not mean really;
but as to their thoughts, they are not
on the clouds. They do not look up, but
down. It is the very thing God points
out in contrasting the land of Canaan
with the land of Egypt, that Canaan, Israel's portion, drinks in the water and rain
of heaven. Canaan is a land of dependence. Egypt is a land of independence.

"And that is the serious character of our
natural condition, alas! what is natural to
us now—that we are independent of God!
God indeed supplies the streams of plenteous blessing, and none else than He; but
they come so regularly, so constantly, we
speak wisely (?) of natural laws, and shut
God out. Just as they have been sending
men for long, long years to explore the
sources of that river in Egypt, so men have
been constantly seeking to explore the
sources of natural supply, and they have
hardly succeeded yet.

"Egypt worshipped her river. The river
came to her so constantly that she was
practically independent of heaven; yet
heaven was the source of her supply. She
did not see the blue hills which shed down
upon them what themselves received. And
they worshipped but the river. It is our
state of nature away from God. God was
far off to us. We did not realize the
blessed hand from which all things came,
and we took the blessings in wilful ignorance of the hand upon which both they
and we in reality depended.

"But this Egypt was remarkable in other
ways. It was remarkable, as you know, as
the abode of science and civilization. To
that very wonderful country people go
now to study her monuments and admirable architecture. Egypt built as if she
had eternity before her to enjoy it in. Her
buildings were made to outlast by ages the
people of the day who builded them: they
could not make the people last, yet they
tried their best at that. They embalmed
their dead; and sent their dead down to the
generations yet to come, side by side with
what their hands had made, as if solemnly
saying: 'Here are the mighty works of
those over whom a mightier has triumphed'.
What a comment upon all her grandeur!

Her main literary memorial is a 'book of the dead'. In her monuments death is stereotyped. The desert, after all, has vanquished the river. The land of science and art is a land of death, and not of life.

"And that is the history of the world itself. Death is what is stamped upon it everywhere. It is the stamp of 'vanity' upon a fallen creation. It is more; it is the stamp of Divine reprobation. For 'in His favor is life'. Could He repent and unmake, unless we had given Him cause for repentance? Surely He could not. What a solemn thing that we should have given Him a reason! When God is able to rest in His love, as He will bye and bye, that will necessitate the eternity of the condition in which He can rest. All that, in view of which He can rest, will be stamped as eternal.

"The religion of Egypt was very remarkable. They had a religion in which were embalmed the relics of another religion, the dead tradition of a life that had been. There is no doubt about that. It is very remarkable in fact, according to what they say, that the very expression which God employs to Moses when He tells Moses His name, 'I am that I am,' you find attributed to God in the monuments of Egypt. And yet, with all that, what did Egypt everywhere worship? Emphatically and universally, the creature and not the Creator. Egypt which testified of the true God took up everything which was His total opposite, and deified a hundred beastial objects, the images, in fact, of their own lusts, and debased themselves by the service of these. Their worship was a deification,—as all heathen worship is—of their own lusts and passions. And that is everywhere what controls men naturally as his god. You remember in the garden of Eden, Satan says to the woman, 'Ye shall be as gods'. It was the *bait* he presented to her: and man has found that true in an awful way. As the apostle says of some, even professing Christians, their "god is their belly". That is, there is a craving in man's heart for something that will satisfy; and not being able to find satisfaction in God, and not being able to trust God's love and care, lust and care devour him. He worships himself, in a way continually more and more brutalizing and degrading."

And how did the descendants of Abraham first get into Egypt? Let the chapter before us make answer, and note its typical significance: "Every man and his household came with Jacob" (v. 1). They came into the land of bondage with *their father* Jacob: he was the one who brought them there. Mark, too, the name here given to him—"Jacob", which speaks of the natural man, the "supplanter"; not "Israel" which was his new name, given in sovereign grace. How clearly this speaks to us. We, too, entered the place of spiritual bondage with *our father*, Adam. This was not the place he first occupied: in Eden he was free to eat of all the trees of the garden, with but a single restriction; but alas! he sinned, and this caused him to be driven from the garden, and it was *outside* Eden that all his children were born. They came into the place of bondage with him!

"And the children of Israel were fruitful, and increased abundantly, and multiplied, and waxed exceeding mighty; and the land was filled with them" (v. 7). This was the fulfillment of God's promise to Jacob, made as the patriarch was journeying from Canaan to Egypt—"And he said, I am God, the God of thy father: fear not to go down into Egypt; for I will *there* make of thee a *great* nation". And this was but a repetition of what God had declared to Abraham long years before (see Gen. 12:2). How comforting is this to the children of God today. Unto us are given "exceeding great and precious promises", and these are the promises of Him who can not lie. Rest, then, with implicit confidence on the sure Word—forever settled in heaven—of the Lord our God.

"Now there arose up a new king over Egypt, which knew not Joseph" (v. 8). To understand this we need to turn the light of other scriptures upon it. This "new" king belonged not merely to a new dynasty, but was of a different nationality: he was by birth an Assyrian, not an Egyptian. In Acts 7:18 we read, "Till another king arose, which knew not Joseph". As one has pointed out there are in the Greek two different words for "another": allos, which means "another of the same kind"; heteros, which signifies "another of a different kind". It is the latter word which is used in Acts 7:18. By turning back to Isa. 52:4 we learn what this other kind (in this case, another nationality) actually was. There we read, "For thus saith the Lord God, My people went down aforetime into Egypt to sojourn there; and *the Assyrian* oppressed them without cause". Our purpose in calling attention to this is to remind the reader of the great importance of comparing scripture with scripture, and to show how scripture is self-interpreting.

"And he said unto his people, Behold, the people of the children of Israel are more and mightier than we" (v. 9). The light afforded by the scriptures we have just looked at should remove what has long been a difficulty in this verse. That the children of Israel (who probably numbered about two millions all told, at this time) should be more numerous than the Egyptians seems unthinkable. But this is not what v. 9 states at all. Mark attentively its wording. "And he (the "new" king) said to *his* people", not "*the* people". His people would be the Assyrians who had conquered Egypt, and particularly those in that land policing the country. Note the repetition of "*his* people" in v. 22.

"And he said unto his people, Behold, the people of the children of Israel are more and mightier than we: Come on, let us deal wisely with them; lest they multiply, and it come to pass, that, when there falleth out any war, they join also unto our enemies (that is, lest the Hebrews should unite forces with the Egyptians against the Assyrian invaders), and fight against us and so get them up out of the land. Therefore they did set over them taskmasters to afflict them with their burdens" (vv. 9-11). This was the proud reasoning of the carnal mind, which is enmity against God. It was the finite pitting itself against the Infinite. In thus oppressing and afflicting the children of Israel we have an illustration of the world's hatred for the people of God (John 15:18, 19). How true it is that "the tender mercies of the wicked are cruel" (Prov. 12:10)! How much, then, dear reader, do we owe to the restraining power of God, which holds in check the evil passions of men, and thus allows us to live a quiet and peaceable life! Let the withholding hand of God be withdrawn for a short season, and even now, His people would be sorely "afflicted" too.

"But the more they afflicted them, the more they multiplied and grew" (v. 12). This proves how thoroughly vain it is to fight against the purpose of Him who hath sworn, "My counsel shall stand, and I will do all My pleasure" (Isa. 64:10). Pharaoh might purpose to "deal wisely",

but "the wisdom of this world is foolishness with God" (1 Cor. 3:19). God hath declared, "I will destroy the wisdom of the wise, and will bring to nothing the understanding of the prudent" (1 Cor. 1:19). So it proved here—"the more they afflicted them the more they grew". This also illustrates a principle which has been exemplified again and again in the history of Christendom. Times of severest trial have always been seasons of blessing to the people of God. The more fiercely have burned the fires of persecution the stronger has faith waxed. So, too, it should be, and often has been, in individual lives. Opposition should cast us back more and more upon God. Persecution results in separating us from the world. Suffering ought to refine. The experience of the Psalmist was, "Before I was afflicted I went astray: but now' have I kept Thy Word" (Psa. 119:67). May it prove true of writer and reader that "the more we are afflicted" the more shall we "grow" in grace and in the knowledge of the Lord.

"And the king of Egypt spake to the Hebrew midwives, of which the name of the one was Shiphrah, and the name of the other Puah: And he said, when you do the office of a midwive to the Hebrew women, and see them upon the stools; if it be a son, then ye shall kill him; but if it be a daughter, then she shall live" (vv. 15, 16). It is not difficult to peer behind the scenes and behold one who was seeking to use Pharaoh as an instrument with which to accomplish his fiendish design. Surely we can discover here an outbreaking of the Serpent's enmity against the Seed of the woman. Suppose this effort had succeeded, what then? Why, *the channel* through which the promised Redeemer was to come had been destroyed. If all the male children of the Hebrews were destroyed there had been no David, and if no David, no David's Son. Just as Rev. 12: 4 gives us to behold Satan working behind and through the wicked edict of Herod, so we may discern him here working behind and through Pharaoh.

But once more Egypt's king was foiled, and again was Satan's attacks repulsed: "but the midwives feared God, and did not as the king of Egypt commanded them, but saved the men children alive" (v. 17). Better might a worm withstand the tread of an elephant than the puny creature resist the Almighty. "There is no wisdom, nor understanding, nor counsel against the Lord" (Prov. 21:30). What comfort and confidence should this impart to the believer! If God be for us, it matters not who are against us.

"Therefore God dealt well with the midwives: and the people multiplied, and waxed very mighty. And it came to pass, because the midwives feared God, that He made them houses" (vv. 20, 21). Here we have one more illustration of the law of sowing and reaping. These Hebrew midwives, who through fear of God had overcome the fear of Pharaoh, dealt kindly with the male children of the Israelites, and they were rewarded accordingly—"God dealt well" with them. God is not unrighteous to forget any work and labor of love which is showed toward His name or ministered to His people (Heb. 6:10). His promise is "For them that honor Me, I will honor" (1 Sam. 2:30). They "saved the men children alive", and God "made them houses", which, in the light of 2 Sam. 7:11, 1 Kings 2:24, etc., must mean that He, in turn, gave them husbands and blessed them with children.

"And Pharaoh charged all his people, saying, Every son that is born ye shall cast into the river, and every daughter ye shall save alive" (v. 22). We do not have to look far beneath the surface in order to discover here the malignity of one more vile than Pharaoh. Just as the twelfth of Revelation shows us that it was the Dragon himself who moved Herod to attempt the death of the Christ Child, so here he was employing the king of Egypt to destroy the channel through which He was to come. At the beginning, God declared He would put "enmity" between the woman and her Seed (Gen. 3:15), and in the light of subsequent scriptures it is abundantly clear that "the woman" is Israel—the one who was to bear the Messiah. Here in the passage before us we have a forceful illustration of the Serpent's "enmity". Had his effort succeeded, had all the *male* children of the Hebrews been slain, the channel through which the Saviour was to come had been destroyed.

"And Pharaoh charged all his people, saying, every son that is born ye shall cast into the river, and every daughter ye shall save alive" (v. 22). How this reminds us of the words of Eccl. 8:11: "Because sentence against an evil work is not executed speedily, therefore the heart of the sons of men is fully set in them to do evil". God bears with *much long-suffering* the vessels of wrath fitted to destruction. Every opportunity is given them to repent; the day of mercy is graciously prolonged for them; and if in the end they die in their sins, then is their blood, unmistakeably, on their own heads. How God frustrated this last move of Pharaoh we shall see in our next paper.

CHAPTER 3

THE EARLY DAYS OF MOSES

EXODUS 2

From Adam to Christ there is none greater than Moses. He is one of the few characters of Scripture whose course is sketched from his infancy to his death. The fierce light of criticism has been turned upon him for generations, but he is still the most commanding figure of the ancient world. In character, in faith, in the unique position assigned him as the mediator of the old covenant, and in achievements, he stands first among the heroes of the Old Testament. All of God's early dealings with Israel were transacted through Moses. He was a prophet, priest, and king in one person, and so united all the great and important functions which later were distributed among a plurality of persons. The history of such an one is worthy of the strictest attention, and his remarkable life deserves the closest study.

"The life of Moses presents a series of striking antitheses. He was the child of a slave, and the son of a queen. He was born in a hut, and lived in a palace. He inherited poverty, and enjoyed unlimited wealth. He was the leader of armies, and the keeper of flocks. He was the mightiest of warriors, and the meekest of men. He was educated in the court, and dwelt in the desert. He had the wisdom of Egypt, and the faith of a child. He was fitted for the city, and wandered in the wilderness. He was tempted with the pleasures of sin, and endured the hardships of virtue. He was backward in speech, and talked with God. He had the rod of a shepherd, and the power of the Infinite. He was a fugitive from Pharaoh, and an ambassador from heaven. He was the giver of the Law, and the forerunner of grace. He died alone on Mount Moab, and appeared with Christ in Judea. No man assisted at his funeral, yet God buried him." (Dr. I. M.

Haldeman).

Exodus 2 furnishes us with a brief account of the infancy of Moses. The king of Egypt was determined to check the rapid growth of the Hebrew people. First, he had them placed under taskmasters, who were given orders to "afflict them with their burdens". But this measure failed entirely: "The more they afflicted them, the more they multiplied and grew". Next, the king gave orders to the Hebrew midwives that whenever a male Israelite was born, he should be killed. But once more the evil designs of Pharaoh came to nought. The mid-wives feared God, "and did not as the king of Egypt commanded them, but saved the men children alive". Finally, we are told, "And Pharaoh charged all his people, saying, every son that is born ye shall cast into the river, and every daughter ye shall save alive" (1: 22). It was during this time and under such conditions that the future deliverer of Abraham's descendants was born.

"And there went a man of the house of Levi, and took to wife a daughter of Levi. And the woman conceived, and bare a son: and when she saw him that he was a goodly child, she hid him three months. And when she could not longer hide him, she took for him an ark of bulrushes, and daubed it with slime and with pitch, and put the child therein; and she laid it in the flags by the river's brink" (Ex. 2:1-3). Much of a sentimental nature has been written on these verses. Commentators have reasoned that it was mother-love and the beauty of the child which caused Jochebed to act as she did. But this will not stand the test of Holy Writ. Scripture informs us that it was neither affection nor infatuation but *faith* which was the mainspring of action. Heb. 11:23 declares, "By *faith* Moses, when he was born, was hid

16

three months of his parents, because they saw he was a proper child; and they were not afraid of the king's commandment." Faith "cometh by *hearing*" (Rom. 10:17): the parents of Moses must, therefore, have received a direct communication from God, informing them of what should happen and instructing them what to do. And they believed what God had told them and acted accordingly.

It was faith which saw that the child was "goodly" (in the sight of God), as it was faith which made them defy "the king's commandment"—first by hiding the child, later in placing him in the ark of bulrushes. It is true that in this instance grace did not run counter to natural affection; nevertheless, it was not by feelings but "by faith" they acted. When commanded to do so, we are to obey God against our natural affections. Thus it was with Abraham when called to go out from the land of his birth and leave all his kindred behind; and so later, when called upon to offer up Isaac.

Should it be asked, Wherein is the faith of Moses' parents to be seen? The answer is: In overcoming the fear of the king and in trusting God's protection for the preservation of the child. And is not the strength of their faith evidenced by the selection of the place where the young child was put, after he could be no longer hid in the home? Surely the parents of Moses took him to the very last spot which carnal reasoning would have suggested. The mother laid him "in the flags by the river's brink"! But that was the very place where the babies were drowned! Ah, is not *that* the last location we had chosen? Would not *we* have carried him as far away from the river as possible? It is to be noted that in Heb. 11:23 the faith of both parents is spoken of, while that of the mother's is singled out here in Ex. 2, but his father receives particular mention by Stephen in Acts 7:20. It is blessed to see this concurrence between them. Husband and wife should go hand in hand to the throne of grace and act together in every good work.

Ere passing from our notice of the faith of Amram and Jochebed there are two other points which deserve notice. Though faith vanquished fear, yet *lawful means were used* to overcome danger: the mother "hid" the child, and later, had recourse to the ark. It is not faith but fanaticism which deliberately courts danger. Faith never tempts God. Even Christ, though He knew full well of the Father's will to preserve Him, yet withdrew from those who sought His life (Luke 4:30; John 8:59). It is not lack of faith to avoid danger by legitimate precautions. It is no want of trust to employ means, even when assured by God of the event (Acts 27:31). Christ never supplied by a miracle when ordinary means were to hand (Mk. 5:43).

Another important truth which here receives illustration and exemplification is, that civil authorities are to be defied when their decrees are contrary to the expressed mind of God. The Word of God requires us to obey the laws of the land in which we live and exhorts us to be "subject unto the powers that be" (Rom. 13), and this, no matter how wise and just, or how foolish and unjust those laws appear to us. Yet, our obedience and submission to human authorities is plainly qualified. If a human government enacts a law and compliance with it by a saint would compel him to disobey some command or precept of God, then the human must be rejected for the Divine. The cases of Moses' parents, of Daniel (6:7-11) and of the apostles (Acts 5:29), establishes this unequivocally. But if such rejection of human authority be necessitated, let it be performed not in the spirit of carnal defiance, but in the fear of God, and then the issue may safely be left with Him. It was "by *faith*" the parents of Moses "were not afraid of the king's commandment". May Divine grace work in us "like precious faith" which overcomes all fear of man.

In the opening verses of our chapter we have a lovely picture of salvation. The infant Moses was placed on the brink of the river, the place of death—the last spot we had selected. It is so in salvation. Death is the wages of sin, and from this there can be no escape. Having flagrantly broken God's holy law, justice demands the execution of its penalty. But is not this to close the door of hope against us, and seal our doom? Ah, it is just at this point that the Gospel announces God's gracious provision and tells us (what we had never conceived for ourselves) that life comes to us through death.

Though Moses was brought to the place of death, he was made secure *in the ark*. And this speaks to us of Christ* who went

---

*It is significant that the Hebrew word is used only here and in connection with the ark of Noah, which so clearly typified Christ.

down into death for us. The righteousness of God made imperative the payment of sin's awful wages, and so his spotless Son "died the just for the unjust that He might bring us to God" (1 Pet. 3:15). Thus, *in Christ* our Substitute, we too *have been* in the place of death as was the infant Moses. And note that as it was *"faith"* which placed him there, it is faith which identifies us with Christ. Again; just as Moses was brought out of the place of death, so when Christ rose again, we rose with Him (Eph. 2:5,6). The typical picture may be followed still farther. In the merciful provision which the providence of God arranged for the infant Moses (Ex. 2:4) we have illustrated the tender care of our heavenly Father for every babe in Christ. And, later, in the entrance of Moses into the household and palace of Pharaoh, we have foreshadowed the "mansions" on high, which are now being prepared for us!

"And the daughter of Pharaoh came down to wash herself at the river; and her maidens walked along by the river's side; and when she saw the ark among the flags, she sent her maid to fetch it. And when she had opened it, she saw the child: and, behold, the babe wept. And she had compassion on him, and said, This is one of the Hebrews' children. Then said his sister to Pharaoh's daughter. Shall I go and call to thee a nurse of the Hebrew women, that she may nurse the child for thee? And Pharaoh's daughter said to her, Go. And the maid went and called the child's mother. And Pharaoh's daughter said unto her, Take this child away, and nurse it for me, and I will give thee thy wages. And the woman took the child and nursed it" (Ex. 2:5-9). It was neither by chance nor accident that Pharaoh's daughter went down to the river that day, for there are no accidents nor chance happenings in a world presided over by the living God. Whatsover happens in time is but the outworking of His eternal decrees— "for Whom are all things, and *by* Whom are all things" (Heb. 2:10). God is behind the scenes, ordering everything for His own glory; hence our smallest actions are controlled by Him. "O Lord, I know that the way of man *is not in himself:* it is not in man that walketh to direct his steps" (Jer. 10:23). It is because that whatsoever happens in time is the outworking of God's eternal decrees, that "all things

are working together (the verb is in the present tense) for good to them that love God, who are the called according to His purpose." Big doors often swing on small hinges. God not only directs the rise and fall of empires, but also rules the fall of a sparrow. It was *God* who put it into the heart of this Egyptian princess to go to the river to bathe, and to that particular spot where the ark lay amid the flags; as it was He who caused her to be moved with compassion (rather than with indignation at the defiance of her father's authority) when she beheld the weeping child. And it was God who caused this daughter of the haughty monarch to yield submissively to the suggestion of Miriam, and made the princess willing for its own mother to care for the little child. Only here can the mind repose in unruffled peace. What a haven of rest is this—to know that "of Him, and through Him, and to Him, *are all things:* to whom be glory for ever" (Rom. 11:36).

"And Pharaoh's daughter said unto her, Take this child away, and nurse it for me, and I will give thee thy wages. And the woman took the child, and nursed it" (v. 9). This whole incident of the Divine safeguarding of the infant life of Moses supplies a striking and blessed illustration of God's preservation of His elect during their unregeneracy—a fact that few believers are as thankful over as they should be. We believe it is this which explains a point that has been a sore puzzle to many commentators in Jude 1: "Jude, the servant of Jesus Christ, and brother of James, to them that are sanctified by God the Father, and preserved in Jesus Christ, and called". The *order* of the verbs here is most significant. The "sanctification" by the Father manifestly speaks of our eternal election, when before the foundation of the world God, in His counsels, *separated* us from the mass of our fallen race, and appointed us to salvation. The "calling" evidently refers to that inward and invincible call which comes to each of God's elect at the hour of their regeneration (Rom. 8:30), when the dead hear the voice of the Son of God and live (John 5:25). But observe that in Jude 1 it is said they are "preserved" in Jesus Christ, and "called." Clearly the reference is to *temporal preservation prior to salvation.* As the writer looks back to his unregenerate days he recalls with a shudder a number of occasions when he was in imminent peril, brought face to face with death. But even then, even while in his sins, he was (because in Christ by eternal election) miraculously preserved. What cause for gratitude and praise is this! Doubtless, each Christian reader will recall similar deliverances out of danger. It is this which Ex. 2:6-9 so beautifully illustrates. Even in his unregenerate days, as a babe, the Angel of the Lord encamped round about the infant Moses and delivered him!

"And the child grew, and she brought him unto Pharaoh's daughter, and he became her son. And she called his name Moses: and she said, Because I drew him out of the water". (v. 10) This is a striking illustration of Job 5:13—"He taketh the wise in their own craftiness: and the counsel of the froward is carried headlong". Pharaoh proposed to "deal wisely" with the Israelites, and this, in order that they might not "get them up out of the land" (1:10); and yet, in the end, God compels him to give board, lodging, and education, to the very man which accomplished the very thing that Pharaoh was trying to prevent! Thus was Pharaoh's wisdom turned to foolishness, and Satan's devices defeated.

There are two passages in the New Testament which throw light on the interval passed over between verses 10 and 11 in Ex. 2. In Acts 7:22 we read, "And Moses was learned in all the wisdom of the Egyptians, and was mighty in words and in deeds". But his heart was not in these things. There was something which had a more powerful attraction for him than the honors and comforts of Egypt's court. Doubtless his believing parents had acquainted him with the promises of Jehovah to his forefathers. That the time was not far distant when the Hebrews were to be delivered from their bondage and should journey to the land given to Abraham, Moses had heard, and hearing he believed. The result of his faith is described in Heb. 11:24-26: "By faith Moses, when he was come to years, refused to be called the son of Pharaoh's daughter; Choosing rather to suffer affliction with the people of God, than to enjoy the pleasures of sin for a season; esteeming the reproach of Christ greater riches than the treasures in Egypt: for he had respect unto the recompense of the reward". Upon the character of his faith

and this remarkable renunciation we can only comment briefly.

The first thing to be observed is *the nature of his renunciation:* he "refused to be called the son of Pharaoh's daughter". Josephus tells us that Pharaoh had no other children, and that his daughter, Thermutis, had no children of her own. So, most probably Moses would have succeeded to the throne. That some *offer* was made to Moses, after he had reached manhood, is clearly implied by the words "he *refused*". What he refused then was wealth, honors, power, and, most likely, a throne. Had he accepted, he could readily have mitigated the sufferings of His own people, and lightened their heavy burdens. But he "refused".

Second, note *the character of his choice:* he "chose rather to suffer affliction with the people of God, than to enjoy the pleasures of sin for a season". It was not that suffering was thrust upon him, but that he voluntarily elected it. It was not that there was no escape from it but he deliberately determined to throw in his lot with a despised and persecuted people. He preferred hardship to comfort, shame and reproach rather than fame and honor, afflictions rather than pleasures, the wilderness rather than the court. A remarkable choice was this, and mark it, this was the choice not of a child, but of a full-grown man; not of a fool, but of one skilled in all the wisdom of the Egyptians.

Third, observe *the satisfaction he enjoyed:* "esteeming the reproach of Christ greater riches than the treasures in Egypt". The place Moses volunteered to occupy was a hard one, in every respect the very opposite of that in which he had been reared. Yet Moses did not repine or murmur. So far from being dissatisfied with his bargain, he valued the "reproach" which it brought him. So far from complaining at the affliction, he prized it. He not only endured suffering, but he esteemed it as of more worth than the wealth of the greatest and richest country on earth. In this he puts many of us to shame!

Fourth, mark *the motive spring of his actions:* "By faith Moses....refused....chose....esteemed". As another has said, "He must have *heard* from God that he was not to accept this high privilege. Inasmuch as 'faith cometh by hearing', Moses must have *heard!* And, inasmuch as this hearing cometh by the Word of God', God must have spoken or communicated His will to Moses; for Moses heard, Moses believed, Moses obeyed. God had other counsels and purposes with regard to Moses. Moses must have been told that 'God, by His hand, would deliver' Israel from Egypt's bondage. The 'things to come' had been revealed to him. The 'things of Christ' had been made known 'in part'. He knew God. He knew that Jehovah had a people, and that they were in sore bondage in Egypt. He knew that they were to be delivered. How, then, could he accept the position of heir to Egypt's throne?".

Finally, attend to *the object set before him:* "for he had respect unto the recompense of the reward". Moses must have "heard" of "the eternal weight of glory", and therefore he looked not at the "things that are seen". The pleasures of sin were of brief duration—only for "a season"; but, in view of the eternity of the glory, the "affliction" seemed brief—but "for a moment," and therefore, "light". Moses, then, walked by faith and not by sight; he had his eyes on the invisible, not the tangible; he was occupied with the future rather than the present; and, consequently, it was an easy matter to exchange the palace for the wilderness, and the pleasures of sin for the reproach of Christ. May like precious faith be vouchsafed reader and writer.

Returning to the narrative we are next told, "And it came to pass in those days, when Moses was grown, that he went out unto his brethren, and looked on their burdens: and he espied an Egyptian smiting an Hebrew, one of his brethren. And he looked this way and that way, and when he saw that there was no man, he slew the Egyptian, and hid him in the sand" (Ex. 2:11, 12). One of the features of Scripture which constantly impresses the writer is the absolute fidelity with which the lives of Bible heroes are described. Unlike so many human biographies, the characters of Scripture are painted in the colors of nature and truth. They are described as they actually were. An instance of this is before us here. Moses was truly a wonderful character, and endowed with no ordinary faith; yet, the Holy Spirit has not concealed his defects. Moses was in too big a hurry. He was running before the Lord. God's time had not yet come to deliver Israel. Another forty years must yet run their weary course. But Moses waxed impatient and acted in the energy of the flesh. Some writers have sought to vindicate him, but the words "he *looked* this way and that, and when he *saw* there was no man, he slew the Egyptian" make it evident that he was then walking by sight, rather than by faith; and the fact that we are told he "hid him in the sand" brings out his fear of being discovered. Thus we see that, like ourselves, Moses was one who offended in many things (Jas. 3:2, R.V.).

"And when he went out the second day, behold, two men of the Hebrews strove together: and he said to him that did the wrong, Wherefore smitest thou thy fellow? And he said, Who made thee a prince and a judge over us? Intendest thou to kill me, as thou killedst the Egyptian? And Moses feared, and said, Surely this thing is known. Now when Pharaoh heard this thing, he sought to slay Moses. But Moses fled from the face of Pharaoh, and dwelt in the land of Midian" (2:13-15). This confirms our interpretation of the verses immediately preceding. Moses' eye was not on God but on man, and the fear of man bringeth a snare. Apprehensive that Pharaoh might take vengeance upon him, he fled to Midian. And yet while this is true from the human side, we ought not to ignore the over-ruling Providence of God. The *Lord's* time for delivering Israel had not yet arrived; and what is more to the point, the act of Moses was not at all in accord with the methods which *He* proposed to employ. Not by insurrection on their part, nor by a system of assassination, were the Hebrews to be delivered from the house of bondage. God, therefore, caused this deed of Moses (which he believed had passed unwitnessed) to become known, both to his own brethren and to the king. Thus did He teach a salutary lesson to this one who was yet to be employed as His servant. And is there not also a needed lesson here for us? When a servant of God is not permitted to perform a certain service for Him, on which his heart is set, it does not necessarily follow that this is due to some failure in the servant himself; it may be because *God's* time for the proposed service is not ripe. Such was the case with David who, prompted only by an ardent desire for God's glory, was not permitted to build Jehovah a "house"; yet in the end this "house" was built, though not by David or in David's time.

"Now the priest of Midian had seven daughters: and they came and drew water, and filled the trough to water their father's flock. And the shepherds came and drove them away: but Moses stood up and helped them, and watered their flock. And when they came to Reuel their father, he said, How is it that ye are come so soon today? And they said, an Egyptian delivered us out of the hand of the shepherds, and also drew water enough for us, and watered the flock. And he said unto his daughters, And where is he? Why is it that ye have left the man? Call him, that he may eat bread. And Moses was content to dwell with the man: and he gave Moses Zipporah his daughter" (2:16-21). Here again we may discern *God* working behind the scenes. That Moses should have "stood up" against those shepherds, single-handed, shows plainly that the Lord was on his side; and in thus befriending the daughters of Reuel, Moses was enabled to win the esteem of their father. The sequel shows how the Providence of God thus opened to Moses a home during his long exile frcm Egypt. Thus did God make all things work together for his good.

CHAPTER 4

MOSES AT THE BURNING BUSH

EXODUS 3

In our last article we saw how Moses' attempt to deliver Israel was inopportune, for God's time had not arrived. Moreover, the leader himself was not fully prepared, nor were the Hebrews themselves ready to leave Egypt. The impetuosity of Moses caused him to act with a zeal which was not according to knowledge and this, as is usually the case, brought him into serious trouble. The king sought his life, and to escape him, Moses fled into Midian. So much for the human side. Turning to the Divine, we are made to wonder at and worship before the infinite wisdom of Him who maketh the wrath of man to praise Him and who bringeth good out of evil.

God had an important work for Moses to do and for this he must be prepared. That work was to lead His people out of Egypt, and conduct them unto the promised inheritance. And for this work Moses was not yet equipped. It is true that this one who had become the adopted son of Pharaoh's daughter had received a thorough education, for he was "learned in *all* the wisdom of the Egyptians". Nor was he any longer a youth, but now forty years of age—in the very prime of life. Nor was he only a student or theorist—he was "mighty in words and deeds" (Acts 7:22). What, then, was lacking? Surely here was one who possessed all the necessary qualifications for leadership. Ah, how different are God's thoughts from ours! "That which is highly esteemed among men is abomination in the sight of God" (Luke 16:15). What we have enumerated above were but natural attainments and acquirements; and the natural man is set aside before God, for no *flesh* can glory in *His* presence (1 Cor. 1:29).

The "wisdom of the Egyptians", profound as men esteem it, was, after all, only "the wisdom of the world"; and that is "foolishness with God". The colleges of this world cannot equip for the Divine service; for *that* we must be taught in the school of God. And that is something which the natural man knows nothing about—"And the Jews marvelled, saying, How knoweth this man letters, having never learned?"—in *their* academies (John 7:15). To learn in the school of God, then, Moses must turn his back on the land of the Pharaoh's. It is so still. The heart must be separated, the spirit divorced from the world, if progress is to be made in spiritual things. "The hand of man can never mould a vessel 'meet for the Master's use'. The One who is to use the vessel can alone prepare it".

"Now Moses kept the flock of Jethro his father-in-law, the priest of Midian: and he led the flock to the backside of the desert, and came to the mountain of God, even to Horeb" (Ex. 3:1). From Egypt to "the backside of the desert", from the palace to the sheepfold, was a radical change for this man who was yet to fill so important a role. Tending flocks seems a strange preparation for one who was to be the liberator of a nation of slaves. And again we are reminded of how different are God's thoughts and ways from man's. And the ways of God are not only different from ours, but they are obnoxious to the flesh: as Gen. 46:31 tells us, "Every *shepherd* is an abomination to the Egyptians". Thus God leads His servants to take that very place which is hateful to worldlings.

"The 'backside of the desert' is where men and things, the world and self, present circumstances and their influences, are all valued at what they are really worth. There it is, and there alone, that you will find a Divinely-adjusted balance in which to weigh all within and all around. There

22

are no false colors, no borrowed plumes, no empty pretensions. The enemy of your souls cannot gild the sand of that place. All is reality there. The heart that has found itself in the presence of God at 'the backside of the desert', has right thoughts about everything. It is raised far above the exciting influences of this world's schemes. The din and noise, the bustle and confusion of Egypt, do not fall upon the ear in that distant place. The crash in the monetary and commercial world is not heard there; the sigh of ambition is not heard there; this world's fading laurels do not tempt there; the thirst for gold is not felt there; the eye is never dimmed with lust, nor the heart swollen with pride there; human applause does not elate, nor human censure depress there. In a word, everything is set aside save the stillness and light of the Divine presence. God's voice alone is heard, His light enjoyed, His thoughts received. This is the place to which all must go to be educated for the ministry; and there all must remain if they would succeed in the ministry" (C. H. M.).

What strikes us as even more strange is that Moses should have to remain *forty years* in Midian. But God is in no hurry; nor should we be—"He that believeth shall not make haste" (Isa. 28:16). There is much here which every servant of God needs to ponder, particularly the younger ones. In this day it is the common custom to pitchfork new converts into Christian activities without any serious inquiry as to their fitness for such solemn and moment-ous duties. If a person is "mighty in words and deeds" that is considered all that is necessary. *"Not a novice,* lest being lifted up with pride he fall into the condemnation of the Devil" (1 Tim. 3:6) might as well not be in the Bible, for all the weight it has with most of our moderns.

In a place of *retirement* Moses spent the second forty years of his life; a place where every opportunity for *communion* with God was afforded. Here he was to learn the utter vanity of human resources and the need for entire dependence on God Himself. To be much alone with God is the first requisite for every servant of His. But why is it that no details are recorded of God's dealings with His servant during this interval? Practically nothing is told us of the experiences through which he passed, the discipline of which he was the subject, the heart exercises he suffered.

As in the case of the training of the proph-ets, John the Baptist, Paul in Arabia, this is passed over in silence. Is it because God's dealings with one of His servants are not fitted to another? Are there not some things we can learn neither by precept nor example? Certain it is that there is *no uniform curriculum* in the school of God. Each servant is dealt with according to his individual needs and disciplined with a view to the particular work which God has for *him* to do.

"And he led the flock to the backside of the desert, and came to the mountain of God, even to Horeb" (v. 1). Horeb was the name of a mountain range; Sinai, the "mount of God" (see Ex. 24:12, 13), was a particular peak in that range. It was in this same mount that, centuries later, the Lord met with and commissioned Elijah (1 Kings 19:4-11), as, perhaps, it was also at the same place He gave the Gospel of His glory to the apostle Paul (Gal. 1:17; 4:25).

"And the angel of the Lord appeared un-to him in a flame of fire out of the midst of a bush: and he looked, and, behold, the bush burned with fire, and the bush was not consumed. And Moses said, I will now turn aside, and see this great sight, why the bush is not burnt" (Ex. 3:2, 3). Here was a wonder which all the magicians of Pharaoh could not produce. Here was some-thing which must baffle all the wisdom of the Egyptians. Here was a manifestation of God Himself. The Hebrew word here for "bush" occurs in only one other pas-sage, namely, Deut. 33:16, where we read, "And for the precious things of the earth and fulness thereof, and for the good will of Him that *dwelt* in the bush". In this verse the word for "dwelt" is "shah-chan". It was, then, the *Shekinah* glory which was now displayed before the wondering eyes of Moses. This, we take it, is the meaning of "the angel of the Lord *appeared* unto him in *a flame*" here manifested in the Shekinah-glory.

The "Angel of the Lord" was none oth-er than the Lord Jesus in theophanic mani-festation, for in v. 4 He is denominated "Lord" and "God". This sets forth a truth of vital moment to the servant of God. Be-fore Moses can be sent forth on his im-portant mission he must first behold the in-effable glory of the Lord. To serve ac-ceptably we must work with an eye single to God's glory, but to do this we must first gaze upon that glory. It was so here with

Moses. It was thus with Isaiah (Isa. 6). It was the same in the case of the great apostle to the Gentiles (Acts 9:3, etc.). Make no mistake fellow-laborer, a vision of the glory of God is an essential prerequisite if we are to serve Him acceptably.

Ere considering the Lord's words to Moses, let us first turn aside and view the "great sight" of the Burning Bush. We are satisfied that there is much here of deep significance; may God grant us discernment to understand and appreciate.

Spiritually the Burning Bush speaks of the Gospel of God's grace. The symbol used was unique and startling. A bush burned with fire, and yet the bush (in that arid desert a most imflammable object) was not burnt. Here was a mysterious phenomenon, but it set forth a mystery far more profound—the former natural, the latter moral. Fire in Scripture is uniformly the emblem of Divine judgment, that is, of God's holiness in active opposition against evil. The final word on the subject is, "Our God is a consuming fire" (Heb. 12:29). Here, then, is the deeper mystery: How can God, who is 'a consuming fire'—burning up all that is contrary to His holy nature—reveal Himself without consuming? Or, to put it in another form: How can He who is "of purer eyes than to behold evil and canst not look on iniquity" (Hab. 1:13) have to do with men, other than in judgment! Nothing but the Gospel contains any real solution to this problem. The Gospel tells of how grace reigns, not at the expense of righteousness, but "through righteousness, unto eternal life, through Jesus Christ our Lord" (Rom. 5:21).

And how has this been accomplished? By the Holy One of God being made a "curse" for us (Gal. 3:13). It is deeply significant that the word "seneh" means *"thorny* bush", for thorns are the lasting reminder of the curse (Gen. 3:18). Into the place of the curse entered our blessed Substitute. The fierce flames of holy wrath engulfed Him, but, being "mighty" (Psa. 89:19), they did not, and could not, consume Him. The "Root out of a dry ground" perished not. It was not possible that death should hold the Prince of life. Three days only did He remain in the tomb: on the third day He came forth triumphant, and is now alive for evermore. And it is as the God of *resurrection* He now saves. Note how this, too, comes out in our type. Said the Saviour to the Sadducees, "Now that the dead are raised, even

Moses showed *at the bush,* when he called the Lord the God of Abraham, and the God of Isaac, and the God of Jacob. For He is not a God of the dead, but of the living: for all live unto Him" (Luke 20: 37, 38). And how perfect this type is: it was not until after the Deliverer (Moses) had been rejected by Israel (Ex. 2:14) that God thus revealed Himself at the bush!

But there is a *dispensational* significance as well. Equally clear it is that the Burning Bush was a figure of *the nation of Israel.* At the time the Lord appeared here to Moses, the Hebrews were suffering in "the iron *furnace* of Egypt" (Deut. 4:20), but fiercely as the flames had burned against them for fully forty years, they had not been consumed. And so also has it proven all through these many centuries since then. The fires of persecution have blazed hotly, yet have they been marvelously, miraculously sustained. And why? Ah, does not our type make answer? God Himself was in the Burning Bush; and so He has been with Israel. Just as He was there with the three Hebrews in the midst of Babylon's furnace, so has He been with the Jews all through their checkered history. In the day to come this will be fully owned, for then shall it appear, "in all their affliction *He* was afflicted, and the Angel of His presence saved them" (Isa. 63:9).

While the miraculous preservation of Israel during all their fiery trials is no doubt the prominent thought here, there are others equally significant. The symbol selected by God was most suggestive. It was not in a majestic tree of the forest that God appeared to Moses, but in a humble acacia, or thorn-bush of the desert. And how fitly this represented both the lowly origin of the Hebrew people—"A Syrian ready to perish was my father" (Deut. 26:5); and their subsequent history—a separated nation, dwelling as it were in the desert. Nor is this all. This humble bush, which possessed neither beauty nor comliness, became, temporarily, the abode of Jehovah, and from it He revealed Himself to Moses. And has it not been thus with Israel: it is from *their midst* God has manifested Himself. Finally, the fact that it was an acacia bush burning with fire, represented in a forceful figure the *spiritual* history of Israel—bearing thorns rather than fruit, and in consequence, being chastened of God. Naturalists tell us that thorns are abortive branches, which if developed would bring forth leaves and fruit.

"And when the Lord saw that he turned aside to see, God called unto him out of the midst of the bush, and said, Moses, Moses. And he said, Here am I. And He said, Draw not nigh hither: put off thy shoes from off thy feet, for the place whereon thou standest is holy ground" (vv. 4, 5). How this helps to interpret for us the moral meaning of the "flame of fire"—the activities of Divine holiness. The Shekinah-glory which abode upon the mercy-seat over the ark was not only the evidence of Jehovah's presence in Israel's midst, but was the manifest emblem of His *holiness*—abiding in the Holy of Holies. It was in holiness God was about to deal both with the Egyptians and with His own people, and of this Moses needed to be instructed. He must put off the shoes of every day walk and life, and draw near in the spirit of true worship. Another important lesson is this for the servant of God today. Each laborer in the vineyard needs to keep constantly before him the fact that the One with whom he has to do, and whom he serves, is holy, thrice holy. A realization of this would check the lightness and levity of the flesh.

"Moreover He said, I am the God of thy father, the God of Abraham, the God of Isaac, and the God of Jacob. And Moses hid his face; for he was afraid to look upon God" (v. 6). Thus the Lord stood revealed before Moses as the covenant-keeping God, the God of all grace. When God picked up Abraham, Isaac and Jacob, and made them the fathers of His chosen people, it was not because of any excellence in them, seen or foreseen; rather was it His pure sovereign benignity. So, too, now that He is about to redeem the Hebrews from the land of bondage, it is not because of any good in them or from them. It is as the God of Abraham—the sovereign Elector; the God of Isaac—the almighty Quickener; the God of Jacob—the long-suffering One; who is about to bare His arm, display His power and deliver His people. And in this *same* threefold character does He act today. The God of Abraham is our God the One who sovereignly chose us in Christ before the foundation of the world. The God of Isaac is our God—the One who by His own miraculous power made us new creatures in Christ. The God of Jacob is our God—the One who bears with us in infinite patience, who never forsakes us, and

who has promised to perfect that which concerns us (Psa. 138:8).

"And the Lord said, I have surely seen the affliction of My people which are in Egypt, and have heard their cry by reason of their taskmasters; for I know their sorrows" (v. 7). Mark carefully the condition of these Hebrews: crushed by the cruel oppression of Egypt's slavery; groaning beneath the iron rod of Pharaoh. And how this pictures the condition of the natural man, the bond-slave of sin, the captive of the Devil. This is true not only of the slave of lust or the helpless victim of drugs, but of the moral and refined. They, too, are in bondage to gold, pleasure, ambition, and a dozen other things. The "affliction" which sin has brought is everywhere to be seen, not only in physical suffering, but in mental restlessness and heart discontent. The varied "lusts of the flesh" are just as merciless as the Egyptian taskmasters of old; and the "sorrows" of sin's slaves to-day just as acute as those of the Israelites midst the iron furnace of Egypt. What woe there really is behind the fair surface of society! How fearful the misery which has come on the whole race of man through sin! How great the need for the Saviour! How terrible the guilt of despising Him now that He has come!

"And the Lord said, I have surely *seen* the affliction of My people which are in Egypt, and have *heard* their cry by reason of their taskmasters; for I know their sorrows" (v. 7). The One speaking here is termed in the second verse "the Angel of the Lord". This we know from Mal. 3:1, and other scriptures, was Christ Himself, in theophanic manifestation. It is very helpful and instructive to trace Him as "the Angel of the Lord" all through the Old Testament. The first time He is thus brought before us is in Gen. 16:13: "And she called the name of the Lord (the "Angel of the Lord", see vv. 9, 10) that spake unto her, Thou God *seest* me: for she said, Have I also here looked after Him that *seeth* me?" The second occurrence is in Gen. 21:17 "And the Angel of God called to Hagar out of heaven, and said unto her, What aileth thee, Hagar? Fear not; for God hath *heard* the voice of the lad where he is". Thus, in the third reference here in Ex. 3, we have combined the "seeth" and "heard" which are the central things in the first two. Let the interested reader follow out the other references for himself. How blessed for us to know that there is One above who never slumbers nor sleeps, but "hears" and "sees" all *our* afflictions!

"For I know their sorrows" (v. 7). With this should be compared Ex. 2:23: "And it came to pass in process of time, that the king of Egypt died: and the children of Israel *sighed* by reason of the bondage, and they *cried*, and their cry came up unto God by reason of the bondage." The tenderness of the original is hidden by this rendering. The R. V. gives it: "And it came to pass in the course of *those many days*, that the king of Egypt died", etc. How these words throb with Divine compassion. There were between fourteen and fifteen thousand "days", during that forty years of Moses' sojourn in Midian; and each of them were days of anguish for them. But God had not ignored them, nor been indifferent to their hard lot—"I know their sorrows". How blessed for us, in times of stress and distress to remember that there is One above who takes notice. This was how Job consoled himself (see Job 23:10). The Call Moses received and his Responses thereto we r e s e r v e for separate consideration.

CHAPTER 5

MOSES CALLED AND HIS RESPONSE

EXODUS 3

In our last article we contemplated Moses in Midian and pondered the significance of God appearing to him in the burning bush. It was there he received his call and commission to act as Jehovah's favored instrument in delivering His people from their hard bondage. As Moses turned aside to behold the amazing sight of the bush burning and yet not being consumed, the voice of God addressed him. First, God reminded Moses of His holiness (v. 5). Next, He revealed Himself in covenant-relationship (v. 6). Then, He expressed His compassion (v. 7). Then He declared His purpose: "I am come down to deliver them out of the hand of the Egyptians", etc. (v. 8). Finally, He addressed Himself to His servant: "Come now therefore, and I will send thee unto Pharaoh, that thou mayest bring forth My people the children of Israel out of Egypt" (v. 10).

Ere considering Moses' Call, let us weigh what is recorded in verses 7 and 8: "And the Lord said, I have surely seen the affliction of My people which are in Egypt, and have heard their cry by reason of their taskmasters; for I know their sorrows; And I am come down to deliver them out of the hand of the Egyptians, and to bring them up out of that land unto a good land and a large, unto a land flowing with milk and honey". Notice the *completeness* of this statement. First, the Lord said, "I have surely *seen the affliction* of My people which are in Egypt". Second, "And have *heard their cry* by reason of their taskmasters". Third, "For I *know their sorrows*". Fourth, "And *I am come down to deliver them*". Fifth, "Out of the hand of the Egyptians". Sixth, "And to bring them up out of that land *unto a good land*", etc. Seventh, "Unto a good land and a large, unto *a land flowing with milk and honey*".

Second, observe the *definiteness* and *positiveness* of Jehovah's assertions. There were no "perhaps's" or "peradventure's". It was no mere invitation or offer that was made to Israel. Instead, it was the unconditional, emphatic declaration of what the Lord would do—"I am come down *to deliver*". So it is now. The Gospel goes forth on no uncertain errand. God' Word *shall not* return unto Him void, but "it *shall* accomplish that which He pleases, and it *shall* prosper in the thing whereunto He sends it" (Isa. 55:11).

Finally, admire the blessed *typical picture* here, a prophetic picture of the Divine Incarnation. First, the Divine compassion which *prompted* the unspeakable Gift: "I have surely seen the affliction of My people which are in Egypt"—God contemplated the wretched condition of sinners and their need of deliverance. Second, the *Incarnation itself*: "I am *come down*". Thus it was fifteen hundred years later, when Jehovah–Jesus left His Father's House on high and came down to these scenes of sin and suffering. Third, the *purpose* of the Incarnation: to "deliver" His people and "bring them up out of that land", which symbolizes the world. Fourth, the *beneficent design* of the Incarnation: to "bring them into a good land and large, unto a land flowing with milk and honey"—to bring us on to resurrection ground, where there would be everything to satisfy and rejoice the heart.

"Come *now* therefore, and I will send thee unto Pharaoh, that thou mayest bring forth My people the children of Israel out of Egypt" (Ex. 3:10). Notice the little word which we have placed in italics. God is not to be rushed: our business is not (irreverently) to seek to hurry God, rather is it to *wait on Him* and *for Him*. For

27

many long years had the groans and cries of the distressed Hebrews gone up; but the heavens were silent. Forty years previously, Moses had become impatient at the delay, and thought to take matters into his own hands, only to discover that the time for deliverance was not yet ripe. But "now". *Now* the four hundred years of servitude and affliction (Gen. 15:13) had run their ordained course. *Now* the hour for Divine intervention had struck. *Now* the time for Jehovah to deal with the haughty oppressor of His people had arrived. *Now* the children of Israel would be in a condition to appreciate the promised inheritance. The pleasant pastures of Goshen and the carnal attractions of Egypt had, no doubt, quelled all longings for Canaan, but *now* that their afflictions were fast becoming unbearable, the land flowing with milk and honey would be a pleasing prospect.

And now that the time for deliverance had arrived, what is the method of Divine procedure? A captive people is to be emancipated; a nation of slaves is to be liberated. What, then, is the first move toward this? Had God so chosen He could have sent forth His angels, and in a single night destroyed all the Egyptians. Had He so pleased He could have appeared before the Hebrews in person and brought them out of their house of bondage. But this was not His way. Instead, *He appointed a human ministry to effect a Divine salvation.* To Moses He said, "I will send *thee* . . . . . . that *thou* mayest bring forth My people . . . . out of Egypt". There is little need to apply this to ourselves. God's way then, is God's way now. Human instrumentality is the means He most commonly employs in bringing sinners from bondage to liberty, from death to life.

"Come now therefore, and *I will send* thee unto Pharaoh, that thou mayest bring forth *My people* the children of Israel out of Egypt" (v. 10). What, then, is the response of our patriarch? Surely he will bow in worship before the great I am at being thus so highly honored. Surely he will ask, in fullest submission, "Lord, *what* would'st Thou have me to do?" But how did Moses reply? "And Moses said unto God, Who am I, that I should go unto Pharaoh, and that I should bring forth the children of Israel out of Egypt?" (v. 11).

Moses at eighty was not so eager as at forty. Solitude had sobered him. Keeping sheep had tamed him. He saw difficulties in himself, in the people, and in his task. He had already tried once and failed, and now for long years he had been out of touch with his people. But while all this was true, it was *God* who now called him to this work, and *He* makes no mistakes.

"And Moses said unto God, Who am I, that I should go unto Pharaoh, and that I should bring forth the children of Israel out of Egypt?" (v. 11). This brings out a principle in connection with Divine service which is strikingly illustrated in Luke 9. In v. 57 we read, "And it came to pass, that, as they went in the way, a certain man said unto him, Lord, I will follow Thee whithersoever Thou goest". In response our Lord said, "Foxes have holes, and birds of the air have nests; but the Son of Man hath not where to lay His head". Then we read, "And He said unto another, Follow Me. But he said, Lord, suffer me first to go and bury my father. Jesus said unto Him, Let the dead bury their dead: but go thou and preach the kingdom of God. And another also said, Lord, I will follow Thee; but let me first go bid them farewell, which are at home at my house". The principle is this: When the will of man acts in self-appointed service, he does not feel the difficulties in the way; but when there is a true call from God these *are* felt. Thus it was with Moses. When he went forth in the energy of the flesh (Ex. 2:11, etc.) he was full of confidence in the success of his mission. This comes out clearly in Acts 7:25: "For he supposed his brethren would have understood how that God by his hand would deliver them: but they understood not". But now that he is called of God to this work he is very conscious of the difficulties in the way. The discipline of the "backside of the desert" had not been in vain. Shepherding had chastened him.

The Lord, therefore, graciously encourages him by promising to be with him and assuring him of the ultimate success of his mission. "And He said, Certainly I will be with thee; and this shall be a token unto thee, that I have sent thee: When thou hast brought forth the people out of Egypt, ye shall serve God upon this mountain" (v. 12). This was very comforting. God did not ask Moses to go forward alone: an all-mighty One would accompany him. And this is still the Divine promise to each Divinely-called servant. I doubt not that the apostles must have felt much like Moses when the risen Saviour commissioned them to go and preach the Gospel to every creature—Who am I that I should go? If so, their hearts were reassured with the same promise Moses received—"Lo I am with you alway". And fellow-worker, if the Lord has manifestly called *you* to some task for which you feel utterly insufficient, rest on this precious promise—"Certainly I will be with thee". This is a word that every one engaged in Christian service needs to take to heart. When we think of what is involved in bringing a soul out of darkness into light; when we encounter the fierce opposition of the devil; when we face the frowns and sneers of the world, little wonder that we hesitate, and ask, "Who is sufficient for these things?" But take courage faint-heart, and remember the unfailing promise, "Certainly I will be with thee".

"And Moses said unto God, Behold, when I come unto the children of Israel, and shall say unto them, The God of your fathers hath sent me unto you; and they shall say to me, What is His name? What shall I say unto them?" (v. 13). Let us not be too quick to condemn Moses here—the Lord did not! This was no small difficulty for Moses. No visible presence would accompany him. He was to go alone to the enslaved Hebrews and present himself as the Divinely-sent deliverer. He was to tell them that the God of their fathers had promised to free them. But, as we shall see later, this was not likely to make much impression upon a people who were, most of them at least, sunk in the idolatries of the Egyptians. He felt that they would quickly want to know, Who is this God? What is His character? Prove to us that He is worthy of our confidence. And does not a similar difficulty arise before us! We go forth to tell lost sinners of a God they have never seen. In His name we bid them trust. But cannot we anticipate the response—"Show us the Father, and it sufficeth us" is still, in substance, the demand of the doubting heart. Moses felt this difficulty; and so do we.

"And God said unto Moses, I AM THAT I AM: and He said, Thus shalt thou say unto the children of Israel, I AM hath sent me unto you" (v. 14). At first sight this may strike us as strange and mysterious, yet a little reflection should discover its profound suggestiveness to us. "I am" is the great Jehovistic name of God. Dr. Pentecost says, "It contains each tense of the verb 'to be', and might be translated, I was, I am, and I shall always continue to be". The principle contained in this word of Jehovah to Moses contains timely instruction for us. We are to go forth declaring the name and nature of God as He has been revealed. No attempts are to be made to prove His existence; no time should be wasted with men in efforts to reason about God. Our business is to *proclaim* the Being of God as He has revealed Himself in and through Jesus Christ. The "I am" of the burning bush now stands fully declared in the blessed Person of our Saviour who said, "*I am* the bread of life", "*I am* the good Shepherd", "*I am* the door". "*I am* the light of the world", "*I am* the way, the truth and the life", "*I am* the resurrection and the life", "*I am* the true vine". He is the eternal "I am"—"the Same, yesterday, and today, and forever".

"And God said unto Moses, I AM THAT I AM: and He said, Thus shalt thou say unto the children of Israel, I AM hath sent me unto you" (v. 14). There is a depth here which no finite mind can fathom. "I am that I am" announced that the great God is self-existent, beside whom there is none else. Without beginning, without ending, "from everlasting to everlasting" He *is* God. None but He can say "I am *that* I am"—always the same, eternally changeless. The apostle Paul could say "By the grace of God I am *what* I am" —what grace has made me, but he could not say "I am *that* I am".

"And God said moreover unto Moses, Thus shalt thou say unto the children of Israel, The Lord God of your fathers, the God of Abraham, the God of Isaac, and the God of Jacob, hath sent me unto you: this is My name forever, and this is My memorial unto all generations" (v. 15). This was most blessed. Here was indeed something which ought to win the hearts of the Hebrews when Moses repeated it to them. The God of Abraham, Isaac and Jacob, was the God of sovereign grace, who had singled out these men from the mass of fallen humanity, and made them His high favorites. The God of Abraham, Isaac and Jacob, was the God of unconditional promise, who had pledged to give to them and their seed the land of Canaan for their inheritance. The God of Abraham, Isaac and Jacob, was the covenant-keeping God; for with Abraham God entered into solemn covenant, and with Isaac and Jacob He confirmed it. Note, also, the *threefold* repetition of God—"*The God* of Abraham, *the God* of Isaac, and *the God* of Jacob". Was there not here something more than a hint of the Holy Trinity!

In the remaining verses of Ex. 3 we learn how God further re-assured His servant by declaring what should be the results of his mission (see vv. 16-22). And mark once more the positive terms used: "*I will* bring you up out of the affliction of Egypt . . . . And *they shall* hearken to thy voice . . . . *I am sure* that the king of Egypt will not let you go . . . . And *I will* smite Egypt with all My wonders . . . . and *I will* give this people favor in the sight of the Egyptians", etc. Everything is definitely determined. There is no possibility of the Divine purpose failing. There are no contingencies; no 'I will do my part, *if* you do yours'. The Lord has sworn, "My counsel shall stand, and I will do *all* My pleasure" (Isa. 46:10). Let this be the ground of our confidence. Though all the powers of evil array themselves against us, whatever *God* hath called us to do will issue precisely as He has appointed. It is true that these promises of God to Moses were not made good in a day. It is true that there was much in the sequel to severely test the faith of Moses, ere the children of Israel *were* delivered from Egypt. And it is also true that with two exceptions the six hundred thousand men who left Egypt perished in the wilderness, and thus Moses died *without seeing* the complete fulfillment of Israel's actually reaching the land flowing with milk and honey—for God's promises were made to Israel *as a nation,* not to any particular generation of that nation. Nevertheless, in the end, every word of Jehovah was made good. So, too, God may commission us to a work for Him, and we may die before the determined issue appears; but notwithstanding, the Divine purpose *will be* realized.

"And they shall hearken to thy voice: and thou shalt come, thou and the elders of Israel, unto the king of Egypt, and ye shall say unto him, The Lord God of the Hebrews hath met with us: and now let us go, we beseech thee, three days' journey into the wilderness, that we may sacrifice to the Lord our God. And I am sure that the king of Egypt will not let you go, no, not by a mighty hand" (vv. 18, 19). This presented another test to Moses' faith. Had he stopped to reason about the commission God was giving him, it probably would have appeared foolishness to him. Here was he ordered to go, accompanied by the elders of Israel, unto Pharaoh, and present to Him the message of Jehovah. He was to request that the Hebrews should be allowed to go a three days' journey into the wilderness that they might worship God. And, yet, before he starts Jehovah assures him, "I am *sure* that the king of Egypt *will not* let you go". He might have asked, What, then, is the use of me wasting my breath on him? But it is not for the servant to question his master's orders: it is for him to obey. But not yet was Moses ready to respond to God's call.

"And Moses answered and said, But, behold, they will not believe me, nor hearken unto my voice: for they will say, The Lord hath not appeared unto thee" (4:1). Were it not that we were acquainted in some measure with our own desperately-wicked hearts, it would appear to us well-nigh unthinkable that Moses should continue objecting and cavilling. But the remembrance of our own repeated and humiliating failures only serves to show how sadly true to life is the picture here presented before us. The Lord had favored His servant with the awe-inspiring sight of the burning bush, He had spoken of His tender solicitude for the afflicted Hebrews, He had promised to be with Moses, He had expressly declared that He would deliver Israel from Egypt and bring them into Canaan. And yet all of this is not sufficient to silence unbelief and subdue the rebellious will. Alas! what is man that the Almighty should be mindful of him! Nothing but Divine power working within us can ever bring the human heart to abandon all creature props and trust in God.

"And Moses answered and said, But, behold, they will not believe me, nor hearken unto my voice". Awful presumption was this. The Lord had emphatically declared, "They *shall* hearken to thy voice" (3:18), and now Moses replies, They *will not.* Here was the servant daring to contradict his Lord to His face. Fearfully solemn is this; the more so, when we remember that *we* are made of precisely the same material that Moses was. There is in us the same evil, unbelieving, rebellious heart, and our only safeguard is to cast ourselves in the dust before God, beseeching Him to pity our helplessness and to keep down, subdue, overcome, the desperate and incurable wickedness which indwells us.

How what has been before us repudiates the modern sophistry that God only uses those who are fully consecrated to Him! How often Arminian teachers insist that the measure of our faith and faithfulness will determine the measure of our success in the Lord's service. It is true that every servant of Christ *ought* to be "a vessel unto honor, sanctified, and *meet* for the Master's use" (2 Tim. 2:21), nevertheless, God is *not limited* by our failure at this point, and clearly does this come out in the passage before us. Moses was timid, hesitant, fearful, unbelieving, *and yet God used him!* Nor does he stand by any means alone in this respect. God used the mercenary Balaam to give one of the most re-

markable prophecies to be found in the Old Testament. He used a Samson to deliver Israel from the Philistines. He used a Judas in the apostolate. If God were to wait until He found a human instrument that was *worthy* or *fit* to be used by *Him*, He would go on waiting until the end of time. God is sovereign in this, as in everything. The truth is that God uses whom He pleases.

Not yet was Moses ready to respond to Jehovah's Call. There were other difficulties which the fertile mind of unbelief was ready to suggest, but one by one Divine power and long-sufferance overcame them. Let us take this lesson throughly to heart, and seek that grace which will enable us to place God between us and our difficulties, instead of putting difficulties between God and us. In our next paper we shall dwell upon the three "signs" which God gave to Moses; let the interested reader give these much prayerful meditation as he studies Ex. 4, and thus be prepared to test our exposition.

CHAPTER 6

THE SIGNIFICANCE OF THE SIGNS

EXODUS 4

In our last lesson we dwelt upon the response which Moses made to the call he received from God. After forty years in the backside of the desert he was visited by the Lord, who declared that it was His purpose to send him unto Pharaoh (3:16). Instead of bowing in wonderment and gratitude at the condescension of the Almighty in deigning to employ him in so important and honorous an errand, he answered, "Who am *I*, that I should go unto Pharaoh?". In response to this God assured Moses that *He* would be with him. Moses next enquired in whose name he should address Israel, and then it was that God revealed Himself as the great "I am", the God of Abraham, the God of Isaac, and the God of Jacob. The Lord promised that He would deliver His people from the affliction of Egypt and bring them unto the land of Canaan, and bade His servant appear before Pharaoh with the demand that the king allow the Hebrews to go a three days' journey into the wilderness that they might hold a feast unto the Lord their God. But the Lord informed Moses He was sure that Pharaoh would not grant this request, yet, notwithstanding, He would show forth such wonders that in the end the king *would* let them go; and not only so, but that He would give His people favor in the eyes of the Egyptians so that they would be enriched and go not out empty-handed. Yet notwithstanding these gracious re-assurances Moses continued to be occupied with difficulties and to raise objections: "Behold, they will not believe me, nor hearken unto my voice; for they will say, The Lord hath not appeared unto thee" (4: 1). Our present lesson resumes the sacred narrative at this point.

In response to the third difficulty raised by Moses, the Lord endued His recalcitrant servant with the power to perform three wonders or signs, which were to be wrought before his fellow-countrymen for the purpose of convincing them that Moses was Jehovah's accredited ambassador. That there is a deep meaning to these three signs, and that they were designed to teach important lessons both to Moses, to Israel, and to us, goes without saying. At the beginning of Israel's history it was God's method to teach more by signs and symbols, than by formal and explicit instruction. The fact, too, that these three signs are the *first* recorded in Scripture denotes that they are of prime importance and worthy of our most careful study.

"And the Lord said unto him, What is that in thine hand? And he said, A rod. And He said, Cast it on the ground. And he cast it on the ground, and it became a serpent; and Moses fled from before it. And the Lord said unto Moses, Put forth thine hand, and take it by the tail. And he put forth his hand, and caught it, and it became a rod in his hands: That they may believe that the Lord God of their fathers, the God of Abraham, the God of Isaac, and the God of Jacob hath appeared unto thee" (Ex. 4:2-5). The first of these signs was the turning of the rod into a serpent, and that back again into a rod. But three verses are devoted to the description of this wonder, but marvellously full are they in their spiritual suggestiveness and hidden riches. We purpose to study this miracle from seven different angles, considering in turn: its practical lessons, its doctrinal meaning, its evidential value, its evangelical message, its historical significance, its dispensational forecast, and its typical purport. May the Lord give us eyes to see and ears to hear.

(1) There can be no doubt that the first design of God in connection with this sign was to teach Moses himself *a practical les-*

son. What this was it is not difficult to discover. The sign had to do with the rod in his hand. This rod or staff (as the Hebrew word is sometimes translated) was his *support*. It was that which gave him aid as he walked, it was that on which he leaned when weary, it was a means of defence in times of danger. Now in the light of Psa. 23:4 we learn that, spiritually considered, the "rod" speaks of the upholding, strengthening, protecting *grace of God*. Here, then, is the first lesson the Lord would teach His servant: while Moses continued dependent *(supporting* himself) on God, all would be well; but let him cast his "rod" to the ground, that is, let him renounce God's grace, let him cast away his confidence in Jehovah, let him attempt to stand alone, and he would at once find himself helpless before that old Serpent, the Devil. Here, then, we say, was the great practical lesson for Moses, and for us: the secret of overcoming Satan lies in *leaning* in simple dependency and conscious weakness on our "staff", i. e., the power of God!

(2) But this first sign was also designed to teach Moses, and us, a great *doctrinal* lesson, a doctrine which as the priority of this sign suggests is one of *fundamental* importance. Nor are we left to guess at what this may be. Just as the twenty-third Psalm enables us to interpret its practical meaning, so the second Psalm supplies the key to its doctrinal significance.

In Psa. 2:9 (cf Rev. 2:27) we learn that during the Millennium the Lord Jesus will rule the nations with a *rod* of iron. The "rod", then, speaks of *governmental power*. But what is signified by the "casting down" of the rod *to the ground?* Surely it speaks of God *delegating* governmental power to the rulers *of earth*. And what has been the uniform history of man's use of this delegated power? The answer is, Exactly what the "serpent" suggests: it has been employed in the service of Satan! Thus it proved with Adam, when his Maker gave him "dominion" over all things terrestrial. Thus it proved with the nation of Israel after they became the conquerors of Canaan. So, too, with Nebuchadnezzar, after earthly sovereignty was transferred from Jerusalem to Babylon. And so it has continued all through the Times of the Gentiles. But it is blessed to note that the "serpent" no more succeeded in *getting away* from Moses than the rod had *slipped*

out of his hand. Moses—as God's *representative* before Israel—took the "serpent" by the tail (the time for its head to be "bruised" had not yet come) and it was transformed into a "rod" in his hand again. This tells us that Satan is no 'free agent' in the popular acceptation of that term, but is completely under God's control, to be used by Him in fulfillment of His inscrutable counsels as He sees fit. Thus would Jehovah assure His servant at the outset that the enemy who would rage against him was unable to withstand him!

(3) This sign was to be wrought by Moses before the Hebrews as a proof that God had called and endowed him to be their deliverer. The *evidential value* of this wonder is easily perceived. To see the rod of Moses become a serpent before their eyes would at once evidence that he was endowed with supernatural power. To take that serpent by the tail and transform it again to a rod, would prove that Moses had not performed this miracle by the help of Satan. Moses was to show that he was able to deal with the serpent at his pleasure, making the rod a serpent, and the serpent a rod as he saw fit. Thus in performing a wonder that altogether transcended the skill of man, and a wonder that plainly was not wrought by the aid of the Devil, he demonstrated that he was commissioned and empowered by God.

(4) This sign which Moses wrought before the children of Israel also carried an *evangelical message,* though perhaps this is more difficult to discern than the other meanings it possessed. The rod cast to the ground became a "serpent", and we are told "Moses *fled* from before it". Clearly this speaks of the helplessness of man to cope with Satan. The sinner is completely under the Devil's power, "taken captive by him at his will" (2 Tim. 2:26). Such was the condition of Israel at this time. They were subject to a bondage far worse and more serious than any that the Egyptians could impose upon them, and what is more, they were as unable to free themselves from the one as from the other. Nothing but Divine power could emancipate them, and this is just what this sign was fitted to teach them. Moreover, this power was placed in the hands of a *mediator*—Moses, the one who stood between Israel and God. He, and he only, was qualified to deliver from the serpent. His power over the serpent was manifested by taking it by the tail

and reducing it to nothing—it disappeared when it became a rod again. Beautifully does this speak to us of the Lord Jesus, the One Mediator between God and men, of whom Moses was a type. In Him is your only hope, dear reader; He alone can deliver you from the power of that old Serpent, the Devil.

(5) Let us consider next the *historical significance* of this wonder. The "sign" itself consisted of three things: a rod held in the hand of Moses (God's representative), the rod thrown down to the ground and becoming a serpent, the serpent transformed into a rod again. These three things accurately symbolized *the early history of Israel*. From the Call of Abraham to the going down of his descendants into Egypt, Israel had been held (miraculously supported) in the hand of God, until, in the person of Joseph, they had attained to the position of *rule* over Egypt. But then a king arose who "knew not Joseph", and the Hebrews were then "cast down to the ground"—humiliated by severe and cruel bondage, until at the time of Moses it seemed as though they were completely at the mercy of Satan. But the time for deliverance had now drawn nigh, and the Lord assures them by means of this "sign" that they should remain in the place of oppression no longer, but would be delivered. And not only so, the last part of the sign gave promise that they should be raised to the place of rulership again. This was realized when they reached the promised land and subjugated the Canaanites. Thus the sign prefigured the three great stages in the early history of Israel.

(6) But this sign also provided a *dispensational forecast*. Not only did it accurately prefigure the *early* history of Israel, but it also anticipated in a most striking way the whole of their *future* history. The rod held in the hand contemplated them in the position of authority in Canaan. This portion Judah (the *ruling* Tribe) retained till Shiloh came. But following their rejection of Christ the "rod" was cast down to the ground, and for nineteen centuries Israel have been the prey and sport of the Serpent. But not forever are they to continue thus. The time is coming when Israel shall be raised out of the dust of degradation and, in the hand of a greater than Moses, shall be made the head of the nations (Deut. 28:13). Thus did this mar-

vellous sign prefigure both the past and the future fortunes of the Chosen Nation.

(7) Deeper still lies the *typical purport* of this sign. We believe that its ultimate reference was to Christ Himself, and that the great mysteries of the Divine Incarnation and Atonement were foreshadowed. In Psa. 110:2 the Lord Jesus is called the *Rod* of God: "The Lord shall send the Rod (it is the same Hebrew word as here in Ex. 4) of Thy strength out of Zion: rule Thou in the midst of Thine enemies". The reference in Psa. 110 is to the second advent of Christ when His governmental authority and power shall be fully displayed. But when He was on earth the first time, it was in weakness and humiliation, and to this the casting-down of the "rod" on the ground points. But, it will be objected, surely there is no possible sense in which the Rod became a "serpent"! Yes there was, and none other than the Lord Jesus is our authority for such a statement. The "serpent" is inseparably connected with the Curse (Gen. 3), and on the Cross Christ was "made a curse" for His people (Gal. 3: 10-13). Said He to Nicodemus, "*As* Moses lifted up *the serpent* in the wilderness, *even so* must the Son of Man be lifted up" (John 3:14). But blessed be God that is all past: the Lord Jesus (the Rod) is now exalted to God's right *hand*, and soon will He take to Himself His power and reign over the earth. Marvellously full then was the meaning of this first sign. Equally striking was the second, though we cannot now treat of it at the same length.

"And the Lord said furthermore unto him, Put now thine hand into thy bosom. And he put his hand into his bosom: and when he took it out, behold, his hand was leprous as snow. And he said, Put thine hand into thy bosom again. And he put his hand into his bosom again; and plucked it out of his bosom, and behold, it was turned again as his other flesh. And it shall come to pass, if they will not believe thee, neither hearken to the voice of the first sign, that they will believe the voice of the latter sign" (vv. 6-8). The significance of this second sign is not difficult to discern. "Leprosy" is the well-known emblem of sin —its loathsomeness, its contagiousness, the terrible rapidity with which it spreads, its insidious nature (commencing with a seemingly harmless spot), and its incurability so far as the wisdom of man is concerned, all witness to the accuracy of the figure. Lev. 13 and 14 are the two chapters of the Bible where leprosy is treated of at greatest length. Here in the passage before us we read that Moses put his hand into his bosom—the abode of the heart—and when he drew it forth, behold, it was leprous. In response to God's command he replaced his hand in his bosom, and on plucking it thence the leprosy had disappeared. This second "sign" also admits of various applications.

(1) The sign of the leprous hand was, no doubt, designed first for the instruction of Moses. It was intended to teach him the marvelous *power* of his Lord: that he should be thus smitten instantaneously with leprosy, that it should be confined to his hand, and that it should be cured immediately, without the use of means, was an astounding wonder. It manifested the perfect ease with which God could suddenly inflict such a disease and as quickly cure it: and this evidenced how simple a matter it was for Him to deliver His people out of the hand of the Egyptians.

(2) The "hand" speaks of energy: it is the instrument for work. Moses was God's instrument for doing a wonderful work in Egypt. But the Lord here shows him that *the flesh is set aside;* it is not the energy of the natural man which is the mainspring of action in God's service. How can it be, when the flesh is corrupt and under God's curse?—here symbolized by the hand becoming leprous. By nature, man's "hand" is *unfit* to be used by God. But Divine grace interposes in cleansing power, and that which is weak becomes strong; yet in such a way that what, under God, is now accomplished by that hand is manifestly because of the Lord's power.

(3) But the principal effect which this sign was calculated to have on Moses himself was a *humbling* one. Lest he become puffed up by the power of the rod, he is forcibly reminded of the sink of iniquity, the corrupt heart, within him. Therefore whatever Jehovah was pleased to accomplish by him must be attributed alone to sovereign grace.

(4) Moses is also to be viewed here as *the representative of the Hebrews,* for he was one of them, and what was here enacted before his eyes, vividly portrayed the condition of his people. In themselves they differed nothing from the Egyptians. They too were defiled and needed cleansing. No mere outward reformation would avail, for the seat of the trouble lay within their bosoms. Strikingly accurate were the details of this sign. It was not the hand which affected the heart, but the heart which affected the hand! How this disposes of an error which has been popular in every age. How often we hear it said that such an one may be weak and wayward, but he has *a good heart.* Not so: "Out of the heart", said the One who alone knew it, "proceed evil thoughts, murders, adulteries, fornications, thefts, false witness, blasphemies". So too, cleansing must begin with the heart—here signified by the leprous hand being thrust into the bosom before the loathsome disease was removed. And how is this brought about? By the power of God. True, from the Divine side; but what of the human? The answer is at once to hand. The leprous heart symbolizes sin hidden, the leprous hand, sin exposed (F. W. G.) It was the hand plucked out of the bosom which made manifest what was within! And it is precisely this which God demands from the sinner. What is so hateful to Him and so fatal to us, is for the sinner to *deny* his ruined and lost condition. Whilever man seeks to conceal the iniquity within, whilever he **disguises** himself and pretends to be other than a guilty, undone sinner, there is no hope for him. Seeking to *hide* their shame was one of the first acts of Adam and Eve after their fall. All the false religions of human devising have the same object in view. But to come out into the light, to own our lost condition, to confess our sins, is the first essential (from the human side) in salvation. *This* is evangelical repentance.

(5) Once more we are shown a solemn foreshadowing of that which was vital and central in the great work of Redemption. Moses here prefigures the great Deliverer of God's people. First, Moses is seen as whole, then as leprous, then whole again. Precisely such is the view which Scripture gives us of the Saviour. Ineffably holy in Himself: He had no sin (Heb. 4:15), did no sin (1 Pet. 2:22), knew no sin (2 Cor. 5:21). But in infinite grace He took our place—all praise to His peerless name—and "was made sin for us" (2 Cor. 5:21). "He bare our sins in His own body on the tree" (1 Pet. 2:24). Because of this He was, at that time, in the sight of God what the lep-

er was—defiled, unclean; not inherently so, but by imputation. The leper's place was *outside* the Camp (Lev. 13:46), *away from* where God dwelt. And on the Cross Christ was separated for three terrible hours from the holy God. But after the awful penalty of sin had been endured and the work of atonement was *finished,* the Forsaken One is seen again in communion with God— *"Father* into *Thy* hands I commit My spirit" evidences that. And it was as "the *Holy One"* (Psa. 16:10) He was laid in the sepulchre. Thus, after Moses thrust his leprous hand into his bosom, he drew it forth again perfectly whole—every trace of defilement gone. In their foreshadowings of Christ, then, the first sign intimated that the great Deliverer would "destroy the works of the Devil" (1 John 3:8), while the second signified that He would "take away our sins" (1 John 3:5).

"And it shall come to pass, if they will not believe also these two signs, neither hearken unto thy voice, that thou shalt take of the water of the river, and pour it upon the dry land: and the water which thou takest out of the river shall become blood upon the dry land" (v. 9). Upon this verse Dr. Urquhart has some helpful comments: "The Nile was Egypt's life. Its waters, in the annual inundation, pouring over its banks and spreading the fertilizing mud over the ground, prepared the way for the harvest. But the sign shows that God could turn that blessing into a fearful scourge. Instead of life he might make the river bring forth death: instead of fruitfulness, corruption. The unusual form (in the Heb.) 'shall be and shall be', conveys the strong and solemn assurance that this means of blessing shall certainly be turned into a vehicle of judgment—a threatening which was afterwards fulfilled in the first two plagues".

"And it shall come to pass, if they will not believe also these two signs, neither hearken unto thy voice, that thou shalt take of the water of the river, and pour it upon the dry land: and the water which thou takest out of the river shall become blood upon the dry land" (v. 9). This third "sign" is unspeakably solemn. Its position in the series supplies the key to its interpretation. This third sign was to be wrought only if the testimony of the first two was refused. It therefore tells of the *consequences* of refusing to believe what the other signs so plainly bore witness to. If man rejects the testimony of God's Word that he is under the dominion of Satan and is depraved by nature, and refuses the One who alone can deliver from the one and cleanse from the other, nothing but Divine judgment awaits him. The water turned into blood speaks of life giving place to death. It anticipates "the second death", that eternal death, "The Lake of Fire", which awaits every Christ rejector. Be warned then, unsaved reader, and flee to Christ for refuge ere the storm of Divine wrath overtakes thee. "Believe on the Lord Jesus Christ and thou shalt be saved".

CHAPTER 7

LESSONS IN SERVICE

EXODUS 4

Our present lesson deals with the concluding stage of the Lord's interview with Moses, and of the deliverer starting forth on his mighty errand. It is important to note that Moses was the *first* man that was ever formally called of God to engage in His *service,* and like the first notice of anything in Scripture this hints at all that is fundamental in connection with the subject. First, we are shown that no *training* of the natural man is of any avail in the work of God. Neither the wisdom of Egypt, in which Moses was thoroughly skilled, nor the solitude of the desert, had fitted Moses for spiritual activities. Forty years had been spent in Egypt's court, and another forty years in Midian's sheepfolds; yet, when the Lord appeared to him, Moses was full of unbelief and selfwill. How this shows that the quietude of monastic life is as impotent to destroy the enmity of the carnal mind as is the culture of high society or the instruction of the schools. It is true that Moses had been much sobered by his lengthy sojourn at "the backside of the desert", but in faith, in courage, in the spirit of obedience, he was greatly deficient—grace, not nature, must supply these.

In the second place, we are shown how the Lord *prepared* His servant. God dealt personally and directly with the one He was going to honor as His ambassador: there was a manifestation of His holiness, the avowal of His covenant-relationship, an assurance of His compassion for the suffering Hebrews, and the declaration of His self-sufficiency as the great "I am"; in short, there was a full revelation of His person and character. In addition, Moses received a definite call from Jehovah, the guarantee that God would be with him, an intimation of the difficulties that lay before him, and the promise that, in the end, God's purpose should be realized. These have

ever been, and still are, the vital prerequisites for effectiveness in God's service. There must be a personal knowledge of God for ourselves: a knowledge obtained by direct revelation of God to the soul. There must be a definite call from God to warrant us engaging in His service. There must be a recognition of the difficulties confronting us and a confident resting on God's promise for ultimate success.

In the third place, the Lord *endowed* His servant for the work before him. This endowment was the bestowal upon him of power to work three miracles. The first two of these were designed to teach important lessons to God's servant: he was shown the secret of overcoming Satan, and he was reminded of the corruption of his own heart—things of vital moment for every servant to understand. Moreover, these miracles or signs had a voice for the Hebrews: they showed them their *need* of being delivered from the dominion of the Devil and the pollution of sin—things which every servant must continue pressing on those to whom he ministers. The third miracle or sign spoke of the *judgment* awaiting those who received not God's testimonies—another thing which the faithful servant must not shun to declare.

In the fourth place, we are made acquainted with the *response* which Moses made to God's call. Here again we have something more than what is local and transient. The difficulties felt by Moses and the objections which he raised are those which have, in principle and essence, been felt and raised by all of God's servants at some time or other—the perfect Servant alone excepted. If they have not been expressed by lip, they have had a place in the heart. The first three objections of Moses we have noticed in previous papers: they may be summed up as: self-occupation (3:11), fear (3:13), unbelief (4:1). The fourth, which savored of *pride,* will now engage our attention.

"And Moses said unto the Lord, O my Lord, I am not eloquent, neither heretofore, nor since Thou hast spoken unto Thy servant: but I am slow of speech, and of a slow tongue" (4:10). How many of the Lord's servants (and others who ought to be engaged in His service) regard this as a fatal defect. They suppose that the gift of oratory is a prime pre-requisite for effective ministry. Those who are being "trained for the ministry" must, forsooth, have a course in rhetoric and elocution: as though men dead in sins can be quickened by the enticing words of men's wisdom; as though carnal weapons could have a place in spiritual warfare. Sad it is that such elementary matters are so little understood in this twentieth century. Have we forgotten those words of the apostle Paul, "And I, brethren, when I came to you, *came not* with excellency of speech or of wisdom, declaring unto you the testimony of God" (1 Cor. 2:1)!

"And the Lord said unto him, Who hath made man's mouth? or who maketh the dumb, or deaf, or the seeing, or the blind? Have not I the Lord?" (v. 11). This was manifestly a rebuke. Even though he was not "eloquent", did Moses suppose that the Lord knew not what He was about in selecting *him* to act as His mouthpiece in Pharaoh's court? God was only demonstrating once more how radically different are His ways from man's. The wisdom of this world is foolishness with God (1 Cor. 3:19), and that which is highly esteemed among men, is abomination in His sight (Luke 16:15). The instrument through whom God did the most for Israel, and the one He used in bringing the greatest blessing to the Gentiles, was each unqualified when judged by the standards of human scholarship!—see 2 Cor. 10:1 and 11:6 for the apostle Paul as a speaker.

"And the Lord said unto him, Who hath made man's mouth? or who maketh the dumb, or deaf, or the seeing, or the blind? Have not I the Lord?". It seems evident from this that, in the previous verse, Moses was referring to some impediment in his speech. In reply, the Lord tells him that *He* was responsible for that. The force of what Jehovah said here seems to be this: As all the physical senses, and the perfection of them, are from the Creator, so are

the imperfections of them according to His sovereign pleasure. Behind the law of heredity is the Law-giver, regulating it as He deems best.

"Now therefore go, and I will be with thy mouth, and teach thee what thou shalt say" (v. 12). What a re-assuring word was this! Better far, infinitely better, is the teaching of the Lord and *His* control of the tongue than any gift of "eloquence" or any of the artificialities of speech which human training can bestow. It is just these substitutes of human art which has degraded too many of our pulpits from places where should be heard the simple exposition of God's Word into stages on which men display their oratorical abilities. Little room for wonder that God's blessing has long since departed from the vast majority of our pulpits when we stop to examine the "training" which the men who occupy them have received. All the schooling in the world is of no avail whatever unless the Lord is "with the mouth" of the preacher, teaching him *what* he shall say; and if the Lord *is* with him, then, "eloquence" and rhetorical devices are needless and useless. Note it is *"what"* the preacher has to say, not *how* he says it, which matters most. God has used the simple language of unlettered Bunyan far more than He has the polished writings of thousands of University graduates!

"And he said, O my Lord, send, I pray Thee, by the hand of him whom Thou wilt send" (v. 13). That is, Send any one, but not me! Moses was still unwilling to act as the Lord's ambassador, in fact he now asked God to select another in his place. How fearful are the lengths to which the desperately-wicked heart of man may go! Not only distrustful, but rebellious. The faithfulness of Moses in recording his own sins, and the "anger" of the Lord against him, is a striking proof of the Divine veracity of the Scriptures: an un-inspired writer would have omitted such serious reflections upon himself as these.

"And he said, O my Lord, send, I pray Thee, by the hand of him whom Thou wilt send. And the anger of the Lord was kindled against Moses, and He said, Is not Aaron the Levite thy brother? I know that he can speak well. And also, behold, he cometh forth to meet thee: and when he seeth thee, he will be glad in his heart. And thou shalt speak unto him, and put words in his mouth: and I will be with thy mouth, and with his mouth, and will teach you what ye shall do. And he shall be thy spokesman unto the people: and he shall be, even he shall be to thee instead of a mouth, and thou shalt be to him instead of God. And thou shalt take this rod in thine hand, wherewith thou shalt do signs" (vv. 13-17). "Although there was nothing gained in the way of power, although there was no more virtue or efficacy in one mouth than in another, although it was Moses after all who was to speak unto Aaron, yet was Moses quite ready to go when assured of the presence and co-operation of a poor feeble mortal like himself; whereas he could not go when assured, again and again, that Jehovah would be with him.

"Oh! my reader, does not all this hold up before us a faithful mirror in which you and I can see our hearts reflected? Truly it does. We are more ready to trust anything than the living God. We move along with bold decision when we possess the countenance and support of a poor frail mortal like ourselves; but we falter, hesitate, and demur when we have the light of the Master's countenance to cheer us, and the strength of His omnipotent arm to support us. This should humble us deeply before the Lord, and lead us to seek a fuller acquaintance with Him, so that we might trust Him with a more unmixed confidence, and walk on with a firmer step, as having Him *alone* for our resource and portion" (C.H.M.).

Though God's anger was kindled against Moses, His wrath was tempered by mercy. To strengthen his weak faith, the Lord grants him still another sign that He would give him success. As Moses returned to Egypt he would find Aaron coming forth to meet him. What an illustration is this that when God works, He works at *both* ends of the line! The eunuch and Philip, Saul and Ananias, Cornelius and Peter supply us with further illustrations of the same principle.

"And Moses went and returned to Jethro his father in law, and said unto him, Let me go, I pray thee, and return unto my brethren which are in Egypt, and see whether they be yet alive. And Jethro said to Moses, Go in peace" (v. 18). This act of Moses was very commendable. Jethro had taken him in while a fugitive from Egypt, had given him his daughter to wife,

and had provided him with a home for forty years. Moreover, Moses had charge of his flock (3:1). It would, then, have been grossly discourteous and the height of ingratitude had Moses gone down to Egypt without first notifying his father-in-law. This request of Moses manifested his thoughtfulness of others, and his appreciation of favors received. Let writer and reader take this to heart. Spiritual activities never absolve us from the common amenities and responsibilities of life. No believer who is not a gentleman or a lady is a true Christian in the full sense of the word. To be a Christian is to practise Christliness, and Christ ever thought *of others*.

"And Moses went and returned to Jethro his father in law, and said unto him, Let me go, I pray thee, and return unto my brethren which are in Egypt, and see whether they be yet alive". We are sorry that we cannot speak so favorably of Moses' words on this occasion. His utterance here was quite Jacob-like. Moses says nothing about the Lord's appearing to him, of the communication he had received, nor of the positive assurance from God that He would bring His people out of Egypt into Canaan. Evidently Moses was yet far from being convinced. This is clear from the next verse: "And the Lord said unto Moses in Midian, Go, return into Egypt: *for* all the men are dead which sought thy life". The Lord repeated His command, and at the same time graciously removed the fears of His servant that he was venturing himself into that very peril from which he had fled forty years before. How long-suffering and compassionate is our God!

"And Moses took his wife and his sons, and set them upon an ass, and he returned to the land of Egypt: and Moses took the rod of God in his hand . . . . and it came to pass by the way in the inn, that the Lord met him, and sought to kill him" (vv. 20, 24). At last Moses starts out on his epochmaking mission. In obedience to God's command he goes forth rod in hand, and accompanied by his wife and his sons, returns to the land of Egypt. But one other thing needed to be attended to, an important matter long neglected, before he is ready to act as God's ambassador. Jehovah was about to fulfill His covenant engagement to Abraham, but the sign of that covenant was circumcision, and this the son of Moses had not received, apparently because of the objections of the mother. Such an ignoring of the Divine requirements could not be passed by, and Moses is forcibly reminded anew of the holiness of the One with whom he had to do.

"And it came to pass by the way in the inn, that the Lord met him, and sought to kill him. Then Zipporah took a sharp stone, and cut off the foreskin of her son, and cast it at his feet, and said, Surely a bloody husband art thou to me. So He let him go: then she said, A bloody husband thou art, because of the circumcision" (vv. 24-26). Whether it was the Lord Himself in theophanic manifestation who now appeared to Moses, or whether it was an angel of the Lord with sword in hand, as he later stood before Balaam, we are not told. Nor do we know in what way the Lord sought to kill Moses. It seems clear that he was stricken down and rendered helpless, for his wife was the one who performed the act of circumcision on their son. This is all the more striking because the inference seems unescapeable that Zipporah was the one who had resisted the ordinance of God—only thus can we explain her words to Moses, and only thus can we account for Moses here sending her back to her father (cf 18:2). Nevertheless, it was Moses, the *head* of the house (the one God ever holds primarily responsible for the training and conduct of the children), and not Zipporah, whom the Lord sought to kill. This points a most solemn warning to Christian fathers today. A man may be united to a woman who opposes him at every step as he desires to maintain a scriptural discipline in his home, but this does not absolve him from doing his duty.

Let us also observe how the above incident teaches us another most important lesson in connection with *service*. Before God suffered Moses to go and minister to Israel, He first required him to set his own house in order. Not until this had been attended to was Moses qualified for his mission. There must be faithfulness in the sphere of his own responsibility before God would make him the channel of Divine power. As another has said, "Obedience at home must precede the display of power to the world". That this same principle obtains during the Christian dispensation is clear from 1 Tim. 3, where we are told that among the various qualifications of a "bishop" (elder) is that he must be "one that ruleth his own house well, having his children in subjection with all gravity" (v. 14). As a general rule God refuses to use in public ministry one who is lax and lawless in his own home.

"And the Lord said to Aaron, Go into the wilderness to meet Moses. And he went, and met him in the mount of God, and kissed him. And Moses told Aaron all the words of the Lord who had sent him, and all the signs which He had commanded him" (vv. 27, 28). This is another example of how when God works, He works at *both* ends of the line: Moses was advancing toward Egypt, Aaron is sent to *meet* him. By comparing this verse with what is said in v. 14 it seems clear that the Lord had ordered Aaron to go into the wilderness *before* Moses actually started out for Egypt, for there we find Him saying to Moses, "Behold, he (Aaron) *cometh* forth to meet thee". What an encouragement was this for Moses. Ofttimes the Lord in His tenderness gives such encouragements to His servants, especially in their earlier days; thus did He to Eliezer (Gen. 24:14, 18, 19); to Joseph (Gen. 37:7, 8); to the disciples (Mark 14:13); to Paul (Acts 9:11, 12); to Peter (Acts 10:17).

It is a point of interest and importance to note the *meeting-place* of these brothers: it was "in the mount of God". There it was that Jehovah had first appeared to Moses (3:1), and from it Moses and Aaron now set forth on their momentuous errand. The "mount" speaks, of course, of *elevation*, elevation of spirit through communion with the Most High. An essential prerequisite is this for all effective ministry. It is only as the servant has been in "the mount" with God that he is ready to go forth and represent Him in the plains! Again and again was this illustrated in the life of the perfect Servant. Turn to the four Gospels, and note how frequently we are told there of Christ retiring to "the mount", from which He came forth later to minister to the needy. This is indeed a lesson which every servant needs to learn. I must first commune *with* God, before I am fitted to work *for* Him. Note this order in Mark 3:14 in connection with the apostles: "He ordained twelve that they should be *with* Him, *and* that He might send them forth to preach"!

"And Moses and Aaron went and gathered together all the elders of the children of Israel: And Aaron spake all the words which the Lord had spoken unto Moses, and did the signs in the sight of the people. And the people believed: and when they heard that the Lord had visited the children of Israel, and that He had looked upon their affliction, then they bowed their heads and worshipped" (vv. 29-31). The "elders" are always to be viewed as the representatives of the people: they were the heads of the tribes and of the leading families. Unto them Aaron recited all that Jehovah had said unto Moses, and Moses performed the two signs. The result was precisely as God had fore-announced (3: 18). Moses had said, "They will not believe me" (4:1); the Lord had declared they *would*, and so it came to pass. They believed that Moses was sent of God, and that he would be their deliverer. Believing this, they bowed their heads and worshipped, adoring the goodness of God, and expressing their thankfulness for the notice which He took of them in their distress.

In the favorable response which Moses received from the elders of Israel we may discern once more the tender mercy and grace of the Lord. At a later stage, the leaders came before Moses and Aaron complaining they had made the lot of the people worse rather than better. But here, on their first entrance into Egypt, the Lord inclined the hearts of the people to believe. Thus He did not put too great a strain upon their faith at first, nor lay upon them a burden greater than what they were able to bear. It is usually thus in the Lord's dealings with His servants. The real trials are kept back until we have become accustomed to the yoke. We heartily commend this fourth chapter of Exodus to every minister of God, for it abounds in important lessons which each servant of His needs to take to heart.

CHAPTER 8

MOSES AND AARON BEFORE PHARAOH

EXODUS 5

"And afterward Moses and Aaron went in, and told Pharaoh, Thus saith the Lord God of Israel, Let My people go, that they may hold a feast unto Me in the wilderness" (5:1). Let us endeavor to place ourselves in the position occupied by these two ambassadors of the Lord. Moses and Aaron were now required to confront Pharaoh in person. His temper toward their race was well known, his heartless cruelty had been frequently displayed; it was, therefore, no small trial of their faith and courage to beard the lion in his den. The character of the message they were to deliver to him was not calculated to pacify. They were to tell him in peremptory language that the Lord God required him to let that people whom he held in slavery go, and hold a feast unto Jehovah in the wilderness. Moreover, the Lord had already told His servants that He would harden Pharaoh's heart so that he *would not* let the people go. Notwithstanding these discouraging features, Moses and Aaron "went in and told Pharaoh". A striking example was this of God's power to overcome the opposition of the flesh, to impart grace to the trembling heart, and to demonstrate that our strength is made perfect in weakness.

"And afterward Moses and Aaron went in, and told Pharaoh, Thus saith the Lord God of Israel, Let My people ·go, that they may hold a feast unto Me in the wilderness". Careful attention should be paid to the *terms* of this request or demand upon Pharaoh. Jehovah had already promised Moses that he and his people should worship God on Mount Sinai (3:12), and that was much more than a three days' journey from Egypt—compare 12:37; 14: 2; 15:22 and 19:1; yea, He had declared that He would bring them "unto Canaan" (3:8). Why, then, did not Moses tell

Pharaoh plainly that he must relinquish *all* claim on the Hebrews, and give permission for them to leave his land for good? Mr. Urquhart has ably answered this difficult question:

"God is entering upon a controversy with Pharaoh and with Egypt. He is about to judge them; and, in order that they may be judged, they must first be revealed to themselves and to all men. Had they been asked to suffer the Israelites to depart from Egypt, so large a demand might have seemed to others, and certainly would have appeared to the Egyptians themselves, as so unreasonable as to justify their refusal. A request is made, therefore, against which no charge of the kind can be brought. A three days' journey into the wilderness need not have taken the Israelites much beyond the Egyptian frontier. It was also perfectly reasonable, even to heathen notions, that they should be permitted to worship their God after the accepted manner. The heart of Pharaoh and of his people was, therefore, revealed in their scornful refusal of a perfectly reasonable request. In this way they committed themselves to what was manifestly unjust; and in proceeding against them God was consequently justified even in their own eyes. Conscience was stirred. Egypt knew itself to be in the wrong; and a pathway was made there for return to the living God—the God of the conscience—for all who desired to be at peace with Him whom they had offended.

"Has God ever judged a people whom He has not first dealt with in that very way? National judgments have been preceded by some outstanding transgression in which the heart of the nation has been manifested. Carlyle traces the fearful blow which fell upon the clergy and the aristocracy in the French Revolution to the massacre of St. Bartholomew. France had sought to crush the Reformation as Egypt had sought to crush Israel. Spain dug the grave for her greatness and her fame in the establishment of her Inquisition, and in her relentless wars against a people who desired to remove from the Church what were glaring, and largely confessed scandals.

"But we have to go farther to find the full explanation of that request. The demand was indeed limited. It was seemingly a small matter that was asked for. But what was asked for set forth and inscribed in flaming characters Israel's mission. This conflict was to be waged on ground chosen by the Almighty. The battle was not one merely for Israel's deliverance from bitter bondage. It was not fought and won solely that Israel might be able to go forth and possess the land promised to her fathers. The one purpose, to which every other was subsidiary and contributory, was that Israel should dwell in God's Tabernacle. She was redeemed to be His people. Her one mission was and is to serve Jehovah. No other demand would have adequately stated the claim that God was now making and urging in the face of humanity. No other could have so set forth God's claim as against the claim of Pharaoh. Pharaoh said: 'The people is mine; I will not let them go.' God said: 'The people is Mine; thou must let them go; they have been created and chosen that they may serve Me'. The conflict was being waged over the destiny of a race, its place in history and in the service of humanity. Was Israel to be slave, or priest? Egypt's beast of burden, or the anointed of Jehovah? That was the question; and was it possible that God could have done other than put that question, written large and clear, in the forefront of this great controversy?

"And let me add that the demand was prophetic. Israel is in this matter also the type of God's people. When Christianity began its conflict with the Roman Empire, what was the one question over which the great debate proceeded? We all know now what God intended. The nations were to abandon their idols so that their very names, as the household words of the peoples, were to perish. But no demand was made by the Christian Church that

the temples should be closed, and that the heathen priesthoods should be abolished. One thing only was asked, and that apparently one of the slightest. It was freedom to worship the living God—*the very demand made for Israel in Egypt*. Over that the battle raged for centuries. The triumph came when that was won. It was not for any claim the Christians made to direct the worship of the Roman Empire: it was not for their rights as citizens: it was for liberty to worship God in accordance with His demand. That claim kept them, and when the triumph came it consecrated them, as the people of God" (The Bible: Its Structure and Purpose: Vol. IV).

"And afterward Moses and Aaron went in, and told Pharaoh, Thus saith the Lord God of Israel, Let My people go, that they may hold a feast unto Me in the wilderness". So far as Pharaoh was concerned, this was God addressing *his* responsibility, giving him opportunity for obedience, speaking to him in grace. Not yet does He launch His judgments on the haughty king and his subjects. Before He dealt in wrath, He acted in mercy. This is ever His way. He sent forth Noah as a preacher of righteousness and Enoch as a herald of the coming storm, before the Flood descended upon the antediluvians. He sent forth one prophet after another unto Israel, before He banished them into captivity. And later, He sent forth His own Son, followed by the apostles, before His army destroyed Jerusalem in A. D. 70. So it is with the world today. God is now dealing in grace and long-suffering, sending forth His servants far and wide, bidding men flee from the wrath to come. But this Day of Salvation is rapidly drawing to a close, and once the Lord rises from His place at God's right hand, the door of mercy will be shut, and the storm of God's righteous anger will burst.

"And Pharaoh said, Who is the Lord, that I should obey His voice to let Israel go? I know not the Lord, neither will I let Israel go" (v. 2). Here then was Pharaoh's response to the overtures of God's grace. Unacquainted with God for himself, he defiantly refuses to bow to His mandate. The character of Egypt's king stood fully revealed: "I know not the Lord, neither will I let Israel go". Precisely such is the reply made (if not in word, plainly expressed by their attitude) by many of those who hear God's authoritative fiat, "Repent! Believe!", through His servants today. First and foremost the Gospel is not an invitation, but a *declaration* of what God demands from the sinner—"God now *commandeth* all men everywhere to repent" (Acts 17:30); "And this is His *commandment*, that we should believe on the name of His Son, Jesus Christ" (1 John 3:3). But the response of the unbelieving and rebellious heart of the natural man is "Who is the Lord that I should obey His voice?". Thus speaks the pride of the man who hardens his neck against the Blessed God. "I know Him not" said Pharaoh, and "I know Him not" expresses the heart of the sinner today; and what makes it so dreadful is, he desires not to correct this ignorance. For these two things God will yet take vengeance when Christ returns. He will be revealed "in flaming fire taking vengeance on them that *know not* God, and that *obey not* the Gospel of our Lord Jesus Christ" (2 Thess. 1:8).

"And they said, The God of the Hebrews hath met with us: let us go, we pray thee, three days' journey into the desert, and sacrifice unto the Lord our God; lest He fall upon us with pestilence, or with the sword" (v. 3). By comparing these words of Moses with his first utterance to Pharaoh a number of interesting and important points will be seen the more clearly. First, the demand of Jehovah was, "Let My people go, that they may hold *a feast* unto Me in the wilderness" (v. 1). This speaks from the *Divine* side. The request of Moses was, "Let us go, we pray thee, three days' journey into the desert, and *sacrifice* unto the Lord our God". This speaks from the *human* side. The one tells of what God's heart sought, the other of what man's sin needed. The "feast" points to rejoicing, the "sacrifice" to what makes rejoicing possible. In the second place, observe the *ground* upon which Moses here bases the Hebrews' *need* of a "sacrifice"—"lest He fall upon us with pestilence, or with the sword". It is impossible to evade the plain implication of this language. Israel were confessedly guilty, and therefore deserving of punishment, and the only way of escape was through an atonement being made for them. God must be placated: blood must be shed: the Divine justice must be propitiated. Only thus could God be reconciled to them. Finally, observe a *"three days'* journey" was necessary before the Hebrews could sacrifice to Jehovah. Profoundly significant is this in its typical suggestiveness. "Three days" speaks of the interval between death and resurrection. It is only on resurrection-ground, as made alive from the dead, that we can hold a feast unto the Lord!

"And the king of Egypt said unto them, Wherefore do ye, Moses and Aaron, let (hinder) the people from their works? get you unto your burdens. And Pharaoh said, Behold, the people of the land now are many, and ye make them rest from their burdens" (vv. 4, 5). It seems clear from this that Pharaoh had already heard of the conference which Moses and Aaron had held with the "elders" of Israel, and knew of the signs which had been wrought before them. These had created, no doubt, a considerable stir among the rank and file of the Hebrews, and instead of going about their regular drudgery they had, apparently, expected the Lord to act on their behalf without delay. This, we take it, is what Pharaoh had in mind when he charged Moses and Aaron with hindering the people from their work. When he added "Get you unto your burdens" he referred to the whole of the people, the representatives of whom had accompanied God's two servants into the king's presence (cf 3:18).

"And Pharaoh commanded the same day the taskmasters of the people, and their officers, saying, Ye shall no more give the people straw to make brick, as heretofore: let them go and gather straw for themselves. And the tale of the bricks, which they did make heretofore, ye shall lay upon them; ye shall not diminish ought thereof: for they be idle; therefore they cry, saying, Let us go and sacrifice to our God. Let there more work be laid upon the men, that they may labor therein; and let them not regard vain words" (vv. 6-9). This is ever the effect of rejecting God's testimony. To resist the light means increased darkness: to turn from the truth is to become more thoroughly than ever under the power of him who is the arch-liar. The same sun which melts the wax hardens the clay. Instead of allowing the Hebrews to go and sacrifice to Jehovah, Pharaoh orders that their lot shall be made harder. So it is with the sinner who disobeys the Gospel command. The one who refuses to repent becomes more impenitent, more defiant, more lawless, until (with rare exceptions) the Lord abandons him to his own ways and leaves him to suffer the due reward of his iniquities.

The *unbelief* of Pharaoh comes out plainly here: "Let there more work be laid upon the men, that they may labor therein; and let them not regard *vain words*". Where God Himself is unknown His words are but idle tales. To talk of sacrificing unto Him is meaningless to the man of the world. Such are the Holy Scriptures to the sinner today. The Bible tells man that he is a fallen creature, unprepared to die, unfit for the presence of a holy God. The Bible tells him of the wondrous provision of God's grace, and presents a Saviour all-sufficient for his acceptance. The Bible warns him faithfully of the solemn issues at stake, and asks him how he shall escape if he neglects so great salvation. The Bible tells him plainly that he that believeth not shall be damned, and that whosoever's name is not found written in the book of life shall be cast into the Lake of Fire. But these solemn verities are but "vain words" to the skeptical heart of the natural man. He refuses to receive them as a message from the living God addressed to his own soul. But let him beware. Let him be warned by the awful case of Pharaoh. If he continues in his unbelief and obstinacy, Pharaoh's fate shall be his—God will surely bring him into judgment.

"And the taskmasters of the people went out, and their officers, and they spake to the people, saying, Thus saith Pharaoh, I will not give you straw. Go ye, get you straw where ye can find it: yet not ought of your work shall be diminished. So the people were scattered abroad throughout all the land of Egypt to gather stubble instead of straw. And the taskmasters hasted them, saying, Fulfill your works, and your daily tasks, as when there was straw. And the officers of the children of Israel which Pharaoh's taskmasters had set over them, were beaten, and demanded, Wherefore have ye not fulfilled your task in making brick both yesterday and today, as heretofore?" (vv.

10-14). The severe measures which Pharaoh ordered to be taken upon the Hebrews illustrate the malignant efforts of Satan against the soul that God's grace is dealing with. When the Devil recognizes the first advances of the Holy Spirit toward a poor sinner he at once puts forth every effort to retain his victims. At no place is the frightful malevolence of the Fiend more plainly to be seen than here. No pains are spared by him to hinder the deliverance of his slaves. Satan never gives up his prey without a fierce struggle. When a soul is convicted of sin, and brought to long after liberty and peace with God, the Devil will endeavor, just as Pharaoh did with the Israelites, by increased occupation with material things, to expel all such desires from his heart.

A solemn example of what we have in mind is recorded in Luke 9:42: "And as he was yet a coming, the demon threw him down, and tare him". This obscessed youth was coming to Christ, and while on the way, Satan's emissary sought to rend him to pieces. So long as a person has no desire after Christ the Devil will leave him alone, but once a soul is awakened to his need of a Saviour and begins to seriously seek Him, Satan will put forth every effort to hinder him. This is why so many convicted souls find that their case gets worse before it is bettered. So it was here with the Hebrews. Just as hope was awakened, the opposition against them became stronger: just when deliverance seemed nigh, their oppression was increased.

"Then the officers of the children of Israel came and cried unto Pharaoh, saying, Wherefore dealest thou thus with thy servants? There is no straw given unto thy servants, and they say to us, Make bricks: and, behold, thy servants are beaten; but the fault is in thine own people" (vv. 15,16). How true to human nature is this! Instead of crying unto the Lord these leaders of the Israelites turned unto Pharaoh for relief. Doubtless they hoped to appeal to his pity or to his sense of justice. Surely they could show him that his demands were unreasonable and impossible of fulfillment. Alas, the natural man ever prefers to lean upon an arm of flesh than be supported by Him who is invisible. Just so is it with the convicted sinner: he turns for help to the evangelist, his pastor, his Sunday School teacher, his parents, any one rather than the Lord Himself. God is generally our *last* resource! Deeply humbling is this! And amazing is the grace which bears with such waywardness. Grace not only has to begin the work of salvation, it also has to continue and complete it. It is *all* of grace from first to last.

"But he said, Ye are idle, ye are idle: therefore ye say, Let us go and do sacrifice to the Lord. Go therefore now, and work; for there shall no straw be given you, yet shall ye deliver the tale of bricks" (vv. 17, 18). Little good did it do Israel's "officers" in appealing to Pharaoh. He, like the master of the poor sinner, was absolutely pitiless and inflexible. Probably these officers supposed that the brutal "taskmasters" had acted without the king's knowledge. If so, they were quickly disillusioned. Instead of expressing indignation at the taskmasters, and relieving the officers of the people, Pharaoh insulted them, charging them with sloth and duplicity, arguing that it was not so much the honor of God they regarded, as that they might escape from their work. So, too, the awakened sinner accomplishes little good by turning to human counsellors for relief. When the prodigal son began to be in want he went and joined himself to a citizen of the far country, but being sent into the fields to feed swine was all he got for his pains (Luke 15:15). The poor woman mentioned in the Gospels "suffered many things of many physicians", and though she spent all that she had, she was "nothing bettered, but rather *grew worse*" (Mark 5:26). O unsaved reader, if a work of grace has already begun in your heart so that you realize your wretchedness and long for that peace and rest which this poor world is unable to give, fix it firmly in your mind that One only can give you what you seek. Allow no priest—either Roman Catholic or Protestant—to come in between you and Christ. Cease ye from man, and "seek ye *the Lord* while He may be found".

"And the officers of the children of Israel did see that they were in evil case, after it was said, Ye shall not minish ought from your bricks of your daily task. And they met Moses and Aaron, who stood in the way, as they came forth from

Pharaoh: And they said unto them, The Lord look upon you, and judge; because ye have made our savor to be abhorred in the eyes of Pharaoh, and in the eyes of His servants, to put a sword in their hand to slay us" (vv. 19-21). Poor Moses! His troubles now were only commencing. He had been prepared for the rebuff which he had himself received from Pharaoh, for the Lord had said plainly that He would harden the king's heart. But, so far as the inspired record informs us, nothing had been told him that he would meet with discouragement and opposition from his own brethren. A real testing was this for God's servant, for it is far more trying to be criticized by our own brethren, by those whom we are anxious to help, than it is to be persecuted by the world. But sufficient for the servant to be as his master. The Lord Himself was hated by his own brethren according to the flesh, and the very ones to whom He had ministered in ceaseless grace unanimously cried "Crucify Him".

"And Moses returned unto the Lord, and said, Lord, wherefore hast Thou so evil entreated this people? why is it that Thou hast sent me? For since I came to Pharaoh to speak in Thy name, he hath done evil to this people; neither hast Thou delivered Thy people at all" (vv. 22, 23). Moses did well in turning to the Lord in the hour of trial, but it was most unseemly and irreverent of him to speak in the way that he did—alas that we, in our petulant unbelief, are so often guilty of asking similar questions. It is not for the servant to take it upon him to dictate to his master, far less is it for a worm of the earth to dispute with the Almighty. These things are recorded faithfully for *"our* admonition". There was no need for Jehovah to hurry. His delay in delivering Israel and His permitting them to endure still greater afflictions accomplished many ends. It furnished fuller opportunity for Pharaoh to manifest the desperate wickedness of the human heart. It gave occasion for the Lord to demonstrate how that He "bears with *much* long-suffering the vessels of wrath fitted to destruction". It served to show more clearly how righteous God was in visiting Pharaoh and his subjects with sore judgment. And, too, Israel needed to be humbled: they also were a stiff-necked people, as is clear from the words of their leaders to Moses and Aaron on this occasion. Moreover, the more they were afflicted the more would they appreciate the Lord's deliverance when His time came. Let, then, the writer and reader take this to heart: the Lord always has a good reason for each of His *delays*. Therefore, let us recognize the folly, yea, the wickedness of murmuring at His seeming tardiness. Let us daily seek grace to "Rest in the Lord, and *wait patiently* for Him".

We may add that what has been before us supplies a striking picture of that which awaits Israel in a coming day. The grievous afflictions which came upon the Hebrews in Egypt just before the Lord emancipated them from their hard and cruel bondage, did but foreshadow the awful experiences through which their descendants shall pass during the "time of Jacob's trouble", just prior to the coming of the Deliverer to Zion. Pharaoh's conduct as described in our chapter—his defiance of Jehovah, his rejection of the testimony of God's two witnesses, his cruel treatment of the children of Israel—accurately typifies the course which will be followed by the Man of Sin. Thus may we discern once more how that these pages of Old Testament history are also prophetic in their forecastings of coming events. May it please the Lord to open our eyes so that we may perceive both the application to ourselves and those who are to follow us.

CHAPTER 9

JEHOVAH'S COVENANT

EXODUS 6

Our previous chapter closed with Moses turning unto the Lord in most unbecoming petulancy and daring to call into question the Divine dispensations. The Lord's servant had been severely tried: he had gone in unto Pharaoh and demanded him to let the Hebrews go so that they might sacrifice unto their God. But not only had the haughty king refused this most reasonable request, he had also given orders that his slaves should have additional burdens laid upon them. The officers of the children of Israel had interviewed Pharaoh, but had been mocked for their pains. They then sought out Moses and Aaron and called down a curse upon them, for this we take it is the force of their words, "The Lord look upon you, and *judge;* because ye have made our savor to be abhorred in the eyes of Pharaoh" (5:21). Moses then "returned unto the Lord" and poured out his heart before Him. The reference seems to be to the fact that he had committed his way unto the Lord before he had interviewed the king, and now after his seeming failure, he turns again to the throne of grace.

The discouragements which Moses had met with were more than flesh could stand, and he asks Jehovah, "Wherefore hast Thou so evil entreated this people? and why is it that Thou hast sent me?", ending by saying "For since I came to Pharaoh to speak in Thy name, he hath done evil to this people; neither hast Thou delivered Thy people at all." Moses was right in tracing the afflictions which had come upon the Hebrews to God Himself, for all things are "of Him and through Him" (Rom. 11:36); but He certainly did wrong in questioning the Almighty and in murmuring against the outworking of His counsels. But it is written, "He knoweth our frame; He remembereth that we are

dust", and again, "The Lord is merciful and gracious, slow to anger, and plenteous in mercy" (Psa. 103:14, 8). Fully was that manifested on this occasion. Instead of chastising His servant, the Lord encouraged him; instead of setting him aside, He renewed his commission; instead of slaying him. He revealed Himself in all His grace.

"Then the Lord said unto Moses, Now shalt thou see what I will do to Pharaoh: for with a strong hand shall he let them go, and with a strong hand shall he drive them out of his land" (v. 1). The Lord made no answer to Moses' impatient queries but re-affirmed His immutable purpose. The defiant Pharaoh might insist I will *not* let Israel go (5:2), but the Most High declared that he *should,* nay, that he would even drive them out of his land. There was no need for Moses to be alarmed or even discouraged: the counsel of God *would* stand, and He would do *all* His pleasure (Isa. 46:10). This is a sure resting-place for the heart of every servant, and for every Christian too. No matter how much the Enemy may roar and rage against us, he is quite unable to thwart the Almighty—"There is *no* wisdom, nor understanding, nor counsel against the Lord" (Prov. 21:30). This is the high ground that the Lord first took in encouraging the drooping heart of His despondent servant. Said He, "With a strong hand *shall* he (Pharaoh) let them go, and with a strong hand *shall* he drive them out of the land". There were no "ifs" or "perhaps" about it. The event was absolutely certain, and therefore invincibly necessary, because Deity had eternally decreed it. Similar is the assurance God gives His servants today: "So shall My word be that goeth forth out of My mouth. It *shall not* return unto Me void, but *it shall* accomplish that which I please, and *it shall* prosper in the thing whereto I sent it" (Isa. 55:11).

It is also to be noted that in strengthening the heart of His servant the Lord pointed Moses forward *to the goal*—"Now shalt thou see what I will do to Pharaoh". There was much that was to happen in between, but the Lord passes over all that would intervene, and speaks of the last act in the great drama which was just opening. He bids Moses consider the successful outcome, when the great enemy of His people should be vanquished. There is much for us, to learn in this. We defeat ourselves by being occupied with the difficulties of the way. God has made known to us the triumphant outcome of good over evil, and instead of being harassed by the fiery darts which the Evil One now hurls against us, we ought to rest on the assuring promise that "the God of peace *shall* bruise Satan under your feet shortly" (Rom.' 16:20).

"And God spake unto Moses, and said unto him, I am the Lord: And I appeared unto Abraham, and unto Isaac, and unto Jacob by the name of God Almighty, but by My name JEHOVAH was I not known to them" (vv. 2, 3). These verses have been a sore puzzle to many Bible students. "Jehovah" is the very name which is translated "the Lord" scores of times in Genesis. Abraham knew "the name" of Jehovah, for we read that he "called on *the name of the Lord*" (Gen. 13:4). Of Isaac, too, we read, "And he built an altar there, and called upon *the name of the Lord*" (Gen. 26:25) And of Jacob we read of him praying, "O God of my father Abraham, and God of my father Isaac, *the Lord* which saidst unto me, Return unto thy country, and to thy kindred, and I will deal well with thee, I am not worthy of the least of all Thy mercies", etc. (Gen. 32:9, 10). It is, therefore, clear that the patriarchs *were* acquainted with God's name of Jehovah. What, then, did the Almighty mean when He said here to Moses, "by My name JEHOVAH was I *not known* to them"? It is clear that this is one of many scriptures which cannot be interpreted absolutely, but must be understood relatively. We believe that the key to the difficulty is supplied by what follows, where the Lord says, "I have also established My *covenant* with them".

The Divine-titles are a most important subject of study for they are inseparably connected with a sound interpretation of the Scriptures. Elohim and Jehovah are not employed loosely on the pages of Holy Writ. Each has a definite significance, and the distinction is carefully preserved. Elohim (God) is the name which speaks of the Creator and Governor of His creatures. Jehovah (the Lord) is His title as connected with His people by covenant relationship. It is this which explains the verses now before us. Abraham, Isaac, and Jacob were acquainted with the Jehovistic title, but they had no experimental acquaintance with all that it stood for. God has entered into a "covenant" with them, but, as Heb. 11:13 tells us, "These all died in faith, *not having received* the promises". But now the time had drawn nigh when the Lord was about to fulfill His covenant engagement and Israel would witness the faithfulness, the power, and the deliverance which His covenant-name implied. God was about to manifest Himself as the faithful *performer* of His word, and as such the descendants of the patriarchs would *know* Him in a way their fathers had not.

"And I have also established My covenant with them, to give them the land of Canaan, the land of your pilgrimage, wherein they were strangers" (v. 4). Here then was the next encouragement which the Lord set before His fearful servant. He reminds him how that He had *established* His covenant with the patriarchs, to whom He had pledged Himself to give them the land of Canaan. How impossible was it, then, that the Egyptians should continue to hold them as slaves. How foolish and how wicked Moses' unbelieving fears. If Jehovah had established a covenant it *must be* fulfilled, for that covenant was an unconditional one. A similar ground of assurance have we to stay our hearts upon in the midst of the trials of this scene. Says our God, "Incline your ear, and come unto Me: hear, and your soul shall live; and I will make an everlasting covenant with you, even the sure mercies of David", i. e. "the Beloved" (Isa. 55:3)—note how the apostle Paul quotes from this very verse in his sermon at Antioch (Acts 13:34). There are those who say that the saints of this dispensation are not related to God by covenant bonds, but this is a mistake. They are, as Heb. 13:20 makes abundantly clear, for there we read of "the blood of the *everlasting* covenant". Before time began the

Father entered into a covenant with our glorious Head, (cf Titus 1:2) and that covenant was sealed by blood. And just as the covenant God made with Abraham guaranteed "an heritage" (Ex. 6:8), so the covenant which the Father made with the Son (cf Heb. 7:22) has an inheritance connected with it, even an inheritance which is "incorruptible and undefiled, and that fadeth not away, reserved in heaven" for us (1 Pet. 1:4). May our faith so lay hold upon it that even now we shall live in the enjoyment of it.

"And I have also heard the groaning of the children of Israel, whom the Egyptians keep in bondage; and I have remembered My covenant" (v. 5). Additional comfort was this for God's servant. Moses had told the Lord how that since he had spoken to Pharaoh he had done evil to the Hebrews (5:23). The Lord needed not to be told this. He was neither oblivious nor indifferent to their sufferings. *He* had heard the "groaning of the children of Israel". And, fellow-Christian, thou who art tried beyond endurance, the Lord has heard thy groanings; every tear has been recorded in His book (Psa. 56:8); and what is more, He *sympathizes* with thee, and is *touched* with the feeling of thine infirmities (Heb. 4:15). Though there may be much of unfathomable mystery as to *why* God permits our "groanings", nevertheless, here is much cause for comfort —*God* "hears them"!

"Wherefore say unto the children of Israel, I am the Lord, and (1) *I will bring you* out from under the burdens of the Egyptians, and (2) *I will rid you* out of their bondage, and (3) *I will redeem you* with a stretched out arm, and with great judgments: And (4) *I will take you* to Me for a people, and (5) *I will be to you* a God: and ye shall know that I am the Lord your God, which bringeth you out from under the burdens of the Egyptians. And (6) *I will bring you* in unto the land, concerning the which I did sware to give it to Abraham, to Isaac, and to Jacob; and (7) *I will give it you* for an heritage: I am the Lord" (vv. 6-8). Observe that these verses commence with the word "Therefore" which looks back to the closing words of the previous verse: "I have *remembered My covenant*". The contents of these verses, then, grow out of the covenant which the Lord made with Abraham, and confirmed to Isaac and Jacob. It will

be noted that in them the Lord makes seven promises, prefacing them with the declaration "I will".

In Gen. 17 we find recorded another seven "I will's" of Jehovah: "And (1) *I will make thee* exceeding fruitful, and (2) *I will make nations of thee*, and kings shall come out of thee. And (3) *I will establish* My covenant between Me and thee and thy seed after thee in their generations for an everlasting covenant, to be a God unto thee, and to thy seed after thee. And (4) *I will give* unto thee, and to thy seed after thee, the land wherein thou art a stranger, all the land of Canaan, for an everlasting possession; and (5) *I will be their God* . . . . and (6) *I will establish* My covenant with him for an everlasting covenant, and with his seed after him. But My covenant (7) *I will establish* with Isaac" (vv. 6, 7, 8, 19, 21). With these passages should be compared the "new covenant" recorded in Jer. 31:33, 34. Here, too, we find *seven promises from the Lord:* "After those days, saith the Lord, (1) I will put My law in their inward parts, and (2) write it in their hearts; and (3) will be their God, and (4) they shall be My people. And (5) they shall teach no more every man his neighbour, and every man his brother, saying, Know the Lord: for they shall all know Me, from the least of them unto the greatest of them, saith the Lord: and (6) I will forgive their iniquity, and (7) I will remember their sin no more". Let us now consider, though briefly, each of the seven promises which God here made to Moses:

(1) "I will bring you out from under the burdens of the Egyptians. This speaks of God's gracious purpose. His people were groaning beneath the intolerable demands made by their cruel taskmasters. For many weary years they had toiled under a load which was becoming more and more unendurable. Was there then no eye to pity, no hand to deliver? There was. The covenant God of their fathers had promised that at the end of four hundred years' affliction they should be emancipated (see Gen. 15:13-16). And now the time had come for God to make good His word. He declares, therefore, that He *will* bring them out from under their burdens. So, too, this is what God does for each of His elect today. The first thing of which we are conscious in the ap-

plication of salvation to our souls is deliverance from the burdens of our lost condition, of conscious guilt, of our unpreparedness to die.

(2). "And I will rid you out of their bondage". As another has said, "This was something far more than mere relief from their burdens: it was a complete severance from their previous condition. A slave may be sold to a kind master, and his burden removed, but he would remain a slave still; and Israel's burdens might have been removed, and they still remain captives in Egypt. But this was not God's way. He would rid them clean out of the land of bondage. Instead of them toiling in the kilns of Egypt, He would have them out in the wilderness, in communion with Himself. This is still God's way. The one who receives Christ as his Saviour is delivered from the bondage of sin, of Satan, of the fear of death".

(3) "I will redeem you". To redeem means to purchase and set free. Evangelical redemption is by price and by power. The price is the shedding of atoning blood: the power, the putting forth of an all-mighty hand. It was thus God would deliver Israel. First the slaying of the paschal lamb and then the display of Divine omnipotence at the Red Sea. Thus it is with the Christian: we have been redeemed, not with corruptible things as silver and gold, but with the precious blood of the Lamb (1 Pet. 1:18, 19); we are not our own, but "bought with a price" (1 Cor. 6:20). Almighty power was put forth at our regeneration, for we read of "the exceeding greatness of His power to usward who believe" (Eph. 1:19).

(4) "And I will take you to Me for a people". For Israel this meant that henceforth they, as a nation, would occupy an unique relationship to God: they would be His peculiar treasure, the objects of His special care and favor. Marvellous indeed was it that the great Jehovah should own as *His* a down-trodden nation of slaves. But He did! And on what ground? The ground of *redemption*. He had redeemed them *unto Himself*. The same blessed truth is set forth on the pages of the New Testament. We, too, belong to God as His peculiar people. Utterly unfit and unworthy in ourselves, yet precious in the sight of God for *Christ's* sake—"Accepted in the Beloved".

(5) "And I will be to you a God". How fully was this exemplified in the sequel! Who but *God* could have made a way through the Sea so that His redeemed passed over dry shod; and who but He could have caused that Sea to turn back and drown the hosts of the Egyptians? Who but *God* could have guided His people through that trackless desert by a pillar of cloud by day and a pillar of fire by night? Who but *God* could have quenched their thirst from a rock, and fed a hungry multitude for forty years in a wilderness? Truly He was a "God" unto Israel. And such is His promise to us: "I will be *their God,* and they shall be My people" (2 Cor. 6:16). And daily does every believer receive a performance of this promise. None but *God* could preserve to the end a people so ignorant, so weak, so fickle, so sinful, as each of us is.

(6) "I will bring you in unto the land". Not only did the Lord bring His people out of the land of bondage, but He also brought them into the land which He had sworn to give unto Abraham, Isaac, and Jacob. It is true that many, many individuals fell in the wilderness, but nevertheless, the *nation* of Israel God brought into Canaan. They were not consumed by the Amalekites (Ex. 17). Sihon, king of the Amorites, and Og king of Bashan, might "gather all his people together" and go out against Israel (Num. 21), and Balak might hire Balaam to curse the people of God, but the Lord speedily brought to naught their efforts. God *did* bring Israel into the promised land. And He *will* bring each of us, His blood-bought ones, safely to Heaven. The world, the flesh, and the Devil may array themselves against us, but not a single sheep of Christ shall perish.

(7) "And I will give it you for an heritage". This was the goal toward which God was working. All was done in order that they might *enjoy* that which He had promised to their fathers. Not yet has this been completely fulfilled. It is in the Millennium that Israel shall enter fully into their covenanted portion. In like manner, the full enjoyment of our heritage is future. Already we have "the *earnest* of our inheritance" (Eph. 1:14); soon shall we have the portion itself. And note this is a *gift*. It is not by works of merit, but solely by sovereign grace.

"Note how these seven 'I will's' are enclosed in a framework of Divine assurance. They are prefaced and summed up with the words, 'I am Jehovah'. As if God would fix their eyes on Himself as the Almighty One, before He utters a single 'I will'; and then, at the close of the unfolding of His wondrous purposes, He would still keep their eye on the fact that it is He, *the Almighty,* who speaks. Every doubt and difficulty would vanish if faith but grasped the fact that it is 'I am' who has pledged His word. Faith remembers with calm and unruffled peace, in spite of circumstances, that 'With God all things are possible'" (Dr. Brookes).

"And Moses spake so unto the children of Israel; but they hearkened not unto Moses for anguish of spirit, and for cruel bondage" (v. 9). How this exposes the heart of the unregenerate! The condition of the poor sinner is vividly portrayed in these earlier chapters of Exodus. First, groaning in bondage; second, ignorant of that grace which God had in store for them; and now unable to value the precious promises of Jehovah. While we are in bondage to sin and Satan, even the promises of God fail to bring us any relief. Relief never comes until the shed blood of the "lamb" is applied! It was so with Israel; it is equally true with men today.

"And the Lord spake unto Moses, saying, Go in, speak unto Pharaoh king of Egypt, that he let the children of Israel go out of his land" (vv. 10, 11). Moses was not to be afraid of the haughty monarch, but must interview him again, and speak plainly and boldly, not in a supplicatory, but in an authoritative way, in the name of the King of kings. This was before the Lord proceeded to punish Pharaoh for his disobedience, that His judgments might appear more manifestly just and right.

"And Moses spake before the Lord, saying, Behold, the children of Israel have not hearkened unto me; how then shall Pharaoh hear me, who am of uncircumcised lips?" (v. 12). Why did Moses refer again to the impediment in his speech? Was it because that he thought the Lord ought to have removed it, and because he

was dissatisfied at having Aaron to act as his mouthpiece?

"And the Lord spake unto Moses and unto Aaron and gave them a charge unto the children of Israel, and unto Pharaoh king of Egypt, to bring the children of Israel out of the land of Egypt" (v. 13). The Lord having previously answered this same objection of Moses (4:10-12) makes no further reply to it now, but instead, gives him a charge unto his own people—to comfort and direct them how they should conduct themselves in the interval before God's deliverance arrived—and unto Pharaoh.

From vv. 14-37 we have a list of genealogies brought in here to show us the ancestors of God's ambassadors, and also to demonstrate the Lord's sovereign grace. Only those genealogies of the Hebrews are here given which concern the offspring of the first three of Jacob's sons. The sons of Reuben and of Simeon are named, but not from either of them did God select the honored instrument of deliverance. The order of grace is not the order of nature. It was from the tribe of Levi which, along with Simeon, lay under *a curse* (Gen. 49:5-7) that God called Moses and Aaron. And here too we may see grace exemplified by giving Moses, the younger, the precedency over Aaron, the senior. It should also be noted that Levi was the *third* son of Jacob—the number which ever speaks of *resurrection*—that the deliverer came!

The last three verses of our chapter connect the narrative with v. 10. As another has said, "The objection of Moses in v. 30 is evidently the same as in v. 12. And yet there is a reason for its repetition. In chapters 3 and 4 Moses makes five difficulties in reply to the Lord; here in the 6th, are two, making *seven* altogether. It was therefore the *complete* exhibition of the weakness and unbelief of Moses. How it magnifies the grace and goodness of the Lord; for in His presence man is revealed; it also brings to light what *He* is in all the perfections of His grace, love, mercy and truth" (E. Dennett).

CHAPTER 10

A HARDENED HEART

EXODUS 7

The seventh chapter begins the second literary division of the book of Exodus. The first six chapters are concerned more particularly with the *person of the deliverer*, the next six with an account of the *work of redemption*. In the first section we have had a brief description of the deadly persecution of Israel, then an account of Moses' birth and his miraculous preservation by God, then his identifying of himself with his people and his flight into Midian. Next, we have learned how God met him, commanded him to go down into Egypt, overcame his fears, and equipped him for his mission. Finally, we have noted how that he delivered Jehovah's message to the Hebrews and then to Pharaoh, and how that the king refused to heed the Divine demand, and how in consequence the people were thoroughly discouraged by the increased burdens laid upon them. Moses himself was deeply dejected, and chapter 6 closes with the Lord's servant bemoaning the seeming hopelessness of his task. Thus the *weakness* of the instrument was fully manifested that it might the better be seen that the *power* was of Jehovah alone, and of Jehovah acting not in response to faith but in covenant faithfulness and in sovereign grace.

From chapter 7 onwards there is a marked change: Moses is no more timid, hesitant and discouraged. The omnipotence of the Lord is displayed in every scene. The conflict from this point onwards was one not of words but of deeds. The gauntlet had been thrown down, and now it is open war between the Almighty and the Egyptians. It hardly needs to be pointed out that what is before us in these early chapters of Exodus is something more than a mere episode in ancient history, something more than what was simply of local interest. A thrilling drama is unfolded to our view, and though its movements are swift, yet is there sufficient detail and repetition in principle for us to discern clearly its great design. It spreads before us, in vivid tableau, *the great conflict between good and evil* as far as this comes within the range of human vision.

So far as Scripture informs us the Great Conflict is being fought out *in this world,* hence this historical drama, with its profound symbolic moral meaning, was staged in the land of *Egypt.* The great *mystery* in connection with the Conflict is forcibly shown us in the prosperity of the wicked and the adversity of the righteous. The Egyptians held the whip hand: the Hebrews groaned under unbearable oppression. The leading characters in the tableau are Moses as the vicegerant of *God,* and Pharaoh as the representative and emissary of *Satan.* The powerful and haughty king takes fiendish delight in persecuting the Lord's people, and openly defies the Almighty Himself. To outward sight *the issue* seemed long in doubt. The kingdom of Pharaoh was shaken again and again—as has the kingdom of Satan been during the course of the ages, in such events as the Flood, the destruction of the Canaanites the Advent of the Son of God, the day of Pentecost, the Reformation, etc.,—but each fresh interposition of Jehovah's power and the withdrawal of His judgments only issued in the hardening of Pharaoh's heart. The *prolongation* of the Egyptian contest gave full opportunity for the complete testing of human responsibility, the trying of the saints' faith, and the manifestation of all the perfections and attributes of Deity—apparently the three chief ends which the Creator has in view in suffering the entrance and *continuance* of evil in His domains. The great drama *closes* by showing the absolute triumph of Jehovah, the com-

53

pleted redemption of His people, and the utter overthrow of His and their enemies. Thus we have revealed to the eye of faith the Glorious Consummation when God's elect—through the work of the Mediator—shall be emancipated from all bondage, when every high thing that exalteth itself against the Almighty shall be cast down, and when God Himself shall be *all in all*. We shall now follow step by step the various stages by which this end was reached.

"And the Lord said unto Moses, See, I have made thee a god to Pharaoh: and Aaron thy brother shall be thy prophet" (7:1). This presents a startling contrast from what was before us at the close of Ex. 6. There we read of Moses' complaint before the Lord, "I am of uncircumcised lips, and how shall Pharaoh hearken unto me?". That was a confession of feebleness, but it sprang from unbelief. Here we find Jehovah acting according to His sovereign power and dealing in wondrous grace with His poor servant.

"I have made thee *a god* to Pharaoh", that is, Jehovah had selected Moses to act as His ambassador, had invested him with Divine authority, and was about to use him to perform prodigies which were contrary to the ordinary course of nature. But mark the qualification, "I have made thee a god *to Pharaoh*". Acting in God's stead, Moses was to *rule over* Egypt's proud king, commanding him what he should do, controlling him when he did wrong, and punishing him for his disobedience, so that Pharaoh had to apply *to him* for the removal of the plagues.

"And Aaron thy brother shall be *thy prophet*". If this be compared with 4:15, 16 we shall find a Divine definition of what constitutes a prophet. There we find the Lord promising Moses concerning Aaron that "thou shalt speak unto him, and put words in his mouth: and I will be with thy mouth, and with his mouth, and will teach you what ye shall do. And he shall be thy spokesman unto the people: and he shall be, even he shall be to thee instead of a mouth, and thou shalt be to him instead of God." God's prophet then is God's spokesman: he acts as God's mouthpiece, the Lord putting into his lips the very *words* he would utter. Thus Moses was a "god to Pharaoh" in this additional way, in that he had one who acted as *his* prophet.

"Thou shalt speak all that I command thee: and Aaron thy brother shall speak unto Pharaoh, that he send the children of Israel out of his land" (v. 2). This injunction was very definite. Moses was not free to make a selection from Jehovah's words and communicate to Aaron those which *he* deemed most advisable to say unto Pharaoh, but he was to speak *all* that had been commanded him. A similar charge is laid upon God's servant today: he is to "preach the Word" (2 Tim. 4:3) and to "hold fast *the form* of sound words" (2 Tim. 1:13), and is warned that "If any man teach otherwise, and consent not to wholesome words, even the words of our Lord Jesus Christ, and to the doctrine which is according to godliness; he is a fool, knowing nothing" (1 Tim. 6:3, 4). But alas! how few, how very few there are, who faithfully shun not to declare "the *whole* counsel of God".

"And I will harden Pharaoh's heart, and multiply My signs and My wonders in the land of Egypt" (v. 3). This verse brings before us one of the most solemn truths revealed in the Holy Scriptures—the Divine hardening of human hearts. At no point, perhaps, has the slowness of man to believe *all* that the prophets have spoken been more lamentably manifested than here. The hardening of Pharaoh's heart by God has been eagerly seized by His enemies to make an attack upon the citadel of truth. Infidels have argued that if Pharaoh's subsequent crimes were the result of his heart being hardened by Jehovah, then that makes God the author of his sins; and, furthermore, God must be very unrighteous in punishing him for them. The sad thing is that so many of the profest servants of God have, instead of faithfully maintaining the integrity of God's Word, attempted to blunt its keen edge in order to make it more acceptable to the carnal mind. Instead of acknowledging with fear and trembling that God's Word *does* teach that the Lord actually hardened the heart of Pharaoh, most of the commentators have really argued that He did nothing of the kind, that He simply *permitted* the Egyptian monarch to harden his own heart.

That Pharaoh *did* harden his own heart the Scriptures expressly affirm, but they *also* declare that THE LORD hardened his heart too, and clearly this is not one and the same thing, or the two *different* expressions would not have been employed.

Our duty is to believe *both* statements, but to attempt to show the philosophy of their reconciliation is probably, as another has said, "to attempt to fathom infinity". In Psa. 105:25 it is said, "He turned their hearts to hate His people, to deal subtilly with His servants". Nothing could be stronger or plainer than this. Are we to deny it because *we* cannot explain the way in which God did it? On the same ground we might reject the doctrine of the Trinity. I may be asked how God could in any sense harden a man's heart without Him being the Author of sin. But the most assured belief of the fact does not require that an answer should be given by me to this question. If *God* has not explained the matter (and He has not), then it is not for us to feign to be wise above what is written. I believe many things recorded in Scripture not because I can *explain* their rationale, but because I know that God cannot lie. Calvin was right when he represented those as *perverting* the Scriptures who insist that no more is meant than a bare *permission* when God is said to harden the hearts of men. Is it nothing more than passive permission on His part when God *softens* men's hearts? Is it not, rather, by His active agency? Let us remember that it is no part of our business to vindicate God in justifying the grounds of His procedure; our responsibility is to believe *all* that He has revealed in His Word, on the sole ground of His written testimony. Our business is to "preach the Word" in its purity, not to tone it down or explain away its most objectionable portions in order to render it acceptable to the depraved reason of worms of the dust. The Lord will vindicate Himself in due time, silencing all His critics, and glorifying Himself before His saints.

It should be pointed out that the case of Pharaoh and the Egyptians does not by any means stand alone in the Holy Scriptures. In Deut. 2:30 Moses records the fact that "Sihon king of Heshbon would not let us pass by him: for the Lord thy God *hardened his spirit,* and *made his heart obstinate,* that He might deliver him into thy hand". The reference is to Num. 21:21-23 where we read, "And Israel sent messengers unto Sihon king of the Amorites, saying, Let me pass through thy land: we will not turn into the fields, or into the vineyards; we will not drink of the waters of the ground: but we will go along

by the king's highway, until we be passed thy borders. And Sihon would not suffer Israel to pass through his borders". The verse in Deut. explains to us the reason of Sihon's obstinacy. Clearly it was no mere *judicial* hardening, instead it was a solemn illustration of what we read of in Rom. 9:18, *"whom He will* He hardens". So, too, in Joshua 11:19, 20 we are told "There was not a city that made peace with the children of Israel, save the Hivites the inhabitants of Gibeon: all other they took in battle. For it was of the Lord *to harden their hearts,* that they should come against Israel in battle, that He might destroy them utterly". Such solemn passages as these are not to be reasoned about, but must be accepted in childlike faith, knowing that the Judge of all the earth does nothing but what is *right.*

"But Pharaoh shall not hearken unto you, that I may lay My hand upon Egypt, and bring forth Mine armies, and My people the children of Israel, out of the land of Egypt by great judgments, and the Egyptians shall know that I am the Lord, when I stretch forth Mine hand upon Egypt, and bring out the children of Israel from among them" (vv. 4, 5). These verses supply us with one reason *why* the Lord hardened the hearts of Pharaoh and the Egyptians: it was in order that He might have full opportunity to display His mighty power. A dark background it was indeed, but a dark background is required to bring out the white light of Divine holiness. Similarly we find the Lord Jesus saying, "It *must needs be* that offences come, but woe to that man by whom the offence cometh" (Matt. 18:7). What Jehovah's "great judgments" were we shall see in the chapters that follow.

"And Moses and Aaron did as the Lord commanded them, so did they" (v. 6). Why are we told this here? We believe the answer is, To point a contrast from what we find at the beginning of Ex. 5. In the opening verse of that chapter we learn that Moses "went in, and told Pharaoh, Thus saith the Lord God of Israel, Let My people go". This was the Lord's peremptory *demand.* Then we read of Pharaoh's scornful refusal. Now note what follows: "And they said, The God of the Hebrews hath met with us: let us go, *we pray thee,* three days' journey into the desert, and sacrifice unto the Lord our God" It is plain that Moses and Aaron *changed* the Lord's words. They *toned down* the offensive message. Instead of occupying the high ground of God's ambassadors and *commanding* Pharaoh, they descended to the servile level of *pleading* with him and making a *request* of him. It is for this reason, we believe, that in 7:1 we find Jehovah saying to Moses, *"See* (that is, mark it well) I have made thee *a god* to Pharaoh": it is not for you to go and *beg* from him, it is for you to demand and command. And then the Lord added, "Thou shalt speak all that I *command thee"*. This time the Lord's servants obeyed to the letter, hence we are now told that they "did *as* the Lord commanded them, *so* did they".

"And Moses was fourscore years old, and Aaron fourscore and three years old, when they spake unto Pharaoh" (v. 7). This reference to the ages of Moses and Aaron seems to be brought in here in order to magnify the power and grace of Jehovah. He was pleased to employ two *aged* men as His instruments. No doubt the Holy Spirit would also impress us with the *lengthiness* of Israel's afflictions, and the long-sufferance of Jehovah before He dealt in judgment. For over eighty years the Hebrews had been sorely oppressed.

"And the Lord spake unto Moses and unto Aaron, saying, When Pharaoh shall speak unto you, saying, Show a miracle for you: then thou shalt say unto Aaron, Take thy rod, and cast it before Pharaoh, and it shall become a serpent. And Moses and Aaron went in unto Pharaoh, and they did so as the Lord had commanded: and Aaron cast down his rod before Pharaoh, and before his servants, and it became a serpent. Then Pharaoh also called the wise men and the sorcerers: now the magicians of Egypt, they also did in like manner with their enchantments. For they cast down every man his rod, and they became serpents: but Aaron's rod swallowed up their rods" (vv. 8-12). The reason why Pharaoh asked Moses and Aaron to perform a miracle was to test them and prove whether or not the God of the Hebrews had really sent them. The miracle or sign selected we have already considered at length in Article 6. Its meaning and message in the present connection is not easy to determine. From an evidential viewpoint it demonstrated that Moses and Aaron were supernaturally endowed. Probably, too, the rod becoming a serpent was designed to speak to the conscience of Pharaoh, intimating that he and his people were under the dominion of Satan. This seems to be borne out by the fact that nothing was here said—either by the Lord when instructing Moses (v. 9), or in the description of the miracle (vv. 10-12)—about the serpent being turned into a rod again. It is also very significant that the second sign—the restoring of the leprous hand—which accredited Moses before the Israelites, was not performed before Pharaoh. The reason for this is obvious: the people of God, not the men of the world, are the only ones who have *revealed* to them the secret of deliverance from the defilement of sin.

The response of Pharaoh to this miracle wrought by Moses and Aaron was remarkable. The king summoned his wise men and the sorcerers—those who were in league with the powers of evil—and they duplicated the miracle. It is indeed sad to find almost all of the commentators *denying* that a real miracle was performed by the Egyptian magicians. Whatever philosophical or doctrinal difficulties may be involved, it ill becomes us to yield to the rationalism of our day. The scriptural account is very explicit and leaves no room for uncertainty. First, the Holy Spirit has told us that the magicians of Egypt "also did *in like manner* (as what Moses and Aaron had done) with their enchantments." These words are not to be explained away, but are to be received by simple faith. Second, it is added, "for they cast down every man his *rod,* (not something else which they had substituted by sleight of hand) and they (the rods) *became* serpents". If language has any meaning then these words bar out the idea that the magicians threw down serpents. They cast down their rods, and these *became* serpents. Finally, we are told, "but Aaron's rod swallowed up their rods", i. e., Aaron's rod, now turned into a serpent, swallowed up their rods, now become serpents. That the Holy Spirit has worded it in this way is evidently for the express purpose of forbidding us to conclude that anything other than "rods" were cast to the ground.

If it should be asked, How was it possible for these Egyptian sorcerers to perform this miracle? the answer must be, By the power of the Devil. This subject is admittedly mysterious, and much too large a one for us to enter into now at length. As remarked at the beginning of this paper, what is before us here in these earlier chapters of Exodus adumbrates the great conflict between good and evil. Pharaoh acts throughout as the representative of Satan, and the fact that he was able to summon magicians who could work such prodigies only serves to illustrate and exemplify the mighty powers which the Devil has at his disposal. It is both foolish and mischievous to under-estimate the strength of our great Enemy. The one that was permitted to transport our Saviour from the wilderness to the temple at Jerusalem, and the one who was able to show Him "all the kingdoms of the world *in a moment of time*" (Luke 4:5), would have no difficulty in empowering his emissaries to transform their rods into serpents.

"They cast down every man his rod, and they became serpents: but Aaron's rod swallowed up their rods" (v. 12). This is very striking. The magicians appeared in the name of their "gods" (cf Ex. 12:12 and 18:11), but this miracle made it apparent that the power of Moses was *superior* to their sorceries, and *opposed* to them too. This "sign" foreshadowed the end of the great conflict then beginning, as of every other wherein powers terrestrial and infernal contend with the Almighty. "The symbols of their authority have disappeared, and that of Jehovah's servants alone remained" (Urquhart).

"And He hardened Pharaoh's heart (literally, Pharaoh's heart was hardened) that he hearkened not unto them; as the Lord had said" (v. 13). Here again the commentators offend grievously. They insist, almost one and all, that this verse signifies that Pharaoh hardened his own heart, and that it was not until later, and *because* of Pharaoh's obduracy, that the Lord "hardened" his heart. But this very verse unequivocally repudiates their carnal reasonings. This verse emphatically declares that Pharaoh's heart was hardened, that he hearkened not unto them, *as the Lord had said*". Now let the previous chapters

be read through carefully and note *what* the Lord *had* said. He had said *nothing whatever* about Pharaoh hardening his own heart! But He *had* said, "*I will* harden his heart" (4:21), and again, "*I will* harden his heart" (7:3). This settles the matter. God had expressly declared that He *would* harden the king's heart, and now we read in 7:13 that "Pharaoh's heart *was* hardened (not, "was hard"), that he harkened not unto them, AS *the Lord had said*". Man ever reverses the order of God. The carnal mind says, Do good in order to be saved: God says, You must be saved before you can do any good thing. The carnal mind reasons that a man must believe in order to be born again; the Scriptures teach that a man must first have spiritual life before he can manifest the activities of that life. Those who follow the theologians will conclude that God hardened Pharaoh's heart because the king had *first* hardened his heart; but those who bow to the authority of Holy Writ (and there are *very* few who *really* do so), will acknowledge that Pharaoh hardened his heart *because* God had first hardened it.

What is said here of Pharaoh affords a most solemn illustration of what we read of in Prov. 21:1: "The king's heart is in the hand of the Lord, as the rivers of water: *He* turneth it *whithersoever He will*". The hardening of Pharaoh's heart is not one whit more appalling than what we read of it Rev. 17:17: "For *God hath put in their hearts* to fulfill His will, and to agree, and give their kingdom unto the Beast". Here we find ten kings in league with the Antichrist, the Man of Sin, and that it is God Himself who puts it into their hearts to give their kingdom unto him. Again we say that such things are not to be philosophized about. Nor are we to call into question the righteousness and holiness of God's ways. Scripture plainly tells us that *His* ways are "*past* finding out" (Rom. 11:33). Let us then tremble before Him, and if in marvelous grace He has softened *our* hearts let us magnify His sovereign mercy unceasingly.

CHAPTER 11

THE PLAGUES UPON EGYPT

EXODUS 7-11

For over eighty years, and probably much longer, the Egyptians had oppressed the Hebrews, and patiently had God borne with their persecution of His people. But the time had arrived when He was to interpose on behalf of His "firstborn" (4:22) and take vengeance on those who had reduced Israel to the most servile bondage. The Lord is slow to anger and plenteous in mercy, but, "He will not always chide; neither will He keep His anger forever" (Ps. 103:9). A succession of terrible judgments therefore now decended upon Pharaoh and upon his land, judgments which are known as "the Plagues of Egypt". They were ten in number. First, the waters of the Nile were turned into blood (7:14-25). Second, frogs covered the land and entered the homes of the Egyptians (8:1-5). Third, lice was made to attack their persons (8:16-19). Fourth, swarms of flies invaded the houses of the Egyptians and covered the ground (8:20-24). Fifth, a grievous disease smote the cattle (9:1-7). Sixth, boils and sores were sent on man and beast (9:8-12). Seventh, thunder and hail were added to the terrors of these Divine visitations (9:18-35). Eighth, locusts consumed all vegetation (10:1-20). Ninth, thick darkness, which might be felt, overspread the land for three days (10:21-29). Tenth, the firstborn of man and beast were slain (11, 12). A frightful summary is found in Psalm 78: "He cast upon them the fierceness of His anger, wrath, and indignation, and tribulation, by sending evil angels among them. He made a way to His anger; He spared not their soul from death, but gave their life over to the pestilence, and smote all the firstborn in Egypt, the chief of their strength in the tabernacle of Ham" (vv. 49-51 and cf. Ps. 105:27-36).

That there is much for us to learn from the record of these judgments cannot be doubted. That they set forth many important lessons of a practical, typical, and prophetic nature, we are fully satisfied. Their order, their arrangement, their number, their nature, their purpose, their effects, each call for careful and separate study. Little or no attempt has been made (so far as we are aware) to supply a detailed interpretation of their significance, so that there is small help to be obtained from the commentaries. This must cast us back the more on the Lord Himself, who never fails a dependent soul that turns to Him for aid. Let the little light which has been granted the writer stir up the reader to earnestly seek, at the Throne of Grace, more for himself. In this article we shall generalize; in the next we shall enter more into detail.

1 The *purpose* of these plagues was manifold. First, they gave a public manifestation of the mighty power of the Lord God (see 9:16). This, the very magicians were made to acknowledge—"then the magicians said unto Pharaoh, This is the finger of God" (8:19).

Second, they were a Divine visitation of wrath, a punishment of Pharaoh and the Egyptians for their cruel treatment of the Hebrews. This the haughty monarch was compelled to admit—"Then Pharaoh called for Moses and Aaron in haste; and he said, I have sinned against the Lord your God, and against you" (10:16).

Third, They were a judgment from God upon the gods (demons) of Egypt. This is taught in Numbers 33:4—"For the Egyptians buried all their firstborn which the Lord had smitten among them; upon *their gods* also the Lord executed judg-

58

ments".

Fourth, they demonstrated that Jehovah was high above all gods. This was confessed later by Jethro—"And Jethro said, Blessed be the Lord who hath delivered you out of the hand of the Egyptians, and out of the hand of Pharaoh, who hath delivered the people from under the hand of the Egyptians. *Now I know* that the Lord *is greater* than all gods; for in the thing wherein they dealt proudly He was above them."

Fifth, They furnished a complete testing of human responsibility. This is indicated by their *number*, for one of the leading signification of *ten*, is full responsibility—compare the *ten* Commandments, e. g.

Sixth, They were a solemn warning to other nations, that God would curse those who curse the Israelites (Gen. 12:3). This was plainly realized by Rahab of Jericho —"And she said unto the men, I know that the Lord hath given you the land, and that your terror is fallen upon us, and that all the inhabitants of the land faint because of you. *For we have heard* how the Lord dried up the water of the Red Sea for you when ye came out of Egypt" etc. (Josh. 2:8, 9). It was also felt by the Philistines—"Woe unto us! who shall deliver us out of the hand of these mighty Gods? these are the Gods that smote the Egyptians with all the plagues in the wilderness" (1 Sam. 4:8).

Finally, these miraculous plagues were evidently designed as a series of testings for Israel. This is taught in Deut. 4:33, 34, where Moses asked Israel, "Did ever people hear the voice of God speaking out of the midst of the fire, as thou hast heard, and live? or hath God assayed to go and take Him a nation from the midst of another nation, *by temptations,* by signs, and by wonders, and by war, and by a mighty hand, and by stretched out arms, and by great terrors, according to all that the Lord your God did for you in Egypt before your eyes?" The *outcome* of these testings was expressed in the following words—"who is like unto Thee, O Lord, among the gods? who is like Thee, glorious in holiness, fearful in praises, doing wonders?" (Ex. 15:11)!

2 The *arrangement* of the plagues plainly manifests Divine order and design. The tenth is separated from all the others be-

cause of its special relation to Israel and their redemption. The other nine are arranged in groups of three's. "They form three divisions, each division consisting of three plagues. That these dividing lines are drawn by the Scripture itself will be plain when we note one remarkable feature. A warning precedes, in each instance, the first and the second plagues; but with the third in each series no warning is given. Thus Moses is commanded to meet Pharaoh before the waters of Egypt are turned into blood. So again (8:1) when the frogs are to cover the land, Moses is to go in unto Pharaoh and announce what God is about to do. But when the dust is smitten and it becomes lice throughout the land of Egypt there is no command to seek Pharaoh's presence. So it is with the sixth plague, when the ashes of the furnace are used, and it becomes boils upon man and beast; and so also is it with the ninth plague, when the land was covered with darkness as with the pall of death. In none of these three cases is there any announcement to Pharaoh. It was a reminder that God would not always strive; and that warning, repeated but unheeded, will be followed by judgment sudden and terrible" (Urquhart). Murphy in his commentary on the book of Exodus has also called attention to the fact that "in the first three plagues, Aaron uses the rod; in the second and third, it is not mentioned; in the third three, Moses uses it, though in the last of them only his hand is mentioned. All these marks of order lie on the face of the narrative, and point to a deep order of nature and reason out of which they spring."

There is a striking *Introversion* to be observed in connection with the plagues. Thus, in the first, the waters of the Nile were turned into blood—the symbol of *death;* while in the tenth there was actual blood-shedding, in the death of all the first-born. In the second plague, the frogs which are creatures of the night, that is, *of darkness,* came forth; while in the ninth plague there was actual darkness itself. In the third plague, the magicians were forced to exclaim, This is the finger of God (8: 19); while in the eighth (the balancing number according to the Introversion) Pharaoh said, "I have sinned against the Lord your God" (10:16). In the fourth plague we are specifically informed that

God *exempted* the land of Goshen—"no swarms of flies shall be there" (8:22) ; so also in connection with the seventh plague we read, "only in the land of Goshen, where the children of Israel were, was there no hail". While that which was common to both the fifth and the sixth plagues was the fact that in each of them the *cattle* of the Egyptians were attacked (see 9:3 and 9:9). Thus we see again the Divine hand in the arrangement and order of these different plagues.

3 The *progressive nature* of these plagues is easily perceived. There was a marked gradation, a steady advance in the *severity* of the Divine judgments. The first three interfered merely with the *comfort* of the Egyptians: the first, depriving them of water to drink and to wash in; the second, invading their homes with the frogs; the third, the lice attacking their persons. In the second three the Lord's hand was laid on their *possessions;* the first, the "flies" corrupting their land (8:24) ; the second, destroying their cattle; and the third, attacking their persons again, this time in the form of "boils" and "blains" (sores). The last three brought *desolation and death,* more plainly evidencing the direct hand of God; the hail destroyed both the herbage and the cattle; the locusts consuming what vegetation was not ruined by the hail; the darkness arresting all activity throughout the land of Egypt. All of this served to illustrate a principle which is very marked in all of the Divine dealings; as in nature, so in grace and also in judgment, there is first the blade, then the ear, then the full corn in the ear!

4 The *moral significance* of these plagues is very striking. They furnish a most solemn and complete description of the world-system (which Egypt accurately portrayed) in its dominant features. The water turned into blood tells of how death broods over this scene. The frogs, by their very inflation, suggest the pride and self-sufficiency of the children of this world. The plague of lice speaks of the uncleanness and filth which issue from the lusts of the flesh. The swarms of flies announces how that the wicked are of their father the Devil, i. e. "Beelzebub", which means "Lord of flies". The murrian of cattle (beasts of burden)—tells us that the service of the natural man is corrupted at its source. The boils and blains make us think of that awful description of the unregenerate given through the prophet Isaiah—"From the sole of the foot even unto the head there is no soundness in it; but wounds and bruises, and putrifying sores" (1:6). The hail (accompanied by fearful lightnings which ran along the ground) symbolized that the wrath of God abideth on the disobedient. The locusts which ate up all the vegetation, pictured the spiritual barrenness of this world—a desolate waste so far as the soul is concerned. The dense darkness shows how that the world is alienated from Him who is Light. The death of all the firstborn (representative of the family) foretells that Second Death which awaits all whose hearts are hardened against God.

5 The plagues were *designed to establish the faith of the Israelites.* For four hundred years they had dwelt in a land of idolatry, where Jehovah was entirely unknown. Moreover, the priests of Egypt were able to perform deeds which could not be explained apart from supernatural agency. The Lord therefore was pleased to so manifest Himself now that all impartial observers (whose minds were not blinded by Satan) must recognize the existence and omnipotence of the true God, in contradistinction from the impotency of the false gods of their heathen neighbors. In the plagues, the presence and power of Jehovah were demonstrated, so that He stood discovered to His people as the Living God. This comes out the more clearly when it is recognized that these displays of the Lord's power were so many judgments directed against the false confidences and idolatrous objects of the Egyptians (see 12:12). The sign which authenticated the mission of Moses to Pharaoh furnished more than a hint—the "serpent" was an object of worship among the Egyptians, and when Aaron's serpent-transformed rod swallowed those of the magicians, a plain warning was given that their god would be unable to save them from the forthcoming storm.

Others have described in detail the particular "gods" against which the different plagues were directed, so that it is unnecessary for us to say more than a few words upon this phase of our subject. The first plague smote the Nile, an object regarded with profound veneration by the

Egyptians. Its waters were held as sacred as is the Ganges by the Hindoos. A fearful blow then was it to their system of worship when its waters were turned to blood and its dead fish made to stink. In the second plague, the Nile was made to send forth myriads of frogs, which invaded the homes of the Egyptians and became a nuisance and torment to the people. In the third plague, lice were sent upon man and beast, and, "if it be remembered", says Gleig, "that no one could approach the altars of Egypt upon which so impure an insect harbored; and, that the priests to guard against the slightest risk of contamination, wore only linen garments, and shaved their heads and bodies every third day, the severity of this miracle as a judgment upon Egyptian idolatry may be imagined. Whilst it lasted no act of worship could be performed, and so keenly was this felt that the very magicians explained, 'this is the finger of God' ".

The fourth plague was designed "to destroy the trust of the people in Beelzebub, or the Fly-god, who was reverenced as their protector from visitation of swarms of ravenous flies, which infested the land generally about the time of the dog-days, and removed only as they supposed at the will of their idol. The miracle now wrought by Moses evinced the impotence of Beelzebub and caused the people to look elsewhere for relief from the fearful visitation under which they were suffering. The fifth plague, which consumed all the cattle, excepting those of the Israelites, was aimed at the destruction of the entire system of brute worship. This system, degrading and bestial as it was, had become a monster of many heads in Egypt. They had their sacred bull, and ram, and heifer, and goat, and many others, all of which were destroyed by the agency of the God of Moses, thus, by one act of power, Jehovah manifested His own supremacy and destroyed the very existence of their brute idols" (Dr J. B. Walker). And so we might continue.

6. The *conduct of the magicians* in connection with the plagues is deserving of notice. It has already been intimated in a previous article that we have no patience with those who would reduce the miracles wrought by these men to mere slight-of-hand-deceptions. Not only is there no hint whatever in the sacred narrative of

any deception practiced by them, not only does the inspired account describe what they wrought in precisely the same terms as it refers to the wonders performed by Moses and Aaron, but there are other insuperable objections against the conjuring theory. It is therefore deeply distressing to find men whose names command respect, pandering to that rationalism which seeks to deny everything supernatural. Have such men forgotten those words in Revelation 16:14—"they are the spirits of demons *working miracles*"!

If Jehovah was to make a public display of Himself before the Egyptians and the Israelites, it was necessary (in the fitness of things) that He should suffer the sorcerers of Egypt to enter into conflict against Himself. The magicians, appearing in the name of their gods, were completely routed, for not only was it evidenced that the power of God working through Moses was superior to their sorceries, but it was also shown that He was hostile to them and their idolatrous worship. Three times were the magicians allowed to display their powers—in the changing of their rods to serpents (7:12) in turning water into blood (7:22), and in bringing forth frogs (8:12). Beyond this they did not go. The three things which they *did* do were very significant; the first spoke of Satanic power, the second of death, and the third of pride and uncleanness. Concerning the fourth plague, we are told, "and the magicians did so with their enchantments to bring forth lice, but *they could not*". (8:18). Here is further proof that the wonders wrought by the magicians were no mere feats of legerdemain. If they were really exhibiting slight-of-hand tricks it would have been far simpler to substitute lice for dust, than it would be to substitute serpents for rods! The fact that they *could not* duplicate the miracle of the lice is proof positive that something more than a conjuring performance is in view here.

If we bear in mind that these earlier chapters of Exodus bring before us a symbolic tableau of the great conflict between good and evil, we shall easily perceive the reason why the Lord permitted Pharaoh's sorcerers to work these miracles. They serve to illustrate the activities of Satan, and this, not only as describing the character of his works, but also, as exposing both the methods he pursues and the limits of his success. The Devil is ever an *imitator,* as the parable of the tares following that of the wheat (Matt. 13) plainly shows. The aim of Pharaoh was to *nullify* the miracles of Moses. The Lord's servant had performed miracles—very well, the king would summon his magicians and show that they could do likewise. This exemplifies an unchanging principle in the workings of Satan. First, he seeks to oppose with force (persecution, etc.), as he had the Hebrews by means of their slavery. When he is foiled here he resorts to subtler methods, and employs his wiles to deceive. The one is the roaring of the "lion" (1 Pt. 5:8); the other the cunning of the "serpent" (Gen. 3:1).

There is a striking verse in the New Testament which throws light on the subject before us. In 2 Tim. 3:8, we read, "Now as Jannes and Jambres withstood Moses, so do these also resist the truth; men of corrupt minds, reprobate concerning the faith." Here we learn the names of two of the magicians (doubtless the principal ones) who worked miracles in Egypt. Jannes and Jambres *withstood* Moses. They did this not by having him turned out of the king's palace, not by causing him to be imprisoned or slain, but by duplicating his works. And, says the Holy Spirit, there are those now who similarly resist the servants of God—"*as* Jannes and Jambres withstood Moses, *so* do these (the ones mentioned in vv. 5 and 6) *also* resist the truth". This is one of the Divinely-delineated characteristics of the "perilous times". The reference is to men (and women) supernaturally endowed by Satan to work miracles. Such are found to-day, we believe, not only among Spiritualists and Christian Scientists, but also in some of the leaders of the Faith-healing cults. There are men and women now posing as evangelists of Christ who are attracting large crowds numbered by the thousand. Their chief appeal is not the message they bear, but their readiness to "anoint" and pray over the sick. They claim that "Jesus" (they never own Him as "the Lord Jesus"), in response to their faith, has through them removed paralysis, healed cancers, given sight to the blind. When their claims are carefully investigated it is found that most of the widely-advertised "cures" are impos-

tures. But on the other hand, there *are* some cases which are genuine healings, and which cannot be explained apart from supernatural agency. So it was with the miracles wrought by the magicians of Pharaoh; though limited by God they *did* perform prodigies.

7 These plagues furnished a most striking *prophetic forecast* of God's future judgments upon the world. This is, to us, one of the most remarkable things connected with God's judgments upon Egypt. The analogies furnished between those visitations of Divine wrath of old and those which the Scriptures predict, and announce for the future, are many and most minute. We here call attention only to a few of the more striking ones; the diligent student may discover many more for himself if he will take the necessary trouble:—

(1) During the Time of Jacob's Trouble Israel shall again be sorely oppressed and afflicted (Isa. 60:14 and Jer. 30:5-8).

(2) They will cry unto God, and He will hear and answer (Jer. 31:18-20).

(3) God will command their oppressors to, Let them go (Isa. 43:6).

(4) God will send two witnesses to work miracles before their enemies (Rev. 11:3-6).

(5) Their enemies will also perform miracles (Rev. 13:13-15)

(6) God will execute sore judgments upon the world (Jer. 25:15, 16).

(7) God will protect His own people from them (Rev. 7:4; 12:6, 14-16).

(8) Water will again be turned into blood (Rev. 8:8; 16:4, 5).

(9) Satanic frogs will appear (Rev. 16:13).

(10) A plague of locusts shall be sent (Rev. 9:2-11).

(11) God will send boils and blains (Rev. 16:2).

(12) Terrible hail-stones shall descend from heaven (Rev. 8:7).

(13) There shall be awful darkness (Isa. 60:2; Rev. 16:10).

(14) Just as Pharaoh hardened his heart so will the wicked in the day to come (Rev. 9:20, 21).

(15) Death will consume multitudes (Rev. 9:15).

(16) Israel will be delivered (Zech. 14: 3, 4; Rom. 11:26).

Thus will history repeat itself, and then will it be fully demonstrated that the plagues of Jehovah upon Egypt of old portended the yet more awful judgments by which the earth shall be visited in a day now very near at hand.

CHAPTER 12

THE PLAGUES UPON EGYPT
(Continued)

EXODUS 7-11

In our last article we made a number of general observations upon the judgments which the Lord God sent upon Pharaoh and his people. The subject is admittedly a difficult one, and little light seems to have been given on it. This should make *us* seek more fervently for help from above, that *our* eyes may be opened to behold wondrous things in this portion of the Word. We shall now offer a few remarks upon each plague separately according to our present understanding of them.

1. The first plague is described in Exodus 7:14-25—let the reader turn to the passage and ponder it carefully. This initial judgment from the Lord consisted of the turning of the waters into blood. Blood, of course, speaks of death, and death is the wages of sin. It was, therefore, a most solemn warning from God to Egypt, a warning which intimated plainly the doom that awaited those who defied the Almighty. Similarly will God give warning at the beginning of the Great Tribulation, for then shall the moon "become as blood" (Rev. 6:12). The symbolic significance of this first plague is easily discerned. Water is the emblem of the Word (John 15:3; Eph. 5:26), and the water turned to blood reminds us that the Word is "a savor of death unto death" (2 Cor. 2:16) as well as "of life unto life".

The striking contrast between this first plague and the first miracle wrought by the Lord Jesus has been pointed out by others before us. The contrast strikingly illustrates the great difference there is between the two dispensations; "The law was given by Moses, but *grace* and truth came by Jesus Christ" (John 1:17). All that the Law can do to its guilty transgressor is to sentence him to death, and this is what the Water turned into blood symbol-

ized. But by the incarnate Word the believing sinner is made to *rejoice,* and this is what the turning of the water into wine speaks of.

Before passing on to the next plague we would offer a word of explanation upon a point which may have troubled some of our readers. The Lord's command to Moses was, "Say unto Aaron, Take thy rod and stretch out thine hand upon the waters of Egypt, upon their streams, upon their rivers, and upon their ponds, and upon *all* their pools of water, that they may become blood" (Ex. 7:19). And yet after this we are told, "And the magicians of Egypt did so with their enchantments" (v. 22). Where then did they obtain *their* water? The answer is evidently supplied in verse 24; "And all the Egyptians *digged* round about the river for water to drink".

2. The second plague is described in Ex. 8:1-7. An interval of "seven days" (7:25) separated this second plague from the first. Full opportunity was thus given to Pharaoh to repent, before God acted in judgment again. In view of the fact that the Flood commenced on the *seventh* day (see Gen. 7:10 margin), that is, the holy Sabbath, the conclusion is highly probable that each of these first two plagues were sent upon Egypt on the *Sabbath* day, as a Divine judgment for the Egyptians' desecration of it.

This second plague, like the former, was Divinely directed against the idolatry of the Egyptians. The river Nile was sacred in their eyes, therefore did Jehovah turn its waters into blood. The frog was an object of worship among them, so God now caused Egypt to be plagued with frogs. Their ugly shape, their croaking noise, and their disagreeable smell, would make these frogs peculiarly obnoxious. Their abounding numbers marked the severity of this judgment. Escape from this scourge was impossible, for the frogs not only "covered the land of Egypt" but they invaded the homes of the Egyptians, entered their bed-chambers, and defiled their cooking-utensils.

The moral significance of these "frogs" is explained for us in Rev. 16:13—the only mention of these creatures in the New Testament. There we read "And I saw three *unclean* small spirits *like frogs* come out of the mouth of the Dragon, and out of the mouth of the Beast, and out of the mouth of the False Prophet". Frogs are used to symbolize the Powers of evil and stand for *uncleanness*. The turning of the waters into blood was a solemn reminder of the "wages of sin". The issuing forth of the frogs made manifest the character of the Devil's works—uncleanness.

Concerning this second plague we read, "And the magicians did so with their enchantments and brought forth frogs upon the land of Egypt" (8:7). This is most suggestive. The magicians were unable to remove the frogs, nor could they erect any barriers against their encroachments. All they could do was to bring forth more frogs. Thus it is with the Prince of this world. He is unable to exterminate the evil which he has brought into God's fair creation, and he cannot check its progress. All he can do is to multiply wickedness.

3. The third plague is described in Ex. 8:16-19. This judgment decended without any warning. The dust of the ground suddenly sprang into life, assuming the most disgusting and annoying form. This blow was aimed more directly at the persons of the Egyptians. Their bodies covered with lice, was a sore rebuke to their pride. Herodotus (2:37) refers to the cleanliness of the Egyptians: "So scrupulous were the priests on this point that they used to shave their heads and bodies every third day, for fear of harboring vermin while occupied in their sacred duties". As another has said, "This stroke would therefore humble their pride and stain their glory, rendering *themselves* objects of dislike and disgust".

The key to the moral significance of this third plague lies in the *source* from which the lice proceeded. Aaron smote the *dust* of the land "and it became lice in man

and beast" (8:16). In the judgment which God pronounced upon disobedient Adam we read that He said, "*Cursed* is the *ground* for thy sake" (Gen. 3:17), and again, "for *dust* thou art, and unto dust shalt thou return" (Gen. 3:19). When Aaron *smote* the "ground", and its "dust" became lice, and the lice came upon the Egyptians, it was a graphic showing-forth of the awful fact that man by nature is *under the curse* of a holy God.

Concerning this plague we read, "and the magicians did so with their enchantments to bring forth lice, but *they could not*" (8:18). How small a matter the Lord used to bring confusion upon these magicians! As soon as God restrained them, they were helpless. Turn water into blood, and bring forth frogs, they might, by God's permission; but when He withheld permission they were impotent. Thus it is with Satan himself. His bounds are definitely prescribed by the Almighty, and beyond them he cannot go. Death he can inflict (by God's permission), and uncleanness he can bring forth freely—as the "magicians" illustrated in the first two plagues; but with the Curse (which the "dust" becoming lice so plainly speaks of) he is not allowed to tamper with.

The admission of the magicians on this occasion is noteworthy: "Then the magicians said unto Pharaoh, This is the finger of God" (8:19). These are their *last* recorded words. In the end they were obliged to acknowledge the hand of God. So will it be in the last Great Day with the Devil himself, and with all his hosts and victims. They, too, will have to bow before the Lord, and publicly confess the supremacy of the Almighty.

There is a striking correspondency between this third plague and what is recorded in the eighth chapter of John's Gospel. There we find a similar contest—between the Lord and His enemies. The Scribes and the Pharisees, using the woman taken in adultery as their bait, sought to ensnare the Saviour. His only response was to stoop down and write *on the ground*. After saying to them, "He that is without sin among you, let him first cast a stone at her", we read that "Again He stooped down and wrote on the ground". The effect was startling: "They which heard, being convicted by their conscience, went out one by one . . . . and Jesus was left alone, and the woman standing in the midst". What was this but the enemy of the Lord acknowledging that it was *"the finger of God"* as He wrote in *the dust*!

4. The next plague is described in Ex. 8:20-32. This plague marked the beginning of a new series. In the first three, the magicians had opposed, but their defeat had been openly manifested. No longer do they appear upon the stage of action. Another thing which evidences that this fourth plague begins a new series is the fact that God now made "a division" between His own people and the Egyptians. The Israelites too had suffered from the first three judgments, for they also merited the wages of sin, were subject to the debasing influences of Satan, and were under the curse. But now that the Lord was about to destroy the property of the Egyptians, He spared the Israelites.

It will be noted by the student that the words "of flies" are in italics, supplied by the translators. the word "swarms" being given for the original term. The Hebrew word signifies, literally, "mixture", being akin to the term *"mixed* multitude" in Ex. 12:38. Apparently these "swarms" were made up of not only flies, but a variety of insects. As we are told in Ps. 78:45, "He sent *divers sorts* of flies". Moreover, this verse in the Psalms informs us of their devastating effects—they "devoured them"; the Hebrew signifying "ate up". This was, therefore, worse than the plague of lice. The lice annoyed, but the "divers sorts of flies" preyed upon their flesh.

The deeper meaning of this plague may be gathered from the nature of its effects, and also from the fact that the Israelites were exempted from it. This judgment had to do with *the tormenting of the bodies* of the Egyptians, thus looking forward to the eternal judgment of the lost, when their bodies shall be tormented forever and ever in the Lake which burneth with fire and brimstone. In this the people of God will have no part.

5. The next plague is described in Ex. 9: 1-7. This judgment was directed against the possessions of the Egyptians. A grievous disease smote their herds so that "all the cattle of Egypt died". But once more Jehovah exempted His own people—"of the cattle of the children of Israel died not one" (9:6). This afforded a striking demonstration of the absolute rulership of God. He completely controls every creature He has made. Disease strikes only when and where He has decreed. The herds of the Egyptians might be dying all around them, but the cattle of Israel were as secure as though there had been no epedemic at all.

The spiritual meaning and application of this judgment is not difficult to perceive. The cattle are man's servants. He harnesses them to do the hardest portion of his work. The destruction of all the "horses, asses, camels, oxen and sheep" of the Egyptians tells us that God will not accept the labors of the unregenerate—"the plowing of the wicked is sin" (Prov. 21: 4). This world and all its works will yet be burned up—destroyed as completely as were the beasts of Egypt. The sparing of the cattle of the Israelites intimates that the works of the new nature in the believer *will* "abide" (I Cor. 3:14).

6. The plague of the boils is recorded in Ex. 9:8-12. Like the third plague, this one was sent without any warning. Moses was instructed to take "handfuls of ashes of the furnace, and sprinkle it toward heaven in the sight of Pharaoh" (9:8). The definite article implies that some particular "furnace" is meant, and that Pharaoh was near it, suggests it was no mere heating apparatus. The Companion Bible says of this furnace: "i.e., one of the altars on which human sacrifices were sometimes offered to propitiate their god *Typhon* (the evil Principle). These were doubtless being offered to avert the plagues, and Moses, using the ashes in the same way produced another plague instead of averting it." Just as the previous plague signified the worthlessness of all the *works* of the natural man, so this teaches the utter vanity of his *religious* exercises.

7. The next plague is described in Ex. 9:18-35. It marks the beginning of a third series. We quote from the Numerical Bible; "We are now, in the third stage, to see, man being what he is, what the attitude of Heaven must be toward him. The three plagues that follow all distinctly point to heaven as their place of origin. Here too the rod, which in the last three, had not been seen, appears again,—a thing which the typical meaning alone, as it would seem, accounts for. For it will be seen that the middle plagues, to men, seem scarcely Divine inflictions; they proceed

more from man himself, although, in fact, the government of God may truly be seen in them. But now we come again, as in the first plagues, to direct, positive influences". In other words, the last three plagues brought out, emblematically, the *state* of the natural man; the swarms of flies breeding from filthiness; the murrian of the cattle and the boils on man, telling of impurities within, which, through the corruption of sin breaks out in moral diseases; reminding us of that graphic but awful picture of the sinner drawn by Isaiah—"From the sole of the foot even unto the head, there is no soundness in it; but wounds and bruises, and putrifying sores" (1:6).

The *severity* of this plague is marked by several particulars. It was "a very grievous hail" (9:18). It was "such as hath not been in Egypt since the foundation thereof even until now". The hail was accompanied by an electric storm of fierce intensity, so that "the fire ran along upon the ground". The effects were equally striking: "The hail smote throughout *all* the land of Egypt *all* that was in the field, both man and beast; and the hail smote every herb of the field and brake every tree of the field". This judgment was expressive of the *wrath* of a holy and sin-hating God. Similar expressions of His anger will be witnessed during the Great Tribulation—see Rev. 8:7; 16:21.

8. The eighth plague is recorded in Ex. 10:1-20. Locusts are one of the terrors of the East. They prey upon the crops, and consume all vegetation. This plague, coming on the top of the destruction of the cattle, seriously threatened the food-supplies of Egypt. Referring to this plague, the Psalmist says, "He spake and the locusts came, and caterpillars, and that without number and did eat up all the herbs in their land, and devoured the fruit of their ground" (Ps. 105:34, 35). They came at the bidding of God, and they departed at His bidding. So does every creature, the feeblest as well as the mightiest, fulfill the secret counsels of their Creator. In Joel 2:11, which speaks of a yet future judgment in the Day of the Lord, the locusts are termed, "*His* army".

We are not quite sure about the deeper meaning and spiritual significance of this eighth plague. It is clear, that like the previous one, it definitely manifested the *wrath* of God. But there would seem to be an additional line of thought suggested by these "locusts". The second chapter of Joel and the ninth of Revelation should be carefully studied in this connection. In these two chapters we have a species of *infernal* "locusts" brought to our view. They issue from the Bottomless Pit, and the Anti-Christ, is said to be their "king". It would seem then that the plaguing of Pharaoh and the Egyptians with the "locusts" points to the yet future punishing of the lost in the company of *infernal beings*: as the Lord said, "They shall be cast into everlasting fire, prepared for the Devil and his angels" (Matt. 25:41).

9. The plague of darkness is described in Ex. 10:21-29. "In Egypt the sun was worshipped under the title of Ra: the name came conspicuously forward in the title of the kings, Pharaoh, or rather Phra, meaning 'the sun'" (Wilkinson's "Ancient Egypt"). "Not only therefore was the source of light and heat eclipsed for the Egyptians, but the god they worshipped was obscured and his powerlessness demonstrated—a proof, had they but eyes to see, that a mightier than the sun, yea the Creator of the sun, was dealing with them in judgment." (Ed. **Dennett**).

This ninth plague formed a fitting climax to the third series. It is easily interpreted. God is Light: darkness is the withdrawal of light. Therefore, this judgment of darkness, gave plain intimation that Egypt was now *abandoned by God*. Nothing remained but death itself. The darkness continued for three days—*full manifestation* of God's withdrawal. So fearful was this "thick darkness" that the Egyptians "saw not one another, neither rose any from his place". Striking is the contrast presented in the next sentence: "But all the children of Israel *had* light in their dwellings." This light was as supernatural as the darkness. It emanated, most probably, from the Shekinah glory. The Egyptians had a darkness which they could not light up: Israel a light which they could not put out. Thus it is upon earth to-day. The people of God are "children of light" (Eph. 5:8), because God "who commanded the light to shine out of darkness, hath shined in our hearts to give *the light* of the knowledge of the glory of God in the face of Jesus Christ" (2 Cor. 4:6). But "the way of the wicked *is as darkness*:

they know not at what they stumble" (Prov. 4:19), and this because they are "without God in the world" (Eph. 2:12).

The three days of darkness which brooded over the land of Egypt remind us of the three hours of darkness over all the earth when the Saviour hung upon the cross—outward expression of God's abandonment. There the Holy One of God was being "made sin" (2 Cor. 5:21) for His people, and He Who is "of purer eyes than to behold evil, and canst not look upon iniquity" (Hab. 1:13), turned away His face from the One who was being punished in our stead. It was this turning away of God from Him which caused the Saviour to cry, "My God, my God, why hast Thou *forsaken* Me?".

Finally, this three days of dense darkness upon Egypt utters a solemn warning for all who are now out of Christ. Unsaved reader, if you continue in your present course, if you go on slighting the mercy of God, if you refuse to heed His warning to flee from the wrath to come, you shall be finally cast into "the outer darkness" (Matt. 8:12)—the "blackness of darkness forever" (Jude 13). Neglect, then, thy soul's salvation no longer. Turn even now unto Him who is "the *Light* of the world", and in His light thou shalt see light.

10. The final plague upon Egypt is recorded in Ex. 11 and 12. Comments upon this we will reserve for our next papers. In this last plague, the Lord did that to which all the other plagues were logically and irresistibly leading up—the slaying of the first-born. Terrible climax was this. Disease, desolation, and darkness had visited Pharaoh's land; now *death* itself was to do its work.

The study of these plagues shows plainly the *character* of Him with whom we all have to do. The Lord is not indifferent to sin, nor can He be defied with impugnity. He bears with much longsuffering the vessels of wrath, but in the end His righteous judgments descend upon them. What point do these plagues give to that solemn word, "It is a *fearful thing* to fall into the hands of the living God" (Heb. 10:31)! Be warned, then, dear reader. To-day, if you will hear His voice, harden not *your* heart. Remember what befell Pharaoh for hardening his! Flee then to the Divinely-appointed Refuge. Believe on the Lord Jesus Christ and thou shalt be saved.

CHAPTER 13

PHARAOH'S COMPROMISES

Our plan in this series of papers is not to furnish a verse by verse exposition of the book of Exodus, but rather to treat its contents topically, singling out the more important incidents and concentrating our attention upon them. The most serious disadvantage of this method is, that after we have followed out one topic to its conclusion, we are obliged to retrace our steps to begin a new one. Yet, perhaps, this is more than offset by the simplicity of the present plan and by the help afforded the reader to remember, substantially, the contents of this second book of Scripture. It is much easier to fix details in the mind when they are classified and conveniently grouped. Having gone over the ten plagues, we are now to contemplate the effect which they had upon Pharaoh. This will require us to go back to the earlier chapters.

In the course of the revelation which Jehovah made to Moses at the burning bush, we find Him saying, "And thou shalt come, thou and the elders of Israel, unto the king of Egypt, and ye shall say unto him, The Lord God of the Hebrews hath met with us; and now let us go, we beseech thee, three days' journey into the wilderness, that we may sacrifice to the Lord ,our God" (3:18). And while Moses was responding to the Divine call, the Lord said unto him again, "When thou goest to return into Egypt, see that thou do all these wonders before Pharaoh, which I have put in thine hand; but I will harden his heart, that he shall not let the people go. And thou shalt say unto Pharaoh, Thus saith the Lord, Israel is My son, even My firstborn; And I say unto thee, Let my son go, that he may serve Me" (4:21-23). In this last-quoted scripture the Lord furnished a reason *why* He desired His people to go into the wilderness to serve Him—"Israel is My son, My firstborn". Two truths were here enunciated. To Israel pertained "the adoption" (Rom. 9:4). This adoption was not individual (as with us), but as a nation. The use of this term denoted that Israel had been singled out as the objects of God's special favors—"I am a Father to Israel, and Ephraim is My *firstborn*" ·(Jer. 31:9). The title of "firstborn" speaks of dignity and excellency (see Gen. 49:3; Ps. 89:27). Israel will yet occupy the *chief* place among the nations, and be no more the "tail", but the "head". The place of the "firstborn", then, is that of honor and privilege. To the firstborn belonged a double portion.

The *terms* of this demand upon Pharaoh call for careful consideration. First, God had said that His people must go a three days' journey into the wilderness that they might *"sacrifice* to the Lord their God" (3:18). Then the Lord added, "that he (His "firstborn") may *serve* Me" (4:23). Finally, when Moses and Aaron delivered their message unto Egypt's king, we find them, saying, "Thus saith the Lord God of Israel, Let My people go that they may *hold a feast unto Me* in the wilderness" (5:1). The *order* of these three statements is very significant. The thought of "sacrifice" comes first! This is required to avert God's judgment. Only as the sinner places *blood* between himself and the thrice holy God, can he stand in His august presence. Nothing but simple faith in an accomplished atonement enables the heart to be quiet before Him. "Without shedding of blood is no remission (Heb. 9:22)· Following this, comes *service*. None can serve God acceptably till they are reconciled to Him. "Whose I am, *and* whom I serve" (Acts 27:23) is the Divine order. Following this, comes "the feast", which speaks of *fellowship* and *gladness*. But this cannot be until the will is broken and the "yoke" has been received—for *this* is what true "service" implies. These three things, in the same beautiful order are strikingly illustrated in connection with the Prodigal Son. First the wayward one was reconciled, then he took his proper place—"make me as one of Thy hired *servants*"; and then came the feasting, over the "fatted calf".

When God's demand was first presented to Pharaoh, the king repulsed it in most haughty fashion; "And Pharaoh said, Who is the Lord, that I should obey His voice to let Israel go? I know not the Lord, neither will I let Israel go" (5:2). How the "enmity" of the carnal mind is evidenced here! How the awful depravity of the unregenerate heart was displayed! The natural man knows not the Lord, neither does he hear or heed His voice. And, too, can we not clearly discern here the Arch-rebel, the "god of this world", whom Pharaoh so strikingly adumbrated? Surely we can; and as we shall yet see, this is by no means the only trace of the Adversary's footprints which are to be detected on the face of this record.

The answer of God to this defiant refusal of Pharaoh was to visit his land with sore judgments. As pointed out in a previous paper, the first three plagues fell upon Israel as well as the Egyptians. But in the fourth God said, "I will sever in that day the land of Goshen, in which My people dwell, that no swarms of flies shall be there" (Ex. 8:22). This seems to have deeply impressed the king, for now, for the first time, he pays attention to Jehovah's demand.

1. "And Pharaoh called for Moses and Aaron and said, Go ye, sacrifice to your God in the land" (8:25). At first sight it would appear that at last Pharaoh was amenable to reason, recognizing the futility of fighting against the Almighty. But a closer glance at his words will show that he was far from being ready to comply with Jehovah's requests. God's command was couched in no uncertain terms. It called for the *complete separation* of His people unto Himself. Three things made this clear. First, "The God of the *Hebrews*" said Moses, "hath met with us" (5:3). This title always calls attention to the separate character of His people (cf. 9:1; 9:13; 10:3). Second, "Let us go *three*

days' journey". From Genesis 1 onwards, the third day speaks of resurrection. God would have His people completely delivered from the land of darkness and death. Third, "Let My people go, that they may hold a feast unto Me *in the wilderness*", that is, apart from Egypt, which speaks of the world. Only one sacrifice was offered to the Lord in Egypt, namely, The Passover, and that was to deliver from death in Egypt; all others were reserved for the tabernacle in the wilderness.

The original response of Pharaoh was, "Wherefore do ye, Moses and Aaron, hinder the people from their work? Get you unto your burdens" (5:4). As another has said, This is "typical of the world's attitude towards spiritual service. The 'burdens of Egypt' are far more important than the service of the Lord, and even among the Lord's people Martha finds more imitators than Mary, so much of Egypt do we all carry with us".

But now, when the fifth plague fell upon Egypt, Pharaoh said, "Go ye, sacrifice to your God *in the land* (8:25). The Lord had said, A three days' journey into the wilderness. Pharaoh temporized. He grants Israel permission to worship *their* God; he does not insist that they bow down to *his;* but he suggests there is no need for them to be extreme: "sacrifice to your God *in the land*".

This proffer was very subtile and well calculated to deceive one who was not acquainted with the character of God. "It might with great plausibility and apparent force, be argued: Is it not uncommonly liberal on the part of the king of Egypt to offer you toleration for your peculiar mode of worship? Is it not a great stretch of liberality to offer your religion a place on the public platform? Surely you can carry on your religion here as well as other people. There is room for all. Why this demand for separation? Why not take common ground with your neighbors? There is no need, surely, for such extreme narrowness." (C.H.M.)

Writing to the Corinthians, the apostle said, "We are not ignorant of his (Satan's) devices" (2 Cor. 2:11). Nor need any Christian be with the Word of Truth in his hands. One merciful reason why God has given to us the Scriptures is to inform us of Satan's wiles, uncover his subtility and expose his methods of attack. They are to be sought not only in those verses where he is referred to by name, but also in passages where he is only to be discovered working behind the scenes. Referring to some incidents in the history of Israel, the apostle declared, "Now all these things happened unto them for types; and they are written for our admonition" (1 Cor. 10:11). In the light of these scriptures, then, we are fully justified in regarding these compromises of Pharaoh as samples of the temptations which the Devil now brings to bear upon the people of God.

"Sacrifice to your God *in the land*", that is, Egypt. And Egypt represents the *world*. But God's people have been delivered "from this present evil world" (Gal. 1:4). Said the Lord to His apostles, "Ye are not of this world, but I have chosen you out of the world". (John 15:19). And again, "They are not of the world, even as I am not of the world". (John 17:14). "The friendship of the world is enmity with God" (James 4:4), how then can believers worship God "in the land"? They cannot. God *must be* worshipped "in spirit and in truth" (John 4:24), and to worship God "in spirit" means to worship Him through the new nature. It means to take our place, by faith, *outside* of the world which crucified the Son of God! It means "going forth without the camp, bearing His reproach" (Heb. 13:13). It means being separated, in spirit, from all that is of the flesh.

This is just what Satan hates. He aims to get the believer to *mix* the world and the church. Alas! how well he has succeeded. Professing Christians have, for the most part, so assimilated their worship to Egyptian patterns, that instead of being hated by the world, they have taught the men of the world to join in with them. Thus far has the offense of the cross ceased. Of few indeed can it now be said, "the world *knoweth us not*, because it knew Him not (1 John 3:1).

Insidious was Pharaoh's proposal. Moses was not deceived by it. His answer was prompt and uncompromising: "And Moses said, It is not meet so to do; for we shall sacrifice the abomination of the Egyptians to the Lord our God: lo, shall we sacrifice the abomination of the Egyptians before their eyes and will they not stone us?" (8:26). It is *not meet* or proper for God's people to worship Him in the midst of His enemies: "Come out from among them,

and be ye separate, saith the Lord" (2 Cor. 6:17) has ever been His demand. Moreover, to worship God "in the land" would be to "sacrifice the abomination of the Egyptians". Light is thrown upon this expression by what we are told in Genesis 46:34—"For every shepherd is an abomination unto the Egyptians". If every "shepherd" was an abomination to the Egyptians, certainly to present a *lamb* in sacrifice to God would be equally abominable to them. Nor have things changed since then. Christ crucified—which condemns the flesh, and makes manifest the total depravity of man—is still a "stumbling-block". Again; "shall we sacrifice the abomination of the Egyptians before their eyes, will they not stone us?" Press upon men the Divine need of the Cross—God's judgment of sin (Rom. 8:3); announce that by the Cross of Christ believers are crucified to the world (Gal. 6:14), and the world's enmity is at once aroused. Said the Lord Jesus, "If ye were of the world, the world would love his own; but because ye are not of the world, but I have chosen you out of the world, therefore the world hateth you. Remember the word that I said unto you, The servant is not greater than his Lord. If they have persecuted Me, they will also persecute you; if they have kept My saying, they will keep yours also" (John 15:19, 20).

One more reason Moses gave why he would not accept Pharaoh's proposal; "We will go three days' journey into the wilderness and sacrifice to the Lord our God, *as He shall command us*" (8:27). Here Moses reveals the real point of the Enemy's attack—it was the Word of God which he sought to neutralize. The Lord had said "in the wilderness". To have worshipped God "in the land" would, therefore, have been rank disobedience. When God has spoken, that settles the matter. No room is left for debating or reasoning. It is vain for us to discuss and dispute. Our duty is to submit. The *Word* itself must regulate our worship and service, as well as everything else. Human opinions, human traditions, custom, convenience, have nothing to do with it. Divine revelation is our only Court of Appeal.

2. His first compromise firmly repulsed, Pharaoh resorts to another, even more subtle. "And Pharaoh said, I will let you go, that you may sacrifice to the Lord your

God in the wilderness". (8:28). Ah, that sounded promising. It appeared as though the king was now ready to yield. But mark well his closing and qualifying words— "*only* ye shall not go very far away". Pharaoh was ready to lengthen the chain, but it *was* still *a chain*. Complete liberty he was not ready to grant the Israelites. The point at issue was the *complete separation* of God's people from Egypt (the world), and *this* Pharaoh (representing Satan) contested to the bitter end.

"Only ye shall not go very far away" is one of the favorite and most successful of the Devil's temptations. Avoid extremes; do not be fanatical; be sane and sensible in your religious life; beware of becoming narrow-minded, are so many different ways of expressing the same thing. If you really must be a Christian, do not let it spoil your life. There is no need to cut loose from your old friends and associations. God does not want you to be long-faced and miserable. Why then abandon pleasures and recreations innocent in themselves? With such whisperings Satan beguiles many a soul. Young believers especially need to be on the guard here.

"Not very far away" is incompatible with the first law of the Christian life. The very purpose for which the Lord sent Moses to Pharaoh was to lead His people out of Egypt, and to bring them into the land of Canaan. And in this Moses was a type of the Lord Jesus. The Son of God left heaven for earth that He might take a people from earth to heaven.—bring them there first in spirit and heart, later in person. "Set your affection upon things above (Col. 3:1) is God's call to His children. "Holy (separated) brethren, partakers of the heavenly calling" (Heb. 3:1) is one of our many titles, and Heaven *is* "very far away" from the world! Separation from this world in our interests, our affections, our ways, is the first law of the Christian life. "Love not the world, neither the things which are in the world. If any man love the world the love of the Father is not in him" (1 John 2:15).

But how can the Christian be happy if he turns his back upon all that engaged his mind and heart in the unregenerate days? The answer is very simple: By being occupied with that which imparts a deeper, fuller, more lasting and satisfying joy than anything which this poor world has to offer. By being absorbed with the infinite perfections of Christ. By meditating upon the precious promises of the Word. By serving the Lord. By ministering to the needy. God did not propose to bring His people out of Egypt and give them nothing in return. He would lead them into the wilderness in order that they might "hold a *feast* unto the Lord". True, the "feast" (fellowship) is now "in the wilderness", but the wilderness is Heaven begun when we are delighting ourselves with Christ; in *His* presence there is "fulness of joy".

After all, Pharaoh was only dissembling. As soon as the plague of flies was removed, he "hardened his heart . . . . neither would he let the people go" (8:32). But he reckoned without God. Heavier judgments were now sent upon his land, which brought the king to his knees, yet not in genuine repentance and submission.

3. "And Moses and Aaron were brought again unto Pharaoh; and he said unto them, Go, serve the Lord your God; but *who* are they that shall go? And Moses said, We will go with our young and with our old, with our sons and with our daughters, with our flocks and with our herds will we go; for we must hold a feast unto the Lord. And he said unto them, Let the Lord be so with you, as I will let you go, and your little ones; look to it; for evil is before you. *Not so;* go now ye that are *men,* and serve the Lord; for that ye did desire. And they were driven out from Pharaoh's presence" (Ex. 10:8-11).

This was surely a cunning wile of Satan—professing willingness to let the men go if they would but leave their little ones behind in Egypt! Thereby he would have falsified the testimony of the Lord's redeemed ones, and retained a most powerful hold upon them through their natural affections. For how could they have done with Egypt as long as their children were there? Satan knew this, and hence the character of this temptation. And how many Christians there are who become entangled in this snare! Professing to be the Lord's, to have left Egypt, they allow their families to remain behind. As another has said, "Parents in the wilderness, and their children in Egypt—terrible anomaly! This would only have been a half deliverance; at once useless to Israel, and dishonoring to Israel's God. This could not be. If the children remained in Egypt, the parents could not possibly be said to have left it, inasmuch as their children were part of themselves. The most that could be said in such a case was, that in part they were serving Jehovah, and in part Pharaoh. But Jehovah could have no part with Pharaoh. He should either have all or nothing. This is a weighty principle for Christian parents. . . . . It is our happy privilege to count on God for our children and to bring them up in the nurture of the Lord! These admirable words should be deeply pondered in the presence of God. For nowhere does our testimony so manifestly break down as in our families. Godly parents, whose walk is blameless, are seduced into permitting their children practices which they would not for one moment allow in themselves, and thus to flood their houses with the sounds and sights of Egypt" (Ed. Dennett).

Be a Christian, says Satan, if you really must, but do not force religion upon the members of your family, and especially do not tease your children with it. They are too young to understand such things. Let them be happy now; time enough for serious concerns when they grow up. If you press spiritual things upon them to-day, you will nauseate them, and drive them to infidelity. Thus the Devil argues, and only too many professing Christians heed his siren voice. Family discipline is relaxed, the Scriptures are not given their proper place, the children are allowed to chose their own companions, and no real effort is made to bring them out of Egypt.

The training of children is a most solemn responsibility, and in these days of laxity and lawlessness, an increasingly serious problem. No little grace is needed to defy the general trend of our day, and to take a firm stand. But the Word of God is plain and pointed. "Train up a child in the way he *should* go" (Prov. 22:6). For this the parent needs to be daily cast upon God, seeking wisdom and strength each hour from Him. The "training" cannot start too early. Just as a wise gardener begins, while the trees are young and tender to train the branches along the wall, so should we begin with our children in their most tender years. God has declared, "Them that honor Me, I will honor" (1 Sam. 2:20). The first lines the Christian's children should be taught are not nursery rhymes and fairy tales, but short and appropriate verses of Scripture. The first truths which need to be pressed upon the

little one are the claims that God has upon all His creatures—that He should be revered, loved, obeyed. That the child is a lost sinner, in need of a Saviour, cannot be taught him too early. If it be objected that he is too young to understand such things, the answer is, Salvation does not come to any through *understanding,* but— through FAITH, and faith cometh by hearing, and hearing by the Word of God. And to give the children God's Word is the binding and daily duty of every parent. You cannot lawfully transfer this duty to someone else. Not the Sunday-School teacher but *the parent* is the one whom *God* holds responsible to teach the children.

"While on this subject of training children, we would, in true brotherly love, offer a suggestion to all Christian parents, as to the immense importance of inculcating a spirit of *implicit obedience.* If we mistake not, there is a very widespread failure in this respect, for which we have to judge ourselves before God. Whether through a false tenderness, or indolence, we suffer our children to walk according to their own will and pleasure, and the strides which they make along this road are alarmingly rapid. They pass from stage to stage, with more than railroad speed, until at length they reach the terrible goal of despising their parents altogether, throwing their authority entirely overboard, and trampling beneath their feet the holy order of God, and turning the domestic circle into a scene of godless misrule and confusion.

"How dreadful this is we need not say, or how utterly opposed to the mind of God, as revealed in His Holy Word. But have we not ourselves to blame for it? God has put into the parent's hands the reins of government and the rod of authority; but if parents through indolence suffer the reins to drop from their hands, and if through false tenderness or moral weakness, the rod of authority is not applied, need we marvel if the children grow up in utter lawlessness? How could it be otherwise? Children are, as a rule, very much what we make them. If they are *made* to be obedient, they *will* be so; and if they are allowed to have their own way, the result will be accordingly" (C.H.M.)

Here, then, in part at least, is what is signified by the believer leaving his children behind in Egypt. It is permitting them to have their own way. It is allowing them to be "conformed to this world". It is bringing them up without the fear of God upon them. It is neglecting their *soul's* interests. It is ignoring the command of God to "bring them up in the nurture and admonition of the Lord" (Eph. 6:4). It is failure to follow in the steps of "our father Abraham," of whom the Lord said. "For I know him, that he will command his children, and his household after him, and they shall keep the way of the Lord" (Gen. 18:19). The standard which God sets before Christian parents now is certainly not a lower one than what He placed before Israel of old, and to them He said, "And these words, which I command thee this day, shall be in thine heart; And thou shalt teach them diligently unto thy children, and shalt talk of them when thou sittest in thy house, and when thou walkest by the way, and when thou liest down, and when thou riseth up" (Deut. 6:6,7). May Divine grace be earnestly sought and freely granted those of our readers who are fathers and mothers to enable them to turn a deaf ear to Satan who pleads that the little ones may be left behind in Egypt!

4. "And Pharaoh called unto Moses, and said, Go ye, serve the Lord; only let your flocks and your herds be stayed" (Ex. 10:24). "With what perseverance did Satan dispute every inch of Israel's way out of the land of Egypt! He first sought to keep them *in* the land, then to keep them *near* the land, next, to keep *part* of themselves in the land, and finally, when he could not succeed in any of these three, he sought to send them forth without any ability to serve the Lord. If he could not keep the servants, he would seek to keep their ability to serve, which would answer much the same end. If he could not induce them to sacrifice in the land, he would send them out of the land without sacrifices"! (C.H.M.)

"And Pharaoh called unto Moses and said, Go ye, serve the Lord, *only* let your flocks and your herds be stayed". This was Pharaoh's last compromise. Mark the word "only" again! The distraction of a divided heart, the vain effort to serve two masters, the miserable attempt to make the best of both worlds are suggested here. Demas was caught in this snare (II Tim. 4:10) ; so also were Ananias and Sapphira.

The danger is very real. Where our treasure is, there will our hearts be also (Matt. 6:21). If our possessions remain in Egypt, so will our affections.

The application of the spiritual principle contained in this fourth compromise is not hard to discover. The flocks and herds of this pastoral people constituted the principle part of what they owned down here. They speak then of our earthly possessions. The issue raised is whether or not God has a title to all that we have. In the light of the Word the issue is decisively settled. Nothing that we have is really ours : all is committed to us as *stewards*. And it is right here that so many of us fail. "Give yourselves to God if you must; but do not consecrate your possessions to His service" is the Devil's final plea. And multitudes of professing Christians heed it. Look at the wealth of those who bear the name of Christ. How it has piled up! And where is it all? Surely in Egypt! How much of it is held as a sacred trust for Christ?. Is not the greater part of it used to gratify self! Of old, God charged His people with *robbing* Him of His tithes and offerings (Mal. 3:8). And the same charge can justly be laid against most of us to-day.

The answer made by Moses, to this temporizing of Pharaoh is very striking: "And Moses said, Thou must give us also sacrifices and burnt offerings, that we may sacrifice unto the Lord our God. Our cattle also shall go with us; there shall not an hoof be left behind; for thereof must we take to serve the Lord our God; and we know not with what we must serve the Lord until we come thither" (10:25,26). Observe two things; "Not an hoof" must be left behind. The spiritual application of this is far reaching. We may place our money at the Lord's disposal but reserve our time for ourselves. We may be ready to pray but not to labor; or labor and not pray. "Not an hoof" means, that all that I have and am is held at the disposal of the Lord. Finally, it is striking to observe that Israel would not know the full Divine claims upon their responsibility until they reached the wilderness. The mind of God could not be discerned so long as they remained in Egypt!

We might easily have enlarged upon these compromises of Pharaoh at much greater length, but sufficient has been said, we trust, to put each Christian reader upon his guard against the specious temptations which the great Enemy of souls constantly brings to bear upon us. Let us faithfully recognize the fulness of God's claims upon us, and then seek daily grace to walk worthy of the vocation wherewith we have been called.

CHAPTER 14

THE DEATH OF THE FIRSTBORN

EXODUS 11

The contest between Pharaoh and Jehovah was almost ended. Abundant opportunity had been given the king to repent him of his wicked defiance. Warning after warning and plague after plague had been sent. But Egypt's ruler still "hardened his heart". One more judgment was appointed, the heaviest of them all, and then not only *would* Pharaoh "let" the people go, but he would *thrust* them out. Then would be clearly shown the folly of fighting against God. Then would be fully demonstrated the uselessness of resisting Jehovah. Then would be made manifest the impotence of the creature and the omnipotence of The Most High. "There are many devices in a man's heart; nevertheless the counsel of the Lord, that *shall* stand. (Prov. 19:21.)

"For the Lord of hosts hath purposed, and who shall disannul it? and His hand is stretched out, and who shall turn it back?" (Isa. 14:27). No matter though it be the king of the most powerful empire upon earth, "Those that walk in pride God is able to abase" (Dan. 4:21.) Pharaoh might ask in haughty defiance, "Who is the Lord, that I should obey His voice to let Israel go?" He might blatantly declare, "I know not the Lord, neither will I let Israel go" (5:2). But now the time had almost arrived when he would be *glad* to get rid of that people whose God had so sorely troubled him and his land. As well might a worm seek to resist the tread of an elephant as for the creature to successfully defy the Almighty. God can grind to powder the hardest heart, and bring down to the dust the haughtiest spirit.

"And the Lord said unto Moses, Yet will I bring one plague more upon Pharaoh, and upon Egypt; afterwards he will let you go hence; when he shall let you go, he shall surely thrust you out hence altogether"

(11:1). "One plague more". The severest of them all was this, directed as it was against "the chief of their strength" (Psl. 78:51). A mightier king than Pharaoh would visit the land of Egypt that night. The "king of terrors" would lay his unsparing hand upon the firstborn. And with all their wisdom and learning Pharaoh and his people would be helpless. The magicians were of no avail in such an emergency. There was no withstanding the Angel of Death! Neither wealth nor science could provide deliverance. Those in the palace were not one whit more secure than the occupants of the humblest cottage. Longsuffering God had surely shown Himself, but now His holy anger was to burst forth with irresistable might, and bitter and widespread would be the resulting lamentations.

"Speak now in the ears of the people, and let every man borrow of his neighbor, and every woman of her neighbor, jewels of silver, and jewels of gold" (11:2). This and the verse that follows are to be regarded as a parenthesis. The night on which the first-born were slain came between the fourteenth and fifteenth days of the month Nisan. And yet in 12:3 we find the Lord telling Moses to instruct Israel to take them every man a lamb on the *tenth* day of the month. Similarly, here in Ex. 11, the body of the chapter is concerned with what took place on the Passover night, verses 2 and 3 coming in parenthetically as a brief notice of what had happened previously.

That which is recorded in verse 2 has been seized upon by enemies of God's truth and made the ground of an ethical objection. The word "borrow" implies that the article should later be returned. But there was no thought of the Israelites giving back these "jewels" to the Egyptians. From this it is argued that God was teaching His peo-

76

ple to practice deception and dishonesty. But all ground for such an objection is at once swept away if the Hebrew word here translated "borrow" be rendered correctly. The Hebrew word is "Sha'al". It occurs 168 times in the Old Testament, and 162 times it is translated "ask, beg or require". The Septuagint (the Greek translation of the O. T.) gives "aites" (ask). Jeromes' Latin version renders it by "postulabit" (ask, request). The German translation by Luther reads "Fordern" (demand). The mistake has been corrected by the English Revisers, who give "ask" rather than "borrow".

While the substitution of "ask" for "borrow" removes all ground for the infidel's objection that Israel were guilty of a fraudulent transaction, there is still a difficulty remaining—felt by many a devout mind. Why should the Lord bid His people "ask" for anything from their enemies? In receiving from the Egyptians, they were but taking what was their own. For long years had the Hebrews toiled in the brick-kilns. Fully, then, had they earned what they now asked for. Lawfully were they entitled to these jewels. Yet we believe that the real, more satisfactory answer, lies deeper than this. Every thing here has a profound typical meaning. The world is greatly indebted to the presence of God's people in it. Much, very much, of the benevolence practiced by the unregenerate is the outcome of this. Our charitable institutions, our agencies for relieving suffering, are really biproducts of Christianity: hospitals, and poor-houses are unknown in lands where the light of the Gospel has not shone! When, then, God took His people out of Egypt He made its inhabitants *feel* the resultant loss. In like manner when the saints are all raptured at the descent of Christ into the air, the world will probably be made to feel that all true blessing and enlightenment has departed from it.

"And the Lord gave the people favor in the sight of the Egyptians" (11:3). This was the fulfillment of the promise made by the Lord to Moses at the burning bush: "And *I will* give this people favor in the sight of the Egyptians: and it shall come to pass, that, when ye go, ye shall not go empty" (3:21). And it was also the fulfillment of one of the promises which Jehovah made to Abraham four hundred years earlier: "And also that nation, whom they shall

serve will I judge: and afterward *shall* they come out *with great substance*" (Gen. 15:14). This is very blessed. No word of God can fail. For many long years the Hebrews had been a nation of slaves, and as they toiled in the brick-kilns there were no *outward* signs that they were likely to leave Egypt "with great substance". But the people of God are not to walk by sight, but by faith. How this fulfillment of God's ancient promise to Abraham should show the *certainty* of Him making good all His promises *to us!*

"And the Lord gave the people favor in the sight of the Egyptians" (11:3). Herein Jehovah manifested His absolute sovereignty. From the natural standpoint there was every reason why the Egyptians should *hate* the Israelites more than ever. Not only were they, as a pastoral people, an "abomination unto the Egyptians" (Gen. 46:34), but it was the God of the Hebrews who had so severely plagued them and their land. It was therefore due alone to God's all-mighty power, moving upon the hearts of the Egyptians which caused them to now regard His people with *favor*. Similar examples are furnished by the cases of Joseph and Potiphar (Gen. 39:3), Joseph and the prison-keeper (Gen. 39:21) Daniel and his master (Dan. 1:9) etc. Let us learn from these passages that when we receive kindness from the hands of the unregenerate it is because *God* has given us favor in their sight.

"And Moses said, Thus saith the Lord, About midnight will I go out into the midst of Egypt", (11:4). Moses was still in the Court. 11:1, 4 should be read straight on from 10:28, 29. The seeming interval between the two chapters disappears if we read 11:1 (as the Hebrew fully warrants) "the Lord *had* said unto Moses." God's servant, then, was still in Pharaoh palace, though the king and his courtiers were unable to see him because of the "thick darkness" which enveloped the land of Egypt. If further proof be required for this the 8th verse of our chapter supplies it, for there we read, "And all these thy servants shall come down unto me, and bow down themselves unto me, saying, Get thee out, and all the people that follow me: and after that I will go out. And he *went out from* Pharaoh in a great anger". The fourteenth day of Nisan had arrived, and after delivering the Divine ultimatum, Moses left forever the palace of the Pharaohs'.

"And Moses said, Thus saith the Lord, About midnight will I go out into the midst of Egypt: And all the firstborn in the land of Egypt shall die, from the firstborn of Pharaoh that sitteth upon his throne, even unto the firstborn of the maidservant that is behind the mill; and all the firstborn of beasts. And there shall be a great cry throughout all the land of Egypt, such as there was none like it, nor shall be like it anymore". (11:4-6). How this reminds us of that solemn word in Rom. 11:22, "Behold therefore the goodness and severity of God: on them which fell, severity; but toward thee, goodness!" In exempting His own people from this heavy stroke of judgment we behold the "goodness" of the Lord; in the slaying of all the firstborn of the Egyptians we see His "severity". But why, it may be asked, should the *"firstborn"* be destroyed? At least a twofold answer may be returned to this. It commonly happens that in the governmental dealings of God the sins of the fathers are visited upon the children. In the second place, Rom. 9:22 teaches us that the "vessels of wrath" are made by God for the express purpose of showing His wrath and making known His power. The slaying of the children rather than their parents served to accomplish this the more *manifestly*. Again, the death of the *first born* was a *representative* judicial infliction. It spoke of the judgment of God coming upon *all* that is of the natural man; the firstborn like "the firstfruits" being a *sample* of all the rest. But why slay the firstborn of *all* the Egyptians, when Pharaoh only was rebellious and defiant? Answer: It is clear from Ex. 14:17 that the rank and file of the Egyptians were far from being guiltless.

"But against any of the children of Israel shall not a dog move his tongue against man or beast: that ye may know how that the Lord *doth put a difference* between the Egyptians and Israel (11:7). Marvelous example was this of the absolute sovereignty of Divine grace. As we shall yet see, the Israelites, equally with the Egyptians, fully merited the wrath of God. It was not because of any virtue or excellence in them that the Hebrews were spared. They, too, had sinned and come short of the glory of God. It was simply according to His own good pleasure that God made this difference:. "For He saith to Moses I will have mercy *on whom I will* have mercy, and I will have compassion *on whom I will* have compassion" (Rom. 9:15). And this was no isolated instance. It was characteristic of the ways of God in every age. It is the same to-day. Some are in Christ; many are out of Christ: *sovereign grace* alone has made the difference. There can be only one answer to the apostle's question" who maketh thee to differ from another?" (1 Cor. 4:7)—it is *God.* It is not because *our* hearts (by nature) are more tender, more responsive to the Holy Spirit, than the hearts of unbelievers; it is not that *our* wills are more pliable and less stubborn. Nor is it because of any superior mental acumen which enabled us to see *our* need of a Saviour. No; grace, distinguishing grace, sovereign grace, is the discriminating cause. Then let us see to it that we give God *all* the glory for it!

"But against any of the children of Israel shall not a dog move his tongue". Striking proof was this that every creature is beneath the *direct control* of the great Creator! It was nighttime when the Angel of death executed God's sentence. Moreover, "thick darkness" shrouded the land. On every side was the weeping and howling of the Egyptians, as they discovered that their firstborn had been smitten down. Moreover, there was the movement of the Israelites, as by their hundreds of thousands they proceeded to leave the land of bondage. There was, then, every reason why the "dogs" *should* bark and howl, yea, why they should rush upon the Hebrews. But not a single dog moved his tongue! An invisible Hand locked their jaws. Just as Babylon's lions were rendered harmless by God, when Daniel was cast into their den, so Egypt's dogs were stricken dumb when Jehovah's people set out for the promised land. What comfort and assurance is there here for the believer to-day. Not so much as a fly can settle upon you without the Creator's bidding, any more than the demons could enter the herd of swine until Christ gave them permission.

It now remains for us to say something about the spiritual condition of this people here so signally favored of God. Comparatively little is told us in the earlier chapters of Exodus concerning the relations which Abraham's descendants sustained toward Jehovah, but one or two details of information are supplied in the later scriptures.

We propose, then, to bring these together that we may contemplate, briefly, the picture which they furnish us of the moral state of the Children of Israel at the time that the Lord delivered them from the House of Bondage.

In Lev. 17:7 we read, "And they shall no more offer their sacrifices unto demons unto whom they have gone a whoring". Mark the words "no more": the implication is plain that *previously* to coming out into the wilderness, Israel *had* practiced idolatry. Plainer still is Joshua 24:14, "Now therefore fear the Lord and serve Him in sincerity and in truth: and put away the gods which your fathers served on the other side of the flood, *and in Egypt;* and serve ye the Lord". Here we learn that the patriarchs served false gods before Jehovah called them, and that their descendants did the same thing in Egypt.

"In the day that I lifted up my hand unto them, to bring them forth of the land of Egypt into a land that I had espied for them, flowing with milk and honey, which is the glory of all lands; Then said I unto them, Cast ye away every man the abominations of his eyes, and defile not yourselves with *the idols of Egypt;* I am the Lord your God. But they rebelled against Me, and *would not hearken unto Me;* they did not every man cast away the abominations of their eyes, neither did they forsake the idols of Egypt; then I said, I will pour out My fury upon them, to accomplish My anger against them, in the midst of the land of Egypt. But I wrought for My name's sake that it should not be polluted before the heathen, among whom they were, in whose sight I made Myself known unto them, in bringing them forth out of the land of Egypt" (Eze. 20:6-9). Very pointed is this, supplying us with information that is not furnished in the book of Exodus. First, this passage tells us that Israel worshiped the idols of Egypt. Second, it shows how God expostulated with them. Third, it informs us that Israel heeded not God's reproval, but instead, blatantly defied Him. Fourth, it intimates how that the earlier plagues were also visitations of judgment upon the Hebrews, as well as the Egyptians. Fifth, it shows that the Lord delivered Israel, not because of any worthiness or fitness He found in them, but simply for His name's sake.

As we turn to the book of Exodus—everything in it being typical in its significance —we find how accurately the physical condition of the Israelites symbolized their spiritual state. First, they are seen in bondage, at the mercy of a cruel king,—apt portrayal of the condition of the natural man, the "captive" of the Devil (2 Tim. 2:26). Second, we read that they "sighed by reason of their bondage, and they cried" (2:23). But nothing is said about them crying *unto God!* They were conscious of their hard lot, but not yet did they know the Source from which their deliverance must proceed. How like the natural man, when he is first awakened by the Holy Spirit! His spiritual wretchedness, his lost condition, make him to sigh and groan, but as yet he is unacquainted with the Deliverer. Beautiful is it to mark what follows in 2:23: "And their cry *came up unto God* by reason of the bondage". Yes, God *heard* their cry, even though it was not addressed to Himself. And God "remembered His covenant". Ah, *that* was the ground of His action. Not their faith, for they had none. Nor was it pity for their wretchedness, for there were many others in different parts of the earth equally wretched, whom God ignored. God had respect to them for His *covenant's* sake. And it was precisely thus with us, Christian readers. God made a covenant with Christ before the foundation of the world and it was *this,* which made Him have "respect" unto us!

And what do we next read of in Exodus? This: that all unknown to the enslaved and groaning Israelites, God had raised up for them a saviour. Ex. 3 records the appearing of Jehovah to Moses at the burning bush, and the appointing of him to be the deliverer of God's people. But at that time Israel knew it not; they were in total ignorance of the wondrous grace which God had in store for them. How truly accurate the picture!. When we were first made conscious of our woeful condition, when our consciences groaned beneath the intolerable load of guilt, at that time we knew nothing of God's appointed Deliverer.

Next we are told of the Lord sending Aaron into the wilderness to meet his brother, and together they entered Egypt, gather the elders of Israel, and tell them of God's promised deliverance. We are told, "And the people believed; and when they heard that the Lord had visited the children of Israel, and that He had looked upon their affliction, then they bowed their heads and worshipped" (4:31). But it is clear from what follows that this was not a genuine *heart* believing, and their worship was evidently very superficial. Nor does the analogy fail us here. How many of us became very religious when the Deliverer was first presented to our view! But, alas, how superficial was our response!

The sequel is very striking! As soon as Pharaoh learned of God's intentions toward Israel he at once increases their burdens and says, "Let more work be laid upon the men" (5:9). How clearly Pharaoh foreshadows Satan here! As soon as the great Enemy of souls discerns the spirit of God commencing His operations of grace within the sinner, he makes the spiritual lot of that one more miserable than ever. He sets the poor soul *to work* the harder. He tells such an one that he must labor with increased zeal if ever he is to find favor with God. "They were in evil case" says the record (5:19), and so is the poor guilt-burdened, conscience-smitten, convicted sinner.

Next, we read that the people came to Moses complaining of their increased misery. Even now they did not put their trust in the Lord, but instead, leaned upon the arm of flesh. So, too, the convicted sinner —with very rare exceptions—instead of turning at once to Christ for relief, seeks out the sunday-school teacher, the evangelist, or the pastor. Similarly did the "prodigal son" act. When he "began to be in want", he did not return at once to the Father, but "went and joined himself to a citizen of that country". How slow, how pathetically slow, is man to learn the great truth that God alone is able to meet his deep, deep need!

Moses sought the Lord, and the Lord in tender patience bade His servant to go unto the Israelites and say, "I am the Lord and *I will* bring you out from under the burdens of the Egyptians, and *I will* rid you of their bondage, and *I will* redeem you with stretched out arm, and with great judgments; And *I will* take you to Me for a people, and I will be to you a God: and ye shall know that I am the Lord your God, which bringeth you out from under the burdens of the Egyptians, and *I will* bring you in unto the land, concerning the which I did swear to give it to Abraham, to Isaac, and to Jacob; and *I will* give it you for an heritage: I am the Lord" (6:6-8). Wondrous grace was this! Sad indeed is what follows: "And Moses spake so unto the children of Israel, *but they hearkened not* unto Moses for anguish of spirit, and for cruel bondage" (v. 9). How this goes to show that their earlier bowing down and "worshipping" (4:31) was merely an evanescent thing of the moment. And again we say, How true to life is the picture presented here! While Israel groaned under the burdens of the brick-kilns of Egypt, even *the promises of God* failed to give relief. So it was with each of us. While we continued to justify ourselves by our own works, while we sought to weave a robe of righteousness by our own hands, even the promises of the Gospel failed to comfort us. Ah, it is not until the soul turns away from everything of self and puts his trust alone in the Finished Work of Christ, that peace will be obtained. "To him that *worketh not,* but believeth on Him that justifieth the ungodly, his faith is counted for righteousness" (Rom. 4:5).

"And Moses spake so unto the children of Israel: but they *hearkened not* unto Moses for anguish of spirit and for cruel bondage". This is the *last* thing which we are told about the Israelites before the Angel of Death visited the land of Egypt. How clear it is then, that when the Lord "put a difference between the Egyptians and the Israelites" it was not because of any merit which He discovered in the latter. They, too, were idolaters, rebellious and unbelieving. The more clearly we perceive the spiritual wretchedness of Israel at this time, the more shall we recognize the absolute *sovereignty* of that grace which redeemed them. So, too, the more fully we are acquainted with the teaching of Scripture concerning the utter corruption and total depravity of the natural man, the more shall we be made to marvel at the infinite mercy of God toward such worthless creatures, and the more highly shall we value that wondrous love that wrought salvation for us. May the Holy Spirit impart to us an ever-deepening realization of the terrible extent to which sin has "abounded", and make us perceive with ever-increasing gratitude and joy the "super-abounding" of grace.

CHAPTER 15

THE PASSOVER

EXODUS 12

In Exodus 11:4-7 we read, "Thus saith the Lord, About midnight will I go out into the midst of Egypt: And all the firstborn in the land of Egypt shall die, from the firstborn of Pharaoh that sitteth upon his throne, even unto the firstborn of the maidservant that is behind the mill; and all the firstborn of beasts. And there shall be a great cry throughout all the land of Egypt, such as there was none like it, nor shall be like it anymore. But against any of the children of Israel shall not a dog move his tongue against man or beast, that ye may know how that the Lord doth put a difference between the Egyptians and Israel". Notice carefully the exact wording of v. 5: it was not "all the firstborn *of* the land of Egypt shall die, but "all the firstborn *in* the land of Egypt". This Divine sentence of judgment included the Israelites equally with the Egyptians. Yet in the seventh verse we are told "not a dog shall move his tongue against any of the children of Israel, for the Lord "put *a difference* between the Egyptians and Israel". Here is what the infidel would call 'a flat contradiction!' But as we are fully assured that there can be *no* contradictions in "the Word of *Truth*", so we know there must be an interpretation which brings out the harmony of this passage. *What that is,* no mere human wisdom could have devised. The sentence of universal condemnation proceeded from the *righteousness* of God; the "difference" which He put between the Egyptians and Israel was the outflow of His *grace*. But how can justice and mercy be reconciled? How can justice exact its full due without excluding mercy? How can mercy be manifested except at the expense of justice? This is really the problem that is raised here. The solution of it is found in Ex. 12. *All* the firstborn *in* the land of Egypt *did die,* and yet the firstborn of Israel were *delivered* from the An-

gel of Death! But how could this be? Surely both could not be true. Yes they were, and therein we may discover a blessed illustration and type of the contents of the Gospel.

Ex. 12 records the last of the ten plagues. This was the death of the firstborn, and inasmuch as death is "the wages of sin", we have no difficulty in perceiving that it is the question of SIN which is here raised and dealt with by God. This being the case, both the Egyptians and the Israelites alike were abnoxious to His righteous judgment, for both were sinners before Him. This was dealt with at some length in our last paper. In this respect the Egyptians and the Israelites were alike: both in nature and in practice they were sinners. "There is no difference: for *all* have sinned and come short of the glory of God (Rom. 3: 22, 23). It is true that God had purposed to redeem Israel out of Egypt, but He would do so only on a *righteous basis*. Holiness can never ignore sin, no matter where it is found. When the angels sinned God "spared them not" (2 Pt. 2:4). The elect are "children of *wrath* even as others" (Eph. 2:3). God made no exception of His own blessed Son: when He was "made sin for us" (2 Cor. 5:21)—He spared Him not (Rom. 8:32).

But all of this only seems to make the problem more impossible of solution. The Israelites were sinners: their guilt was irrefutably established: a just God can "by no means clear the guilty" (Ex. 34:7): sentence of death was passed upon them (Ex. 11:5). Nothing remained but the carrying out of the sentence. A reprieve was out of the question. Justice *must* be satisfied; sin *must* be paid its wages. What, then? Shall Israel perish after all? It would seem so. Human wisdom could furnish no solution. No; but man's extremity is God's opportunity, and He did find a solution. "Where sin a b o u n d e d, grace did much more abound" (Rom. 5:20), and yet grace was not shown at the expense of righteousness. Every demand of justice *was* satisfied, every claim of holiness *was* fully met. But how? By means of *a substitute*. Sentence of death *was* executed, but it fell upon an innocent victim. That which was *"without* blemish" died in the stead of those who had *"no* soundness" (Isa. 1:6) in them. The "difference" between the Egyptians and Israel was not a moral one, but was made solely by the blood of the pascal lamb! It was in the blood of the Lamb that mercy and truth met together and righteousness and peace kissed each other (Psl. 85:10).

The whole value of the blood of the pascal lamb lay in its being a type of the Lord Jesus—"Christ our Passover is sacrificed for us: therefore let us keep the feast" (1 Cor. 5:7, 8). Here is Divine authority for our regarding the contents of Ex. 12 as typical of the Cross-work of our blessed Saviour. And it is this which invests every detail of our chapter with such deep interest. May our eyes be anointed so that we shall be able to perceive some, at least, of the precious unfoldings of the truth which are typically set forth in our chapter.

The first great truth to lay hold of here is what we are told in the 11th verse: "It is *the Lord's* passover". This emphasizes a side of the truth which is much neglected to-day in evangelical preaching. Gospellers have much to say about what Christ's death accomplished for those who believe in Him, but very little is said about what that Death accomplished *Godwards*. The fact is that the death of Christ glorified God if never a single sinner had been saved by virtue of it. Nor is this simply a matter of theology. The more we study the teaching of Scripture on this subject, and the more we lay hold by simple faith of what the Cross meant to God, the more stable will be our peace and the deeper our joy and praise.

The particular aspect of truth which we now desire to press upon the reader is plainly taught in many a passage. Take the very first (direct) reference to the "Lamb" in Scripture. In Gen. 22:8 we read that Abraham said to his son, "God will provide Himself a lamb for a burnt offering". It was not simply God would "provide" a lamb, but that He would "provide *Himself* a lamb". The Lamb was "provided" to glorify God's character, to vindicate His throne, to satisfy His justice, to magnify

His holiness. So, too, in the ritual on the annual Day of Atonement, we read of the two goats. Why *two?* To foreshadow the two great aspects of Christ's atoning work —Godwards and usward. "And he shall take the two goats and present them before the Lord at the door of the Tabernacle of the congregation. And Aaron shall cast lots upon the two goats; one lot *for the Lord,* and the other for the scapegoat" (Lev. 16: 7, 8). It is *this* aspect of truth which is before us in Rom. 3:24-26, "Being justified freely by His grace through the redemption that is in Christ Jesus. Whom God hath set forth to be *a propitiation* through faith in His blood to declare *His righteousness* . . . that He might be *just,* and the justifier of him which believeth in Jesus". In 1 Cor. 5:7 we read, "Christ *our* Passover". He is now *our* Passover, because He was first *the Lord's* Passover (Ex. 12: 11).

If further confirmation of what we have said above be needed it is supplied by another term which is used in Ex. 12:27. Here we are expressly told that the Passover was a "sacrifice"—"It is *the sacrifice* of the Lord's passover". Nor is this the only verse in the Scriptures where the Passover is called a sacrifice. In Ex. 34: 25 we read that God said unto Israel, "Thou shalt not offer the blood of My sacrifice with leaven; neither shall *the sacrifice* of the feast of the Passover be left unto the morning". Again, in Deut. 16:2 we read, "Thou shalt therefore *sacrifice the Passover* unto the Lord thy God". So also in the New Testament, it is said, "Christ our Passover is *sacrificed* for us" (1 Cor. 5:7). We emphasize this point because it has been *denied* by many that the Passover *was* a "sacrifice". Objectors have pointed out that the pascal lamb was not slain by the priest, nor was it offered upon the altar, for there was no altar which God could own in Egypt. But such an objection is quickly removed if reference be made to the later Scriptures on the subject. *After the Exodus* the "passover" was never allowed to be killed anywhere except in the place which God had chosen. This is abundantly clear from Deut. 16:4, 5, "And there shall be no leavened bread seen with thee in all thy coasts seven days, neither shall there any thing of the flesh, which thou sacrificedst the first day at even, remain all night until the morning. Thou mayest not sacrifice the passover within any of *thy* gates, which the Lord thy God giveth thee; but *at the place* which the Lord thy God shall choose to place His name in, *there* thou shalt sacrifice the passover at even, at the going down of the sun, at the season that thou camest forth out of Egypt". The Israelites were here expressly forbidden to kill the passover in their own homes, and were commanded to sacrifice it *only* "at the place which the Lord Thy God shall choose to place His name in". What *that* "place" was we may learn from Deut. 12:5,6 and similar passages—it was the Tabernacle, afterwards the Temple.

That the Passover was a *"sacrifice"*, a priestly offering, is further proven by the fact that in Numbers 9:6, 7, 13, it is specifically designated a "corban", and it is certain that nothing was ever so called except what was brought and offered to God in the Tabernacle or the Temple. Furthermore, there is definite scripture to show that the blood of the pascal sacrifice was poured out, sprinkled, offered at the altar by *the priests*. "Thou shalt not *offer* the blood of My sacrifice with leavened bread; neither shall the fat of My sacrifice remain until the morning" (Ex. 23:18)—only *the priests* "offered" the blood. Plainer still is the testimony of 2 Chron. 30:15, 16, "Then they killed the passover on the fourteenth day of the second month and *the priests and the Levites* were ashamed, and sanctified themselves, and brought in the burnt offerings into the house of the Lord. And they stood in their place after their manner according to the Law of Moses the man of God; *the priests* sprinkled the blood". And 2 Chron. 35:11, "And they killed the passover and *the priests* sprinkled the blood". So again Ezra 6:20, "For the priests and the Levites were purified together, all of them were pure, and killed the passover for all the children of the captivity and for their brethren the priests, and for themselves". Note "the priests and Levites" killed the passover *for* all the children of the captivity!

Now there are two lines of thought associated with *sacrifices* in Scripture. First, a sacrifice is a propitiatory satisfaction rendered unto God. It is to placate His holy wrath. It is to appease His righteous hatred of sin. It is to pacify the claims of His justice. It is to settle the demands of His law. God is "light" as well as "love". He is of "purer eyes than to behold evil, and canst not look on iniquity" (Hab. 1:13). This truth is denied on every side today. Yet this should not surprise us; it is

exactly what prophecy foretold (2 Tim. 4:3, 4). Plain and pointed is the teaching of Scripture on this subject. Following the rebellion and destruction of Korah, we read that all the Congregation murmured against Moses and Aaron saying, "Ye have killed the people". What was God's response? This: "The Lord spake unto Moses saying, "Get you up from among this congregation, that I may consume them as in a moment" (Num. 16:45). How was the consuming anger of God averted? Thus: "And Moses said unto Aaron, Take a censer and put fire therein off the altar, and put on incense and go quickly unto the congregation and make an *atonement* for them; *for* there is *wrath* gone out from the Lord; the plague is begun. And Aaron took as Moses commanded and ran into the midst of the congregation; and, behold, the plague was begun among the people; and he put on incense, and made an atonement for the people. And he stood between the dead and the living; and *the plague* was stayed" (Num. 16:46-48)! A similar passage is found in the last chapter of Job. There we read, "The Lord said to Eliphaz the Temanite, My *wrath* is kindled against thee and against thy two friends; for ye have not spoken of Me the thing that is right, as My servant Job hath. *Therefore* take unto you now seven bullocks and seven rams and go to My servant Job, and offer up for yourselves a *burnt offering;* and My servant Job shall pray for you: for him will I accept; lest I deal with you after your folly."

Here, then, is the primary thought connected with "sacrifice". It is a bloody offering to appease the holy wrath of a sin-hating and sin-punishing God. And *this* is the very word which is used again and again in connection with the Lord Jesus the Great Sacrifice. Thus, Eph. 5:2: "Christ also hath loved us, and hath given Himself for us an offering and *a sacrifice to God* for a sweet-smelling savor." Again, "Once in the end of the world hath He appeared to put away sin *by the sacrifice* of Himself", (Heb. 9:26). And again, "This man, after He had offered one *sacrifice* for sins forever sat down on the right hand of God (Heb. 10:12). The meaning of these passages is explained by Rom. 3:25, 26,: Christ was unto God a "propitiation", an appeasement, a pacification, a legal satisfaction. Therefore could the forerunner of the Redeemer say, "Behold the Lamb of God which taketh away the sin of the world" (John 1:29).

The second thought associated with "sacrifice" in the Scriptures is that of *thanksgiving and praise* unto God; this being the effect of the former. It is because Christ has propitiated God on their behalf that believers can now offer "a sacrifice of praise" (Heb. 13:15). Said one of old, "And now shall mine head be lifted up above mine enemies round about me; therefore will I offer in His tabernacle *sacrifices of joy*" (Psl. 27:6). Said another, "I will sacrifice unto Thee with a voice of thanksgiving" (Jonah 2:9). This is why, after being told that "Christ our Passover hath been sacrificed for us", the exhortation follows "therefore let us keep *the feast*" (1 Cor. 5:7). The pascal lamb was first a sacrifice unto God; second, it then became the food of those sheltered beneath its blood.

The ritual in connection with the Passover in Egypt was very striking. The lamb was to be *killed* (Ex. 12:6). Death must be inflicted either upon the guilty transgressor or upon an innocent substitute. Then its *blood* was to be taken and sprinkled upon the door-posts and lintel of the house wherein the Israelites sheltered that night. "Without *shedding* of blood is no remission" (Heb. 9:22), and without *sprinkling* of blood is no salvation. The two words are by no means synonymous. The former is for *propitiation;* the latter is faith's *appropriation*. It is not until the converted sinner *applies* the blood that it avails *for him*. An Israelite might have selected a proper lamb, he might have slain it, but unless he had *applied* its blood to the outside of the door, the Angel of Death would have entered his house and slain his firstborn. In like manner to-day, it is not enough for me to know that the precious blood of the Lamb of God was shed for the remission of sins. A Saviour *provided* is not sufficient: he must be *received*. There must be *"faith* in His blood" (Rom. 3:25), and faith is a *personal* thing. *I* must exercise faith. I must by faith take the blood and shelter beneath it. I must place it between my sins and the thrice Holy God. I must rely upon it as the sole ground of my acceptance with Him.

"For I will pass through the land of Egypt this night and will smite all the firstborn in the land of Egypt, both man and beast; and against all the gods of Egypt I will execute judgment; I am the Lord. And the blood shall be to you for a token upon the houses where ye are; and when I see the blood I will pass over you, and the plague shall be not upon you to destroy you, when I smite the land of Egypt" (Ex. 12:12, 13). When the executioner of God's judgment saw the blood upon the houses of the Israelites, he entered not, and why? Because death had already done its work there! The innocent *had died* in the place of the guilty. And thus justice was satisfied. To punish twice for the same crime would be unjust. To exact payment twice for the same debt is unlawful. Even so those within the blood-sprinkled house were secure. Blessed, blessed truth is this. It is not merely God's mercy but His *righteousness* which is now on the side of His people. Justice itself *demands* the acquittal of every believer in Christ. Herein lies the glory of the Gospel. Said the apostle Paul, "I am not ashamed of the Gospel of Christ; for it is the power of God unto salvation to every one that believeth; to the Jew first, and also to the Greek (Rom. 1:16). And *why* was he not "ashamed" of the Gospel? Hear his next words, *"For* therein is *the righteousness of God* revealed from faith to faith".

"And when I see the blood I will pass over you". God's eye was not upon the house, but on the blood. It might have been a lofty house, a strong house, a beautiful house; this made no difference; if there was no blood there judgment entered and did its deadly work. Its height, its strength, its magnificence availed nothing, if the blood was lacking. On the other hand, the house might be a miserable hovel, falling to pieces with age and decay; but no matter; if *blood* was upon its door, those within were perfectly safe.

Nor was God's eye upon those within the house. They might be lineal descendants of Abraham, they might have been circumcised on the eighth day, and in their outward life they might be walking blamelessly so far as the Law was concerned. But it was neither their genealogy, nor their ceremonial observances, nor their works, which secured deliverance from God's judgments. It was their personal application of the shed blood, and of that alone.

"And the blood shall be to you for a token upon the houses where ye are; and when I see the blood, I will pass over you" (v. 13). To the mind of the natural man this was consummate folly. What difference will it make, proud reason might ask, if *blood* be smeared upon the door? Ah! "The natural man receiveth not the things of the Spirit of God: for they are *foolishness* unto him (1 Cor. 2:14). Supremely true is this in connection with God's way of salvation—"For the preaching of the cross is to them that perish *foolishness;* but unto us which are saved it is the power of God . . . But we preach Christ crucified, unto the Jews a stumbling-block, and unto the Greeks foolishness" (1 Cor. 1:18, 23). It is faith, not reasoning, which God requires; and it was faith which rendered the Passover-sacrifice effective; "Through *faith* he kept the passover, and the sprinkling of blood lest he that destroyed the first-born should touch them" (Heb. 11:28).

"To realize what this faith must have been, we have to go back to 'that night', and note the special circumstances, which can alone explain the meaning of the words 'by faith'. God's judgments had been poured out on Egypt and its king, and its people. A crisis had arrived; for, after nine plagues had been sent, Pharaoh and the Egyptians still remained obdurate. Indeed, Moses had been threatened with death if he ever came again into Pharaoh's presence (Ex. 10:28, 29). On the other hand, the Hebrews were in more evil case than ever; and Moses, who was to have delivered them, had not made good his promises.

"It was at such a moment that Moses heard from God what he was to do. To sense and sight it must have seemed most inadequate, and quite unlikely to accomplish the desired result. Why should this last plague be expected to accomplish what the nine had failed to do with all their accumulating terrors? Why should the mere sprinkling of the blood have such a marvelous effect? And if they were indeed to leave Egypt 'that same night' why should the People be burdened with all those minute ceremonial observances at the moment when they ought to be making preparation for their departure? Nothing but 'faith' could be of any avail here. Everything was opposed to human understanding and human reasoning.

"With all the consciousness of ill-success upon him, nothing but unfeigned faith in the living God and what he had heard from Him, could have enabled Moses to go to the people and rehearse all the intricacies of the Pascal observances, and tell them to exercise the greatest care in the selection of a lamb on the tenth day of the month, to be slain on the fourteenth day, and eaten with (to them) an unmeaning ceremony. It called for no ordinary confidence in what Moses had *heard* from God to enable him to go to his brethren who, in their deep distress, must have been ill-disposed to listen; for, hitherto, his efforts had only increased the hatred of their oppressors, and their own miseries as bondmen. It would to human sight be a difficult if not impossible task to persuade the people, and convince them of the absolute necessity of complying with all the minute details of the observance of the Passover ordinance.

"But this is just where *faith* came in. This was just the field on which it could obtain its greatest victory. Hence we read that, *"through faith* he kept the passover, and the sprinkling of blood" (Heb. 11:28), and thus every difficulty was overcome, and the Exodus accomplished. All was based on 'the hearing of faith'. The words of Jehovah *produced* the faith, and were at once the cause and effect of all the blessing" (Dr. Bullinger)

"And the blood shall be to you for a token upon the houses where ye are: and when I see the blood, I will pass over you, and the plague shall not be upon you to destroy, when I smite the land of Egypt" (v. 13). In connection with this it is deeply important that we should distinguish between two things; the *foundation* of *security* and the proof *basis* of *peace.* That which provided a safe refuge from judgment was the *death* of the lamb and *sprinkling* of the blood. That which offered a stay to the heart was the *promise* of Him who cannot lie. So many err on this second point. They want to make their experience, their feelings, something within themselves, the basis of their assurance. This is a favorite device of Satan, to turn the eye downwards upon ourselves. The Holy Spirit ever directs the eye *away from ourselves* to God and His Word.

Let us suppose a case. Here are two households on that Passover night. At the head of the one is an unbelieving father who has refused to heed the Divine warning and avail himself of the Divine provision. Early that evening his firstborn says, "Father I am very uneasy. Moses has declared that at midnight an Angel is to visit this land and slay all the firstborn, except in those houses which are protected by the blood of a lamb". To still the fears of his son, the father lies, and assures him that there is no cause for alarm seeing that he *has* killed the lamb and applied its blood to the door. Hearing this, the son is at rest, all fear is gone, and in its place he is filled with peace. *But it is a false peace!*

In the second home the situation is reversed. At the head of this house is a God-fearing man. He has heard Jehovah's warning message through Moses, and hearing, has believed and acted accordingly; the lamb has been slain, its blood placed upon the lintel and posts of the door. That evening the firstborn says, "Father, I feel very uneasy. An Angel is to smite all the firstborn to-night and how shall I escape?" His father answers, "Son, your alarm is groundless; yea, it is dishonoring to God. The Lord has said, 'when I see the blood, *I will* pass over you'". "But", continues the son, "while I know that you have killed the lamb and applied its blood, I cannot be but terrified. Even now I hear the cries of terror and anguish going up from the houses of the Egyptians. O that morning would come! I shall not feel safe 'till then". *But his fears were groundless.*

Now observe. In the first case supposed above we have a man full of happy feelings, yet he perished. In the second case, we have one full of fears yet was he preserved. Examine the *ground* of each. The oldest son in the first house was happy because he made *the word of man* the ground of his peace. The oldest son in the second house was miserable because he *failed* to rest on the sure Word *of God*. Here, then, are two distinct things. *Security* is by the applied blood of the Lamb. *Assurance and peace* are to be found by resting on the Word of God. The *ground* of both is *outside* of ourselves. Feelings have nothing to do with either. Deliverance from judgment is by the Finished Work of Christ, *and by that alone*. Nothing else will avail. Religious experiences, o r d i n a n c e s, self-sacrifice, Church-membership, works of mercy, cultivation of character, avail *nothing*. The first thing for me, as a poor lost sinner, to make sure of is, Am I *relying* upon what Christ did *for* sinners? Am I *personally* trusting in His shed blood? If I am not, if instead, under the eloquence and moving appeals of some evangelist, I have decided to turn over a new leaf, and endeavor to live a better life, and I have "gone forward" and taken the preacher's hand, and if *he* has told me that I am now saved and ready to "join the church," and doing so I feel happy and contented—*my peace is a false one,* and I shall end in the Lake of Fire, unless God in His grace disillusions me.

On the other hand, if the Holy Spirit has shown me my lost condition, my deep need of the Saviour, and if I have cast myself upon Christ as a drowning man clutches at a floating spar; if I have really *believed* on the Lord Jesus Christ (Acts 16:31), and *received* Him as my own personal Saviour (John 1:12), and yet, nevertheless, I am still lacking in assurance of *my acceptance* by God, and have no *settled peace* of heart; it is because I am failing to rest in simple faith on the *written Word*. GOD SAYS, "Believe on the Lord Jesus Christ and thou shalt be saved". That is enough. That is the Word of Him who cannot lie. Nothing more is needed. "Verily, verily, I say unto you, He that heareth My Word, and believeth on Him that sent Me, hath everlasting life, *and shall not come into condemnation;* but is passed from death unto life" (John 5:24). Never mind about your feelings; do not stop to examine your repentance to see if it be deep enough. It is CHRIST that saves; not your tears, or prayers, or resolutions. If you *have* received Christ, then you *are saved*. Saved now, saved forever.—"For by one offering He hath perfected *forever* them that are set apart" (Heb. 10:14). How may you *know* that you are saved? In the same way that the firstborn Israelite could know that *he* was secure from the avenging Angel—by *the Word* of God. "When I see the blood *I will* pass over you". God is saying the same to-day. If you are under the blood, then you are eternally secure. Neither the Law, nor the Devil, can harm you. "It is God that justifieth, who is he that condemneth?" (Rom. 8:33, 34). Receive Christ for salvation. Rest on God's Word for assurance and peace!

Nor are we to be occupied with our *faith,* any more than with our feelings. It is not the *act* of faith which (instrumentally) saves us, but *the TRUTH itself,* which faith lays hold of. If no blood had been placed on the door, no believing it *was* there would have delivered from the avenger. On the other hand, if the blood *had been* placed on the door, and those within doubted its efficacy, peace would have been destroyed but not their security. It is faith in God's promise which brings assurance. For *salvation,* faith is simply the hand that receives the gift. For *assurance,* faith is "setting to our seal that God is true" (John 3:33). And this is simply receiving "*His* testimony".

In this paper we have only sought to develop that which is central and vital in connection with our salvation and peace.

In our next we shall, God willing, take up some of the many interesting details of Exodus 12. May the Lord be pleased to use what we have written to establish His own.

CHAPTER 16

THE PASSOVER (Continud)

EXODUS 12

The institution and ritual of the Passover supply us with one of the most striking and blessed foreshadowments of the cross-work of Christ to be found anywhere in the Old Testament. Its importance may be gathered from the frequency with which the title of "Lamb" is afterwards applied to the Saviour, a title which looks back to what is before us in Exodus 12. Messianic prediction contemplated the suffering Messiah "brought as a Lamb to the slaughter" (Isa. 53:6). John the Baptist hailed Him as "Behold the Lamb of God which taketh away the sin of the world" (John 1:29). The apostle speaks of Him as "a Lamb without blemish and without spot" (1 Pt. 1:19). While the one who leaned on the Master's bosom employs this title no less than twenty-eight times in the closing book of Scripture. Thus, an Old Testament prophet, the Lord's forerunner, an apostle, and the Apocalyptic seer unite in employing this term of the Redeemer.

There are many typical pictures of the sacrificial work of Christ scattered throughout the Old Testament, yet it is to be doubted if any single one of them supplies so complete, so many-sided a portrayal of the person and work of the Saviour as does the one before us. The Passover sets forth both the Godward and the manward aspects of the Atonement. It prefigures Christ satisfying the demands of Deity, and it views Him as a substitute for elect sinners. Hardly a single vital phase of the Cross, either in its nature or its blessed results, but what is typified here. That which is central and basic we contemplated in our last paper; here we shall confine our attention to details.

1. Following the order of the contents of Ex. 12, the first thing to be noted is that the institution of the Passover changed Israel's calendar: "*This* month shall be unto you the beginning of months; *it* shall be the first month of the year to you" (12:2). Deeply significant is this. Passover-month was to *begin* Israel's year; only from this point was their national existence to be counted. The type is accurate down to the minutest detail. The new year did not begin exactly with the Passover-night itself, for that fell between the fourteenth and fifteenth of Nisan. Now the pascal lamb was a type of the Lord Jesus, and the chronology of the civilized world is dated back to the birth of Christ. Anno Mundi (the year of the world) has given place to Anno Domini (the year of our Lord). The coming of Christ to this earth changed the calendar, and the striking thing is that the calendar is now dated not from His death, but from His birth. By common consent men on three Continents reckon time from the Babe of Bethlehem; thus, the Lord of Time has written His signature upon time itself!

But there is another application of what has just been before us. The Passover speaks not only of Christ offering Himself as a sacrifice, a sin-offering to God, but it also views the believing sinner's appropriation of this unto himself. The slaying of the "lamb" looks at the Godward side of the Cross; the sprinkling of the blood tells of faith's application. And it is *this* which changes our relationship to God. But *our* appropriation of Christ's atoning sacrifice is not the first thing. Preceding this is a Divine work of grace *within* us. While we remain dead in trespasses and sins, there is no turning to Christ; nay, there is no discernment, and no capacity *to* discern, our *need* of Him. Except a man be born again he "cannot *see* the kingdom (things) of God" (John 3:3). Regeneration is the cause, faith's application of the sacrifice of Christ, the effect. The new birth is the beginning of the new life. Hence, Israel's new calendar dated not from the Passover itself, but from the *beginning* of the month in which it occurred. The truth here typified is both blessed and solemn. All the years we lived before we became new creatures in Christ are not reckoned to our account. The past is blotted out. Our unregenerate days were so much lost time. Our past lives in the service of sin and Satan, were *wasted*. But when we became new creatures in Christ "*old* things passed away" and all things became *new*.

2. "Speak ye unto all the congregation of Israel, saying, In the tenth day of this month they shall take to them every man a lamb, according to the house of their fathers, a lamb for an house" (v. 3). This is the first thing in connection with the "lamb": it was singled out from the flock, separated, appointed unto death four days before it was actually slain. We believe that two things were here foreshadowed. In the antitype, Christ was marked out for death *before* He was actually slain: "Redeemed with the precious blood of Christ, as of a lamb without blemish and without spot, who verily was *foreordained* before the foundation of the world" (1 Pet. 1:19, 20). It is to this that the singling out of the lamb *four* days before its slaying points, for four is the number of *the world*.

The second application of this detail, which has also been pointed out by others before us, has reference to the fact that *four years* before His crucifixion the Lord Jesus was singled out for death. At the beginning of His public ministry (which lasted between three and four years—cf. Num. 14:34; Ezek. 4:6, a year for a day) John the Baptist cried, "Behold *the Lamb of God* which taketh away the sin of the world." It was then that the Lamb was singled out from the flock—"the lost sheep of the House of Israel"! In the Numerical Bible Mr. Grant has called attention to the fact that Christ was about thirty years old at that time, and 30 is 10 x 3: 3 being the number of manifestation and 10 of human responsibility. This shows us *why* God commanded the Israelites to single out the lamb on the *tenth* day. Not until He had reached the age which, according to its numerical significance, spoke of human responsibility fully manifested, did the Lord Jesus enter upon His appointed work which terminated at Calvary.

3. "Your lamb shall be without blemish" (v. 5). With this should be compared Lev. 22:21, 22. "And whosoever offereth a sacrifice of peace offerings unto the Lord to accomplish his vow, or a freewill offering in beeves or sheep, it shall be *perfect* to be accepted; there shall be *no* blemish therein. Blind, or broken or maimed, or having a wren or scurvy, or scabbed, ye shall not offer these unto the Lord". The moral significance of this is obvious. Nothing but a *perfect* sacrifice could satisfy the requirements of God, who Himself is perfect. One who had sin in himself could not make an atonement for sinners. One who did not himself keep the Law in thought and word and deed, could not magnify and make it honorable. God could only be *satisfied* with that which *glorified* Him. And where was such a sacrifice to be found? Certainly not among the sons of men. None but the Son of God incarnate, "made under the law" (Gal. 4:4) could offer an acceptable sacrifice. And before He presented Himself as an offering to God, the Father testified, "This is My beloved Son, in whom I am well pleased". He was the antitype of the "perfect" lamb. As Peter tells us, Christ was "a lamb *without* blemish and *without* spot" (1:19).

4. "Your lamb shall be without blemish, *a male of the first year*" (v. 5). "The age of the sacrifice is prescribed. It is to be a male of the first year. The Hebrew phrase is 'a male, the son of a year'; that is, it is to be one year old. The lamb was not to be too young or too old. It was to die in *the fulness* of its strength. If we ask how that might apply to Christ, we note that this particular may be fully sustained as a description of Him. For He died for us, not in old age, nor in childhood, or boyhood, or in youth, but in the fulness of His opening manhood" (Urquhart). In the language of Messianic prediction, Christ was cut off "in the midst" of His days (Psl. 102:24).

Before passing on to the next verse we would call attention to a striking gradation here. In v. 3 it is "*a lamb*"; in v. 4 "*the* lamb"; in v. 5. "*your* lamb". This order is most instructive, corresponding to the enlarged apprehension of faith. While in our unregenerate state, Christ appeared to us as nothing more than *a* Lamb; we saw in Him no beauty that we should desire Him. But when the Holy Spirit awakened us from the sleep of death, when He made us see our sinful and lost condition, and turned our gaze toward Christ, then we behold Him as *the* Lamb. We perceived His uniqueness, His unrivaled perfections. We learned that "neither is there salvation in any other; for there is none other Name under heaven given among men whereby we must be saved, (Acts 4:12). Finally, when God in His sovereign grace gave us faith whereby to receive Christ as our own personal Saviour, then could He be said to be *your* Lamb, *our* Lamb. Each elect and believing sinner can say with the apostle Paul, "Who loved *me* and gave Himself for *me*" (Gal. 2:20).

5. "And ye shall keep it up until the four- teenth day of the same month; and *the whole assembly* of the congregation of Is- rael shall kill it in the evening (v. 6). This is very solemn. The *whole* congregation of Israel was to slay the "lamb". Not that every particular individual, man, woman and child, shared in the act itself, but they did so *representatively*. The head of the household stood for and acted on the be- half of each member of his family. It was not simply Moses and Aaron or the Levites who slew the Lamb, but the entire people, as represented by the heads of each house- hold. The fulfillment of this aspect of our type is plainly brought out in the Gospels. It was not simply the chief priests and elders, nor the scribes and Pharisees only, who put the Lord Jesus to death. When Pilate decided the issue as to whether Barabbas or Christ should be released, he did so by the popular vote of the common people, who *all* cried "crucify Him" (see Mark 15:6-15). In like manner it is equally true that it was the sins of each individual believer which caused our Saviour to be put to death: He bare *our* sins in His own body on the tree.

6. "And ye shall keep it up until the *four- teenth* day of the same month; and the whole assembly of the congregation of Is- rael shall kill it *in the evening*" (v. 6). Here we have defined the exact time at which the pascal lamb was to die. It was to be "kept up" or tethered until the fourteenth day of Nisan, and then killed in the evening, or more literally, "between the evenings", that is between the fourteenth and fif- teenth days of the month. To point out precisely the antitypical fulfillment of this would necessitate an examination of quite a number of N. T. passages. Only by a most minute comparison of the statements in each of the four Gospels can we discover the fact that the Lord Jesus died "between the evenings" of the fourteenth and fif- teenth of Nisan. Others before us have performed this task, the best of which, per- haps, is to be found in vol. 5 of the Com- panion Bible. But if the reader will prayer-

fully study the closing chapters of each of the Gospels it will be seen that the Lamb of God died at the very time that the pascal lambs were being slain in the temple.

7. "And the whole assembly of the con- gregation of Israel shall kill *it* in the even- ing". (v. 6). Here the type passes to the Antitype. This point is very striking in- deed. Many thousands of lambs were to be slain on that memorable night in Egypt, yet the Lord here designedly used the singu- lar number when giving these instructions to Moses—Israel shall kill *it*, not "them"! It is indeed remarkable that never once is the plural "lambs" used throughout the 12th chapter of Exodus. "There was only one before God's mind—The Lamb of Calvary" (Urquhart).

8. "And they shall eat the flesh in that night, roast with fire, and unleavened bread; and with bitter herbs they shall eat it" (v. 8). Not only was the lamb to be killed, but its flesh was to be eaten. This was God's provision for those *inside* the house, as the blood secured protection from the judgment *outside*. A journey lay be- fore Israel, and food was needed to strengthen them first. "Eating" signifies two things in Scripture: appropriation and fellowship. The "lamb" spoke of the *per- son* of Christ, and *He* is God's *food* for His people—"The *Bread* of Life". Christ is to be the object before our hearts. As we feed upon Him our souls are sustained and He is honored.

"It is *death* here which God ordains as the food of life. We are so familiar with this we are apt by the very fact to miss its significance. How we see nature thus eve- rywhere instructing us, if we have but learned to read her lessons in the deepest lesson of God's wisdom! The laying down of life becomes the sustenance of life. For men this did not begin until after the Del- uge; at least it is only after this we read of Divine permission for it. And when we see in that Deluge with its central figure, the ark of salvation, bearing within it the neucleus of the new world, the pregnant figure of how God has saved us and brought us in Christ into a new creation, how its similitude in what we have here bursts upon us! It is only as sheltered and saved from death—from what is alone truly such—that we can feed upon death; that Samson's riddle is fulfilled, and 'out of the eater comes forth meat, and out of the strong sweetness! Death is not merely vanquished and set aside; it is in the Cross the sweet and wonderful display of Divine love and power in our behalf accomplished in the mystery of human weakness. Death is become the food of life—yea, of a life which is eternal." (F. W. Grant).

But mark carefully the lamb is to be eaten with "unleavened bread and bitter herbs". In Scripture "leaven" uniformly symbolizes *evil*. The lesson taught here is of vital importance. It is only as we are *separated* from what is repugnant to Divine holiness that we can really feed upon Christ. While we are indulging known sin there can be no communion with Him. It is only as we "walk in the light as He is in the light" that the blood of God's Son cleanseth us from all sin and "we have *fellowship* one with another" (1 John 1:7). The *"bitter* herbs" speak of the remorse of conscience in the Christian. We cannot have "fellowship with His sufferings" (Phil. 3: 10) without remembering *what* it was that made those sufferings needful, namely, *our sins;* and the remembrance of these cannot but produce a chastened spirit.

9. "Eat not of it raw, nor sodden at all with water, but roast with fire" (v. 9). How very explicit—rather, how carefully God preserved the accuracy of the type! In the previous verse we read, "eat the flesh in that night, roast with fire", here, "eat not of it raw". The Israelites were to feed not only upon that where *death* had done its work, but upon that which had been subjected to the *fire*. Solemn indeed is this. "It is appointed unto men once to die, and after this the judgment" (Heb. 9: 27). These are two separate things. For the lost, *death* is not all, nor even the worst that awaits them. *After* death is "judgment," the judgment of a sin-hating God. Therefore if Christ was to take the place of His sinful people and suffer what was righteously due them, He must not only die, but pass under and through the *judgment* of God. "Fire" here, as ever, speaks of the *wrath* of a holy God. It tells of Christ being "made sin for us" (2 Cor. 5:21), and consequently being "made a curse for us" (Gal. 3:13) and as such, enduring the judgment of God. Speaking anticipatively by the Spirit, through the prophet Jeremiah, the Saviour said, "Is it nothing to you, all ye that pass by? behold, and see if there be any sorrow like unto My sorrow, which is done unto Me, wherewith the Lord hath afflicted Me in the day of His fierce anger. From above hath He sent *fire* into My

bones". It was this which caused Him to also say through the Psalmist, "My moisture is turned into the *drought* of summer" (Psl. 32:4). And this it is which, in its deepest meaning, explains His cry from the Cross—"I thirst". His "thirst" was *the effect* of the agony of His soul in the fierce heat of God's wrath. It told of the *drought* of the land where the living God is not. "Not sodden (boiled) at all with water", because water would have *hindered* the direct action of the fire.

"His head with his legs, and with the purtenance (inwards) thereof" (v. 9). "The head, no doubt, expresses the thoughts and counsels with which the walk (the legs) keep perfect company. The inwards are those affections of His heart which were the motive-power impelling Him upon the path He trod. In all, the fire brought forth nothing but sweet savor; for men, it prepared the food of their true life; all is absolutely perfect; and. all is ours to appropriate. Occupation with the person of Christ is thus impressed upon us; we need this. Not the knowledge of salvation alone will suffice us; it is the One who saves whom we need. Christ for our hearts alone keeps and sanctifies them, (Mr. Grant).

10. "And ye shall let nothing of it remain until the morning." (v. 10). The lamb must be eaten the same night as it was slain. Communion must not be separated from the sacrifice on which that communion was founded. Communion is based upon redemption accomplished. We find the same truth brought before us again at the close of Christ's parable of the prodigal son. As soon as the lost son enters the Father's house and is suitably attired, the word goes forth "Bring hither the fatted calf, and kill; and let us *eat* and be merry" (Luke 15:23).

Another thought is also suggested here by the words "ye shall let nothing of it remain until the morning". "The sacrifice in all its ceremonial was to be completed within a single night. The rising sun was thus to see no trace of the slain lamb. In like manner the atoning work of Christ is not a progressive but a completed thing. It is not in process of being accomplished; it has been accomplished definitely and eternally. As a fragrant and hallowed *memory* Calvary's costly sacrifice abides with God and the redeemed forever; but the sacrifice *itself* is past and completed. For God's suffering Lamb the dark night of judgment is no more, and He lives on high in the eter-

nal sunshine of Divine favor and love"
(Mr. W. W. Fereday).

11. "And *thus* shall ye eat it; with your
loins girded, your shoes on your feet, and
your staff in your hand; and ye shall eat it
in haste; it is the Lord's Passover" (v. 11).
The little word "thus" is very emphatic. It
defines for us the accessories, what should
accompany feeding upon Christ; four
things are mentioned. First, their dress;
"loins girded". "Having your loins girt
about with *truth*", says the apostle. "The
garments are spiritually what we may des-
ignate by the old word for them—'*habits*'.
They are the moral guise in which we appear before men,—what they identify with
us at least, if they are not, after all, *ourselves*. And if not just 'ourselves' we may
be in many ways *read in them;* pride or
lowliness, boldness or unobtrusiveness, sloth
or diligence, and many another thing.
"The long robes of the East, as we are
all aware, required the girdle in order that
there might be no hindrance in the way of
a march such as Israel now had before
them. If they were allowed to flow loose,
they would get entangled with the feet and
overthrow the wearers; and the dust of the
road would get upon them and defile them.
The *truth* it is which is to be our girdle,
keeping us from the loose and negligent
contact with ever-ready defilement in a
world which the lust of the flesh, the lust
of the eyes, and the pride of life characterizes, and from the entanglement to our
feet which lax habits prove.
"Garments *un*-girded are thus practically
near akin to the 'weights' (Heb. 12:2)
which the apostle bids us 'lay aside', and
which are not things in themselves sinful,
and yet nevertheless betray us into sin.
Have you noticed *the connection* in that exhortation of his 'lay aside every weight and
the sin which doth so easily beset us'? If
you had a pack of wolves following you,
you would understand very quickly. why- if
carrying a weight you would be indeed
'easily beset'. And herein, many a soul may
discern, if he will, why he has so great and
so little successful conflict. The 'weight'
shows, like the flowing garment that whatever else we may be, we are not *racers*. . . .
Fit companions then with unleavened bread
and bitter herbs are these girt loins. We
must arise and depart for this is not our
rest" (Mr. Grant).
"Your shoes on your feet". This, again,
was in view of the journey which lay before
them. It tells of preparation for their walk.

There is a most interesting reference to
these "shoes" in Deut. 29:5, where at the
close of his life, Moses said, "I have led
your forty years in the wilderness; your
clothes are not waxen old upon you, and
thy *shoe* is not waxen old upon thy foot",
And again he reminded them, "Neither did
thy foot swell these forty years" (Deut.
8:4). Remarkable was this. For forty
years Israel had wandered up and down the
wilderness, yet their shoes were neither
torn to pieces nor did their feet suffer. How
this tells of the *sufficiency* of that provision
which God has graciously provided for the
walk of His saints! When the prodigal son
came to His Father, there was not only the
best robe for his body, and the ring for his
hand, but there were also "shoes for his
feet" (Luke 15:22)! The significance of
these "shoes" is explained for us in Eph.
6:15—"Your *feet shod* with the preparation
of the Gospel of peace".
"Your staff in your hand". The staff is
the sign of *pilgrimage*. As they journeyed
to the Promised Land, Israel were to pass
through a wilderness in which they would
be strangers and pilgrims. So it is with
Christians as they pass through this world.
Their *home* is not here: "Our citizenship
is in heaven" (Phil. 3:20). Therefore does
God say, "I beseech you *as* strangers and
pilgrims" (1 Pet. 2:11). Staff in hand signifies that as Israel journeyed they were to
lean on something *outside* of themselves.
Clearly this is the written Word, given us
for a stay and support. The dependent soul
who leans hard upon it can say with the
Psalmist, "Thy rod and *Thy staff* they comfort me" (23:4).
"And ye shall eat it in haste". "They
were to eat it in haste because they expected that any moment the Lord might come
and pass over them; any moment they
might be called to arise and go out of the
land of bondage. They expected the imminent Coming of the Lord. That is to say,
because the Coming of the Lord *was* imminent they expected it". (Dr. Haldeman).
12. "When I see the blood, I will pass
over you" v. 13. Upon this Mr. Urquhart
has made some illuminating remarks. "The
term rendered Passover '*pesach*' does not
seem to have that meaning. It is entirely
different from the Hebrew verb, *a-bhar*, or
ga-bhar, so frequently used in the sense of
'to pass over'. *Pasach* (the verb) and *pesach*
(the noun) have no connection with any
other Hebrew word. They closely resemble,
however, the Egyptian word *pesh*, which

means 'to spread the wings over,' 'to protect'. The word is used—we may say explained—in this sense in Isa. 31:5: "As birds flying, so will the Lord of Hosts *defend* Jerusalem; defending also He will deliver it; and passing over (pasoach, participle of pasach) He will *preserve* it'. The word has, consequently, the very meaning of the Egyptian term for 'spreading the wings over', and 'protecting'; and *pesach,* the Lord's Passover, means such sheltering and protection as is found under the outstretched wings of the Almighty. Does not this give a new fulness to those words of our Saviour, 'O Jerusalem! Jerusalem! .... how often would I have gathered thy children together, as a hen does gather her brood under her wings, and ye would not' (Luke 13:34)? Jesus of Nazareth was her PESACH, her *shelter* from the coming judgment; and she knew it not! Quite in keeping with this sense of protecting with outstretched wings is the fact that this term *pesach* is applied (1) to the ceremony, 'It is the Lord's Passover' (Ex. 12:11), and (2) to the lamb (v. 21); 'draw out and take you a lamb according to your families and kill the Passover'. The slain lamb, the sheltering behind its blood and the eating of its flesh, constituted the *pesach,* the protection of God's chosen people beneath the sheltering wings of the Almighty". This interpretation is clearly established by what we read in verse 23: "For the Lord will pass through to smite the Egyptians; and when He seeth the blood upon the lintel and upon the two side posts, the Lord will pass over the door, *and will not suffer the Destroyer to come in unto your houses to smite you*". It was not merely that the Lord passed by the houses of the Israelites, but that He stood on guard *protecting* each blood-sprinkled door!

13. "And this day shall be unto you for a memorial; and ye shall keep it a feast to the Lord throughout your generations; ye shall keep it a feast by an ordinance forever" (v. 14). It is interesting to trace Israel's subsequent response to this command. Scripture records just *seven* times when this Feast was kept. The first in Egypt, here in Ex. 12. The second in the Wilderness (Num. 9). The third when they entered Canaan (Joshua 5). The fourth in the days of Hezekiah (2 Chron. 30). The fifth under Josiah (2 Chron. 35). The sixth after the return from the Captivity (Ezra 6). Just six in the O. T. The *seventh* was celebrated by the Lord Jesus and His apos-

tles immediately before the institution of "the Lord's Supper, (Luke 22:15, etc.). In that last Passover the true Lamb of God is seen, who had been prefigured by the preceding pascal lambs. "It should also be observed, that Jesus Christ, who celebrated the last Passover, had been Himself in Egypt, where the first had been observed. As the passover came from Egypt, so Jesus Christ, who is the true Passover was called out of Egypt (Matt. 2:15)" (Robert Haldane: Evidence and Authority of Divine Revelation).

14. "And ye shall take a bunch of hyssop and dip it in the blood that is in the basin, and strike the lintel and the two side posts with the blood that is in the basin" (v. 22). This gives us a marvelous typical picture of the sufferings of our blessed Lord upon the Cross, though the picture is marred by translating here, the original word, "basin". Once more we avail ourselves of the scholarly help of Dr. Urquhart. The word rendered 'basin' is *sap,* which is an old Egyptian word for the step before a door, or the threshold of a house. The word *is* translated 'threshold' in Judges 19:27 and 'door' in 2 Kings 12:9—apparently for the sole reason that the sense 'basin', favored by lexicographers and translators, could not possibly be given to the word in these passages. . . .No direction was given about putting the blood upon the threshold, for the reason that the blood *was already there.* The lamb was evidently slain at the door of the house which was protected by its blood". We may add that the Septuagint gives "para ten thuran", which means along the door-way! While the Vulgate reads, "in sanguine qui est limine"—in the blood which is on the threshold. This point is not simply one of academic interest, but concerns the accuracy of the type. The door of the house wherein the Israelite was protected had blood on the lintel (the cross piece), on the side posts and on the step.* How marvelously this pictured Christ on the Cross; blood above, where the thorns pierced His brow; blood at the sides, from His nail-pierced hands; blood below, from His nail-pierced feet!!

15. The blood was to be applied with "a bunch of hyssop" (v. 22). Nothing in the Word is meaningless: the smallest detail

The objection that blood on the step would cause the Israelite to walk upon it, is obviated by Jehovah's instructions. *"And none of you shall go out at the door* until the morning" (v. 22)!

has its due significance. Nor are we ever left to guess at anything; Scripture is ever its own interpreter. The "hyssop" was not connected with the "lamb", but with the application of its blood. It speaks, then, not of Christ but of the sinner's appropriation of His sacrifice. The "hyssop" is never found in connection with any of the offerings which foreshadowed the Lord Jesus Himself. It is beheld, uniformly, in the hands of the sinner. Thus in connection with the cleansing of the leper, Lev. 14; and the restoration of the unclean, Num. 19. From Psl. 51:7 we may learn that "hyssop" speaks of *humiliâtion of soul,* contrition, repentance. Note that in 1 Kings 4:33 "hyssop" is contrasted with "the cedars", showing that "hyssop" speaks of *lowliness.*

Perhaps a word should be added concerning the Feast of Unleavened Bread which followed the Passover: "And ye shall observe the Feast of Unleavened Bread; for in this selfsame day have I brought your armies out of the land of Egypt; therefore shall ye observe this day in your generations by an ordinance forever. In the first month, on the fourteenth day of the month, at even, ye shall eat unleavened bread, until the one and twentieth day of the month at even. Seven days shall there be no leaven found in your houses; for whosoever eateth that which is leavened, even that soul shall be cut off from the congregation of Israel, whether he be a stranger or born in the land. Ye shall eat nothing leavened; in all your habitations shall ye eat unleavened bread" (vv. 17-20). The interpretation of this for us is supplied in 1 Cor. 5:7,8: "Purge out *therefore* the old leaven, that ye may be a

new lump, as ye are unleavened. For even Christ our passover is sacrificed for us; *therefore* let us keep the feast not with old leaven, neither with the leaven of malice and wickedness; but with the unleavened bread of sincerity and truth".

Upon the above we cannot do better than quote from Mr. C. H. MacIntosh: the Feast spoken of in this passage is that which, in the life and conduct of the Church, corresponds with the Feast of unleavened bread. This lasted seven days (a complete circle of time A. W. P.); and the Church collectively, and the believer individually, are called to walk *in practical holiness,* during their days, or the entire period of their course here below; and this, moreover, as the direct *result* of being washed in the blood, and having communion with the sufferings of Christ.

"The Israelite did not put away leaven in order to be saved, but because he was saved; and if he failed to put away leaven it did not raise the question of security through the blood, but simply of fellowship with the assembly. The cutting off of an Israelite from the Congregation answers precisely to the suspension of Christian fellowship, and if he be indulging in that which is contrary to the holiness of the Divine presence. God cannot tolerate evil. A single unholy thought (entertained: A. W. P.) will interrupt the soul's communion; and until the soil contracted by any such thought is got rid of by confession, founded on the advocacy of Christ, the communion cannot possibly be restored (see 1 John 1:5-10)".

May the Lord stir us up to a more diligent and prayerful study of His wonderful Word.

CHAPTER 17

THE ACCOMPANIMENTS OF THE
PASSOVER

EXODUS 12, 13

Though we have entitled this paper "the Accompaniments of the Passover", other things will come before us. The instructions which Jehovah gave to Israel concerning the observance of the Feast of Unleavened Bread are found part in Ex. 12 and part in Ex. 13. Therefore as these two chapters are to be the portion for our study, we must not pass by other incidents recorded in them. First, then, a brief word upon the carrying out of the death-sentence upon the Egyptians.

"And it came to pass, that at midnight the Lord smote all the firstborn in the land of Egypt, from the firstborn of Pharaoh that sat on his throne unto the firstborn of the captives that was in the dungeon; and all the firstborn of cattle. And Pharaoh rose up in the night, he, and all his servants, and all the Egyptians; and there was a great cry in Egypt; for there was not a house where there was not one dead" (12: 29, 30). The very first message which the Lord commanded Moses to deliver to Egypt's ruler was, "Thus saith the Lord, Israel is My son, even My firstborn; And I say unto thee, Let My son go, that he may serve Me; and if thou refuse to let him go, behold, *I will slay thy son, even thy first-born*" (4:22, 23). It is evident from the sequel that Pharaoh did not believe this message. In this he accurately represented the men of this world. All through this Christian dispensation the solemn word has been going forth, "Except ye repent ye shall all likewise perish" (Luke 13:3) : "He that believeth not shall be damned" (Mark 16: 16). But, for the most part, the Divine warning has fallen on deaf ears. The vast majority do not believe that God means what He says. Nevertheless, though oftentimes men's threats are mere idle words and empty bombast, not so is it with the threatenings of Him who cannot lie. It is true that God is "slow to anger" and long

does He leave open the door of mercy, but even *His* long-sufferance has its limits. It was thus with Pharaoh and his people. Pharaoh received plain and faithful warning and this was followed by many appeals and preliminary judgments. But the haughty king and his no less defiant subjects only hardened their hearts. And now the threatened judgment from heaven fell upon them, and neither wealth nor poverty provided any exemption—"there was not a house where there was not one dead". A most solemn proof is this unto rebels against God to-day, that in a short while at most, unless they truly repent, Divine wrath *shall* smite *them*.

"Now the sojourning of the children of Israel, who dwelt in Egypt, was four hundred and thirty years. And it came to pass at the end of the four hundred and thirty years, even the selfsame day it came to pass, that all the hosts of the Lord went out from the land of Egypt" (12:40,41). It is very striking to observe the accuracy of the type here. It was not until the day following the Passover-night that Israel was delivered from Egypt. As we have gone over the first twelve chapters of Exodus we have witnessed the tender compassion of God (2: 23-25) ; we have seen the appointment of a leader (3:10) ; we have listened to the Divine promises (6:6-8) ; and we have beheld remarkable displays of Divine power (in the plagues), and yet not a single Israelite was delivered from the house of bondage. It was not until the blood of the "lamb" was shed that redemption was effected, and as soon as it *was* shed, even the very next morning, Israel marched forth a free people—remarkable is the expression here used : "All the hosts *of the Lord* (not "of Israel") went out from the land of Egypt" (12:41). They were the Lord's by purchase—"bought with a price", and that price "not corruptible things as silver and

95

gold, but with the precious blood of a Lamb"!

The same thing is to be seen in the Gospels. Notwithstanding all the blessed display of grace and power in the life and ministry of the Lord Jesus, at the close of His wonderful works of mercy among men, had there been nothing more, He must have remained alone. Listen to His own words; "Verily, verily, I say unto you, Except a corn of wheat fall into the ground and die, it abideth *alone;* but if it die, it bringeth forth much fruit (John 12:24). As another has well said, "Blessed as was that ministry, great as were His miracles, heavenly as was His teaching, holy as was His life, yet had He not died, the Just for the unjust, not one of all the sons of Adam could possibly have been saved. What a place this gives to redemption!" (Mr. C. Stanley). How sadly true. Though Christ *"spake* as never man spake" (John 7:46), and though men confessed "He hath *done* all things well; He maketh both the deaf to hear and the dumb to speak (Mark 7:37), yet at the close we read, even of His apostles, "they *all* forsook Him and fled". But how different after His precious blood had been shed! Then He is no longer "alone". Then, for the first time, He speaks of the disciples as His "brethren" (John 20:17)!

The *order* of truth in Ex. 12, like every other chapter in the Bible, is according to *Divine* wisdom, yet the writer has to confess dimness of vision in *perceiving* the purpose and beauty of the arrangements of its contents. One thing is very clear, it evidences plainly that it was not of Moses' own design. Here, as ever, God's thought and ways are different from ours. A trained mind, accustomed to think in logical sequence, would certainly have reversed the order found here. Yet we have not the slightest doubt that *God's* order is infinitely superior to that of the most brilliant human intellect. These remarks are occasioned by what is found in verses 43-50. After telling us in verse 41 that "The selfsame day it came to pass, that all the hosts of the Lord went out from the land of Egypt", vv. 43 to 50 give us the *"ordinance* of the Passover", and then in v. 51 it is repeated that "The Lord did bring the children of Israel out of the land of Egypt". The strange thing is that this ordinance was for Israel's guidance in the *future,* hence one would naturally have expected to find these instructions given at a later date, as a part of the ceremonial law. But though, at present, we can offer no satisfactory explanation of this, several points of interest in the "ordinance" itself are clear, and these we will briefly consider.

"And the Lord said unto Moses and Aaron, This is the ordinance of the Passover; There shall no stranger eat thereof; but every man's servant that is bought for money, when thou hast circumcised him, then shall he eat thereof. A foreigner and an hired servant shall not eat thereof" (vv. 43-45). Here we learn that three classes of people were debarred from eating the Passover. First, no *stranger* was to eat thereof. This Feast was for Israel alone, and therefore no foreigner must participate. The reason is obvious. It was only the children of Abraham, the family of faith, who had participated in God's gracious deliverance, and they alone could commemorate it. Second, no *hired servant* should eat the Passover. This too is easily interpreted. An "hired" servant is an outsider; he is actuated by self-interest. He works for pay. But no such principle can find a place in that which speaks of redemption: "To him *that worketh not* but believeth on Him that justifieth the ungodly, his faith is counted for righteousness" (Rom. 4:5). Third, *no uncircumcised person* should eat thereof. (v. 48). This applies to Israel equally as much as to Gentiles. "Circumcision" was the sign of the Covenant, and only those who belonged to the Covenant of Grace can feed upon Christ. Circumcision was God's sentence of death written upon nature. Circumcision has its antitype in the Cross. (Col. 2:11, 12).

"But every man's servant that is bought for money when thou hast circumcised him, then shall he eat thereof. . . . and when a stranger shall sojourn with thee, and will keep the Passover to the Lord, let all his males be circumcised, and then let him come near and keep it; and he shall be as one that is born in the land: for no uncircumcised person shall eat thereof" (vv. 44, 48). A wall was erected to shut out enemies, but the door was open to receive friends. No hired servant could participate in the Feast, but a *bond*-servant who had been purchased and circumcised, and who was now one of the household, could. So, too, the foreigner who *sojourned* with Israel, provided he would submit to the rite of circumcision. In this we have a blessed foreshadowing of Grace reaching out to the Gentiles, who though by nature were "aliens from the commonwealth of Israel and strangers to the covenants of promise", are now, by grace "no more strangers and foreigners, but fellow-citizens with the saints and of the household of God" (Eph. 2:12, 19).—a statement which manifestly looks back to Ex. 12.

"In one house shall it be eaten; thou shalt not carry forth ought of the flesh abroad out of the house; neither shall ye break a bone thereof (v. 46). "The lamb was to be eaten under the shelter of the atoning blood, and there alone. Men may admire Christ, as it is the fashion very much to do, while denying the whole reality of His atoning work, but the Lamb can only be eaten really where its virtue is owned! Apart from this, He cannot be understood or appreciated. Thus the denial of His *work* leads to the denial of His *person*. Universalists and Annihilationists slip naturally into some kind of Unitarian doctrines as is evidenced on every hand.

"Thus this unites naturally with the commandment 'Neither shall ye break a bone thereof'. God will not have the perfection of Christ disfigured as it would be in type by a broken bone. With the bones perfect a naturalist can show the construction of the whole animal. Upon the perfection of the bones depends the symmetry of form. God will have this preserved with regard to Christ. Reverent, not rash handling, becomes us as we seek to apprehend the wondrous Christ of God. And looking back to what is in connection with this, how suited a place to preserve reverence, the place 'in the house' under the shelter which the precious blood has provided for us! With such a one, so sheltered, how could rationalism or irreverence, we might ask, be found? And yet, alas, the injunction, we know too well is not unneedful" (Mr. Grant).

It is indeed blessed to mark how God guarded the fulfillment of this particular aspect of the type. That there might be no uncertainty that Christ Himself, the Lamb of God, was in view here, the Spirit of prophecy also caused it to be written (in one of the Messianic Psalms), "He keepeth all His bones; not one of them is broken" (34:20). And in John 19 we behold the antitype of Ex. 12 and the fulfillment of Psl. 34. "The Jews therefore, because it was the preparation that the bodies should not remain upon the Cross on the Sabbath day (for that Sabbath day was an high day), besought Pilate that their legs *might be broken*, and that they might be taken

away" (v. 31). Here was Satan, in his malignant enmity attempting to falsify and nullify the written Word. Vain effort was it. "Then came the soldiers and brake the legs of the first, and of the other which was crucified with Him" (v. 32). Thus far might the agents of the Roman empire go, but no farther—"But when they came to Jesus and saw that He was dead already, *they brake not His legs,*" (John 19:33). Here we are given to see the Father "*keeping*" (preserving) all the bones of His blessed Son. Pierce His side with a spear a soldier might, and this, only that prophecy might be fulfilled, for it was written, "They shall look on Him whom they *pierced,*" (Zech. 12:10). But brake His legs they could not, for "a bone of Him *shall not* be broken", and *it was not!*

"And the Lord spake unto Moses saying, Sanctify unto Me all the firstborn, whatsoever openeth the womb among the children of Israel both of man and of beast it is Mine" (13:1, 2). "The narrative of the Exodus from Egypt is suspended to bring in certain consequences,—responsible consequences for the children of Israel—consequences which flowed from their redemption out of the land of bondage. For, although, they are still in the land, the teaching of the chapter is founded upon their having been brought out, and it is indeed anticipative of their being in Canaan. If God acts in grace toward His people, He thereby establishes claims upon them, and it is these claims that are here unfolded" (Ed. Dennett).

A redeemed people become the property of the Redeemer. To His New Testament saints God says, "Ye are not your own; for ye are bought with a price" (1 Cor. 6:19, 20). It is on this same principle that Jehovah here says unto Moses, "Sanctify unto Me all the firstborn". The reference to the "firstborn" here should be carefully noted. It was the *firstborn* of Israel who had been redeemed from the death-judgment which fell upon the Egyptians, and now the Lord claims these for Himself. Typically this speaks of practical holiness, setting apart unto God. Thus the first exhortation in Romans which follows the doctrinal exposition in chapters 1 to 11 is, "I beseech you therefore, brethren, by the mercies of God, that ye present your bodies a living sacrifice, holy, acceptable unto God, which is your reasonable service" (12:1). Personal devotedness is the first thing which God has a right to look for from His blood-bought people.

"Seven days thou shalt eat unleavened bread, and in the seventh day shall be a feast to the Lord. Unleavened bread shall be eaten seven days; and there shall no leavened bread be seen with thee, neither shall there be leaven seen with thee in all thy quarters" (13:6,7). Typically this shows the nature of sanctification. Throughout Scripture "leaven" is the symbol of evil, evil which spreads and corrupts everything with which it comes into contact, for "a little leaven leaveneth the whole lump" (1 Cor. 5:6). To eat "unleavened bread" signifies separation from all evil, in order that we may feed upon Christ. That this Feast lasted "seven days", which is a *complete* period, tells us that this is to last throughout our whole sojourn on earth. It is to this that 1 Cor. 5:7,8 refers. "Purge out therefore the old leaven, that ye may be a new lump, as ye are unleavened. For even Christ our Passover is sacrificed for us; Therefore let us keep the feast not with old leaven, neither with the leaven of malice and wickedness; but with the unleavened bread of sincerity and truth." Because we are saved by *grace*, through the sprinkled blood of Christ, it is not that we may now indulge in sin without fear of its consequences, or that grace may abound. Not so. Redemption by the precious blood of Christ imposes an additional responsibility to separate ourselves from all evil, that we may now show forth the praises of Him who has called us out of darkness into His marvelous light. Carelessness of walk, evil associations, worldliness, fleshly indulgences are the things which hinder us from keeping this Feast of *unleavened* Bread.

But much more is included by this figure of "leaven" than the grosser things of the flesh. We read in the N. T. of "the *leaven* of the *Pharisees,* (Matt. 16:6). This is superstition, the making void of the Word of God by the *traditions* of men. Formalism and legality are included too. Sectarianism and ritualism as well are the very essence of Phariseeism. Then we read of "the *leaven* of the Sadducees" (Matt. 16:6). The Sadducees were materialists, denying a spirit within man, and rejecting the truth of resurrection, (Acts 23:8). In its present-day form, Higher Criticism, Rationalism, Modernism answers to Sadduceeism. We also read of "the *leaven* of *Herod* (Mark 8:15). This is worldliness, or more specifically, the friendship of the world, as the various statements made about Herod in the Gospels will bear out. All of these things must be rigidly excluded. The allowance of any of them makes it impossible to feed upon Christ. Is it not because of our failure *to* "purge out the old leaven" that so few of the Lord's people enter upon "the *feast* of unleavened bread"!

"And thou shall show thy son in that day, saying, this is done because of that which the Lord did unto me when I came forth out of Egypt" (13:8). Striking indeed is this. The basis of this Feast was what the Lord had done for Israel in delivering them from the land of bondage. In other words, its foundation was redemption accomplished, entered into, known, enjoyed. No soul can really *feast* upon Christ while he is in doubt about his own salvation. "Fear hath torment" (1 John 4:18) and this is the opposite of joy and salvation, of which *"feasting"* speaks. Little wonder then that there are so many joyless professing Christians. How could it be otherwise? "Rejoice" said Christ to the disciples, "that your names *are* written in heaven" (Luke 10:20). Until this joy of assurance is ours there cannot be, we say again, any *feasting* upon Christ.

"And it shall be for a sign unto thee upon thine hand, and for a memorial between thine eyes, that the Lord's law may be in thy mouth; for with a strong hand hath the Lord brought thee out of Egypt". (13:9). The Feast was a "sign" upon the *hand,* that is, it signified that their *service* was consecrated to God. It was also a "memorial between the eyes", that is, upon the forehead, where all could see; which being interpreted, signifies, *an open manifestation* of separation unto God. Finally, it was to be accompanied with "the Lord's law in their mouth". The correlative of "law" is obedience. God's redeemed are not a lawless people. Said the Lord Jesus, "If ye love Me, keep My *commandments*" (John 14: 15); and as John tells us, "His commandments are not grievous" (1 John 5:3). Those who insist so urgently that in no sense are Christians under Law evidence a sad spirit of insubordination; it shows how much they are affected and infected, with the spirit of *lawlessness* which now, alas, is so prevalent on every side and in every realm.

"And it shall be when the Lord shall bring thee into the land of the Canaanites, as He sware unto thee and to thy fathers, and shall give it thee, That thou shalt set apart unto the Lord all that openeth the matrix and every firstling that cometh of a beast which thou hast; the males shall be the Lord's. And every firstling of an ass thou shalt redeem with a lamb; and if thou wilt not redeem it, then thou shalt break his neck; and all the firstborn of man among thy children shalt thou redeem". (13:11-13). The deep significance of this cannot be missed if we observe the connection—that which precedes. In Ex. 12 we have had the redemption of the "firstborn" of *Israel,* here it is the redemption of the "firstling" of an *ass.* In the second verse of chapter 13 the two are definitely joined together—"Sanctify unto Me all the firstborn, whatsoever openeth the womb of the children of Israel, both of man *and* of beast; it is Mine". That there may be no mistaking what is in view here, the Lord gave orders that the firstling of the ass was to be redeemed with a lamb, just as the firstborn of Israel were redeemed with a lamb on the passover night. Furthermore, the ass was to have its neck broken, that is it was to be destroyed, unless redeemed; just as the Israelites would most certainly have been smitten by the avenging Angel unless they had slain the lamb and sprinkled its blood. The conclusion is therefore irresistible: God here compares the natural man with the ass! Deeply humbling is this!

The "ass" is an *unclean* animal. Such is man by nature; shapen in iniquity conceived in sin. The "ass" is a most *stupid and senseless* creature. So also is the natural man. Proudly as he may boast of his powers of reason, conceited as he may be over his intellectual achievements, the truth is, that he is utterly devoid of any *spiritual intelligence.* What saith the Scriptures? This: "Walk not as other Gentiles walk in the vanity of their mind, having the understanding darkened, being alienated from the life of God through the ignorance that is in them" (Eph. 4:17, 18). Again; "If our Gospel be hid, it is hid to them that are lost; in whom the god of this world (Satan) has *blinded* the minds of them which believe not" (2 Cor. 4:3, 4). How accurately, then, does the "ass" picture the natural man! Again; the "ass" is *stubborn and intractable,* often as hard to move as a mule. So also is the natural man. The sinner is rebellious and defiant. He *will not* come to Christ that he might have life (John 5:40). It is in view of these things that Scripture declares, "For vain man would be wise, though *man be born like a wild ass's colt"* (Job 11:12).

It is instructive to trace the various references to the "ass" in Scripture. The first mention of the "ass" is in Gen. 22; from it we learn two things. "Abraham rose up early in the morning and *saddled* his "ass". (v. 3). The "ass" is not a free animal. It is a beast of burden, *saddled.* So, too, is the sinner—"serving divers lusts". Second, "And Abraham said unto his young men, *Abide ye here with the ass;* and I and the lad will go yonder and worship" (Gen. 22:5). The "ass" did not accompany Abraham and Isaac to the place of worship. Nor can the sinner worship God. Third, in Gen. 49:14 we read, "Issachar is a strong ass, couching down *between two burdens".* So, too, is the sinner—*heavily* "laden" (Matt. 11-28). Fourth, God forbade His people to plow with an ox and ass together (Deut. 22:10). The sinner is shut out from the service of God. Fifth, in 1 Sam. 9:3 we are told, "And the asses of Kish Saul's father were *lost",* and though Saul and his servant sought long for them they recovered them not. The sinner, too, is lost, away from God, and no human power can restore him. Sixth, In Jer. 22:19 we read, "He shall be buried with the burial of an ass, drawn and *cast forth beyond* the gates of Jerusalem". Fearfully solemn is this. The carcass of the ass was cast forth *outside* the gates of the holy city. So shall it be with every sinner who dies outside of Christ; he shall not enter the New Jerusalem, but be *"cast* into the Lake of Fire". The final reference to the "ass" is found in Zech. 9:9 "Rejoice greatly O daughter of Zion; shout, O daughter of Jerusalem, behold, thy King cometh unto thee, He is just, and having salvation; lowly, and *riding upon an ass".* Most blessed contrast is this. Here we see the "ass" *entering Jerusalem,* but only so as it was beneath the controlling hand of the Lord Jesus! Here is the sinner's only hope—to submit to Christ!

In Gen. 16:12 we have a statement which is very pertinent in this connection, though its particular force is lost in the A. V. rendering; we quote therefore from the R. V., "And he shall be a *wild-ass* man among men; his hand shall be against every man, and every man's hand against him". Those were the words of the Lord to Sarah. They were a prophecy concerning Ishmael. From Gal. 4 we learn that Ishmael stands for *the natural man,* as Isaac for the believer, the seed of promise. In full accord, then, with all that we have said above is this striking description of Sarah's *"firstborn";* he was a *wild-ass* man. The Bedowin Arabs are his descendants, and fully do they witness to the truth of this ancient prophecy. But solemn is it to find that here we have *God's* description of the natural man. And more solemn still is what we read of Ishmael in Gal. 4; he *"persecuted* him that was born after the Spirit" (v. 29), and in consequence had to be "cast out" (v. 30).

In view of what has been said above, how marvelous the *grace* which provided *redemption for* "the firstling of an ass"! "But God commendeth His love toward us, in that, *while we were yet sinners,* Christ died for us" (Rom. 5:8). Ah, dear reader, have you taken *this place* before God? Do you own that the "ass" is an accurate portrayal of all that you are in yourself—unclean, senseless, intractable, fit only to have your neck broken? Do the words of the apostle suitably express the real sentiments of your heart—"Christ Jesus came into the world to save sinners; *of whom I am chief"* (1 Tim. 1:15)? Or, are you like the self-righteous Pharisee, who said, "God, I thank Thee, that *I am not* as other men are, extortioners, unjust, adulterers" (Luke 18:11)? Christ came not to call the righteous but *sinners* to repentance, (Luke 5:32). He came "To seek and to save *that which was lost"* (Luke 19:10). Again, we ask, Have you taken this place before God? Have you come to Him with all your wretchedness—undone, corrupt, guilty, lost? Have you abandoned all pretentions of worthiness and merit, and cast yourself upon His undeserved mercy? Have you seen your own need of the *sinner's* Saviour, and thankfully received Him? If you *have,* then will you gladly "set to your seal that God is true", and acknowledge that the "ass" *is* a suitable figure to express what you were and still are by nature. And, then, too, will you praise God for the matchless grace which redeemed you, not with corruptible things as silver and gold, "but with the precious blood of Christ, as of a Lamb without blemish and without spot" (1 Peter 1:19). Thank God for the *Lamb* provided for the *ass.* The more fully we realize the accuracy of this figure, the more completely we are given to see how *ass-like* we are in ourselves, the deeper will be our gratitude and the more fervent our praise for the redemptive and perfect Lamb.

CHAPTER 18

THE EXODUS FROM EGYPT

EXODUS 12-14

"And the Egyptians were urgent upon the people, that they might send them out of the land in haste; for they said, We be all dead men. And the people took their dough before it was leavened, their kneading-troughs being bound up in their clothes upon their shoulders. And the children of Israel did according to the word of Moses; and they borrowed of the Egyptians jewels of silver, and jewels of gold, and raiment. And the Lord gave the people favour in the sight of the Egyptians so that they lent unto them such things as they required. And they spoiled the Egyptians" (Ex. 12: 33-36). At last was fulfilled the promise made by Jehovah to Abraham more than four hundred years before. He had said, "Know of a surety that thy seed shall be a stranger in a land that is not theirs, and shall serve them; and they shall afflict them four hundred years" (Gen. 15:13). Literally had this been fulfilled. The experiences of Abraham's seed in Egypt was precisely as God had said. But He had also declared to Abraham, "And also that nation, whom they shall serve, will I judge; and afterward shall they come out with great substance" (Gen 15:14). This, too, was now made good. There were no provisos, no ifs or peradventures. "Afterward shall they come out with great substance." So God had decreed, so it came to pass. So had God promised, so He now made good His word.

"And it came to pass at the end of the four hundred and thirty years, even the self-same day it came to pass that all the hosts of the Lord went out from the land of Egypt" (12:41). Upon this verse we commented briefly in our last paper. Those who went forth from the land of bondage are here termed "the hosts *of the Lord."* Israel were the Lord's hosts in a threefold way: first, by covenant purpose, by the eternal choice of a predestinating God; second, by creation, who had made them

for Himself; third, by purchase, for He had redeemed them by precious blood.

"And it came to pass the selfsame day, that the Lord did bring the children of Israel out of the land of Egypt by their armies" (12:51). The last three words in this quotation show that Israel did not issue from Egypt as a disorderly mob. How could they, seeing that it was *the Lord* who "brought them out!" God is not the author of confusion. There is a supplementary word in 13:18 which brings this out in further detail: "The children of Israel went up *by five in a rank* (margin) out of the land of Egypt." A similar example of Divine *orderliness* is to be observed in connection with our Lord feeding the hungry multitude. In Mark 6:29 we are told that Christ commanded the disciples to "make all sit down *by companies* upon the green grass." And we are told "they sat down *in ranks,* by hundreds, and by fifties." The fact that Israel went forth by *"five in a rank"* exemplified and expressed God's *grace,* for five in Scripture ever speaks of grace or favour.

There is another word in Psalm 105:37 which adds a beautiful touch to the picture here before us. There we are told, "He brought them forth also with silver and gold; and *there was not one feeble person* among their tribes." How this illustrates the need of diligently *comparing* Scripture with Scripture if we would obtain the *full* teaching of the Word on any subject! Nothing is said of this in the historical narratives of Exodus; it was reserved for the Psalmist to tell us of this Divine miracle, for miracle it certainly was, that not a single one in all that vast host was sickly or infirm.

"And Moses took the bones of Joseph with him; for he had straitly sworn the children of Israel, saying, God will surely visit you; and ye shall carry up my bones away hence with you" (13:19). This was no ancestor or relic worship, but an

101

act of faith, the declaration of Joseph's belief that the destination of Israel was to be the land which God had promised to give to Abraham and his seed, which promise the faith of Joseph had firmly laid hold of. During their long bondage in Egypt this commandment which Joseph gave concerning "his bones" must have often been the theme of converse in many of the Hebrew households; and now, by taking with him the embalmed remains, Moses showed his sure confidence that a grave would be found for them in the land of promise. Nor was his confidence misplaced, as Joshua 24:33 shows: "And the bones of Joseph, which the children of Israel brought up out of Egypt, buried they in Shechem."

Hebrews 11:22 tells us that this commandment which Joseph gave was "by *faith*," and here, hundreds of years after, we behold God's *response* to the faith of His servant. Moses had much to occupy him at this time. An immense responsibility and undertaking was his—to organise the "armies of Israel" and lead them forth in orderly array. But in simple dependence Joseph had put his dying trust in the living God, and it was impossible that he should be disappointed. Therefore did Jehovah bring to the mind of Moses this command of Joseph, and caused him to carry it out. Blessed demonstration was it of the *faithfulness* of God.

But what, we may ask, is the *typical* lesson in this for *us?* Every other detail in the exodus of Israel from Egypt, as well as all that preceded and followed it, has a profound significance and spiritual application to us. What, then, is foreshadowed in Israel carrying the bones of Joseph with them as they commenced their journey across the wilderness toward the promised land? If we bear in mind that Joseph is a type of Christ the answer will not be difficult to discover. 2 Cor., 4:10 gives us the N.T. interpretation: "Always bearing about in the body *the dying of* the Lord Jesus, that the life also of Jesus might be made manifest in our bodies." It is the power of the cross applied to the mortal body which ever craves present ease and enjoyment. It is only by "keeping under" the body that the *life* of Jesus (the new nature) is manifested by us.

"And the children of Israel journeyed from Rameses to Succoth, about six hundred thousand on foot that were men, beside children" (12:37). "Rameses means 'child of the sun.' It was a fortress the Israelites, as slaves, had helped to build for the Egyptians. It was named after one of their great kings, whose remains, as a mummy, are now in the British Mu-

seum. He was the Pharaoh who oppressed Israel so cruelly, and the father of the Pharaoh who pursued the Israelites and was drowned in the Red Sea. He was a great warrior; he conquered Ethiopia and other lands." Typically, Rameses speaks of that system: 'This present evil world,' from which the grace and power of God delivers His elect, that system over which the mighty fallen angel, Satan, presides as Prince.

"So here, on the very threshold of their journey, we have a strange and wonderful parable—a picture that everyone who knows the rudiments of astronomy can appreciate. As the literal Israel was called out of the domains of the 'child of the sun' to journey to a land unknown to them, so is the spiritual Israel—the Church—called out from the realm described in the book of Ecclesiastes as 'under the sun'—all this kingdom in which the planets ('wanderers') move in their never-ceasing revolutions around the sun—to go to that undiscovered realm, in which, because what of it is visible to the eye is at such an inconceivable distance from us that their movements can hardly be detected at all, we call them fixed stars—that calm, immovable heaven of heavens that we see gazing at us every night, unperturbed and untouched by anything that can occur in our solar system of wanderers, where our earth, like the rest, is a poor restless wanderer in a path that never arrives anywhere. How graphically Solomon describes all our life 'under the sun', its mirths, its cares, its toils, its joys, and its sorrows, as unceasing 'vanity and vexation of spirit'! . . . . 'The thing that hath been is that which shall be, and that which *is* done is that which *shall be* done; and there is no new thing under the sun' (Ecc. 1:9).

"To that 'third heaven,' as Paul calls it (2 Cor., 12), that Paradise altogether beyond and free from any of the influences of our planatary system, the believer is going. We belong not to the world. Chosen in Christ before this world's foundation, we belong to an eternal realm beyond and apart from all men's ambitions, schemes, philosophies, religions (Eph. 1:4-10).

"Such a calling *is* mysterious. No wonder Paul, even when in the very act of trying to explain it to us, lifts up an earnest prayer that a spirit of wisdom and revelation might be given us, so that we might be able to *"know"* what is the hope of His calling' (Eph. 1:18). It is all so new; it is all so *un*-earthly; its doctrines, its maxims, its hopes and fears, its rules of conduct, are all so different to what is *'under* the sun'" (C. H. Bright).

"And the children of Israel journeyed

from Rameses to Succoth." "Succoth" means "booths" or "tents." This spoke plainly of the *pilgrim* character of the journey which lay before them. This was one of the great lessons learned by the first pilgrim: *"Here* have we no *continuing city"* (Heb. 13:14); for "by faith he sojourned in the land of promise, as in a strange country, dwelling in *tents* with Isaac and Jacob, the heirs with him of the same promise." (Heb. 11:3). *Booths* are all that we have down here, for "our citizenship is in heaven" (Phil. 3:20). But, blessed be God, the day is now near at hand when we shall exchange our temporary "tents" for the eternal "mansions" of the Father's House.

"And a mixed multitude went up also with them" (12.38). Very solemn is this; it was a wily move of the Enemy. Scripture presents him in two chief characters—as the roaring lion and as the cunning serpent. The former was exemplified by the cruel oppressions of Pharaoh; the latter, in what is here before us. Satan tried hard to keep some, at least, of the Israelites in Egypt; failing in this, he now sends some of the Egyptians to accompany Israel to Canaan! This "mixed multitude" would doubtless be made up of Egyptians and others of different nations who resided in Egypt. A variety of causes and motives might prompt them. Some, through intermarriages with the Israelites (Lev. 24:10), and now loth to part with their relatives; others, because afraid to remain any longer in a land so sorely afflicted with Divine judgments, and now rendered desolate and untenable; others, because quick to perceive that such wonders wrought on behalf of the Hebrews plainly marked them out as a people who were the favourites of Heaven, and therefore deemed it good policy to throw in their lot with them (c.f. 9:20). But it was not long before this "mixed multitude" proved a thorn in the side of Israel. It was this same "mixed multitude" who first became dissatisfied with the manna and influenced Israel to murmur. (See Num. 11:4.)

It has been well said that "when a movement of God takes place men are wrought upon by other motives than those by which the Holy Spirit stirs the renewed heart, and a mass attach themselves to those who are led forth." Witness the fact that when God "called Abraham *alone"* (Isa. 51:2), Terah (his father) and Lot (his nephew) accompanied him (Gen. 11:31). Witness the Gibeonites making a league with Joshua (Jos. 9). So, too, we find that after the Jewish remnant returned from the captivity "a mixed multitude" joined themselves to Israel (Neh. 5:17), though later "they *separated* from Israel all the mixed multitudes" (Neh. 13:3). So, too, we read of the Pharisees and Sadducees coming to John the Baptist (Matt. 3:7)! And these things are recorded for *our* "learning." This fellowshiping of believers with unbelievers, this sufferance of the ungodly among the congregation of the Lord, has been the great bane of God's saints in every age, the source of their weakness, and the occasion of much of their failure. It is because of this the Spirit of God says, "wherefore come out from among them and *be ye separate"* (2 Cor. 6:17).

"And it came to pass when Pharaoh had let the people go that God led them not through the way of the land of the Philistines, although that was near; for God said, Lest peradventure the people repent when they see war and they return to Egypt" (13:17). How this reminds us of Psl. 103: 13, 14: "Like as a father pitieth his children, so that Lord pitieth them that fear Him. For He knoweth our frame; He remembereth that we are dust." This people who had spent many long years in slavery were now starting out for the promised land, and it is beautiful to see this tender concern for them. It exemplifies a principle of general application in connection with the Lord's dealings with His people. The Lord is not only very compassionate, but His mercies are "tender" (James 5:11). The Lord does not suffer His "babes" to be tested as severely as those who are more mature; witness the various trials to which He subjected Abraham—the command for him to offer Isaac was not the first but the *last* great test which he received. It was so here with Israel. Later, there would be much *fighting* when Canaan was reached, but at the beginning He led them not the way of the land of the Philistines, for that would have involved warfare. He had respect unto their weakness and timidity. "The Lord, in His condescending grace, so orders things for His people that they do not, at their first setting out, encounter heavy trials, which might have the effect of discouraging their hearts and driving them back." (C.H.M.)

"God led them not through the way of the land of the Philistines." This is the *first* thing noticed by the Holy Spirit after Israel left the land of Egypt—*God* chose the way for His people through the wilderness. Unspeakably blessed is this. "The *steps* of a good man are ordered by the Lord, and He delighteth in his way (Psl. 37:23). We are not left alone to choose our own path. "As many as are *led* by the Spirit of God they are the sons of God"

(Rom. 8:14). And what is it that the Spirit uses in His leading of us to-day? In this, as in everything, it is the written Word—"Thy Word is a lamp unto my feet," to reveal the pitfalls and obstacles of the way, "and a light unto my path"— to make clear the by-paths to be avoided (Psl. 119:105). What a full provision has been made for us! Nothing is left to chance, nothing to our own poor reasoning—"we are His workmanship, created in Christ Jesus unto good works, which God hath before ordained *that we should walk in them*" (Eph. 2:10).

"But God led the people about through the way of the wilderness of the Red Sea (13:8). It is often said that the "wilderness" had no place in the *purpose* of God for Israel. But this is certainly erroneous. It was *God* Himself who led the people round about "the way of the wilderness of the Red Sea." It was God's original intention that Israel *should* take exactly the route which they actually followed. Not only is this evident from the fact that the Pillar of Cloud *led* them each step of their journey to Canaan, but it was plainly intimated by the Lord to Moses *before* the exodus took place. At the very first appearing of Jehovah to His servant at Horeb (Ex. 3:1—see our note on this in Article 4), He declared, "When thou has brought forth the people out of Egypt ye shall serve God upon *this mountain*." God's purpose in leading Israel to Canaan through the wilderness, instead of via the land of the Philistines, was manifested in the sequel. In the first place, it was in order that His marvellous power might be signally displayed on their behalf in bringing them safely through the Red Sea. In the second place, it was in order that Pharaoh and his hosts might there be destroyed. In the third place, it was in order that they might receive Jehovah's laws in the undisturbed solitude of the desert. In the fourth place, it was in order that they might be properly organised into a Commonwealth and Church-state (Acts 7:53) prior to their entrance into and occupation of the land of Canaan. Finally, it was in order that they might be humbled, tried, and proved (Deut. 8:2, 3), and the sufficiency of their God in every emergency might be fully demonstrated.

"And they took their journey from Succoth, and encamped in Etham, on the edge of the wilderness. And the Lord went before them by day in a pillar of a cloud, to lead them the way; and by night in a pillar of fire, to give them light; to go by day and night" (13:20, 21). Very precious is this. Just as Jehovah—the *covenant* God, the *promising* God, the One who heard the groanings of Israel, the One who raised up a deliverer for them—reminds us of *God the Father,* just as the Lamb—without spot and blemish, slain and its blood sprinkled, securing protection and deliverance from the avenging angel—typifies *God the Son;* so this Pillar of Cloud—given to Israel for their guidance across the wilderness—speaks to us of *God the Holy Spirit.* Amazingly full, Divinely perfect, are these O.T. foreshadowings. At every point the teaching of the N.T. is anticipated. But the anointed eye is needed to perceive the hidden meaning of these primitive pictures. Much prayerful searching is necessary if we are to discern their spiritual signification.

This "pillar" was the visible sign of the Lord's presence with Israel. It is called "a pillar of cloud" and "a pillar of fire." Apparently its upper portion rose up to heaven in the form of a column; its lower being spread out cloudwise, over Israel's camp. Note how in Ex. 14:24 the two descriptive terms are combined, showing that the "pillar" did not change its form, as a "cloud" by day and a "fire" by night as is popularly supposed; but, as stated above, it was one—a "pillar of fire" in its upper portion, a "cloud" below." It is clear, though, from subsequent scriptures (Num. 14:14, etc.), that the whole "cloud" was illuminative by night-time "to give them light in the way wherein they should go" (Neh. 9:12). Let us now consider some of the points in which the Cloud typified the Holy Spirit.

1. The "Cloud" was not given to Israel until they had been delivered from Egypt. First, the slaying of the Pascal Lamb, then the giving of the Cloud. This is the order of the N.T. First, the death of God's Lamb, followed by His resurrection and ascension, and then the public descent of the Holy Spirit on the day of Pentecost. So, also, is it in Christian experience. There is first the sinner appropriating by faith the death of Christ, and then the coming of the Holy Spirit to indwell that soul. It is on the ground of Christ's shed blood— not because of *any* moral fitness in us— that the Spirit of God seals us unto the day of redemption. Strikingly is this order observed in the epistle to the Romans— the great doctrinal treatise of the N.T. There, as nowhere else so fully, is unfolded God's method of salvation. But it is not until *after* the believing sinner is "justified" (5:1) that we read of the Spirit of God. In 2:4-10 we get repentance; in 3:22-28, faith; and then in 5:5 we read,

"the love of God is shed abroad in our hearts by *the Holy Spirit which is given unto us!*"

2. The "Cloud" was God's gracious *gift* to Israel. No word is said about the people *asking* for this Guide. It came to them quite unsought, as a tender provision of God's mercy. Do we not find the same thing in the Gospels? At the close of His mission the Lord Jesus told the disciples of His departure, of His return to the Father. And though we read of them being troubled and sorrowful, yet there is no hint that any of the apostles *requested* Him to send them another Comforter. The purpose to do this proceeded alone from Himself—"I will pray the Father, and He shall give you another Comforter" (John 4:16).

3. The Cloud was given to *guide* Israel through their wilderness journey. What a merciful provision was this—an infallible Guide to conduct them through the tractless desert! "The Lord went before them by day in a pillar of cloud, *to lead* them the way" (Ex. 13:21). In like manner, the Holy Spirit has been given to Christians to direct their steps along the Narrow Way which leadeth unto life. "As many as are *led* by the Spirit of God, they are the sons of God" (Rom. 8:14).

4. The Cloud gave *light.* "And by night in a pillar of fire to *give them light*" (Ex. 13:21). Beautifully does Nehemiah remind their descendants of this hundreds of years later: "Thou leadest them in the day by a cloudy pillar and in the night by a pillar of fire, *to give them light* in the way wherein they should go" (Neh. 9:12). By day or by night Israel was "thoroughly furnished." For a similar purpose is the Holy Spirit given to Christians. He is. "the Spirit of wisdom and understanding, the Spirit of counsel and might, the Spirit of knowledge and of the fear of the Lord" (Isa. 11:2). Said the Lord to His apostles, "When He, the Spirit of truth, is come, He will *guide* you into all the truth" (John 16:13).

5. The Cloud was given *for a covering*: "He spread a cloud for a covering" (Psl. 105:39). This Cloud was for Israel's protection from the scorching heat of the sun in the sandy desert where there was no screen. Beautifully has this been commented upon by one who knew from an experience of contrast the blessedness of this merciful provision of God for Israel: "To appreciate what the cloud was to Israel, we must transport ourselves in imagination to a rainless country like Egypt. We lived many years on the coast of Peru —hundreds of miles as rainless as Egypt.

We recalled with horror that some English hymn writer had sung the glories of a "cloudless sky, a waveless sea." In a small schooner, becalmed under a tropical sun off the coast of Equador, we tasted the awfulness of a waveless sea, and in Peru for half the year we had a cloudless sky, and rainless always. How beautiful the distant clouds looked, away off there on the peaks of the lofty Andes. We could not but feel, 'What must be the soothingness of being under a cloud like those Indians who lived up there in that happy fertile region of clouds amid the valleys and mountains!' Therefore, that cloud must have been a welcome sight to those ex-slaves, accustomed to labour in the fields under the sun of Egypt. It was a proof to them of the *all*-mighty power of Jehovah. He could give them a cloud where there was nothing in Nature to form clouds. He could furnish a shelter to *His* people when no other people had a shelter (C. H. Bright). So, too, is the Holy Spirit our Protector—we are "*sealed* unto the day of redemption" (Eph. 4:30).

6. God *spake* from the Cloud: "He spake unto them *in the cloudy pillar* (Psl. 99:7). The Psalmist is here referring back to such passages as Ex. 33:9—"And it came to pass, as Moses entered into the tabernacle, the cloudy pillar descended, and stood at the door of the tabernacle, and the Lord *talked* with Moses" (Num. 12:5). In like manner the Holy Spirit is to-day the Spokesman for the Holy Trinity, "He that hath an ear, let him hear what *the Spirit* saith unto the churches" (Rev. 2, 3).

7. This Cloud was *darkness to the Egyptians*: "And it came between the camp of the Egyptians and the camp of Israel, and it was a cloud *and darkness to them*" (14:20). Fearfully solemn is this. God not only reveals, but He also conceals: "At that time Jesus answered and said, I thank Thee, O Father, Lord of Heaven and Earth, because *Thou hast hid* these things from the wise and prudent" (Matt. 11:25). It is so with the Holy Spirit— "The Spirit of truth whom the world *cannot* receive" (John 14:17).

8. This Cloud rested upon the Tabernacle as soon as it was erected. "So Moses finished the work. *Then* a cloud covered the tent of the congregation, and the glory of the Lord filled the Tabernacle, and Moses was not able to enter into the tent of the congregation because the cloud abode thereon, and *the glory* of the Lord filled the Tabernacle" (Ex. 40:33-35). How strikingly this foreshadowed the coming of the Holy Spirit upon that Blessed One who tabernacled among men, of Whom it

is written, "We beheld His *glory* (John 1:14). So, too, the Holy Spirit came upon the twelve apostles on the day of Pentecost and they were all *filled* with the Holy Spirit" (Acts 2:4).

9. All through Israel's wilderness wanderings this Cloud *was never taken away from them*: "Yet Thou in Thy manifold mercies forsookest them not in the wilderness; the pillar of the cloud *departed not* from them" (Neh. 9:19). Despite all Israel's failures—their murmurings, their unbelief, their rebellion—God never withdrew the Cloudy Pillar! So, too, of the Holy Spirit given to believers the sure promise is, "He shall give you another Comforter, that He may (should) abide with you *forever*" (John 14:16).

10. It is blessed to learn that the Cloud shall once more descend upon and dwell among Israel. When God regathers His scattered people, when He resumes His covenant relationship with them, and brings them to a saving knowledge of their Messiah-Redeemer, then shall be fulfilled the ancient promise, "When the Lord shall have washed away the filth of the daughters of Zion, and shall have purged the blood of Jerusalem from the midst thereof by the spirit of judgment, and by the spirit of burning. And the Lord will create upon every dwelling-place of mount Zion, and upon her assemblies, a Cloud and smoke by day and a shining of *a flaming fire* by night; for upon all the Glory shall be a defence" (Isa. 4:6). What a truly marvellous type of the person and ministry of the Holy Spirit was the fiery and cloudy "pillar!"

CHAPTER 19

CROSSING THE RED SEA

EXODUS 14

In this lesson we are to have for our consideration one of the most remarkable miracles recorded in the O.T., certainly the most remarkable in connection with the history of Israel. From this point onwards, whenever the servants of God would remind the people of the Lord's power and greatness, reference is almost always made to what He wrought for them at the Red Sea. Eight hundred years afterwards the Lord says through Isaiah, "I am the Lord thy God, that divided the sea, whose waves roared; the Lord of hosts in His name" (Isa. 51:15). Nahum announced, "The Lord hath His way in the whirlwind and in the storm, and the clouds are the dust of His feet. He rebuketh the sea, and *maketh it dry*." (Nahum 1:3, 4). When the Lord renewed His promise to Israel, He takes them back to this time and says, "According to the days of thy coming *out of the land of Egypt* will I show unto him marvellous things" (Mich. 7:15 and cf. Joshua 24:6, 7: Neh. 9:9; Psl. 106:7, 8; Jer. 31:35, etc.). It was *this* notable event which made such a great impression upon the enemies of the Lord: "For we have *heard* how the Lord dried up the water of the Red Sea for you, when ye came out of Egypt; and what ye did unto the two kings of the Amorites, that were on the other side Jordan, Sihon and Og, whom ye utterly destroyed, and as soon as we have heard these things, *our hearts did melt*, neither did there remain any more courage in any man because of you; for the Lord your God, He is God in heaven above, and in earth beneath" (Josh. 2:10, 11).

The miracle of the Red Sea occupies a similar place in the O.T. scriptures as the *resurrection* of the Lord Jesus does in the New; it is appealed to as a standard of measurement, as the supreme demonstration of God's power (cf. Eph. 1:19, etc.). Little wonder, then, that each generation of infidels has directed special attacks against *this* miracle. But to the Christian, miracles occasion no difficulty. The great difference between faith and unbelief is that one brings in God, the other shuts Him out. With *God* all things are possible. Bring in God and supernatural displays of power are to be expected.

Before we consider the miracle of the parting of the Red Sea, we must first give a brief notice to what preceded it. Exodus 14 opens by telling us, "And the Lord spake unto Moses, saying, Speak unto the children of Israel that they turn and encamp before Pi-hahiroth, between Migdol and the sea, over against Baalzephon; before it shall ye encamp by the sea" (vv. 1, 2). In this word God commanded Israel to turn off from the route they were following, and encamp before the Red Sea. Many attempts have been made to ascertain the precise location, but after such a lapse of time and the changes incident upon the passing of the centuries it seems a futile effort. The third verse tells us all that it is necessary for us to know, and the information it supplies is far more accurate and reliable than any human geographies Israel were "shut in by the wilderness," and the Red Sea stretched before them. Thus Israel were so placed that there was no human way of escape. In the mountain fastnesses they might have had a chance; but surrounded by the wilderness, it was useless to flee before the cavalry and chariots of Egypt.

"Speak unto the children of Israel, that they turn and encamp before Pihahiroth, between Migdol and the sea, over against Baal-zephon; before it shall ye encamp by the sea" (14:2). Here, as everywhere in Scripture, these names are full of meaning. They are in striking accord with what follows. "Pi-hahiroth" is rendered by Ritchie "Place of Liberty." Such indeed it proved to be, for it was here that Israel were finally delivered from those who had long held them in cruel bondage. "Migdol" signifies "a tower" or "fortress." Such did Jehovah demonstrate Himself to be unto His helpless and attacked people. Newberry gives "Lord of the North" as the meaning of "Baal-zephon," and in

Scripture the "north" is frequently associated with *judgment* (cf. Joshua 8:11, 13; Isa. 14:31; Jer. 1:14, 4:6; 6:1 · Eze. 1:4, etc.). It was as the Lord of Judgment that Jehovah was here seen at the Red Sea.

"For Pharaoh will say of the children of Israel, They are entangled in the land, the wilderness hath shut them in" (14:3). How this brings out the inveteracy of unbelief! How it demonstrates the folly of human reasoning! Granting that Israel *were* "entangled in the land," that they *were* "shut in" by the wilderness, that they *were* trapped before the Red Sea, did Pharaoh suppose that they would fall easy victims before his onslaught? What of Israel's God? Had He not already shown Himself strong on their behalf? Had He not already shown Egypt that those who persecuted His covenant people "touched the apple of His eye" (Zech. 2:8)! What a fool man is? How he disregards every warning? How determined he is to destroy himself? So it was here with Pharaoh and his army. Notwithstanding the ten plagues which had swept his land, he now marches out against Jehovah's redeemed to consume them in the wilderness.

"And I will harden Pharaoh's heart, that he shall follow after them; and I will be honoured upon Pharaoh, and upon all his hosts; that the Egyptians may know that I am the Lord. And they did so" (14:4). Here was God's reason for commanding Israel to "encamp by the sea." "Terrible as Egypt's chastisements had been, something more was still needed to humble her proud king and his arrogant subjects under the felt hand of God, and to remove from Israel all further fear of molestation. There was one part of Egypt's strength, their chief glory, which had so far escaped. Their triumphant army had not been touched. Moses is told that, when Pharaoh's spies carried the tidings to him that the Israelites had gone down by the Egyptian shore, it would seem to the king that his hour for vengeance had come. A force advancing rapidly upon the rear of the Israelites would block their only way of escape, and so the helpless multitude would be at his mercy" (Urquhart).

"And it was told the king of Egypt that the people fled; and the heart of Pharaoh and of his servants was turned against the people, and they said, Why have we done this, that we have let Israel go from serving us? And he made ready his chariot, and took his people with him; and he took six hundred chosen chariots, and all the chariots of Egypt, and captains over every one of them. And the Lord hardened the heart of Pharaoh, king of Egypt, and he pursued after the children of Israel; and the children of Israel went out with an high hand But the Egyptians pursued after them, all the horses and chariots of Pharaoh and his horsemen and his army, and overtook them encamping by the sea, beside Pi-hahiroth, before Baal-Zephon" (vv. 5-9). All happened as God had foretold. Pharaoh and his courtiers became suddenly alive to their folly in having permitted Israel to go, and now a splendid opportunity seems to be afforded them to retrieve their error. The army is summoned in hot haste, Pharaoh and his nobles arm and mount their chariots. The famous cavalry of Egypt sally forth with all their glory. Not only the king, but his servants also, the very ones who had entreated him to let Israel go (10:7), are urgent that Israel should be pursued and captured. The judgments of God being no more upon their land, and recollecting the great service the Hebrews had rendered them, the advantages of having them for slaves, and the loss sustained by parting with them, they are now anxious to recover them as speedily as possible.

"And when Pharaoh drew nigh, the children of Israel lifted up their eyes and behold the Egyptians marched after them; and they were sore afraid; and the children of Israel cried out unto the Lord. And they said unto Moses, because there were no graves in Egypt hast thou taken us away to die in the wilderness? Wherefore hast thou dealt with us, to carry us forth out of Egypt? Is not this the word that we did tell thee in Egypt, saying, Let us alone, that we may serve the Egyptians? For it had been better for us to serve the Egyptians, than that we should die in the wilderness" (vv. 10-12). This was a sore trial of faith, and sadly did Israel fail in the hour of testing. Alas! that this should so often be the case with us. After all God had done on their behalf in Egypt, they surely had good reason to trust in Him now. After such wondrous displays of Divine power, and after their own gracious deliverance from the Angel of Death, their present fear and despair were inexcusable. But how like ourselves! Our memories are so short. No matter how many times the Lord has delivered us in the past, no matter how signally His power has been exerted on our behalf, when some new trial comes upon us we forget God's previous interventions, and are swallowed up by the greatness of our present emergency.

"And when Pharaoh drew nigh, the children of Israel lifted up their eyes, and, behold, the Egyptians marched after them. (v. 10). Their eyes were upon the Egyptians, and in consequence they were 'sore afraid.' It is always thus. The only cure for fear is for the eye to remain steadfastly fixed on the Lord. To be occupied with our circumstances and surroundings is fatal to our peace. It was so in the case of Peter as he started to walk on the waters to Christ. While he kept his gaze upon the Lord he was safe; but as soon as he became occupied with the winds and the waves, he began to sink.

"And they were sore afraid; and the children of Israel cried out unto the Lord" (v. 10). Had they prayed unto God in this their distress for help and assistance, protection and preservation, with a holy yet humble confidence in Him, their crying had been right and laudable; but it is clear from the next two verses that theirs was the cry of complaint and despair, rather than of faith and hope. It closely resembles the attitude and action of the disciples in the storm-tossed ship as they awoke the Master and said, "Carest Thou not that we perish?" How solemn it is to see that such unbelief, such despair, such murmuring, can proceed from the people of God! How the realisation that *we* have the same evil hearts within us should humble us before Him.

"And they said unto Moses, Because there were no graves in Egypt, hast thou taken us away to die in the wilderness? wherefore hast thou dealt thus with us to carry us out of Egypt?" (v. 11). How absurd are the reasonings of unbelief! If death at the hands of the Egyptians was to be their lot, why had Jehovah delivered them from the land of bondage? The fact that He had led them out of Egypt was evidence enough that He was not going to allow them to fall before their enemies. Besides, the Lord had promised they should worship Him in Mount Horeb (3:12). How, then, could they now perish in the wilderness? But where faith is not in exercise, the promises of God bring no comfort and afford no stay to the heart.

Israel had been brought into their present predicament by God Himself. It was the Pillar of Cloud which had led them to where they were now encamped. Important truth for *us* to lay hold of. We must not expect the path of faith to be an easy and smooth one. Faith must be tested, tested severely. But, why? That we may learn the *sufficiency* of our God! That we may prove from experience that He *is* able to supply our every need (Phil. 4:19), make a way of escape from every temptation (1 Cor. 10:13), and do for us exceedingly abundantly above all that we ask or think.

"Is not this the word that we did tell thee in Egypt, saying, Let us alone that we may serve the Egyptians? For it had been better for us to serve the Egyptians than that we should die in the wilderness" (v. 12). Behind the rage of Pharaoh and

his hosts who were pursuing the Israelites, we are to see the enmity of Satan against those whom Divine grace has delivered from his toils. It is not until a sinner is saved that the spite of the Devil is directed against him who till recently was his captive. It is now that he goes forth as a roaring lion seeing to devour Christ's lamb. Beautiful it is to see here the utter failure of the enemy's efforts. Now that the Divine righteousness had been satisfied by the blood of the Lamb, it was solely a question between God and the Enemy. Israel had to do no fighting —*God* fought *for* them, and the enemy was utterly defeated. This is one of the outstanding lessons of Ex. 14—"If God be for us who can be against us?"

Vitally important it is for the believer to lay firm hold on this soul-sustaining truth. How often it occurs (exceptions must surely be few in number) that as soon as a sinner has fled to Christ for refuge, Satan at once lets fly his fiery darts. The young believer is tempted now as he never was in his unregenerate days; his mind is filled with evil thoughts and doubts, and he is terrified by the roaring of the "lion," until he wonders who is really going to gain possession of his soul—God or Satan. This was precisely the issue raised here at the Red Sea. It *looked* as though Jehovah had deserted His people. It *seemed* as though they must fall victims to their powerful and merciless foes. But how deceptive are appearances? How quickly and how easily the Lord Almighty reversed the situation? The sequel shows us *all* Israel *safe* on the other side of the Red Sea, and *all* the Egyptians *drowned* therein! But how was this brought about? Of deep moment is every word that follows.

"And Moses said unto the people, Fear ye not, stand still, and see the salvation of the Lord, which He will show to you to-day; for the Egyptians whom ye have seen to-day, ye shall see them again no more forever" (v. 13). The first word was, "Fear not." The servant of God would quieten their hearts and set them in perfect peace before Him. "Fear not" is one of the great words recurring all through the Scriptures. "Fear not" was what God said to Abraham (Gen. 15:1). "Fear not, neither be thou dismayed" was His message to Joshua (8:1). "Fear not" was His command to Gideon (Judges 16: 23). "Fear not" was David's counsel to Solomon (1 Chron. 28:20). This will be the word of the Jewish remnant in a day to come: "Be strong, fear not, behold, your God will come" (Isa. 35:4). "Fear not" was the angel's counsel to Daniel (10: 12). "Fear not little flock" is the Lord's message to us (Luke 12:32). "I will fear no evil" said the Psalmist (23:4), "for Thou art with me." But how is this to be attained? *How* is the heart to be established in peace? Does not Isa. 26:3 sum it all up—"Thou wilt keep him in perfect peace whose *mind is stayed in Thee* because He trusteth in Thee."

"Stand still" was the next word of Moses to Israel. All attempts at self-help must end. All activities of the flesh must cease. The workings of nature must be subdued. Here is the right attitude of faith in the presence of a trial—"*stand still.*" This is impossible to flesh and blood. All who know, in any measure, the restlessness of the human heart under anticipated trial and difficulty, will be able to form some conception of what is involved in standing still. Nature must be *doing* something. It will rush hither and thither. It would feign have some hand in the matter. And although it may attempt to justify and sanctify its worthless doings, by bestowing upon them the imposing and popular title of " a legtimate use of means," yet are they the plain and positive fruits of unbelief, which always shut out God, and sees nought save every dark cloud of its own creation. Unbelief creates or magnifies difficulties, and then sets us about removing them by our own bustling and fruitless actions, which, in reality, do but raise a dust around us which prevents our seeing God's salvation. "Faith, on the contrary, raises the soul above the difficulty, straight to God Himself, and enables one to 'stand still.' We gain nothing by our restless and anxious efforts. We cannot make one hair white or black, nor add one cubit to our stature, What could Israel do at the Red Sea! Could they dry it up? Could they level the mountains? Could they annihilate the hosts of Egypt? Impossible! There they were, enclosed within an impenetrable wall of difficulties, in view of which nature could but tremble and feel its own impotency. But this was just the time for God to act. When unbelief is driven from the scene, then God can enter; and in order to get a proper view of His actings, we must 'stand still.' Every movement of nature is, so far as it goes, a positive hindrance to our perception and enjoyment of Divine interference on our behalf" (C.H.M.).

"And see the salvation of the Lord." It is surprising how many have missed the point here. Most of the commentators regard this word as signifying that Israel were to remain passive until the waters of the Red Sea should be cleft asunder. But this is clearly erroneous. Heb. 11:29 tells us that it was "by *faith* they passed through the Red Sea," and faith is the

opposite of sight. The mistake arises from jumping to the conclusion that "*see* the salvation of the Lord" refers to *physical* sight. It was *spiritual sight* that Moses referred to, the exercising of the eyes of the heart. Faith is a looking not at the things which are seen, but a *looking* "at the things which are not seen" (2 Cor. 4:18)—strange paradox to the natural man! As we read in Heb. 11:13, "These all died *in faith,* not having received the promises, but having *seen* them afar off." And of Moses we read, "he endured *as seeing* Him who is invisible" (Heb. 11:13)—that is, seeing Him with the eyes of faith. To "*see* the salvation of the Lord", we must first "stand still"—all fleshly activity must cease. We have to be *still* if we would *know* that God *is* God (Psl. 46:10).

"For the Egyptians whom ye have seen to-day, ye shall see them again no more forever. The Lord shall fight for you, and ye shall hold your peace" (vv. 13, 14). Notice the repeated use of the future tense here: "He *will* show you . . . . ye *shall* see them again no more . . . . the Lord *shall* fight for you." How this confirms what we have just said. Jehovah's "salvation" had first to be seen by the eye of faith before it would be seen with the eye of sense. That "salvation" must first be revealed to and received by "the hearing of faith." "Which He *will* show you to-day" was the *ground* of their faith. Striking are the closing words of v. 14: "and ye shall hold your peace," or, as some render it, "ye shall keep silence." Six hundred thousand men, besides women and children, were to remain motionless in the profound silence which befitted them in a scene where so unparalleled a drama was to be enacted, moving neither hand, foot, nor tongue! How well calculated was such an order to draw the trembling heart of Israel away from a fatal occupation with its own exigencies to faith in the Lord of hosts!

"And the Lord said unto Moses, Wherefore criest thou unto Me? Speak unto the children of Israel that they go forward" (v. 15). "Go forward" does not contradict, but complements the "stand still." This is ever the spiritual order. We are not ready to "go forward" until we have first "stood still" and *seen* the salvation of the Lord. Moreover, before the *command* was given to "Go forward" there was first the *promise*, "see the salvation of the Lord which He *will* show you to-day." Faith must be based on the Divine promise, and obedience to the command must spring from the faith thus produced. Before we are ready to "go forward" faith must *see* that which is invisible, namely, the "salvation of the Lord," and this, be-

fore it is *actually* wrought for us. Thus "by *faith* Abraham went out, not knowing whither he went" (Heb. 11:8).

"But lift thou up thy rod and stretch out thine hand over the sea, and divide it: and the children of Israel shall go on dry ground through the midst of the sea . . . And Moses stretched out his hand over the sea: and the Lord caused the sea to go back by a strong east wind all that night, and made the sea dry land, and the waters were divided. And the children of Israel went into the midst of the sea upon the dry ground; and the waters were a wall unto them on their right hand and on their left hand" (vv. 16:21, 22). The best commentary upon this is Heb. 11:29: "*By faith* they passed through the Red Sea as by dry land." From this it is very clear that the waters of the Red Sea did not begin to divide until the feet of the Israelites came to their very brink, otherwise they would have crossed by sight, and not "by faith." Equally clear is it that the sea was not divided throughout at once. As another has said, "It does not require faith to begin a journey when I can see all the way through; but to begin when I can merely see the first step, this is faith. The sea opened as Israel moved forward, so that every fresh step they needed to be cast upon God. Such was the path along which the redeemed of the Lord moved, under His own directing hand." So it was then; such is the true path of faith now. It is beautiful to observe another word in Hebrews 11:29— "The children of Israel *walked* upon dry land in the midst of the sea." They did not rush through at top speed. There was no confusion. With absolute confidence in the Lord they crossed in orderly procession.

"And the Egyptians pursued, and went in after them into the midst of the sea, even all Pharaoh's horses, his chariots, and his horsemen. And it came to pass, that in the morning watch the Lord looked unto the host of the Egyptians through the pillar of fire and of the cloud, and troubled the host of the Egyptians, and took off their chariot wheels, that they drove them heavily: so that the Egyptians said, Let us flee from the face of Israel; for the Lord fighteth for them against the Egyptians. And the Lord said unto Moses, Stretch out thine hand over the sea, that the waters may come again upon the Egyptians, upon their chariots, and upon their horsemen. And Moses stretched forth his hand over the sea, and the sea returned to his strength when the morning appeared; and the Egyptians fled against it; and the Lord overthrew the Egyptians in the midst of the sea. And the waters returned, and covered the chariots, and the horsemen, and all the host of Pharaoh that came into the sea after them; there remained not so much as one of them" (vv. 23:28). The practical lesson to be learned from this is very plain: Those who attempt to do without faith, what believers succeed to do by faith—those who seek to obtain by their own efforts, what believers obtain by faith —will assuredly fail. By faith, the believer obtains peace with God; but all of the unbeliever's efforts to obtain peace by good works, are doomed to disappointment. Believers are sanctified by the truth (John 17:19); those who aim to arrive at holiness without believing are following a will o' the wisp. In the little space that remains let us summarise some of the many lessons our passage sets forth.

Typically the crossing of the Red Sea speaks of Christ making a way through death for His people. "The Red Sea is the figure of death—the boundary-line of Satan's power" (Ritchie). Note the words of God to Moses: "Lift thou up *thy rod*, and stretch out thine hand over the sea, and divide it; and the children of Israel shall go on dry ground through the midst of the sea" (v. 16). Moses is plainly a type of Christ, the "rod" a symbol of His power and authority. The Red Sea completely destroyed the power of Pharaoh (Satan) over God's people. Heb. 2:14 gives us the antitype—"That *through death* He might destroy him that had the power of death, that is, the Devil." The *effect* of Moses lifting up his rod and stretching forth his hand is blessed to behold—"And the children of Israel went into the midst of the sea upon the dry ground; and *the waters were a wall unto them* on their right hand, and on their left" (v. 22). Not only had that which symbolised *death* no power over Israel, but it was now a *defence* to them! This very sea, which at first they so much feared, became the means of their deliverance from the Egyptians; and instead of proving their enemy became their friend. So if death overtakes the believer before the Lord's return it only serves to bring him into the presence of Christ—"Whether Paul or Apollos, or Cephas, or the world, or life, *or death*, or things present, or things to come; *all are yours*" (1 Cor. 3:22). But deeply solemn is the other side of the picture: "By faith they passed through the Red Sea as by dry land: *which the Egyptians assaying to do, were drowned*," for the natural man to meet death in the power of human confidence is certain destruction.

"*Evangelically* the crossing of the Red Sea tells of the completeness of our salvation. It is the sequel to the Passover-night, and *both* are needed to give us a full view of what Christ has wrought for us. In Heb. 9:27 we read, "It is appointed unto men once to die, but after this the judgment." For the believer this order is reversed, as it was with his Substitute. It was during the three awful hours of darkness, while He hung on the cross, that the Lord Jesus endured the "judgment" of God against our sins. Having passed through the fires of God's wrath, He then "yielded up the spirit." So in our type. On the Passover-night, we see Israel sheltered by blood from the judgment of God —the avenging angel; here at the Red Sea, we behold them brought safely through the place of death. The order is reversed for the unbeliever. 'After death, the judgment" for him.

"*Doctrinally* the passage through the Red Sea sets forth the believer's union with Christ in His death and resurrection. "I am crucified *with Christ*" (Gal. 2:20), refers to our judicial identification with our Substitute, not to experience. That Israel passed *through* the Red Sea, and emerged safely on the far side, tells of resurrection. So we read in Rom. 6:5, "If we have been planted together in the likeness of His death, we snall be also in the likeness of His resurrection." And again, "When we were dead in sins, hath quickened us together with Christ, and raised us up together" (Eph. 2:5 6).

Practically the deliverance of Israel from the Red Sea illustrates the absolute sufficiency of our God. The believer to-day may be hemmed in on every side. A Red Sea of trial and trouble may confront him. But let him remember that Israel's God is *his* God. When His time comes, it will be an easy matter for Him to cleave a way through for you. Take comfort from His promise: "When thou passeth through the waters, *I will be with thee;* and through the rivers, they shall not overflow thee" (Isa. 43:2). God can protect His people in the greatest difficulties and dangers and make a way of deliverance for them out of the most desperate situations.

Dispensationally the passing of Israel through the Red Sea foreshadows the yet future deliverance and restoration of the Jews. The "sea" is a well-known figure of *the Gentiles* (Psalm 65:7; Daniel 7:2; Revelation 17:15) Among the Gentiles the seed of Abraham have long been scattered, and to the eye of sense it has seemed that they would be utterly swallowed up. But marvellously has God preserved the Jews all through these many centuries. The "sea" *has not* consumed them. They still dwell as "a people apart" (Num. 23:9), and the time is coming when Jehovah will fulfil the promises made to their fathers (Ezek. 20:34; 37:21, etc.). When these promises are fulfilled our type will receive its final accomplishment. Israel shall be brought safely *out of* the "sea" of the Gentiles, into their own land.

CHAPTER 20

ISRAEL'S SONG

EXODUS 15

Exodus 15 contains the first song recorded in Scripture. Well has it been said, "It is presumably the oldest poem in the world, and in sublimity of conception and grandeur of expression, it is unsurpassed by anything that has been written since. It might almost be said that poetry here sprang full-grown from the heart of Moses, even as heathen mythology fables Minerva come full-armed from the brain of Jupiter. Long before the ballads of Homer were sung through the streets of the Grecian cities, or the foundation of the Seven-hilled metropolis of the ancient world was laid by the banks of the Tiber, this matchless ode, in comparison with which Pindar is tame, was chanted by the leader of the emancipated Hebrews on the Red Sea shore; and yet we have in it no polytheism, no foolish mythological story concerning gods and goddesses, no gilding of immorality, no glorification of mere force; but, instead, the firmest recognition of the personality, the supremacy, the holiness, the retributive rectitude of God. How shall we account for all of this? If we admit the Divine legation and inspiration of Moses, all is plain; if we deny that, we have in the very existence of this Song, a hopeless and insoluble egnima. Here is a literary miracle, as great as the physical sign of the parting of the Sea. When you see a boulder of immense size, and of a different sort of stone from those surrounding it, lying in a valley, you immediately conclude that it has been brought hither by glacier action many, many ages ago. But here is a boulder-stone of poetry, standing all alone in the Egyptian age, and differing entirely in its character from the sacred hymns either of Egypt or of India. Where did it come from? Let the rationalist furnish his reply; for me it is a boulder from the Horeb height whereon Moses communed with the great I AM—when he saw the bush that burned but yet was not consumed—and left here as at once a witness to his inspiration, and the nations' gratitude" (W. M. Taylor, Moses the Law-giver).

This first Song of Scripture has been rightly designated the Song of Redemption, for it proceeded from the hearts of a redeemed people. Now there are two great elements in redemption, two parts to it, we may say: redemption is by *purchase* and by *power*. Redemption therefore differs from ransoming, though they are frequently confounded. Ransoming is but a part of redemption. The two are clearly distinguished in Scripture. Thus in Hosea 13:14 the Lord Jesus by the Spirit of Prophecy declares, "I will *ransom* them from the power of the grave; I will *redeem* them from death." And again we read, "For the Lord hath redeemed Jacob *and* ransomed him from the hand of him that was stronger than he" (Jer. 31:11). So in Eph. 1:14 we read, "which is the earnest of our inheritance until *the redemption* of *the purchased* possession."

Ransoming is the payment of the price; redemption, in the full sense, is the *deliverance* of the persons for whom the price was paid. It is the latter which is the all-important item. Of what use is the ransom if the captive be not released? Without actual emancipation there will be no song of praise. Who would ever thank a ransomer that left him in bondage? The Greek word for "Redemption" is rendered *"deliverance"* in Heb. 11:35—"And others were tortured not accepting deliverance." "Not accepting *deliverance*" means release from their affliction, i.e., not accepting it on the terms of their persecutors, namely, upon condition of apostacy. The twofold nature of Redemption is the key to that wondrous and glorious vision described in Rev. 5. The "book" there, is the Redeemer's title-deeds to the earth. Hence his dual character; "Lamb"—the Purchaser; "Lion"—the powerful Emancipator.

On the Passover-night Israel were secured from the *doom* of the Egyptians; at the Red Sea they were delivered from the *power* of the Egyptians. Thus delivered—"redeemed"—they sang. It is

113

only a redeemed people, conscious of their deliverance, that can really praise Jehovah, the Deliverer. Not only is worship impossible for those yet dead in trespasses and sins, but intelligent worship cannot be rendered by professing Christians who are in doubt as to their standing before God. And necessarily so. Praise and joy are essential elements of worship; but how can those who question their acceptance in the Beloved, who are not *certain* whether they would go to Heaven or Hell should they die this moment,—how could such be joyful and thankful? Impossible! Uncertainty and doubt beget fear and distrust, and not gladness and adoration. There is a very striking word in Psalm 106:12 which throws light on Ex. 15:1— *"Then believed* they His words; they sang His *praise."*

"Then sang Moses and the children of Israel this song unto the Lord" (15:1). "Then." When? When "the Lord saved Israel that day out of the hand of the Egyptians; and Israel saw the Egyptians dead upon the sea shore" (14:30). A close parallel is met with in the book of Judges. At the close of the 4th chapter we read, "So God subdued on that day Jabin the King of Canaan before the children of Israel. And the hand of the children of Israel prospered, and prevailed against Jabin the king of Canaan, until they had destroyed Jabin king of Canaan" (vv. 23, 24). What is the immediate sequel to this deliverance of Israel from Jabin? This: *"then* sang Deborah and Barak the son of Abinoam on that day, saying, Praise ye the Lord for the avenging of Israel" (5:1). An even more blessed example is furnished in Isaiah. The 53rd chapter of this prophecy (in its *dispensational* application) contains the confession of the Jewish remnant at the close of the Tribulation period. Then will their eyes be opened to see that the One whom their nation "despised and rejected" was, in truth, the Sin-Bearer, the Saviour. Once their *faith* lays hold of this, once they have come under the virtue of Christ's atoning sacrifice, everything is altered. The very first word of Isa. 54 is, *"Sing* O barren thou that didst not bear; break forth into singing."

"Then *sang* Moses and the children of Israel." What a contrast is this from what was before us in the earlier chapters! While in the house of bondage no joyful strains were upon the lips of the Hebrews. Instead, we read that they *"sighed* by reason of the bondage, and they *cried* . . . . and God heard their *groaning."* But now their sighing gives place to singing; their groans to praising. They

are occupied no longer with themselves, but with the Lord. And what had produced this startling change? Two things: the blood of the Lamb, and the power of the Lord. It is highly significant, and in full accord with what we have said above, that we never read in Scripture of *angels* "singing." In Job 38:7 they are presented as "shouting," and in Luke 2:13 they are seen "praising" God,· while in Rev. 5:11, 12 we hear them "saying," Worthy is the Lamb. Only the redeemed "sing!"

"Then sang Moses and the children of Israel this song unto the Lord." And what did they sing about? Their song was entirely about Jehovah. They not only sang *unto* the Lord, but they sang *about* Him! It was all concerning Himself, and nothing about themselves. The word "Lord" occurs no less than twelve times within eighteen verses! The pronouns "He," "Him," "Thy," "Thou," and "Thee" are found thirty-three times!! How significant and how searching is this! How entirely different from modern hymnology! So many hymns to-day (if "hymns" they deserve to be called) are full of maudlin sentimentality, instead of Divine adoration. They announce *our* love to God instead of *His* for us. They recount our experiences, instead of His mercies. They tell more of human attainments, instead of Christ's Atonement. Sad index of our low state of spirituality! Different far was this Song of Moses and Israel: "I will exalt *Him"* (v. 3), sums it all up.

"I will sing unto the Lord, for He hath triumphed gloriously: the horse and his rider hath He thrown into the sea" (v. 1). How many there are who imagine that the first thing for which we should praise God is our *own* blessing, what He has done for *us!* But while that is indeed the *natural* order, it is not the *supernatural.* Where the Spirit of God is fully in control He always draws out the heart unto God. It was so here. So much was self forgotten, the Deliverer *alone* was seen. "Out of the abundance of the heart the mouth speaketh," and where the heart is really occupied with the Lord, the mouth will tell forth *His* praises. *"The Lord* is my strength and song." Beautiful and blessed was this first note struck by God's redeemed. O that *our* hearts were so set upon things above that *He* might be the constant theme of our praise—"singing and making melody in your hearts *unto the Lord"* (Eph. 5:19).

"I will sing unto the Lord, *for* He hath triumphed gloriously; the horse and his rider hath He thrown into the sea." The *theme* of this song is what the Lord had done: He had delivered His people and destroyed their enemies. Israel began by magnifying the Lord because in overthrowing the strength of Egypt He had glorified Himself. This is repeated in various forms: "Thy right hand O Lord, is become glorious in power: Thy right hand, O Lord, hath dashed in pieces the enemy. And in the *greatness of Thine excellency* Thou hast overthrown them that rose up against Thee" (vv. 6, 7). Joy is the spontaneous overflowing of a heart which is occupied with the person and work of the Lord. It ought to be a *continuous* thing—"Rejoice in the Lord *alway*"—in the Lord, not in your experiences nor circumstances; "and again I say, Rejoice" (Phil. 4:4).

"The Lord is my strength *and* song" (v. 2). The connecting of these two things is significant. Divine strength and spiritual song are inseparable. Said Nehemiah, "The joy of the Lord is your strength" (8:10). Just as assurance leads to rejoicing, so rejoicing is essential for practical holiness. Just in proportion as we are rejoicing in the Lord shall we have power for our walk.

"And He is become my salvation" (v. 2). Not until now could Israel, really, say this. Not until they had been brought right out of the Enemy's land and their foes had been rendered powerless by death, could Israel sing of salvation. It is a very striking thing that never once is a believer found saying this in the book of Genesis. Not that Abel, Enoch, Noah, Abraham, were not saved; truly they were; but the Holy Spirit designedly reserved this confession for the book which treats of "Redemption." And even here we do not find it until the Red Sea is reached. In 14.13 Moses said, "Fear ye not, stand still and see the salvation of the Lord, which He *will* show to you to-day." And now Jehovah *had* "shown" it to them, and they can exclaim, "The Lord *is become* my salvation."

"He is my God, and I will prepare Him an habitation" (v. 2). Beautiful is this. A spirit of true devotion is here expressed. An "habitation" is a dwelling-place. It was Jehovah's *presence* in their midst that their hearts desired. And is it not ever thus with the Lord's redeemed—to enjoy *fellowship* with the One who has saved us! True, it is our happy privilege to enjoy communion with the Lord even now, but nevertheless the soul pants for the time when everything that hinders and spoils our fellowship will be forever removed—"Having a desire to depart. and *to be with Christ;* which is far bettter" (Phil. 1:23). Blessed beyond words will be the full realisation of our hope. Then shall it be said, "Behold *the Tabernacle of God* is

with men, and He will *dwell with* them. and they shall be His people, and God Himself shall be with them and be their God. And God shall wipe away all tears from their eyes; and there shall be no more death, neither sorrow, nor crying, neither shall there be any more pain; for the former things are passed away" (Rev. 21:3, 4).

"The Lord is a man of war: The Lord is His name" (v. 3). This brings before us an aspect of the Divine character which is very largely ignored to-day. God is "light" (1 John 1:5) as well as "love;" holy and righteous, as well as longsuffering and merciful. And because He *is* holy, He hates sin; because He *is* righteous, He must punish it. This is something for which the believer should *rejoice;* if he does not, something is wrong with him. It is only the sickly sentimentality of the flesh which shrinks from believing and meditating upon these Divine perfections. Far different was it here with Israel at the Red Sea. They praised God *because* He had dealt in judgment with those who so stoutly defied Him. They looked at things from the Divine viewpoint. They referred to Pharaoh and his hosts as *God's* enemies, not as *their's.* "In the greatness of Thine excellency Thou hast overthrown them that rose up *against Thee*" (v. 7). The same thing is seen in Rev. 18 and 19. Immediately after the destruction of Babylon by the fearful plagues of God, we read, "And after these things I heard a great voice of much people in heaven, saying, Alleluia; Salvation, and glory, and honor, and power, unto the Lord our God; for true and righteous are His judgments; for He hath judged the great whore which did corrupt the earth with her fornication, and hath avenged the blood of His servants at her hand. And *again* they said, *Alleluia*" (Rev. 19:1-3).

Far different were the sentiments of Israel here than those which govern most our moderns. When they magnified Jehovah as a Man of War their meaning is clearly expressed in the next words of their song: "Pharaoh's chariots and his hosts hath *He* cast into the sea; his chosen captains also are drowned in the Red Sea. The depths have covered them; they sank into the bottom as a stone." They did not regard this Divine judgment as a reflection upon God's character; instead, they saw in it a display of His perfections. "He hath triumphed *gloriously . . .* Thy right hand, O Lord, is become *glorious* in power . . . in the greatness of Thine *excellency* Thou hadst overthrown them (vv. 6, 7) was their confession. The "modernists" have not hesitated to criticise Israel severely, yea, to condemn them in unmeasured terms, for their "vindictive glee." Such a conception of the Lord as Israel here expressed was worthy, we are told, of none but the most ferocious of the Barbarians. But that Israel were not here *mis*-representing God, that they were not giving utterance to their own carnal feelings, is abundantly clear from Rev. 15:3, where we read of saints *in Heaven* singing "The *Song of Moses* the servant of God, and the Song of the Lamb." Certainly there will be no manifestations of the flesh in Heaven!

Strikingly does the Song of Exodus 15 set forth the *perfect ease* with which the Almighty overthrew His enemies: "The Enemy said, I will pursue you, I will overtake, I will divide the spoil; my lust shall be satisfied upon them; I will draw my sword, my hand shall destroy them. Thou didst *blow* with Thy wind, the sea covered them; they sank as lead in the mighty waters" (vv. 9, 10). The Lord had promised to bring His redeemed into Canaan, the haughty Egyptians thought to resist the purpose of the Most High. With loud boastings of what *they* would do, they followed Israel into the parted waves of the Red Sea. With one breath of His mouth the Lord overthrew the marshalled forces of the enemy, in their mightiest array, as nothing more than a cob-web which stood in the pathway of the onward march of His eternal counsels.

Well might Israel cry, "Who is like unto Thee, O Lord, among the gods? who is like Thee, glorious in holiness, fearful in praises, doing wonders?" (v. 11). And well may we ask to-day, "Who is like Thee, O God of the Holy Scriptures, among the 'gods' of Christendom?" How entirely different is *the Lord*—omnipotent, immutable, sovereign, triumphant—from the feeble, changeable, disappointed and defeated "god" which is the object of "worship" in thousands of the churches! How few to-day *glory* in God's "holiness!" How few *praise* Him for His "fearfulness!" How few are acquainted with His "wonders!"

"Thou in Thy mercy hast led forth the people which Thou hast redeemed. Thou hast guided them in Thy strength unto Thy holy habitation" (v. 13). This was a *new standing*—brought nigh to God, into His very presence. This is what redemption effects. This is the *position* of all believers in the Lord Jesus Christ. "For Christ also hath once suffered for sins, the just for the unjust, that He might *bring us to God*" (1 Peter 3:18). God's redeemed are a people whom He has purchased for Himself, to be with Himself forever—

"that where *I am*, there *ye* may be also." "Thou hast guided them in Thy strength unto Thy holy habitation." "This is our place as His redeemed. That is, we are brought to God according to all that He is. His whole moral nature having been completely satisfied in the death of Christ, He can now rest in us in perfect complacency. The hymn therefore does but express a Scriptural thought which says—'So near, so very near to God, I nearer cannot be, For in the person of His Son, I am as near as He.' The place indeed is accorded to us in grace, but none the less in righteousness; so that not only are all the attributes of God's character concerned in bringing us there, but He Himself is also glorified by it. It is an immense thought, and one which, when held in power, imparts both strength and energy to our souls—that we are even now *brought to God*. The whole distance—measured by the death of Christ on the cross, when He was made sin for us—has been bridged over, and *our* position of nearness is marked by the place *He* now occupies as glorified by the right hand of God. In Heaven itself we shall not be nearer, as to our position, because it is *in Christ*. It will not be forgotten that our *enjoyment* of this truth, indeed our apprehension of it, will depend upon our *present* condition. God looks for a state corresponding with our standing, i.e., our responsibility is measured by our privilege. But until we know our place there cannot be an answering condition. We must first learn that we are brought to God if we would in any measure walk in accordance with the position. State and walk must ever flow from a *known relationship*. Unless therefore we are taught the truth of our standing before God, we shall never answer to it in our souls, or in our walk and conversation" (Ed. Dennett).

"The people shall hear, and be afraid; sorrow shall take hold on the inhabitants of Palestina. Then the dukes of Edom shall be amazed; the mighty men of Moab, trembling shall take hold upon them; all the inhabitants of Canaan shall melt away. Fear and dread shall fall upon them; by the greatness of Thine arm they shall be as still as a stone; till Thy people pass over, O Lord, till the people pass over, which Thou hast purchased. Thou shalt bring them in, and plant them in the mountain of Thine inheritance, in the place, O Lord, which Thou hast made for Thee to dwell in, in the Sanctuary, O Lord, which Thy hands have established" (vv. 14-17). What firm confidence do these words breathe! What God had wrought at the Red Sea was the guaranty to Israel that He who had begun a work for them, would finish it. They were not counting on their own strength—"By the greatness of *Thine* arm they (their enemies) shall be as still as a stone." Their trust was solely in the Lord—"*Thou* shalt bring them in," blessed illustration of the first outflowings of simple but confident faith! Alas, that this early simplicity is usually so quickly lost. Alas, that so often it is displaced by the workings of an evil heart of unbelief. Oh, that we might ever *reason* as did Israel here, and as the apostle Paul—"Who *delivered* us from so great a death, and *doth* deliver; in whom we trust that He *will yet* deliver (2 Cor. 1:10)."

"Fear and dread shall fall upon them; by the greatness of Thine arm they shall be as still as a stone" (v. 16). Opposition there would be, enemies to be encountered. But utterly futile would be their puny efforts. Impossible for them to resist successfully the execution of God's eternal counsels. Equally impossible is it for *our* enemies, be they human or demoniac, to keep us out of the promised inheritance. "Who shall separate us from the love of God in Christ Jesus?" Who, indeed! "For I am persuaded, that neither death, nor life, nor angels, nor principalities, nor powers, nor things present, nor things to come, nor height, nor depth, nor any other creature, shall be able to separate *us*" (Rom. 8:38, 39). Thus the end is sure from the beginning, and we may, like Israel, sing the Song of Victory *before* the first step is taken. in the wilderness pathway!

Israel's confidence was not misplaced. A number of examples are furnished in later Scriptures of how tidings of Jehovah's judgments on Israel's behalf became known far and wide, and were used by him to humble and alarm. Jethro, the Midianite, comes to Moses and says, "Blessed be the Lord, who hath delivered you out of the hand of the Egyptians and out of the hand of Pharaoh . . . now I *know* that the Lord is greater than all gods" (Ex. 18, 10, 11). Rahab of Jerico declared to the two spies, "I know that the Lord hath given you the land and that *your terror* is fallen upon us, and that all the inhabitants of the land faint because of you. For *we* have *heard* how the Lord dried up the water of the Red Sea for you," etc. (Jos. 2:9, 10). Said the Gibeon-ites to Joshua, "From a very far country thy servants are come because of the name of the Lord thy God; for *we have heard* the fame of Him and all that He did in Egypt" (Josh. 9:9). Hundreds of years later the Philistines said, "Who shall deliver us out of the hand of these mighty Gods? these are the Gods that smote the Egyptians with all the plagues in the wilderness" (1 Sam. 4:8)!

"The Lord shall reign forever and ever" (v. 18). And here the Song ends—the next verse is simply the inspired record of the historian, giving us the cause and the occasion of the Song. The Song ends as it began—with "The Lord." Faith views the eternal future without a tremor. Fully assured that God is *sovereign*, sovereign because omnipotent, immutable, and eternal, the conclusion is irresistible and certain that, "The Lord *shall* reign *forever and ever.*"

"And Miriam the prophetess, the sister of Aaron, took a timbral in her hand; and all the women went out after her with timbrals and with dances. And Miriam answered them, Sing ye to the Lord, for He hath triumphed gloriously; the horse and his rider hath He thrown into the sea" (vv. 20, 21). "The women's voices, with their musical accompaniments, take up the refrain. It is the seal of *completeness*. Sin had come in through the women; now her heart is lifted up in praise, which testifies in itself of victory over it. The mute inanimate things also become responsive in the timbrals in her hand. The joy is full and universal in the redeemed creation" (Numerical Bible). Blessed witness to the final fruits of Redemption.

Some persons have experienced a difficulty here in that Miriam also *led* in this Song of Victory. It seems to clash with the teaching of the New Testament, which enjoins the subordination of women to the men in the assembly. But the difficulty is self-created. There is nothing here which in anywise conflicts with 1 Cor. 14-34. Observe two things: it was *only* the "women" (v. 20) whom Miriam led in song! Second, this was *not* in the presence of the men—"*all* the women *went out* after her!" Thus Divine order was preserved. May the Lord grant a like spirit of subordination to His daughters to-day.

CHAPTER 21

IN THE WILDERNESS

EXODUS 15

"So Moses brought Israel from the Red Sea, and they went out into the wilderness of Shur" (15:22). When God separates a people unto Himself, it is not only needful that that people should be redeemed with "precious blood," and then brought near as purged worshippers, but it is also part of God's wise purpose that they should pass through the wilderness ere they enter into the promised inheritance. Two chief designs are accomplished thereby. First, the trials and testings of the wilderness make manifest the evil of our hearts, and the incurable corruption of the flesh, and this in order that we may be humbled— "to hide pride" from us; and that we may prove by experience that entrance into the inheritance itself is also and solely a matter of sovereign grace, seeing that there is *no worthiness,* yea, *no* "good thing" in us. Second, inasmuch as when Jehovah leads His people into the wilderness He goes with them and makes His presence and His love manifest among them. Inasmuch as it is His purpose to display His power in saving His redeemed from the consequences of their failures, and thus make their need the opportunity of lavishing upon them the riches of His grace, we are made to see not only Israel, but God *with* them and *for* them in the waste howling desert.

Trial and humiliation are not "the end of the Lord" (James 5:11), but are rather the occasions for fresh displays of the Father's long-sufferance and goodness. The wilderness may and will make manifest the weakness of His saints, and, alas! their failures, but this is only to magnify the power and mercy of Him who brought them into the place of testing. Further: God has in view our ultimate wellbeing— that He may "do thee good at thy *latter* end" (Deut. 6:18); and when the trials are over, when our faithful God has supplied our *"every* need," *all,* all shall be found to be to *His* honour, praise, and

glory. Thus God's purpose in leading His people through the wilderness was (and is) not only that He might try and prove *them* (Deut. 8:2-5), but that in the trial He might exhibit what *He* was for them in bearing with their failures and in supplying their need. The "wilderness," then, gives us not only a revelation of *ourselves,* but it also makes manifest the *ways* of God.

"So Moses brought Israel from the Red Sea, and they went out into the wilderness of Shur." This is the first time that we read of them being *in* "the wilderness." In 13:18 we are told that "God led the people about *the way of* the wilderness," but that they had not then actually entered it is clear from v. 20—"And they took their journey from Succoth, and encamped in Etham, in *the edge of* the wilderness." But now they "went out *into* the wilderness." The *connection is very striking and instructive.* It was their passage through the Red Sea which introduced God's redeemed to the wilderness. Israel's journey through the Red Sea speaks of the believer's union with Christ in His death and resurrection (Rom. 6:3, 4): Typically, Israel were now upon resurrection-ground. That we may not miss the force of this, the Holy Spirit has been careful to tell us that "Moses brought Israel from the Red Sea, and they went out into the wilderness of Shur; and they went *three days* in the wilderness." Here, as in many other passages, the "three days" speaks of *resurrection* (1 Cor. 15:4).

It is only when the Christian's faith lays hold of his oneness with Christ in His death and resurrection, recognising that he is a "new creature" in Him, that he becomes conscious of "the wilderness." Just in proportion as we apprehend our new standing before God and our portion in His Son, so will this world become to us a dreary and desolate *wilderness.* To the

118

natural man the world offers much that is attractive and alluring; but to the spiritual man all in it is only "vanity and vexation of spirit." To the eye of sense there is much in the world that is pleasant and pleasing; but the eye of faith sees nothing but death written across the whole scene —"change and decay in *all* around I see." It has much which ministers to "the lust of the flesh, the lust of the eye, and the pride of life," but nothing whatever for the new nature. So far as the spiritual life is concerned, the world is simply a *wilderness*—barren and desolate.

The wilderness is the place of *travellers,* journeying from one country to another; none but a madman would think of making his *home* there. Precisely such is this world. It is the place through which man journeys from time to eternity. And *faith* it is which makes the difference between the way in which men regard this world. The unbeliever, for the most part, is content to *remain* here. He settles down as though he is to stay here for ever. "Their inward thought is, their houses shall continue *forever,* and their dwelling-places to all generations; they call their land after their names" (Pel. 49:11). Every effort is made to prolong his earthly sojourn, and when at last death claims him, he is loath to leave. Far different is it with the believer, the *real* believer. *His* home is not here. He looks *"for* a city which hath foundations whose builder and maker is God" (Heb. 11:10). Consequently, he is a stranger and pilgrim here (Heb. 11:13). It is of *this* the "wilderness" speaks. Canaan was the country which God gave to Abraham and his seed, and the wilderness was simply a strange land through which they passed on their way to their inheritance.

"And they went three days in the wilderness, *and found no water"* (v. 22). This is the first lesson which our wilderness-life is designed to teach us. There is nothing down here which can in anywise minister to that life which we have received from Christ. The pleasures of sin, the attractions of the world, no longer satisfy. The things which formerly charmed, now repel us. The companionships we used to find so pleasing have become distasteful. The things which delight the ungodly only cause us to groan. The Christian who is in communion with his Lord finds absolutely nothing around him which will or can *refresh his thirsty soul.* For him the shallow cisterns of this world

have run dry. His cry will be that of the Psalmist: "O God, Thou art my God; early will I seek Thee; my soul thirsteth for Thee, my flesh longeth for Thee, *in a dry* and *thirsty* land, where no water is" (Psl. 63:1). Ah, here is the believer's Resource: *God* alone can satisfy the longings of his heart. Just as he first heeded the gracious words of the Saviour, "If any man thirst, let him come unto *Me,* and *drink"* (John 7:37), so must he *continue to go* to Him who alone has the Water of Life.

"And when they came to Marah they could not drink of the waters of Marah, for they were bitter; therefore the name of it was called Marah" (v. 23). A sore trial, a real test, was this. Three days' journey in the hot and sandy wilderness without finding any water; and now that water *is* reached, behold, it is *"bitter!"* "How often this is the case with the young believer, aye, and with the old one, too. We grasp at that which we think will satisfy, and only find bitter disappointment. Has it not proved so? Have you tried the pleasures, or the riches, or the honours of the world, and only found them *bitter?* You are invited to a gay party. Once this would have been very delightful; but now, how bitter to the taste of the *new nature!* How utterly disappointed you return home. Have you set your heart on some earthly object? You are permitted to obtain it; but how empty! Yea, what you expected to yield such satisfaction only brings sorrow and emptiness" (C. Stanley).

Israel were now made to feel the bareness and bitterness of the wilderness. With what light hearts did they begin their journey across it? Little prepared were they for what lay before them. To go three days and find no water, and when they reached some to find it bitter! How differently had they expected from God! How natural for them, after experiencing the great work of deliverance which He had wrought for them, to count on Him providing a smooth and easy path for them. So, too, is it with young Christians. They have peace with God and rejoice in the knowledge of sins forgiven. Little do they (or did we) anticipate the tribulations which lay before them. Did not we expect things would be agreeable here? Have we not sought to make ourselves happy in this world? And have we not been disappointed and discouraged, when we found "no water," and that what there is was "bitter?" Ah, we enter the wilderness without understanding what it is! We thought, if we thought at all, that our gracious God would screen us from sorrow. Ah, dear reader, it is at *God's right hand,* and not in this world, that there are "pleasures for evermore."

As we have said, the "wilderness" accurately symbolises and portrays this world, and the *first* stage of the journey forecasts the whole! Drought and bitterness are all that we can expect in the place that owns not Christ. How could it be otherwise? Does God mean for us to settle down and be content in a world which hates Him and which cast out His beloved Son? Never! Here, then, is something of vital importance for the young Christian. I ought to start my wilderness journey *expecting* nothing but dearth. If we expect peace instead of persecution, that which will make us merry rather than cause us to groan, disappointment and disheartenment at not having our expectations realised, will be our portion. Many an experienced Christian would bear witness that most of his failings in the wilderness are to be attributed to his starting out with a wrong view of what the wilderness is. Ease and rest are not to be found in it, and the more we look for these, the keener will be our disappointment. The first stage in our journey must proclaim to us, as to Israel, what the true nature of the journey is. *It is Marah.*

"And the people *murmured* against Moses, saying, What shall we drink?" (v. 24). Very solemn is this. Three days ago this people had been singing, now they are murmuring. Praising before the Red Sea gives place to complaining at Marah! A real trial was this experience, but how sadly Israel failed under it. Just as before, when they saw the Egyptians bearing down upon them at Pihahiroth, so now once more they upbraid Moses for bringing them into trouble. They appeared to have overlooked entirely the fact that they had been *led* to Marah by the Pillar of Cloud (13:22)! Their murmuring against Moses was, in reality, murmuring against the Lord. And so it is with us. Every complaint against our circumstances, every grumble about the weather, about the way people treat us, about the daily trials of life, is directed *against* that One Who "worketh *all* things after the counsel of *His Own* will (Eph. 1:11). Remember, dear reader, that what is here recorded of Israel's history is "written for *our admoni-*

tion" (1 Cor. 10:11). There is the same evil heart of unbelief and the same rebellious will within us as were in the Israelites. Therefore do we need to earnestly seek grace that the one may be subdued and the other broken.

And what was the *cause* of their "murmuring?" There can be only one answer: their eye was no longer upon God. After the wonders of Jehovah's power which they had witnessed in Egypt, and their glorious deliverance at the Red Sea, it ought to have been unmistakably evident to them that *He* was *for* and *with* them in very truth. But so far from recognising this, they do not seem to have given *Him* a single thought. They speak as if they had to do with Moses only. And is it not frequently so with us? When we reach Marah, do we not charge some fellow-creature with being responsible for *our* hard lot? Some friend in whom we trusted, some counsellor whose advice we respected, some arm of flesh on which we leaned has failed us, and we *blame them* because of the "bitter waters!"

"And he cried unto the Lord" (v. 25). Moses did what Israel ought to have done—he took the matter to God in prayer. This is what our "Marah's" are for— to drive us to the Lord. I say *"drive,"* for the tragic thing is that most of the time we are so under the influence of the flesh that we become absorbed with His blessings, rather than with the Blesser Himself. Not, perhaps, that we are entirely prayerless, but rather that there is so little *heart* in our prayers. It is sad and solemn, yet nevertheless true, that it takes a "Marah" to make us cry unto God *in earnest.* "They wandered in the wilderness in a solitary way; they found no city to dwell in. Hungry and thirsty their soul fainted in them. *THEN they cried unto the Lord in* their trouble, and He delivered them out of their distresses. . . . Therefore He brought down their heart with labour; they fell down, and there was none to help. *THEN they cried unto the Lord* in their trouble, and He saved them out of their distresses. . . . Their soul abhorreth all manner of meat; and they drew near unto the gates of death, *THEN they cry unto the Lord* in their trouble, and He saveth them out of their distresses. . . . They reel to and fro, and stagger like a drunken man, and are at their wits' end. *THEN they cry unto the Lord* in their trouble, and He bringeth them out of their distresses" (Psl. 107:4, 5, 12, 13, 18, 19, 27, 28). Alas that this is so often true of writer and reader.

"And he cried unto the Lord; and the Lord showed him a tree, which, when he had cast into the waters, the waters were made sweet" (v. 25). Moses did not cry unto God in vain. The One who has provided redemption for His people is the God of all grace, and with infinite long-sufferance does He bear with them. The faith of Israel might fail, and instead of trusting the Lord for the supply of their need, give way to murmuring; nevertheless, He came to their relief. So with us. How true it is that "He hath not dealt with us *after* our sins, nor rewarded us *according to* our iniquities" (Psl. 103:10). But *on what ground* does the thrice Holy One deal so tenderly with His erring people? Ah, is it not beautiful to see that at this point, too, our type is perfect—it was in response to the cries of an *interceding mediator* that God acted. In His official character Moses is seen all through as the one who came between God and Israel. It was in response to *his* cry that the Lord came to Israel's relief! And blessed be God there is also One who "ever liveth to make intercession for us" (Heb. 7:25), and on *this* ground God deals tenderly with us as we pass through the wilderness: "If any man sin we have an *Advocate* with the Father, Jesus Christ the Righteous" (I. John 2:1).

The form which God's response took on this occasion is also deeply significant and instructive. He showed Moses "a tree." The "tree" had evidently been there all the time, but Moses *saw* it not, or at least knew not its sweetening properties. It was not until the Lord *"showed him"* the tree that he learned of the provision of God's grace. This shows how *dependent* we are upon the Lord, and how blind we are in ourselves. Of Hagar we read, "And God *opened her eyes,* and she saw a well of water" (Gen. 21:19). So in 2 Kings 6:17 we are told, "And the Lord *opened the eyes* of the young man, and he saw; and, behold, the mountain was full of horses and chariots of fire round about Elisha." Clearly "the hearing ear, and *seeing eye,* the Lord hath made even both of them" (Prov. 20:12).

And *what* was it that the Lord "showed" Moses? It was "a tree." And what did this "tree" which sweetened the bitter waters, typify? Surely it is the person and work of our Blessed Saviour—the two are inseparably connected. There are several Scriptures which present Him under the figure of a "tree." In the 1st Psalm it is said, "He shall be *like a tree* planted by the rivers of water, that bringeth forth His fruit in His season, His leaf also shall not wither; and whatsoever He doeth shall prosper" (v. 3). Again, in Song of Solomon 2:3 we read, *"As the apple tree* among the trees of the wood, *so* is my Beloved among the sons. I sat down under His shadow with great delight, and His fruit was sweet to my taste." Here is the second great lesson of our wilderness-life—nothing can sweeten the bitter cup of our earthly experiences except reposing under the shadow of Christ! Sit down at *His* feet, dear reader, and *you* shall find His fruit "sweet" unto your taste, and His words sweeter than the honey or the honey-comb.

But the "tree" also speaks of the *cross* of Christ: "Who His own self bare our sins in His own body *on the Tree"* (I. Pt. 2:24), "The cross of Christ is that which makes what is naturally bitter sweet to us. It is *the fellowship of His sufferings* (Phil. 3:10), and the knowledge of its being that, what suffering can it not sweeten! . . . . Let us remember here that these sufferings of which we speak are therefore sufferings which are peculiar to us *as Christians.* This 'bitterness' of death in the wilderness is not simply the experience of what falls to the common lot of man to experience. It is not the bitterness simply of being in the body—of enduring the ills which, they say, flesh is heir to. It is the bitterness which results from being linked with Christ in His own path of suffering here. 'If we suffer with Him we shall also reign with Him.' Marah then is sweetened by this 'tree'; the cross, the cross of shame; the cross which was the mark of the world's verdict as to Him—the cross it is that sweetens the struggles. If we endure shame and rejection for Him, as His, we can endure it, and the sweet reality of being linked with Him makes Marah itself drinkable" (Mr. Grant). A beautiful illustration is furnished in Acts 16. There we see Paul and Silas in the prison of Philippi; they were cruelly scourged, and then thrown into the innermost dungeon. Behold them in the darkness, feet fast in the stocks, and backs bleeding. That was *"Marah"* for them indeed. But how were they employed? They *"sang praises,"* and sang so lustily that the other prisoners heard them (Acts 16:25). There we see the "tree" sweetening the bitter waters. How was it possible for them to sing under such circumstances? Because they rejoiced that they were "counted worthy to suffer shame for *"His name"* (Act 5:41)! This, then, is *how we are to use* the Cross in our daily lives—to regard our Christian trials and afflictions as opportunities for having fellowship with the sufferings of the Saviour.

"There He made for them a statute and an ordinance, and there he proved them and said, If thou wilt diligently hearken to the voice of the Lord thy God and wilt do that which is right in His sight, and wilt give ear to His commandments, and keep all His statutes, I will put none of these diseases upon thee, which I have brought upon the Egyptians" (vv. 25, 26). It is very important to mark the context here. Nothing had been said to Israel about Jehovah's "statutes and commandments" while they were in Egypt. But now that they were redeemed, now that they had been purchased for Himself, God's governmental claims are pressed upon them. The Lord was dealing with them in wondrous grace. But grace is not lawlessness. Grace only makes us the more indebted to God. Our obligations are increased not cancelled thereby. Grace reigns "through righteousness," not at the expense of it (Rom. 5:21). The obligation of obedience can never be liquidated so long as God *is* God. Grace only establishes *on a higher basis* what we most emphatically and fully OWE to Him as His redeemed creatures.

This principle runs throughout the Scriptures and applies to every dispensation: blessing is dependent upon obedience. Israel were to be immune from the diseases of Egypt only so long as they hearkened diligently to the voice of the Lord their God and did that which was right in His sight! But let us be clear on the point. The keeping of God's commandments has *nothing* to do with our salvation. Israel here were *already* under the blood and had been, typically, brought through death on to resurrection-ground. Yet *now* the Lord reminds them of His commandments and statutes. How far wrong, then, are they who contend that *the law* has *nothing* to do with Christians? True, it has nothing to do with their salvation. But it *is* needful for the regulation of their walk. Believers, equally with unbelievers, are subject to God's government. Failure to recognise this, failure to conform our daily lives to God's statutes, failure to obey His commandments, will not forfeit our salvation, but it *will* bring down upon us the chastening "plagues" of our *righteous* Father (John 17:25).

A separate word is called for upon the closing sentence of verse 26: "For I am the Lord that *healeth* thee." This has been seized upon by certain well-meaning people whose zeal is "not according to knowledge." They have detached this sentence of Scripture and "claimed" the Lord as their *Healer.* By this they mean that in response to their appropriating faith God recovers them from sickness *without* the use of herbs or drugs. From it they deduce the principle that it is *wrong* for a believer to have recourse to any doctor or medical aid. The Lord is *their* Physician, and it is distrust of Him to consult an earthly physician. But if this scripture be examined in its context, it will be found that instead of teaching that God *disdains* the use of means in the healing of His people, *He employs them.* The bitter waters of Marah were healed not by a peremptory fiat from Jehovah, but by a "tree" being cast into them! Thus, in the *first* reference to "healing" in the Bible we find God deliberately choosing to *employ means* for the healing and health of His people. Similarly, did He bless Elisha in the use of means (salt) in healing the waters at Jericho (2 Kings 2:19-22). Similarly did God instruct His servant Isaiah to use means (a fig-poultice) in the healing of Hezekiah. So also in Psl: 104:14 we read, "He causeth the grass to grow for the cattle and *here* for the service of *man;* that he may bring forth good out of the earth." So we find the apostle Paul exhorting Timothy to take a little wine for his stomach's sake (1 Tim. 5:23). Even on the new earth God will use *means* for healing the bodies of the nations which have lived through the millenium without dying and being raised in glorified bodies: "The leaves of the tree were for *the healing* of the nations" (Rev. 22:2).

"And they came to Elim, where were twelve wells of water, and three-score and ten palm trees, and they encamped there by the waters" (v. 27). This does not conflict with our remarks upon the previous verses. Elim is the complement to Marah, and this will be the more evident if we observe their order. First, the bitter waters of Marah sweetened by the tree, and then the wells of pure water and the palm trees for shade and refreshment. Surely the interpretation is obvious: when we are walking in fellowship with Christ and the principle of His cross is faithfully applied to our daily life, not only is the bitterness of suffering for His sake sweetened, but we enter into the pure joys which God has provided for His own, even down here. "Elim" speaks, then, of the satisfaction which God gives to those who are walking with Him in obedience. This joy of heart, this satisfaction of soul, comes to us through *the ministry of the Word*—hence the significance of the *twelve* "wells" and the *seventy* "palm trees"; the very numbers selected by Christ in the sending forth of His apostles. (See Luke 9:1-10:1!) May the Lord grant that we shall so heed the lesson of Marah that Elim will be our happy lot.

CHAPTER 22

THE MANNA

EXODUS 16

Not for long were Israel permitted to enjoy the grateful refreshment and shade of the wells and palm trees of Elim (15: 27). The first verses of our chapter tell us, "And they took their journey from Elim, and all the congregation of the children of Israel came unto the wilderness of Sin." If we compare Num. 33, which records the various stages or stopping-places in Israel's journeys, we find that "they removed from Elim, and encamped by the Red Sea" (v. 10). Most probably this was some bay or creek of the Sea, where for a short time their camp was now pitched, perhaps with the design of them looking once more at those waters through which they had passed dry-shod, but which had overwhelmed their enemies. Evidently their stay there was a short one, and as nothing of importance happened, it is omitted in Ex. 16.

The leading of Israel into the Wilderness of Sin brings out the strength of Moses' faith. Here, for the first time, the full privation of desert life stared the people fully in the face. Every step they took was now leading them farther away from the inhabited countries and conducting them deeper into the land of desolation and death. The isolation of the wilderness was complete, and the courage and faith of their leader in bringing a multitude of at least two million people into such a howling waste, demonstrates his firm confidence in the Lord God. Moses was not ignorant of the character of the desert. He had lived for forty years in its immediate vicinity (3:1), and, therefore, he knew full well that only a miracle, yea, a series of daily miracles, could meet the vast needs of such a multitude. In this his faith was superior to Abraham's (Gen. 12:10).

"And they took their journey from Elim, and all the congregation of the children of Israel came unto the Wilderness of Sin, which is between Elim and Sinai, on the fifteenth day of the second month after their departing out of the land of Egypt" (v. 1). Why, we may ask, such particularity in noting the *time-mark* here? As a matter of mere history it seems of little interest or importance. What difference does it make to us to-day *which* month and *what* day of the month it was when Israel entered the Wilderness of Sin? It was on "the fifteenth day of the second month" after their leaving Egypt that Israel came unto this wilderness. The very fact that the Holy Spirit *has* recorded this detail is sufficient proof it is not meaningless. There is nothing trivial in the Word *of God*. Even the numerals are there used with Divine purpose and significance. And herein we may discover the answer to our question. It was the "second month," and in Scripture "two" speaks of *witness* or *testimony* (cf. Rev. 11:3, etc.). It was the "fifteenth day" of the month, and the factors of 15 are five and three. In Scripture "five" signifies *grace or favour* (Gen. 43: 34, etc.), and "three" is the number of *manifestations*—hence the number of resurrection, when life is fully manifested. By combining these definitions we learn that God was now to give unto Israel a witness and manifestation of His grace. How fully the sequel bears this out is most apparent.

In order for grace to shine forth there must first be the dark background of sin. Grace is unmerited favour, and to enhance its glory the demerits of man must be exhibited. It is where *sin* abounded that *grace* did much more abound (Rom. 5:21). It was so here. The very next thing that we read of is, "And the whole congregation of the children of Israel *murmured* against Moses and Aaron in the Wilderness: And the children of Israel said unto them, Would to God we had died by the hand of the Lord in the land of Egypt, when we sat by the flesh-pots, and when we did eat bread to the full; for ye have brought us forth into this wilderness to kill this whole assembly with hunger" (vv.

2, 3). A darker background could scarcely be imagined.

Here was the self-same people who had been divinely spared from the ten plagues on Egypt, who had been brought forth from the land of bondage, miraculously delivered at the Red Sea, Divinely guided by a Pillar of Cloud and Fire, day and night, —now "murmuring," complaining, rebelling! And it was not a few of the people who did so; the "*whole* congregation" were guilty. It was not simply that they muttered among themselves, but they murmured *against* their Divinely-chosen leader. Their sin, too, was aggravated by an oath; they took the Divine name "in vain"— "would *to God* we had died by the hand of the Lord in the land of Egypt." It is also evident that in their hot-headed insubordination they *lied*, for as slaves of the merciless Egyptians there is no ground whatever for us to suppose that they "sat by the flesh-pots" or "ate bread to the full." Finally, their wicked unbelief comes out in the words, "for *ye* have brought us forth into this wilderness to *kill* this whole assembly with hunger." It was *Jehovah*, not simply Moses and Aaron, who had brought them forth; and He had promised they should worship Him at Sinai (Ex. 3:12). It was not possible, then, for them to die with hunger in the wilderness.

What, then, was the Lord's response to this awful outbreak of rebellious unbelief? Verse 4 tells us: "Behold, I will rain"— what: "fire and brimstone that ye may be consumed"? No; "Behold, I will rain *bread from heaven for you.*" Marvellous grace was this; sovereign, unmerited favour! The very first word here is designed to arrest our attention. In Scripture, "behold" is the Holy Spirit's exclamation mark. "Behold"—mark with worshipful wonder. Here, then, is the blessed force of the *time-mark* in verse 1. The raining (which speaks of a *plentiful* supply) of bread from Heaven for these murmuring Israelites was indeed a *witness* to the *grace* of God *fully manifested!*

That which follows here in Exodus 16 is deeply important. Every detail in it speaks loudly *to us*, if only we have ears to hear. The manna which Jehovah provided for Israel is a beautiful type of *the food which God has provided for our souls*. This food is His own Word. This food is both His written Word and His incarnate Word. We propose to consider these separately. In the remainder of this article we shall trace some of the many points of analogy between the manna and the Scriptures as the heavenly food for God's people. In our next paper we shall view the manna

as a type of the Lord Jesus, the Heavenly One come down to earth.

1. *The manna was a supernatural gift.* "Then said the Lord unto Moses, Behold, I will rain *bread from heaven* for you" (v. 4). This is the first great lesson which the manna is designed to teach us. The manna was not a product of the earth; it was not manufactured by man; it was not something which Israel brought with them out of Egypt—there was no manna there. Instead, it came down from heaven. It was a gift from God.

Various attempts have been made to explain away the supernatural in connection with the manna. Some have declared that it grew on a certain tree found in the wilderness; but they fail to explain how it grew in winter as well as summer; how that it was obtainable in every part of the wilderness, no matter where Israel's camp was pitched; or, how that sufficient was to hand to feed upwards of two million souls for almost forty years! How foolish is man's infidelity. The only possible explanation of the manna is to see in its continued supply *a miracle.* It was furnished by God Himself. So it is with that which the manna prefigured—the written Word. The Scriptures are the spiritual manna for our souls, and at every point they manifest their supernatural origin. Many efforts have been made to account for the Bible, but on this point man's reasonings are as ridiculous as when he attempts to explain the manna on natural lines. The Bible is a miraculous production. It was given by Divine Inspiration. It has come from heaven. It is the gift of God.

It is striking to note how the supernatural is evidenced in connection with the giving of the manna. In Ex. 16:16 we read, "This is the thing which the Lord hath commanded; gather of it every man according to his eating, *an omer for every man*, according to the number of your persons; take ye every man for them which are in his tents." Now, a conservative estimate of the total number of Israelites who came out of Egypt would be two million, for they had six hundred thousand men able to go forth to war" (See Num. 1:45, 46). An "omer" was to be gathered for every one of these two million souls, and an "omer" is the equivalent of six pints. There would be twelve million pints, or nine million pounds gathered daily, which was four thousand five hundred tons. Hence, ten trains, each having thirty cars, and each car having in it fifteen tons, would be needed for a *single* day's supply. Over a *million tons* of manna were gathered annually by Israel. And let it be remembered this continued for forty years! Equally wonderful, equally miraculous, equally Divine is the Bible.

2. The manna came right to where the people were.

"And in the morning the dew lay *round about the host;* and when the dew that lay was gone up, behold, upon the face of the wilderness there lay a small round thing" (vv. 13, 14). No long journey had to be taken in order to secure the manna. The Israelites did not have to cross the wilderness before they could secure their needed food. It was right to hand; before their eyes. There, just outside their tent door, lay the manna on the ground. So it is with the Word of God. It is blessedly accessible to all of us. I often think that if it were harder to procure a Bible than it is some of us would prize it more than we do. If we had to cross the ocean and journey to the other side of the world to obtain a copy of the Holy Scriptures we would value them far more than we do now!

But the very accessibility of the manna only added to the responsibility of Israel. Its very nearness measured their obligation. By virtue of the fact that it lay on the ground just outside their tents they *had to* do something with it. They *must* either gather it or trample it beneath their feet! And my reader, this is equally true of God's Word. The very fact that it *is* right here to your hand determines your responsibility. You are *obliged* to do one of two things with it: show your appreciation by gathering it unto your soul, or despise and trample it beneath your feet by a criminal neglect.

3. The manna was small in size.

"And when the dew that lay was gone up, behold, upon the face of the wilderness there lay a *small* round thing, as *small* as the hoar frost on the ground" (v. 14). Who would have imagined that a complete and perfect revelation *from* God and *of* God could be comprised within the compass of a comparatively small volume? Think of it—the sum total of God's revealed Truth in a book which can be carried in your pocket! All that is needed to make us wise unto salvation; all that is needed to sustain our souls throughout our earthly pilgrimage; all that is needed to make the man of God "perfect" (complete), within the compass of the Bible!

Observe that not only is the size but also the shape of the manna is given. It was "a small *round thing*." It had no angles, and no rough edges. Continuing to regard the manna as a symbol and a type of the Word of God, what does this teach us? Why, surely, it prefigured the beautiful symmetry of Scripture. It tells us that the Bible is a perfect whole, complete and entire.

4. The manna was white in colour.

"And the house of Israel called the name thereof manna: and it was like coriander seed, *white*" (v. 31). Everything here has a spiritual significance. The Holy Spirit had a good reason for telling us the particular colour of the manna. There is nothing meaningless in Scripture anywhere. Everything in God's Word has a value and message for us.

Now "white" is the emblem of *purity.* Thus we have emphasised the absolute purity of the Word of God. Let us link together three Scriptures. "The words of the Lord are *pure words;* as silver tried in a furnace of earth, purified seven times" (Psl. 12:6): they are pure morally and they are pure spiritually. They are like the "pure river of the water of life" which proceedeth out of the throne of God and of the Lamb—they are "clear as crystal" (Rev. 22:1). Again, we read in Psl. 119: 140, "Thy Word is *very pure*: therefore Thy servant loveth it." The Scriptures are termed the *"Holy* Scriptures" because they are separated off from all other writings by virtue of their exalted spirituality and Divine purity. Once more, in Prov. 30:5, we read, *"Every word* of God *is pure."* There is *no* admixture of error in God's Word. In it there are no mistakes, no contradictions, no blemishes.

5. The manna was to be eaten.

This brings us to the central and most important point in connection with our type. The manna was not given simply to look at, or admire; but to be eaten. It was for food. It was God's provision to meet the bodily need of His people Israel. It is thus with the spiritual manna. God's Word is to be turned to practical account. It is given to provide food for our souls. But in order to derive from it the nutriment we require we need to learn *how* to feed on the Bread of Life. Just as a neglect of suitable diet or proper feeding in the natural sphere results in a low condition of bodily health, so to neglect our spiritual food or to ignore the laws of spiritual dietetics results in a sickly state of soul. In all correct eating there are three things: appropriation, mastication, assimilation. Let us consider each one separately.

Appropriation. This is a point so obvious

that many may think it is unnecessary to develop it. And yet it is just here that so many of God's children fail. When I sit down to a well-spread table it is apparent that I cannot begin to eat everything before me. Nor is that required. The first thing necessary is to appropriate to myself *a portion* of the food before me. No matter how excellent the quality of the food may be, or how tastily prepared, it will avail me nothing to sit and admire it. I need to have a certain portion of it placed upon my own plate, and then to eat it.

It is so with the spiritual manna. The Word of God is exhaustless in its contents. In it is stored sufficient for the people of God in all ages. There is far more in it than ever I can possibly assimilate. What I must do is make an appropriation to my own soul's needs. And this must be done just as definitely as the eating of my material food. We are anxious to be of real help here to all our readers, so let us be very simple.

Our first need is to *appropriate*. To appropriate means to take unto ourselves, to *make our own*. This was the initial lesson in connection with our salvation. The difference between an unbeliever and a believer is in the employment of the personal pronoun. An unbeliever may speak of *the Saviour,* but only the believer can truthfully say *"my* Saviour." Faith appropriates unto ourselves. Faith personalises. When I read in Isa. 53 concerning Christ that "He was wounded for *our* transgression," faith individualises it and says, "He was wounded for *my* transgressions." This is what we mean by appropriation. We appropriated Christ when we *took Him as our own* personal Saviour.

Now, just as we appropriated the Saviour, so we need to appropriate the *promises* and the *precepts* of God's Word. For example, when I read in Matt. 7:7, "Ask, and it shall be given you; speak, and ye shall find; knock, and it shall be opened unto you," faith makes it personal, and applying to myself what I read there, I say—"Ask, and it shall be given *me;* seek, and *I* shall find; knock, and it shall be opened unto *me."* And again, I read in Rom. 8:32, "He that spared not His own Son, but delivered Him up for us all, how shall He not with Him also freely give *us* all things," and faith takes this to myself. I apply it to my *own* case, and read, "How shall He not with Him also freely give *me* all things?"

A Scottish pastor once called on an aged saint of God. At once she handed the minister the Bible and asked him to read

some portion to her—would that we had more like her to-day; many a pastor's heart would be rejoiced if, when he called on his members, they desired him to read and pray with them instead of wanting him to discuss the gossip and scandal of the town. As the minister turned the pages he noticed that in the margins had been written the letters T. and T.P. He asked the old lady what these letters signified. She answered, Observe that they are always placed opposite some *promise* of God. T. means "tried," and T.P., "tried and proven." She had learned to *feed* on God's Word. She had appropriated the promises unto *herself.* Have you learned this lesson yet, dear reader? God's promises will afford *you* no comfort, and minister no strength to you until you make them *your own.* For example, I read in Phil. 4:19, "My God shall supply all *your* need according to His riches in glory by Christ Jesus," and when I really *appropriate* this to myself I shall say, "My God shall supply all Arthur Pink's need."

It must be the same with the *precepts* of Scripture. The commands, the exhortations, the admonitions of the Bible, are not so many abstractions. No; they are a revelation of Gods will *for me.* I must read the Scriptures as addressed to me *personally.* When I come to some word of God which condemns my ways, I must not pass it over, but be honest and take it unto myself. May God give all of us grace to daily appropriate *both* His promises *and* precepts.

Mastication. After a certain portion of the food spread before me had been placed on my own plate and in my mouth, the next thing is to *chew* it, to chew it slowly and thoroughly. But in this matter most of us are serious offenders. We bolt our food. We swallow it *before* it has been properly masticated. We eat too hurriedly. That is the chief reason why so many suffer from dyspepsia—they give their stomachs the work to do which the teeth were intended to perform. A little food thoroughly masticated will supply far more nutrition to the system than a lot of food swallowed almost whole, and our general health would be much better, too.

This is equally true spiritually. Thousands of God's children are grievous offenders here. They have never learned to use their *spiritual teeth.* The Bread of Life must be *chewed* if we are to derive from it the sustenance we so much need. What do I mean? This: *meditation stands to reading as mastication does to eating.* Re-read, and ponder this last sentence.

Dear reader, you will derive far more benefit from a single verse of Scripture read slowly and prayerfully, and duly meditated upon, than you will from ten chapters read through hurriedly!

Meditation is well-nigh a lost art. And it is at the root of most of our troubles. How many complain that they find it so difficult to *remember* passages of Scripture, passages which they have read perhaps many times. But this is easily explained. It is because the passage was not turned over in the mind; it was not duly "pondered" (Luke 2:19). Did you ever notice that the "Blessed Man" of Psl. 1 "*meditated*" in God's Law day and night? Meditation is a wonderful aid to fixing in our minds verses and passages of Scripture.

Let us give an illustration of what we mean by *meditation*. We select one of the most familiar verses in all the Bible (Psl. 23:4), "Yea, though I walk through the valley of the shadow of death I will fear no evil, for Thou art with me; Thy rod and Thy staff they comfort me." Now, as I begin to meditate upon this I take *each* word or expression *separately* and then *ask* them questions. The first thing that strikes my attention is the way in which the verse opens. It does not say "*When I shall* walk through the valley," but "*Yea, though* I walk." I ponder this over. I ask it a question; I say, *why* this indefinite language? Is it not certain that one day I *shall* be called on to walk through the valley of shadows? And then I remember that blessed word in 1 Cor. 15:51, "We shall *not all* sleep, but we shall all be changed." Then I see *why* the Holy Spirit caused this Psalm to open thus.

Next I turn to the central thing in this verse—"the valley of the shadow of death," through which the believer, who *does* die, passes. I ask, *Why* is dying likened to walking through a "valley"? What are the thoughts suggested by *this* figure? As I turn this question over in my mind it soon occurs to me (as it should to anyone who gives it a little thought). Why, a "valley" suggests peacefulness, fertility beauty, and particularly, *easy travel.* A "valley" is the antithesis of a "mountain," which is *difficult and dangerous* to climb. In contradistinction, then, from climbing a mountain which is arduous and hazardous, death is likened to walking through a valley which is *delightful and safe!*

Then I go back to the beginning of the verse, and note thoughtfully each single word. As the believer comes to the end of his earthly pilgrimage he learns that death is simply like passing through a valley. Note he *walks*, not runs, as though afraid. Then, observe, "though I walk *through.*" He does not *stay in* the "valley," but walks through it. Death is only *a door* through which the believer passes from these scenes of sin and sorrow to the realm of glory and bliss.

Next I observe that this "valley" is called the "*shadow* of death." Why is this? I must not hurry, or I shall be the loser. Let me continue pondering each word separately, so that I may extract its own peculiar sweetness. What is a "shadow"? Ah, how often it terrifies! How many of us, especially during childhood, were *frightened* by shadows! But if we had only walked right up to them we should have quickly discovered they were powerless to injure us. And how many a believer has filled the valley of death with terrifying phantoms! How fearfully has he contemplated these images of his own unbelief! O fellow-believer there is nothing, absolutely nothing, for thee to *fear* in death should it overtake you before the Lord Jesus returns. This valley is called "the valley of the *shadow* of death" because a "shadow" is the most *harmless* thing there is!

And now, as though at last the believer has fully grasped the blessedness of these beautiful figures, having discovered that Death is not a difficult and dangerous mountain to climb, but a "valley"—peaceful and easy-going—to pass through; having learned that in this valley there is nothing more terrifying than a "shadow" he now cries with exulting confidence, "I will fear *no evil*, for Thou art with me."

Here, then, is an example of what we mean by *feeding* on God's Word. *Meditation stands to reading as mastication does to eating.* Take a single verse of Scripture at the beginning of the day; write it out on a slip of paper, and carry it with you wherever you go. Refresh your memory as opportunity occurs by re-reading it. Pray over it, and ask God to give *you* a blessing out of this verse; to reveal to you its beauty and preciousness. Then ponder each word separately. Ask the verse questions and seek to discover its deeper meaning. Suppose you are meditating on Psl. 34:7. "The angel of the Lord encampeth round about them that fear Him, and delivereth them." Ask such questions as these: Why "*the* angel"? *who* is it? "Encampeth"; note the perfect tense (continuous)—*what* is suggested by this figure? "Round about"—what is meant by this? "Them that fear Him"—am I one of them? "And *delivereth* them"—*from what?*—find answer from other Scriptures which speak of "deliver" and "deliverance."

Assimilation. This is the result of appropriation and mastication, and the chief end in view. The food which I eat is to supply the waste of the body. The food which I have masticated and digested is now taken up into my system, and is transmuted into blood and tissue, thereby affording health and strength. The food thus assimilated appears in the vigour of my step, the strength of my arm, the glow on my face. And now equipped, my system is able to ward off the disease germs which attack my body. All of this has its counterpart in the spiritual man. The food which I have taken into my soul, if properly digested, will build up the new nature. It will nourish faith, and supply the needed strength for my daily walk and service. Moreover, it will be a safeguard against the germs of temptation which assail me— "Thy Word have I hid in mine heart, *that I might not* sin against Thee" (Psl. 119: 11).

Here, then, is the grand end in view. God's Word is given us to feed upon, and this feeding is for the purpose of translating the Scriptures into the terms of daily living. The principles and precepts of the Bible must be incorporated into my life. The Word has not been assimilated until it has become the regulator of my walk and the dynamo of my service.

6. *The manna was gathered daily.*

Then said the Lord unto Moses, "Behold I will rain bread from Heaven for you; and the people shall go out and gather a certain rate *every day*" (v. 4). The manna which Israel gathered to-day would not suffice them for to-morrow. A new supply must be secured each day. The spiritual application of this is very evident. The soul requires the same systematic attention as does the body, and if this be neglected and our spiritual meals are taken irregularly, the results will be equally disastrous. But how many fail at this very point! What would you think of a man who sat down to his Sunday dinner and tried to eat sufficient then, at one meal, to last him for the whole week? And yet that is precisely the method followed by multitudes of people with their spiritual food. The only time they get an adequate spiritual meal is on Sunday, and they make *that* last them for the remainder of the week. Is there any wonder that so many Christians are weak and sickly! O let us face the fact that our souls are in urgent need of a *daily* supply of the Bread of Life. Whatever else be left undone let us see to it that we regularly feed on the spiritual manna. Remember, it is not the amount of time spent, but the amount of *heart* which is put into the time which counts.

7. *The manna was gathered in the morning.*

"And *in the morning* the dew lay round about the host. And when the dew that lay was gone up, behold, upon the face of the wilderness there lay a small round thing" (vv. 13, 14). Here is a lesson which all of us need to seriously take to heart. It was in the early morning, *before other things had time to occupy their attention*, that God's people of old gathered their daily supply of the manna. And this is recorded "for our learning." The Divine Word must not be given a secondary place if we would have *God's* blessing upon us. What a difference it would make in many a Christian life if *each* day was BEGUN in God's presence! How many, now weak and sickly, would become strong in the Lord and in the power of His might if they formed the *habit* of feeding each *morning* on the Bread of Life! If the soul was fed at the time of "the dew," strength would be obtained and we should be equipped for the duties that lay before us and girded for the temptations which confronted us throughout the day!

Let no reader complain that he has not the time. You may not have time for the careful study of a *whole* chapter each morning, though even that is to be seriously questioned, but certain it is that you *have* time to prayerfully select one verse of Scripture and write it out on a piece of paper and attempt to commit it to memory, consulting it during your spare minutes through the day, on the train, or the street-car, if needs be—the writer memorised the whole epistle of Ephesians on the street-car, a verse at a time. Certain it is that you *do* have time to meditate on this one verse throughout the day, and to ponder each word separately. And after the labours of the day are over you may sit down (if only for five minutes) and look up the parallel passages, given in the marginal references. If you will do this daily you will be surprised and delighted at the incalcuable blessing it will bring to your soul. "Seek ye *first* the kingdom of God and His righteousness" (Matt. 6:33).

8. *The manna was obtained by labour.*

"We are reminded by the gathering of it, of the Lord's words, 'Labour for the meat.' They did not indeed labour to bring it from Heaven; their labour was to gather it when rained down to them from thence. And here we find that they had to use diligence. It would not keep; they could not lay up a stock for the future: every day they had afresh to be employed with it. If they were not out early and the sun rose upon it, it melted. And here is where diligence on our part is so much needed. Would that we understood this, beloved brethren, better! Manna *did not fall into their mouths,* but around their tent. They had to use diligence to gather it. Do we understand the necessity of diligence in the apprehension of Divine things? Do we understand that the character of the Word of God is such, as that however plain in a sense it may be, yet it ministers in fact its fulness only to those who have *earnestness* of heart to seek it. Only 'if thou criest after knowledge' says the wise man, 'and lifted up thy voice for understanding; if thou *seekest* her as silver, and *searchest* for her as for hid treasures; then shalt thou understand the fear of the Lord and find the knowledge of God.' And yet He adds for the Lord giveth wisdom.' But He gives it according to the rules of His own holy government.

"*Labour* is here, therefore, very specially needed; not that the labour simply by itself is anything; not that man's efforts only can ever here procure for himself what God alone supplies, but still God seeks from us that *diligence* which shows our apprehension of the treasure that His Word is. He does not give to carelessness or indolence of soul, nor is faith simply a receiver here, but a *worker with God.*" (Mr. Grant.) Before "an omer" could be gathered *much* labour was entailed, for them manna was "a *small* round thing."

9. *The manna was gathered by stooping*

It grew not upon the trees, but fell upon the ground. In order to obtain it the Israelites had to go down on their knees. How significant, and how accurate the type! Diligence on our part is required if we are to appropriate from the Word that which our souls need. But something more than diligence is necessary. There must be *dependence* upon God, the Author of the Word. There must be a *seeking from Him.* We must get down on our knees and cry, "Open Thou mine eyes, that I may behold wondrous things out of Thy Law."

10. *Some gathered more, some less.*

"And the children of Israel did so, and gathered some *more,* some *less*" (v. 17). How like what we find around us to-day! Some Christians confine themselves to the Psalms and the Gospels, rarely referring to any other section of the Bible. Others study the Church Epistles, but neglect the prophetical portions. A few study the Old Testament, as well as the New, and derive immeasurable delight in the wonderful types to be found there on almost every page. It is also true with the spiritual manna that some "gather more, some less."

11. *What was gathered must be used.*

"Let no man leave of it till the morning" (v. 19). Divine truth is not to be hoarded up, but turned to present profit. We are to use what God has given us. We are first to walk in the truth ourselves, and then to recommend it to others.

As the Lord gives us opportunities it is our happy privilege to pass on to others what He has given us. It is in this way that Christian fellowship becomes most helpful—when we spend an hour, or even a few minutes, with a fellow-believer and discuss together the things of God, instead of the things of the world.

12. *The manna was incomprehensible to the natural man.*

"And when the children of Israel saw it they said one to another it is manna: *for they wist* (knew) *not* what it was" (v. 15). There was something about this manna which the Israelites could not understand. It was different from anything else they had ever seen. They possessed no knowledge of it. The very word "manna" means "What is it"? "They wist not what it was." Thus it is also with that which the manna prefigured. The unregenerate are unable to comprehend the Scriptures: "The natural man receiveth not the things of the Spirit of God for they are foolishness unto him; neither can he know them because they are spiritually discerned" (1 Cor., 2:14).

13. *The manna was despised by the mixed multitude.*

"And the mixed multitude that was among them fell a lusting and the children of Israel also wept again, and said, Who shall give us flesh to eat? We remember the fish which we did eat in Egypt freely: the cucumbers, and the melons, and the leeks, and the onions, and the garlic: But now our soul is dried away: there is nothing at all, besides this manna before our eyes" (Num. 11:4-6). Israel were not alone as they came forth from Egypt. They were accompanied by "A mixed multitude" which had, doubtless, been deeply impressed by Jehovah's plagues and interventions on Israel's behalf, but who had no knowledge of God for themselves. Just so it is to-day; side by side with the wheat grows the tares. There is a "mixed multitude" in the Christian profession, and these like their ancient forefathers, despise the manna. They have no relish for spiritual things. They may own a Bible, perhaps one with an expensive binding and beautifully gilded; but its contents are dry and incipid to them.

13. *The manna was preserved in the Ark.*

"And Moses said unto Aaron, 'Take a pot, and put an omer full of manna therein, and lay it up before the Lord to be kept for your generations.' (v. 33). Heb. 9:4 tells us that it was a 'golden pot.' This is very striking. The manna was not to be stored up in the tents of the Israelites for a single day; yet here we see it preserved for almost forty years in the Tabernacle. It was to be kept for the land of Canaan. And so with the antitype: while we cannot feed on yesterday's experience and make that satisfy the need of to-day, nevertheless, our experiences from day to day in the wilderness will be found again with rich and blessed fruitage. The 'golden pot' in which the manna was stored tells of what a *high value* God sets upon that which it typified. The fact that the manna was kept in the ark till Canaan was reached, tells of how God has *preserved* the Scriptures all through the ages.

15. *The manna lasted until Canaan was reached.*

"And the children of Israel did eat manna forty years until they came to a land inhabited: they did eat manna until they came unto the borders of the land of Canaan" (v. 35). This tells of what an *inexhaustible supply* God has for His people. To the end of the wilderness journey the manna continued. And thank God this is true of the spiritual manna. The grass withereth and the flower fadeth, but the Word of the Lord endureth forever. We may be in the "last days" of this age; the "perilous times" may be upon us; but we still have God's blessed word. May we prize it more highly, read it more carefully, study it more diligently.

Here is the grand secret of a healthy and vigorous spiritual life. It is by earnestly desiring the sincere (pure) milk of the Word, that we grow thereby. It is by daily feeding on the Bread of Life that we obtain the strength which we need. It is through having God's Word in our hearts that we are kept from sinning against Him. And it is in this way that we should be able to say with Jeremiah, "Thy words were found *and I did eat them;* and Thy Word was unto me the joy and rejoicing of mine heart." (15:16).

CHAPTER 23

MANNA—A TYPE OF CHRIST

EXODUS 16

In our last paper we considered the "manna" with which Jehovah supplied the bodily need of Israel in the wilderness as a type of the Food which God had so graciously provided for the sustenance of our souls. That Food is His own blessed Word. But "the Word" is used both of the Scriptures and of the Lord Jesus Christ. The two are most intimately related. "In the volume of the Book," said Christ, "it is written of *Me*" (Psl. 40:7); and again, "Search the Scriptures . . . they are they which testify *of Me*" (John 5:39). Almost everything that can be postulated of the one can be predicted of the other. But the chief value of the written Word is to set forth the perfections and bring us into communion with the incarnate Word. It is only as we feed upon *Christ Himself* that we truly feed upon the written Word. Therefore in this article we shall confine our attention to the manna typifying the person and perfections of the Lord Jesus Christ.

Beneath many a figure and behind innumerable shadows and symbols the anointed eye may discern the glories of our blessed Lord. It should be our chief delight as we read the O.T. Scriptures to prayerfully search for that which foreshadows Him of whom "Moses and the prophets" did write. All doubt is removed as to whether or not the manna pointed to the incarnate Son by His own words in John 6:32, 33. There we find the Saviour saying, "Verily, verily, I say unto you, Moses gave you not that bread from Heaven; but My Father giveth you the true Bread from Heaven. For the Bread of God is He which cometh from Heaven and giveth life unto the world." May the Spirit of God now condescend to open our sin-blinded eyes as we earnestly desire to behold "wondrous things" out of His perfect Law.

1. *The Occasion of the giving of the Manna* is both striking and solemn. After being the recipients of wondrous mercies from the Lord, Israel arrived in the Wilderness of Sin. But no sooner had they come thither than we find that the whole congregation of the children of Israel *murmured* against Moses and Aaron, saying, "Would to God we had died by the hand of the Lord in the land of Egypt, when we sat by the flesh-pots, and when we did eat bread to the full; for ye have brought us forth into this wilderness, to kill this whole assembly with hunger" (v. 3). A more fearful exhibition of unbelief, ingratitude, and rebellion could scarcely be imagined. The marvel is that the fiery judgments of God did not consume them there and then. But instead of pouring upon them His wrath, He dealt with them in marvellous grace by raining bread from Heaven for them.

Strikingly does this picture the condition of that world into which the Lord of Glory descended. For four thousand years the temporal and governmental mercies of God had been showered upon the human race, making His sun to rise on the evil and on the good, sending His rain on the just and the unjust (Matt. 5:45). And what had been man's response? "When they knew God, they glorified Him not as God, neither were they thankful; but became vain in their imaginations, and their foolish heart was darkened. Professing themselves to be wise, they became fools, and changed the glory of the uncorruptible God into an image made like to corruptible man, and to birds, and to four-footed beasts, and creeping things" (Rom. 1:21-23). Little better was it with Israel, as a glance at their O.T. history will show. What wonder, then, if God had abandoned the whole race! But no; in matchless, wondrous grace, He sent forth His own beloved Son to a world wherein every human creature had forfeited every possible claim upon His goodness and mercy.

2. *The Place where the Manna fell* is also deeply significant. It was in the

131

"Wilderness of Sin" (16:1) that the "bread from Heaven" first fell. Surely it were impossible to select a more fitting title to accurately describe the character of that world into which the Son of God descended. Verily, a *wilderness of sin* was this world to the Holy One of God! A *wilderness!* What is a "wilderness"? It is a *homeless* place. No one would think of building a house there. And a homeless place was this world to the Son of God. No room in the inn at His birth; not where to lay His head during the days of His public ministry; a borrowed grave for His crucified body, sums it all up. A wilderness *of sin!* Never was that more apparent than when the Sinless One was here. How the Light exposed the hidden things of darkness! How the murder of the Saviour demonstrated the sinfulness of Jew and Gentile alike!

3. *The Glory of the Lord was linked with the giving of the Manna.* "And it came to pass as Aaron spake unto the whole congregation of the children of Israel that they looked toward the wilderness, and, behold, *the glory* of the Lord appeared in the Cloud" (v. 10). This is very striking indeed. It is the *first time* we read of the appearing of "the glory of the Lord," not only in connection with Israel, but in Scripture. Marvellously accurate is this detail of our type. Not until the Son of God became incarnate was "the glory of the Lord" fully revealed. But when the eternal Word became flesh and tabernacled among men, then, as the beloved apostle declares, "We beheld His *glory, the glory* as of the Only-begotten of the Father" (John 1:14). The "glory of God" is seen *"in the face of Jesus Christ"* (2 Cor. 4:6).

4. *The Manna came down from Heaven.* "Then said the Lord unto Moses, Behold I will rain bread from Heaven for you." The manna was not a product of this earth. It grew neither in the wilderness nor in Egypt. It was neither produced by human efforts nor manufactured by human skill. It descended from God. It was a gift from Heaven come down to earth. So our Lord Jesus was no native product of this earth. As we read in Eph. 4:10, "He that *descended* is the same also that ascended up far above all heavens." The first man (Adam) was of the earth, earthy; but the second Man (Jesus Christ) was "The Lord from Heaven" (1 Cor. 15:48).

5. *The Manna was a free gift from God.* "And Moses said unto them, This is the bread which the Lord hath *given* you to eat" (v. 15). No charge was made for this manna. It was neither a wage to be

earned nor a prize to be won, but was a token of God's grace and love. No payment was demanded for it. It was without money and without price. "For God so loved the world that He *gave His only begotten Son,* that whosoever believeth in Him should not perish, but have everlasting life" (John 3:16). Let us join with the apostle in saying, "Thanks be unto God for His unspeakable Gift" (2 Cor. 9:15).

6. *The Manna was sent to the Israelites.* "Behold I will rain bread from Heaven *for you;* and *the people* shall go out and gather a certain rate every day" (v. 4). Two truths are here illustrated. First, the Manna was God's provision for His elect people, and for none others. We do not read of God raining manna upon Egypt nor upon Canaan. It was given to Israel in the wilderness and to them alone, just as the Pascal lamb was for them and not for the Egyptians. So, too, Christ is God's Provision for those whom He "ordained unto eternal life." Listen to His own words in John 17:19: "For *their sakes* I sanctify Myself"—set Myself apart unto death. It was for "the sheep," not the goats, that He gave His life (John 10:11).

But second, this manna was also sent to a needy and foodless people. Whatever food Israel had brought with them out of Egypt was, by this time, all consumed. From the human side, they seemed in imminent danger of starving to death. Had not God met their need they *would* have perished in the wilderness. But from the Divine side everything was sure. God had purposed to bring Israel to Sinai (3.12), and His counsel cannot fail. A complete provision did He make for His needy people. It is the same now. By nature, the elect of God are "children of wrath, even as others" (Eph. 2.3). Shapen in iniquity and conceived in sin, their lot is indeed a desperate one. But praise be to God, full provision is made for them. The Bread of Life is their all-sufficient supply. Even before His birth it was announced, "Thou shalt call His name Jesus, *for* He shall His *people* from their sins" (Matt. 1:21).

7. *The Manna came right down to where the Israelites were.* The Israelites were in immediate danger of starving to death, but as we have seen, God graciously made provision to supply their need and now we would notice that no long journey had to be taken in order to secure that which would satisfy their hunger—the manna fell all around the camp. "And in the morning the dew lay *round about the host;* and when the dew that lay was gone up, behold, upon the face of the wilderness there lay a

small round thing" (vv. 13, 14). Here we have foreshadowed the blessed fact that, to the sinner conscious of his need and anxious to meet with the Saviour, God says, "Say not in thine heart Who shall ascend into Heaven? (that is to bring Christ down from above) or, Who shall descend into the deep? (that is, to bring Christ again from the dead). But what saith it? *The Word is nigh thee."* And out of this very nearness springs the sinner's responsibility. All around each tent door lay the manna. Something had to be done with it. It must either be gathered or trodden under foot! Sinner, what are you doing with the Christ of God? Remember His searching words, "He that is not with Me is against Me."

8. *The Manna must be gathered by each individual.* "This is the thing which the Lord hath commanded, Gather of it *every man* according to his eating" (v. 16). It is so spiritually. Receiving Christ (John 1:12) is a personal matter. No one can believe for another. There is no salvation by proxy. The gospel of Christ is, "the power of God unto salvation to *every one that believeth"* (Rom. 1:16), and "he that believeth not shall be damned" (Mark 16 16). Saving faith is that act whereby each awakened sinner appropriates Christ unto himself. It is true that Christ loved the Church as a whole, and gave Himself for *it* (Eph. 5:25), but it is also the happy privilege of each member of that Church to say with the Apostle Paul, "Who loved *me* and gave Himself for *me"* (Gal. 2:20). Have *you*, dear reader, believed on the Lord Jesus Christ?

9. *The Manna met a daily need.* "Then said the Lord unto Moses, Behold, I will rain bread from heaven for you; and the people shall go out and gather a certain rate *every day"* (v. 4). The manna which they gathered to-day would not suffice them for to-morrow. They needed to obtain a fresh supply each day. It is just here that so many of the Lord's people fail. We, too, need to feed upon Christ *"every* day." Just as in the physical realm the food which I ate yesterday will not nourish me to-day, so my past experiences and attainments will not meet the exigencies of the present. Christ must be kept constantly before the heart. "Give us day by day our *daily bread,"* should be the prayer of every child of God.

10. *Appetite determined the amount gathered.* "This is the thing which the Lord hath commanded. Gather of it every man according to his eating, an omer for every man, according to the number of your persons take ye every man for them

which are in his tents. And the children of Israel did so and gathered, some *more,* some *less"* (vv. 16, 17). Thus we see that the appetite governed the amount gathered. How strikingly and how solemnly true is this of the believer, "We all have as much of Christ as we desire, no more, no less. If our desires are large, if we open our mouth wide, He will fill it. We cannot desire too much, nor be disappointed when we desire. On the other hand, if we are but feebly conscious of our need, a little only of Christ will be supplied. The measure, therefore, in which we feed upon Christ as our wilderness food, depends entirely upon our felt spiritual need—upon our affections" (Ed. Dennett).

11. *The Manna was despised by those who were not the Lord's people.* "And the mixt multitude that was among them fell a lusting, and the children of Israel also went again, and said, Who shall give us flesh to eat? We remember the fish, which we did eat in Egypt freely; the cucumbers, and the melons, and the leeks, and the onions, and the garlic. But now our soul is dried away; there is nothing left at all, beside this manna, before our eyes" (Num. 11:4-6). How these words remind us of the language of Isa. 53— "And when we shall see Him there is no beauty that we should desire of Him. He is despised and rejected of men." The sin-blinded eyes of the natural man are incapable of perceiving the attractiveness of the Lord Jesus; His wondrous perfections he is unable to discern. So, too, he sees not his deep need, and how Christ alone is able to meet that need. Hence he neither comes to Christ nor desires Him.

12. *The Manna fell upon the dew, not upon the dust of the ground.* "And when the dew fell upon the camp in the night, the manna fell *upon it"* (Num. 11:9). Everything in the Scriptures has a spiritual meaning and application. What, then, is the significance of the above? Gen. 3:19 throws light on this passage—"dust thou art and unto dust thou shalt return." These words were spoken to fallen man and called attention to the corruption which sin had worked in him. "Dust," here, and onwards, speaks of *fallen humanity.* Now the manna *fell* not upon "the dust," but upon the dew. How clearly this foreshadowed the uniqueness and incorruptibility of our Lord's humanity! The Word became flesh, but in His humanity the Lord Jesus shared not our corrupt nature. He took upon Him the form of a servant, but the body which was prepared for Him (Heb. 10:5) belonged not to the "dust" of this earth. Before He was born the angel

announced unto His mother, "The Holy Spirit shall come upon thee and the power of the Highest shall overshadow thee; therefore also that *holy thing* which shall be born of thee shall be called the Son of God" (Luke 1:35).

13. *The Manna was white in colour.* We read in Ex. 16:31, "And the house of Israel called the name thereof manna; and it was like coriander seed, *white.*" This speaks of the spotless purity of our Lord as manifested outwardly in His daily walk. He "knew no sin" (2 Cor. 5:21). "He was without sin" (Heb. 4:15). "He did no sin" (1 Pt. 2:22). He was "holy, harmless, undefiled, *separate from sinners*" (Heb. 7:26). In 1 Peter 1:19 we are told that He was a lamb "without spot and without blemish." The former expression referring to the absence of outward pollution, the latter to the absence of inward defect. In His walk through this scene of corrupiton He contracted no defilement. He only could touch the leper without becoming contaminated. He was "without spot," pure, white.

14. *The Manna was sweet to the taste.* "And the taste of it was like wafers of honey" (v. 31). We need to go to the Song of Solomon for the interpretation of this. There we read, "As the apple tree among the trees of the wood, so is my Beloved among the sons. I sat down under His shadow with great delight, and His fruit was *sweet* to my taste" (2:3). And again, "His cheeks are as a bed of spices, as *sweet* flowers; His lips like lillies, dropping *sweet* smelling myrrh . . . . His mouth is *most sweet;* yea, He is altogether lovely" (5:13, 16). The Lord grant that *our* "meditation of Him shall be sweet" (Psl. 104:34).

15. *The Manna was ground and baked.* "And the people went about and gathered it, and *ground it* in mills, or *beat* it in a mortar, and *baked* it in pans, and made cakes of it" (Num. 11:8). How this speaks to us of the *sufferings* of our blessed Lord! Such expressions as "He groaned for their hardness of heart," He "sighed" because of their unbelief, He "wept" over Jerusalem, and many others, tell of the *grinding* of the manna. His treatment at the hands of the Jews and the brutal soldiers in Herod's judgment-hall show us the *beating* of the manna. On the Cross we behold Him subjected to the fierce *fires* of God's wrath. Thus we learn that the manna, ground and beaten, speaks to us of Him who "was *bruised* for our iniquities."

16. *The Manna was preserved on the Sabbath.* "And he said unto them, This is that which the Lord hath said, to-morrow is the rest of the holy Sabbath unto the Lord, bake that which ye will bake, and seeth that ye will seeth, and that which remaineth over, lay up for you *to be kept until the morning.* And they laid it up till the morning, as Moses bade; and it did not stink, neither was there any worm therein" (vv. 23, 24). On the Sabbath day the manna was preserved, and in this, too, it speaks to us of our blessed Lord. He is the only one who was preserved through death. He lay in the tomb on the Sabbath day and was "kept," for God had said, "Neither wilt Thou suffer Thine Holy One *to see corruption*" (Psl. 16:10).

17. *The Manna was laid up before the Lord.* "And Moses said unto Aaron, Take a pot and put an omer full of manna therein, and lay it up before the Lord (v. 33). Concerning the anti-type, we read, "For Christ is not entered into the holy place made with hands which are the figures of the true; but into Heaven itself, now to appear in the presence of God for us" (Heb. 9:24). The golden pot in which the manna was preserved tells of how God is glorified in Him whom it foreshadowed. "Although the Son of Man it is that gives it to us; although it is humanity here that we know, and humanity in the form in which we shall not find it when we shall reach Him above, yet it *is* humanity in which God is glorified now, and so He will be glorified in it forever. We shall find in the One upon the Throne of Glory, though no longer 'with a face marred more than any man's,' and a form more than the sons of men—the very One whose face *was* marred—the very One whose heart put Him into the sorrow in which we, of necessity there, learned to know Him thus" (Mr. Grant).

18. *The Manna is called angel's food.* We read in Psl. 78:25, man did eat *angel's* food; He gave them meat to the full"; the reference here is to the giving of manna to Israel in the wilderness. The anti-type of this is brought before us in several passages in the last book of Scripture. Christ not only feeds the souls of those of His people who are upon earth, but He also satisfies the hearts of celestial beings. The unfallen angels find their chief delight in feeding upon Christ. They worship Him, they serve Him, and they tell forth His praises.

19. *The Manna was given in the night.* It was during the hours of darkness that the manna was sent to the Israelites. It is while they were asleep (picture of man's helplessness, for we are never so helpless as when we are asleep) that the bread was given from Heaven. So, too, it was when we were in darkness and unbelief impotent, "without strength," that Christ

came to us. Moreover, it will be at the close of this world's night, when "the darkness shall cover the earth, and gross darkness the people," that the Bread of God shall return and give Life to the world.

20. *The Manna is now hidden.* In Rev. 2:17 we read, "To him that overcometh will I give to eat of the hidden manna." So, too, Christ, of whom the manna continually speaks, is now "hidden." Unseen by the eye of sense, He remains in Heaven till that day when He shall be manifested before all the world. "We shall not only 'see' the Heavenly manna, but we shall 'eat' of it again. Fresher than ever will be our realisation of His love and the perfection of the grace which is manifested toward us. It is then in fact, when we come to be there, that we shall have the full enjoyment; knowing as we are known, of all the experiences, which though they be experiences of the wilderness, yet, wait for the land to which we are hastening to find their full interpretation and blessing. The meat *endures* to everlasting life. The meat itself endures. We are enjoying that which shall be our joy for eternity. We are feeding on that which shall be our food for eternity" (Mr. Grant).

We are conscious that our treatment of this wonderful and precious type is most inadequate and unworthy. But if it leads our fellow-believers to a more careful study of the written Word, and to a deeper longing to become better acquainted with the incarnate Word, our feeble efforts will be well repaid.

CHAPTER 24

THE SMITTEN ROCK

EXODUS 17

"And all the congregation of the children of Israel journed from the Wilderness of Sin" (v. 1). Mark that this chapter opens with the word "And," connecting it with the one preceding. So, too, chapter 16 begins with "And," linking it on to the closing verses of 15. "And" is a little word, but we often miss that which is of much importance and value through failing to weigh it carefully. There is nothing trivial in *God's* Word, and each word and syllable has its own meaning and worth. At the close of Ex. 15 (v. 23) Israel came to Marah, and they could not drink of the waters there because they were bitter. At once we find the people *murmuring* against Moses, saying, "What shall we drink?" (v. 24). Sad, sad was this, after all that the Lord had done for them. Moses cried unto God, and in long-suffering grace He at once came to the relief of the people. The Lord showed him a tree, which when cast into the bitter waters, at once sweetened them. After this experience they reached Elim, where were twelve wells of water. There Ex. 15 closes.

Ex. 16 opens with "And." Why? To connect with what has just preceded. But for what purpose? To show us the inexcusableness and to emphasise the enormity of the conduct of Israel immediate following; as well as to magnify the marvellous patience and infinite mercy of Him who bore so graciously with them. Israel had now entered the wilderness, the Wilderness of Sin, and it furnished no food for them. How, then, do they meet this test of faith? After their recent experience at Marah, one would suppose they promptly and confidently turned unto their Divine Benefactor and looked to Him for their daily bread. But instead of doing this we read, once more, "The whole congregation of the children of Israel *murmured* against Moses and Aaron" (16:3), and not only so, they "spake against God; they said, Can God furnish a table in the wilderness?" (Psl. 78:19). Yet, notwithstanding their petulency and unbelief, the Lord

again came to their relief and rained down bread from Heaven. The remainder of the chapter is occupied with details concerning the manna.

Now, once more, the chapter before us for our present study, begins with "And." The opening verse presents to us a scene very similar to that which is found at the beginning of the previous chapter. Israel are once again face to face with a trial of faith. Their dependency upon God is tested. This time it is not lack of food, but absence of water. How this illustrates the fact that the path of faith is a path of trial. Those who are led by God must expect to encounter that which is displeasing to the flesh, and also a constant and real testing of faith itself. God's design is to wean us from everything down here, to bring us to the place where we have no reliance upon material and human resources, to cast us completely upon Himself. O how slow, how painfully slow we are to learn this lesson! How miserably and how repeatedly we fail! How *long*-suffering the Lord is with us. It is *this* which the introductory "And" is designed to point. Here in Exodus 17 it is but a tragic repetition of what it signifies at the beginning of chapter 16.

"And there was no water for the people to drink." What of that? This presented no difficulty to Him who could part the sea asunder and then make its waves return and overwhelm their enemies. It was no harder for Jehovah to provide water than it was for Him to supply them with food. Was not He their Shepherd? If so, shall they want? Moreover, had not the Lord Himself *led* Israel *to* Rephidim? Yes, for we are here expressly told, "The children of Israel journeyed according to *the commandment of the Lord*, and pitched in Rephidim." *He* knew there was *no* water there, and yet He directed them to this very place! Well for *us* to remember this. Ofttimes when we reach some particularly hard place, when the streams of creature-comfort are dried up, we blame

136

ourselves, our friends, our brethren, or the Devil perhaps. But the first thing to realise in *every* circumstance and situation where faith is tested, is, that the Lord Himself has *brought us* there! If this be apprehended, it will not be so difficult for us to trust Him to *sustain* us while we remain there.

"Wherefore the people did chide with Moses, and said, Give us water that we may drink" (v. 2). The word "chide" signifies that the people expostulated with Moses in an angry manner for bringing them hither, reproaching and condemning him as the cause of their trouble. When they said to him, "Give us water that we may drink," it was either that they petulantly demanded *he* should give what God only could provide, signifying that he was under obligations to do so, seeing that he was the one who had brought them out of Egypt into the wilderness; or, because they had seen him work so many wonders, they concluded it was in *his* power to miraculously obtain water for them, and hence, insisted that he now do this.

"And Moses said unto them, Why chide ye with *me?* Wherefore do ye tempt *the Lord?*" (v. 2). Moses at once reminded the Israelites that in criticising him they arraigned the Lord. The word "tempt" in this verse seems to signify try or test. They tried His patience, by once more chiding His servant. They called into question both His goodness and faithfulness. Moses was their appointed leader, God's representative to the people; and therefore to murmur against him was to murmur against the Lord Himself.

"And the people thirsted there for water; and the people murmured against Moses, and said, Wherefore is this that thou hast brought us up out of Egypt, to kill us and our children and our cattle with thirst?" (v. 3). As their thirst increased they grew more impatient and enraged, and threw out their invectives against Moses. "Had Israel been transported from Egypt to Canaan they would not have made such sad exhibitions of what the human heart is, and, as a consequence, they would not have proved such admirable ensamples or types for us; but their forty years' wandering in the desert furnish us with a volume of warning, admonition, and instruction, fruitful beyond conception. From it we learn, amongst many other things, the unvarying tendency of the heart to distrust God. Anything, in short, for it but God. It would rather lean upon a cobweb of human resources than upon the arm of an omnipotent, all-wise, and infinitely gracious God; and the smallest cloud is more than sufficient to hide from its view the light of His blessed countenance. Well, therefore, may it be termed 'an evil heart of unbelief,' which will ever show itself ready to 'depart from the living God'" (C.H.M.).

"And Moses cried unto the Lord, saying, What shall I do unto this people? they be almost ready to stone me" (v. 14). It is beautiful to see that Moses made no reply to the cruel reproaches which were cast upon him. Like that Blessed One whom he in so many respects typified, "When He was reviled, He reviled not again; when He suffered, He threatened not; but committed Himself to Him that judgeth righteously" (I Peter, 2:23). This is what we see Moses doing here. Instead of returning an angry and bitter rejoinder to those who falsely accused him, he sought the Lord. Blessed example for us. This was ever his refuge in times of trouble (cf. 15:25, etc.). The fact that we are told Moses "*cried* unto the Lord" indicates the earnestness and vehemance of his prayer. "What shall I do?" expressed a consciousness of his own inability to cope with the situation, and also showed his confidence that the Lord would come to his and their relief. How often should we be spared much sorrowful regret later, if, instead of replying on the spur of the moment to those who malign us, we first sought the Lord and asked, "What shall I do?"

"And the Lord said unto Moses, Go on before the people, and take with thee of the elders of Israel; and thy rod, wherewith thou smotest the river, take in thine hand, and go. Behold, I will stand before thee there upon the rock in Horeb; and thou shalt smite the rock, and there shall come water out of it, that the people may drink. And Moses did so in the sight of the elders of Israel" (v. 5, 6). This brings before us one of the many Old Testament types of the Lord Jesus, one for which we have New Testament authority for regarding it as such. In I Cor. 10:1-4 we read, "Moreover, brethren, I would not that ye should be ignorant, how that all our fathers were under the cloud, and all passed through the sea; And were all baptised unto Moses in the cloud and in the sea; And did all eat the same spiritual meat; And did all drink the same spiritual drink; for they drank of that spiritual Rock that followed them: And *that Rock was Christ.*"

The "Rock" is one of the titles of Jehovah, found frequently on the pages of the O.T. In his "song," Moses laments that Israel forsook God and "lightly esteemed the *Rock* of his salvation" (Deut. 32:15). In his song, we also hear the sweet singer of Israel saying, "The Lord is my *Rock*, and my Fortress, and my Deliverer" (2 Sam. 22:2). The Psalmist bids us make a "joyful noise to the *Rock* of our salvation" (95:1). While the prophet Isaiah tells us "And a Man shall be as an hiding place from the wind, and a covert from the tempest as rivers of water in a dry place, as the shadow of a *Great Rock* in a weary land" (32:2). In the N.T. we get that memorable and precious word, "Upon *this Rock* (pointing to Himself, not referring to Peter's confession) I will build My church" (Matt. 16:18).

The first thing that impresses one when we see a rock is its *strength and stability*, a characteristic noted in Scripture in the question of Bildad to Job, "Shall the rock be removed out of his place?" (Job. 18:4). This is a most comforting thought to the believer. The Rock upon which he is built cannot be shaken: the floods may come, and the winds may beat upon it, but it will "stand" (Matt. 7:25).

Another prominent characteristic of rocks is their *durability*. They outlast the storms of time. Waters will not wash them away, nor winds remove them, from their foundations. Many a vessel has been dashed to pieces on a rock, but the rock stands unchanged; and it is a deeply solemn thought that those who are not *built* upon The Rock, will be *shattered* by it—"And whosoever shall fall on this Stone shall be broken," said Christ, pointing to Himself, "but on whomsoever it shall fall, it will grind him to powder" (Matt. 21:24). A third feature that may be mentioned about a rock is its *elevation*. It towers high above man and is a landmark throughout that part of the country where it is situated. Some rocks are so high and so steep that they cannot be scaled. Each of these characteristics find their application to and realisation in the Lord Jesus. He is the strong and powerful One—"The *mighty* God" (Isa. 9:6). He is the durable One—"the *Same* yesterday and to-day and forever." He is the elevated One, exalted to the Throne of Heaven, seated at the right hand of the Majesty on high.

The first thing to be noted here in our type is that the rock was to be *smitten*. This, of course, speaks of the death of the Lord Jesus. It is striking to note the *order* of the typical teaching of Ex. 16 and 17. In the former we have that which speaks of the incarnation of Christ; in the latter, that which foreshadowed the crucifixion of Christ. Ex. 17 is supplementary to chapter 16. Christ must descend from Heaven to earth (as the manna did) if He was to become the Bread of life to

His people; but He must be smitten by Divine judgment if He was to be the Water of life to them! Here is another reason for the opening "And."

There are three details here which enable us to fix the interpretation of the smiting of the rock as a type of *the death* of the Lord Jesus. First, it was to be smitten by the *rod* of Moses. The "rod" in the hand of Moses had been the symbol of *judgment*. The *first* reference to it definitely determines that. When he cast it on to the ground it became a "serpent" (4:3) —reminder of the *curse*. With his rod the waters of the Nile were smitten and turned into blood (7:17), and so on. Second, only the "elders of Israel" witnessed the smiting of the rock. This emphasises the *governmental* character of what was here foreshadowed. Third, Jehovah Himself stood upon the rock while it was smitten. *"Behold, I will stand before thee there* upon the rock in Horeb" (v. 6)—marvellous line in the picture was this. Putting these things together what spiritual eye can fail to see here a portrayal of our Substitute being smitten by the rod of Divine justice, held in the hand of the Governor of the Universe. Doubtless that word in Isa. 53:4, 5 looks back to this very type—"*Smitten* of God . . . . by His *stripes* we are healed." How solemn to behold that it was the people's *sin* which led to the smiting of the rock!

Out from the smitten rock flowed the water. Beautiful type was this of the *Holy Spirit*—gift of the crucified, now glorified, Saviour. May not this be one reason why the Holy Spirit is said to be *"poured out"* (Act. 2:18)?—speaking in the language of this very type. The gift of the Holy Spirit was consequent upon the crucifixion and exaltation of the Lord Jesus. This is clear from His own words from John 7:37, 38: "Jesus stood and cried, saying, If any man thirst, let him come unto Me, and drink. He that believeth on Me, as the Scripture hath said, out of his belly shall flow rivers of living water." Now mark the interpretation which is given us in the very next verse: "But this spake He *of the Spirit*, which they that believe on Him should receive: for the Holy Spirit was not yet given because that Jesus was not yet glorified."

The Holy Spirit has given us a supplementary word through the Psalmist which enhances the beauty of the picture found in Exodus 17. There we are told, "He opened the rock, and the waters gushed out; they ran in the dry places like a river. *For He remembered* His holy promise (to) Abraham His servant" (105:41, 42). It was because of His covenant to Abraham that God gave the water to Israel. So, too, we read of God *promising* to give eternal life to His elect *"before* the world began" (Titus 1:1, 2), and this, on the basis of "the everlasting covenant" (Heb. 13:20).

1 Cor., 10, also supplements Ex. 17. In the historical narrative we read of Moses striking the rock in the presence of "the elders" of Israel, but nothing is there said about the people drinking of the streams of water that flowed from it. But in 1 Cor., 10:4, we are told, "And did *all* drink the same spiritual drink." This is an important word. It affirms, in type, that *all* of God's people have received the Holy Spirit. There are some who deny this. There are those who teach that receiving the Holy Spirit is a *second* work of grace. This is a serious error. Just as *all* the children of Israel (God's covenant people) drank of the water from the smitten rock, so in the anti-type, *all* of God's children are made partakers of the Holy Spirit, gift of the ascended Christ—"And because ye are sons, God had sent forth the Spirit of His Son into your hearts, crying, Abba, Father" (Gal. 4:6). There is no such thing as a believer in Christ who has not received the Holy Spirit: "If any man have not the Spirit of Christ, he is none of Him" (Rom. 8:9).

Much of the blessedness of our type will pass unappreciated unless we note carefully *the occasion* when the stream of living water gushed from the smitten rock. It was not when Israel were bowed in worship before the Lord, it was not when they were praising Him for all His abundant mercies toward them. No such happy scene do the opening verses of Ex. 17 present to our view. The very reverse is what is there described. Israel were murmuring (v. 3); they were almost ready to stone God's servant (v. 4); they were filled with unbelief, saying, "Is the Lord among us, or not?" v. 7). The giving of the water, then, was God acting according to His marvellous grace. Where sin abounded, grace did much more abound. But, be it well noted, it was grace acting on a *righteous* basis. Not till the rock was *smitten* did the waters flow forth. And not till the Saviour had been bruised by God was the Gospel of His grace sent forth to "every creature." What, my reader, is the response of your heart to this amazing and rich mercy of God? Surely you say, out of deepest gratitude, "thanks be unto God for His unspeakable Gift" (2 Cor. 9:15).

This paper would not be complete were we to close without a brief word upon Num. 20, where we again find Moses smiting the rock. "And the Lord spake unto Moses, saying, Take the rod, and gather thou the assembly together, thou, and Aaron, thy brother, and speak ye unto the rock before their eyes, and it shall give forth His water, and thou shall bring forth to them water out of the rock; *so* thou shalt give the congregation and their beasts drink" (vv. 7, 8).

What is recorded in Num. 20 occurred forty years later than what has been before us in Ex. 17. Almost everything here is in sharp contrast. The rock in Ex. 17 foreshadowed Christ on the cross; the rock in Num. 20 pictured Him on high. The Hebrew word for "rock" is not the same. The word used here in Num. 20 means an *elevated* rock, pointing plainly to the Saviour in His exaltation. Next, we notice that Moses was *not* now bidden to "strike" the rock, but simply to *speak* to it. In Ex. 17 the rock was smitten before the "elders" of Israel; here Moses was bidden to "gather the assembly together." And while Jehovah bade him take a rod, it was not the rod used in Ex. 17. On the former occasion Moses was to use his *own* rod—"Thy rod, wherewith thou smotest the river." That was the rod of judgment. But here he was to take *"The* rod" (Num. 20:8), namely, the rod of Aaron. This is clear from verse 9, "And Moses took the rod *from before the Lord,* as He commanded him" if we compare it with Num. 17:10—"And the Lord saith unto Moses, Bring *Aaron's* rod again *before the testimony* (viz., the Ark in the Holy of Holies), to be kept for a token against the rebels." This, then, was the *priestly* rod. Mark also how this aspect of truth was further emphasised in the type by the Lord bidding Moses, on this second occasion, to take *Aaron* along with him—Aaron is *not* referred to at the first smiting of the rock!

The interpretation of the typical meaning of Num. 20:8 is therefore abundantly clear. The rock must not be *smitten* a second time, for that would spoil the type. "Knowing that Christ being raised from the dead *dieth no more;* death hath no more dominion over Him. For in that He died, He died unto sin *once; but in that He liveth, He liveth unto God."* (Rom. 6:9, 10). "But now *once* in the end of the world hath He appeared to put away sin by the sacrifice of Himself . . . . So Christ was *once* offered to bear the sins of many" (Heb. 9:26, 28). Streams of spiritual refreshment flow to us on the ground of *accomplished* redemption and in connection with Christ's *priestly ministry.*

How solemn the sequel here. The servant of the Lord failed—there has been but one *perfect* "Servant" (Isa. 42:1). The meekest man upon earth became angry at the repeated murmurings of Israel. He addressed the covenant people of God as "Ye rebels." He asked them, "Must *we* fetch you water out of the rock?" He "*smote* the rock *twice*"—indicating the heat of his temper. And because of this God suffered him not to lead Israel into Canaan. He is very jealous of the types—more than one man was slain because his conduct marred them.

It is striking to note that though Moses smote the rock instead of speaking to it, nevertheless, the refreshing waters gushed forth from it. How this should warn us against the conclusion that a man's *methods* must be right if the Lord is pleased to *use* him. Many there are who imagine that the methods used in service *must* be pleasing to God if His blessing attends them. But this incident shows plainly that it is not safe to argue thus. Moses' methods were *wrong;* notwithstanding, God gave the blessing! But how this incident also manifests, once more, the wondrous grace of God. In spite of (not because of) Israel's murmuring, and in spite of Moses' failure, water *was* given to them, their every need was supplied. Truly, our God *is* the "God of *all* grace." May the realisation of this draw out our hearts in adoring worship, and may our lives rebound more and more unto His glory.

CHAPTER 25

AMALEK

EXODUS 17

One thing that impresses the writer more and more in his studies in and meditations upon the contents of this book of Exodus is the wonderful variety and the comprehensive range of truth covered by its typical teachings. Not only do its leading events and prominent characters foreshadow that which is spiritual and Divine, but even the smallest details have a profound significance. Moses is a type of Christ, Pharoah of Satan, Egypt of the world. Israel groaning in bondage pictures the sinner in his native misery. Israel delivered from their cruel task-masters speaks of our redemption. Their journey across the wilderness points to the path of faith and trial which we are called on to walk. And now we are to see that the history of Israel also adumbrated the conflict between the two natures in the believer.

Our previous studies have already shown us that the experiences of Israel in the wilderness were a series of trials, real* testings of faith. Now we are to see another aspect of the Christian's life strikingly set forth : Israel were called upon to do some fighting. It is very striking indeed to note the occasion of this, the stage at which it occurred in Israel's history. Not only is there a wondrous variety and comprehensiveness about the typical teachings of this second book of scripture, but the order in which they are given equally displays the Divine hand of their Author.

*Compare our comments on this striking feature about the types in the first book of Scripture : "Gleanings in Genesis," Vol. 2, pages 45 and 139.

*God is the God of order ;. Satan of confusion. The thoughless reader of the Scriptures loses much by failing to observe the perfect arrangement of everything in them.

In our last article we contemplated the smiting of the rock, from which flowed the stream of water and of which all the people drank. This, as we saw, typified the smiting of our blessed Saviour by the hand of Divine justice, and the consequent gift of the Holy Spirit to those who are His. But after the Holy Spirit comes to take up His abode within the believer, after a new and holy nature of His creating has been implanted, a strange conflict is experienced, something hitherto unknown. As we read in Gal. 5 : 17, "The flesh lusteth against the spirit, and the spirit against the flesh ; and these are contrary the one to the other." It is this which the scripture to be before us so accurately depicts.

The typical scene which we are about to study is of great practical importance. Ignorance of what it sets forth, the truth which it illustrates, has resulted in great loss and has been responsible for untold distress in many souls. How many a one has thought, and how many have been taught, that when a sinner really receives Christ as his Saviour, that God will change his heart, and that henceforth he will be complete victor over sin. But "a change of heart" is nowhere spoken of in Scripture. God never changes anything. The old is set aside or destroyed, and something altogether new is created or introduced by Him. It is thus with the Christian. The Christian is one who has been "born again," and the new birth is neither the removal of anything from a man, nor the changing of anything within ; but the impartation of something new to him. The new birth is the reception of a new nature : "that which is born of the Spirit, is Spirit" (John 3 : 6).

At the new birth a spiritual, Divine nature is communicated to us. This new nature.is created by the Holy Spirit ; the "seed" (1 John 3 : 9) used is the Word of God.

141

(I Pet. 1 : 23). This explains John 3 :5 : "Born of water and of the Spirit." The "water" is the emblem of the pure and refreshing Word of God (cf. Eph. 5 : 26). This is what is in view, typically, in the first half of Ex. 17. But when the new nature is communicated by God to the one born again, the old sinful nature remains, and remains unchanged till death or the coming of Christ, when it will be destroyed, for then "this corruptible shall put on incorruption" (I Cor. 15 : 53). In the Christian, then, in every Christian, there are two natures : one sinful, the other sinless ; one born of the flesh, the other born of God. These two natures differ from each other in origin, in character, in disposition and in the activities they produce. They have notning in common. They are opposed to each other. This is what is in view, typically in the second half of Ex. 17.

The two natures in the Christian are illustrated in the life of Abraham. He had two sons : Ishmael and Isaac. The former represents that which is "born of the flesh ;" the latter, that which is "born of the Spirit." Ishmael was born according to the common order of nature. Isaac was not. Isaac was born as the result of a miracle. God supernaturally quickened both Abraham and Sarah, when the one had passed the age of begetting and the other was too old to bear children. Ishmael, born first, was of "the bond-woman" ; Isaac of the "free-woman" (Gal. 4 : 22). But after Isaac entered the household of Abraham, there was a conflict : "And Sarah saw the son of Hagar the Egyptian which she had born unto Abraham, mocking." (Gen. 21 : 9). That what we have just heard said about the two sons of Abraham is no fanciful or strained interpretation of ours, will be seen by a reference to Gal. 4 : 29, where the Spirit of God has told us, "But as then he that was born after the flesh persecuted him that was born after the Spirit even so it is now."

The two natures in the Christian are also illustrated in the life of Isaac's son, Jacob. Jacob had two names : one which he received from his earthly parents, ane one which he received from God. The Lord called him "Israel" (Gen. 32 : 28). From that point onwards the history of Jacob-Israel presents a series of strange paradoxes. His life exhibited a dual personality. At one moment we see him trusting God with implicit confidence, at another we behold him giving way to an evil heart of unbelief. If the student will read carefully through chapters 33 to 49 of Genesis he

will notice how that sometimes the Holy Spirit refers to the patriarch as "Jacob," at other times as "Israel." When "Jacob" is referred to it is the activities of the old nature which are in view, when "Israel" is mentioned it is the fruits of the new nature which are evidenced. For example ; when Joseph's brethren returned to their father from Egypt and told him that his favorite son was yet alive and was now governor over all the land of Egypt, we are told, "And Jacob's heart fainted for he believed them not" (45 : 26). But "They told him all the words of Joseph, which he had said unto them; and when he saw the wagons which Joseph had sent to carry him, the spirit of Jacob their father revived : And Israel said, It is enough ; Joseph my son is yet alive" (45 : 48) ! It is blessed to note the closing words concerning him : "When Jacob had made an end of commanding his sons, he gathered up his feet into the bed, and yielded up the spirit . . . and the physicians embalmed Israel" (49 : 33 ; 50 : 2) ! "Jacob" died ; "Israel" was embalmed. At death only the new nature will be preserved !

But that which we particularly emphasise here is, that during the Christian's life on earth there is a conflict between the two natures. Just as Ishmael "persecuted" Isaac, and just as the Jacob-nature frequently set aside the Isaac-nature, so it is in the Christian : "the flesh lusteth against the spirit, and the spirit against the flesh ; and these are contrary the one to the other ; so that ye cannot do the things that ye would." (Gal. 5 : 17). What, then, is the remedy ? Is there no way by which the flesh may be subdued ? Has God made no provision for the believer to walk in the spirit so that he may not fulfill the lusts of the flesh ? Certainly He has ; and absence of victory is due entirely to our failure to use the means of grace which God has put in our hands. What these are, and how the victory should be gained are clearly set forth in our type.

"Then came Amalek, and fought with Israel in Rephidim" (17 : 8). In the light of Gen. 21 : 25 ; 26 : 19, 20 ; Ex. 2 : 17; Num. 20 : 19 ; Judges 5 : 11, where we learn that the possession of water (wells, etc.) was frequently a bone of contention among the ancients, it is evident that the spread of the news that a river of water was now gushing from the rock in Rephidim, caused the Amalekites to attempt to gain possession. To do this meant they must first dispossess Israel ; hence their attack.

The first thing to note here is the

Identity of Israel's enemy. It was Amalek. "Amalek" signifies "Warlike," apt name for that whose lusts ever **war** against the soul' " (1 Peter 2 : 11). Amalek was the grandson of Esau (Gen. 36 : 12) : 'Who for one morsel of meat sold his birthright, and when he would have inherited the blessing was rejected,' is thus surely a representative of the 'old man' "(F.W.G.). Very striking in this connection is the prophetic word of Balaam : "And when he looked for Amalek, he took up his parable, and said, Amalek was the first of the nations that warred against Israel : but his **latter end** shall be that he perish forever" (Num. 24 : 20). The **character** of Amalek comes out plainly in the words of Moses concerning him at a later date—"He feared not God" (Deut. 25 : 17, 18)—such is "the flesh."

The second thing to be noted is the **time** when Amalek made his assault upon Israel : "then came Amalek and fought with Israel." The Holy Spirit has called our attention to the **time** when this occurred. It was when Moses smote the rock and the waters were given. Then, for the first time, Israel was called upon to do some fighting—contrast 13 : 17. They had done no fighting in the house of bondage, nor had the Lord called upon them to fight the Egyptians at the Red Sea. But now that that which typified the Holy Spirit had been given, their warfare commenced; yea, it was that which typified the Holy Spirit that **caused** the Amalekites to attack Israel ! Wonderfully accurate is the type.

It is not until the Christian has been made partaker of the Divine nature (2 Peter 1 : 4) that the inward conflict begins. Previous to the new birth, he was dead in trespasses and sins ; and therefore quite insensible to the claims of God's holiness. Until the Holy Spirit begins to shed abroad His light upon our wicked hearts, we do not realise the depths and power of the evil within us. Ofttimes the believer is astounded by the discovery of the tendencies and desires within him, which he never knew before were there. The religious professor knows nothing of the conflict between the two natures nor of the abiding sense of inward corruption which this experience conveys. The unregenerate man is entirely **under the dominion** of the flesh, he serves its lusts, he does its will. The "flesh" does not fight its subjects ; it **rules** over them. But as soon as we receive the new nature the conflict begins.

It is striking to note that it was not Israel who attacked Amalek, but Amalek that attacked Israel. The new nature in the believer delights to feed upon the Word, to commune with God, and be engaged with spiritual things. But the flesh will not let him live in peace. The Devil delights to rob the believer of his joy, and works upon the flesh to accomplish his fiendish designs. The antitype is in perfect accord. Note how that in Gal. 5 : 17 it is first said that "The flesh lusteth against the spirit," and not vice versa.

Next, let us note carefully the record of **how** Israel engaged Amalek in fight : "And Moses said unto Joshua, Choose us out men, and go out, fight with Amalek ; to-morrow I will stand on the top of the hill with the rod of God in mine hand. So Joshua did as Moses had said to him, and fought with Amalek ; and Moses, Aaron, and Hur went up to the top of the hill. And it came to pass, when Moses held up his hand that Israel prevailed ; and when he let down his hand, Amalek prevailed. But Moses' hands were heavy ; and they took a stone and put it under him, and he sat thereon ; and Aaron and Hur stayed up his hands, the one on one side and the other on the other side ; and his hands were steady until the going down of the sun. And Joshua discomfited Amalek and his people with the edge of his sword" (vv. 9-13).

There is considerable difference of opinion among the commentators concerning the typical application of the above scripture. Some regard Moses at the top of the hill with hands uplifted toward heaven as the figure of Christ interceding for us on High. But that cannot be. And this for two reasons : Moses was **accompanied** by Aaron and Hur ; furthermore, his hands grew heavy. It is grossly dishonoring to the perfect Word of God to say that the type is imperfect at this point—far better to confess our ignorance than to cast such reflections upon the Scriptures. Others regard Joshua as the type of Christ in this incident, but that cannot be, because Israel did not gain a complete victory over Amalek. Rather is it evident that the respective actions of Moses and Joshua point out **the provisions** which God has made for **us** to combat the flesh.

The first thing to note here is that Israel's success against Amalek was determined by the uplifted hand of Moses : "And it came to pass, when Moses held up his hand, that Israel prevailed ; and when he let down his hand Amalek prevailed" (v. 11). The significance of

Moses' attitude is clearly defined in several scriptures. The uplifted hand was emblematic of **prayer,** the supplicating of God: "Hear the voice of my supplications, when I cry unto Thee, when I lift up my hands toward Thy holy oracle" (Psl. 28 : 2); "I will therefore that men **pray** everywhere, **lifting up holy hands,** without wrath and doubting" (1 Tim. 2 : 8).

Second, observe that "Moses' hands grew heavy." Here is where the real and beautiful accuracy of our type is to be seen. How soon we grow weary of supplicating God! "Men ought always to pray and **not to faint**" (Luke 18 : 1), said our Lord. But how sadly we fail. How quickly our **hearts** get "heavy"! And as soon as we lose the spirit of dependency upon God **the flesh prevails.**

Third, but Moses was not left to himself. Blessed it is to mark this. Aaron and Hur were with him, and "Stayed up his hands, the one on one side and the other on the other side." Here again we discover the beautiful accuracy of our type. Surely there is no difficulty in interpreting this detail. Aaron was the head of Israel's priesthood, and so speaks plainly of our great High Priest. "Hur" means "light"—the emblem of Divine holiness, and so points to the Holy Spirit of God. Thus God in His grace has fully provided for us. Supported on **either side,** both the earthly and the heavenly. "Likewise the Spirit also helpeth our infirmities. For we know not what we should pray for as we ought; but the Spirit Himself maketh intercession for us with groanings which cannot be uttered" (Rom. 8 : 26) ; this is on the earthly side. "And another angel (Christ as "the Messenger of the Covenant") came and stood at the altar having a golden censer; and there was given unto Him much incense, that He should offer it with the prayers of all saints upon the golden altar which was before the throne" (Rev. 8 : 3) : this is on the heavenly side—Christ receiving our supplications and offering them to God, as accompanied by the sweet fragrance of His own perfections.

Fourth, the typical picture is completed for us by what is said in v. 13 : "And Joshua discomfited Amalek and his people with the edge of the sword." The "sword" here points to the Holy Scriptures (see Heb. 4 : 12). It is not by prayer alone that we can fight the flesh. The Word, too, is needed. Said the Psalmist, "Thy Word have I hid in mine heart that I might not sin against Thee" (Psl. 119 : 11).

Some may object to what we have just said above about the Christian fighting the flesh. We are not unmindful of Rom. 6 : 11 and 2 Tim. 2 : 22 and much that has been written thereon. But there are scriptures which present **other phases** of our responsibility. There is a fight to be fought (see 1 Tim. 6 : 12; 2 Tim. 4 : 7 etc.). And this fight has to do with **the flesh.** Said the Apostle, "So fight I, not as one that beateth the air; but I keep under my body, and bring it into subjection" (I Cor. 9 : 26; 27).

Another thing which is important to note here is the fact that Amalek was not destroyed or completely vanquished on this occasion. We only read that "Joshua **discomfited** Amalek." Here too, the type is in perfect accord with the antitype. There is no way of destroying or eradicating the evil nature within us. Though discomforted it still survives. Why, it may be asked, does God permit the evil nature to remain in us? Many answers may be given, among them these· That we may obtain a deeper and personal realisation of the awful havoc which sin has wrought in man, the total depravity of our beings, and thereby appreciate the more the marvellous grace which has saved such Hell-deserving wretches. That we may be humbled before God and made more dependent upon Him. That we may appropriate to ourselves His all-sufficient grace and learn that His strength is made perfect in our weakness. That we may appreciate the more His keeping-power, for left to ourselves, with such a sink of iniquity within, we should surely perish.

A very helpful word and one which we do well to take to heart, is found in Deut. 25 : 17, 18 : "Remember what Amalek did unto thee by the way, when ye were come forth out of Egypt; How he met thee by the way and smote **the hindmost** of thee, even all that were feeble behind thee, **when** thou wast faint and weary; and he feared not God." How this should stir us up to watchfulness! It was the "hindmost"—those farthest away from their leader—that were smitten. The flesh cannot smite us while we are walking in close communion with God! And note that it was **when Israel** were "faint and weary" that Amalek came down upon them. This too is a warning word. What is the remedy against faintness? This: "He giveth power to the faint; and to them that have no might He increaseth strength. Even the youths shall faint and be weary, and the young men shall utterly fail; But **they that wait upon** the Lord shall renew their strengtn, they shall mount up with wings as eagles ; they shall run and not be weary; they shall walk, and not faint" (Isa. 40 30, 31).

Very blessed are the closing words of Ex. 17 : "And the Lord said unto Moses, Write this for a memorial in a book, and rehearse it in the ears of Joshua ; for I will utterly put out the remembrance of Amalek trom under heaven. And Moses built an altar, and called the name of it Jehovah-Nissi : For he said, Because the Lord hath sworn that the Lord will have war with Amalek from generation to generation" (vv. 14-16). God here promised that in the end He would utterly annihilate Amalek. In the confident assurance of faith Moses anticipated God's final victory by erecting an altar and calling it "The Lord, our Banner." How blessed to know that at the end the Saviour shall "change our vile body, that it may be fashioned like unto His glorious body according to the working whereby He is able even to subdue all things unto Himself." (Phil. 3 : 21).

CHAPTER 26

MOSES' WIFE

EXODUS 18

The chapter before us contains two distinct sections: the first, covering verses 1 to 12, presents to us a beautiful typical picture; the second, verses 13 to 27 contains important moral lessons. Ex. 18 is a parenthesis, interrupting the chronological order of the book. In Ex. 17 Israel is seen at Rephidim; in chapter 19 they are viewed at Sinai. The incident recorded in Ex. 18 occured just as Israel were about to leave Sinai and enter the wilderness of Paran. It was in the third month after leaving Egypt that Israel reached the Mount of the Law; it was eleven months later that Jethro came to Moses bringing his wife and children. The proof for this is conclusive.

In Num. 10:11, 12 we read "And it came to pass on the twentieth day of the second month, in the second year, that the cloud was taken up from off the tabernacle of the testimony. And the children of Israel took their journeys out of the wilderness of Sinai, and the cloud rested in the wilderness of Paran." Following this we are told "And Moses said unto Hobab, the son of Raguel, the Midianite, Moses father-in-law, We are journeying unto the place of which the Lord said I will give it you; come thou with us, and we will do thee good; for the Lord hath spoken good concerning Israel. And he said unto him, I will not go; but I will depart to my own land, and to my kindred" (vv. 29, 30)—compare with this the last verse of Ex. 18. Now it was after the departure of Jethro (18:24, 25) that Moses carried out the suggestion of his father-in-law to select men to assist him in the work of governing Israel—see Num. 11:11-17. Further confirmation of this is supplied in Deut. 1. Note "in Horeb" (v. 6) and then Moses' words to Israel, "I spake unto you at that time, saying, I am not able to bear you myself alone . . . Take you wise men

and understanding, and known among your tribes, and I will make them rulers over you" (vv. 9, 13). Finally; if Ex. 18 be read attentively there will also be found evidences therein that God had already given Israel the law when Jethro came to Moses. For instance, note the mention of "The Mount of God" in v. 5; Moses' statement that the people now came unto him "to inquire of God" (v. 15); his declaration that he "made them know the statutes of God and His laws" (v. 16).

"When Jethro, the priest of Midian, Moses' father-in-law, heard of all that God had done for Moses, and for Israel his people, and that the Lord had brought Israel out of Egypt; then Jethro, Moses' father-in-law, took Zipporah, Moses' wife, after he had sent her back, and her two sons; of which the name of the one was Gershom, for he said I have been an alien in a strange land; and the name of the other was Eliezer; for the God of my father, said he, was mine help, and delivered me from the sword of Pharaoh; And Jethro, Moses' father-in-law, came with his sons and his wife unto Moses into the wilderness, where he encamped at the Mount of God; and he said unto Moses, I thy father-in-law Jethro, am come unto thee, and thy wife, and her two sons with her." (vv. 1-6). The dispensational scene which is here foreshadowed is very beautiful, and the place which this one has in the series of typical pictures, in which the book of Exodus abounds, evidences once more the hand of God, not only in their production, but also in arranging their order. In Ex. 16 the manna speaks of the incarnate Son, come down from heaven to earth. In the first part of Ex. 17, the smiting of the rock views the Lord Jesus stricken of God. In the issuing forth of the water, we get a lovely emblem of the Holy Spirit ministering to the people of God. In the second half

146

of Ex. 17, where we find Amalek attacking Israel, and the defeat of the former through the supplications of Moses—upheld by Aaron and Hur—we have adumbrated the believer's conflict with the flesh, and him sustained in that conflict by the joint intercession of Christ and the Holy Spirit. This goes on to the close of the Church age. Here in Ex. 18 we are carried forward to the next dispensation and are furnished with a blessed foreshadowment of millennial conditions.

Zipporah restored to Moses is a perfect type of Israel brought back to the Lord. Some see in Zipporah a type of the Church, but nowhere in the Old Testament is the Church (as such—a corporate whole) ever seen—Col. 1:26, 27, etc., makes this very plain. Moreover, the details of our type here should forbid such an interpretation.

In the first place, Zipporah had been separated from her husband. Now if Zipporah figures the Church, and the Church is the prospective wife of Christ, the type fails us here completely. Those who believe that the Church is the Bride of the Lamb acknowledge that the "marriage" is yet future, occurring after the Rapture. If this be so, when, following the Rapture, will the Church ever be separated from Christ? When, indeed! But the type does not fail. It is perfectly accurate. Zipporah is the figure of Israel, the wife of Jehovah (see Isa. 54:6; Jer. 31:32, etc.), now alienated from Him (Hosea 2:2, etc.), Yet to be restored to His favour (Isa. 54:4-8, etc.).

In the second place, mark carefully the cause and occasion of Zipporah's separation from her husband. This is found recorded near the close of Ex. 4. When Moses started for Egypt to bring God's people out of the house of bondage his wife accompanied him. The Lord met him and sought to kill him. The reason for this was his failure in not having circumcised his son. The sequel suggests that the cause of this failure lay in his wife. At once Zipporah herself performed the operation on her son, and then, in hot anger, reproached Moses in the words: "A bloody husband thou art" (4:25), which is repeated in the very next verse. How plain, how accurate the type! The disobedience of Zipporah in the matter of circumcising her son points unmistakably to the failure of Israel under the Law. The separation of Zipporah from Moses, because he was a "bloody hus-

band," or literally, "a husband of bloods," tells of Israel's alienation from God through the offence of the Cross. "We preach Christ crucified; unto the Jews a stumbling-block" (1. Cor. 1:23). It was blood-shedding which was the "stumbling-block" to Zipporah!

In the third place, note the fruit of her marriage. She bore Moses "two sons" (18:3). Those who regard Zipporah as a type of the Church ignore this detail, and conveniently so, for they can make nothing of it. But that is no way to treat the Word of God. Whenever we come across anything in it which fails to fit in with any of our views either of doctrine, prophecy or the types, that should show us that something is wrong with our views, that they need to be, revised or enlarged. This line in our present picture is also found in several of its companions. Joseph's wife also bore him two sons. So did Isaac's. What then was typified thereby? The wife contemplated Israel when first espoused to Jehovah—at Sinai. The fruit of the marriage points to a later period in their history. What that period is we are not left in doubt. The outstanding point in Israel's later history was in the days of Rehoboam, when the kingdom was rent asunder and divided into two—the kingdom of Israel and the kingdom of Judah. Thus the "wife" was succeeded by her "two sons."

In the fourth place, the names of Zipporah's sons are profoundly significant. The firstborn was "Gershom," which means "a stranger there." The reason for Moses giving him this name was, "I have been a stranger in a strange land" (2:22). Appropriately does this speak of Israel in their dispersion, away from their land. The second son was named "Eliezer," which means, "God is my helper." Though scattered throughout the world, Israel has been marvellously helped of God—He has preserved them all through the centuries, preventing them from being either annihilated or assimilated by the Gentiles. Many of the Jews fail to recognise how God is helping them, and it is most significant that the name of this second son of Zipporah is not given until Ex. 18, where we have the Millennium in view. Gershom is referred to in Ex. 2, not so Eliezer; not until Israel has been restored to God will they recognise how marvellously He has helped them!

Fifth, notice the time when Zipporah

and her sons were restored to Moses. It was "When Jethro, the priest of Midian, Moses' father-in-law, heard of all that God had done for Moses, and for Israel His people, that the Lord had brought Israel out of Egypt; Then Jethro . . . took Zipporah . . . and ner two sons . . and came unto Moses." It was not while Moses was presenting Jehovah's demands before Pharoah, nor in the morning following the Passover-night; but it was when Moses had become Israel's leader and law-giver! In like manner, Israel will not be restored to God until their rejected Messiah is manifested on earth as their King and Lord.

Sixth, in striking accord with what we have just noted is the place where Moses was when the reconciliation took place: "he encamped at the Mount of God, (v. 5). Here, as always, the "mount" speaks of the kingdom, of governmental authority (Psl. 2:6; Isa. 2:3 etc.) It was from the summit of this same Mount that Jehovah gave the Ten Commandments to Moses. It was while seated upon a Mount that the Lord Jesus gave the laws of His Kingdom (Matt. 5.). It was on the Mount that He was transfigured, which was a miniature of His Kingdom-glory. It is to the Mount that He shall return (Zech. 14:4). The "Mount of God" (v. 5) speaks, then, of the governmental glory of God. And it is when the governmental glory of God shall be displayed in the person of His Son on earth that Israel shall be restored to Him!

Seventh, let us now observe that Zipporah and her sons were brought to Moses by a Gentile, for Jethro was a Midianite. There are many types of Israel as Jehovah's wife—espoused, divorced and restorea—but each one has its own distinctive features. Here we have that which, so far as the writer is aware, is not found elsewhere in the types, though it is the direct subject of prophecy. In Isa. 18 there is a remarkable prediction. A Divine call goes forth to some land "beyond the rivers of Ethiopia," a maritime power, most probably Great Britain. This land is bidden to send forth her ships as swift messengers to "A nation scattered and peeled. To a people terrible from their beginning hitherto; a nation meted out and trodden down." Clearly this oppressed people is Israel. In a coming day the maritime Gentile power shall carry the dispersed Hebrews back to the land of their fathers: "In that time shall the present be brought unto the Lord of hosts of a people scattered and peeled . . . to the place of the name of the Lord of hosts, the mount Zion" (Isa. 18:7). Note the words we have placed in black and compare the language of Ex. 18.

That which followed the reconcilation of Zipporah to her husband is equally interesting and meaningfull. First, we are told that "Moses told his father-in-law all that the Lord had done unto Pharoah and the the Egyptians for Israel's sake, and all the travail that had come upon them by the way, and how the Lord delivered them" (v. 8). Jethro, the Midianite, represents the Gentiles in the Millennium, who will then learn fully, how wondrously the Lord had preserved Israel not only through the vicissitudes of the centuries, but also through the birth-pangs of the Tribulation.

Next we are told that, "Jethro rejoiced for all the goodness which the Lord had done to Israel, whom He had delivered out of the hand of the Egyptians" (v. 9). In the millennium the jealousy and hatred of the Gentiles against the Jews will be removed. The confession of Jethro on this occasion is most noteworthy: "Now I know that the Lord is greater than all gods: for in the thing wherein they dealt proudly He was above them" (v. 11). Such will be the confession of the Gentiles when they learn of what the Lord has done for His ancient people.

Finally, in verse 12 we are told, "And Jethro, Moses' father-in-law took a burnt offering and sacrifices for God: and Aaron came, and all the elders of Israel, to eat bread with Moses' father-in-law before God." Very blessed is this. Here is a plain foreshadowing of what we read of in Isa. 2:2, 3 and other Scriptures: "And it shall come to pass in the last days, that the mountain of the Lord's house shall be established in the top of the mountains, and shall be exalted above the hills; and all nations shall flow unto it. And many people shall go and say, Come ye, and let us go up to the mountain of the Lord, to the house of the God of Jacob."

The second half of Ex. 18, though being mainly of a practical rather than a typical nature (so far as the writer is able to discern), adds one beautiful line to this picture of the millennium · "And Moses chose able men out of all Israel, and made them heads over the people, **rulers** of thousands. rulers of hundreds, rulers of fifties, and rulers of tens," (v. 25). Does not this plainly foreshadow what is promised to us in Rev. 3 : 21, "To him that overcometh will I grant to sit with me **in My throne."**

The passage is too lengthy for us to quote in full, but let each reader turn to and read carefully Ex. 18 : 13-27. These verses record the failure of Moses and are written for our admonition. Several most important lesson are here plainly inculcated.

Moses had been appointed **by the Lord** as the leader and head of His people. As Jethro witnessed the exacting duties of his son-in-law, advising the people from morn to eve, he felt that Moses was undertaking too much. Jethro feared for his health, and suggested that his son-in-law appoint some assistants. In listening to Jethro, Moses did wrong. From a natural standpoint Jethro's counsel was **kindly and well-meant.** It was the amiability of the flesh. It presented a subtle temptation, no doubt. But the man of God is not to be guided by **natural** principles ; only that which is spiritual should have any weight with him. Nor should he heed any human counsel when he is engaged in the service of the Lord ; he is to take his orders **only** from the One who appointed him.

One thing that this passage does is to warn God's servant's against following the advise of their relatives according to the flesh. Jethro's eye was not upon God, but upon Moses. It was not the eternal glory of Jehovah which was before him, but the temporal welfare of his son-in-law—**"Thou** wilt surely wear away, both thou and this people that is with thee ; for this thing is too heavy for **thee** ; thou art not able to perform it thyself alone" (v. 18). A parallel case is found in connection with our Saviour. In Mark 3 : 20 we read, "And the multitude cometh together again, 'so that they **could not so much as eat bread."** The Lord Jesus knew what it was to "spend and be spent." But those related to Him by fleshly ties did not appreciate this ; for we are told in the very next verse that, "When His friends heard of it, they went out to lay hold on Him ; for they said, **He is beside Himself."** Very solemn is this and very necessary for the servant of God to heed. The flesh (in us) must be mortified in connection with our service just as much as in our daily walk.

When the Lord Jesus announced to His disciples for the first time that "He must go unto Jerusalem, and suffer many things of the elders and chief priests and scribes to be killed," we are told "then Peter took Him and began to rebuke Him, saying, **Pity Thyself,** Lord : this shall not be unto thee." (Matt. 16 : 21, 22). Here again we behold the amiability of the flesh. It was what men would call 'the milk of human kindness.' But it ignored the will and glory of God. The answer of our Lord on this occasion is very solemn : "He turned, and said unto Peter, Get thee behind Me, Satan ; thou art **an offence** unto Me : for thou **perceivest not** the things that be of God, but those that be of men." That was the severest thing that Christ ever said to one of His own. What a solemn warning against being influenced by the natural affections of our friends !

Subtle as was the temptation presented to Moses, if he had remembered the **Source** of his strength, as well as his office, he would not have yielded to it. "Hearken now unto **my counsel**" said Jethro (v. 19). But that was the very thing which Moses had no business to do. "So shall it be **easier for thyself**" (v. 22) pleaded the tempter. But was not God's grace sufficient! It is sad to see the effect which this specious suggestion had upon Moses. In Num. 11 we find that Moses complained to the Lord—"I am not able to bear all this people alone, because it is too heavy for me" (v. 14). Does some servant of God reading these lines feel much the same to-day ? Then let him remember that he is not called upon to bear any people **alone.** Has not God said, "Fear thou not ; for I am with thee, be not dismayed for I am thy God, **I will** strengthen thee; yea, **I will** help thee; yea, **I will** uphold thee with the right hand of My righteousness" (Isa. 41 : 10) ! And if the burden is "too heavy" for thee, remember that it is written, "Cast thy burden **upon the Lord,** and He shall sustain thee" (Psl. 55 : 22).

"It is here the servant of Christ constantly fails ; and the failure is all the more dangerous because it wears the appearance of humility. It seems like distrust of one's self, and deep lowliness of spirit, to shrink from heavy responsibility ; but all we need to enquire is, Has God imposed that responsibility ? If so, He will assuredly be with me in sustaining it ; and having Him with me, I can sustain anything. With Him, the weight of a mountain is nothing; without Him, the weight of a feather is overwhelming. It is a totally different thing if a man, in the vanity of his mind, thrust himself forward and take a burden upon his shoulder which God never intended him to bear, and therefore never fitted him to bear it: we may then surely expect to see him crushed beneath the weight, but if God lays it upon him, He will qualify and strengthen him to carry it.

"It is never the fruit of humility to depart from a 'Divinely-appointed' post. On the contrary, the deepest humility will express itself by remaining there in simple dependence upon God. It is a sure evidence of being occupied about self when we shrink from service on the ground of inability. God does not call us unto service on the ground of our ability, but of His own: hence, unless, I am filled with thoughts about myself, or with positive distrust of Him, I need not relinquish any position of service or testimony because of the heavy responsibilities attaching thereto. All power belongs to God, and it is quite the same whether that power acts through one agent or through seventy—the power is still the same: but if one agent refuse the dignity, it is only so much the worse for him. God will not force people to abide in a place of honor if they cannot trust Him to sustain them there" (C.H.M.)

Strikingly was this seen in the sequel. Moses complained to God of the burden, and the Lord removed it; but in the removal went the high honour of being called to carry it alone. "And the Lord said unto Moses, Gather unto Me seventy men of the elders of Israel, whom thou knowest to be the elders of the people, and officers over them; and bring them unto the tabernacle of the congregation, that they may stand there with thee. And I will come down and talk with thee there; and I will take of the spirit which is upon thee, and will put it upon them; and they shall bear the burden of the people with thee, that thou bear it not thyself alone" (Num. 11:16, 17). Nothing was really gained. No fresh power was introduced; it was simply a distribution of the "spirit" which had rested on one now being placed on seventy! Man cannot improve upon God's appointments. If he persists in acting according to the dictates of 'common

sense' nothing will be gained, and much will be lost.

A word should be said upon the closing verse of our chapter: "And Moses let his father-in-law depart; and he went his way into his own land" (v. 27). This receives amplification in Num. 10: "And Moses said unto Hobab, the son of Raguel the Midianite, Moses' father-in-law, We are journeying unto the place of which the Lord said, I will give it you; come thou with us and we will do thee good: for the Lord had spoken good concerning Israel. And he said unto him, I will not go; but I will depart to mine own land, and to my kindred"(vv. 29-30). How this revealed the heart of Jethro (here called Hobab). The ties of nature counted more with him than the blessings of Jehovah. He preferred his "own land" to the wilderness, and his own "kindred" to the people of God. He walked by sight, not faith; he had no respect unto "the recompense of the reward" of the future, but preferred the things of time and earth. How ill-fitted was such a one to counsel the servant of God!

In concluding this article we would point out how that Jethro's departure from Moses in no wise mars the typical picture presented in the earlier part of this chapter; rather does it give completeness to it. Jethro returned to his own land and kindred because he had no heart for the Lord and his people. A similar tragedy will be witnessed at the end of the Millennium. In Psl. 18 we read, "Thou hast delivered me from the strivings of the people; and Thou hast made me the head of the heathen (Gentiles); a people whom I have not known shall serve Me. As soon as they hear of Me they shall obey Me; the strangers shall yield feigned obedience unto Me. The strangers (Gentiles) shall fade away" (vv. 43-45). This will find its fulfillment in the Millennium. Many Gentiles will turn to the Lord, but their hearts are not won by Him. At the end, when Satan is released, they will quickly flock to his banner (see Rev. 20:7-9).

May the Lord grant us stedfastness of heart, and keep us from being drawn away by the things of time and sense.

CHAPTER 27

ISRAEL AT SINAI

EXODUS 19

"In the third month, when the children of Israel were gone forth out of the land of Egypt, the same day came they into the wilderness of Sinai. For they were departed from Rephidim, and were come to the desert of Sinai, and had pitched in the wilderness; and there Israel camped before the mount" (vv. 1, 2). Thus was fulfilled God's promise to Moses. When he appeared to him at the burning bush He had declared, "Certainly I will be with thee: and this shall be a token unto thee, that I have sent thee: When thou hast brought forth the people out of Egypt, ye shall serve God upon this mountain." (3:12). Many difficulties had stood in the way, but they had disappeared before the irresistible execution of God's counsels like the dew before the morning sun. Israel had been made willing to depart from Egypt, and their masters had been glad to let them go. The waters of the Red Sea had parted asunder so that the covenant-people went through dryshod. The wilderness of Etham had been crossed so too had the Wilderness of Sin, and though two whole months had passed since they left the land of Pharaoh, not an Israelite had perished with hunger or died through sickness. "Ye shall serve God upon this mountain" (3:12), and they did. No word of God can fail. No matter how the enemy may rage, "the counsel of the Lord shall stand" (Prov. 19:21).

"In the third month . . . the selfsame day . . . . Israel camped before the mount." The time-mark here is important. It supplies a key to what follows. Three is ever the number of manifestation. Jehovah was now to give His people a wondrous manifestation of Himself. Previously, they had seen His judgments upon Egypt; they had beheld His power displayed at the Red Sea, they had witnessed His guiding-hand in the pillar of Cloud and Fire; they had experienced His mercies in the providing of the manna and the giving of

water from the smitten rock; but they were now to behold His exalted majesty suitably was this displayd from the mount.

"And Moses went up unto God, and the Lord called unto Him out of the mountain, saying, Thus shalt thou say to the house of Jacob, and tell the children of Israel; Ye have seen what I did unto the Egyptians and how I bore you on eagles' wings and brought you unto Myself. Now, therefore, if ye will obey My voice indeed, and keep My covenant, then ye shall be a peculiar treasure unto Me above all people, for all the earth is Mine" (vv. 3-5). These verses have suffered much from the hands of certain commentators. Most erroneous conclusions have been drawn from them. Men well versed in the Scriptures have strangely overlooked other passages in the previous chapters which plainly contradict their assertions. One respected expositor begins his remarks on Ex. 19 and 20 as follows:—"A new dispensation is inaugurated in these chapters. Up to the close of chapter 18, as before indicated, grace reigned, and hence characterised all God's dealing with His people, but from this point they were put, with their own consent, under the rigid requirements of law." In this he is followed by others of the school to which he belongs. A wide influence has been exerted by this school, and to-day thousands blindly accept the dicta of its leaders as though they were infallible. Indeed, one will at once court suspicion of his orthodoxy if he dares to challenge their ex cathedra utterances. Nevertheless, it is our bounden duty to test by the Word all that men have to say upon it.

So far as our own light goes, we know of nothing in Scripture which warrants the assertion that "a new dispensation" began when the children of Israel reached Sinai. John 1:17 is often appealed to in proof:—"The law was given by Moses, but grace and truth came by

151

Jesus Christ." But this verse is far from proving what is assumed. The Lord does not here say that a "new dispensation began" with the giving of the law: that is what men have read into it. If "the law was given by Moses" signifies that the Jewish dispensation began at that point, then the second clause—"but grace and truth came by Jesus Christ"—must mean that the Christian dispensation began with the coming of Jesus Christ. But it did not. The Christian dispensation did not begin, and could not, till after the death of our Saviour. John 1 : 17 contrasts the ministries of Moses and Jesus Christ.

When, then, did the Mosaic dispensation begin? If not when Israel reached Sinai, at what other point in their history? Without any hesitation we answer, on the Passover night; it was from that night their national history is to be dated, and that the Mosaic dispensation commenced. Previous to that night they had no existence as a nation, no corporate existence; they were a disorganised crowd of slaves. But that night everything was changed for them. Then, for the first time, were they termed an "assembly" (Ex. 12 : 6). That the Passover marked not only the beginning of their national existence but also the commencement of the Mosaic dispensation, is abundantly clear from the fact that their calendar was then changed by Divine order (Ex. 12 : 2)!

The new dispensation (the Mosaic) began by the establishment of a new relationship between Jehovah and His people. They were now His redeemed. As we have shown in a previous paper, redemption is two-fold—by purchase and by power. Israel were purchased to God by the blood of the "lamb," they were delivered from their enemies by His power at the Red Sea. If, as some able expositors contend, the crossing of the Red Sea was three days after the Passover night, then the analogy between the beginning of the Mosaic dispensation and the beginning of the Christian dispensation is perfect. In one sense the Christ-dispensation began at the death of Christ, with the "rending of the veil"; in another sense, it began three days later, at His resurrection from the dead.

The leaders of the "school" referred to above teach that, prior to Sinai, God dealt with Israel in pure grace, but that at Sinai they, for the first time, came under law. Such a mistake is even more excuseless than the statement that a "new dispensation" began then. Israel were under law before they reached the Mount of God. Listen to the testimony of Ex. 15 : 25-26, "And he cried unto the Lord; and the Lord showed him a tree, which when he had cast into the waters, the waters were made sweet; there He made for them a statute and an ordinance and there He proved them. And He said, If thou wilt diligently hearken to the voice of the Lord thy God, and wilt do that which is right in His sight, and wilt give ear to His commandments, and keep all His statutes, I will put none of these diseases upon thee, which I have brought upon the Egyptians." Surely this is plain enough; reference is made to both God's "commandments" and His "statutes." But lest the quibble be raised that this was prospective, i.e., in view of the Law which He was shortly to give them, we beg the reader to weigh carefully our next reference. In Ex. 16 : 4 we read that God said, "Behold, I will rain bread from heaven for you; and the people shall go out and gather a certain rate every day, that I may prove them, whether they will walk in My law, or no." The meaning of this is explained in v. 23, "This is that which the Lord had said, Tomorrow is the rest of the Holy Sabbath unto the Lord; bake that which ye will bake to-day and seethe that ye will seethe; and that which remaineth over lay up for you to be kept until the morning." Israel's response to this is given in v. 27 "And it came to pass, that there went out some of the people on the seventh day for to gather, and they found none." Now mark attentively the next verse, "And the Lord said unto Moses, How long refuse ye to keep My commandments and My laws?" Certainly this was not "prospective." It was retrospective. It furnishes indubitable proof that Israel were under law before they reached Sinai.

That there was a marked change in Jehovah's dealings with Israel after Sinai cannot be denied, and we suppose it is from this premise that the erroneous conclusion has been drawn that a new dispensation then began. Before Sinai was reached, when Israel "murmured," God bore with them in greatest long-sufferance, but after Sinai their murmurings were visited with summary chastisements. How then, is this to be explained? If it was not the giving of commandments and statutes which introduced the change in God's dealings with His people, what was it? We answer, it was because of the covenant which Israel there solemnly entered into. Prior to Sinai, God dealt with Israel on the ground of the Abrahamic covenant; but from Sinai onwards, He dealt with them, nationally, according to the terms of the Sinaiatic covenant. As this is of vital importance to the understanding of the later Scriptures we must dwell upon it in a little more detail.

Gen. 15 records the covenant which God made with Abraham, confirmed later to Isaac and Jacob. We cannot now attempt an exposition of the second half of Gen. 15, though it is of deep importance. Briefly the facts are these In verse 6 we read for the first time of Abraham's justification. Following this, the Lord bids Abraham prepare Him a sacrifice. This Abraham does, dividing each animal "in the midst." Then a deep sleep fell upon Abraham, and while asleep, God promised to bring His descendants, of the fourth generation, into Canaan. Then we read of the Shekinah-glory passing between the pieces of Abraham's sacrifices—an action which symbolically signified the making of a covenant, see Jer. 34:18, 19. Following which, we are told, "In the same day the Lord made a covenant with Abraham saying, Unto thy seed have I given this land" (Gen. 15:18).

Three things should be carefully noted. First, there was only one party to this covenant—Jehovah himself. Abraham was asleep. Its fulfilment therefore, turned alone on the Divine faithfulness. There were no conditions attached to it which man had to meet. Second, it was based upon a sacrifice. Third, it was a covenant of pure grace. Mark "unto thy seed have I given this land." Contrast from this Gen. 13:15. "For all the land which thou seest to thee will I give it!" But now a sacrifice had been offered, blood had been shed, the purchase-price had been paid, a solemn covenant had been made; hence the change from "I will" to "I have."

Now it is of the very first moment to observe that God's deliverance of Israel from Egypt was on the ground of His covenant with Abraham. Proof of this is furnished in Ex. 2:24 where we read "And God heard their groaning, and God remembered His covenant with Abraham, with Isaac and with Jacob." Again, in 6:3, 4, we find God reminding Moses of this: "And I appeared unto Abraham, unto Isaac and unto Jacob, by the name of God Almighty, but by My name Jehovah was I not known to them. And I have also established My covenant with them to give them the land of Canaan, the land of their pilgrimage wherein they were strangers."

It was on the ground of this covenant that the Lord dealt with Israel up to the time they reached Sinai! The last thing recorded before Israel reached Sinai was the giving of water from the smitten rock, and mark how the Psalmist refers to this, "He opened the rock, and the waters gushed out: they ran in the dry places like a river. For He remembered His holy promise to Abraham His servant" (Psl. 105:41,42). But at Sinai Jehovah's relationship to Israel was placed upon a different basis.

In Ex. 19:5 we find God, from the Mount, bidding Moses say unto His people, "Now therefore, if ye will obey My voice indeed, and keep My covenant, then ye shall be a peculiar treasure unto Me above all people; for all the earth is Mine; and ye shall be unto Me a kingdom of priests, and an holy nation." There has been much confusion upon this and much consequent error. The Lord was not here referring to His covenant with Abraham (that patriarch is not mentioned at all in the chapter). This is made unmistakably clear from His words, "If ye will obey My voice indeed and keep My covenant." There was nothing about God's covenant with Abraham that Israel could "keep." There were no conditions attached to it, no stipulations, no provisos. It was unconditional so far as Abraham and his descendants were concerned. But here at Sinai, God proposed to make another covenant, a covenant, to which there should be two parties—Himself and Israel; a covenant of works, a covenant whch Israel must "keep" if they were to enjoy the conditional blessings attached to it.

What were the terms of the Siniatic covenant, and what were the conditions and blessings attached to it? The answer to these questions is plainly stated in the Scriptures. In Ex. 34:27, 28, we read, "And the Lord said unto Moses, Write thou these words: for after the tenor of these words I have made a covenant with thee and with Israel. And he was there (on the Mount) with the Lord forty days and forty nights; he did neither eat bread, nor drink water. And he wrote upon the tables the words of the covenant, THE TEN COMMANDMENTS." Forty years later, Moses reminded Israel, "And He declared unto you His covenant, which He commanded you to perform, ten commandments; and He wrote them upon two tables of stone" (Deut. 4:13).

Returning to Ex. 19, we learn there that in response to Jehovah's proposal to enter into a legal covenant with them, Israel unanimously and heartily accepted the same: "All the people answered together, and said, All that the Lord hath spoken we will do" (v. 8). These words were repeated by the people after Moses had made known to them the details of the covenant, "And Moses came and told the people all the words of the Lord, and all the judgments; and all the people answered with one voice, and said, All the words which the Lord hath said will we do" (24 : 3). Then the covenant was solemnly ratified by blood. See Ex. 24 : 4-8.

Now it was on the ground of this Siniatic covenant, not on the ground of the Abrahamic, that Israel entered Canaan in the days of Joshua; and it was on the ground of this Siniatic covenant that God dealt with Israel during their occupancy of the land. This was made apparent right from the beginning. As soon as it became evident that there was an Israelite who had broken the eighth commandment, the Lord declared, "Israel hath sinned, and they have also **transgressed My covenant** which I commanded them; **for** they have even taken of the accursed thing, and have also **stolen**, and dissembled also, and they have put it even among their own stuff ... And it shall be that he that is taken with the accursed thing shall be burnt with fire, he and all that he hath; **because he** hath **transgressed the covenant of the Lord**, and because he hath wrought wickedness in Israel" (Josh. 7 : 11, 15). Accordingly we find that Achan and all his family were stoned to death. At a later date, we read, "And it came to pass, when the judge was dead, · that they returned and corrupted themselves more than their fathers, in following other gods to serve them, and to bow down unto them; they ceased not from their own doings, nor from their stubborn ways. And the anger of the Lord was hot against Israel; and He said, **Because** that this people hath **transgressed My covenant** which I com-manded their fathers, and have not hearkened unto My voice; I also will not henceforth drive out any from before them of the nations which Joshua left when he died" (Judges 2 : 19, 21). The rending of the kingdom was because Solomon failed to keep this covenant (1 Kings 11 : 11). Throughout Israel's occupation of Canaan, God dealt with them on the ground of the Siniatic covenant. See Jer. 11.

A few words upon the **circumstances** attending the Siniatic covenant must suffice. In verses 10 and 11 we read, "And the Lord said unto Moses, "Go unto the people, and sanctify them to-day and to-morrow, and let them wash their clothes, and be ready against the third day; for the third day the Lord will come down in the sight of all the people upon Mount Sinai." Here we have emphasised what was noted upon the opening verse of the chapter. It was in the **third** month when the children of Israel were gone forth out of the land of Egypt that they arrived at Sinai; and it was on the **third** day of this month (twice repeated) that the Lord declared He would "come down in the sight of His people." Clear-ly, then, what we have here is a **mani-festation** of the Lord Himself. cf. Deut. 5 : 24. And everything that followed was in perfect keeping with that fact bearing in mind the typical character of that Dispensation.

The people were to "sanctify" themselves, even to the point of washing their clothes. How plainly this inti-mated that God would draw nigh only to a people who were clean—that it is sin which separates the Creator from His creatures.

"And thou shalt set bounds unto the people round about, saying, Take heed to yourselves, that ye go not up into the mount or touch the border of it; whosoever toucheth the mount shall be surely put to death" (v. 12). Much has been made of this in the endeavour to prove that a "new dispensation" had begun, that God was no longer dealing with Israel in grace. But it is only another example of men reading their own pre-conceived ideas into Scripture. Moreover, it is, in this instance, to ig-nore what has gone before. Months earlier when Jehovah had appeared to Moses at the burning bush and Moses had said, "I will now turn aside, and see this great sight," God at once called to him and said, "draw **not nigh** hither put off thy shoes from off thy feet, for the place whereon thou standest is holy ground" (3 : 5)!

"And it came to pass on the third day in the morning that there were thunders and lightnings, and a thick cloud settled upon the mount, and the voice of the trumphet exceeding loud; so that all the people that was in the camp trembled" (v. 16). This, too, has been twisted to mean something quite different from its obvious import. These were the awe-spiring attendants of the awful majesty of Jehovah, upon whose face none could look and live.

Were these phenomena intended to show that Israel had done wrong in entering into this covenant? Or were they designed to manifest the dignity, the holiness, the greatness of the One with whom they were making the covenant? Surely the latter. If proof of this be required it is furnished in 20 : 20. "And Moses said unto the people, "Fear not, for God has come to prove you, and that His fear may be before your faces that ye sin not" and cf. Deut. 5 : 24. Let it not be forgotten that in heaven itself the apocalytic seer is given to behold a Throne out of which "proceeded lightnings and thunderings and voices" (Rev. 4 : 5)—the identical things witnessed on Sinai!

There is a passage in Deuteronomy which should forever settle the question as to whether or not Israel acted wisely in entering into the Siniatic covenant, as to whether they did right or wrong in promising to do all that the Lord had said, and as to whether God was pleased or displeased with them. This passage is found in the fifth chapter of that book. Moses is there reviewing what took place at Sinai. He declares, "These words, the Lord spake unto all your assembly in the mount out of the midst of the fire of the cloud, and of the thick darkness, with a great voice and He added no more. And He wrote them on two tables of stone, and delivered them unto me." (v. 22). He then reminds Israel of the response which they made, "And it came to pass, when ye heard the voice out of the midst of the darkness, (for the mountain did burn with fire), that ye came near unto me, even all the heads of your tribes, and your elders: and ye said, Behold, the Lord our God hath showed us His glory and His greatness, and we have heard His voice out of the midst of the fire; we have seen this day that God doth talk with man, and he liveth. Now therefore, why should we die? For this great fire will consume us; if we hear the voice of the Lord our God any more, then shall we die. For who is there of all flesh, that hath heard the voice of the living God speaking out of the midst of the fire as we have, and live? Go thou near, and hear all that the Lord our God shall say; and speak thou unto us all that the Lord our God shall speak unto thee; and we will hear it and do it" (vv. 23, 27). And then in v. 28 we are told, "And the Lord heard the voice of your words, when ye spake unto me; and the Lord said unto me, I have heard the

voice of the words of this people, which they have spoken unto you; they have well said all that they have spoken." Nothing could be plainer than this. God was not displeased with Israel for their avowal of allegiance, any more than he was displeased with Joshua when he said, "But as for me and my house, we will serve the Lord" (Josh 24 : 15).

Finally, it must not be forgotten that Ex. 24 completes what is before us in Ex. 19. There we read of the ratification of the covenant. There we are told, "And he took the book of the covenant, and read in the audience of the people, and they said, All that the Lord hath said will we do, and be obedient" (24 : 7). Now what is of special importance to note is the words which immediately follow, "And Moses took the blood and sprinkled it on the people, and said, 'Behold the blood of the covenant' which the Lord hath made with you concerning all these words." The application of the blood to the people plainly signified that God would deal graciously with them. What, then, was the outstanding lesson which Jehovah taught Israel at Sinai? This, that His grace towards them would henceforth "reign through righteousness" (Rom. 5 : 21).

In closing, let us make practical application of what has been before us. Such a view of God's majesty as Israel were favoured with at Sinai is the crying need of our day. The eye of faith needs to see Him not only as our "Father," as "The God of all grace," but also as the "High and Lofty One that inhabiteth eternity" (Isa. 57 : 15), as the "Great and Dreadful God" (Dan. 9 : 4), as the One who has said, "Behold, the nations are as a drop in a bucket, and are counted as the small dust of the balance; behold, He taketh up the isles as a very little thing . . . all nations before Him are as nothing; and they are counted to Him less than nothing, and vanity" (Isa. 40 : 15, 17), read the whole of Isa. 40. If we beheld Him thus, then should we work out our own salvation with "fear and trembling." Let it not be forgotten that the God of the Old Testament and the God of the New Testament is one and the same; He is a God into whose hands it is a fearful thing to fall. May His Holy Spirit so reveal Him to us, as the One to be reverenced, obeyed and worshipped.

CHAPTER 28

THE LAW OF GOD

EXODUS 20

In His Olivet discourse the Lord Jesus prophesied that "Because iniquity (Greek, **lawlessness**) shall abound, the love of many shall wax cold." (Matt. 24 : 12). Surely no anointed eye can fail to see that this prediction is now being fulfilled. Law'essness **abounds** on every side. Men are bent on pleasing themselves. Authority is openly flouted. Discipline is becoming a thing of the past. Parental control is rarely exercised. Marriage has, for the most part, degenerated into a thing of convenience. Nations regard their solemn treaties as 'scraps of paper.' In the U.S.A. the 18th Amendment is despised on every side. Yes, "lawlessness" **is** abounding. And God's own people have not escaped the chilling effects of this; the love of **many** of them has waxed cold.

The supreme test of love is the desire and effort to please the one loved, and this measured by conformity to his known wishes. Love to God is expressed by **obedience** to His will. Only One has **perfectly** exemplified this, and of Him it is written, "I will delight to do Thy will, O My God : yea, Thy law is within My heart." (Psa. 40 : 8). But we ought so to walk even as He walked (1 John 2 : 6). Simple but searching is that word of His, "He that hath My **commandments** and **keepeth** them he it is that **loveth** Me"(John 14 : 21). And again it is written, "By this we know that we love the children of God, when we love God, and keep **His commandments.** For this is the love of God, that we **keep** His commandments : and His commandments **are not grievous."** (1 John 5 : 2-3). The "waning" of **love**, then, means departing from, failing to keep, God's commandments !

The prophecy of Christ in Matt. 24 : 12 does not stand alone. In the book of Jude, that treats of conditions which are to obtain in the closing days of the history of Christendom, apostates are described as those who **"despise domi-**nion, and spake evil of dignities" (v. 8). The despising of dominion is the essence of lawlessness. Those latter-day apostates are also referred 'to in the second Epistle of Peter : "While they promise them liberty they themselves are the slaves of corruption" (2 : 19). Their slogan is, emancipation from authority, deliverance from all law.

While we cannot but deplore the lawlessness which abounds in the world and the effect which it is having on many who bear the name of Christ, far more sad and solemn is it to hear their teachers giving out that which can only foster and further this evil spirit. Reputable Bible teachers are declaring that the Law of God is not binding on men to-day least of all on Christians. They say that the Law was only for Israel. They insist that this is the Dispensation of Grace, and that Law is the enemy of Grace. They affirm that when we become members of the new creation, all the responsibilities attaching to the old creation automatically cease. They argue that because a Christian is indwelt by the Holy Spirit, he needs no law. They brand as legalists the few who press the claims of God's Law upon the consciences of men. They regard with scornful pity men mightily used of God in the past who taught that the Law of God **is a rule of** life, a standard for **moral conduct.**

Now it is of first importance that we obtain a Scriptural view of the **nature** of the Law. The very fact that it is the law **of God** should at once show us that it cannot contain anything inimical to man's welfare. Like every thing else that God has given, the Law is an expression of His love, a manifestation of His mercy, a provision of His grace. The Law of the Lord was Christ's delight (Psa. 1 : 2) ; so also was it the apostle Paul's (Rom. 7 : 22). In Rom. 7, the Holy Spirit has expressly affirmed, "Wherefore the

156

Law is **holy,** and the commandment holy, and just, and **good"** (v. 12) ; yea more, He has declared "The Law is **spiritual"** (v. 15). How terrible then for men to despise that Law and speak evil of it ! What state of soul must they be in who **wish to be delivered from it !**

Above, we have said that the Law expressed God's love. This comes out clearly in Deut. 33 : "The Lord came from Sinai, and rose up from Seir unto them ; He shined forth from Mount Paran, and He came with ten thousands of saints : from His right hand went a fiery law for them. **Yea, He LOVED the people."** (vv. 2-3). Love is the **fulfilling** of the law from the human side and love **provided** the Law from the Divine side. What, then, ought to be our response to such a Law ? Surely that of David : "O **how love I Thy Law :** it is my meditation all the day" (Psa. 119 : 97).

While Divine love provided the Law, the prime purpose of God in giving it was that His **authority** should be maintained. Israel must be brought to see that they were under His **government.** And this of necessity. The creature must be made to recognise the rights of his Creator. No sooner did the Lord God place man in the Garden which He had planted for him, than He **commanded** him—note how in Gen. 3 God pressed this both upon Eve and Adam (vv. 11, 17). The very ground of the sentence passed upon them was that they had repudiated His creatorial claims.

Now what we have in Ex. 19 and 20 is the enforcement of God's claims upon **double** one. They belonged to Him not Israel. His claim upon them was a only because He had made them but also because He had purchased them : they were not only His creatures, but they were also His redeemed people. It was this **second** relationship which is now pressed upon them both in Ex. 19 and 20. In the former He says, "Ye have **seen** what I did unto the Egyptians, and how I bare you on eagles' wings, and brought you unto Myself. Now **therefore,** if ye will obey My voice indeed, and keep My covenant, then ye shall be a peculiar treasure unto Me above all people : for all the earth is Mine" (vv. 4-5). In the latter, He prefaces the Ten Commandments with the statement, "I am the Lord thy God, which have brought thee out of the land of Egypt, out of the house of bondage" (v. 2). But it should be carefully noted that in Ex. 20 He presses both of His claims upon Israel. In the first verse it is, "And God

(the Creator) spake all these words" ; while in v. 2, He reminds them, that as **the Lord** their God He had brought them out of the land of Egypt.

Now what we would particularly emphasise here, is the fact that redemption does not cancel the claims which God has upon men **as His creatures.** Instead, these claims are still enforced, but, the new relationship into which redemption introduces, imposes **additional** responsibilities, or, more accurately speaking, supplies an additional **motive** for recognising and meeting God's claims upon us. In the previous chapters we have witnessed God dealing in marvellous grace with Israel, bearing with them in tender patience, supplying their every need. But now the point has been reached when they must be taught that God has righteous claims upon them, that His Throne must be established over them, that His authority must be owned, that His will is supreme and must be made the regulator of their lives, and that as His redeemed they were under the deepest possible obligations to fear, obey, and serve Him. Notice how Moses pressed this upon Israel near the close of his life: "The Lord thy God **redeemed** thee, **therefore I command** thee this thing to-day" (Deut. 15 : 15).

"The laws which God gave unto Israel fall into three classes : the moral, the ceremonial and the civil. The people of Israel may be considered three ways. First, as **rational creatures,** depending upon God, as the Supreme Cause, both in a moral and natural sense. And thus the **law of the decalogue** was given them ; which, as to its substance is one and the same with the law of nature (the work of which is written on man's heart. A.W.P.) binding man as such. Second, as the **Church of the Old Testament,** who expected the promised Messiah, and happy times when He should make every thing perfect. And in that character they received the **ceremonial** law, which really shewed the Messiah was not yet come, and had not perfected all things by His satisfaction (sacrifice), but that He would come and make all things new. Third, as a **peculiar people,** who had a policy of government suited to their genius and disposition in the land of Canaan : a republic constituted not so much according to those forms which philosophers have delineated, but which was in a peculiar manner, a **theocracy** as Josephus significantly calls it, God Himself holding the reins of government therein—Judges 8 : 23. Under this view God prescribed their political laws" (Dr. Herman Witsius, 1680— a deeply-taught theologian from whom our moderns might learn much).

We heartily concur with the remarks of the late Mr. D. L. Moody in "Weighed and Wanting"—"The commandments of God given to Moses in the mount at Horeb are as binding to-day as ever they have been since the time when they were proclaimed in the hearing of the people. The Jews said the Law was not given in Palestine (which belonged to Israel), but in the wilderness, because the Law was for all nations." We believe that the Ten Commandments are binding on all men, and especially upon Christians, and that for the following reasons :—

First, because it is both right and meet that the great Creator's **authority** should be proclaimed by Him and acknowledged by His creatures. This was the demand which He made upon Adam, and every sober mind will acknowledge it was a righteous one. Even the unfallen angels are beneath a regime of law : of them it is said, "Bless the Lord ye His angels that excel in strength, that do His **commandments**, hearkening unto the voice of His word" (Psa. 103 : 20). Only a spirit of lawlessness can inveigh against the statement that every human creature is responsible to keep the law of God.

Second, because the Ten Comamndments have never been repealed. The very fact that they were written by the finger of God Himself, written not upon parchment, but on tables of **stone,** argues conclusively their permanent nature. If it was contrary to the mind of God that those living during the Christian dispensation should regard the Ten Commandments as binding upon them, then surely He would have said so in plain language. But the New Testament will be searched in vain for a single word which announces their cancellation.

Third, because we need them. Has human nature so improved, is man so much better than he was three thousand years ago, that he no longer stands in need of the Divine Law ? If the covenant people of old required to have such statutes are the Gentiles to-day any less self-sufficient ? Are men now so little prone to idolatry that they need not the Divine command "Thou shalt have **no other gods before Me ?** Has the **enmity of** the carnal mind been so refined that it is no longer timely to say "Thou shalt not take the name of the

Lord thy God in vain ?" Are the children of this twentieth century A.D. so devoted to their parents and so marked by the spirit of obedience that it is superfluous to say to them "Honour thy father and thy mother ?" Is human life now held in such reverence that it is idle to say "Thou shalt not kill?" Has the marriage-relationship come to be so sacredly regarded that "Thou shall not commit adultery" is an impertinence ? And is there now so much honesty in the world that it is a waste of breath to remind our fellows that God says "Thou shalt not steal ?" Rather is it not true that in the light of present-day conditions the Ten commandments need to be thundered forth from every pulpit in the land ?

Fourth, because the Lord Jesus Christ Himself respected them. Gal. 4 : 4 tells us that **He** was, "made under the Law." On entering this world He declared "I delight to do Thy will, O My God : yea, **Thy Law** is within My heart." (Psa. 40 : 8), and the record of His earthly life fully bears this out. When the ruler asked Him, "What shall I do to inherit eternal life ?" He answered, "Thou knowest the commandments—'Do not commit adultery,' " etc. Whatever may have been our Lord's reason for returning such a reply, one thing is clear—He **honored** the holy Law of God ! When the lawyer tempted Him by asking, "Which is the greatest commandment in the Law ?" (Matt. 22 : 36), His answer once more shows Him maintaining the authority of God's Law.

Fifth, because of our Lord's teaching on the subject. In the Sermon on the Mount we find Him saying, "Think not that I am come to destroy the Law, or the Prophets : I am not come to destroy, but to fulfil. For verily I say unto you till heaven and earth pass, one jot or one tittle shall in nowise pass from the Law, till all be fulfilled. Whosoever therefore shall break one of these least commandments, and shall teach men so, he shall be called the least in the kingdom of heaven : but whosoever shall do and teach them, the same shall be called great in the kingdom of heaven" (Matt. 5 : 17-19). What could be clearer than this ? So far from affirming that He had come to cancel the Law, He declared that He would fulfil it. Yea, more, He insisted that the Law shall remain, and remain intact so long as the earth remained. His words that not "one jot or tittle of the Law should pass away (become obsolete) proves conclusively that the fourth commandment (on the Sabbath) would remain in force equally with the other nine! Finally, He solemnly warns us that the one who should teach men to break one of these commandments, shall suffer loss in a coming day.

Sixth, because of the teaching of the New Testament Epistles. In them we find the Ten Commandments recorded and enforced. At the close of Romans 3, where the apostle treats of Justification, he raises the question, "Do we then make void the Law through faith?" and the emphatic answer is "God forbid: yea, we **establish** the Law." In the same Epistle he declares again after quoting five of the Commandments. "Love is the fulfilling of the Law" (13 : 10), and love **could not** "fulfil" the Law if it had been abrogated. Once more, in I Cor. 9 : 21, Paul says, "Being **not** without Law to God, but **under** the Law to Christ."

Seventh, because God has threatened to chastise those Christians who disregard His Law. In the 89th Psa. there is a striking prophetic passage which brings this out plainly. In vv. 27-29 God declares of Christ, "I will make Him My Firstborn, higher than the kings of the earth. My mercy will I keep for Him for evermore, and My covenant shall stand fast with Him. His seed also will I make to endure for ever, and His throne as the days of heaven." And then God solemnly adds, "If His children **forsake My Law,** and walk not in My judgments; If they break My statutes, and **keep not** My commandments; **then** will I visit their transgression with **the rod,** and their iniquity with **stripes."** The writer often wonders how much of the afflictions that so many Christians are now groaning under are explained by this scripture!

The Ten Commandments have been rightly designated **the moral law,** inasmuch as they enunciate a rule or standard for human conduct. Their application is race wide. Even Mr. Darby admitted in his Synopsis (Vol. 1, p. 86),

"such is the character of the Law, a rule sent out to **man,** taken in its **largest** character." (italics ours). While dissenting from the expression "moral law," and while denying that the Law was a "rule of life," for the believer, nevertheless Mr. Darby did not go to the lengths of Antinomianism to which some of his followers have gone in their teachings. In Vol. 10 of his "Collected writings" he said," If I make of the law a moral law (including therein the principle of the New Testament and all morality in heart and life), to say a Christian is delivered from it **is nonsense,** or utter **monstrous wickedness:** certainly it is not Christianity. Conformity to the Divine will, and that as **obedience to commandments** is alike the **duty of the renewed mind.** I say obedience to commandments. Some are afraid of the word, as if it would weaken love, and the idea of a new creation : Scripture is not. Obedience, and keeping the commandments of one we love, is the proof of that love, and the delight of the new nature." As to Mr. Darby's **consistency** in arguing that the believer nevertheless is not under the Law in any sense, we leave the reader to judge.

It is not our intention to refute the objections which have been made against the truth that the Ten Commandments are not binding on men to-day, and that believers especially are in no sense under the Law. We have dealt with these, and expounded the scriptures which are supposed to support the objections, in our booklet on "The Saint and the Law." Suffice it now to point out that in the Word a sharp distinction is drawn between "the law of **Moses"** and "The Law of **God :"** the former was for Israel only: the latter is for all men. The Lord grant that writer and reader may be able to truthfully say with the Apostle Paul. "I **delight** in the Law of God after the inward man" (Rom. 7 : 22) ; and again, "So then with the mind I myself **serve** the Law of God ; but with the flesh the law of sin" (Rom. 7 : 25).

CHAPTER 29

THE TEN COMMANDMENTS

EXODUS 20

Much confusion prevails to-day among those who speak of "The law." This is a term which needs to be carefully defined. In the New Testament there are three expressions used which require to be definitely distinguished. First, there is "The law of God" (Rom. 7 : 22, 25, etc.). Second, there is "The law of Moses" (John 7 : 2-, Acts 13 : 39, 15 : 5, etc.). Third, there is "the law of Christ" (Gal. 6 : 2). Now these three expressions are by no means synonymous, and it is not until we learn to distinguish between them, that we can hope to arrive at any clear understanding on the subject of "The law."

The "law of God" expresses the mind of the Creator, and is binding upon all rational creatures. It is God's unchanging moral standard for regulating the conduct of all men. In some places the "law of God" may refer to the whole revealed will of God, but usually it has reference to the Ten Commandments, and it is in this restricted sense we shall here use the term. The Law was impressed on man's moral nature from the beginning, and though now fallen, he still shows the work of it written on his heart. This Law has never been repealed, and, in the very nature of things, cannot be. For God to abrogate the moral law would be to plunge the whole universe into anarchy. Obedience to the law of God is man's first duty. This is why the first complaint that Jehovah made against Israel after they left Egypt was "How long refuse ye to keep My commandments and My laws ?" (Ex. 16 : 2, 27). That is why the first statutes which God gave to Israel after their redemption were the Ten Commandments, i.e., the moral law. That is why in the first discourse of Christ recorded in the New Testament, He declared, "Think not that I am come to destroy the Law, of the Prophets : I am not come to destroy, but to fulfil" (Matt. 5 : 17), and then proceeded to expound and enforce the moral law. And that is why in the first of the Epistles, the Holy Spirit has taught us at length the relation of the Law to sinners and saints, in connection with salvation and the subsequent walk of the saved : the word "law" occurs in Romans no less than seventy-five times, though, of course, not every reference is to the law of God. And that is why sinners (Rom. 3 : 19), and saints (Jas. 2 : 12), shall be judged by this law.

The "law of Moses" is the entire system of legislation, judicial and ceremonial, which Jehovah gave to Israel during the time they were in the wilderness. The "law of Moses, as such, is binding upon none but Israelites. The "law of Moses" has not been repealed, for it will be enforced by Christ during the Millennium "Out of Jerusalem shall go forth the Law, and the Word of the Lord from Jerusalem" (Isa. 2 : 3). That the "law of Moses" is not binding on Gentiles is clear from Acts 15.

The "law of Christ" is God's moral law in the hands of a Mediator. It is the law that Christ Himself was "made under (Gal. 4 : 4). It is the law which was "in His heart" (Psa. 40 : 8).. It is the law which He came "fulfil" (Matt. 5 : 17). The "law of God" is now termed "the law of Christ" as it relates to Christians. As creatures we are under bonds to "serve the law of God" (Rom. 7 : 25) : as redeemed sinners we are "bondslaves of Christ" (Eph. 6 : 6); and as such it is our bounden duty to "serve the Lord Christ" (Col. 3 : 2b). The relation between these two appellations, "the law of God" and "the law of Christ," is clearly intimated in 1 Cor. 9 : 21, where the apostle states that ne was not "without law to God," for he was "under the law to Christ." The meaning of this is very simple. As a human creature, the Apostle was still under obligations to obey the Moral Law of God, his Creator; but as a saved man, he now belongs to Christ, the Mediator, by redemption. Christ had purchased him: he was His, therefore was he under the "law of Christ." The "law of Christ," then, is just the moral of law of God now in the hands of the Mediator—cf. Ex. 34 : 1 and what follows !

Should any one object against our definition of the distinction drawn between God's **moral law** and "The law of Moses" we request them to attend closely to what follows. God took special pains to show us the clear line of demarcation which He Himself has drawn between the two. The Moral Law became incorporated in the Mosaic law, yet was it sharply distinguished from it :—

In the first place, the Ten Commandments, and **they alone,** of all the laws which God gave unto Israel, were **promulgated** by the voice of God, amid the most solemn manifestations and tokens of the Divine presence. Second, the Ten Commandments and they alone of all Jehovah's statutes to Israel, were **written directly** by the finger of God, written upon **tables of stone, and written thus** to denote their lasting and imperishable nature. Third, the Ten Commandments were distinguished from all the other laws which had merely a local application to Israel by the fact that **they alone were laid up in the ark**. A tabernacle was prepared by the special direction of God, and within it an ark was placed, in which the two tables of stone were deposited. The ark, formed of the most durable wood, was overlaid with gold within and without. Over it was placed the mercy seat, which became **the throne** of Jehovah in the midst of His redeemed people. Not until the tabernacle had been erected and the Law placed in the ark, did Jehovah take up His abode in Israel's midst. Thus did the Lord signify to Israel that the Moral Law was **the basis** of all His governmental dealings with them !

It is therefore clear beyond room for doubt that the Ten Commandments are to be sharply distinguished from the "law of Moses." The "law of Moses," excepting the Moral Law incorporated therein, was binding upon none but Israelites or Gentile proselytes. But the "Law of God," unlike the Mosaic, is binding upon **all men**. Once this distinction is perceived, many minor difficulties are cleared up. For example: someone says, If we are to keep the Sabbath-day holy, as Israel did, why must we not observe the other "sabbaths"—the Sabbatic year, for instance ? The answer is, Because the Moral Law **alone** is binding upon Gentiles and Christians. But why, it may be asked,

does not the death-penalty attached to the desecration of the Sabbath day (Ex 31 : 14, etc.) still obtain ? The answer is, Because though that was a part of the **Mosaic** law, it was not a part of the Moral Law, i.e., it was not inscribed on the tables of stone : therefore it concerned none but Israelites. Let us now consider separately, but briefly, each of the Ten Commandments.

The **order** of the Commandments is most significant. The first four concern human responsibility **Godwards**; the last five our obligations **manwards** : while the fifth suitably bridges the two, for in a certain sense parents occupy to their children the place of God. We may also add that the substance of each commandment is in perfect keeping with its numerical place in the Decalogue. One stands for **unity** and **supremacy** so in the first commandment the absolute sovereignty and pre-eminency of the Creator is insisted upon. Since God is who He is, He will tolerate no competitor or rival : **His** claims upon us are paramount.

1. "Thou shalt have no other gods before Me" (Ex. 20 : 3). If this first Commandment received the respect it demands, obedience to the other nine would follow as a matter of course. "Thou shalt have no other gods before Me" means, Thou shalt have no other object of worship: thou shalt own no other authority as absolute : thou shalt make Me **supreme** in your hearts and lives. How much this first commandment contains ! There are other "gods" besides idols of wood and stone. Money, pleasure, fashion, fame, gluttony, and a score of other things which make self supreme, usurp the rightful place of God in the affections and thoughts of many. It is not without reason that even to the saints the exhortation is given, "Little children keep yourselves from idols" (1 John 5 : 21).

2. "Thou shalt not make unto thee any graven image, or any likeness of any thing that is in heaven above, or that is in the earth beneath, or that is in the water under the earth : Thou shalt not bow down thyself to them, nor serve them for I the Lord thy God am a jealous God, visiting the iniquity of the fathers upon the children unto the third and fourth generation of them that hate Me ; and showing mercy unto thousands of them that love Me, and keep My commandments" (vv. 4-6). Two is the number of **witness**, and in this second commandment man is forbidden to attempt any visible representation of Deity, whether furnished by the skill of

the artist or the sculptor. The first commandment points out the one only object of worship; the second tells us how He is to be worshipped—in spirit and in truth, by faith and not by images which appeal to the senses. The design of this commandment is to draw us away from carnal conceptions of God, and to prevent His worship being profaned by superstitious rites. A most fearful threat and a most gracious promise are attached. Those who break this commandment shall bring down on their children the righteous judgment of God; those who keep it shall cause mercy to be extended to thousands of those who love God. How this shows us the vital and solemn importance of parents teaching their children the unadulterated truth concerning the Being and Character of God!

3. "Thou shalt not take the name of the Lord thy God in vain: for the Lord will not hold him guiltless that taketh His name in vain" (v. 7). God requires that the majesty of His holy name be held inviolably sacred by us. His name must be used neither with contempt, irreverently, or needlessly. It is striking to observe that the first petition in the prayer the Lord taught His disciples is, "Hallowed be Thy name!" The name of God is to be held profoundly sacred. In our ordinary speech and in our religious devotions nothing must enter that in anywise lowers the sublime dignity and the high holiness of that Name. The greatest sobriety and reverence is called for. It needs to be pointed out that the only time the word "reverend" is found in the Bible is in Psa. 111 : 9 where we read, "Holy and reverend is His name." How irreverent then for preachers to style themselves "reverend"!

4. "Remember the Sabbath day to keep it holy. Six days shalt thou labour and do all thy work, but the seventh day is the sabbath of the Lord thy God: in it thou shalt not do any work, thou, nor thy son nor thy daughter, thy manservant, nor thy maidservant, nor thy cattle, nor the stranger, that is within thy gates; For in six days the Lord made heaven and earth, the sea, and all that in them is, and rested the seventh day: wherefore the Lord blessed the Sabbath day and hallowed it" (vv. 8-11). There are two things enjoined here: First, that man should work six days of the week. The same rule is plainly enforced in the New Testament: "And that ye study to be quiet, and to do your own business, and to work with your own hands, as we commanded you"

(1 Thess. 4 : 11). "For even when we were with you this we commanded you, that if any would not WORK, neither should he eat" (2 Thess. 3 : 10)! The second thing commanded is, that on the seventh day all work must cease. The Sabbath is to be a day of rest. Six days work: one day for rest. The two must not be separated: work calls for rest; rest for work.

The next thing we would observe is that the Sabbath is not here termed "the seventh day of the week." Nor is it ever so styled in Scripture! So far as the Old Testament is concerned any day which was used for rest, and which was followed by six days of work was a Sabbath! It is not correct, then, to say that the "Sabbath" can only be observed on a Saturday. There is not a word of Scripture to support such a statement.

In the next place, we emphatically deny that this Sabbath law has ever been repealed. Those who teach it has, are guilty of the very thing which the Saviour so pointedly condemns in Matt. 5 : 19. There are those who allow that it is right and proper for us to keep the other nine Commandments, but they insist that the Sabbah has passed away. We fully believe that this very error was anticipated by Christ in Matt. 5: 19 : "Whosoever shall break one (not "any one") of these least commandments, and shall teach men so, he shall be called the least in the kingdom of heaven." Heb. 4 : 9 tells us that Sabbath-keeping remains: it has not become obsolete.

The Sabbath (like all the other Commandments) was not simply for Israel but for all men. The Lord Jesus distinctly declared "the Sabbath was made for MAN" (Mark 2 : 27) and no amount of quibbling can ever make this mean Jews only. The Sabbath was made for man: for man to observe and obey; also for man's well-being, because his constitution needed it. One day of rest each week is requisite for man's physical, mental, and spiritual good.

"But we must not mistake the means for the end. We must not think that the Sabbath is just for the sake of being able to attend meetings. There are some people who think they must spend the whole day at meetings or private devotions. The result is that at nightfall they are tired out and the day has brought them no rest. The number of church services attended ought to be measured by the person's ability to enjoy them and get good from them, without being wearied. Attending meetings is not the only way to observe the Sabbath. The Israelites were commanded to keep it in their dwellings as well as in holy convocation. The home, that centre of so great influence over the life and character of the people, ought to be made the scene of true Sabbath observance" (The late Mr. D. L. Moody).

5. "Honour thy father and thy mother: that thy days may be long upon the land which the Lord thy God giveth thee" (v. 12). The word "honor" means more than obey, though obedience is necessarily included in it. To "honor" a parent is to give him the place of superiority, to hold him or her in high esteem, to reverence him. The Scriptures abound with illustrations of Divine blessing coming upon those who honored their parents, and the Divine curse descending on those who honoured them not. The supreme example is that of the Lord Jesus. In Luke 2 : 52, we read "And He went down with them and came to Nazareth, and was subject unto them." On the Cross we see the Saviour honoring His mother by providing a home for her with His beloved disciple John.

It is indeed sad to see the almost universal disregard of this fifth Commandment in our own day. It is one of the most arresting of the many "signs of the times." Eighteen hundred years ago it was foretold, "In the last days perilous times shall come. For men shall be lovers of their own selves, covetous, boasters, proud, blasphemous, disobedient to parents, unthankful, unholy, without natural affection" (2 Tim. 3 : 1, 3). Unquestionably, the blame for most of this lies upon the parents, who have so neglected the moral and spiritual training of their children that (in themselves) they are worthy of neither respect nor honor. It is to be noted that the promise attached to the fulfilment of this Commandment as well as the command itself is repeated in the New Testament—see Eph. 6 : 1, 3.

6. "Thou shalt not kill" (v. 13). The simple force of this is, Thou shalt not murder. God Himself has attached the death-penalty to murder. This comes out plainly in Gen. 9 : 5, 6, "And surely your blood of your lives will I require ; at the hand of every beast will I require it, and at the hand of man ; at the hand of every man's brother will I require the life of man. Whoso sheddeth man's blood, by man shall his blood be shed, for in the image of God made He man." This statute which God gave to Noah has never been rescinded. In Matt. 5 : 21, 22, we have Christ's exposition of this sixth commandment : He goes deeper than the letter of the words and gives

the spirit of them. He shows that murder is not limited to the overt act, but also pertains to the state of mind and the angry passion which prompts the act —cf., 1 John 3 : 15.

In this sixth Commandment, God emphasises the sacredness of human life and His own sovereignty over it—He alone has the right to say when it shall end. The force of this was taught Israel in connection with the cities of refuge. These provided an asylum from the avenger of blood. But they were not to shelter murderers, but only those who had killed "unwittingly" (R.V.). It was only those who had unintentionally taken the life of a fellow-creature who could take refuge therein ! .And this, be it observed, was not regarded as a light affair : even the man who had taken life "unawares" was deprived of his liberty till the death of the high priest !

7. "Thou shalt not commit adultery" (v. 14). This respects the marriage relationship which was instituted in Eden—"Therefore shall a man leave his father and his mother, and shall cleave unto his wife : and they shall be one flesh" (Gen. 2 : 24). The marriage-relationship is paramount over every other human obligation. A man is more responsible to love and care for his wife than he is to remain in the home of his childhood and take care of his father and mother. It is the highest and most sacred of human relations. It is in view of this relationship that the seventh Commandment is given. "Thou shalt not commit adultery" means, Thou shal not be unfaithful to the marriage obligations.

Now in Christ's exposition of this Commandment we find Him filling it out and giving us its deeper meaning : "I say unto you, That whosoever looketh on a woman to lust after her hath committed adultery with her already in his heart" (Matt. 5 : 28). Unfaithfulness is not limited to the overt act, but reaches to the passions behind the act. In Christ's interpretation of the law of divorce He shows that one thing only can dissolve the marriage relationship, and that is unfaithfulness on the part of the husband or the wife. "I say unto you, Whosoever shall put away his wife, except for fornication, and shall marry another, committeth adultery : and whoso marrieth her which is put away doth commit adultery" (Matt. 19 : 9). Fornication is the general term ; adultery the specific : the former includes the latter. 1 Cor. 7 : 15 supplies no exception : if one depart from the other, except it be on the ground of unfaithfulness, neither is free to marry again. Separation is not divorce in the scriptural sense. "If she depart, let her remain unmarried" (1 Cor. 7 : 11).

8. "Thou shalt not steal" (v. 15). The design of this Commandment is to inculcate honesty in all our dealings with men. Stealing covers more than pilfering. "Owe no man anything" (Rom. 13 : 8), "Providing for honest things, not only in the sight of the Lord, but also in the sight of men" (2 Cor. 8 : 21). I may steal from another by fraudulent means, without using any violence. If I borrow a book and fail to return it, that is theft—it is keeping what is not my own. How many are guilty here ! If I misrepresent an article for sale, the price which I receive over and above its fair market-value is stolen ! The man who obtains money by gambling, receives money for which he has done no honest work, and is therefore a thief ! "Parents are woefully lax in their condemnation and punishment of the sin of stealing. The child begins by taking sugar, it may be. The mother makes light of it at first and the child's conscience is violated without any sense of wrong. By and by it is not an easy matter to check the habit, because it grows and multiplies with every new commission" (Mr. D. L. Moody).

9. "Thou shalt not bear false witness against thy neighbour" (v. 16). The scope of these words is much wider than is generally supposed. The most flagrant form of this sin is to slander our neighbours—a lie invented and circulated with malicious intentions. Few forms of injury done by one man to another is more despicable than this. But equally reprehensible is tale-bearing where there has been no careful investigation to verify the evil report. False witness may be borne by leaving a false impression upon the minds of people by a mere hint or suggestion. "Have you heard about Mr. —— ?" "No." "Ah ! Well, the least said the soonest mended." Again, when one makes an unjust criti-

cism or charge against another in the hearing of a third party, and that third party remains silent, his very silence is a breach of this ninth Commandment. The flattering of another, exaggerated eulogy, is a false witness. Rightly has it been said, "There is no word of the Decalogue more often and more unconsciously broken than this ninth Commandment, and men need perpetually and persistently to pray 'Set a watch, O Lord, before my mouth ; keep the door of my lips.' "

10. "Thou shalt not covet thy neighbour's house, thou shalt not covet thy neighbour's wife, nor his manservant, nor his maidservant, nor his ox, nor his ass, nor any thing that is thy neighbour's" (v. 17). This Commandment differs from all the others in that while they prohibit the overt act, this condemns the very desire to act. The word "covet" means desire, and the Commandment forbids us to covet any thing that is our neighbour's. Clear proof is this that these Commandments are not of human origin. The tenth Commandment has never been placed on any human statute book ! It would be useless to do so, for men could not enforce it. More than any other, perhaps, does this Commandment reveal to us what we are, the hidden depths of evil within. It is natural to desire things, even though they belong to others. True; and that only shows the fallen and depraved state of our nature. The last Commandment is especially designed to show men their sinfulness and their need of a Saviour. Believers, too, are exhorted to "beware of coveteousness" (Luke 12 : 15). There is only one exception, and that is stated in 1 Cor. 12 : 31 : "Covet earnestly the best gifts."

May the Holy Spirit of God fasten these Commandments upon the memory of both writer and reader, and may the fear of God make us tremble before them.

CHAPTER 30

THE DECALOGUE AND ITS SEQUEL

EXODUS 20

The Ten Commandments expressed the obligations of man in his original state, while enjoying free and open communion with God. But the state of innocence was quickly departed from, and as the offspring of fallen Adam, the children of Israel were sinners, unable to comply with the righteous requirements of God. Fear and shame therefore made God's approach terrible, as He appeared in His holiness, as a consuming fire. The effects upon Israel of the manifestation of Jehovah's majesty at Sinai are next given: "And all the people saw the thunderings, and the lightnings, and the noise of the trumpet, and the mountain smoking: and when the people saw it, they removed, and stood afar off. And they said unto Moses, Speak thou with us, and we will hear; but let not God speak with us, lest we die" (20:18, 19).

Here was a plain acknowledgment from Israel that they were **unable** to deal with God directly on the ground of the Decalogue. They felt at once that some provision needed to be made for them. A **mediator** was necessary: Moses must treat with God on their behalf. This was alright so far as it went, but it failed to meet fully the requirements of the situation. It met the need from **their** side, but not from God's. The Lawgiver was holy, and His righteous requirements must be met. The transgressor of His Law could not be dealt with simply through a mediator as such. **Satisfaction** must be made: sin must be expiated: only thus could the inexorable demands of Divine justice be met. Accordingly this is what is brought before us in the sequel. The very next thing which is here mentioned in Exodus 20 is an ALTAR!

The "altar" at once tells of the provision of Divine **grace,** a provision which fully met the requirements of

God's governmental claims, and which made it possible for sinners to approach Him without shame, fear, or death; a provision which secured an agreement of peace. On **such a basis** was the Siniatic covenant ratified. Not that this rendered null and void what Jehovah had said in Ex. 19:5, "Now therefore, if ye will **obey** My voice indeed, and **keep** My covenant, then ye shall be a peculiar treasure unto Me above all people." The Siniatic covenant was an agreement wherein God proposed to deal with Israel in blessing on the ground of **their obedience.** Governmentally this was never set aside. **But provision was made for their failure,** and this, right from the beginning! Israel's failure to appropriate God's gracious provision only rendered the more inexcusable their subsequent wickedness.

We read of no "altar" in Eden. Man in his innocence, created in the image and likeness of God, needed **none. He** had no sin to be expiated upon an altar: he had no sense of shame, and no fear of God in coming into his Maker's presence and communing with Him directly. It was man's **sin** which made necessary an "altar," and it was Divine **grace** which provided one. There are two things to bear in mind here in Ex. 20: Jehovah was not dealing with Israel on the **alone** ground of His righteousness, but **also** according to His rich mercy!

It is vitally important to see the relation between the two great subjects of our chapter: God giving the **Law** and God furnishing instructions concerning **the altar.** If it was impossible for Israel to enter **directly** into the Siniatic covenant (a mediator being necessary), and if they (as sinners) were unable to keep the Decalogue, why propose the one and give the other? Three answers may be returned First, **to show to Israel** (and the race)

165

that man is a sinner. A fixed standard which definitely defined man's fundamental relations both with God and his fellows, a standard holy and just and good in all its parts, revealed to man his want of conformity to God's Law". I had not known sin (its inner workings as lust) but by the Law . . . that sin by the commandment might become exceeding sinful" (Rom. 7 : 7. 13). Second, **to bring to light man's moral inability.** The Law with its purity and its penalty, disclosed the fact that on the one hand, man was **unable** (because of his corrupted nature) to keep the Law ; and on the other hand, unable to atone for his transgressions of it— "Sin taking occasion by the commandment wrought in me all manner of concupiscence . . . For I was alive without the Law once ; but when the commandment came, sin revived and I died. And the commandment, which was ordained to life, I found to be unto death" (Rom. 7 : 8, 10). Third, **to show man his need of the Saviour.** "Wherefore then serveth the Law ? It was added because of transgressions, till the Seed should come to whom the promise was made . . . . But before faith came, we were kept under the law, shut up unto the faith which should afterwards be revealed. Wherefore the Law was our schoolmaster unto Christ, that we might be justified by faith" (Gal. 3 : 19, 23 24).

It is therefore abundantly clear that the Ten Commandments were never given to men or to Israel as a means of salvation, i.e., being saved through obeying them. They were not given in **statutory form** till after man had become a sinner, and his nature so corrupted that he had neither ability nor desire to keep them. The Law was not a way of life, but a rule of conduct. The writing of the Ten Commandments on tables of stone long after man had become a fallen being, was to show that God's claims upon His creatures had not been cancelled, any more than has the **right** of a creditor to collect though the debtor be **unable** to pay. Whether unfallen, or fallen, or saved, or glorified, it ever remains true that man **ought** to love God with all his heart and his neighbour as himself. While ever the distinction between right and wrong holds good, man is under obligation to keep God's Law. This is what God was enforcing at Siani—**His** righteous claims upon Israel, first as His creatures, then as His redeemed. It is true that Israel were unable to meet those claims, therefore did God in His

marvellous grace, make provision both for **their** failure and the upholding of **His** claims. This we see in the "altar."

Before we examine the typical significance of the "altar" we would call attention to a most lovely thing not found here in Exodus 20, but given in a later scripture. As Israel beheld the fearful phenomena which manifested the presence of Jehovah upon the Holy Mount, they said unto Moses, "Speak thou with us, and we will hear: but let not God speak with us lest we die" (20 : 19). Now it is exceedingly blessed to mark God's **response** to this. But not to the careless reader is this discovered. It is only by prayerfully and diligently comapring scripture with scripture that its exquisite perfections are revealed, and only thus are we able to obtain a **complete** view of many a scene. In Deut. 5 : 22, 27 Moses reviews the giving of the Law at Sinai and the effects which that had upon the people. Then he says, "And the Lord heard the voice of your words, when ye spake unto me, and the Lord said unto me, I have heard the voice of the words of this people, which they have spoken unto thee : **they have well said ALL that they have spoken."** Now if we compare with this Deut. 18 : 17, 18, we discover the full response which the Lord made to Israel's request : "And the Lord said unto me, They have well spoken that which they have spoken. **I will raise them up a Prophet** from among their brethren, like unto thee, and I will put My words in His mouth ; and He shall speak unto them all that I shall command Him." The desire of Israel for a **mediator,** for one of their own number to act as God's mouthpiece unto them was to be realised, eventuaiiy, in the great Mediator, the chief Prophet or Spokesman of God. How blessedly does this reveal to us the thoughts of **grace** which Jehovah had unto Israel even at Sinai ! How refreshing to turn away from the miserable perversions of many of the modern commentators and learn what the Scriptures have to say concerning that memorable day at Sinai!

"And the people stood afar off, and Moses drew near unto the thick darkness where God was" (v. 21). In the above paragraph we have sought to point out a part, at least, of the precious revelation which Jehovah made to Moses in the "thick darkness." Following this, Moses returned to the people with this message from the Lord: "Ye have seen that I have talked with you from heaven. Ye shall not make with Me gods of silver, neither shall ye make unto you gods of gold" (vv. 22, 23). Idolatry was expressly forbidden. It was God, once more, insisting upon His unrivalled supremacy. And then immediately after this, instructions are given concerning the "altar."

"An altar of earth shall thou make unto Me, and shalt sacrifice thereon thy burnt offerings, and they peace offerings, thy sheep and thine oxen" (v. 24). The Tabernacle had not yet been erected. Clearly then, what we have here were Divine instructions for Israel's immediate compliance: an altar was to be built at the foot of Sinai! It was not the future which was in view, but the present. All doubt as to the correctness of this conclusion is forever removed by what we read of in Exodus 24 : 4—what intervenes being a connected account of what Jehovah made known unto Mones on the Mount to be communicated unto the people. Here we are told, "And Moses wrote all the words of the Lord, and rose up early in the morning, and builded an altar under the hill, and twelve pillars, according to the twelve tribes of Israel." That there may be no possibility of failure to identify this "altar," it is immediately added, "And he sent young men of the children of Israel, which offered **burnt offerings** and sacrificed **peace offerings** of oxen unto the Lord. Here then was the "altar" (of earth), and here were the "burnt offerings" and the "peace of offerings." And why has the Holy Spirit been so careful to record these details here in Exodus 24 ? Why, if not to show us the fulfilment of Jehovah's word unto Pharoah : "Thus saith the Lord God of Israel, Let My people go, that they may hold a feast unto Me in the wilderness" (5 : 1) ! The "**peace**-offering" is the one offering of all others specially connected with feasting : "And Solomon awoke; and, behold it was a dream. And he came to Jerusalem, and stood before the ark of the covenant of the Lord, and offered up burnt offerings and offered **peace** offerings, and made **a feast** to all his servants (1 Kings 3 : 15, cf. 8 : 64, 65, etc).

"In all places where I record My name I will come unto thee, and I will bless thee" (v. 24). Plainly this begins a **new** sentence and is connected with what follows, as the first words of v. 25 clearly show. Jeremiah 7 : 12 affords an illustration of what is meant by God

recording His name in a place : "But go ye now unto My place which was in Shiloh, where I set My name at the first." Let the interested reader look up the various references to "Shiloh." Compare also "Bethel" and "Zion" where God's name was also recorded.

"And if thou wilt make Me an altar of stone,, thou shalt not build it of hewn stone : for if thou lift up thy tool upon it thou hast pollutted it" (v. 25). The connection between this and the last clause of v. 24 is most significant and important. God had promised to "come unto" Israel and "bless" them in all places where His name was recorded. But if Israel were to come unto Jehovah an "altar" must be erected, an altar where blood should flow and fire consume : blood to propitiate God ; fire to signify His acceptance of the sacrifice.

The first thing to notice about this altar (like the one in the previous verse) is its extreme simplicity and plainness. This was in marked contrast from the "gods of silver" and "gods of gold" (v. 23) of the heathen The altar which Israel was to erect unto God must not be made of that which man had manufactured, nor beautified by his skill : there should be in it no excellence which human hand had imparted. Man would naturally suppose that an altar to be used for **Divine** sacrifices should be of gold, artistically designed and richly ornamented. Yes, but that would only allow man to glorify **himself** in his handiwork. The great God will allow "no" flesh to glory in **His** presence" (1 Cor. 1 : 29). Solemn indeed are the words "If thou liftest up thy tool upon it, thou hast **polluted** it." "Not by works of righeousness which we have done" (Titus 3 : 5) is the New Testament equivalent. Sinfulness cannot approach the thrice holy God with any thing in hand which his own labours have produced. That is why the Lord had not respect unto the offering which Cain brought to Him : Cain presented the fruits of the ground, the product of his own labours ; and God rejected them. And God **still rejects** all the efforts of the natural man to propitiate Him, All the attempts of the sinner to win the notice and merit the respect of God by his efforts at self-improvement are worse than vain. What God demands of His fallen creatures is that they should take the place of **lost sinners** before Him, coming empty-handed to receive **undeserved** mercy.

"Neither shalt thou go up by steps unto Mine altar" (v. 26). The meaning of this is not difficult to perceive. It is parallel in principle to what was before us in the previous verse. "Steps" are a human contrivance to avoid the strain of rising from a lower level to a higher. Man cannot climb up to God by any steps of his own making. What God requires from the sinner is, that he shall take his true place before Him —in the dust. **There God will meet with him.** It is true that morally **and spiritually man is separated from God by a distance, a distance far too great for man to ever bridge. But though** man cannot climb up to God, God, in the person of His Son, has come down all the way to the poor sinner. The second chapter of Philippians describes that marvellous and gracious descent of the Lord of glory. **Five** distinct "steps" are there marked—the number of **grace.** He who was in the form of God, and thought it not robbery to be equal with God (1) "made Himself of no reputation," (2) "took upon Him the form of a servant," (3) "and was made in the likeness of men." (4) "Being found in fashion as a man He humbled Himself," (5) "and became obedient unto death, even the death of the cross." Self-evident is it then that there are no "steps" for man to climb !

"Neither shalt thou go up by steps unto Mine altar, that thy nakedness be not discovered thereon" (v. 26). The very efforts of men to climb up to God only expose their own shame. Remarkably is this brought out in the very chapter which records the entrance of of sin into this world. As soon as Adam and Eve had eaten of the prescribed fruit we are told. "And the eyes of them both were opened, and they knew that they were naked ; and they sewed fig leaves together, and made themselves aprons" (Gen. 3 : 7). But of what avail were these aprons before Him who can read the innermost secrets of the heart ? The very next thing we read is "And they heard the voice of the Lord God walking in the garden in the cool of the day, and Adam and his wife **hid themselves** from the presence of the Lord God amongst the trees of the garden." Their fig-leaf "aprons" did not now even satisfy themselves ! But that is not all : "and the Lord God called unto Adam, and said unto him, Where art thou ?" And what was our guilty forefather's response ? This : "And he said I heard Thy voice in the garden, and I was afraid, because I was naked; and I hid myself." The apron of fig-leaves only served to make manifest and emphasise the fact that he **was** naked—naked even with the "apron" on ! How true, then, that man's very efforts to climb up to God do but expose his shame !

It should be pointed out, in conclusion, that the two "altars," the one of "earth" and the other of "stone," both point to the person of the Lord Jesus, bringing out His varied perfections. On this we cannot do better than let Mr. Grant interpret for us :—

"The material which God accepts for His altar, then, is either earth or stone, things which are in contrast with one another ; 'earth' deriving its name from its crumbling character (**eratz, from, ratz,** to crumble away, says Parkhurst of the Hebrew word) ; and 'stone,' which resists pressure, and is characterised by its hardness and durability. Of the dust of the earth man is made, and as this is fertile as it **yields** to the hand that dressed it, so is man to God, as he yields himself to the Divine hand. Earth seems thus naturally to stand for the creature in its frailty,—conscious of it, and accepting the place of weaknses and subjection, thus to the bringing forth of fruit to God. While 'stone' stands for the strength that is found in another, linked with and growing out of the consciousness of weakness: 'When I am weak, then am I strong.'

"Now in both respects He who was perfect, who came down to all the reality of manhood, to know both its weakness and the wondrous strength which is wrought out of weakness, thus waiting upon and subject to God. It was thus in endurance He yielded Himself up, and endured by yielding Himself to His Father's will."

The "earth" then, corresponds in thought to the "fine flour" of the meal offering (Lev. 2), speaking of the perfect **yieldedness** of Christ's to the Father's will. Most blessedly was this evidenced in Gethsemane, where we hear Him saying, "Nevertheless, not My will, but Thine be done." The "stone" points to the same thing as the "brass" in the Tabernacle altar. It showed there was that in Christ (and in Him alone) capable of **enduring** the fearful fires of God's wrath. The fact that the stones of this altar must not be "hewn," shaped by human chisel, shows once more how jealously God guarded the accuracy of these types. The stones must be left just as the Creator had made them—man must not change their form. The antitype of this would be that Christ, as it were, retained the "form" which God had given Him. And all the pressure of circumstances and all the efforts of men and Satan could not alter it. When the Lord announced the Cross (the "altar" on which the great Sacrifice was to be offered), Peter said, Spare Thyself" : that was Satan, through man, attempting to "hew" the "stone' "; but the Lord suffered it not.

May God stir up writer and reader to a more diligent and prayerful **searching of the Scriptures.**

CHAPTER 31

THE PERFECT SERVANT

EXODUS 21:1-6

The law of Moses had three grand divisions : the moral the civil, and the ceremonial. The first is to be found in the Ten Commandments; the second (mainly) in Ex. 21-23 ; the third (principally) in the book of Leviticus. The first defined God's claims upon Israel as human creatures ; the second was for the social regulation of the Hebrew commonwealth ; the third respected Israel's religious life. In the first we may see the governmental authority of God the Father; in the second, the sphere and activities of God the Holy Spirit—maintaining order among God's people; in the third, we have a series of types concerning God the Son.

"Now these are the judgments which thou shalt set before them. If thou buy an Hebrew servant, six years he shall serve : and in the seventh he shall go out free for nothing. If he came in by himself, he shall go out by himself: if he were married, then his wife shall go out with him. If his master has given him a wife, and she have borne him sons or daughters ; the wife and her children shall be her master's, and he shall go out by himself. And if the servant shall plainly say, I love my master, my wife, and my children, I will not go out free : Then his master shall bring him unto the judges ; he shall also bring him to the door, or unto the doorpost ; and his master shall bore his ear through with an aul : and he shall serve him forever" Ex. 21 : 1-6). This passage begins the series of "judgments" or statutes which God gave unto Israel for the regulation of their social and civil life. Its chief value for us to-day lies in its spiritual application to the Lord Jesus Christ. We have here a most beautiful and blessed foreshadowment of His person and work: Psalm 40 : 6 compared with Ex. 21 : 6 proves this conclusively. In that great Messianic Psalm the Lord Jesus, speaking in the spirit of prophecy, said, "Sacrifice and offering Thou didst not desire; Mine ears hast Thou digged."

The passage before us pertained to the servant or slave. It brings out, in type, the Perfect Servant. Messianic prophecy frequently viewed Him in this character : "Behold, My Servant, whom I uphold" (Isa. 42 : 1). "Behold, I will bring forth My Servant, the Branch" (Zech. 3 : 8). "Behold, My Servant shall deal prudently. He shall be exalted and extolled, and be very high" (Isa. 52 : 13). "By His knowledge shall My righteous Servant justify many for He shall bear their iniquities" (Isa. 53 : 11).

In Phil. 2 we are exhorted, "Let this mind be in you which was also in Christ Jesus" (v. 5). This is enforced as follows : "Who, being in the form of God thought it not robbery to be equal with God : But made Himself of no reputation, and took upon Him the form of a Servant, and was made in the likeness of man : And being found in fashion as a man He humbled Himself, and became obedient unto death, even the death of the cross." Marvellous stoop was this : from the place of highest authority, to that of utmost dependency ; from honor and glory, to suffering and shame. The Maker of heaven and earth entering the place of subjection. The One before whom the seraphim veiled their faces being made lower than the angels. May we never lose our sense of wonderment at such amazing condescension ; rather may we delight in reverently contemplating it with ever-deepening awe and adoration.

One whole book in the New Testament is devoted exclusively to setting before us the service of the perfect Servant. The design of Mark's Gospel is to show us how He served : the spirit which actuated Him, the motives and principles which regulated Him, the excellency of all that He did.*

*This has been treated of in our book. "Why Four Gospels".

"Lo, I come, to do Thy will, O God" (Heb. 10 : 9), was His utterance when He took the Servant form. "Wist ye not that I must be about My Father's business" (Luke 2 : 49) are His first recorded words after He came here. "I came down from heaven, not to do Mine own will, but the will of Him that sent Me" (John 6 : 38) summed up the whole of His perfect life while He tabernacled among men. As the perfect Servant, He was dependent upon the pleasure of His Master. He "pleased not Himself" (Rom. 15 : 3). "I am among you as He that **serveth**" (Luke 22 : 27) were His words to the apostles.

The servanthood of Christ was perfectly voluntary. The passages cited above prove that. And herein we behold the uniqueness of it. Who naturally chooses to be a **servant**? How different from the first Adam! He was given the place **of a servant**, but he **forsook** it. He was required to be in subjection to his Maker, but he revolted. And what was it that lured him from the place of submission? "Ye shall be as God" was the appealing lie which caused his downfall. With the Lord Jesus it was the very reverse. He **was** "as God," yea, He was God; yet did He make Himself of **"No reputation."** He voluntarily laid aside His eternal glory, divested Himself of all the insignia of Divine majesty, and took the servent form. And when the Tempter approached Him and sought to induce Him to repudiate His dependency on God, "make these stones bread," He announced His unfaltering purpose to live in subjection to the Father of spirits. Never for a moment did He deviate from the path of complete submission to the Father's will.

"If thou buy an Hebrew servant, six years he shall serve" (v. 2). The first thing to be noted here is the service of the servant. His master had a certain definitely defined claim upon him: "six years he shall serve him." Six is the number of **man** (Rev. 13 : 18), therefore what is in view here is the measure of **human responsibility** what **man** owes to his lawful Owner. The Owner of man is God, **what**, then, does man owe to his Maker? We answer, unqualified submission, complete subjection, implicit obedience to His known will. Now the will of God for man is expressed in the Law, conformity to which is all summed up in the words "Thou shalt love the Lord thy God with all thy heart . . . . and thy neighbour as thyself." **This**, every descendent of fallen Adam **has failed to do. The Law has brought in all the world guilty before God** (Rom. 3 : 19).

Now the Lord Jesus came down to this world to honour God in the very place where He had been universally dishonoured. He came here to "magnify the Law and make it honourable." Therefore was He "made under the Law" (Gal. 4 : 4). Therefore did He formally announce, "Think not that I am come to destroy the law, or the prophets: I am not come to destroy but to fulfill" (Matt. 5 : 17). God's Law was within His heart (Psa. 40 : 8). In it He meditated day and night (Psa. 1 : 2). From beginning to end, in thought, word, and deed, He kept the Law. Every demand of God upon man was fully met by the Perfect Man: every claim of God completely upheld. Christ is the only man who ever fully discharged human responsibility Godwards and manwards.

"And in the seventh he shall go out free for nothing" (v. 2). After the Hebrew servant had served for six years, his master had no further claim upon him. When the seventh year arrived (which tells of **service completed**) he was at liberty to go out, and serve no more. This was also true of the Lord Jesus, the anti-type. The time came in His life when, as Man, He had fulfilled every jot and tittle of human responsibility, and when the Law had, therefore no further claim upon Him. We believe that this point was reached when He stood upon the "holy mount," when in the presence of His disciples He was transfigured, and when there came a voice from the excellent glory proclaiming Him to be the One in whom the Father delighted. This, we believe, was the Father bearing witness to the fact that Christ was the faithful "Hebrew Servant." Right then He could (so far as the Law was concerned) have stepped from that mount to the Throne of Glory. He had perfectly fulfilled every righteous claim that God had upon man: He had loved the Lord with all His heart and His neighbour as Himself.

"If he came in by himself, he shall go out by himself: if he were married, then his wife shall go out with him. If his master has given him a wife, and she have borne him sons and daughters; the wife and her children shall be her master's and he shall go out by himself" (vv. 3, 4). We shall confine our remarks on these verses to the antitype. The Lord Jesus had no wife when He entered upon "His service," for Israel had been divorced (Isa. 50 : 1). Now although He was entitled by the Law to "go out free," the same Law required that He should go out **alone**—"by himself." This points us to something about which there has been much confusion. There was no **union** possible with the Lord Jesus in the perfections of His human life: "Verily, verily, I say unto you, Except a corn a wheat fall into the ground and die, it abideth **alone**" (John 12:24). Nothing could be plainer than this. The very perfections of the Servant of God only served to emphasise the more the distinction between Him and sinful man. It is only on **resurrection**-ground that **union** with Christ is possible, and for that death must intervene. It was on the resurrection-morning that He, for the first time, called His disciples **"brethren."** Does, then, our type fail us here? No, indeed. These typical pictures were drawn by tne Divine Artist, and like Him, they are perfect. The next two verses bring this out beautifully.

"And if the servant shall plainly say, I love my master, my wife, and my children, I will not go free: Then his master shall bring him unto the judges; he shall also bring him to the door, or unto the door posts; and his master shall bore his ear through with an aul; and he shall serve him for ever" (vv. 5, 6). Most blessed is this. It was **love** which impelled him to forego the freedom to which He was fully entitled by the Law—a threefold love: for His Master, his wife, and his children. But mark it well: "if the servant **shall plainly say,** I love my master," etc. When was it that the perfect Servant said this? Clearly it must have been just after the Transfiguration, for as we have seen, it was then that He had fulfilled every requirement of the Law, and so could have gone out free. Equally plain is it that we must turn to the **fourth** Gospel for the avowal of His love for it is there, as nowhere else, His love is told forth by the apostle of love. Now in John's Gospel there is no account of the Transfiguration, but there is that which closely corresponds to it: John 12 gives us the parallel and the sequel to Matthew 17. It is here that we find Him saying, "The hour is come that the Son of Man should be glorified. Verily, verily: I say unto you, Except a corn of wheat fall into the ground and die, it abideth alone" (John 12:23, 24), and then He added "But if it die, it bringeth forth much fruit." Mark carefully what follows: **"Now** is My soul troubled; and what shall I say? Father save Me from this hour?" Ah, He answered His own question: "But for this cause came I unto this hour: Father, glorify Thy name" (vv. 27, 28).

"What led Him to say that? Love! Love that thinks not of self at all; love that places itself entirely at the disposal of the loved ones. No matter what that terrible 'hour' contained, and He knew it all, He would go through it in His love to His Father and to us" (J. T. Mawson). Love led Him to undertake a service that the Law did not lay upon Him, a service that involved **suffering** (as the "bored" ear intimates) a service which was to last **forever.**

Every detail in this truly wondrous type calls for separate consideration. "If the servant shall plainly say, I love my master." This, be it noted, comes **before** the avowal of his love for his wife and children. This, of itself, is sufficient to establish the fact that what we have here **must** be of more than local application, for when and where was there ever a servant who put the love of his "master" **before** that of his wife and children? Clearly we are **obliged** to look for someone who is "Fairer than the children of men." And how perfectly the type answers to the antitype! There is no difficulty here when we see that the Holy Spirit had the Lord Jesus in view. Love to His **Father,** His "Master;" was ever the controlling motive in the life of the perfect Servant. His first recorded utterance demonstrated this. Subject to Mary and Joseph He was as a child, yet even then the claims of His Father's "business" were paramount. So too, in John 11, where we read of the sisters of Lazarus (whom He loved) sending Him a message that their brother was sick. Instead of hastening at once to their side, He "abode two days still in the same place where He was!" And why, "For the glory of God" (v. 4). It was not the affection of His human heart, but the will of His Father that moved Him. So, once more, in John 12, when He contemplated that awful 'hour' which troubled His soul, He said, "Father, glorify **Thy** name." The Father's glory was His first concern, At once, the answer came, "I have both glorified (**Thee**) and will glorify (Thee) again" (v. 28). What is meant by the "again"? The Father's name had already been glorified through the perfect fulfilment of His Law in the life of the Lord Jesus, as well as in that which was infinitely greater—the revelation of Himself to men. But He would also glorify Himself in the death and resurrection of His Son, and in the fruits thereof.

"I love . . . my wife." In the type this was said prospectively. The Lord Jesus is to have a Bride. The "wife" is here carefully distinguished from His "children." The "wife," we believe, is redeemed millennial Israel. Both the "wife" and the "children" are the fruit of His death. The two are carefully distinguished again in John 11 : "But being high priest that year, he (Caiaphas) prophesied that Jesus should die for (1) that nation ; and not for that nation only, but that (2) also He should gather together in one the children of God that were scattered abroad" (vv. 51 : 52). Looking forward to the time when Christ shall see of the travail of His soul and be satisfied, the Holy Spirit says to Israel, "Fear not, for thou shalt not be ashamed : neither be thou confounded ; for thou shalt not be put to shame : for thou shalt forget the shame of thy youth, and shalt not remember the reproach of **thy widowhood** any more. For thy Maker is **thine Husband** : the Lord of hosts is His name; and thy Redeemer the Holy One of Israel ; the God of the whole earth shall He be called. For the Lord hath called thee as **a woman forsaken** and grieved in spirit, and **a wife of youth,** when thou wast refused, saith thy God. For a small moment, have I forsaken thee ; but with great mercies will I gather thee. In a little wrath I hid My face from thee for a moment ; but with everlasting kindness will I have mercy on thee, saith the Lord, thy Redeemer" (Isa. 54 : 4-8).

"I love . . . My children." Christ's love was not limited to Israel, even though here, as ever, it is the Jew **first.** No; not only was He to die for **"that** Nation" not "this Nation," the then present nation of Israel, but "that" **future** Nation, which shall be born "at once," (Isa. 66 : 8), but also He should "gather together in one (family) **the children** of God that were scattered abroad." "Children of God" is never applied in Scripture to Israel. These "children" were to be the fruit of His dying travail. Blessed is it to hear Him say, "Behold I and the children which God hath given Me" (Heb. 2 : 13).

"Then his master shall bring him unto the judges ; he shall also bring him to the door, or unto the door post, and his master shall bore his ear through with an aul" (v. 6). The boring of the **ear** marked the entire devotedness of the servant to do His Master's will. "The door-post was the sign of personal limits: by it the family entered, and none else had the right. It was not therefore a thing that might pertain to a stranger, but pre-eminently that which belonged to that household. This too was the reason why it was on the door-post that the blood of the paschal lamb was sprinkled; it was staying the hand of God, so far as that house was concerned, on the first-born there, but on no one else. So here" (Mr. W Kelly). Important truth is this. Christ died not for the human race why should He when half of it was already in Hell ! He died for the Household of God, His "wife" and "children," and for none else : John 11 : 51, 52 proves that cf., also Matt 1 : 21; John 10 :11; Heb. 2 : 17, 9 : 28, etc. Significant too is this : when his master took his servant and bored his ear, so long as he lived that servant carried about in his body the mark of his servitude. So, too, the Lord Jesus wears forever in His body the marks of the Cross ! After He had risen from the dead, He said to doubting Thomas, "Reach hither thy finger, and behold My hands ; and reach hither thy hand, and thrust it into My side" (John 20 : 27). So, too, in Rev. 5 the Lamb is seen, **"as** it had been slain" (v. 6).

"And his master shall bore his ear through with an aul, and he shall serve him **forever"** (v. 6). Very wonderful is this in its application to the Antitype. The service of the Lord Jesus did not terminate when He left this earth. Though He has ascended on high, He is still ministering to His own. A beautiful picture of this is found in John 13, though we cannot now discuss it at any length. What is there in view is a parabolic sample of His work for His people since He returned to the Father. The opening verse of that chapter supplies the key to what follows : "When Jesus knew that His hour was come that He should depart out of this world unto the Father." So, too, in the fourth verse : "He riseth from supper (which spoke of His death) and laid aside His garments," which is literally what He did when He left the sepulchre. In John 13, then, from v. 4 onwards, we are on **this** side of the resurrection. The washing of the disciples feet tells of Christ's present work of maintaining the walk of His own as they pass through this defiling scene. The towel and the basin speak of the love of the Servant-Saviour in ministering to the needs of His own. Even now that He has returned to the glory He is still serving us.

"But "he shall serve him **forever."** Will this be true of the Lord Jesus ? It certainly will. There is a remarkable passage in Luke 12 which brings this out : "Blessed are those servants, whom the Lord when He cometh shall find watching : verily I say unto you that He shall **gird** Himself, and make them to sit down to meat, and will come forth and **serve** them" (v. 37). Even in the Kingdom He will still serve us. But how can that be ? Our feet will not require washing ; we shall no longer have any need to be met. True, gloriously true. But if there is no need on our part, there is **love** on His, and love ever delights to minister unto its beloved. Surpassingly wonderful is this : "He will come forth and serve **them**." How great the condescension ! In the kingdom He will be seated upon the Throne of His Glory, holding the reigns of government; acknowledged as the King of kings and Lord of lords ; and yet He will delight to minister unto our enjoyment. And too,

He will serve "forever" : it will be the eternal activity of Divine love delighting to minister to others.

Thus in this wondrous type we have shown forth the love of God's faithful Servant ministering to His Master, His wife, and His children, in His life, His death, His resurrection, and in His kingdom. The **character** of His service was perfect, denoted by the six years and **seventh** "go out free." The **spring** of His service was **love,** seen in His **declining** to go out free. The **duration** of His service, is "for ever" ! The Lord enable us to heed that searching and needful word, "Let **this** mind be in **you,** which was also in Christ Jesus" (Phil. 2 : 5).

CHAPTER 32

THE COVENANT RATIFIED

EXODUS 24

The twenty-fourth chapter of Exodus introduces us to a scene for which there is nothing approaching a parallel on all the pages of inspired history prior to the Divine Incarnation and the tabernacling of God among men. It might suitably be designated the Old Testament Mount of Transfiguration, for here Jehovah manifested His glory as never before or after during the whole of the Mosaic economy. Here we witness Moses and Aaron, Nadab and Abihu, and seventy of the elders of Israel in the very presence of God, and not only are we told that "He laid not His hand-on them," but they were thoroughly at ease in His presence, for they did "eat and drink" before Him! Before endeavouring to contemplate such a glorious scene let us offer a brief remark on its occasion and setting.

In Exodus 19 we behold Jehovah proposing to enter into a covenant of works with Israel, making their national blessing contingent upon their obedience to His commandments (vv. 5,6). To the terms of this covenant the chosen people unanimously and heartily agreed (v. 8). Following their purification. of themselves, three days later God came down to the summit of Sinai and spake to Moses, charging him to go and again warn the people assembled at its base not to break the barrier which had been erected. After which God spake all that is recorded in Exodus 20 to 23. Concerning the Ten Words in chapter 20 and the typical significance of the "judgment" regarding slaves at the beginning of 21, we have already commented; the re mainder of those chapters we now pass over as not falling within the scope of our present work, which is to concentrate upon that which is more obvious in the typical teachings of Exodus. That there is much spiritual teaching as well as moral instruction in Exodus 22 and 23 we doubt not, but so far as we are aware God has not yet been pleased to enlighten any of His servants thereon. Let the student, however, read carefully through them, noting how just, comprehensive and perfect were the laws which the Lord gave unto Israel.

"And He said unto Moses, Come up unto the Lord, thou and Aaron, Nadab and Abihu, and seventy of the elders of Israel and worship ye afar off" (v. 1). In the light of what precedes, this is most significant and solemn. It tells us in language too plain to be misunderstood that man cannot approach unto God on the ground of his own works. Mark that this was said by the Lord before the legal covenant had been confirmed, and therefore before a single failure had been recorded against Israel under that economy. Even had there been no failure, no disobedience, yet the keeping of God's commandments cannot secure access into the Divine presence as the "afar off" plainly denoted. For any man to come unto the Father, tne work of Christ was indispensable.

"And Moses alone shall come near the Lord; but they shall not come nigh, neither shall the people go up with him" (v. 2). An exception was made in the case of Moses, not because he possessed any superior claim upon God, nor because he was personally entitled to such a privilege, but only because he was the appointed mediator between God and His people, and therefore the type of the Lord Jesus Christ. It is this which gives meaning to and opens for us the typical significance of so much that is recorded about Moses. The repeated prohibition in this verse emphasises what is said in the previous one and confirms our comments thereon; Christ had to suffer for sins, "The Just for the unjust, that He might bring us to God" (Peter 3: 18).

"And Moses came and told the people all the words of the Lord, and all the judgments; and all the people answered with one voice, and said, All the words which the Lord hath said will we do" (v. 3). The "words" refer to the ten commandments recorded in Exodus 20, the "judgments" to what is found in chapters 21 to 23, as the first verse of 21 intimates. It is most important to observe that the Ten Words are here again definitely distinguished from the other "judgments," affording additional confirmation of what we have said thereon in previous articles. Once more the people unanimously registered their acceptance of the covenant of works.

"And Moses wrote all the words of the Lord, and rose up early in the morning, and builded an altar under the hill, and twelve pillars, according to the twelve tribes of Israel. And he sent young men of the children of Israel, which offered burnt offerings, and sacrificed peace offerings of oxen unto the Lord" (vv. 4, 5). That was in obedience to what the Lord had said unto Moses as recorded in 20: 24. The "young men" (probably the "first born" who had been sanctified unto the Lord, 13: 2, etc.) performed this priestly work because the Levites had not yet been set apart to that office. Much confusion has been caused through failing to note the specific character of these sacrifices. It was not the blood of atonement which was here shed, for wherever that is in view it is always for the averting of God's holy wrath against sin. But nothing like that is seen here. What we have before us is that which speaks of thanksgiving and dedication unto God (the "burnt" offering) and that which tells of happy fellowship (the "peace" offering).

"And Moses took half of the blood, and put in basons; and half of the blood he sprinkled on the altar. And he took the blood of the covenant, and read in the audience of the people; and they said All that the Lord hath said will we do, and be obedient" (vv. 6, 7). For a full exposition of the meaning of Moses' act we must refer the reader to Hebrews 9, regretting very much that we cannot here give a detailed interpretation of that most important chapter; it will be noted that vv. 18-20 refer specifically to what is here before us in Exodus 24. Suffice it now to say that, so far as the historical significance of this sprinkling of the blood was concerned, it denoted a solemn ratification of the covenant into which Israel entered with Jehovah at Sinai. Note how the covenant God made with Noah was also preceded by a sacrifice offered to Him: Gen. 8: 20 to 9; so too in connection with the Abrahamic covenant (Gen. 15: 9, 10, 17).

"Then went up Moses and Aaron, Nadab and Abihu, and seventy of the elders of Israel; and they saw the God of Israel" (vv. 9, 10). Precious beyond words is this, showing us the inestimable value of the blood, and the wondrous privileges it procures for those who are sprinkled by it. Note the connecting "then," i.e., when the blood had been applied. A similar example, equally forceful and blessed, is found in Rev. 7: 14, 15, where we read, "And He said to me, These are they which came out of great tribulation, and have washed their robes, and made them white in the blood of the Lamb. Therefore are they before the throne of God, and serve Him day and night in His temple." The "elders" of Exodus 24 were representatives of the Nation. Here then was a blood-sprinkled people, who had not yet broken the covenant, in communion with God. The eating and drinking told of the fulness of their welcome and of the peace which ruled their hearts in the Divine Presence.

"And they saw the God of Israel; and there was under His feet as it were a paved work of a sapphire stone, and as it were the body of heaven in his clearness" (v. 10). The "sapphire stone" speaks of Divine government—the throne of God— as a reference to Ezekiel 1:26 will show: that government which will yet rest upon the shoulders of "the Man" Christ Jesus. But why the "paved work"? May not the reference be to the finished work of the Saviour which forms the basis of His Millennial reign? Christ came here to finish the Father's work (John 5: 17, 17: 4), piecing it all together, that it might be a pavement of glory as the place of His feet. The "body of heaven in his clearness" may speak of the Divine counsels. If we look up to heaven on a clear day all is blue; it is the intensity of the depths of space, infinite—like Jehovah's counsels. But in Christ God has brought His counsels so near that we may contemplate them as the body of heaven in its clearness.

"And upon the nobles of the children He laid not His hand; also they saw God, and did eat and drink" (v. 11). "But yesterday it would have been death to them to 'break through to gaze' but now 'they saw God'! And such was their 'boldness,' due to the blood of the covenant, that 'they did eat and drink' in the Divine presence. The man of the world will ask, How could 'the blood of calves and goats' make any difference in their fitness to approach God? And the answer is, Just in the same way that a few pieces of paper may raise a pauper from poverty to wealth. The bank-note paper is intrinsically worthless, but it represents gold in the coffers of the Bank of England. Just as valueless was that 'blood of slain beasts,' but it represented 'the precious blood of Christ.' And just as in a single day the bank-notes may raise the recipient from pauperism to affluence, so that blood availed to constitute the Israelites a holy people in covenant with God" (Sir Robert Anderson).

There is one thing here that is very solemn, namely, the repeated mention of Nadab and Abihu; vv. 1, 9. "They were both sons of Aaron, and with their father were selected for this singular privilege. But neither light nor privilege can ensure salvation, nor, if believers, a holy and obedient walk. Both afterwards met with a terrible end. They 'offered strange fire before the Lord, which He commanded them not. And there went out fire from the Lord, and devoured them; and they died before the Lord' (Lev. 10: 1, 2). After this scene in our chapter, they were consecrated to the priesthood and it was while in the performance of their duty in this office, or rather because of their failure in it, that they fell under the judgment of God. Let the warning sink deep into our hearts, that office and special privileges are alike powerless to save" (Mr. Dennett).

Israel's history continued for almost fifteen hundred years after this memorable occasion, but never again did their elders "see God," and never again did they eat and drink in His presence. Sin came in; their very next act was to break the holy Law by making and worshipping a golden calf, and the next time we see them drinking, it is of the waters of judgment (32: 20). How unspeakably blessed to remember that what Israel (through their official heads) enjoyed for a brief season, is now ours for ever! A way has been opened for us into the very presence of God, and there, within the vail, we may commune with Him.

In the remainder of our chapter Moses is once again separated from Aaron, Nadab and Abihu and the seventy elders, resuming his mediatorial position, to receive from God the two tables of stone which He had written. For this purpose he is called up to meet the Lord in the Mount—apparently at the summit—where he remained forty days and nights alone with God. During this time the glory of the Lord was displayed before the eyes of Israel for seven days—a glory "like devouring fire" (vv. 15 to 18). "This was not the glory of His grace but the glory of His holiness, as is seen by the symbol of devouring fire—the glory of the Lord in His relationship with Israel on the basis of the law (compare 2 Cor. 3). It was a glory therefore that no sinner could dare approach, for holiness and sin cannot be brought together; but now, through the grace of God, on the ground of accomplished atonement, believers can not only draw near, and be at home in the glory, but with unveiled face beholding the glory of the Lord are changed into the same image from glory to glory, as by the Spirit of the Lord (2 Cor. 3: 18). We approach boldly, and with delight gaze upon the glory, because every ray we behold in the face of Christ glorified is a proof of the fact that our sins are put away, and that redemption is accomplished" (Mr. E. Dennett).

"And Moses went into the midst of the cloud, and gat him up into the mount; and Moses was in the Mount forty days and forty nights" (v. 18). Those forty days, what happened in them, and the typical significance of those happenings, together with the sequel, form one of the most wondrous of the many wonderful types in all the Old Testament. The Holy Spirit now focusses attention on Moses, type of our Lord Jesus Christ. First, he is seen entering the glory, consequent upon his having erected the altar and sprinkled the blood. "And the glory of the Lord abode upon Mount Sinai, and the cloud covered it six days; and the seventh day He called unto Moses out of the midst of the cloud. . . And Moses went into the midst of the cloud" (vv. 16, 18). How beautiful and how perfect the type! After "six days," which speaks of work and toil, on the seventh day, which tells of **rest**, Moses, the mediator, is called by God to enter the glory. So of Him of whom Moses was the type it is written, "He that is entered into His rest, He also hath ceased from His own works (Heb. 4: 10). And what is the character of the "rest" into which He has entered? Does not His own request in John 17: 4, 5, furnish us with the answer: "I have finished the work which Thou gavest Me to do. And now, O Father, glorify Thou Me with Thine own self with the glory which I had with Thee before the world was." Yes, He has entered into the Glory. Moses going up the Mount and entering the cloud to commune with Jehovah is a type of the **Ascension** of Christ, following the triumphant completion of the work which had been given Him to do.

We are not left in ignorance as to what formed the subject of communion between the Lord and Moses during the forty days in the Mount; the next six chapters of Exodus tell us that it was about the marvellous and mysterious Tabernacle, the pattern of which Moses was shown while there on Sinai. As we shall yet see, the Tabernacle and all its parts prefigure the manifold perfections of the Lord Jesus, making known the full provisions of God's grace stored up in His beloved Son—provisions which meet every need of His favoured people. The tabernacle is what meets our eye in Exodus while Moses is up the Mount, for it is not until after it has been fully described that we behold him descending. Thus has the Holy Spirit supplied us with an important key to open the spiritual treasures of this portion of the Word, by intimating that the Tabernacle speaks of what God's grace has furnished for us during the interval of the Mediator's absence from the earth.

And what is the next thing recorded in this book so rich in typical pictures of the Redeemer? Why, the **descent** of Moses, which we have in chapters 32, 33, 34. Moses did not end His days there upon Sinai, but returned unto his people. So also the Lord Jesus who has gone on High is not to remain absent from the earth for ever; the words of the angels to His disciples at His ascension make this indelibly clear—"Ye men of Galilee, why stand ye gazing up into heaven? This same Jesus, which is taken up from you into heaven, shall so come in like manner as ye have seen Him go into heaven" (Acts 1: 11). Yes, shall return to this same earth from which He went to heaven, return in person just as literally and truly as He left it.

But, now, students of prophecy have discovered that the Holy Scriptures divide the second advent of Christ into two distinct stages; the first, when He descends into the air for His saints, to receive them unto Himself (1 Thess. 4: 16, etc.); the second, when He descends to the earth with His saints (Col. 3: 4, etc.). These two stages of His second advent each have a most important bearing upon the Jews; the first will be followed by **judgment**, the second by **blessing**. After the Church has been removed from this world, there follows the time of "Jacob's trouble" (Jer. 30: 7),

when God deals with His earthly people and punishes them for their sins, this period also being known as the **Great Tribulation**. After this period has run its course, the Lord Jesus descends in blessing, purges Israel, and in full manifested glory dwells in their midst—this will be during the Millennium.

What is so striking in the type which we are now engaged with is that these two stages in the second advent of the great Mediator are here vividly foreshadowed. Mark how complete the type is: Moses came down twice from Sinai after he had entered the glory! But let us observe first how Israel were conducting themselves during the time of his absence in the Mount: "And when the people saw that Moses delayed to come down out of the Mount, the people gathered themselves together unto Aaron, and said unto him, Up, make us gods which shall go before us out of the land of Egypt, we wot not what is become of him" (32: 1). Is not this the very condition of the Jews to-day during the Messiah's absence? They are all at sea, knowing not what to think. But that is not all. During Moses' absence they made a calf of gold and worshipped it— and are we not now witnessing the very same thing over again? If there is one thing which characterises the Jew to-day above everything else it is not the love of conquest or of pleasure, as with the Gentiles, but the lust for **gold**.

Now just as Moses at his **first** descent from the Mount found Israel worshipping the golden calf, so at the first stage at the second coming of Christ the Jews will be wholly occupied with their greed for riches. And what was Moses' response? Read Exodus 32: 19-28. He acted in **judgment**. He made them drink a bitter cup of their own providing and gave orders for the sword to do its fearful work among them. Thus will it be right after the first stage of the Descent of Christ—they shall be made to drink of the vials of God's wrath. But though sore will be their desolations the Jews will not be completely destroyed. Blessed is it to mark the sequel here. Moses returned unto the Lord and **interceded** on Israel's behalf (32: 30, 32). So also will the Lord Jesus yet intercede before God on behalf of the Jews: See Zech. 3.

In Exodus 33 and 34 we have the **second** descent of Moses from the Glory. He came down from the Mount with shining face, so that the people were afraid to come near him. But he quickly reassured them. This time he descended not in judgment, but in mercy, and therefore did he place them at ease by talking with them—so that "all the children of Israel **came nigh**" (vv. 30-32). Thus will it be when the Sun of Righteousness rises upon Israel with healing in His wings. Moses now "gave them in commandment all the Lord had spoken with him in Mount Sinai" (v. 32), which was a beautiful type of Millennial conditions: "out of Zion shall go forth the Law and the Word of the Lord from Jerusalem" (Isa. 2: 3).

And what is the remainder of Exodus occupied with? Nothing but the erection of the Tabernacle. Chapters 35 to 39 give us **God's habitation in the midst of** Israel. In the closing chapters we read, "And he reared up the court round about the tabernacle and the altar, and set up the hanging of the court gate. So Moses finished the work. Then a cloud covered the tent of the congregation and the glory of the Lord filled the tabernacle" (vv. 33-34), a lovely type of Christ in the Millenium in the midst of Israel! And there the book of Exodus ends. May the Lord give us eyes to see and hearts to enjoy the wonders fo His own workmanship.

CHAPTER 33

THE TABERNACLE

EXODUS 25-40

We have now arrived at the longest, most blessed, but least read and understood section of this precious book of Exodus. From the beginning of chapter 25 to the end of 40—excepting the important parenthesis in 32 to 34—the Holy Spirit has given us a detailed description of the Tabernacle, its structure, furniture, and priesthood. It is a fact worthy of our closest and fullest consideration that more space is devoted to an account of the Tabernacle than to any other single object or subject treated of in Holy Writ. Its courts, its furniture, and its ritual are described with a surprising particularity of detail. Two chapters suffice for a record of God's work in creating and fitting this earth for human habitation, whereas ten chapters are needed to tell us about the Tabernacle. Truly God's thoughts and ways are different from ours!

How sadly many of God's own people have dishonoured Him and His Word by their studied neglect of these chapters! Too many have seen in the Tabernacle, with its Divinely-appointed arrangements and services, only a ritual of the past—a record of Jewish manners and customs which have long since passed away and which have no meaning for or value to us. But "all Scripture is given by inspiration of God and is profitable" (2 Tim. 3 : 16). The Christian cannot neglect any portion of the Word without suffering loss : "whatsoever things were written aforetime (in the Old Testament) were written for our learning" (Rom. 15 : 4). Again and again in the New Testament the Holy Spirit makes figurative reference to the Tabernacle and its furniture, and much in the Epistle to the Hebrews cannot be understood without reference to the contents of Exodus and Leviticus.

"The tabernacle is one of the most important and instructive types. Here is such a variety of truths, here is such a fulness and manifoldness of spiritual teaching, that our great difficulty is to combine all the various lessons and aspects which it presents. The tabernacle has no fewer than three meanings. In the first place, the tabernacle is a type, a visible illustration, of that heavenly place in which God has His dwelling. In the second place, the tabernacle is a type of Jesus Christ, who is the meeting-place between God and man. And, in the third place, the tabernacle is a type of Christ in the Church—of the communion of Jesus with all believers" (Adolph Saphir).

The first of these meanings is clearly stated in Hebrews 9 : 23-24 : "It was, therefore necessary that the **patterns of things in the heavens** should be purified with these (i.e., sprinklings of blood see Heb. 9 : 21-22) ; but the heavenly things themselves with better sacrifices than these. For Christ is not entered into the holy places made with hands, which are **the figures of the true;** but into Heaven itself, now to appear in the presence of God for us." "The tabernacle was a symbol of God's dwelling. There is a Sanctuary, wherein is the especial residence and manifestation of the glorious presence of God. Solomon, although he confesses that the heaven of heavens cannot contain God, yet prays that the Lord may hear in heaven His dweling-place (2 Chron. 6). Jeremiah testifies, 'A glorious high throne from the beginning is the place of our sanctuary' (17 : 12). The visions of Ezekiel also bring before us the heavens opened and the likeness of a throne, and the appearance of the likeness of the glory of the Lord ; the likeness as the appearance of a man above upon the throne (1 : 26). Of this heavenly locality David speaks, when he asks, 'Who shall abide in Thy tabernacle ? Who shall dwell in Thy holy hill ?' (Psa. 24 : 3). In the book of Revelation we receive still further confirmation of this truth : 'And after that I looked, and, behold, the temple of the tabernacle of testimony in Heaven was opened' (15 : 5) . . . . Almost all expressions which are employed in describing the significance of the tabernacle are also used in reference to Heaven" (A. Saphir).

Secondly, the Tabernacle is a type of the Lord Jesus Himself, particularly of Him here on earth during the days of His flesh. Just as the Tabernacle was Jehovah's dwelling-place in the midst of Israel so are we told that "God was in Christ reconciling a world unto Himself" (2 Cor. 5 : 19); and again, "In Him dwelleth all the fulness of the Godhead bodily" (Col. 2 : 9). Beautifully was this application of our type manifested at the Incarnation. The Tabernacle was not something which originated in the minds of Israel, or even of Moses, but was designed by God Himself. So the Manhood of Christ, which enshrined His Deity, was not begotten by man—"A body hast **Thou** prepared Me" (Heb. 10 : 5), He said. This second aspect of the type will be developed more fully below

But the tabernacle has yet a third aspect. "There God and His people met. The ark of the covenant was not merely the throne where God manifested Himself in His holiness, but it was also the throne of relationship with His people. In all the offerings and sacrifices God was manifested; just as regards sin, merciful as regards the sinner; there also God and the sinner met. So throughout the tabernacle there was the manifestation of God in order to bring Israel into communion with Himself. In the Tabernacle man's fellowship with God was symbolised through manifold mediations, sacrifices, offerings. But in Jesus we have the perfect and eternal fulfilment" (A Saphir). This third aspect of our type is more than hinted at in Rev. 21 : 3 : "Behold, the **tabernacle** of God is with men, and He will **dwell** with them, and thy shall be His people, and God Himself shall be with them, and be their God."

The key to the Tabernacle, then, is **Christ**. In the volume of the Book it is written of Him. As a whole and in each of its parts the Tabernacle foreshadowed the person and work of the Lord Jesus. Each detail in it typified some aspect of His ministry or some excellency in His person. Proof of this is furnished in John 1 : 14 : "And the Word became flesh and **tabernacled** among us." (R. V. margin). The reference here is to the Divine incarnation and first advent of God's Son to this earth, and its language takes us back to the book of Exodus. Many and

varied are the correspondences between the type and the antitype We take leave to quote from our comments on John 1 : 14.

1. The Tabernacle was **a temporary** appointment. In this it differed from the temple of Solomon, which was a permanent structure. The Tabernacle was simply a tent, a temporary convenience, something that was suited to be moved about from place to place during the journeyings of the children of Israel. So it was when our blessed Lord tabernacled here among men. His stay was but a brief one—less than forty years; and, like the type, He abode not long in any one place, but was constantly on the move, unwearied in the activity of His love.

2. The Tabernacle was **for use in the wilderness.** After Israel settled in Canaan, the Tabernacle was superceded by the temple. But during the time of the pilgrimage from Egypt to the promised land, the Tabernacle was God's appointed provision for them. The **wilderness** strikingly foreshadowed the conditions amid which the eternal Word tabernacled among men at His first advent. The wilderness-home of the Tabernacle unmistakeably foreshadowed the manger-cradle, the Nazareth-carpenter's bench, the "nowhere for the Son of man to lay His head," the borrowed tomb for His sepulchre. A careful study of the chronology of the Pentateuch seems to indicate that Israel used the Tabernacle in the wilderness rather less than thirty-five years !

3. The Tabernacle was **mean, humble, and unattractive in outward appearance.** Altogether unlike the costly and magnificent temple of Solomon there was nothing in the externals of the Tabernacle to please the carnal eye. Nothing but plain boards and skins. So it was at the Incarnation. The Divine majesty of our Lord was hidden beneath a veil of flesh. He came, unattended by any imposing retinues of angels. To the unbelieving gaze of Israel He had no form or comeliness; and when they beheld Him their unanointed eyes saw in Him no beauty that they should desire Him.

4. The Tabernacle was **God's dwelling place.** It was there, in the midst of Israel's camp, that He took up His abode. There, between the Cherubim, upon the mercy-seat He made His throne. In the holy of holies He manifested His presence by means of the Shekinah glory. And

during the thirty-three years that the Word tabernacled among men. God had His dwelling-place in Palestine. The holy of holies received its anti-typical fulfilment in the person of the Holy One of God. Just as the Shekinah dwelt between the two Cherubim, so on the mount of transfiguration the glory of the God-man flashed forth from between two men—Moses and Elijah. "We beheld his glory "is the language of the tabernacle-type.

5. The Tabernacle was, therefore, the place where God met with man. It was termed "the Tent of Meeting." If an Israelite desired to draw near unto Jehovah he had to come to the door of the Tabernacle. When giving instruction to Moses concerning the making of the Tabernacle and its furnishings, God said, "And thou shalt put the mercy-seat above upon the ark, and in the ark thou shalt put the testimony that I shall give thee. And there I will meet with thee, and I will commune with thee" (Exodus 25 : 21-22). How perfect is this lovely type ! Christ is the meeting-place between God and man. No man cometh unto the Father but by Him (John 14 : 6). There is but one Mediator between God and men—the Man Christ Jesus (1 Tim. 2 : 5). He is the One who spans the gulf between Deity and humanity, because Himself both God and Man.

6. The Tabernacle was the centre of Israel's camp. In the immediate vicinity of the Tabernacle dwelt the Levites the priestly tribe: "But thou shalt appoint the Levites over the tabernacle of testimony, and over all the vessels thereof ; and over all things that belong to it ; they shall bear the tabernacle and all the vessels thereof ; and they shall minister unto it, and shall encamp round about the tabernacle" (Num. 1 : 50) ; and around the Levites were grouped the twelve tribes, three on either side—see Num. 2. Again ; we read that when Israel's camp was to be moved from one place to another, "then the tabernacle of the congregation shall set forward with the camp of the Levites in the midst of the camp" (Num. 2 : 17). Once more, "And Moses went out, and told the people the words of the Lord and gathered the seventy men of the elders of the people. and set them round about the tabernacle. And the Lord came down in a cloud and spake unto him" (Num. 11 : 24-25). How striking is this ! The Tabernacle was the great gathering-centre. As such it was a beautiful fore-

shadowing of the Lord Jesus. He is our great gathering-centre, and His precious promise is that "where two or three are gathered together in My name there am I in the midst of them" (Matt. 18 : 20).

7. The Tabernacle was the place where the Law was preserved. The first two tables of stone, on which Jehovah had inscribed the ten commandments were broken (Exodus 32 : 19) ; but the second set were deposited in the ark in the tabernacle for safe keeping (Deut. 10 : 2-5). It was only there, within the holy of holies, that the tablets of the Law were preserved intact. How this, again, speaks to us of Christ ! He it was that said, "Lo, I come : in the volume of the book it is written of Me ; I delight to do Thy will. O My God : Yea, Thy Law is within My heart" (Psa. 40 : 8). Throughout His perfect life He preserved in thought, word, and deed the Divine Decalogue, honouring and magnifying God's Law.

8. The Tabernacle was the place where sacrifice was made. In its outer court stood the brazen altar, to which the animals were brought, and on which they were slain. There it was the blood was shed and atonement was made for sin. So it was with the Lord Jesus. He fulfilled in His own person the typical significance of the brazen altar, as of every piece of the tabernacle furniture. The body in which He tabernacled on earth was nailed to the cruel Tree. The Cross was the altar upon which God's Lamb was slain, where His precious blood was shed, and where complete atonement was made for sin.

9. The Tabernacle was the place where the priestly family was fed. "And the remainder thereof shall Aaron and his sons eat : with unleavened bread shall it be eaten in the holy place ; in the court of the tabernacle of the congregation they shall eat it . . . The priest that offereth it for sin shall eat it : in the holy place shall t be eaten" (Lev. 6 : 16-26). How deeply significant are these scriptures in their typical import ! And how they should speak to us of Christ as the Food of God's priestly family to-day, i.e., all believers (1 Peter 2 : 5). He is the Bread of life. He is the One upon whom our souls delight to feed.

10. The Tabernacle was the place of worship. To it the pious Israelite brought his offerings. To it he turned

when he desired to worship Jehovah. From its door the voice of the Lord was heard. Within its courts the priests ministered in their sacred service. And so it was with the antitype. It is by **Him** we are to offer unto God a sacrifice of praise. (Heb. 13 : 15). It is in Him, and by Him, **alone**, that we can worship the Father. It is through Him we have access to the throne of grace.

11. The Tabernacle **had but one door.** Think of such a large building with but a single entrance ! The outer court, with its solid walls of white curtains, was pierced by one gate only ; telling us there is, but one way into the presence of the holy God. How this reminds us of the words of that One who said, "I am the way, the truth, and the life, no man cometh unto the Father but by Me !" Access can be obtained only through Him who declared "I am the Door" (John 10 : 9).

12. The Tabernacle was **approached through the tribe of Judah.** This is a most striking detail not obvious at first sight, but which is clearly established by a comparison of scripture with scripture. Num. 2, records the ordering of the twelve tribes of Israel as they were grouped around the four sides of the Tabernacle, and verse 3 tells us that **Judah** was to pitch on the **east** side. Now Exodus 27 : 12-17 makes it clear that **the door** of the Tabernacle was also on the **east** side. Thus, entrance into the Divine sanctuary was obtained through Judah. The significance of this is easily discerned. It was **through Judah** that the true Tabernacle obtained entrance into this world. Therefore is our Lord designated "the Lion of the tribe of Judah." (Rev. 5 : 5).

13. The Tabernacle **hints at the universal Lordship of Christ.** This may be seen from the fact that every kingdom in nature contributed its share toward buiding and enriching the Tabernacle. The mineral kingdom supplied the metals and the precious stones ; the vegetable gave the wood, linen, oil and spices ; the animal furnished the skins and goats hair curtains, in addition to the multitude of sacrifices which were constantly required. How this reminds us of the words of Him whom the Tabernacle foreshadowed," The silver is Mine, and the gold is Mine" (Hag. 2 : 8) ; and again, "The cattle upon a thousand hills are Mine" (Psa. 50 : 10).

14. The Tabernacle was **ministered**

unto by the Women. Their part was to provide the beautiful curtains and hangings : "And all the women that were wise-hearted did spin with their hands, and brought that which they had spun, both of blue, and of purple, and of scarlet, and of fine linen. And all the women whose hearts stirred them up in wisdom spun goats' hair" (Exodus 35 : 26). How beautifully this foreshadowed the loving devotion of those women mentioned in the Gospels who ministered to Christ of their substance : see Luke 7 : 37 ; 8 : 2-3 ; John 12 : 3 ; Luke 23 : 55-56.

Thus we see how fully and how perfectly the tabernacle of old foreshadowed the person of our blessed Lord, and why the Holy Spirit, when announcing the Incarnation, said, "And the Word became flesh and **tabernacled** among us." It should be pointed out that there is a series of striking contrasts between the wilderness tabernacle and Solomon's temple in their respective foreshadowings of Christ.

(1) The tabernacle foreshadowed Christ in His first advent ; the temple looks forward to Christ at His second advent.

(2) The tabernacle was first historically ; the temple was not built until long afterwards.

(3) The tabernacle was but a temporary erection ; the temple was a permanent structure.

(4) The tabernacle was erected by Moses the **prophet** (which was the office Christ filled during His first advent): the temple was built by Solomon the **king** (which is the office Christ will fill at His second advent).

(5) The tabernacle was used in the **wilderness**—speaking of Christ's humiliation ; the temple was built in Jerusalem, the "city of the great King" (Matt. 5 : 35)—speaking of Christ's future glorification.

(6) The numeral which figured most prominently in the tabernacle was five, which speaks of **grace,** and grace was what characterised the earthly ministry of Christ at His first advent ; but the leading numeral in the temple was twelve, which speaks of **government,** for at His second advent Christ shall rule and reign as King of kings and Lord of lords.

(7) The tabernacle was unattractive in

its externals—so when Christ was here before, He was as "a root out of a dry ground": but the temple was renowned for its outward magnificence—so Christ when He returns shall come in power and great glory.

The careful reader will have noticed that there are two full accounts given in Exodus of the construction of the Tabernacle. This is indeed noteworthy, and evidences once more the accuracy and fulness of the type. First we have a description of the Tabernacle and its furniture as it was given to Moses in the Mount directly by Jehovah Himself. Then, as a parenthesis, in chapters 32, 33, we have the record of Israel's transgressing the holy covenant in the sin of idolatry. Finally, from chapters 35 to the end of the book we have the actual erection of the Tabernacle. What was foreshadowed by this we shall now endeavour to indicate.

First, there is the tabernacle as it was originally planned in Heaven and then shown as a pattern to Moses on the Mount. What did this adumbrate but Christ set forth from eternity in the counsels of the Godhead? The great Sacrifice was no afterthought on the part of God. He was not taken by surprise, nor was His eternal purpose interfered with when Adam transgressed His commandment. The Lamb was "foreordained before the foundation of the world" (1 Peter 1 : 20) ! Then in Jehovah showing to Moses the pattern of the Tabernacle which was to be erected, we have prefigured the successive types and prophecies which God gave to His people before His Son became incarnate. Just as Moses later built the Tabernacle according to the actual model which God had shown him during the forty days on the Mount, so Christ was born, lived and died, in exact accord with the prophetic plan which God gave during the forty centuries that preceded.

Second, in chapters 32 and 33 we are introduced to a dark interval of rebellion, when Israel sinned grievously against their Divine Benefactor. How accurately this depicts the fall and failure of man during the whole of the Old Testament period, and how it witnessed to the need of that redemption which God, in His marvellous grace, had prepared ! "Christ had been already provided, but man must feel the need of the Divine salvation by the actual experience of sin. It is touching beyond degree to know that all the time that man was rebelling against God, God's remedy was

waiting in that mount of grace" (Christ in the Tabernacle, by A. B. Simpson). Despite Israel's fearful transgression in the interval, the Tabernacle was erected; even so the fearful wickedness of men and all their countless abominations did not turn God from His purpose of mercy. When the fulness of time was come, God sent forth His Son. Where sin abounded, grace did much more abound.

Third, in the last six chapters we have the inspired record of **the actual erection** of the Tabernacle. Here we see the counsels of God perfectly executed, and most striking is it to note the provision He made for carrying out His design of a sanctuary. In 35 : 30-31, we read, "And Moses said unto the children of Israel, See, the Lord hath called by name Bezeleel the son of Uri, the son of Hur, of the tribe of **Judah** ; and he hath filled him with the Spirit of God, in wisdom, in understanding, and in knowledge, and in all manner of workmanship." Thus we learn that it was by the gracious agency of **the Spirit of God** that the Tabernacle was brought into existence ! What anointed eye can fail to see here that which made possible and actual the Divine incarnation, namely, the supernatural operations of the Spirit of God—see Luke 1 : 34-35 ! And how remarkable (and yet not remarkable) that the instrument used belonged to the tribe of Judah : so Mary was of the royal stock ! Thus, in type and Antitype, the Divine plan was secured through the operations of the Spirit of God. Thus, also, do we see all the three persons of the Godhead in connection with the Tabernacle.

How unspeakably blessed is the word recorded in 40 : 34 . "Then a cloud covered the tent of the congregation and the glory of the Lord filled the Tabernacle." Mean as was the outward appearance of that Tent, yet within, abode the Divine glory. So it was with the Antitype. When He appeared before men, He had "no form nor comeliness" (Isa. 5. : 2), yet in Him dwelt all the fulness of the Godhead bodily.

What has been said above in no wise conflicts with the closing paragraphs of the preceding article. David was inspired to write "Thy commandment is exceeding **broad**" (Psalm 119 : 96). Well, had it been if expositors and commentators had borne this more in mind. There is not only a depth, but also a fulness to the Scriptures which are worthy of their Divine Author. God's

Word is many-sided in its application. Some times a single parable (that of the Sower, for example) contains important practical lessons, doctrinal instruction, a prophetic forecast and a dispensational picture. How many of the prophecies, perhaps all of them have a double—a minor and a major, a germinal and a terminal—and sometimes a threefold fulfilment. Thus it is also with the types. Some Old Testament characters are equally types of Christ, of Israel, and of the Christian. So with the Tabernacle : many of its details have more than one typical significance. May the Holy Spirit be our Teacher as we endeavour to take them up.

CHAPTER 34

THE TABERNACLE (Continued)

EXODUS 25:1-9

The neglect of typology and the ignorance which prevails to-day concerning the spiritual significance of the Tabernacle is one of the many solemn signs of the times. The pyramids of Egypt and the catacombs of Rome are never-failing objects of interest. The ancient abbeys of England and the temples of heathendom attract thousands every year from the ends of the earth, to admire their architectural designs and to study their historical features. But the Tabernacle of Jehovah, which possesses a charm and a claim unknown to any other building is, like its Antitype, despised and rejected of men. True, it is no longer to be seen on earth in concrete form, yet a Divinely-inspired and detailed account of it has been given to us in the Holy Scriptures. But so widely is the study of typology neglected, comparatively few among the great masses of professing Christians know anything of the Divine wonders and spiritual beauties in which the closing chapters of Exodus abound.

In our day even students of theology leave those fruitful fields to glean elsewhere. Many of them are wasting their time reading through almost countless volumes treating of the authorship of the Pentateuch, instead of poring over the sacred pages themselves. They prefer to wade through the polluted streams which the higher critics have digged, rather than drink from the pure river of the Water of Life. Even where the Divine inspiration of the books of Moses is accepted, comparatively few are occupied with their deeper teachings and blessed foreshadowings. Alas that it is so.

"The typical portions of Scripture are supremely important and as a study vastly interesting. Types are shadows. Shadows imply substance. A type has its lessons. It was the design of Jehovah to express His great thought of redemption to His people Israel in a typical or symbolic manner. By laws, ceremonies, institutions, persons and incidents, He sought to keep alive in Israel's hearts the hope of a coming Redeemer. Christ is therefore the key to Moses' gospel. This then is our advantage, that we can minutely compare type and antitype, and learn thereby the lessons of grace which bringeth salvation" ("Shadow and Substance," by G. Needham).

In our last article we dwelt upon the typical purport of the Tabernacle; here we shall say a few words concerning its doctrinal lessons. One of the chief values which the closing sections of Exodus possesses to the true people of God is that there we have set before us Divine illustrations, concrete representations, vivid pictures of the fundamental verities connected with our "great salvation." God, in His infinite condescension, graciously adapted His instructions to the spiritual intelligence of His children. An abstract statement of truth is much harder to apprehend than a visible representation of it to the eye. Just as in natural things a child is able to grasp the meaning of pictures before it learns to spell and to read, so God has first given us a full description of the Tabernacle and all its contents, setting before the eye that which is found in the N.T. Epistles in the form of doctrinal expositions. Thus by means of material symbols we are assisted to understand better the riches of God's grace in Christ our Saviour.

The Tabernacle—the materials of which it was composed, the seven pieces of furniture, the priesthood who ministered therein, the offerings and sacrifices —is to be regarded as one great object-lesson, setting forth spiritual truth. For this reason, among others, was it designated "the Tent of the Testimony" (Num. 9: 15). There, witness was borne of "good things to come" (Heb. 10: 1). There, was proclaimed the holiness and majesty of the great Jehovah. There, were set forth the terms of communion with Him. There, was revealed the way of approach by blood-shedding. There, was exhibited the imperative need of a Divinely-appointed Mediator. There, was shown the efficacy of atonement by the sacrifice of an innocent victim in the room of the guilty. There, was established the Mercy-seat, from which God communed with the representative of His people.

Our great difficulty in seeking to interpret the portions of Scripture which now lie before us is the multitude of the revelations contained therein. By means of the Tabernacle Jehovah revealed His character and made known His purpose of redemption. There, devouring holiness and righteous indignation against sin declared the fact that God was just even while He justified. The Tabernacle was the place of sacrifice; its most vivid spectacle was the flowing and sprinkling of blood, pointing forward to the sufferings and death of Christ. It was also the place of cleansing; there was the blood for atonement and also the water for washing away the stains of defilement. So Christ "loved the Church and gave Himself for it, that He might sanctify and cleanse it, with the washing of water by the Word; that He might present it to Himself a glorious Church, not having spot or wrinkle, or any such thing, but that it should be holy and without blemish" (Eph. 5: 25-27). The Tabernacle had inner chambers, setting forth the fullness of those blessings which the believer has in Christ. In them was light, bread, and the altar of prayer—all finding their antetypical fulfilment in our blessed Redeemer.

Probably the outstanding lesson taught us through the Tabernacle was the way in which a sinner might approach God. First of all, he was most forcibly reminded that sin had separated him from God. The Tabernacle was God's dwelling-place, and it was enclosed, being encircled by walls of pure white curtains. This at once taught Israel the holiness of the One who had come to dwell in their midst; they were shut out and He was shut in. Their sinfulness unfitted them to enter His holy presence. O my reader, have you ever pondered the ineffable holiness of God, and realised that your sins have placed you at a guilty distance from Him?

But though the sanctuary of Jehovah was enclosed, there was a door through which the Israelite might enter the outer court, though further he might not advance. There, within the outer court,

stood the Tabernacle proper, with its two compartments, surrounded by walls of wooden boards, and only the priests were allowed therein, and they but in the first chamber—the holy place. Beyond, lay the holy of holies, where the Shekinah glory, the visible representation of God's presence, resided between the cherubim on the mercy-seat. Into this compartment none ever entered save Moses the mediator, and Aaron the high priest one day in the year.

Marvellous is the progressive order of teaching in connection with the various objects in the Tabernacle. At the brazen altar sin was judged, and by blood-shedding put away. At the laver purification was effected. In the holy place provision was made for prayer, food and illumination; while in the holy of holies the glory of the enthroned King was displayed. The same principle of progress is also to be seen in the increasing value of the sacred vessels. Those in the outer court were of wood and brass; whereas those in the inner compartments were of wood and gold. So too the various curtains grew richer in design and embellishment, the inner vail being the costliest and most elaborate. Again, the outer court, being open, was illumined by natural light; the holy place was lit up by the light from the golden candle-stick; but the holy of holies was radiated by the Shekinah glory of Jehovah. Thus the journey from the outer court into the holy of holies was from sin to purification, and from grace to glory. How blessedly did this illustrate the truth that "the path of the just is as the shining light, that shineth more and more unto the perfect day" (Prov. 4: 18).

The order in which the Tabernacle and its contents are described is most significant. The first thing mentioned is the ark (25: 10) and its covering—the mercy-seat (25: 17), which was Jehovah's throne in Israel's midst. Then comes the table (25: 23) and the candlestick (25: 31), the curtains (26: 1), and boards (26: 15) of the Tabernacle proper, with the separating veil (26: 31). Last comes the brazen altar (27: 1) and the hangings of the court (27: 9). Thus it will be seen that the order is from the interior to the exterior. It is the order of sovereign grace, God coming from His throne right to the outer door where the sinner was! How this reminds us of the Incarnation; the sinner in his sins could not go from earth to heaven, so God in the person of His Son came from heaven to earth, and died the Just for the unjust "that He might bring us to

God (1 Peter 3: 18). Blessedly was this emphasised by Christ in His teaching—the Shepherd going after the lost sheep (Luke 15: 4), the good Samaritan journeying to where the wounded traveller lay (Luke 10: 33), etc.

"In describing the things that pertain to worship, He commences with the most precious type of all—the breast-plate the high priest wore on his heart (28: 4) and ends with the laver of brass in which Aaron's sons were to wash their hands and feet daily (30: 18). It is thus too in the book that takes up the sacrifices —Leviticus. It commences not with the offerings for sins, but the highest form of all—the burnt offering (Lev. 2: 1). God's glory must be the first object to be established by the work of Christ, and then our need met (Lev. 4). But that which we first apprehend is surely that which meets our need in the sin-offering. And the vast difference in the ancient and it is often years before we understand that it is a "sweet savor" sacrifice that met the need of God's heart and established His glory" (Mr. C. H. Bright in "Pictures of Salvation").

It is very striking to note that in the second description of the Tabernacle, where we have the record of its manufacture and erection, there is a notable variation—instead of beginning with the contents of the holy of holies where Jehovah dwelt, we have described the Tabernacle and curtains of the outer court, which the common people saw. Here the order is from without to within —the experimental order, the order in which Divine truth is apprehended by the soul. This same twofold order may —be seen in the Epistles to the Romans and Ephesians. In the former, the Holy Spirit begins with man's sinfulness, guiltiness, and ruin; goes on to speak of God's provision in Christ, and then closes the doctrinal section by showing us the redeemed sinner in the presence of God, from whom there is no separation. In Ephesians the Spirit begins with God's eternal counsels, choosing us in Christ before the foundation of the world, and then treats of redemption and regeneration and the consequent privileges and responsibilities flowing therefrom. In Romans it is the sinner going in to God; in Ephesians, God coming out the sinner. Such is the double teaching in the twofold order of the description of the Tabernacle.

Before Jehovah gave instructions to Moses concerning the various articles in the Tabernacle, He first ordered him to require of Israel as an offering, the different materials out of which they were to be made. "And the Lord spake unto Moses, saying, Speak unto the children of Israel that they bring Me an offering: of every man that giveth it willingly with his heart ye shall take My offering" (Ex. 25: 1-2). Very beautiful is this. The materials out of which the Tabernacle was to be made were to be provided by the voluntary offerings of devoted hearts. The great Jehovah who inhabiteth the praises of eternity condescended to take up His abode in a boarded and curtained Tent, erected by those who desired His presence in their midst (see 15: 2).

Historically, we may admire the fruit of God's grace working in the hearts of His redeemed so that they willingly offered the required materials. Their offering was so spontaneous and full (see 35: 21-29) that we are told, "And they spake unto Moses, saying, the people bring much more than enough for the service of the work, which the Lord commanded to make. And Moses gave commandment, and they caused it to be proclaimed throughout the camp, saying, Let neither man nor woman make any more work for the offering of the sanctuary, so the people were restrained from bringing. For the stuff they had was sufficient for all the work to make it, and too much" (36: 5-7). But behind the historical we are to look for the spiritual, and behold here a lovely type of the voluntariness and joy of the Lord Jesus, who freely and gladly became flesh, thus providing God with a perfect Sanctuary as He tabernacled among men!

"And this is the offering which ye shall take of them; gold, and silver and brass; and blue, and purple, and scarlet, and fine linen; and goats, and rams skins dyed red, and badgers skins; and shittim wood; oil for the light, spices for anointing oil, and for sweet incense; onyx stones, and stones to be set in the ephod, and in the breastplate" (v. 3-7). Each of these articles tells forth one of the manifold perfections of Christ. The gold, His Divine glory. The silver, the redemption which He wrought and bought for us. The brass, His capacity to endure the wrath of God against our sins. The blue, His heavenly origin. The purple, His royal majesty. The scarlet, His earthly glory in a coming day. The fine linen, His holiness made manifest by His righteous walk and ways. The goats hair, His atonement. The rams skins, His devotedness to God. The badgers skins, His ability to protect

His people. The shittim wood, His incorruptible humanity. The oil for the light, His Divine wisdom. The spices, His fragrance unto God. The precious stones, His priestly perfections. We do not now offer proofs for these definitions nor enlarge upon their blessedness, as, God willing, each one will come before us for fuller consideration in the articles to follow.

With the above verses should be compared Exodus 38: 24-31, where the Holy Spirit has given us the respective weights of the gold, silver and brass. Careful students have estimated there would be fully a ton and a quarter of gold, which at modern value would be worth upwards of one hundred and seventy-five thousand pounds, or eight hundred and sixty thousand dollars, but allowing for present-day purchasing values, worth much more. Of silver there would be fully four tons and a quarter, and worth forty thousand pounds or two hundred thousand dollars. Of brass (more likely, copper) there was also over four tons. In addition, there were the textile fabrics, blue, purple, scarlet and fine twined linen, besides goats' hair, rams and badgers' skins, and large quantities of shittim wood, the amounts of which are not recorded. Last, but not least, were the precious stones for the breastplate of the high priest. All of this indicates the great costliness of the Tabernacle. At modern values its materials would be worth at least a million pounds or five million dollars. How this, in type, told of God's estimate of Christ; how it shows us the Father saying, This is My Beloved Son in whom I am well pleased!

It is noteworthy that there were **fifteen** separate articles specified in the above verses, the factors of which are three and five—almost every numeral connected with the Tabernacle was a division or multiple of one of these. Now three is the number of **manifestation** and therefore of God—in the three Persons of the Trinity. Five is the number of grace. Putting these together, fifteen signifies, in the language of spiritual arithmetic, God's grace manifested. How eminently suited were these numerals as the predominating ones in that dwelling-place of God which pointed forward to His incarnate Son! It was in Christ, come to earth, that the grace of God was fully made known. How this shows us, again, that there is a deep meaning to the minutest detail of Holy Writ!

"And let them make Me a sanctuary; that I may dwell among them" (v. 8). Here is the leading feature to bear in mind concerning the Tabernacle: it was to be Jehovah's "sanctuary," God's dwelling-place. It is important to observe that it was not until He had redeemed a people unto Himself that God dwelt amid them on the earth. He visited Adam in Eden, He appeared to and communed with the patriarchs, He gave communications to Moses even in Egypt, but not until He had redeemed His people out of the house of bondage, not until they had been separated from their enemies at the Red Sea, not until His government over them had been established at Sinai, did He propose the making of a sanctuary, in which He might dwell among His saints.

The Tabernacle then was the pledge and proof that God had graciously brought His redeemed people into relationship with Himself, yea, into a place of nearness to Himself. So we, who once were (because of sin) far off from Him, have been made nigh by the precious blood of Christ (Eph. 2: 13). The awful distance which once separated is now gone; we have been brought "to God" (1 Peter 3: 18). O the wondrous riches of Divine mercy! First bought by Christ, then sought by the Spirit, and in consequence, brought to the Father; and that not as guilty criminals, but as happy children. Blessedly is this illustrated at the close of that wondrous parable in Luke 15. There we are shown that the one who had wasted his substance in the far country, then convicted of his deep need and brought to repentance, finally welcomed by the Father, fitted for His presence and given a seat at His table.

But as at the marriage-feast in Cana of Galilee, the best wine is reserved for the last. "And I saw a new heaven and a new earth; for the first heaven and the first earth were passed away; and there was no more sea. And I, John, saw the holy city, new Jerusalem, coming down from God out of heaven, prepared as a bride adorned for her husband. And I heard a great voice out of heaven saying, Behold, **the tabernacle of God** is with men, and **He will dwell with them**, and they shall be His people, and God Himself shall be with them, and be their God" (Rev. 21: 1-3). "Then the counsels of God's heart will be displayed in their consummated perfection, and, inasmuch as the former things, with all the sorrows connected with them through man's sin, will have passed away, there will be nothing to hinder the full, perfect, and blessed enjoyment arising out of the unhindered flow of God's heart to His people, and their hearts to Him, and from His perfect manifestation and their perfect worship and service" (Mr. Ed. Dennett).

"According to all that I show thee, after the pattern of the Tabernacle, and the pattern of all the instruments thereof even so shall you make it" (v. 9). It is to be noted that Moses not only received implicit instructions as to what materials the tabernacle was to be made from, and (as we shall see later) complete details as to the dimensions, plan, and furnishings thereof; but that a pattern or model was set before him, after which it was to be constructed. That this is a point of importance for us to weigh is evident from the number of times it is repeated in the Scriptures. No less than seven times are we informed that Moses was commanded to make the Sanctuary after the pattern of it which was shown him in the Mount—see Exodus 25: 9; 25: 40; 26: 30; 27: 8; Numbers 8: 4; Acts 7: 44; Heb. 8: 5. Nothing was left to man's wisdom, still less to "chance"; everything was to be in exact accordance with the Divine model. Does not this teach us that everything concerning Christ and His people has been wrought out according to the eternal purpose of Him who worketh all things after the counsel of His own will! May Divine grace enable us to rest there in perfect peace and joyous worship.

CHAPTER 35

THE ARK ✓

EXODUS 25:10-16

Of the seven pieces of furniture which were found in the Tabernacle the Holy Spirit has described first the ark and the mercy-seat. Though these two are intimately related, so intimately that together they formed one complete whole—the mercy-seat being the cover or lid of the ark—yet are they mentioned, and are therefore to be considered, separately. The ark was a wooden chest, slightly over four feet in length and about two and a half feet broad and high. The wood of which it was made was overlaid with gold, both within and without, so that nothing save gold was visible to the eye.

The great importance of the ark is clear from several considerations. When Jehovah gave instructions to Moses concerning the Tabernacle, He began with the ark. It was first in order because first in importance. Before any details were communicated concerning the sanctuary itself, before a word was told Moses about its court and chambers its priesthood and ritual, its furniture and garniture, minute directons were given regarding the ark; without the ark the whole service of the Tabernacle had been meaningless and valueless, for it was upon it, as His throne, that God dwelt. The ark was the object to which the brazen altar pointed, the sacrifice of which gave right of access to the worshipper, who came to the ark representatively in the person of the high priest. It was the first of the holy vessels to be made, and made by Moses himself (Deut. 10 : 1-5). It was the place where the tables of the law were preserved. Its pre-eminence above all the other vessels was shown in the days of Solomon, for the ark alone was transferred from the tabernacle to the Temple.

"The ark was a symbol that God was present among His people, that His covenant blessing was resting upon them.

It was the most sacred and glorious instrument of the sanctuary ; yea, the whole sanctuary was built for no other end, but to be as it were a house, an habitation for the ark (see Exodus 26 : 33). Hence sanctification proceeded unto all the parts of it ; for, as Solomon observed, the places were holy whereunto the ark of God came, 2 Chron. 8 : 11" (A. Saphir). We shall consider the ark in seven connections. ✓

1. Its Significance.

The ark typified the person of our Lord Jesus Christ. This is so obvious that it is hardly necessary to pause and furnish proof. The other two arks, that of Noah, in which he and his family found shelter from the flood ; and that in which the infant Moses was preserved, plainly foreshadowed Christ Himself. The fact that the ark of the covenant was composed of two materials and of two only—the wood and the gold—clearly point to the two natures of our Lord : the human and the Divine. The fact that the two tables of stone were preserved in the ark, and the words of the Saviour, "Thy law is within My heart" (Psa. 40 : 8) supply us with a sure key. The fact that the mercy-seat (where God received the representative of His sinful but blood-cleansed people) rested upon the ark, furnishes additional confirmation.

It is the typical significance of the ark which explains its pre-eminence over the other sacred vessels. Each of them pointed to some aspect of Christ's work, or its effects, but the ark spoke of His person : they of what He has done, this of what HE is. It is the blessed person of Christ which gave value to His work. To-day, in evangelical circles, the emphasis is placed on what the Saviour has done for us, rather than on what He is in Himself. Scripture ever reverses this order. Note how in the typical ritual on the annual day of atonement, the high

191

priest first entered the holy of holies with his hands full of sweet incense (Lev. 16 : 12), before he took in and sprinkled the blood (v. 14)—God would first be reminded of the fragrant perfections of Christ's person, ere that which spoke of His redemptive work was placed before Him ! Mark the order in the announcement of the Lord's forerunner "Behold the Lamb of God" (first His person) which taketh away (second. His work) the sin of the world," (John 1 : 29). So with the apostle Paul, "I determined not to know anything among you save Jesus Christ(His person) and Him crucified"—His work" (1 Cor. 2 : 2). So again, in the apocalyptic visions : 'I beheld . . . and in the midst of the elders, stood a Lamb (His person) as it had been slain"—His work (Rev. 5 : 6). Thus it was in this order of the Tabernacle furniture : first the ark which tells of Christ's person, then the mercy-seat, etc., which point to His work.

2. Its Materials.

The ark was made of "shittim wood," a species of the acacia, which is said by many to be imperishible. It is a tree which is found in the arid desert. The "shittim wood," grown here on earth, typified the humanity of our Saviour. Isaiah 53 : 2 speaks in the language of this type : "For He shall grow up before Him as a tender plant, and as a root out of a dry ground." "There are three things about this shittim-tree which makes it a peculiarly fitting as a type of this. It is the tree now called the acacia seyal—the only tree that grows to any size in the deserts through which Israel passed. First it is a tree that can thrive in a very dry soil. Second, it has very long, sharp thorns Third, it is the tree from which is obtained the gum arabic so largely used in medicinal preparations, which is procured simply by piercing the tree at nightfall, and that which oozes out is, without any preparation, the gum-arabic of commerce. To the spiritual mind these facts are sweetly suggestive of Him who, in a dry and thirsty land, where surely there was naught to sustain His spirit, was in the constant freshness of communion with God, for other than an earthly stream sustained Him. Though indeed crowned now with glory, a crown of thorns was all this world had for Him. And we remember too, that it was He who was pierced for us in that blackest night of guilt, when the blood flowed forth from His side, to be the only balm for the troubled soul and sin-burdened conscience" (Mr. C. H. Bright).

As the shittim-wood was one that never rotted, it was a most appropriate emblem of the sinless humanity of the Lord Jesus. It is indeed striking to find that in the Septuagint (the first translation ever made of the Old Testament—into Greek) it is always translated "incorrupible wood." Now it is of paramount importance that we should hold fast and testify to the fundamental truth conveyed by the "incorruptible wood," namely, the real but absolute untainted humanity of Christ. That Christ was truly Man is clear from His repeated use of the title "the Son of Man," and from the Holy Spirit's appellation "the Man Christ Jesus" (1 Tim. 2 : 5). But His humanity was uncorrupt and incorruptible. In Him was no sin (1 John 3 : 5) for He was the Holy One of God ; and therefore disease and death had no claim upon Him, Begotten by the Holy Spirit, and born of a virgin, His immaculate humanity was pronounced "that holy thing which shall be born" (Luke 1 : 45).

The wood of the ark was overlaid with gold, within and without. This perfigured His **Divine nature.** "While the acacia boards gave **form** and **dimensions** to the ark, the **appearance** was all gold—no wood was visible. Thus our Lord's humanity gives Him the form in which He was and is. Light of light, the Creator and Upholder of all things, He became a Man, and was and is eternally 'the Man Christ Jesus.' But how God guards us from having a single low view of this most lowly One. The gold covers all Look at Him, gaze, as far as finite mind and heart can, upon the the majesty of His being, and all is Divine ! The Divine nature is displayed over the 'form of a servant' and wherever the all-seeing eye of God rests, within that pure and and holy mind, affections and will, as well as without upon that blameless walk, meekness and obedience, He owns Him as His Equal, His co-eternal Son. It is all gold, though the form of the Servant was there, with perfect human faculties and dependence—everything that belongs to man, sin apart. But spread over all this is the gold of His deity. And does not faith see the same?" (Lectures on the Tabernacle by S. Ridout).

Thus, in the wood and the gold together forming the ark we have foreshadowed the great mystery of godliness —God manifest in flesh. Here we see, in symbol the **union** of the two natures in the God-man, a Scriptural conception

The Ark 193

of whom is so important and vital—important, as God has shown us by making the ark to be the first object of contemplation as we take up the study of the Tabernacle; vital, because sound views of Christ are inseparable from our very salvation : "This is life eternal, that they might know Thee the only true God, and Jesus Christ, whom Thou hast sent" (John 17 : 3).

3. Its Dimensions.

The ark was two and a half cubits in length, one and a half in breadth, and one and a half in height. The repeated half at once arrests attention. The word "half" in the Hebrew comes from a root which means to cut in two. Another has pointed out that these half cubits suggest that the knowledge of Christ given to us now is only partial : "Now we know in part" (Cor. 13 : 9). "Those who have the fullest knowledge of Christ are the first to say, in the language of the Queen of Sheba, 'it was a true report that I heard . . and behold, the half was not told me' (1 Kings 10 : 6-7). So with our all-glorious Lord, the scale is reduced—may we say ?—that our finite minds may grasp something of the wondrous fulness of that which passeth knowledge" (Mr. S. Ridout).

Two and a half is half of five, and one and a half is half of three, and both of these numbers have a meaning in Scripture which is deeply significant. Take the latter first. Three is the number of manifestation, that is why it is the number of resurrection, for only in resurrection is life fully manifested ; for the same reason three is the number of Deity, for God is fully manifested in the three persons of the Holy Trinity. How significant then that the breadth and height (which both have to do with the display of an object) of the ark were both half of three. Remembering that the ark speaks of the person of Christ and three is the number of manifestation, do we not find here more than a hint that when Christ came to the earth He would not fully manifest Himself ? Nor did He : Had He completely unveiled His glory men had been blinded as was Saul of Tarsus (Acts 9 : 8), or had fallen at His feet as dead, as did John (Rev. 1 : 17). But blessed be God we shall yet "see Him as He is," and then shall we eat of "the hidden Manna" (Rev. 2 : 17). So, too, with the other number. Five stands for grace, and the length of the ark speaks of the span of God's grace in Christ. That span is

eternal ; but eternity is endless duration both backwards and forwards. Therefore is the five halved for though believers now know of the grace that was given them in Christ before the foundation of the world (2 Tim. 1 : 9), the endless ages yet to come await its future display (Eph. 2 : 7).

It is to be noted that the ark measured the same in height as in breadth, which at once points to the perfections and uniqueness of Christ. The "breadth" would speak of Him in His dealings with man, the "height" His relations Godward. How far our spiritual height falls short of our breadth ! For example how much more cautious are we against displeasing our fellows than God! Not so with the Perfect One. In meeting the needs of men, He never lost sight of the claims of His Father : Mark how in responding to the appeal of Lazarus' sisters, the glory of the Father was His only motive and consideration (John 11 : 4-6).

4. Its Contents.

These are described in Heb. 9 : 4 : "The ark of the covenant overlaid round about with gold, wherein was the golden pot that had manna, and Aaron's rod that budded, and the tables of the covenant." Some have seen a contradiction between this verse and 1 Kings 8 : 9 : "There was nothing in the ark save the two tables of stone." But there is no conflict between the two passages for they are not treating of the same point in time. Hebrews 9 : 4 is speaking of what was in the ark during the days that it was lodged in the Tabernacle, whereas 1 Kings 8 : 9 tells us of what comprised its contents after it came to rest in the Temple. Thus we see how quickly disappeares one of the stock 'contradiction' arguments of infidels !

The distinction noted above between what was inside the ark during its respective sojourns in the Tabernacle and in the Temple supplies the key to the typical significance of its contents. The three articles specified in Heb. 9 : 4 point to God's provisions in Christ while they are journeying through the wilderness. This becomes abundantly clear when we consider the first thing named, "the golden pot that had manna." The manna was the food which Jehovah gave to Israel while they were journeying from the house of bondage to the promised inheritance. It foreshadowed Christ as the Bread of life, the food of His pilgrim people. But most blessed is the added word here. In Exodus 16 : 3, we simply read that Moses said unto Aaron "take a pot and put an omer full of manna therein and lay it up before the testimony, to be kept; whereas in Hebrews 9 : 4, the Spirit tells us it was "a golden pot." The Old Testament could not give us that, it is reserved for the New Testament to bring it out. The Manna was the grace of God meeting the need of His people in the wilderness. Now while the Old Testament makes it plain that Israel's deepest need would be met through the promised Messiah, yet it was by no means clear that the Messiah would be a member of the Godhead; rather was the emphasis thrown upon the fact that He was to be the seed of Abraham and of David. But with the New Testament before us, we have no difficulty in perceiving that naught but a vessel which was holy and Divine was adequate to hold what God had for needy sinners and that that vessel was no other than His beloved Son incarnate. It is in John's Gospel, particularly, that we get the truth of the "golden pot." There we see the Vessel which was capable of holding the grace of God for His people: **"full** of grace and truth" is found only in John!

There is. no doubt, an additional thought connected with the golden pot," which contained the manna. The amount stored therein was "one omer" which, as we learn from Exodus 16 : 16, was the quantity for each man. Thus the amount preserved was the measure of a man; but the **golden** pot which contained it tells us that this Man is now **glorified**, the same thought being found in the "crown of gold which was round about the ark." This is confirmed by a comparison of Exodus 25 · 18 with Heb. 9 : 5, where the cherubim of "gold" are called the cherubim of "glory." It is, then, in the Man Christ Jesus, now crowned with glory and honour, that God's food for His people is to be found. Just as in another type, when the famine stricken people came to Pharaoh for corn, he referred them to the once humbled, but then exalted Joseph.

The second article within the ark was "Aaron's rod that budded." This takes us back to Numbers 17 where we have the historical account of it. In Numbers 16, we read of a revolt against Moses and Aaron headed by Korah, a revolt occasioned by jealously at the authority God had delegated to His two servants. This revolt was visited by summary judgment from on High, and was followed by a manifest vindication of Aaron. The form that this vindication

took is most interesting and instructive. The Lord bade Moses take twelve rods, one for each tribe, writing Aaron's name on the rod for Levi. These rods were laid up before the ark, and the one that should be made to blossom would indicate which had been chosen of God to be the priestly tribe. Next morning it was found that Aaron's rod had "brought forth buds, and blossomed blossoms, and yielded almonds." Afterwards the Lord ordered Moses to bring Aaron's rod before the testimony "to be kept for a token against the rebels." The spiritual and typical significance of this we shall now endeavour to indicate.

The issue raised by Korah and his company was that of priestly ministry—who had the right to exercise it ? In deciding this issue the tribal rods (symbols of **authority**) were laid up before the Lord, to show that the matter was taken entirely out of the hands of man and was to be decided by God alone. Thus the question of the priesthood was determined solely by Jehovah. The manner in which God's mind was made known on this momentous point is very striking. The "rods" were all of them lifeless things, but during the interval that they were laid up before the testimony, unseen by the eye of man, the mighty power of the living God intervened, a miracle was wrought, the dead rod was quickened, and resurrection-life and fruit appeared.

The spiritual eye will have no difficulty in perceiving what all of this pointed forward to. Numbers 16 foreshadowed Israel's rebellion against Him, whom Moses and Aaron jointly prefigured. Moses, the prophet proclaimed the **truth** of God; Aaron, the priest, expressed His **grace**; both were hated without a cause. So He who was full of grace and truth was despised and rejected of men; not only so but put to a shameful death. And what was God's response ? He fully vindicated His beloved Son by raising Him from the dead. Moses entering the Tabernacle on the morrow (Num. 17 : 8) and there beholding the evidences of God's resurrection power, reminds us of the disciples entering the empty sepulchre and beholding the signs that Christ had risen from the dead. Moses bringing out the rods and showing them to the people (v. 9), finds its antitype in the resurrection of Christ established before many witnesses (1 Cor. 15 : 6). In the rod laid up before the Lord, we have a picture of Christ, now hidden, at the right hand of God. But it is with the rod in the ark that we now have to do. All that was in the ark speaks of the wondrous provision which God has made for His people in Christ. Now what is before us in Numbers 17, is not God dealing in judgment, but in grace: "And the Lord said unto Moses, Bring Aaron's rod again before the testimony, to be kept for a token against the rebels; and thou shalt quite **take away** their murmurings from Me **that they die not."** Thus, the priestly ministry of Aaron was to preserve God's people before Him while they were passing through the wilderness. How plain is the type. That which answers to it is found in the ministry of our great High Priest in heaven, who secures our salvation to the uttermost by His constant intercessions for us (Heb. 7:25). Here, then, is God's provision for us in Christ: food to strengthen, priestly grace to sustain.

One other point remains to be considered in connection with Aaron's rod. In Heb 9:4, it is referred to simply as "Aaron's rod that budded," whereas in Numbers 17:8, we are told that it "brought forth buds, and blossomed blossoms, and yielded almonds." We believe that the omission in Heb. 9:11 of the latter part of this statement is most significant. Numbers 17:8 refers to resurrection-life in three stages, all, of course, pointing to Christ. We would suggest that the "budding" of the rod found its fulfilment in the resurrection of Christ Himself; that the "blossomed blossoms" will receive its realisation in the resurrection of "them that are Christ's at His coming"; while the "yielded almonds" points forward to the raising of Israel from the dead who shall then fill the earth with fruit. As the "blossoming" and the "yielding almonds" is yet future, the Holy Spirit has most appropriately omitted these in Heb 9:4.

The third thing in the ark was tne two tables of stone on which were written the ten commandments. The reader will recall that the Lord gave to Moses on two separate occasions tables of stone engraved by His own finger. The first ones Moses dashed to the ground when he beheld the idolatry of the people (Ex. 32), thereby intimating that fallen man is unable to keep the law. But God's counsels cannot be thwarted, neither will He abate the requirements of His righteousness: "At that time the Lord said unto me, Hew thee two tables of stone like unto the first, and come up unto Me into the Mount, and make thee an ark of wood. And I will write in the tables the words that were in the first tables which thou breakest, and thou shalt put them in the ark" (Deut. 10:1-2).

The second set of tables of stone were deposited in the ark. The careful student will observe a notable omission in the above quotation from Deut. 10:1-2, an omission emphasised by its repetition in the next verse—"And I made an ark of shittim wood, and hewed two tables of stone." Nothing is said of the wood being overlaid with gold, nor of the cherubim of glory on its cover. It is simply said that the two tables of stone were to be placed in "an ark of wood." The law which fallen man had broken was to be preserved intact by the perfect **Man.** It was as "the second Man, the Last Adam" that Christ "magnified the law and made it honourable" (Isa. 42:21). How perfect is every jot and tittle of Scripture, even in its omissions!

The fulfilment of this aspect of our type is given in Psalm 40 where, speaking by the Spirit of prophecy, our glorious Surety exclaimed, "Lo, I come: in the volume of the book it is written of Me, I delight to do Thy will O My God · yea **Thy law is within My heart"** (vv. 7, 8). The blesses Substitute of God's elect was "made under the law" (Gal. 4:4), and perfectly did He "fulfil" it (Matt. 5:17). Therefore is it written "By the obedience of One shall many be made righteous" (Rom. 5:19), Christ has answered every requirement of God's law for His people. He has fully discharged all their creature responsibilities. In Christ, as our type plainly shows, and in Christ alone, is found that obedience which meets every demand of God's throne. Therefore may each believer joyfully exclaim **"In the Lord** have I righteousness" (Isa. 45:24). Thus can the whole ransomed Church hail its covenant Head as "The Lord our Righteousness" (Jer. 23:6).

In our next paper, God willing, we shall ponder the coverings of the ark, its various names, and its remarkable history. In the meantime may the Holy Spirit occupy both writer and reader, more and more, with Him whom the ark typified.

CHAPTER 36

THE ARK (*Continued*)

As the Ark is singled out from the seven pieces of furniture in the Tabernacle for special sanctity and prominence, and as so much more is recorded about its history than that of any of the other holy vessels, we felt it needful to devote two articles to its consideration. In the preceding one we pondered its importance; its significance, its materials, its dimensions and its contents. In this we shall deal with its coverings, its varied names or titles, and its remarkable career. May the Holy Spirit, whose office it is to take of the things of Christ and show them to His people, graciously enlighten our sin-darkened understandings and draw out our hearts in adoring worship to Him whom the Ark so strikingly perfigured.

5.—Its Coverings.

The actual cover or lid of the Ark was the mercy-seat, but it is not of this we shall now treat, as that will be the object of contemplation in the next article. The coverings of the Ark which we shall here notice are those which protected it as it was borne from place to place during the journeyings of Israel. These are suitably mentioned in Numbers—the Wilderness book. In Numbers 4: 5, 6, we read, "And when the camp setteth forward, Aaron shall come, and his sons, and they shall take down the covering vail, and cover the Ark of testimony with it: And shall put thereon the covering of badgers' skins, and shall spread over it a cloth wholly of biue, and shall put in the staves thereof."

First, the Ark was wrapped in tne "covering veil"—the most precious of all the curtains. The veil, as we learn from Heb. 10:20, typified the perfect humanity of Christ, rent for His people by the hand of God. This tells us that when God the Son was here in this wilderness-world His Divine glory was hidden from the eyes of men by His flesh, He who was in the form of God having taken upon Himself the form of a servant.

Second, over the covering veil was placed "the covering of badgers' skins." Unlike the skins of other animals,' the lion, tiger,or leopard, the badger's is quite unattractive. In Ezek. 16:10 we read of badgers' skins for making sandals, hence when used symbolically they would speak of lowliness. In our present type the badgers' skins tell of our Lord's humiliation, particularly that aspect of it from which nature turns away, saying, "He hath no form or comeliness, and when we shall see Him there is no beauty that we should desire Him"; but an aspect which those who through sovereign grace are in communion with Him, ever recognise as that which fills them with adoring love.

Third, the external covering of the Ark was "a cloth wholly of blue"—this alone being seen by men as the Ark was carried through the wilderness from place to place. It was this which distinguished the Ark, once more, from the other vessels, for all of them had the badgers' skins for their outer covering. Why, then, was the cloth of blue the external garment of the Ark? Blue is the colour of heaven and is ever employed for the setting forth of celestial things. All heavenly things are not suitable for testimony to the world, but Christ as the God-man is to be borne witness to before all!

6. Its Names.

"His name shall be called Wonderful" (Isa. 9:6) was the language of Messamiac prophecy, and strikingly was this foreshadowed by the different titles of the Ark. They are seven in number, and are wonderful for their variety, dignity and sublimity.

First, the ark was termed "the ark of the Testimony" (Ex. 25:22). This is the name by which it is most frequently called. It was thus designated because it was there that the "two tables of testimony" (31:18) were deposited for safe keeping. The Ark was given this appellation because it testified to the holiness and grace, the majesty and condescension of Jehovah. It was so denominated because Christ, to whom the Ark pointed, is the Centre of all God's counsels.

Second, the Ark was called "the ark of the covenant" (Num. 10:33). This brings before us a most blessed though much neglected subject, upon which we feign would linger, but must not. Christ is expressly termed the "Surety of a better testament" or covenant" (Heb. 7:23); of which He is also the Mediator (Heb. 9:6). This covenant is one into which He entered before the foundation of the world (Heb. 13:20), a covenant "ordered in all things and sure" (2 Sam. 23:5); a covenant in which Christ agreed to discharge all the obligations and responsibilities of His people.

Third, the Ark was named "the ark of the Lord, the Lord of all the earth" (Josh. 3:15). This title was used just after Israel had crossed the Jordan, when the unconquered land of Canaan lay before them. It was, at that time, filled with enemies. But there was the symbol and word of assurance—the Ark which went before them was the Ark of the Lord of all the earth. The antitypical fulfilment of this is yet future. When Christ returns He will find the inheritance occupied with usurpers. But a short work will He make of them: the enemy will be ejected and His own throne securely established—Zech. 14:9!

Fourth, the Ark was denominated "the Ark of God" (1 Sam. 3:3). This is very striking. God never identified Himself with any of the other vessels of the sanctuary. But how appropriate that He should do so with that which, in a special way, symbolized the person of Christ, How this title of the Ark pointed to the absolute Deity of Him who was made in the likeness of men.

Fifth, the Ark was entitled "the Ark of of the Lord God" (1 Kings 2:26)—in the Hebrew, "Adonai Jehovah." "Adonai" always has reference to **headship**, and to God's purpose of blessing. "Jehovah" is God in **covenant** relationship. The connection in which this particular name of the Ark occurs is most interesting and blessed. The first chapter of King's records a conspiracy at the close of David's reign, to prevent Solomon securing the throne. The second chapter tells how the conspirators and their abettors were dealt with after Solomon came to the throne: Adonijah and Joab were slain, but Abiathar, the priest, was spared because **he** had borne the Ark.

Sixth, the Ark was designated "the holy Ark" (2 Chron. 35:3). It was so spoken of by king Josiah, in whose days there was a blessed revival of true godliness. Preceding his reign there had been a long period of awful declension and apostasy, and the Ark was no longer kept in the Temple, therefore one of the first acts of Josiah was to give orders for the placing of the holy Ark in the House which Solomon had built. How this shows us that the holiness and majesty of Christ's person is only appreciated when God is working in power among His people!

Seventh, the Ark was spoken of as "the Ark of Thy strength" (Psa. 132:8). Lovely title was this. How it reminds us of that word: "I have laid help upon One that is mighty" (Psa. 89:19); and again, "Christ the power of God," "and the wisdom of God" (1 Cor. 1:24). Blessed be His name, there is no feebleness in our Redeemer; all power in heaven and earth is His. He is none other than "the migty God" (Isa. 9:6). O that His dear people may draw more and more from His fullness, proving that His strength is made perfect in their weakness.

7. Its Career.

By its career we have particular reference to its journeyings and history. Provision was duly made for the Ark to be carried while the Tabernacle was being borne from one camping place to another. "And thou shalt cast four rings of gold for it, and put them in the four corners thereof; and two rings shall be in the one side of it, and two rings in the other side of it. And thou shalt make staves of shittim wood, and overlay them with gold. And thou shalt put these staves into the rings by the sides of the Ark, that the Ark may be borne with them. The staves shall be in the rings of the Ark: they shall not be taken from it" (Ex. 25: 12-15).

"This shows that God's people were pilgrims in the wilderness, journeying on to the place which God had prepared for them. But the time would come when the inheritance should be possessed, and when the temple, suited in magnificence to the glory of the king of Israel should be built. The staves, which in the desert were not to be taken from the rings of the Ark, should then be withdrawn (2 Chron. 5:9), because the pilgrimage past, the Ark would, with the people, have entered into its rest (Psa. 132:8). The staves in the rings, therefore, speak of Christ with His pilgrim host, as being Himself with them in wilderness circumstances. It is Christ in this world, Christ in all His own perfectness as man—Christ, in a word, in all that He was as the revealer of God; for in truth, He was the perfect presentation of God to man" (Mr. Ed. Dennett).

Before we attempt to trace the actual career of the Ark, there is one other point to be considered concerning its history, namely, that before its journeyings commenced it was anointed. This is recorded in Ex. 30:26, "And thou shalt anoint the Tabernacle of the congregation therewith, and the Ark of the Testimony." The antitype is presented to us in Acts 10:38: "God anointed Jesus of Nazareth with the Holy Spirit and with power: who went about doing good and healing all that were oppressed of the devil." Notice the "anointing" of the Saviour occurred before He "went about doing good," just as the anointing of the Ark preceded its travels. The anointing of our Redeemer with the Holy Spirit took place at His baptism when, at the solemn inauguration of His public ministry, the Spirit came upon Him in the form of a dove (Matt. 3).

(1) "And they departed from the mount of the Lord three days' journey and the Ark of the covenant of the Lord went before them in the three days' journey, to search out a resting place for them" (Num. 10:33). Very blessed and beautiful is this. Lovely type was it of the Good Shepherd going before His sheep (John 10:4), leading them into the green pastures and beside the still waters. But the preciousness of the type here will be lost unless we attend to the context—note the "and" at the beginning of Numbers 10:33!

First, mark Numbers 9:18-20, where we have a notable instance of God's grace, and faithfulness in providing Israel with the cloud to guide them, intimating when they were to move and when to stop. Second, observe the failure of Moses. Forgetful of the Lord's promise to guide them, he desired to lean upon the arm of flesh, and said to his father-in-law, "Leave us not, I pray thee; forasmuch as thou knowest how we are to encamp in the wilderness, and thou mayest be to us instead of eyes" (10:31). Alas, what is man, even the best among men! Third, beautiful is it to see how mercifully the Lord intervened: the Ark was now to go before Israel as their guide—type of Christ as the **Leader** of His pilgrim people. As another has said, "In the path Homeward, the brightest human eyes and the keenest human wisdom are absolutely of no avail." The "three days'

journey" intimate that it is on **resurrection-ground** that the Lord directs His people.

(2) "But they presumed to go up unto the hill top: nevertheless the Ark of the covenant of the Lord and Moses departed not out of the camp" (Num. 14:44). The whole of this chapter is very solemn, recording as it does the judgment of God, which would descend upon a people who feared to follow the counsel of Caleb and Joshua. But the people believed not the Divine warning, and next morning, feeling the folly of their timidity on the previous day, determined to go up, and, in their own strength, disposes the enemy. Nevertheless the Ark and Moses departed not out of the camp. Therefore we need not be surprised at what follows: "Then the Amalekites came down, and the Canaanites which dwelt in that hill, and smote them, and discomfited them, even unto Hormah" (v. 45). What a solemn warning is this for us to-day: unless the Lord Himself is leading us, when we act simply in the energy of the flesh, failure and disaster are the sure consequence.

(3) Joshua 3: 5 to 17. This passage is too long for us to quote here, but let the student please turn to it and read it carefully ere he proceeds with our comments. Here we see Israel crossing the Jordan and the Ark going before them to open up a way through its waters. Though Israel's journey across the wilderness was one long record of unbelief, murmuring and rebelling, the Ark still continued to guide them, and now that the promised land was spread before their eyes conducted them into it. Blessed type was this of the marvellous and matchless long-suffering of God, who, notwithstanding all the sins and miserable failures of His people, has promised, "I will **never** leave thee nor forsake thee."

The Jordan is the river of judgment and a figure of death. The Ark of the Lord's presence entering Jordan, dividing its waters for Israel to pass over dryshod, is a type of the Lord Jesus suffering death for His people. "The fact that the Ark of the Lord had passed before them into Jordan and that its waters had dried up before it, was to be proof positive that the Lord would drive out all their enemies before them: the fact that Jesus entered death for us, received its sting, tasted what real death as the wages of sin is, exhausted its bitterness, is also certain proof to us that no enemy can ever prevent our final entrance into and enjoyment of the Heavenly Canaan. And this fact is of fullest blessing. The king of terrors is disarmed for us; he is powerless that had the power of death, and those are delivered who through fear of death were all their lifetime subject to bondage" (Mr. C. H. Bright). In consequence, those for whom Christ died shall never themselves receive the wages of sin. Fall asleep they may, but die they shall not: "If a man keep My saying, he shall never see death" (John 8:52); "Whosoever liveth and believeth on Me shall never die" (John 11:26).

(4). Joshua 6:4 to 20. Once again we would ask the student to read the Scripture before noting our brief remarks thereon. The one thing which we here single out for mention is that the Ark of the covenant **led the way** as Israel marched around the walls of Jericho. How plainly this teaches us that, if the strongholds of Satan are to fall before the people of God, if proud imaginations and every high thing that exalteth itself against the knowledge of God are to be cast down, it can only be under the immediate leadership of the Captain of our salvation. Notice how the "Ark" is mentioned no less than ten times in Joshua 6! The power was not in the trumpets, nor in the marching or shouting of the people, but in the Ark with its blood-sprinkled mercy-seat going before them; and strikingly did God bear witness to its efficacy.

(5). "And all Israel, and their elders, and officers, and their judges, stood on this side of the Ark and on that side before the priests and Levites, which bear the Ark of the covenant of the Lord, as well the stranger, as he that was born among them; half of them over against Mount Gerizim, and half of them over against Mount Ebal; as Moses the servant of the Lord had commanded before, that they should bless the people of Israel" (Josh. 8:33). Here a lovely scene is presented to us. At their first attempt to capture Ai, Israel had failed miserably, due to their pride and self-sufficiency—see 7:3. Deeply exercised in heart Joshua had sought unto Jehovah, who made known to him the sin of Achan. After that had been dealt with, the Lord assured Joshua (8:1) that He had given Ai into his hands. The sequel made this manifest: the city was burned and its king hanged. Then we are told, Joshua built an altar unto the Lord, upon whose stones He wrote the ten commandments, and then summoning all Israel together, read in their ears all the words of the law. But what is so blessed to behold is, that the Ark formed **the centre.** "And all Israel

. . . . stood on this side of the Ark and on that side." Precious figure was this of Christ in the midst of His assembly, and praise being rendered to Him for the victories He has wrought.

(6). "And the children of Israel inquired of the Lord, **for** the Ark of the covenant of God was there in those days (Judges 20:27). The chapter in which this is found records another of Israel's sad failures into which we must not now enter. The tribe of Benjamin had sinned grievously and the remaining tribes undertook to punish them. Though vastly superior in numbers, Israel was defeated. Then it was that they wept and fasted before the Lord, and inquired of Him. The reference to the Ark here, typically shows us that the mind of God can only be learned through and in **Christ.**

(7). 1 Sam 4: This chapter presents to us the sad spectacle of the Ark of God captured by the Philistines (v. 11)—permitted by God because of the apostasy of His people. Typically, this points to the humiliation of that One whom the Ark ever prefigured, and foreshadowed His being delivered into the hands of **the Gentiles!** Two details here emphasise what we have just said, and exceedingly striking they are. Connected with, yea, synchronising with, the Ark being laid hold of by the Philistines, was **the death of the high priest** (v. 18). According to the eternal counsels of God, the Lord Jesus was delivered into the hands of the Gentiles in order to the death of the great High Priest! Equally noteworthy were the words of Eli's daughter-in-law: "The glory of God is **departed** from Israel, because the Ark of God was taken" (v. 21). So it was with the Anti-type. With the delivering up of Christ into the hands of the Gentiles the glory of God departed from Israel!

(8). 1 Sam 5. This chapter traces the history of the Ark while it was away from Israel in the land of the Philistines. First, they took it into the house of Dagon, and set it before this idol. The sequel was startling: "And when they of Ashdod rose early on the morrow, behold Dagon was **fallen upon his face to the earth before the Ark of the Lord."** How forcibly this reminds us of what is mentioned in John 18: 3-6, when the officers came to arrest Christ they "fell to the ground before Him!" And afterwards God troubled the Philistines so severely they got rid of the Ark by sending it back to Israel. Did not this foreshadow the Gentiles' rejection of Christ, their aspostasy, and the subsequent return of Christ to the Jews!

(9). "And they set the Ark of God upon a new cart and brought it out of the house of Abinadab" (2 Sam. 6:3). In setting the Ark on a new cart (imitating the Philistines—1 Sam 6:7-11) they disregarded the Divine injunction—see Num. 3:27-31. "And when they came to Nachom's threshing floor, Uzzah put forth his hand to the Ark of God, and took hold of it; for the oxen shook it. And the anger of the Lord was kindled against Uzzah: and God smote him there for his rashness; and there he died by the Ark of God" (2 Sam 6: 6, 7). This was God's judgment because of their disobedience to His word. Numbers 4:15 specifically prohibited any from touching the holy things save the Levites, and Num. 1:51 threatened death. "David carried it aside into the house of Obed-edom the Gittite. And the Ark of the Lord continued in the house of Obed-edom three months. And the Lord blessed Obed-edom, and all his household" (vv. 10, 11). This gives us the other side of the typical picture—Divine grace flowing out to the Gentiles while Christ is with them (Acts 15:14).

(10). "So David went and fetched up the Ark of God from the house of Obed-edom into the city of David with gladness" (2 Sam. 6:12): with this should be carefully compared 1 Chron. 15, from which we learn that all was now done according to Divine order. "And they brought in the Ark of the Lord, and set it in his place, in the midst of the Tabernacle that David had pitched for it: and David offered burnt offerings and peace offerings before the Lord" (v. 17). It is exceedingly striking that after the Ark left the Tabernacle in the days of Eli, it is not again found in Jerusalem until the king chosen of God, the man after His own heart, had ascended the throne! In the days of Solomon the Ark was deposited in the Temple, indicative of Christ present in Israel's midst during the Millennium.

May the Lord add His own blessing to this little study and make it as refreshing to others as it has been to us.

CHAPTER 37

THE MERCY SEAT

EXODUS 25:17-22

The Mercy-seat was a solid sheet or slab of pure gold. Though a separate and distinct article in itself, it formed the lid of the Ark, being placed "above upon the Ark"; whose "crown of gold round about" (forming the top of its sides) would support and prevent it from slipping off. The Mercy-seat differed from the Ark in that no wood entered into its composition. There was only one other piece of furniture in the Tabernacle made solely of gold, namely, the candlestick, which was smaller in size and weight; therefore the Mercy-seat, according to its intrinsic worth, was the most valuable of all the holy vessels. How this tells us of the preciousness in the sight of God of that which the Mercy-seat foreshadowed.

The Mercy-seat, or better, the Propitiatory, derived its name from the blood of propitiation which was sprinkled thereon. It was the same length and breadth as the Ark, being two and a half by one cubit and a half. At either end of it was a cherub, not fastened thereto, but beate out of the same one piece of gold of which the Mercy-seat was formed. These symbolic figures had their wings outstretched, thus overshadowing the Mercy-seat, with their faces looking down upon · it. Let us now consider:—

1. Its Significance.

Concerning the typical meaning of the Mercy-seat there is quite a variety of interpretations offered to us. Some writers have been turned aside from the right track by dwelling upon the etymology of the Hebrew word, instead of seeking a definition from its usage in the Scriptures. Others have caused confusion through failing to distinguish between the respective foreshadowings of the brazen altar and the Mercy-seat. The real typical meaning of the Mercy-seat has been Divinely explained to us in Romans 3: 25, though the Authorised Version partly hides this from view: "Being justified freely by His grace through the redemption that is in Christ Jesus: whom God hath set forth to be a Propitiation (better, a "Propitiatory") through faith in His blood, to declare His righteousness for the remission of sins that are past." The Greek word here rendered "propitiation" is the identical one translated "Mercy-seat" in Hebrews 9: 5. Romans 3, then, declares that in the gospel God presents Christ before us as the antitypical Mercy-seat.

It were better, because less ambiguous, if we rendered "Kapporeth" (the Hebrew word) by "Propitiatory" rather than Mercy-seat; the added light from the New Testament not only justifies, but requires this change. Christ is the Mercy-seat, but He is so by virtue of the propitiation which He offered to God. In 1 John 2:2 and 4: 10 the Greek (in a different form from Romans 3: 25) is rightly rendered "propitiation," for in these verses the reference is to the Lord Jesus as the Sacrifice which pacifies God's offended justice; but the word in Romans 3: 25 is the one which is always employed in the Septuagint as the equivalent of "Kapporeth," and is actually translated "Mercy-seat" in Hebrews 9: 5. The Propitiatory was not the place where propitiation was made, but instead, the place where its abiding value was borne witness to before God. It is failure to mark this distinction which has resulted in so much confusion of thought.

The verb "to propitiate" signifies to appease, to placate, to make satisfaction. When, then, we read in Romans 3: 25 that Christ is now set forth a Propitiatory, the evident meaning is that, through the Gospel, God now bears testimony to His blessed Son as the One by whom He was propitiated, the One by whom His holy wrath against the sins of His people was pacified, the One by whom the righteous demands of His law were satisfied, the One by whom every attribute of Deity was glorified. The type of Christ as "the propitiation for our sins" is the bleeding victim on the altar; the type of Christ as God's resting place or Propitiatory is the Mercy-seat within the veil. Christ has become God's rest, in whom He can now meet poor sinners in all the fulness of His grace because of the propitiation made by Him on the cross.

The great propitiation which Christ made, and the propitiatory which is the result of it, were both borne witness to in the ritual of Israel's annual Day of Atonement. This is described for us in Lev. 16. Into the most interesting and important details of this chapter we cannot here enter; the one point bearing on our present theme being found in v. 14: "And he shall take of the blood of the bullock, and sprinkle it with his finger upon the Mercy-seat eastward, and before the Mercy-seat shall he sprinkle of the blood with his finger seven times." The blood (obtained through the death of the animal— type of propitiation) told of judgment already visited upon the innocent substitute; the blood sprinkled on the Propitiatory announced that God had accepted the victim offered to Him; the blood sprinkled before the propitiatory secured a standing-ground in God's presence. Once was sufficient for the eye of God; seven times grace suffered it to be sprinkled before the propitiatory, to assure us (who are so slow of heart to believe) of the perfectness of the standing-ground which Christ has procured for His people!

2. Its Purpose.

In the Tabernacle there was a table, but no chair for Aaron or any of the priests to sit on, because their work was never finished, needing constant repetition—emblematic of the fact that the one great Sacrifice, which would provide rest and satisfaction, was yet to come. But there was one seat, the Mercy-seat, reserved for Jehovah Himself, who sat there between the cherubim. This Mercy-seat, resting upon the Ark, foreshadowed the grand truth that God would find His rest in that perfect work which His incarnate Son should perform. The Mercy-seat, then, was God's throne here on earth. "And thou shalt put the Mercy-seat above upon the Ark; and in the Ark thou shalt put the testimony that I shall give thee. And there I will meet with thee, and I will commune with thee from above the Mercy-seat, from between the two cherubim which are upon the Ark of the testimony, of all things which I will

give thee in commandment unto the children of Israel" (vv. 21, 22).

The fact that the Mercy-seat formed God's throne in the midst of Israel is referred to in quite a number of Old Testament passages. In 1 Sam. 4: 4 we read, "So the people sent to Shiloh, that they might bring from thence the Ark of the covenant of the Lord of hosts, who dwelleth between the cherubim." In 2 Sam. 6; 2 it is said, "And David arose, and went with all the people that were with him from Baale of Judah to bring up from thence the Ark of God, whose name is called by the name of the Lord of hosts that dwelleth between the cherubim." Hezekiah addressed his prayer to Jehovah as "O Lord God of Israel, which dwellest between the cherubim" (2 Kings 19: 15). The Psalmist cried, "Give ear, O Shepherd of Israel, Thou that leadest Joseph like a flock; Thou that dwellest between the cherubim, shine forth." (Psa. 80: 1). In Psalm 99: 1 we are told, "The Lord reigneth; let the people tremble: He sitteth between the cherubim; let the earth be moved."

But now the question arises, How was it possible for the thrice holy God to dwell in the midst of a sinful people? The answer is, On the ground of accepted sacrifice. His throne was a blood-sprinkled one. This is shown us in Lev. 16: 14, already quoted. The blood of the sin-offering was sprinkled upon that Mercy-seat which constituted Jehovah's throne, and there that blood was left under His searching eye, as the abiding witness that the claims of His justice had been met, and that He could righteously dwell in the midst of a people who had broken His law— righteously, because their sin had been put away.

Now it is impossible to over-estimate the importance of thoroughly-settled views of God's satisfaction in Christ. Many Christians never get beyond the fact, though a precious fact it is, that Christ's death has procured and secured their life; and even this, in the case of many, is not maintained. The reason for this is that we listen so often to the dictates of our evil hearts of unbelief, which tell us that self must have a hand in the work of salvation, must contribute something to it—if not works, then feelings! But the truth is that God has entirely set aside ourself, and acted for Himself in saving us. God's glory and our salvation are indissoluably linked together. Accordingly we ought not only to enjoy the assurance of our eternal security, but also enter into a deeper communion with God's revealed thoughts concerning the power of Christ's blood in relation to His Throne in Heaven! It is this which the Mercy-seat or Propitiatory particularly and so blessedly typifies.

The Mercy-seat, which formed God's throne in Israel, then, directs our thoughts to the governmental aspect of the Atonement. Not only is it true that Christ died for sinners, but it is equally true—though in a different sense—that He died for God: He died in the stead of His sinful people, He died on behalf of the thrice holy God. Christ lived and died to make it possible for God to take hell-deserving sinners into fellowship with Himself, and that, consistently with His holiness and justice. He died to vindicate the character of God before all the intelligences of the universe. He died that God's throne might be established: "justice and judgment are the habitation (or "base") of Thy throne" (Psa. 89: 14). God's throne is settled in Christ, because all the claims of God's righteousness have been settled by Christ. The Antitype of this is most gloriously brought before us in Rev. 5: 6: "And I beheld, and, lo, in the midst of the throne. . . stood a Lamb as it had been slain"!!

"Whom God hath set forth a Propitiatory through faith in His blood to declare His righteousness" (Rom. 3: 25). To "declare" here signifies to make manifest, to proclaim and exhibit publicly. Divine righteousness requires that His law should be obeyed, and that its penalty should be enforced where its precepts have been broken. Divine mercy could not be exercised at the expense of justice, The character of God as the Ruler of the universe was involved. But the Antitype of the Mercy-seat sets forth the precious fact that God's avenging holiness was fully satisfied by the shedding of the blood of His Son on the cross. Justice, instead of being reduced to the necessity of taking a part from the bankrupt, has received full payment from the bankrupt's Surety and thus his deliverance is guaranteed. Thus Christ by His life of obedience "magnified the law and made it honourable" (Isa. 42: 21), and by His death glorified all the Divine perfections. God's love, grace, and mercy were manifested at Calvary as nowhere else; equally so were His holiness, justice and righteousness. For this reason, then, the Mercy-seat was made solely of pure gold—the Divine glory displayed. Propitiation has been made, and God points all to His Son, the Propitiatory, as the proof of it; just as the Mercy-seat with the blood sprinkled thereon attested that propitiation had been typically accomplished.

3. Its Dimensions.

It is not without good reason, for there is nothing meaningless or even trivial in God's Word, that the Holy Spirit has been pleased to give us the measurements of the Propitiatory. Its length was two and a half cubits and its breadth one cubit and a half. But nothing is told us of its thickness: does not this designed omission suggest what is recorded in Psalm 103: 112, "For as the heaven is high above the earth so great is His mercy toward them that fear Him"! What, then, are we to learn from the measurements which are recorded? This, its length and breadth were precisely the same as those of the Ark. The dimensions speak clearly of the strict limitations which God has set to His saving grace. As another has said, "It is all very well to say 'there's a wideness in God's mercy like the wideness of the sea,' but it is much better to understand clearly what is signified by the words 'two cubits and a half shall be the length, thereof, and a cubit and a half the breadth thereof.' God's mercy is, indeed, wide enough to take in every sinner who contritely presents himself at the appointed Mercy-seat, but it extends no further than that. The limits are Divinely established, and are unalterable."

There are some who count upon the love of God apart from Christ and His atoning death, which is virtually to devise a Mercy-seat which is wider than the Ark. But this is a vain delusion. God's grace reigns "through righteousness unto eternal life by Jesus Christ our Lord" (Rom. 5 :21). No grace can be shown unto any sinner apart from the redemptive blood of the Lord Jesus. "A just God and a Saviour" (Isa. 45: 21). Saving mercy is extended to none except those for whom Christ met the demands of Divine justice. There is much so-called Evangelism to-day which is condemned by the strictly defined dimensions of the Mercy-seat! Christ died not to make possible the salvation of the whole human race, but to make certain the salvation of God's elect: He made "propitiation for the sins of the people" (Heb. 2: 17. R.V.).

4. Its Ornamentation.

This was in the form of two cherubs, one on either end of the Mercy-seat, with wings outstretched over it, thus overshadowing and as it were protecting God's throne. That there is some profound and important significance connected with the figures of the cherubim is clear from the prominent place which they occupy in the Divine description of the Mercy-seat: if the student will re-read Exodus 25: 17-22 he will find that mention is made of them, either in the single or plural number, no less than seven times. Much has been written on the subject, but nothing we have seen is satisfactory.

The first time the "cherubim" are mentioned in Scripture is in Gen. 3: 24, where they are viewed guarding the way to the tree of life, the "flaming sword," seen in connection with them suggesting that they are associated with the administration of God's judicial authority. In Rev. 4: 6-8 (compare Ezekiel 1: 5-10) we find them related to the throne of God. Rev. 5: 11-14 indicates that the cherubim are the highest among the angelic order of creatures. In the Psalms and in Ezekiel the cherubim come before us in connection with judicial acts, with Divine interference in judgment, and this gives a striking significance to their place here on the Mercy-seat: God's righteousness, nay, His wrath against sin, is seen to be of one piece with His mercy! God's attributes do not conflict: light and love are but two sides of His nature!

On the Mercy-seat the two cherubim stood facing each other, attracted by a common object, heads bowed as in adoration. Their number speaks of competent witness. The subject is too vast for us to even outline here, but there is more than one hint in Scripture that the redemption of the Church is an object lesson unto the angels. 1 Cor. 4: 9 declares that the suffering apostles were "made a spectacle (theatre) unto angels." Eph. 3: 10 tells us that "the manifold wisdom of God is now being made known by (through) the Church unto the principalities and powers in the heavenlies." 1 Peter 1: 11, 12 announces that the sufferings of Christ and His glories which were to follow are "things which the angels desire to look into." We take it, then, that the figures of the two cherubim, with their bowed heads over the Mercy-seat, denote the interest of the angelic hierarchies in the unfolding of God's redemptive purpose.

5. Its Blessedness.

First, this comes out in the fact that the Mercy-seat completely hid from view the tables of stone which were kept in the Ark. As the cherubim stood there with their faces downward, they saw not those holy statutes which condemned their transgressors; instead, they gazed on that which spoke of the glory of God—Deity magnified by sacrifice. There was blood between the law and its Administrator and His executors!

Suppose an Ark with no Mercy-seat: the Law would then be uncovered: there would be nothing to hush its thunderings, nothing to arrest the execution of its righteous sentence. The law expresses God's righteousness, and demands the death of its violator: "Cursed is everyone that continueth not in all things which are written in the book of the Law to do them" (Gal. 3: 10). Such is the inevitable judgment pronounced on all sinners by the inexorable sentence of the law. The only man who could stand before God on the basis of having kept that law was the Man Christ Jesus. He could have been justified by it, enthroned upon it, and from it have pronounced sentence of just doom on all of Adam's guilty race. But He did not do so. No; blessed be His name, instead of coming to earth as the Executioner of the law, He bared His holy bosom to its righteous sword. The same heart which held the law unbroken (Psalm 40: 8) received the penalty which was due His people for having broken it. The storm of wrath having spent itself upon Him, the law can no longer touch those who have fled to Him for refuge. It is of this that the blood-sprinkled Mercy-seat, covering the tables of stone within the Ark, so blessedly speaks.

A nation of transgressors could never stand before the naked law. An uncovered Ark furnishes naught but a throne of judgment. This supplies the key to a passage in the Old Testament that has puzzled many. When the Philistines sent back the Ark, which Jehovah had suffered to fall into their hands, we are told, "And He smote the men of Beth-shemesh, because they had looked into the Ark of the Lord, even He smote of the people fifty thousand and three score and ten men: and the people lamented, because the Lord had smitten many of the people with a gross slaughter. And the men of Beth-shemesh said, Who is able to stand before this holy Lord God?" (1 Sam. 6: 19-20). The sin which God here punished so severely was Israel's daring to uncover what God had covered. In order to "look into the Ark" the Mercy-seat had to be removed, and in removing it they exposed the Law, and thus severed mercy from judgment, the result of which must ever be, death for the guilty. The thrice holy God can only meet the guilty, polluted sinner, in Him by whom "righteousness and peace have kissed each other" (Psa. 85: 9). No man can draw near unto the Father but by Him.

Second, the Mercy-seat was the place where Jehovah met the sinner in the person of His representative: "And he (Aaron) shall take of the blood of the bullock, and sprinkle it with his finger upon the Mercy-seat eastward; and before the Mercy-seat shall he sprinkle of the blood with his finger seven times" (Lev. 16: 14). This tells us that Christ is the one appointed Meeting-place between God and His people, the place where He meets with them not in judgment but in grace. But be it remembered that the typical Mercy-seat was in the holy of holies, hidden from the view of the sinner who desired to approach God. So it is with the Antitype: God's throne of grace is not visible to the eye of sense; it can be approached only by faith. Hence the exhortation of Heb. 10, "Having therefore, brethren, boldness to enter into the holiest by the blood of Jesus, By a new and living way, which He hath newly-made for us, through the veil, that is to say, His flesh; and having an high priest over the house of God; Let us draw near with a true heart in full assurance of faith" (vv. 19-22).

Third, the Mercy-seat is the place of communion: "And there I will meet with thee, and I will commune with Thee from above the Mercy-seat, from between the two cherubim, which are upon the Ark of the testimony" (Ex. 25: 22). A beautiful example of this is furnished in Numbers 7: 89: "And when Moses was gone into the Tabernacle of the congregation to speak with Him, then he heard the voice of One speaking unto him from off the Mercy-seat that was upon the Ark of testimony, from between the two cherubim: and he spake unto Him." Precious indeed is this. It is in the Lord Jesus that Christians have been brought into this place of inestimable blessing. Not only have we been brought nigh to God, but we are permitted to speak to Him and hear Him speaking to us. Having been reconciled to God by the death of His Son, He now says "I will commune with thee." Wondrous grace is this! O that our hearts may enter into and enjoy this blessed privilege. Then "Let us come boldly unto the throne of grace." There is nothing between: no sin, no guilt; and the veil has been rent. We may worship in the Holy of Holies! Then "Let us draw near in full assurance of faith."

CHAPTER 38

THE TABLE

EXODUS 25:23-30

Having described the contents of the innermost chamber of the Tabernacle, the Holy Spirit now conducts us into the Holy-place. In the former the high priest ministered on the annual day of atonement, in the latter the Levites served daily. In this second chamber stood three pieces of furniture: the table, the candlestick, and the altar of incense. The order in which these are brought before us in the sacred narrative is most suggestive, and the very reverse of what would have occurred to us. We had surely put the golden altar of incense first, then the seven-branched candlestick, and last, the table. But God's thoughts and ways are ever the opposite of ours. When we see what the table stood for, perhaps we shall the better appreciate the Divine arrangement.

As it was in the innermost shrine, so it is in the holy place—nought but gold met the eye of him who had entered: it was therefore a scene displaying the Divine glory. Silence reigned in the sacred apartment. No prayers were offered, no songs of praise were sung. The voice of man was still, but the voice of the golden vessels therein mutely, yet eloquently, spoke of Christ; for the light of the knowledge of the glory of God shines "in the face of Jesus Christ" (2 Cor. 4: 6). None but the priestly family ever penetrated this sacred precinct, telling us that only those who, by wondrous grace, are "an holy priesthood," those who by sovereign mercy are "a chosen generation, a royal priesthood" (1 Peter 2: 5, 9), can enter into the spiritual significance of its symbolic contents. Coming now to the Table, let us consider:—

1. Its Meaning.

In seeking to ascertain the spiritual purport of the Table the first thing which arrests our attention in the Divine description of it is the word "also" in Exodus 25: 23—found only once more in

connection with the holy vessels and furnishings of the Tabernacle, see 30: 18. The "also" at the beginning of our present passage suggests a close link of connection with what has gone before. In the preceding verse we read, "And there will I meet with thee, and I will commune with thee from above the Mercy-seat," and then following right after this, "Thou shalt also make a Table." Thus God has graciously hung the key right over the entrance, and told us that the Table has to do with communion. This is in full accord with other scriptures where the "table" is mentioned.

A lovely picture of that blessedness of which the "table" speaks is found in 2 Sam. 9. There we find David asking "Is there yet any that is left of the house of Saul, that I may show him kindness for Jonathan's sake?" (v. 1). A beautiful illustration is this of the wondrous grace of God, showing kindness to those who belong to the house of His enemies, and that for the sake of His Beloved One. There was one, even Mephibosheth, lame on his feet; him David "sent and fetched" unto himself. And then to show that he was fully reconciled to this descendant of his arch-enemy, David said, "Mephibosheth shall eat bread always at my table" (v. 10); showing that he had been brought into the place of most intimate fellowship.

In 1 Cor. 10 we are also taught that the "table" is inseparably connected with communion: "But I say, that the things which the Gentiles sacrifice, they sacrifice to demons, and not to God: and I would not that you should have fellowship with demons. Ye cannot drink the cup of the Lord, and the cup of demons: ye cannot be partakers of the Lord's table, and of the table of demons" (vv. 20, 21). The "Lord's table" is the symbol of fellowship with Christ, in separation from all that owns not His authority and denies His claims and rights.

Returning now to the "also" with which our passage opens and noting its relation to the immediate context, we learn that the blood-sprinkled Mercy-seat speaks of Christ as the **basis** of our fellowship with God, while the Table points to Christ as the **substance** of that fellowship. What we have here is the person of Christ as the Food of God and the One in whom He has communion with His people. The Table sets forth Jehovah's feast of love for His saints and for Himself in fellowship with them. This will be still more evident when we ponder the Contents of the Table, meanwhile let us turn to:—

2. Its Composition.

Like the Ark, the table was made of shittim wood (v. 23), overlaid with pure gold. Both typified the union of Deity and humanity in the person of Christ. It is indeed striking to observe, and important to note, the several points of oneness between the ark and the table. They were both of the same height—the only pieces of furniture that were so. They were both ornamented with a crown of gold. They were both provided with rings and staves. They both had something placed upon them: the one, the Mercy-seat; the other, the twelve cakes of bread. These points of likeness emphasise the truth that it is the person of the God-man which is the basis of all communion with God.

"The natural suggestion of a "table" is a place for food, and the food upon it. 'Thou preparest a table before me in the presence of mine enemies' (Psa. 23: 5). We will find this thought of food linked with our Lord's **person** in the sixth chapter of John: 'Verily, verily, I say unto you, Moses gave you not that bread from heaven; but My Father giveth you the true bread from heaven. For the bread of God is He which cometh down from heaven, and giveth life unto the world (John 6: 32, 33). The One who 'came down from heaven' reminds us of the deity of our Lord; this is the gold.

" 'I am the living bread which came down from heaven: if any man eat of this bread, he shall live forever; and the bread that I will give is My flesh, which I will give for the life of the world. The Jews therefore strove among themselves, saying, How can this man give us His flesh to eat? Then Jesus said unto them, Verily, verily, I say unto you, except ye eat the flesh of the Son of man, and drink His blood, ye have no life in you.'

(John 6: 51, 52). Evidently our Lord here is speaking of His death. But His death presupposes His incarnation. He must become man that He may die. We have in this way the twofold truth of our Lord's deity and His humanity linked together, and put before us in this chapter, where He is presented as the Bread of life. We have thus the gold and the acacia wood which form the table" (Mr. S. Ridout). Let us turn next to:—

3. Its Dimensions.

"Thou shalt also make a table of shittim wood: two cubits shall be the length thereof, and a cubit the breadth thereof, and a cubit and a half the height thereof" (Ex. 25: 23). Thus the Table was the same height as the Ark, though it fell short of its length and breadth. This intimates that though our communion with God rises to the level of our apprehension of the two natures in the person of His beloved Son, yet there is a breadth or fulness of perfection in Him which we fail to realize and enjoy. The length of the Table was two cubits, which supplies an additional hint to the meaning of this piece of furniture, for one of the significations of two is that of communion—"How can two walk together except they be agreed?" (Amos. 3: 3). In breadth the Table was one cubit, which speaks of **unity**, for there can be no fellowship where there is discord.

4. Its Contents.

"And thou shalt set upon the table shewbread before Me alway" (v. 30). This shewbread consisted of twelve loaves or cakes, made of fine flour; baked, and placed in two rows upon the Table, on which was sprinkled pure frankincense for a memorial. Here they remained before the Lord for seven days, when they were removed and eaten by Aaron and his sons, in the holy place—see Lev. 24: 5-9.

There is much difference of opinion as to the precise typical purport of these twelve loaves. One class of commentators see in them a figure of the twelve tribes of Israel presented before the Lord, but these offer no satisfactory interpretation of this bread being eaten afterwards by the priestly family. Others see in the loaves a foreshadowing of Christ as the Food of God and His children, but they are far from clear as to why there should be twelve loaves and why these were placed in two rows of six. Personally we believe there is a measure of truth in each view, but great care needs to be taken in seeking accurate expression.

It is clear that the thoughts suggested by the Table and by the bread placed upon it are intimately related, for later on we find the Table taking its name from the loaves thereon: in Numbers 4: 7 it is called the "Table of Shewbread." But though they are closely connected Heb. 9: 2 teaches us they have a distinctive significance and are to be considered separately. A close parallel to this is found in 1 Cor. 10 and 11: in the former we read of "the Lord's table" (v. 21), in the latter of "the Lord's supper" (v. 20): the one speaking of the character of our fellowship, the other of what forms the substance of our fellowship. This, we believe, supplies the key to the distinction in our type: the Table pointing to the person of Christ as the Sustainer of fellowship between God and His saints, the bread directing our thoughts to Christ as the substance of it.

The bread on the Table points first, as does everything in the Tabernacle, to Christ Himself. The name by which it is called clearly indicates this—"shewbread" is, literally, "bread of faces," faces being put by a figure for presence —pointing to the Divine presence in which the bread stood: "shewbread before Me alway." The fact that the bread was before the face of God always, told of its acceptableness to Him, and foreshadowed the person of Christ as the One in whom the Father has ever found His delight. In Lev. 24: 5 the bread on the Table is described as "twelve cakes," and Young's Concordance gives as the meaning of challoth "perforated" cakes. How solemnly significant! This bread which spoke of Christ had been pierced! The fine flour in the form of cakes, which had therefore been baked, points to the Lord Jesus as having been exposed to the fires of God's holy wrath, when on the cross He was made sin for His people.

But why twelve pierced cakes? Clearly this number has specially to do with Israel and suggests the different tribes being here represented before God. But representation implies a representative, and it is at this point that so many have missed the lesson. That which is here so blessedly symbolized is the Lord Jesus identifying Himself with God's covenant people. There is a striking passage in the New Testament which brings out—under this figure of bread —the identification of the Lord with His people and they with Him, "The cup of blessing which we bless, is it not the communion of the blood of Christ? The bread which we brake, is it not the communion of the body of Christ? For we being many are one bread, and one body: for we are all partakers of that one bread" (1 Cor. 10: 16, 17).

The twelve loaves then speak of Christ in immediate connection with His people. "The marvellous fact that Jehovah condescends to receive into fellowship with himself the people of His choice, is mirrored on every feature of the Tabernacle ritual. They were always before Him on the priestly mitre, breastplate, and shoulder-stones, and on the shewbread table. And surely this Old Testament symbolism finds its prophetic complement in New Testament fact, for by its revelation believers are said to be presented faultless in the presence of His glory, unreproveable and unrebukable in His sight—Col. 1: 22" (Mr. G. Needham).

The cakes were all of the same quality, size and weight, showing that the smallest tribe was represented equally with the greatest. In spreading them out in two rows, instead of piling them up in a heap, each one would be seen equally as much as another. Our acceptance in Christ and our representation by Him admits of no degrees. All of God's covenant people have an equal standing before Him, and an equal nearness to Him.

The cakes were made of "fine flour" (Lev. 25: 5) in which was no grit or unevenness, foreshadowing the moral perfections of the Word as He tabernacled among men. "Pure frankinscence" was placed upon them, emblematic of the active graces of Christ, and assuring us that those who are in Christ are ever before God according to the value and fragrance of His blessed Son. Every Sabbath these cakes were renewed, so that they were "before the Lord continually" (Lev. 24: 8); never was the Table unsupplied. "The loaves being placed on the Table every Sabbath day may accord with the fact that it was when the spiritual sabbath, the rest for our souls, obtained by Christ's atonement, was gained, that He took His place in the presence of God for us" (Mr. C. H. Bright). Each cake contained two "tenth deals" or omers of flour (Lev. 24: 5). This is indeed precious. A double portion is the thought suggested (contrast Exodus 16: 16, 36), foreshadowing the truth that Christ is the Food or delight of both God and His people. In Lev.

21: 21 it is expressly called "The bread of his (the priest's) God.

"And it shall be Aaron's and his sons; and they shall eat it in the holy place" (Lev. 25: 9). This bread which had been before Jehovah seven days, was now enjoyed by the priestly family. It speaks of Christ as the One who delights both the heart of the Father and His beloved people. "Eating" indicates identification and communion with what we feed upon: compare again 1 Cor. 10: 16, 17. The twelve cakes on the Table speak of Christ identified with His covenant people—not simply Israel after the flesh, for note "everlasting covenant" in Lev. 24: 8; the cakes eaten by the priestly family, His people identifying themselves (by faith's appropriation) with Christ! But this eating must be in "the holy place": we can only really feed upon Christ as we are in communion with God. The eating of the twelve cakes on "the Sabbath day" prophetically hints at the literal Israel's appropriation of Christ in the great dispensational Sabbath, the millennium.

5. Its Ornamentation.

"And thou shalt overlay it with pure gold, and make thereto a crown of gold round about. And thou shalt make unto it a border of an hand-breadth round about, and thou shalt make a golden crown to the border thereof round about" (vv. 24, 25). The "crown" speaks of Christ glorified—"a crown of glory" (1 Peter 5: 4)—now at the right hand of God for us, "crowned with glory and honour" (Heb. 2: 9). The crowned border on the top of the Table was for the purpose of protection, guarding whatever was placed upon it. The bread was not removed from the Table even when Israel was on the march (Numbers 4: 7), and the raised border would hold the cakes in place, preventing them from slipping off. This tells of the absolute security of that people with whom the incarnate Son has identified Himself.

First, the Table itself was encircled with "a crown of gold" (v. 24). "It is 'the glory of His grace' (Eph. 1: 6) that is suggested by the loaves of bread held in their place by the crown. It is a glorified Christ who maintains His own, according to all that He is" (S. Ridout). Beautifully is this brought out here in the measurement that is given "a border of an handbreadth round about," which is the more striking because all the other dimensions in the Tabernacle are

cubits or half cubits. How blessedly does this border of the handbreadth round about point to that which guarantees the eternal preservation of all Christ's redeemed: "Neither shall any pluck them out of My hand" (John 10: 28)!

Everything here about the ornamentation speaks of the security of the cakes and of those whom they typified. The Hebrew word "border" means "enclosing," and in 2 Sam. 22: 46 it is rendered "close places." Again, observe that this border of an hand-breadth was, in turn, protected by "a golden crown" (v. 25). This announces that the very glory of God is concerned in the preservation of His people: His honour is at stake:—"He leadeth me in the paths of righteousness for His name's sake" (Psalm 23: 3). How often Moses fell back upon this: see Exodus 32: 11-13; Numbers 14: 13-19, etc.!

The same thought is emphasised and reiterated by the second "crown," for the "border" had one as well as the Table—vv. 24, 25. "Again we are confronted with the precious grace that each believer, all believers, are secured by God. The highest revealed blessings are theirs, and these cannot be alienated, nor the believer removed from the position given him. Christ, the Table, maintains him before God; Christ, the border, secures him there. The border too has a crown as well as the Table. There is a certain glory attaching to our maintenance, and further a glory attaching to our security. If a believer could be lost, if anything could impair his security, if the border could be damaged, the crown must share it, and the very glory of Christ must be sullied. Impossible! 'Neither shall any pluck them out of my hand' (John 10: 28)." (Foreshadowments by E. C. Pressland).

There is one other detail which perhaps falls under this present division of our subject. In v. 29 we read, "and thou shalt make the dishes thereof, and spoons thereof, and covers thereof, and bowls thereof, to cover withal: of pure gold shalt thou make them" (v. 29). The "dishes" would no doubt be used when the bread was removed from the Table and eaten by the priestly family. The "spoons" and the "cover" would be employed in connection with the frankincense. The "bowls thereof to cover withal" should be rendered "the cups to pour out withal"—see margin of Authorised Version. These "cups" were used in connection with the "drink offerings" which were poured out before the Lord "in the holy place" (Num. 28: 7). The "drink-offerings" expressed **thanksgiving**. The fact that the "cups," used in connection with the drink-offerings, were placed upon the Table, tells us that **communion** is the basis of thanksgiving!

6. Its Rings and Staves.

These are described in Exodus 25: 26-28 and tell of provision made for journeying. "The children of Israel were pilgrims in the wilderness and hence the Tabernacle and all its furniture were made for them in this character, and accompanied them in all their wanderings" (Mr. E. Dennett). Thus the particular detail in the type now before us speaks of the provision which God has made for His people in Christ while they pass through this world. That provision is feeding upon Christ Himself in communion with God. Wherever Jehovah led the Hebrews, His Table accompanied them! So wherever the Christian's lot may be cast, even though it be for years in jail like Bunyan, there is ever a precious Christ to feed upon and commune with!

7. Its Coverings.

These are described in Numbers 4: 7, 8. They were three in number. First a cloth of blue draped the Table, its bread and its utensils; over this was spread a cloth of scarlet, and on the outside of all was cast a covering of badger's skins. These were only used while Israel was on the march. The Table standing in the holy place speaks of Christ now on high as God's bread and ours. The Table accompanying Israel in their journeyings, with its threefold covering, reminds us of the varied perfections manifested by Christ as He passed through this wilderness scene, the contemplation of which is an essential part of our food.

First, came the cloth of blue, which points to Christ as the Bread **from Heaven**. Seven times over in John 6 did our Lord thus announce Himself. If Christ be not recognised and enjoyed as wholly above and beyond all that this earth can yield, there will be no true devotion nor any scriptural testimony to Him. But let Him be known as the heavenly portion of the soul and these are secured. It is most significant to note that this first covering was seen only by the eyes of the priestly family.

Second, came the cloth of scarlet. According to its scriptural usage "scarlet" is the emblem of **earthly glory**, as may be seen by a reference to its various occurrences. This colour was so called because it was obtained from a worm, in fact was named after it, the same Hebrew word being variously translated "scarlet" or "worm" as the connection requires. There is something most appropriate in this, for truly the glory of man is that of a perishing worm. How then are these two thoughts, so dissimilar, to be combined, in connection with Christ? Does not Psalm 22: 6—the **cross**-Psalm—tell us? There we find the Saviour saying "I am a **worm** (same word as "scarlet") and no man." Thus the "scarlet" reminds us of the **glory** of the cross (Gal. 6: 14). The Lord Jesus, by becoming a "worm," by His cross brought forth the true glory. Another glory shall be manifested by Him (Col. 3: 3) when He returns to the earth. This second covering also was seen only by the priests!

Third, the external covering was one of badgers' skins, and met the eyes of all as the Table was borne through the wilderness. This typified our Lord's **humiliation**. This covering was provided to **protect** the Table and its inner coverings from the defiling dust and atmosphere of the wilderness. We are thus reminded not only of the unattractiveness to men's eyes of the servant-form which our Saviour took, but also of His personal holiness, repelling all the unholy influences of this defiling world. No speck or stain ever fouled the Holy One of God—He touched the leper without being polluted; nothing of earth could in anywise tarnish His ineffable glory.

It is thus that the Spirit of God would have the saints contemplate Him who is their appointed Food: as the One who is heavenly in His nature and character, as the One who came down to this earth and glorified Himself and the Father by His obedience unto death, and as the One who through His holy vigilance repelled all evil and kept Himself from the path of the Destroyer. Thus contemplated our meditation of Him will be "sweet."

CHAPTER 39

THE LAMPSTAND

EXODUS 25:31-40

The particular piece of the Tabernacle's furniture which is now to engage our attention, is, in our English Bibles termed the "Candlestick," but we believe that this is a very faulty rendition of the Hebrew word. Why term it a "Candlestick" when no candles were burned thereon? It strikes the writer that such a translation is a relic of Romish perversion. "M'nourah" means "lightbearer" or "lampstand," and thus we shall refer to it throughout this article. The fact that it had "seven lamps" (Ex. 25: 25, 37) and that these were fed with "oil" (Lev. 24: 2, 4) is more than sufficient to warrant this correction.

The Lampstand was in the Holy Place. This was the chamber entered by none save the priestly family, and was the place where these favoured servants of Jehovah ministered before Him. It was therefore the place of communion. In keeping with this, each of the three vessels that stood therein spoke of fellowship. The Table, with its twelve loaves, pointed to Christ as the Substance of our fellowship, the One on whom we feed. The Lampstand foreshadowed Christ as the power for fellowship, as supplying the light necessary to it. The Incense-altar, prefigured Christ as maintaining our fellowship, by His intercession securing our continued acceptance before the Father.

The fact that the Lampstand stood within the Holy Place at once shows us that it is not Christ as "the Light of the world" which is typified. It is strange that some of the commentators have erred here. The words of Christ on this point were clear enough: "As long as I am in the world, I am the Light of the world" (John 9: 5)—then only was He manifested here as such. So again in John 12: 35, 36 He said to the people, "Yet a little while is the Light with you . . . while ye have light, believe in the light, that ye may be the children of light." But they loved darkness rather than light. The world rejected the Light, and so far as they were concerned extinguished it. Since He was put to death by wicked hands, the world has never again gazed on the Light. He is now hidden from their eyes.

But He who was put to death by the world, rose again, and then ascended on High. It is there in the Holy Place, in God's presence, the Light now dwells. And while there—O marvellous privilege —the saints have access to Him. For them the veil is rent, and thus the Holy Place and the Holy of Holies are no longer two separate compartments, but one; and, the substance of all that was shadowed forth by the sacred vessels in each is now the wondrous portion of those who, by grace, are "built up a spiritual house, an holy priesthood, to offer up spiritual sacrifices acceptable to God by Jesus Christ" (1 Peter 2: 5).

Black shadows rest upon the world which has cast out the Light of Life: "the way of the wicked is as darkness" (Prov. 4: 19). It is now night-time because the "Dayspring from on High" is absent. The Lampstand tells of the gracious provision which God has made for His own beloved people during the interval of darkness, before the Sun of righteousness shall rise once more and usher in for this earth that morning without clouds. The Lampstand is for the night season! Therefore the illuminating Lampstand speaks of Christ neither in the days of His first advent nor of the time of His second advent, but of the interval between, when those who have access into the true sanctuary walk in the light as He is in the light (1 John 1: 7). Let us now consider:—

1. Its Composition.

"And thou shalt make a Lampstand of pure gold: of beaten work shall the lampstand be made" (v. 31). Unlike the ark and the table of shewbread, no wood entered into the composition of the Lampstand. It was of solid gold. But there is one word here which has been overlooked by almost all the commentators, and by losing sight of it their interpretations have quite missed the mark. The Lampstand, though made of pure gold, was "of beaten work," that is to say, the talent of gold from which it was made was wrought upon by the hammers of skilled workmen until it was shaped into a beautiful and symmetrical form. Only by Divinely-given wisdom could they evolve from a solid talent of gold this richly ornamented vessel with base, shaft and branches, in consistent proportions (Ex. 31: 6).

What is before us now in our present type is the more noteworthy in that the Lampstand was the only vessel or portion of the Tabernacle which was made of "beaten work." It is in striking contrast from the "golden calf" which Aaron made, for that was cast in a mould (Ex. 32: 4). What is idolatrous or according to man's mind, can be quickly and easily cast into shape; but that which has most of all glorified God and secured the redemption of His people was wrought at great cost. Clearly, the "beaten gold" here speaks of a suffering Christ glorified, glorified as the reward of His perfect but painful Work.

That the "pure gold" speaks of the divine side of things is obvious, for the One that is here prefigured was none other than the God-man. It was His deity which sustained His humanity. Had Christ been merely a creature He had completely succumbed to the storm of judgment which burst upon Him. It was His deity which enabled Him to suffer within the compass of a brief span what otherwise would have been the eternal portion of all His people. But after all, the primary thought in the "gold" is glory as Heb. 9: 5 teaches us, and the beaten gold plainly foreshadowed the glorification of Him who was beaten with many stripes on our behalf.

"Of a talent of pure gold shall he make it" (v. 39). This would be worth more than five thousand pounds, upwards of twenty-five thousand dollars. A "talent" was one hundred and twenty lbs., so that sufficient gold was provided to ensure the Lampstand being of a goodly size. Most probably it stood higher than the Table or the Incense-altar, for by its light the priests were enabled to attend to the one and minister at the other. Thus was foreshadowed not only the preciousness of the person of our Redeemer, but also His sufficiency to make manifest the perfections of the Godhead.

2. Its Construction.

The pattern of the Lampstand is described in Ex. 25: 31-36. It consisted of one central stem, with three lateral branches springing from either side. Each branch was adorned with knops, flowers and bowls. The "knops" seem to have been buds, probably of the almond; the "bowls" were for holding the oil which fed the lights. Upon the end of each branch was the bowl or lamp. All was of one piece, beaten out by workmen endowed with divine skill.

The seven lamps while an intrinsic part of the Lampstand itself, may also be contemplated separately. This seems clear from the fact that in Numbers 8: 2 we read, "When thou lightest the lamps, the seven lamps shall give light over against the Lampstand." The accuracy of the type here is most impressive. The sevenfold radiance of the Lampstand speaks of Christ as the "brightness of God's glory" (Heb. 1: 3). It tells of His perfections as the Light. It is worthy of note that when the white light is broken into its varied parts we have just seven colors, as seen in the rainbow. But it is equally clear that the seven "lamps" also symbolise the Holy Spirit in the plenitude of His power and perfections—the "seven Spirits which are before His throne" (Rev. 1: 4). That the type appears to overlap at this point, or rather, has a double application, only shows its marvellous and minute accuracy, for in His ministry toward and in believers, the Spirit works as "the Spirit of Christ" (Rom. 8: 9; 1 Peter 1: 11).

The fact that the seven lamps were supported by the Lampstand foreshadowed the fact that the Spirit, given to us, has come from our glorified Redeemer. There are several scriptures which prove this. The Lord Jesus said to His apostles, "When the Comforter is come, whom I will send from the Father" (John 15: 26). On the day of Pentecost, when explaining the outpouring of the Spirit's gifts, Peter distinctly attributed them to the ascended Christ: "Therefore being by the right hand of God exalted, and having received of the Father the promise of the Spirit He hath shed forth this, which ye now see and hear" (Acts 2: 36). So also in Rev. 3: 1 Christ is spoken of as "He that hath the seven Spirits of God."

3. Its Ornamentation.

"And six branches shall come out of the sides of it; three branches of the Lampstand out of the one side, and three branches of the Lampstand out of the other side: Three bowls made like unto almonds, a knop and a flower in one branch; and three bowls made like almonds in the other branch, a knop and a flower; so in the six branches that come out of the Lampstand." (vv. 32, 33). Mr. S. Ridout has offered an illuminating suggestion that the "knop" might portray the rounded unopened bud, so that the central stem and each of its branches would be ornamented with that which set forth the three stages of the almond—the bud, the flower and the ripened fruit. He has also pointed out how that this suggestion receives confirmation in what is recorded of Aaron's rod in Numbers 17: "Behold, the rod of Aaron for the house of Levi was budded, and brought forth buds, and blossomed blossoms and yielded almonds" (v. 8). Thus the three stages of life were also seen on the branches of the Lampstand—bud, flower, fruit.

The prominence of the "almond" on the Lampstand supplies an important key to its interpretation. It corresponds closely, though it is not exactly parallel in thought with what is foreshadowed in the "acacia (shittim) wood" in the other vessels. The "wood" speaks of the incorruptible humanity of Christ. The "almond" is the emblem of resurrection, here the resurrection of the Lord Jesus, which, of course, presupposes His incarnation. It is not so much the holiness of His humanity which is here foreshadowed, as it is the glory of the Risen One—the "almonds of gold"!

The "almond" is the first of all trees in Palestine to bud, manifesting the new life of spring as early as January. The Hebrew word for "almond" means "vigilent," and is used with this significance in Jer. 1: 11, 12: "And I said, I see a rod of an almond tree. And Jehovah said unto me, Thou hast well seen; for I am watchful over My word to perform it." God has seen to it that His every promise has been vindicated and substantiated in a risen Christ. That the "almond" is the emblem of resurrection is further established in Numbers 17. The twelve rods, cut off from the trees on which they grew, were lifeless things. The budding of Aaron's rod manifested a re-impartation of life—the work of God. Aaron's rod not only exhibited the signs of life, but produced the full results of it, in bud and flower and fruit—and that of the "almond"! So, too, our Saviour was, according to the flesh, "a rod out the stem of Jesse" (Isa. 11: 1) and was "cut off" (Dan. 9: 26) out of the land of the living. But on the third day He rose again from the dead. Mr. Ridout has strikingly pointed out

that just as there was first the bud, then the flower, and then the almond fruit on Aaron's rod, and on each branch of the Lampstand so was there a manifest gradation in the evidences of Christ's resurrection!

"The stone rolled away, the empty tomb, the linen clothes lying in quiet order and the napkin lying by itself—no sign of a struggle, but the witness that the Prince of life had risen from His sleep of death; these may be called the 'buds,' the first signs of His resurrection. The angel who rolled away the stone and sat on it (Matt. 28: 2), the 'young man sitting on the right side' of the tomb (Mark 16: 5, 6), the 'vision of angels' seen by the women which came early to the sepulchre (Luke 24: 23); the two angels in white sitting, the one at the head, the other at the feet, where the body of Jesus had lain (John 20: 12)— these may be called the 'flowers'—the more advanced witnesses of His resurrection. Lastly, His own personal manifestations to Mary Magdalene, to Peter, to the women, to the two disciples at Emmaus, to the gathered disciples in the upper room, to them again when Thomas was present; again at the Sea of Tiberius, and at a mountain in Galilee—these and other 'infallible proofs' might be called the full almond fruit. The empty tomb might have been a precious boon to faith, and was enough for John (John 20: 8); the testimony of the angels would have been stronger testimony; but the crown of all was to behold Him, to hear Him, to see Him eat, hear Him speak, this was indeed the full fruit."

4. Its Position.

As we have already seen, the Lampstand was one of the three pieces of furniture which were in the holy place. But there is a word in Ex. 40: 24 which defined its location still more precisely, "And He put the lampstand in the tent of the congregation over against the table, on the side of the Tabernacle southward."

Like everything else in Scripture the points of the compass are referred to with a moral and spiritual significance. Briefly, we may say that the "west" is the quarter of prosperity and blessing: see Ex. 10: 19; Deut. 33: 23; Josh. 8: 12; Isa. 59: 19. The "east," the opposite quarter, tells of sharp distress and Divine judgment: see Gen. 3: 24, 13: 11, 41: 6; Ex. 10: 13, 14: 21; Isa. 46: 11. The "north"—the Hebrew word means "obscure, dark"—is the direction from which evil comes: see Jer. 1: 14, 4: 6, etc. The sunny "south," the opposite quarter from the north, tells of warmth light, and blessing: see Job 37: 17; Psa. 126: 4; Luke 12: 55; Deut. 33: 3; Acts 27: 13. It is most significant then that the Lampstand was placed on the **south** side of the Tabernacle, the more so when we discover that the Hebrew word for "south" means "bright, radiant"!

5. Its Significance.

There are a number of details which enable us to fix the typical meaning of the Lampstand. First, the fact that it was made of **beaten** gold and was ornamented with **almonds** shows that it is the suffering Christ now risen and glorified which is here foreshadowed. Second, its being set in the Holy Place intimates that it is Christ hidden from the world, enjoyed only by the priestly family. Third, its seven lamps of oil tell of the sufficiency of the Spirit as Christ's **gift** to His people. Fourth, the **time** when the Lampstand was used furnishes another sure key to its interpretation. It was for use in the Holy Place **during the night**: "Aaron and his sons shall order it from evening to morning before the Lord (Ex. 27: 21). It thus typified the maintenance of light within the true Sanctuary during the time that our Lord was absent from the earth, that is, while the nation of Israel is no longer God's witness here below.

That which was most prominent in connection with the Lampstand was its seven branches, supporting the lighted "lamps." These, as we have seen, foreshadowed the person and ministry of the Holy Spirit. It is this which brings out the distinctive aspect of our present type. It is the Spirit as the gift of Christ —the result of His death and resurrection—the "beaten work" and the "almonds" to His people. It is the Spirit shining in their hearts to give them "**the light of** the knowledge of the glory of God in the face of Jesus Christ" (2 Cor. 4: 6). It is the Spirit **within** the Sanctuary, glorifying Christ, taking of the **things of** Christ and showing them to His **people**. It is the operations of the Spirit directed by the glorified Son of God. The several **purposes** which were served by the seven lighted lamps portray the leading aspects of the Spirit's ministry to Christ's people.

First, the lighted lamps revealed the beautiful workmanship of the Lampstand itself: "And thou shalt make the seven lamps thereof: and they shall light the lamps thereof, that they may give light over against the **face of it**" (v. 37) cf. Numbers 8: 2. This tells us of the principal design of the Spirit's ministry to-

ward and in the saints. As the Saviour promised, "He shall glorify Me: for He shall receive of Mine, and shall show it unto you" (John 16: 14). This He does by revealing to us the perfections of Christ, by making Him real to us, by endearing Him to our hearts. It is only by the Spirit that we are enabled to behold and enjoy the excellencies of Him who is "fairer than the children of men." It is in His light alone that we "see light" (Psa. 36: 9).

Second, the Lampstand was placed opposite the Table, so as to cast its light upon its contents: "And he put the Lampstand in the tent of the congregation **over against the Table**" (Ex. 40: 24). The shewbread remained on the Table seven days, when it became the food of Aaron and his sons, who were bidden to "eat in the Holy Place" (Lev. 24: 8,9). There they refreshed themselves with that which had delighted the eye of God. Can we think of them sitting down and enjoying such a feast in darkness? Impossible. Light was a necessity: without it all would have been confusion and disorder. This teaches us that it is only by the ministry and power of the Spirit that Christians can perceive Christ as the Bread of God to sustain His people. It is only by the Spirit we are enabled to feed on Christ and draw from His fulness, that the new man may be nourished and strengthened.

Third, the Lampstand is mentioned in connection with the burning of incense on the Golden-altar: "And Aaron shall burn thereon sweet incense every morning: **when** he dresseth the lamps, he shall burn incense on it. And **when** Aaron lighteth the lamps at even, he shall burn incense upon it" (Ex. 30: 7, 8). Apart from the light furnished by the Lampstand the priests could not have seen the golden altar and would have been unable to minister thereat. This altar speaks both of worship and supplication. Here too the aid of the Spirit is indispensible. **Apart from Him we can** neither praise nor petition Christ as we ought.

Fourth, the Lampstand is said to shed its light "before the Lord" (Ex. 40: 25). The antitype of this is specially brought before us by the Spirit in the closing book of Scripture. There we see Christ vindicating the government of God. There the "seven lamps" which are "the seven Spirits of God" are expressly said to be "burning before the Throne" (Rev. 4: 5), while in Rev. 5: 6 they are seen in connection with the Lamb as He rises to administer judgment. The Lampstand

shining "before the Lord" will find its
accomplishment when Christ overthrows
the foes of God and reigns till He hath
put all enemies under His feet. This will
be during the Millennium when Christ,
in the fulness of the Spirit's power, shall
be manifested as the "Sun of righteousness" (Mal. 4: 2).

There is a very remarkable Scripture
in Isa. 11 which gives us the final antitypical fulfilment of the sevenfold radiance of the Lampstand. There we read,
"there shall come forth a rod out of the
stem of Jesse, and a Branch shall grow
out of his roots: And the Spirit of the
Lord shall rest upon Him: The Spirit of
wisdom and understanding, the Spirit of
counsel and might, the Spirit of knowledge and of the fear of the Lord" (vv.
1, 2). There is here a sevenfold reference of the relation of the Holy Spirit
to Christ during His Millennial reign,
note v. 4. But observe carefully the
arrangement here. Mark the absence
of any "and" between "Him" and "the
Spirit of wisdom," and so between the
second and third and between the third
and fourth mentionings of the Spirit.
The order corresponds exactly with the
construction of the seven - branched
Lampstand "The Spirit of the Lord shall
rest upon Him:" this is separated from
the other six by the absence of a connecting "and" to what follows, reminding
us of the one central stem. The next
six references are arranged in three
pairs (as the "ands" show), like the
three pairs of branches growing out of
the central stem!

6. Its Covering.

"And they shall take a cloth of blue,
and cover the Lampstand of the light,
and his lamps, and his tongs, etc., and
they shall put it and all the vessels
thereof within a covering of badgers'
skins" (Num. 4: 9, 10). This point needs
not to be developed at length as the typical significance of these coverings has
been dealt with in previous articles. In
the "cloth of blue" we have emphasised
the Divine glory of Christ, and are reminded that only saints in priestly communion can recognize and enjoy the
Light of life as the Holy One. As we
see the "blue" folded and concealed in
the "badgers' skins we have a solemn
portrayal of the fact that the ungodly
are without any knowledge of the true
Light: "The way of the wicked is as darkness" (Prov. 4: 19).

7. Its History.

Only twice is the Lampstand referred
to after the Pentateuch is passed, but in
each case the connection is a most striking one. First, in 1 Sam. 3 the Spirit
has informed us that Jehovah revealed
Himself to young Samuel in the Temple
or Tabernacle "ere the lamp of God went
out" (v. 3), and a most solemn communication did He give him. The Lord announced that He would do a thing in
Israel "at which both the ears of every
one that heareth it shall tingle." This
"thing" was the sore judgment which
fell upon the degenerate sons of Eli.
The prophetic and dispensational application of this is obvious. Ere the long
Night of Israel's unbelief is ended, God
will bring upon them the Great Tribulation and judge them for their sins.

The second reference is in Dan. 5.
Here again a night scene is presented to
our view. Belshazzar, attended by his
debauched courtiers and concubines, in
the midst of a drunken revelry, gave orders that the "golden vessels" which had
been taken from the Temple when his
grandfather captured Jerusalem, should
be brought in and drunk out of. Heaven's
response was prompt: "In the same hour
came forth fingers of a man's hand and
wrote over against the Lampstand upon
the plaister of the wall" (v. 5). This time
it was a message of woe pronounced
upon the Babylonians, pointing forward
to the end of the times of the Gentiles,
when the vials of God's wrath shall be
poured out upon this Christ-rejecting
world.

The appropriateness of these two mes-
sages of judgment being linked with the
Lampstand is evident. God is light and
in Him is no darkness at all (1 John
1: 5). "God is light" means, He is ineffably holy, and therefore must punish
sin: it brings before us the other side of
the truth. Light exposes and burns as
well as warms and illumines! For believers the Light is the Light of life; but
for unbelievers it will yet blind and overwhelm: that is why the Judgment-seat in
the great Assize is a "great white Throne.
How thankful should every Christian
reader be that we are "children of light."
Christ is the Light to His people—Prov.
4: 18, 2 Cor. 4: 6; in His people—Eph. 1:
18, 5: 13, 14; through His people—Matt.
5: 14-16.

CHAPTER 40

THE CURTAINED CEILING

EXODUS 26:1-14

Having described the contents of the inner chambers of the Tabernacle, excepting the Golden-altar which is mentioned later in another connection, the Holy Spirit now informs us of what comprised the roof of Jehovah's dwelling-place. This consisted of a number of linen curtains, elaborately embroidered, and joined together; over these was a set of goats' hair curtains; over these was a covering of rams' skins dyed red, and on the outside of all was a covering of badgers' skins. It is noteworthy that the curtained ceiling, which we are now to contemplate, is described before the boards, which formed the framework or sides of the holy structure. Man would naturally have begun with a description of the framework, then the roof, and then the furniture placed within the finished building. But here, as elsewhere, God's thoughts and ways are the opposite of ours.

In this article we shall confine ourselves to the inner ceiling. This was composed of ten white curtains, richly ornamented, each twenty-eight cubits (forty-two feet) in length, and four cubits (six feet) in width. These were coupled together in fives, breadth to breadth, thus giving a total length of forty-two feet and a breadth of sixty feet, which would not only reach across the Tabernacle, which was fifteen feet in width, but would overlap its sides. The two sets of five white curtains were linked together by fifty loops of blue in each, which were fastened with fifty taches or clasps of gold, thus firmly uniting the whole together in one solid piece. There are seven things about these Curtains which we shall now consider:—

1. Their Material.

"Thou shalt make the Tabernacle of ten curtains of fine twined linen" (v. 1). It is striking to note that in 26: 15 we read, "Thou shalt make boards for the Tabernacle": whereas the Curtains were

themselves called "the Tabernacle." Thus what we have before us here is Christ incarnate providing a dwelling-place on earth for God. These spotless Curtains pointed to the person of the Lord Jesus Christ and exhibited the **holiness** of His nature. "The priests were on this account clothed with it (Ex. 28: 39-43); and on the great day of atonement Aaron was dressed in this material (Lev. 16: 4) that he might typify the absolute purity of the nature of the One of whom he was the shadow" (Mr. Ed. Dennett).

The Curtains were made of "fine linen" —not linen merely, but **fine linen**, linen of peculiar excellency. In Rev. 19: 8 we have the Holy Spirit's definition of the significance of this figure, for there the fine linen, "clean and white," is declared to be **"the righteousnesses of the saints."** (R. V.). Thus the leading thoughts are unsullied purity and manifested righteousness. This concept may be the more clearly grasped by noting the contrast presented in Isa. 64:6, "But we are all as unclean, and all our righteousnesses are as filthy rags." This will be the confession of the Jews in a day to come, when they are convicted of their sins and made to mourn before their revealed Messiah. It is also the confession of God's saints to-day. Viewed in ourselves, measured by the standard of Divine holiness, the best efforts of the Christian are comparable only to "filthy rags." The fine white linen, then, typified the **manifested** holiness and righteousness of Christ.

It is in the four Gospels which record the earthly life of our Lord, that the antitypical Curtains are displayed. See Him **as a Boy of twelve.** He had been taken to Jerusalem. Joseph and Mary lost sight of Him for three days. Where did they find Him? In the Temple, and in reply to His mother's question, He said, "Wist ye not that I must be about My Father's business?" (Luke 2: 49). His concern was to be occupied with the things of God. Pertinently has one asked,

216

"Was there ever a child like that, to whom God was Father in such a way that He absorbed His soul?" Behold Him as He went down to Nazareth and was subject to His parents, owning the place of earthly responsibility and manifesting His perfection in this relationship. So, too, we read of Him, in those early days, "Jesus increased in wisdom and stature, and in favour with God and men." "There was the fabric of spotless linen being woven before the eye of God." (Mr. S. Ridout). Follow Him into the wilderness, where for forty days He was tempted of the devil: utterly vain were the efforts of Satan to foul His white robes. Thus may we trace Him all through the inspired record. He eats with publicans and sinners, yet is unsullied by the most polluting atmosphere. He lays His hand on the leper, but instead of contracting defilement, His fingers healed. He touches the bier, but instead of becoming ceremonially unclean, the dead is restored to life.

"Coming to His death, we see the spotless white shining in all its purity. The world puts Him between two thieves. "Ah," says Satan, "I will at least besmirch His whiteness; I will associate Him with malefactors and turn loose the rabble upon Him, railing and casting dust into the air. I will see what will become of His spotlessness! Yes, let us see what will become of His spotlessness. God only brings it out into clearer relief amidst the blackness of human and satanic wickedness. The very thief at His side is constrained to own His sinlessness (Luke 23: 40, 41). The Centurion, too, who presided at the crucifixion, declared Him a righteous Man" (Mr. S. Ridout). The white Curtains, then, foreshadowed the sinless ways and righteous acts of the Holy One of God.

2. Their Colours.

"Of fine twined linen, and blue, and purple, and scarlet" (v. 1). These were used for embroidering the cherubim upon the white Curtains. Each of the colours brings out a separate perfection in the Person of our blessed Redeemer, and was manifested by Him as He passed through this world of sin. "Blue" is the celestial colour—"as it were the body of heaven in its clearness" (Ex. 24: 11). The "blue" upon the white background tells us that He who came down into fathomless depths of humiliation was "the Lord from heaven" (1 Cor. 15: 47).

It is most blessed to go through the Gospels with the object of looking for the "blue" as it was revealed in connection with the second Man. First, we see it at His birth. How carefully God saw to it that testimony should be borne to the heavenly source of that One who then lay in the manger. The angels were sent to announce Him as "Christ the Lord" (Luke 2:11). Later, the wise men from the east came and worshipped the young Child—how beautifully this manifested the "blue"! Those who heard Him asking and answering the questions of the doctors in the Temple, when twelve years of age, were "astonished at His understanding" (Luke 2: 47)—here again we may perceive the heavenly colour. In His words to Nicodemus He spoke of Himself as "The Son of man which is in heaven" (John 3: 13)—as one has said "the One whose whole life here breathed the air of heaven." "Though He was 'very man,' yet He ever walked in the uninterrupted consciousness of His proper dignity, as a heavenly Stranger. He never once forgot whence He had come, where He was, or whither He was going. The spring of all His joys was on High. Earth could neither make Him richer nor poorer. He found this world to be 'a dry and thirsty land, where no water is,' and hence His spirit could only find its refreshment above" (C.H.M.).

"Purple" is emblematic of royalty. This is established by a reference to John 19. When the Roman soldiers expressed their scorn for Israel's Ruler by going through the form of a mock coronation, they placed upon His brow a crown of thorns, and then "put on Him a purple robe" (v. 2). It is in Matthew's Gospel that this second colour comes out most conspicuously. First, the "purple" is seen in the record of the royal genealogy of the Son of David. Next we behold it in the question of the magi, "Where is He that is born King of the Jews?" (Matt. 2: 2). Then we see it in the proclamation of His forerunner, "The kingdom of heaven is at hand" (3: 2)—"at hand," because the King Himself was in their midst. The royal "purple" is plainly evident in the "Sermon" recorded in chapters 5, 6, 7, prefaced by the statement, "He went up into a mountain, and when He was seated . . . He said " etc.—symbolically, it was the King taking His place upon His throne, enunciating the laws of His kingdom. Still more vividly did the "purple" shine when He made His triumphal entry into Jerusalem (21: 1-11). Over His cross was placed the royal banner, "This is Jesus, the King of the Jews" (27: 37).

"Scarlet" is a colour which is used in Scripture with a variety of emblematic significations. From these we select two which seem to bear most closely upon our present type. First, "scarlet," the colour of blood, vividly suggests the **sufferings** of Christ. This is borne out by the fact that the complete Hebrew word for "scarlet" is "tolaath shani," meaning scarlet-worm. Mr. Ridout has pointed out, "It is the 'cocus cacti,' the cochineal, from which the scarlet dye is obtained. In the 22nd Psalm our holy Lord, in the midst of His anguish as a sin-offering on the cross, says 'I am a **worm and** no man' (v. 6). This is the word which is used in connection with scarlet. Thus our Lord, 'who knew no sin,' was 'made sin' for us (2 Cor. 5: 21), taking the place which we deserved. He took the place of being a worm, went down into death, crushed under the wrath and judgment of God, His precious blood shed to put away our scarlet sins."

Thus the "scarlet" speaks first of the **sufferings** of Christ. Side by side with His purity, His heavenly character, and His royal majesty, the Gospel records bring before us the afflictions of the Saviour. We may discern the "scarlet" in the manger-cradle. This colour was also evidenced when Satan assailed Him, for "He **suffered**, being tempted (Heb. 2: 18). He "sighed deeply in His spirit" (Mark 8: 12), "groaning in Himself" (John 11: 38), "weeping over Jerusalem" (Luke 19: 41) are further examples. How tragically the "scarlet" may be seen in Gethsemane, when "His sweat was as it were great drops of blood falling down to the ground" (Luke 22: 44)!

But "scarlet" is also the emblem of glory. The woman seated upon the scarlet-coloured beast in Rev. 17 symbolizes that satanic system which, under Antichrist, will yet ape the millennial glory of Christ. By His sufferings the Saviour has won the place of highest honor and glory. In the coming Age, this world will be the scene of His splendour. The scarlet mantle will then be upon Him whose right it is. It is striking that in the 22nd Psalm—the first part of which describes the Saviour's sufferings—its closing verses depict His royal authority and coming glory: "All the ends of the world shall remember and turn unto the Lord: and all the kindreds of the nations shall worship before Thee," etc. (v. 27). A bright glimpse of the "scarlet" was afforded to the sight of the favoured apostles upon the Mount of Transfiguration.

3. Its Ornamentation.

"With cherubim of cunning work shalt thou make them" (v. 1). The pure white linen was the material on which the various colours were displayed and with which were embroidered the cherubim. Thus, as the priests ministered in the Holy Place and gazed upward, there above their heads were the mystic forms of these highest of all God's creatures—their outstretched wings forming a firmament of feathers upon the ceiling. We believe that reference is made to this sheltering canopy in the following scriptures: "I will abide in Thy Tabernacle forever; I will trust in the covert of Thy **wings**" (Psa. 61: 4); "He shall cover thee with His feathers; and under His **wings** shalt thou trust" (Psa. 91: 4); "Hide me under the shadow of Thy **wings**" (Psa. 17: 8), etc.

As the "cherubim" will come before us again, a brief word thereon must here suffice. They speak of judicial authority, as the first mention of them in the Bible clearly shows: (Gen. 3: 24). A glimpse of what these symbolic figures portrayed in connection with Christ was given by Him when He affirmed, "For the Father judgeth no man, but hath committed all judgment unto the Son. . . and hath given Him authority to execute judgment also because He is the Son of man" (John 5: 22, 27).

4. Their Dimensions.

"The length of one curtain shall be eight and twenty cubits, and the breadth of one curtain four cubits; and every one of the curtains shall have one measure" (v. 2). "Seven is the perfect number, being absolutely indivisible except by itself, and the highest prime number; and four is that of completeness on earth—as seen for example, in the four corners of the earth, four square, four gospels, etc. The dimensions of the Curtains will then betoken perfection displayed in completeness on earth; and such a meaning could only be applied to the life of our blessed Lord. The Curtains of the Tabernacle, consequently, speak of the complete unfolding of His perfections as Man when passing through this scene" (Mr. E. Dennett).

5. Their Meaning.

This has been brought out, more or less, in what has been already before us. The spotless white Curtains, with the beautifully tinted cherubim worked upon them, typified, distinctively, neither the Deity nor the humanity of our Lord, but the **person** of the God-man and the varied glories manifested by Him while He tabernacled among men. It should be noted that in every other instance where we have the four colours mentioned, the blue is first and the white is last. But here the order is reversed. There, it is the Spirit emphasising the heavenly origin of the One who came down to earth; here, it is drawing our attention to the sinlessness and righteousness of the Man who sits now at God's right hand.

The fact that these Curtains formed the inside ceiling of the holy places and were seen, therefore, only by the priestly family, intimates that none but those that had access to God were able to appreciate the perfections of His Son as they were manifested by Him during His earthly sojourn. The rank and file of the Jews saw in Him no beauty that they should desire Him. His moral loveliness was lost upon them; yea, it only served to condemn their moral ugliness, and thus aroused their enmity. But the favoured few, who were the objects of distinguishing grace, exclaimed, "We beheld His glory, the glory as of the only begotten of the Father full of grace and truth" (John 1: 14).

It is the same to-day. Christ is still despised and rejected of men. The unregenerate have no capacity to discern His excellencies. A good Man, the best of men, He is acknowledged to be; but as the Holy One of God (the "white"), the Lord from heaven (the "blue"), the King of kings (the "purple"), and the One who because of His sufferings will yet come back to this earth and reign over it in power and glory (the "scarlet"), He is unknown. But notwithstanding there is even now a company that is "an holy priesthood" (1 Peter 2: 5), and they, having received "an unction," a divine anointing (1 John 2: 20, 27), recognise Him as the altogether Lovely One.

The fact that the Curtains formed the inner ceiling of the Tabernacle suggests that they set before us the One who humbled Himself and became obedient unto death, but who is now exalted and glorified on High. Whenever the worshipper looked up he would see nought but that spotless linen with its rich ornamentations. Does not this announce to us, in accents too plain to be misunderstood, that as God's worshippers enter, in spirit, the heavenly Sanctuary, they are to be occupied with the person and perfections of Him whom, by faith, we now see "crowned with glory and honour" (Heb. 2: 9)! In worship we are occupied not with ourselves—either our failures or our attainments, our needs or our blessings—but with the Father and His blessed Son. It is only as our hearts are absorbed with that which the Curtains and their lovely colours prefigured, that we present to God that which is acceptable in His sight.

6. Their Loops.

Before we take up the distinctive significance of these, let us first consider their use. They were appointed for the joining of the Curtains together. Thus the ten Curtains were arranged in two sets of five each: "The five curtains shall be coupled together one to another; and other five curtains shall be coupled one to another" (v. 3). Now, in Scripture, one of the meanings of "ten" is that of human responsibility. Hence after ten plagues upon Egypt had measured and demonstrated the failure of their responsibility, Pharaoh and his hosts were destroyed at the Red Sea. When Gentile dominion reaches its final form, it will consist of ten kingdoms, and then will be fully manifested the breakdown of its responsibility. When at Sinai God gave a summary of man's duty it was in the form of ten commandments. But these were written upon two tables of stone, or in two sets of fives, similarly to the Curtains here. The first five commandments—joined together by the words "The Lord thy God," which is not found in any of the last five—define our responsibility Godwards; the last five, our responsibility manwards. The ten Curtains, grouped together in two sets of fives, speak of Christ, as the Representative of His people, meeting the whole of their obligations both Godwards and manwards. He loved God with all His heart, and His neighbour as Himself; He was the only one by whom these responsibilities were fully and perfectly discharged.

By this "coupling" of the Curtains together, both their length and breadth would be the better exhibited. " 'Length' is the extension, and may well stand for the whole course of life. It is used this way in Scripture—'length of days' is a familiar expression. 'Breadth' is from a root meaning 'spacious, roomy.' It has a metaphorical use with which we are familiar. King Solomon had great largeness (breadth) of heart (1 Kings, 4: 29). 'Breadth' thus suggests the character of the life and its attendant circumstances. In speaking then of our Lord's life, 'length' would suggest its whole course, and 'breadth' its character and the circumstances in which this was displayed" (Mr. Ridout). How blessed then to behold that each of these ten Curtains was 28 or 7 x 4 cubits long, and 4 broad, telling us that in the discharge of our responsibilites He manifested nought but

perfection here on earth!

"Fifty loops shalt thou make in the one curtain, and fifty loops shalt thou make in the edge of the curtain that is in the coupling of the second; that the loops may take hold one of another" (v. 5) "The loops were blue—the colour of Heaven. Thus the fact that He was from Heaven, lived in Heaven, and was to return to Heaven characterised His whole life of obedience. The mark of Heaven was upon it all. Upon that which spoke of His perfect love and obedience to God were loops of blue, to show that love and obedience were to be united to a life upon earth in which its responsibilities were to be made one with His obedience to God. So the blue loops upon the second set of Curtains show that all was of one with His devotedness to God.

"No life ever was so perfectly given up to God as was His: heart, soul, mind and strength were all and always for God. Yet this devotedness did not make of Him a recluse. There is not the slightest thought of that selfish monasticism with which human self-righteousness has linked the name of Christianity. He loved His Father perfectly, but that was the pledge of His perfect life to man. No hands or heart were ever so filled with love and labour for men; but there was nothing of the sentimental nor merely philanthropic in this. The loops of blue were on all, linking all with His Father's will. He wrought many miracles. . . but we cannot think of these works of love ending there. He was manifesting the works which the Father gave Him to do; 'I must work the works of Him that sent Me'—John 9: 4" (Mr. Ridout).

7. Their Couplings.

"And thou shalt make fifty taches of gold, and couple the curtains together with the taches: and it shall be one Tabernacle" (v. 6). The word "taches" means "couplings": passed through the loops of blue they united the Curtains together. The "loops of blue" and these "hooks of gold" might seem very unimportant, but, without them, there would have been no unity. The beautiful Curtains would have hung apart one from another, and thus one main feature of their manifestation would have been lost.

Significantly were these "couplings" of gold. They tell us that it was the heavenly and Divine character of our Lord which secured the perfect adjustment of His twofold responsibility as Man towards God and His neighbour. These "couplings" fastened the whole of the ten Curtains together so that they were "one Tabernacle." Thus they pointed to that blessed unity and uniformity of the character and life of Christ. "We have here displayed to us in the 'loops of blue' and 'taches of gold' that heavenly grace and divine energy in Christ which enabled Him to combine and perfectly adjust the claims of God and man, so that in responding to both the one and the other He never, for a moment, marred the unity of His character. When crafty and hypocritical men tempted Him with the inquiry, 'Is it lawful to give tribute to Caesar or not?' His wise reply was, 'Render to Caesar the things that are Caesar's, and to God the things that are God's.' Nor was it merely Caesar's, but man in every relation, that had all his claims perfectly met in Christ. As He united in His perfect person the nature of God and man, so He met in His perfect ways the claims of God and man." (C.H.M.).

In the life of the blessed Lord Jesus, and in all the scenes and circumstances of that life, we not only see each distinct phase and feature perfect in itself, but also a perfect combination of all those phases and features by the power of that which was heavenly and divine in Him. The perfect ways and works of our Lord were not only beautiful in themselves, but they were beautifully combined, exquisitely linked together. But it is only those who have been, in some measure, instructed in the holy mysteries of the true Sanctuary who can discern and appreciate these "loops of blue" and "taches of gold" Study the record of His life with this thought in mind. Mark His inflexible righteousness and then His exceeding tenderness; His uncompromising faithfulness in denouncing hypocrisy and then the wondrous compassion for poor sinners; His stern denunciation of error and human traditions, and then the tender patience toward the ignorant and those that were out of the way. Side by side we may see the dignity and majesty of His Godhead and the meekness and lowliness of His Manhood—blessedly united and consistently combined into one, like His robe "without seam"! May the Spirit of truth enable the reader to look for the "loops of blue" and the "taches of gold" as he studies the antitypical Curtains in the New Testament.

CHAPTER 41

THE COVERINGS

EXODUS 26:7-14

As was pointed out at the beginning of our last article, the Tabernacle had four separate Coverings, one over another. The first and innermost was the ten white curtains. These curtains have already been before us. It should be carefully noted that they are themselves designated "the tabernacle," see vv. 1, 6. Over these were placed eleven "curtains of goats' hair," and these are called "the tent," vv. 11, 12. Above these were spread "rams' skins dyed red" and "badgers' skins," v. 14, which are simply called "coverings." That a distinction is drawn between the "Tabernacle" and the "Tent" is clear from several scriptures For example, Numbers 3:25: "The Tabernacle and the Tent." This intimates they are to be contemplated separately.

The above distinction is clearly established in the Hebrew, where two distinct words are employed—"Mishkan" for Tabernacle, "ohel" for Tent. The former signifies "dwelling-place"; the latter, simply "tent." The one refers to the abode of Jehovah, the other to the meeting-place for His people. It is to be regretted that the translators of our English Bible have failed to preserve the difference which is noted in the original. In the A.V. we find the expression "Tabernacle of the congregation" constantly occurring, but in almost every instance the Hebrew has "Tent of the congregation." This holy building was their place of assembly, but it was Jehovah's place of abode: they visited it, He remained there! Looking now, first, at the eleven goats' hair curtains let us note:—

1.—Their Materials.

"And thou shalt make curtains of goats' hair to be a covering upon the Tabernacle" (v. 7). "The word for 'curtains' is yerioth, from a root meaning to tremble or waive, as suspended curtains do. A similar root with a similar primary meaning is the word for 'fear.' How sug-gestively do these thoughts describe the Lord Jesus as He was here. He was the dependent One, not relying upon His own inherent strength, but cleaving ever to His Father. He was perfectly obedient, because perfectly dependent upon the will of God. Thus the true 'fear' of the Lord characterized Him. He was ever moved by the slightest breath of the Spirit. There was thus in the eyes of men entire weakness, for He had no will apart from perfect subjection unto God; therefore the whole character of God with reference to sin, the world and Satan, was manifested. So also He gave fullest expression to God's thoughts and ways of mercy over judgment with reference to man.

"The word 'curtain' is a feminine one, and in speaking of them being joined together 'one to another,' it is 'a woman to her sister.' This, too, is in keeping with the holy place of dependence and subjection taken and kept by our Lord" (Mr. S. Ridout). As though emphasizing this same thought, the Holy Spirit has been careful to tell us that these goats' hair curtains were spun by the women (Ex. 35:26). We may add that this same material was used for making their own tents, and was of a dark colour, as a reference to Song of Sol. 1:5; 6:5 shows.

It is to be noted that the word "hair" in Ex. 26:7 is in italics, which denotes it has been supplied by the translators, and we believe in this case, rightly so. It is not found in the Hebrew of Ex. 35:26, yet the word "spun" clearly implies it. The reason why the word "hair" is omitted from Ex. 26:7 is to direct our attention more particularly to the goats themselves—i.e., to what they typically signified.

2.—Their Number.

"Eleven curtains shalt thou make" (v. 7). As though God anticipated we should experience difficulty with this number,

He has Himself here supplied the very help we need. He has told us that these Curtains were divided into two groups: "Thou shalt couple five curtains by themselves, and six curtains by themselves" (v. 9). Thus in order to discover the spiritual significance of this number eleven, we are thus shown that we are not to consider it by itself as a whole, but as made up of five and six. This simplifies things very much. Five, as we have before had occasion to remark, stands for grace, while six is the number of man. It was on the sixth day that man was created (Gen. 1:26, 31). Six days are the span of man's weekly labour (Ex. 20:9). It is striking how prominent is this numeral in the measures which man uses in connection with his labours: each of the following is a multiple of six. There are twelve inches to the foot; eighteen to the cubit; thirty-six to the yard. It is thus with man's divisions of time. The day has twenty-four hours, each of these is made up of sixty minutes, and these of sixty seconds. It is remarkable there are just six separate words in the Bible for "man"—four in the Hebrew and two in the Greek. How fitting that He who took the place of sinful man was crucified at the sixth hour (John 19:14)! In the indignities man heaped upon the suffering Saviour this same number was stamped upon his vile handiwork: (1) scourging His back; (2) smiting His face with the palms of their hands; (3) spitting upon Him; (4) placing the thorns on His brow; (5) driving the nails into His hands and His feet; (6) plunging the spear into His side. In the light of these examples it is not difficult to trace the significance of the five and the six in the goats' hair Curtains.

3.—Their Dimensions.

"The length of one curtain shall be thirty cubits, and the breadth of one curtain four cubits: and the eleven curtains shall be all of one measure" (v. 8). The width of the Curtains was the same as those which formed the innermost Covering, namely, four cubits—the number which speaks of the earth. But the length of the goats' hair Curtains exceeded those of the white ones: these were thirty cubits, they but twenty-eight. The significance of these larger numbers is always ascertained by the spiritual meaning of their factors. The factors of thirty are either three and ten, or five and six. Three is the number of full manifestation, ten of responsibility. But in view of the fact that the Curtains were divided into two groups of five and six, we probably have there the key to the interpretation of their length. This will come before us more fully when we take up their meaning.

4.—Their Arrangement.

This is by no means obvious at first glance. In v. 9 we are told, "Thou shalt couple five curtains by themselves, and six curtains by themselves and shalt double the sixth curtain in the forefront of the Tabernacle." Then in vv. 12, 13 we read, "And the remnant that remaineth of the curtains of the Tent, the half curtain that remaineth, shall hang over the backside of the Tabernacle. And a cubit on the one side, and a cubit on the other side of that which remaineth in the length of the curtains of the Tent, it shall hang over the sides of the Tabernacle on this side and on that side, to cover it." Now the Tabernacle itself was thirty cubits long, ten cubits broad, and ten cubits high. Thus by taking these Curtains lengthwise and throwing them over the width of the Tabernacle, its two sides and top would be completely covered, for they were just thirty cubits in length. In breadth, joined side by side, they would be forty-four cubits, and thus long enough to cover the rear, stretch right across the length of the top and then over-lap four feet in front. This balance of four cubits in the front was turned back or "doubled" so as to leave eight cubits clear for the entrance.

5.—Their Meaning.

The material of which they were made, supplies the first key to this. The "goat" was pre-eminently the animal used in the sin offerings, in fact, in connection with Israel's great feasts under the law, when the people were collectively represented before God, it was the only one used in their sacrifices for sins. Israel's year began with a commemoration of the Passover. Inseparably connected with this was the ordinance of the feast of unleavened bread: in Luke 22:1 they are identified. During the seven days of this feast, besides other sacrifices, a "goat" was slain for a sin offering (Num. 28:17, 22). The next feast was that of "weeks" or "Pentecost": in this, too, a goat as a sin offering for an atonement was commanded (Lev. 23:15, 19). Then came the feast of Trumpets, and here also the goat for a sin-offering was used (Num. 29:1, 5). Following this was the most solemn of them all, namely, the annual Day of Atonement, when a special sin-offering was appointed. This consisted of two goats: the one being slain, the other having the sins and iniquities of all Israel confessed upon it, then being led away into a land not inhabited (Lev. 16). Finally came the feast of Tabernacles, the feast of ingathering, when Israel rested from their toil and rejoiced in the blessing of God upon their labours. This feast lasted for eight days, and on each one a "goat" was slain as a sin-offering (Num. 29).

In addition to the national convocations when the "goats" alone was used for making atonement, we may observe the prominence of this animal in other sin-offerings. When a ruler sinned, the appointed sacrifice was "a kid of the goats" (Lev. 4:23); so, if one of the common people sinned (Lev. 4:27, 28). At the consecration of the priesthood a "kid of the goats for a sin-offering" was required (Lev. 9:2, 3). At the dedication of the altar each of the "princes" offered "one kid of the goats for a sin-offering" (Num. 7:16). For the sin of ignorance a "kid of the goats" made atonement (Num. 15: 24, 27). At the beginning of each month a special sin-offering was appointed, and this also consisted of "a kid of the goats" (Num. 28: 11, 15). This completes the list where the "goat" was exclusively appointed as the sin-offering. Surely it is more than a coincidence that they are precisely **eleven** in number—corresponding exactly with the eleven Curtains in our type!

It is also very striking to find that where the "goat" is not used in sacrifice, yet is it generally found in an evil connection. Rebekah placed "skins of the kids of the **goats**" upon Jacob's hands and neck for the purpose of deceiving Isaac (Gen. 27:16). So the brethren of Joseph "killed a kid of the **goats**" and dipped his coat in it to aid their deception upon their father (Gen. 37:31). In the trick which Michal imposed upon Saul, a pillow of "goats' hair" was employed (1 Sam. 19:13). So in contrast from the "sheep" (His own people) the Lord likens the wicked unto "**goats**" (Matt. 25:33).

In the light of what has just been before us it is unmistakably plain that the "goats' hair" Curtains pointed to Christ as the great sin-offering for the iniquities of his people. He who knew no sin, was "made sin for us" (2 Cor. 5:21). Of old it was announced "Thou shalt make His soul an offering for sin" (Isa. 53:10), and thus was the fulfilment recorded—

"He hath poured out His soul unto death" (Isa. 53:12). In this connection it is remarkable to note the words of Lev. 4:25: "The priests shall . . . **pour out** his blood at the bottom of the altar." This was only said of the blood of the "sin-offering": of the blood of the burnt-offering we read that it was "sprinkled" only (Lev. 1:5).

The numerals connected with these Curtains confirm our interpretation: they were six, five, and four. Thus we learn that it was the **Manhood** of our blessed Redeemer, in wondrous **grace**, suffering for the sin of His people here on **earth**. But it is the **six** which is doubly prominent, the eleventh Curtain being expressly termed "the sixth" (v. 9), and the thirty cubits in length, has for its factors five and six. Thus, by this emphasis, the Holy Spirit has most graciously pointed out the direction which our thoughts should take. The fact that the "women" spun these goats' hair Curtains still further emphasises the truth that in our present type it is distinctively Christ as the "woman's" Seed (Gen. 3:15)., who is before us. It is true that the God-man suffered and died, and it is true that His two natures are inseparably united; yet, it was His **humanity** which made possible the great sacrifice, for Deity cannot suffer.

Underneath these goats' hair Curtains was the gorgeous tapestry of the cherubim-embroidered white Curtains. But these were seen only by those **inside** the Holy Place, telling us that it is not until we have personally appropriated Christ, by a God-given faith, as our Sin-offering, that we can delight ourselves by being occupied with His personal perfections. Thus, how deeply and how solemnly significant, was the doubled-over curtain, right over the entrance into the Tabernacle. Just above its beautiful gate hung that which would remind the worshipper of the great cost paid by Another to procure entrance for him.

6.—Their Loops and Taches.

"And thou shalt make fifty loops on the edge of the one curtain that is outmost in the coupling, and fifty loops in the edge of the curtain which coupleth the second. And thou shalt make fifty taches of brass, and put the taches into the loops, and couple the Tent together, that it may be one" (vv. 10, 11). Some excellent commentators have insisted that the goats' hair Curtains speak primarily of Christ in His earthly life, and that they pointed to Him as the perfect

Prophet. We think this is a mistake. It is true that "hairy" garments are found connected with false prophets (Heb.. of Zech. 13:5), but no "goats' hair." In the case of John the Baptist we are explicitly told that his raiment was of "camel's hair" (Matt. 3.4).

It will be noted that while the white Curtains were linked together with "gold" taches, the ones now before us were united by "brass" clasps. This important detail both reveals the mistake of others and confirms the interpretation which we have given above. "Brass" in scripture is the symbol of Divine judgment—as this will come before us again in connection with the "Brazen-altar we shall not now adduce the proofs. Now in His prophetic office Christ's ministry was the very reverse of the exercise of judgment—throughout it was marked by grace: John 1: 17; 3; 17. But regarding the goats' hair Curtains as foreshadowing Christ "made sin" for His people, the taches of "brass" are most significant, for they tell us that, while on the Cross, the Saviour suffered the outpoured judgment of God (Isa. 53: 10; Zech. 13:7).

It should also be observed that two little words in connection with the "loops" are here most significantly omitted. The ten white Curtains were linked together through "loops of blue" (26:4); but of the eleven goats' hair Curtains we read, three times over in 26:10, 11, simply of "loops." Had these second Curtains been designed of God to portray Christ in His prophetic office the "blue" had surely been mentioned, for His heavenly Character shone out ceaselessly during His earthly ministry. But when "made sin for us" His heavenly glory was hidden, as the three hours of darkness testified. The minute and wondrous perfection of our type is thus evidenced by the omission of "loops of blue"!

7.—Their Purpose.

These goats' hair Curtains were designed not only as a protection for the white Curtains beneath, but also to cover the golden boards of its sides and rear. These, the under Curtains failed to completely drape. It was a distance of thirty. cubits from the ground on the one side, over the roof, to the ground on the other side. The white Curtains were only twenty-eight cubits in length, leaving one cubit of the golden boards exposed at the bottom on either side. And most fittingly so. As we have seen, the white Curtains, with their lovely colours embroidered upon them, foreshadowed the perfections of Christ's person as He tabernacled among men. During His walk through this world, He did not conceal, but revealed, the glory of God, therefore was there one cubit (one is the number of unity, and thus of God in His essential nature) of the golden boards left uncovered by the white Curtains on either side of the Tabernacle!

But these goats' hair Curtains were thirty cubits long, and thus of sufficient length not only to overlap the white Curtains, but also to completely cover the golden boards on the side of the Tabernacle. By this God intimated the great truth that He could have no tabernacle among men, and could not manifest His beauty and glory in their midst, except as His dwelling-place proclaimed, in every part of it, the fact that sin had been fully met and put away by the sacrifice of His Son!

It remains for us now to offer a brief remark on the outermost Coverings. "And thou shalt make a covering for the tent of rams' skins dyed red, and a covering above of badgers' skins" (v. 14). In a word, these external Coverings, on the outside of the goats' hair Curtains, give us a twofold view of Christ enduring the judgment due the sins of His people: they show how He then appeared to the eye of God and to the eyes of men. The rams' skins presented the Godward aspect first. The "ram" was the victim used at the consecration of the priests (Ex. 29:26), when they were separated unto the service of Jehovah. It spoke, therefore, of devotedness to God. In beautiful accord with this we find that it was a "ram" (Gen. 22:13) which took the place of Isaac when Abraham, in his devotion and obedience to God, had bound him to the altar! "The ram, being the head of the flock, tells of strength and dignity, hence the figurative significance of Psalm 114:3. The skipping and the leaping of the mighty mountains shows the Divine majesty of God, before whom the strongest and mightiest must quail" (Mr. Ridout).

The rams' skins Covering was "dyed red," which plainly expressed devotion unto death. Thus, in the first of these Coverings we have foreshadowed Christ as the Head of His sheep, the Mighty One, living only for God, and manifesting His perfect devotion to the Father by being "obedient unto death, even the death of the cross."

The rams' skins Covering, then, foreshadowed Christ as the Head of His people (the "sheep") perfectly consecrated to God. As a Child it was the Father's business which occupied Him (Luke 2:49). The key-note to His ministry was "I must work the works of Him that sent Me" (John 9:4). Zeal for the Father's honour consumed Him (John 2:17). But the rams' skins were "dyed **red,**" which pointed to bloodshedding. Not only did Christ live entirely for God, but He also laid down His life in obedience to the Father's command (John 10:18). All the varied excellencies of Christ were covered by devotedness to God. At Calvary, men saw only the execution of a condemned criminal, but Heaven looked down upon the unreserved and unparalleled consecration of the Son to the Father.

Over the rams' skins were placed badgers' skins, and this was the outer Covering of all. This alone would be seen by the eyes of men as Israel were in the wilderness. It, therefore, brings before us Christ as He appeared to men. It specially portrays the fact that He "made Himself of no reputation" (Phil. 2:7). Born in a manger; brought up in despised Nazareth; working at the carpenter's bench, were examples of what the rough and unsightly badgers' skins foreshadowed. To such a degree did Christ humble Himself, the glories of His Divine person were hidden from the eyes of sinful creatures. "Is not this the carpenter?" (Mark 6:3), shows their estimation of Him. They could see none of the spiritual grace, the heavenly beauty, or even the moral perfections, which lay beneath the outward form of the despised Jesus of Nazareth. "As for this fellow, we know not from whence He is" (John 9: 29) reveals the fact that they saw only the badger's skins.

As it was with Him during His life, so also was it at His death. Just as the desert tribes through whose territory Israel passed while journeying to Canaan, saw not the lovely Curtains underneath, so the morbid throngs which congregated at Calvary, discerned not the precious significance of what was there transpiring. Many were astonished at Christ because "His visage was more marred than any man's, and His form than the sons of man" (Isa. 52:14). He was regarded as smitten by a curse from God because of blasphemy (Isa. 53:4). They deemed Him utterly helpless, unable to come down from the cross. Thus the rough and unsightly badgers' skins over all, spoke of the shame and humiliation of our precious Saviour before men.

It is most blessed and solemn to observe that, in sharp contrast from the ten white Curtains and the eleven goats' hair Curtains, beneath, **no dimensions** are given of the two outer Coverings. Does not this intimate that that which these Coverings foreshadowed was **beyond** our power to measure! There was a depth and a height both in our Saviour's devotedness to God and in His humiliation before men which it is utterly impossible for us to gauge.

CHAPTER 42

THE BOARDS

EXODUS 26:15-30

That which is now to occupy us is the framework and foundation of the Tabernacle proper. The sides of the Tabernacle were comprised of boards of acacia wood, fitly framed together, standing upon a base of silver sockets. The Tabernacle stood on the west side of the Court, facing the gate. Its solid framework was made up of forty-eight boards, twenty being used on the north side, twenty on the south, six on the west, with a corner-board at each end; the eastern or front side being the entrance, having five pillars between which was suspended an "hanging for the door," which will come before us for separate consideration in a later article (D.V.). Each of the boards was overlaid with gold.

"The north and south sides of the Tabernacle were each composed of twenty boards. Thus the length of the holy building would be thirty cubits (forty-five feet), the boards being a cubit and a half in breadth. Its height was ten cubits (fifteen feet), its width was exactly the same, namely, ten cubits (fifteen feet). Each board was maintained in its place by two tenons, or hands, which again were grasped by two sockets of silver. Then in order to bind the whole in one compact body of strength and security, five bars of shittim wood with gold—same as the boards —ran along the two sides, and also along the end at the west; fifteen bars in all being inserted in rings of gold attached to the boards. The third, or middle bar, stretched across the whole length of the building—forty-five feet; of the length of the other cross-bars we are not informed. The corner-boards at the extreme end — north and south — were coupled together at top and bottom by rings of gold, in addition to the tenons and silver sockets at the base. These corner-boards then would knit the ends so firmly by their fastening of rings,

tenons, and sockets, or blocks of silver, that a breakdown was impossible, while the sides were equally upheld and maintained by the bars. Here then we have the Rock of Ages embodied in the Tabernacle." (Mr. W. Scott.)

There has been much confusion on the part of the commentators concerning the typical import of the Boards and that which secured them together. Many who have seen **Christ** displayed in the Curtains and in the different Vessels, depart from this primary interpretation when they come to the Boards, and regard them as portraying **believers** in their individual and corporate relationships. That much connected with the Tabernacle may have a secondary application to the saints we do not deny, but that everything in it points first and foremost to our Saviour we are fully assured, and it is with Him that our hearts need most to be engaged; so with the **primary** significance of our type we shall now proceed. There are seven things connected with the Boards that claim our careful attention:—

1.—Their Materials.

"And thou shalt make Boards for the tabernacle of shittim wood. . . . . And thou shalt overlay the boards with gold" _(vv. 15, 29). As we have had occasion before to remark, the acacia wood foreshadowed our Lord's humanity, particularly the incorruptibility of it, the Greek version of the O.T. actually translating it "incorruptible wood." It is of paramount importance that we should hold fast to and testify of the fundamental truth conveyed in this typical wood—the real and the untainted Manhood of the Lord Jesus. Error here is most serious and solemn, affecting as it would our estimate of the Saviour's person. There are those who, in their zeal to maintain His absolute Deity, entertain an inadequate conception of His humanity. But His Manhood was just as real as His Godhood. It was not simply that He assumed a human body, but that He became Man in the full sense of that term, having a human spirit and soul and body. "In all things it behoved Him to be made like unto His brethren" (Heb. 2:17). "Forasmuch then as the children are partakers of flesh and blood, He also Himself likewise took part of the same" (Heb. 2:14). Therefore is He called "the Man Christ Jesus" (1 Tim. 2:5).

But in becoming Man, the Lord of glory took unto Himself a spotless and perfect humanity, expressly designated "that Holy Thing" (Luke 1:35). The Son of man "did no sin" (1 Pet. 2:22) and that because "He knew no sin" (2 Cor. 5:21). and that because "in Him was no sin" (1 John 3:5). He ever was and always remained "the Holy One of God." To question this is to cast dishonour both on the Father and on the Son, and undermines the very foundation on which the Christian's peace is based. Some carelessly, or profanely, talk of "Jesus assuming our sinful and our mortal nature," but such could never be, or He had Himself needed a Saviour. Not only did Christ commit no sin, but He was entirely incapable of sinning. Nor were the seeds of death in His Manhood: He did not die from pain and weakness, but laid down His life of Himself (John 10:18), and in death He saw "no corruption" (Acts 2:27). The Virgin-birth and the immaculate nature of the Saviour lie at the very foundation of the Gospel message: without them there would be and could be no announcement of good news for poor sinners.

Inseparable from His humanity is the glorious truth of our Redeemer's Deity. This also is a fundamental part of our faith and underlies all true evangelical testimony. "Unto you is born . . . a Saviour, which is Christ the Lord" (Luke 2:11). None but a Divine Saviour could meet the deep need of fallen creatures: the endurance of God's curse was wholly beyond the resources of human weakness—His Deity alone could sustain the weight of redemption. If the acacia wood foreshadowed the humanity of Christ, the gold spoke of His Divine nature and glory. In the two conjoined we have set before us God manifest in flesh. "The Word was God. . . the Word became flesh" (John 1:1, 14). A profound mystery we grant, yet a blessed truth on which the faith of God's elect rests with unquestioning confidence.

2.—Their Dimensions.

"Ten cubits shall be the length of a board, and a cubit and a half shall be the breadth of one board" (v. 16). "In all structures if there is to be symmetry, there must be accuracy of measurements, and for this there must be a standard. In Scripture it was the cubit, or ammah, from a word meaning 'mother.' It was the length of the 'mother-arm,' the fore-arm, as the chief and prominent part of the arm, from the elbow to the tip of the finger: that which is used in all work. It was thus a standard taken from man, not above him. God's requirements are absolutely reasonable and righteous, not going beyond human capacity. And yet how true it is that not one of the fallen sons of Adam could measure up to that perfect human standard: 'all have sinned and come short of the glory of God.' But God delighted in man, and even the measurement of the heavenly city is by the human standard (Rev. 21:17). If God is to be in any measure apprehended by His creatures, it must be, not in that unutterable glory and infinity which no one knoweth but the Son, but rather in the One who humbled Himself and was found in fashion as a man. How amazing! God is manifested in the flesh, and we are invited to appropriate the standard of measurement (which is in our hands and by which we have been condemned)to Him, and to see how perfectly He has measured up to the fullest requirements of God" (Mr. Ridout).

How profoundly suggestive and significant that in the very unit of measurement which Jehovah ordered Moses to employ, we are reminded of our Lord's incarnation, and that more than a hint is given of His Virgin birth—the word "cubit" being of the feminine gender, not masculine! He was and is God, but He became flesh. So the length of the Boards reiterates and emphasises the same truth. Ten, as we have seen previously, is the number which speaks of the Divine measure of human responsibility. What is here so blessedly foreshadowed, then, is the Son of God become Man, perfectly glorifying His Father in the place of human accountability. Beautiful is it to ponder in this connection the closing words of v. 15: "And thou shalt make boards for the Tabernacle of shittim wood standing up " What a contrast this points! We are all fallen creatures; not so the perfect Man, who was "separate from sinners" (Heb. 7:26). He was upright in all His ways. Ten cubits was the height of every board. Each part of Christ's life was of an unvarying standard. Nothing was out of proportion. Looking at each of the ten commandments we cannot say that Christ kept one more perfectly than the others. Each was fully, constantly, and consistently obeyed by Him.

"A cubit and a half shall be the breadth of each board." This is not the first time that we have had this particular measurement: the Ark was, too, a cubit and a half in breadth and a cubit and a half in height (Ex. 25:10); the Mercyseat was also a cubit and a half in breadth (25:17). Both the Ark and the Mercyseat portray the Lord Jesus in the combined glory of His person as the God-man. Thus the breadth—that which gives form and character to a thing—reminds us that while these Boards prefigure our Saviour in the place of human responsibility, they also tell us that it was One who was more than Man who honored and magnified the Law.

3.—Their Sockets.

"And thou shalt make forty sockets of silver under the twenty boards; two sockets under one board for his two tenons and two sockets under another board for his two tenons" (v. 19). These forty sockets of silver were for the twenty boards on the south side; in vv. 20, 21 we find that the same provision was made for the twenty boards on the north side; while in v. 25 we learn that the eight boards at the western rear had also two sockets each. Thus there were ninety-six in all. Each board was maintained in its place by the two tenons or "hands" which fitted into and were grasped by the silver sockets.

The ninety-six silver "sockets" formed the foundation, and upon them rested the whole fabric of the tabernacle. This tells us, in language too plain to be misunderstood, that redemption is the basis on which Christ has become the meeting-place between the ineffably holy God and His inherently sinful people. It was only through redemption that the perfect humanity and Divine glory of Christ could avail us. Had He not "given Himself a ransom for us," He must have forever remained alone (John 12:24). He was in Himself the "true" and "perfect" Tabernacle, but only by the gift and sacrifice of Himself could He bring us nigh to God. It is because in the Gospel He is set before our eyes "crucified" (Gal. 3:1), that Christians have confidence before God. Reconcilia-

tion rests upon redemption by ransom.

It was the **preciousness of redemption** which was typically expressed in the "sockets of silver." This is definitely established by the fact that all the silver used in connection with the Tabernacle was derived from "the atonement money" (Ex. 30:16). As we hope to deal with this more fully when we come to Ex. 30, a brief summary must here suffice. In Ex. 30:12 we learn that when Moses took the sum of the number of Israel that every man was required to give a ransom for his soul. This ransom consisted of half a shekel (by comparing Ex. 30:13 with Lev. 27:3 it will be found that this was a **silver** coin, in value about 2/6 or 62 cents: the rich might not give more, nor the poor less (v. 15). Concerning this atonement-money God ordered Moses to "appoint it for the service of the Tabernacle (v. 16)—a part of this "service" being to make the silver sockets for its foundations.

It was elsewhere taught Israel that it was the blood "that maketh an atonement for the soul" (Lev. 17:11)—typified by the blood of animals. The blood of their sacrifices came nearest to exhibiting the **mode** of atonement; but in Ex. 30 the silver "atonement-money" proclaimed the **preciousness** of Christ's atonement. The significance of both types may be seen by noting how the Holy Spirit has set each aside, because the Reality has been manifested. Just as we are told in the presence of the **one** "sacrifice for sins" that it was not possible "that the blood of bulls and goats should take away sins" (Heb. 10:4), so we appreciate the design of the atonement-silver when, beholding Him in whom is treasured up all redemption wealth, we read, "Ye were not redeemed with corruptible things as silver and gold" (1 Peter. 1:18).

We must not further enlarge on this fascinating topic, but ere passing from it attention must be called to two most remarkable statements in the Psalms which plainly anticipated the replacing of the shadows by the Substance. In Psa. 49 the costliness of redemption is emphasised by affirming that it lies far beyond the resources of human riches: "They that trust in their wealth, and boast themselves in the multitude of their riches; none of them can by any means redeem his brother, nor give to God a ransom for him: For the redemption of their soul is precious, and it (the type) **ceaseth** forever" (vv. 6-8). This finds its sequel in 1 Peter 1:18, 19. In Psa.

50 we find Jehovah saying "I will take no bullock out of thy house, nor he-goats out of thy folds," which finds its sequel in Heb. 10:4. Thus Psa. 49 disallows the silver and gold which once pointed to the precious ransom, while Psa. 50 disallows the sacrificing of bulls and goats which once foreshadowed the precious blood.

4.—Their Meaning.

The relation of the Boards to the Tabernacle, to its holy vessels, and to the ministrations of the priests therein, supplies the key to their distinctive significance. Without these Boards there had been no tabernacle to house its furniture and no place for the priests to serve in. Moreover, without them the beautiful Curtains could not have been displayed. Upon the golden Boards, held together by the golden bars, resting in their silver sockets, were sustained all the weight of the Curtains and Coverings. So on the God-man was hung all the weight of the Divine government and all the glories of His Father's house. In Him has been completely realised what was typified by Eliakim—read carefully Isa. 22:20-25. It is this which brings out the meaning of the other numerals here. There were forty-eight boards in all and ninty-six sockets: thus we have 6x8 or 4x12 and 12x8. Six is the number of man and eight that of a new order or a fresh beginning. This would point to Christ as "the Second Man" (1 Cor. 15:47), the Head of the new race, the "new man" (Eph. 2:15). Four is the number of earth, and twelve of governmental perfection: so that 4x12 and 8x12 would suggest the governmental claims of God vindicated on earth by the Head of the Church, the "New Man."

That which is foreshadowed in the Boards is the Person of Christ as what sustained His work. The massive framework of the golden Boards was to the Curtains and Coverings, suspended from them, what the poles are to a tent. "They upheld and sustained the glorious display of the blue, purple, scarlet, and fine linen cherubim, as also the goats' hair curtains. Thus what the Lord Jesus Himself was, and is, viz., Son of God, Son of Man, that He has made manifest in His life, and above all, in His death on the cross: and His blessed work there, derives all of its unspeakable value and eternal efficacy from Himself. It is faith in Him that is salvation: 'He that believeth on the Son hath life.' May there not be a tendency to separate too much the work of the Lord Jesus from His person? to preach the death of the blessed Lord without sufficiently preaching also the Lord Himself?

"The boards and bars have the same relation to the Tabernacle itself, as the truth contained in the first two chapters of the Epistle to the Hebrews has to the rest of the Epistle. In the first two chapters, the great foundations of faith are laid. The Lord Jesus Christ is presented to us as the Son; the brightness of God's glory, and the express image of His person; God, the Creator—the Sustainer of all things. He is also presented to us as the Son of Man, partaker of flesh and blood in order to die; the Firstborn from the dead; all things put under Him; anointed above His fellows; not ashamed to call them brethren. On these great truths respecting Christ, depend all the other great verities connected with the value of His sacrifice; the glory and power of His priesthood; the eternal salvation, the eternal redemption, and the eternal inheritance which are obtained for us by His blood" (Mr. G. Soltau).

5.—Their Distribution.

Twenty of the acacia Boards, overlaid with gold, were used for the south side of the Tabernacle (v.18), twenty were used on the north side (v. 20), two boards were used for the corners of the two sides at the rear; and six more completed the back (v. 25). Thus the numeral which is most prominent here is two, one of the scriptural meanings of which is testimony or witness: "in the mouth of two or three witnesses the truth shall be established." So also when Christ sent forth the disciples to bear testimony unto Him it was by two and two. Therefore is the second person of the Godhead called "the faithful and true Witness" (Rev. 3:14). Thus have we another hint here of the distinctive significance of our present type—it is the person of the Lord Jesus with His two natures, Divine and human.

Separate consideration should be given to the two "corner boards" see vv. 23, 24. It was these which gave increased stability to the whole structure. "Our thoughts naturally turn to the two occasions on which the Lord is spoken of in Scripture with reference to the corner; 'Behold, I lay in Zion, for a foundation, a Stone, a tried Stone, a precious corner Stone, a sure foundation' (Isa. 28:16). 'The Stone, which the builders refused, is become the Head-stone of the corner.' (Psa. 118:22). Here we have presented to us, a corner-stone as foundation, and a corner-stone crowning the building: the beginning and the end. The whole strength of the edifice depending on the firmness of the foundation corner-stone; and the whole compactness, and knitting together of the building as one depending on the head-stone of the corner. God laid the foundation in the death of His Son; He completed the building in His resurrection. The walls of living stones rest securely on this Rock of Ages, and are bound everlastingly together on the top-stone. The corner-boards of the Tabernacle may have some reference to these blessed truths." (Mr. G. Soltau).

6.—Their Couplings.

"Two tenons shall there be on one board, set in order one against another: thus shalt thou make for all the boards of the Tabernacle" (v. 17). As the margin informs us, the Hebrew word rendered "tenons" is literally "hands," and it is to be regretted that the translators did not use this word in the text itself. These "hands" grasped the Boards and held them securely in place. Most beautifully did they prefigure the God-man in His voluntary humiliation, dependent upon and in subjection to the Father. As the perfect Servant He was upheld and sustained by the hands of God the Father from above, the Spirit below ministering to Him. Of old the Spirit of prophecy cried "Let **Thy hand** be upon the Man of Thy right hand, upon the Son of Man whom Thou madest strong for Thyself" (Psa. 80:17). So in one of the Messianic Psalms (see v. 5) we find the dependent One saying, "My times are in **Thy hand**" (Psa. 31:15). Beautiful is it to hear Him crying from the cross, "Father, **into Thy hands** I commend My spirit" (Luke 23:46). But how blessed to know that He is now seated on "the **right hand** of the Majesty on high" (Heb. 1:3)! Thus we see, once more, there is a spiritual significance to the minutest detail in these Tabernacle types.

7.—Their Bars.

These are described in much detail in vv. 26-29, to which we would ask the reader to turn. The "bars" were employed to unite the Boards together firmly and solidly. "Each of the boards terminated, as to the lower extremity, in two tenons, which were inserted into mortises in two sockets of silver. The boards were also sustained in their upright position and linked together by five bars of shittim wood, overlaid with gold, which ran through rings or staples of gold inserted in the boards. The middle bar of the five ran the whole length of the Tabernacle, uniting all the twenty boards together; the other four bars, of which two were placed above, and two below the middle bar, are not described as running all the length, but perhaps only extended half the distance, namely, fifteen cubits each. A similiar number of bars coupled the boards composing the north side, and also the west end of the Tabernacle. On the whole therefore there were forty-eight boards and fifteen bars" (Mr. Soltau).

The typical meaning of these "bars" is not difficult to perceive, though they point to that which lies altogether beyond our finite grasp. They served to give unity to the structure by securely linking the Boards together. The wooden Boards, overlaid with gold, portrayed the two natures in Christ: the "bars" pointed to the perfect **union** between them. Though very God of very God, and also very Man of very Man, yet is our Saviour not two persons, but one—the God-man. Though totally distinct, yet are His two natures perfectly and forever joined together, though none of us can say where nor understand how they meet. How significant, then, that these very "bars" which united the boards were themselves made of wood overlaid with gold! May the Spirit of God continue to unfold to us the glories of our Divine Saviour.

CHAPTER 43

THE VEIL

EXODUS 26:31-33

In our last article we had before us the framework of the Tabernacle proper, i.e, the holy place and the most holy. Outside of this, as we shall yet see, D.V., was the court of the Tabernacle, completing its threefold division. Thus there was really a Tabernacle within a tabernacle. Inside the framework of the golden-covered boards, ceiled by the lovely curtains and their coverings, were the two inner rooms. These were separated by another curtain, called "the Veil." It was this which divided the holy place from the holy of holies. The first compartment would thus be thirty feet by fifteen, and the innermost, a separate apartment of fifteen feet by fifteen. In this innermost chamber was Jehovah's throne upon the ark, where the Shekinah-glory dwelt between the two cherubim.

In the verses which form the basis of our present study, we find Jehovah giving instructions to Moses concerning the Veil. He is told of what material it must be made, the manner of its workmanship, and where and how to hang it. Its presence before the holy of holies invested it with a peculiar sanctity and the light from the lampstand shining upon it would reveal its varied beauties. There it hung for five hundred years before the eyes of Israel's priests as they ministered at the table and the golden altar. It announced, in the language of symbolry, that the way of approach to God was not then made known. But inasmuch as it was a curtain and not a wall of stone or metal, there was more than a hint given of its temporary nature, and that ultimately a way of access would be revealed. Seven things will now engage our attention:—

1. Its Material.

"And thou shalt make a veil of blue, and purple, and scarlet, and fine twined linen of cunning work" (v. 31). Like the ten white curtains which formed the inner ceiling of the Tabernacle, the Veil was made of linen, on which the beautiful colours were wrought. But it was not merely linen, but of "fine twined linen;" pointing to the moral excellency of Him who was foreshadowed. The same thought is given in the "fine flour" (Lev. 2:1), and in the "refined gold" (1 Chron. 28:18) and "refined silver" (1 Chron. 29: 4), which was used in the Temple.

The whiteness of the pure linen used in the Veil pointed to the sinless purity of "the Man Christ Jesus" both in His inward thoughts and desires and in His outward ways and works. The eye of God, who is light, could rest upon that Holy One, and find every ray of His own perfect Being reflected in this lowly but lovely Son of man. "The fine linen of the Veil seems, then, especially to present to us 'the Righteous One,' who in His life of toil and sorrow, and most especially in His death of shame and suffering, manifested that unsullied purity, that perfect obedience, and that delight in accomplishing the will of His Father, whereby He has earned for Himself a name, which is above every name, the name of Jesus; 'Who was made sin for us, that we might be made the righteousness of God in Him'" (Mr. Soltau).

Attention should be called to the words "fine twined linen of cunning work," an expression used in connection with the Tabernacle only in the "linen" and the "breastplate." As there is nothing meaningless in Scripture we are assured there is a profound spiritual significance in this detail too. It tells us that this fabric was skilfully wrought: literally, the Hebrew is: "the work of a devisor." Divine wisdom was given for its manufacture and it was copied from a heavenly pattern: its equal never again being found on earth. As this "fine twined linen" foreshadowed the humanity of our Saviour, would not the "cunning work"

231

point to the Divine omniscience in devising for Christ a human nature that was sinless? "A body hast Thou prepared Me" (Heb. 10:5) would give us the antitype. Gabriel's words to Mary betokened the wonder of Immanuel's birth—see Luke 1: 28-35.

2. Its Colours.

"And thou shalt make a veil of blue, and purple, and scarlet, and fine twined linen of cunning work." There is one little variation here from what was before us in 26:1. In connection with the Curtains, the ground-work of "fine twined linen" was mentioned first, ere the colours are specified; but here in the directions for the making of the Veil the colours are referred to first. This seems to intimate that our attention now is to be concentrated more on what was prefigured by the blue and purple and scarlet rather than on what was foreshadowed by the linen itself. The colours told of Heaven, the Cross and the Throne. Probably the colours were used so freely that little of the white linen would be visible.

3. Its Meaning.

This is specifically defined for us by the Holy Spirit in Hebrews 10:19, 20: "Having therefore, brethren, boldness to enter into the holiest by the blood of Jesus, by a new and living way, which He hath newly-made for us, through the veil, that is to say, His flesh." The Veil, then, spoke of the humanity of Christ, of the Son of God incarnate. The one side of it was seen by human eyes, as the Levites ministered in the Sanctuary; the other side was beheld only by Jehovah. The Veil, therefore, was a fitting type that Christ incarnate was perfect God and perfect Man. The colours which were embroidered upon it told of the perfections of His person. Its purpose was to shut out the priests of Israel from the holy of holies, where Jehovah had His earthly throne. The object of a veil is to hide. "Come not" (Lev. 16:2) was the warning which it consistently gave forth. Thus the Veil foreshadowed the moral glories of the Saviour, but at the same time showed, by the very display of such heavenliness of character, how far fallen man was away from God.

The perfect Manhood of Christ exhibited the only humanity which can approach unto God, which can live in His presence, which can dwell in the blazing light of His manifested glory. The perfections of the God-man only served to emphasise the imperfections of fallen man. The

flawless life of Christ made the more evident the awful distance between the thrice holy God and depraved and guilty sinners. "The Incarnation of Christ, while it proclaimed God, shuts out man. Men might admire the beauty of the Veil; as men may to-day admire the human character of Christ after the flesh, and the teaching of His earthly life. But the more perfect we find that humanity, the greater the evidence that it is totally distinct from man's. The Incarnation by itself (apart from the redemption which was the purpose and object of it) neither brings man to God, nor God to men. True, it was ' God with us' just as the Tabernacle was with men: but, when the symbol of God's presence was with men, man could not have access to it. The beautiful Veil was an effectual bar, and its one and only voice was 'Come not.' The life of Christ on earth was an unceasing proclamation of the fact that only His humanity was shone upon by and dwelt in the glory of God. The proclamation of His life ever was: 'Except ye be holy, sinless, spotless, perfect, as I am, ye cannot enter into the presence of God. It was not the object of the Veil to give access to God; for it was that which prevented it. Even so it was not the perfection of Christ's life on earth that brings us into the presence of God" (Dr. E. W. Bullinger).

Typically, the Veil, in O.T. times, announced that the way in to God's presence was not then made manifest. It did not suggest that there was no way, but simply that the way was not then revealed. Subsequently, we find that Jehovah gave instructions as to how Israel's high priests might pass within the Veil, and that was, by the blood of sacrifice (Lev. 16:19). This, too, foreshadowed the coming Substance, yet also bore testimony to the temporary nature of that dispensation. It announced that the way for sinful man to go to God was by sacrifice, yet the one Aaron offered was not that which opened up the real way to God. The Veil unrent signified that the way into the Holiest was not yet revealed. The sacrifice by which Aaron went in once a year foreshadowed the perfect Sacrifice, and his admittance typified the entrance of our Great High Priest into the Heavenly Sanctuary.

"The Veil still unrent declared that if the way in was by sacrifice, the true Sacrifice—the one which really opened up the actual way to the presence of God— had not yet been provided. But if the unrent Veil signified that the true way was not yet made known, it also implied it would be made known. Faith, then, using what was a figure for the time then present, and what had been imposed on Israel until the time of reformation looked forward to the time of the revelation of the true Sacrifice and the manifestation of the true way of approach to God. Turning now to the N.T., we find that when Christ died as a Sacrifice the Veil of the Temple was rent from the top to the bottom. This rending of the Veil declared that the true way to God had been made known. The sacrifice of Christ is the true ground of approach to God. His death, His blood, has opened up the way to His presence. The rending of the Veil of the Temple when Christ died, was the sign that the way to God which faith had been taught to look forward to had been opened up. The Sacrifice which the yearly sacrifice of Lev. 16 had pointed forward to had been made, and the way to God, of which the Veil was a witness, while declaring it to be unmanifested, was now revealed" (Mr. C. Crain).

4. Its Cherubim.

"With cherubim shall it be made" (v. 31). The typical significance of the cherubim here is a double one, accordingly as we view the Veil itself in its twofold aspect. First, the Veil sets forth the excellencies of Christ's person as the incarnate Son of God. In this connection the cherubim would intimate that no matter whether the Lord Jesus be contemplated as the Man from Heaven (1 Cor. 15:47), yet in it (John 3:13), even when on earth (the "blue"); or on the Cross as an expiatory sacrifice (the "scarlet"); or on the Throne (the "purple"), He carries in His own person the judicial authority of the eternal God. Second, the Veil unrent signified that the perfections of Christ only served to emphasise the truth that sinful man had no access to God. This solemn fact would be the more impressively set forth by the cherubim wrought upon it. As the priests gazed on the Veil and saw the mystic figures standing out in vivid colours, would not their thoughts turn at once to what is recorded in Gen. 3:24? When God banished His rebellious creatures from Eden, He placed cherubim at the entrance to the Garden, with flaming sword which turned every way. Here on the Veil these cherubim taught the same lesson; sinful man, as such, cannot approach the ineffably holy God!

5. Its Position.

"And thou shalt hang up the Veil under the taches . . . and the veil shall divide unto you between the holy place and the most holy" (v. 33). The Veil was placed right over the entrance of the holy of holies and thus effectually shut out those who ministered in the holy place. God dwelt behind the Veil. Its very location, then, furnished the key to its significance. As the Veil sets forth the "flesh" of Christ, we are specifically taught that His humanity was the veil of the Godhead. God was enveiled, as well as unveiled, by the Lord Jesus. "God was in Christ reconciling the world unto Himself" (2 Cor. 5:19). And most effectively did the unsullied person of the Son of man bar the sinner's way unto God. This is self evident. If the humanity of Christ is the standard humanity, if it is the humanity in which alone God will dwell, if it is the only humanity which can enter the Glory, then the humanity of Christ is a barrier to the fallen sons of men. So long as Christ walked this earth He witnessed to the separation of the natural man from God.

"He stood forth as the perfect Man, who alone was fit to appear before God; the standard weight of the sanctuary. Any one, weighed against Him, was found wanting. His perfect righteousness placed in dark shade the uncleanness of all men. The measure of His stature declared the utter insignficance of all human attainments. His fulness proved man's emptiness. The white and glistening purity of His character, exceeding white as snow, put to shame the filthiness of all that was born of woman. Thus, the very display of the Perfect One on earth, showed the impossibility of any approach to God, unless some way could be devised whereby the sinner could draw near, clothed in garments unsullied. Man, both Jew and Gentile, had made it plain that he was by nature a sinner, and had come short of the glory of God; and the presence amongst men, of One who was fit for that glory, only rendered the melancholy fact the more apparent. The Veil, as it hung on its golden pillars, precluded entrance into the holiest: the ark and the mercy-seat were hidden, instead of being laid open to public gaze" (Mr. G. Soltau).

6. Its Supports.

"And thou shalt hang it on four pillars of shittim wood overlaid with gold: their hooks shall be of gold, upon the four sockets of silver" (v. 32). The "pillars" of wood and gold, symbolized once more, the two natures in the God-man. They intimated that everything in redemption depended upon the **person** of Christ. Unless He had become Man, it had been impossible for Him to die; unless He had been more than Man, His sacrifice could not have availed. But being both God and Man He was fully competent to make propitation for the sins of His people. The whole value of His work accrues from the peerless excellency of His person. That these "pillars" were four in number, shows it is Christ on earth which was contemplated. It is to be carefully noted that these "four pillars" were without the "fillets" and "chapiters" which adorned the five pillars at the door of the Tabernacle (36:38): thus they lacked the architectural completeness of a pillar. Their abrupt termination pointed to the Saviour "cut off" in the midst of His days" (Isa. 53:8; Psa. 102: 23, 24).

But the **"four** pillars" were for another purpose: they served to display the **Veil** in all its beauty. Between them the Veil was stretched out. Without them, the Veil had hung in folds, and the loveliness of its embroidered designs would not have appeared. The Veil spoke of God the Son **incarnate.** Now the antitype of this is clearly before us in the opening books of the N.T. It is in the **four Gos-**pels that the glories of the God-man are revealed to our eyes. They accomplish exactly the same design as did the "four pillars." In them we have spread out, as it were, the lovely antitypical Veil. There, too, we behold the "cunning work" of the Divine Designer, blending together the varied **perfections of our blessed** Lord, yet severally presenting Him as the Son of David, the flawless Servant, the Son of man, and the Son of God.

"Their hooks shall be of gold": **not** wooden hooks overlaid, but of solid gold. This is very beautiful. In connection with the ephod of the high priest we are told, "He made the ephod of gold, blue and purple, and scarlet, and fine twined linen. And they did beat the gold into thin plates, and cut it into wires, to work it in the blue, and in the purple, and in the scarlet, and in the fine linen" (39:2, 3). And, as we shall yet see, D.V., golden-strands were also woven into other articles. But there were none in the fabric of the Veil. No wires of gold were mingled with the fine linen, which formed the basis of its structure. This could not be, for their presence would have im-

plied that His humanity was commingled with His Deity, which was not the case. Though Deity and humanity were perfectly united in one Person, yet they are not confounded. Nevertheless, the Veil **was** held by "golden hooks" **from above,** thus signifying the Son of man was, throughout His earthly course, sustained and supported from on High!

"Upon the four sockets of silver." It was **in them** that the "four pillars" securely rested. As we saw in our last article, the "silver" was provided by the "atonement-money." How significant then is this detail of our type! The "sockets" conduct us to the foundation, and point to the redemptive-work of Christ on the cross. In perfect accord with this we may note that in Heb. 10:19, 20 the "blood of Jesus" and "the Veil" are brought together. God will never have it forgotten that the Cross is the basis of all blessing.

7. Its Rending.

The Veil unrent shut man out from God. It spoke of separation from Him because of sin. Between the priests and Jehovah stood this Veil. .Between the ordinary worshipper in the outer court and Jehovah was a double partition, for he had no access into the holy place; while between the one outside the court was a threefold barrier between him and Jehovah! The whole ritual of Israel's worship emphasised the distance between God and the creature. Bounds were set about Sinai, so that not even a beast must touch it. One Tribe alone was permitted to encamp, immediately, around the Tabernacle: one family alone of that Tribe was singled out and allowed to enter the holy place: and one man alone of that family had access into the holiest, and that, only once a year, and with such awe-inspiring preparations and ceremonies as must have filled him with fear lest he should incur the judgment of the Most High. Yet, as previously intimated, God did, even then, give a hint, that a way would be made for sinners to approach Him. In Lev. 4:6 we learn that the priest was commanded to take of the blood of the sin-offering and sprinkle it seven times before the Lord, before the Veil of the sanctuary"! Clearer still was what was foreshadowed by the ritual of the Day of Atonement, when the high priest passed within the Veil (Lev. 16: 15). The antitype of this is found in Heb. 4:14; 6:19; 9:12. Christ has passed into Heaven itself, and what is more, He has opened up a way for us to enter too

—Heb. 10:19, 20. But this was consequent upon His death.

"It was not the beauty of the veil which made entrance possible, but the sprinkling of atoning blood before it! That beauty might be admired by the worshipper: he might sing hymns in its praise, and give all sorts of sentimental and endearing names to it. He might use all kinds of poetical language in describing it; he might even copy it, and produce similiar patterns of embroidery, or schemes of colours; but there was only one way of passing to the other side of it, and of standing alive in the presence of God's glory; and that was by sprinkling the blood before it, and taking the blood of the victim beyond it. This blood told of substitution, and acknowledged that he who entered did so as a sinner, who had died, and suffered the wages of sin. By no other means could he stand on the other side of that veil and live.

"The great antitypical lesson for us all is, that it is not by the beautiful life of Christ that we can enter into the presence of God. It is not by any 'imitation of Christ,' not by the observance of any Rules for Daily Living, not by leading a religious and devout life, that we can pass beyond that veil. To attempt it is to confess our ignorance of the very first letter of the Christian's alphabet; and it is to own that we are destitute of the first fundamental lesson of the Christian's life. It is only when the precious blood of that perfect humanity of Christ had been shed that it avails us as our title to enter God's presence. This is why, in 1 John 1:7, when speaking of our entrance into the light of God's presence, and walking therein, that we are at once reminded of that Blood, which alone gives us our title to enter, and preserves us alive when we have entered into that Presence. 'God is light....If we walk in the light as He is in the light, we have fellowship one with another, and the blood of Jesus Christ His Son cleanseth us from all sin!' It is here, in this connection, that the cleansing-power of the blood is mentioned; not in connection with our sin or sinning.

"When it is a case of sin, then it is that we are reminded, not of the atoning blood of Christ, but of our Advocate with the Father! Then it is that we are simply assured of two facts:—(1) that relationship is not broken; God is still our Father; and (2) that Christ is our all-sufficient propitiation (1 John 2:1). But it is in connection with approaching to and walking in the light of God's presence within the veil that we are reminded of the blood which must first be sprinkled before we can have either admission to Him, or preservation when there (1 John 1:7). Hence it is not the life which Christ lived in His spotless humanity (still less our own imperfect copy of it) that gives us liberty to enter, but only when that humanity had been stained by His own blood of atonement. Then it is that we have 'boldness to enter into the Holiest, by the blood of Jesus, by a newly-slain and living way, which He hath newly-made (or opened) for us, through the veil, that is to say, His flesh' Heb. 10:19, 20" (Dr. B. W. Bullinger).

The historical reference to what is referred to in Heb. 10 is given us in the Gospels. There we learn that simultaneous with the death of Christ the veil was rent. (Matt. 27: 45-52.) There are some remarkable resemblances between the shadow and the Substance. First, the veil was rent while hanging between heaven and earth: so Christ was smitten while suspended from the Cross. Second, the veil was rent in twain from the top. this showed it was down by the same Hand as had fallen so heavily on the suffering Substitute—see Psa. 38:2; 42: 7; 88:6, 7; Isa. 53:10; Zech. 13:7. This is the only type where God Himself represented by His own act that it was His hand which smote the Lord Jesus! Third, it was rent "from the top to the bottom" —not an inch of it was left untorn: so the atoning work of Calvary was a complete one, nothing being left for the sinner to do or add. Fourth, it was rent "in the midst" (Luke 23:45), and thus the Mercy-seat in the centre of the holy of holies would be fully revealed: so the believing sinner is not asked to approach God in any roundabout way, or through a side entrance, but has direct access to the Father through the Son. The rending of the veil in the midst, would be such that all within the temple would see it: so the death of Christ was not in a corner, but public and before many eye-witnesses. Fifth, the veil was rent the moment that Christ died (Matt. 27:50), showing that the barrier between God and the contrite sinner was gone. Sixth, as soon as the veil was rent it was changed from a barrier to a gateway: the moment Christ died a "newly-slain and living way" was opened for sinners to God. Seventh, it is deeply significant that the Holy Spirit has linked together the rending of the veil with the opening of the graves (Matt. 27:51, 52), though in time the latter did not occur till after Christ's resurrection. Does not this tell us that, full atonement having been made by Him, a way has been made from the deepest depths into which sin had plunged us, into the highest heaven where grace has placed us!

The purpose of God has now been accomplished. The Corn of wheat, having fallen into the ground and died, now bringeth forth much fruit (John 12:24). The Blood has been shed, the Sacrifice has been offered, the Veil has been rent; and Christ, as the Forerunner of His people, has passed into the Holiest. We then may draw near. Because Christ received the wages of sin which were due us, we share the reward which was due Him. We may boldly enter in. By faith we have unhindered access into the Heavenly Sanctuary. Every barrier having been removed, the believing worshipper may, with perfect liberty, draw near to the Throne of Grace. Then **"let us draw near,** with a true heart, in full assurance of faith, having our hearts sprinkled from an evil conscience" (Heb. 10:22).

CHAPTER 44

THE TABERNACLE DOOR

EXODUS 26:36-37

One important principle which must be observed if the Word of God is to be intelligently studied, is noting carefully the order in which truth is there presented to us. God is a God of order, and infallible wisdom marks all His handiwork; yet His order is often different from ours. In the Scriptures the Holy Spirit frequently ignores the sequence of events and places side by side things which did not immediately follow each other in time. The books of the Bible are not always placed in their historical order: Job takes us back to a period long before the Israelites settled in Canaan. The Psalms and the Proverbs were written centuries before the events described in Nehemiah and Esther. So it is with many of the smaller details in the different books. Take the following as examples. The opening of the graves and the coming forth of many of the saints is mentioned right after the Saviour's death and rending of the Temple's veil (Matt. 27:51-52), yet, as a matter of fact, these occurred after the resurrection of Christ. So in Luke 23.45 the rending of the veil is recorded before the Lord committed His spirit into the hands of the Father.

The arrangement followed by the Holy Spirit varied according to His several designs. Sometimes the chronological order is departed from for a dispensational reason: sometimes details are arranged so as to present a climax: sometimes the order is a moral one: at others, things are placed in juxtaposition to show the relation between cause and effect. Notably is that the case in Matt. 27:51-53: the opening of the graves there attested the efficacy of the Saviour's death and shows it is the ground of the saints' walk in newness of life. Sometimes the design of the Spirit is to point a contrast: such is the case in Luke 23:45. There He has linked together the three hours of darkness and the rending of the Veil: in the former we have Christ shut out from God, in the latter the way is now opened for us into the presence of Him who is Light!

The student of Scripture loses much when he fails to diligently bear in mind this principle. Strikingly is it exemplified in connection with the Tabernacle. It is not always easy to discern the Divine plan, and much prayerful meditation is required to discover the perfections of every detail. That which we are now to contemplate is the Entrance into the Tabernacle, and what we would here particularly take notice of is that this "Door" is mentioned immediately after the description of the Veil. Doubtless there is more than one reason for this; but that which is almost apparent on the surface is that the one points a striking contrast from the other, and the details connected with each bear this out. The Veil had "cherubim" embroidered upon it, the Door had not: the Veil was suspended from four pillars, the hanging for the Door from five: the former had no "chapiters," the latter had; the sockets of the former were made of silver, the latter were of brass. But the outstanding difference between them was this: the Veil was to shut out, whereas the Door was to give admittance: the Veil barred the way into the Holiest, the "hanging" was for the constant entrance of the priests into the Holy Place. Let us now consider:—

1. Its Location.

The Door into God's dwelling-place was no narrow one, but stretched right across the whole of its length, and was ten cubits (fifteen feet) in height. Some of the commentators are in error here through confounding the Door of the Tabernacle (26.36) with the Gate of the Court (27:16). It is important that the student should clearly distinguish between them, for they typically set forth two entirely different lines of truth.

The Door into the Tabernacle spanned the whole of the eastern side. Most significant and most fitting was this, for the east is the quarter of the sun-rising. It is in the east that we discover the evidences of the ending of night and the dawning of another day. Thus a further contrast is here presented. In Gen. 3:24 we read that the Lord God "drove out the man, and he placed at the east of the garden of Eden cherubim, and a flaming sword which turned every way, to keep the way of the tree of life." There, through his sin, man was in the darkness, and in consequence, banished from that place where God had communed with him; and at the east was stationed a flaming barrier. But here, where sin had been typically put away, the priestly family walking in the light, found a door on the eastern side of the Tabernacle which admitted them into Jehovah's dwelling-place!

2. Its Material.

"And thou shalt make an hanging for the door of the tent, of blue, and purple, and scarlet, and fine twined linen, wrought with needlework" (v. 36). The fabric of this hanging for the Door was of the same goods and of the same fine quality that composed the Curtains and the Veil. Fine twined linen formed its basis. It was only as the Son of God became incarnate that the true dwelling-place for Deity on earth was provided. But, as shown in the last article, the Incarnation, though bringing God down to men, did not of itself give men access to God—for that the Veil must be rent, death must come in. Here, too, in the entrance to the Tabernacle, we are shown that it is only through the Man Christ Jesus that God could be approached unto.

There is one added word here in connection with the fine twined linen which claims our notice: it was "wrought with needlework." This was not said in connection with the Curtains or Veil, and is only mentioned elsewhere in the description of the Gate in the outer Court (v. 27:16) and the Girdle of the high priest (v. 28:39). We may add that the Hebrew word here for "needlework" is, in Ex. 35:35, rendered "the work of the embroiderer," in 1 Chron. 29:2 and Ezek. 17:3, "divers colours," and in Psalm 139:15 "curiously wrought." Combining these slightly varied meanings, the term would denote minutely variegated. Thus, it appears, that the Holy Spirit here intimates that attention should be fixed upon the manner in which the different colours were wrought into and interwoven with the fine linen.

3. Its Colours.

The "blue" points to Christ as the Heavenly One, the Son of God; the "scarlet" refers to Him as the Son of man—suffering in the past, glorified on earth in a coming day. The "purple" speaks, distinctively, of the kingship of Christ, but also points to the wonderful union between His Deity and His humanity. The mention of the "blue, and purple, and scarlet," is repeated no less than twenty-four times in connection with the Tabernacle's accessories and priesthood, yet never once is the order varied. This suggests an important truth and lesson in connection with their arrangement. So beautifully has this been brought out by another in a book long-since out of print, we transcribe freely from its most helpful interpretation:—

"If we are to place the blue and the scarlet side by side, without the intervention of some other colour, the eye would be offended with the violent contrast; for, though each is beautiful in itself, and suitable to its own sphere, yet there is such a distinction, we might almost say opposition, in their hues, as to render them inharmonious if seen in immediate contact. The purple interposing remedies this unpleasing effect: the eye passes with ease from the blue to the scarlet, and vice versa, by the aid of this blended colour, the purple. The blue gradually shades off into its opposite, the scarlet; and the gorgeousness of the latter is softened by imperceptible degrees into the blue. The purple is a new colour formed by mingling the two: it owes its peculiar beauty alike to both; and were the due proportion of either absent, its especial character would be lost.,

"The scarlet and the blue are never placed in juxtaposition throughout the fabrics of the Tabernacle. Does not this intimate a truth of an important character? Would the Spirit of God have so constantly adhered to this arrangement had there not been some significant reason for it? Are we not hereby taught a very precious fact respecting the Lord Jesus? He is God and Man; and we can trace in the Gospels all the fulness of the Godhead, as well as the dignity and sympathy of the perfect Man. But besides this, in His thoughts, feelings, ways, words, and actions, there is an invariable blending of the two. . . . In contemplating Christ it is well to remember that the first syllable of His name, as given in Isa. 9:6 is 'Wonderful': and part of this marvel is, that in Him are combined the deep thoughts and counsels of God, with the feelings and affections of man.

"Three instances are recorded in the Gospels of the dead being raised to life by Christ: Jairus's daughter, the widow of Nain's son, and Lazarus of Bethany. Together they afford us a complete display of His mighty power: for, in the first case, death had only just seized its victim; in the second, the sorrowing mother was on her way to commit the body of her only son to the grave; in the third, the corpse had already been deposited sometime, and had become corrupt in the tomb. In each of these scenes the three colours may be traced. We can have no hesitation in recognizing the **blue** in the manifestation of the love of God, when His blessed Son at the entreaty of the sorrowful father, went to the house to heal the dying child. On the way, the message came, 'Thy daughter is dead, why troublest thou the Master any further?' Little did they, who spoke these words, understand who the Master was: or the depths of trouble in which He would be overwhelmed, in order that the dead might live. They knew not that God was present with them, manifest in the flesh: but He at once stilled the fear of the damsel's father; thus doing what none but God could do—commanding peace into his bosom in the very presence of death! Again, the voice of the Mighty God sounds forth to hush the boisterous grief of those who have no hope, saying, 'Weep not: the damsel is not dead, but sleepeth'. But they perceived not who it was that thus spoke. Death was to them a familiar sight; they knew its palor; but they laughed Christ to scorn; ought not the believer to exactly reverse this? In the presence of the Lord, he may well laugh death to scorn. Lastly; were not the power and the grace of the One from Heaven now known, when He spake those words—'Damsel, I say unto thee, arise'!

"Let us now turn to the **scarlet** in this beautiful picture. Who but the Son of man would have pursued the path of kindness and sympathy, notwithstanding the rude scoffs with which His ready love was met? and who but One that knew what hunger and exhaustion were, would have added to this mighty miracle the command, 'Give her something to eat'? And does not this also exhibit to us the **purple**? With sympathy and love for the child, deeper than the mother's, and yet presented in the scene as one who was Lord in it and above it; He can call the dead to life and at the same moment enter into the minutest want of the little maid. The mere human beings who were present, even the very parents, were so over-powered with what they had wit-

nessed, and with the joy of receiving the dead one back to life, that their human sympathies failed. None but God could thus have abolished death; and none but He who was God and Man, could have so **combined** power, majesty, grace, sympathy and tenderest care!

"The next instance, already alluded to, depicts in few but full sentences, the same lovely colours. Unsolicited, the Son of God went to the city where He knew the stroke of death had fallen, and had inflicted another wound upon another heart already stricken with grief. He timed His visit so as to meet, at the gate, the mournful procession, bearing to the grave the only son of a widowed mother. If any hope of God's intervention had at one time cheered her, whilst she watched her dying child, all such hope must now have fled. A little interval only remained and the earth would close over her lost son. But attracted by the very extremity of the case, He, who declared the Father (John 1:18), drew nigh. With the authority of God, He touched the bier, and arrested the bearers in their progress to the tomb. Struck by a sudden consciousness that they were in the presence of One who had a right to stop them on their way, they stood still. They did not, like the attendants on the dead in former case, laugh Him to scorn; and, therefore, they had the blessing of witnessing His mighty act. He commanded the young man to arise from the bier, as He ordered the child to rise from her bed; and in like manner, He was obeyed: 'He that was dead sat up, and began to speak.' Here, then, the **heavenly** colour was evident, so that even they that looked on said, 'God hath visited His people'. But the heart of Christ was occupied with the mother as well as the child. As the voice of the risen youth reached His ear, He knew how the widow felt, as she heard it. Himself undisturbed by the exercise of His life-giving power, yet fully occupied in sympathy and grace with the yearning of the mother to embrace her son, and thus to assure herself of the reality, which even the evidence of her eyes and ears could scarcely credit, He gave completeness to the scene by **delivering him to his mother**. Here was the perfection of human sensibility, such as no man could have exhibited in such circumstances, unless that man were also God.

"But perhaps the most complete manifestation of 'the Word made flesh,' is to be found in John 11, if we except, as we always must do, the Cross, where all was marvellously concentrated. It seemed to the sisters as if the Lord had strangely disregarded their urgent message: for He still abode at a distance, and allowed not only death to bereave them of their brother, but the grave to close upon his remains, His very reply to their announcement ('Lord, he whom Thou lovest, is sick') contained in it a paradox which they were unable to comprehend, and which the subsequent circumstances apparently falsified; for, His answer was 'This sickness is not unto death, but for the glory of God, that the Son of God might be glorified thereby.' And yet He tarried till death had, for four days, retained its victim. Thus, love and truth in Him who is Love, and who is the Truth, for a while appeared to have failed; but in reality the glory of God was the more to shine forth in His Beloved.

"What mingled feelings occupied the heart of Christ, when, seeing the grief of Mary, and of those around, He groaned in the spirit, and was troubled! He grieved over their unbelief and ignorance of Himself; and yet He wept in sympathy with them, and sorrowed for the very sorrow which His presence might have prevented. Who could have shed tears in such circumstances but Christ? Had a mere man been gifted by God with the power to raise the dead, he would be so eager to exhibit that mighty power, and thereby still the mourners' grief, that he would be unable to weep whilst on the way to the grave.. He must be more than man who could display what man in perfection is. The tears of Jesus are precious, because they are those of true human feeling: but they are most precious because they flow from the heart of Him who is the Mighty God. And, when those tears plenteously fell from His eyes, all questions as to His love were at an end; and even the Jews exclaimed, 'Behold, how He loved him!'

"As with authority He had touched the bier, so now He commanded that the stone should be removed. But Martha interposed her objection and though she owned Christ as Lord, and had heard from His lips the wondrous words, 'I am the Resurrection and the Life,' yet she believed not that there could be a remedy for one who had already seen corruption. It was then that Jesus reminded her of the message He had returned when they sent to inform Him of Lazarus's sickness—that it should not be unto death, by answering, 'Said I not unto thee, that, if thou wouldst believe, thou shalt see the glory of God? God's glory was ever His object: and to accomplish that He had been content to bear the questioning of those near to Him, who could not understand why He

had not at once come to their aid.

"The sepulchre was now laid open; and Jesus lifted up His eyes from that receptacle of death to the Heaven above, resting His spirit in the bosom of His Father, and audibly expressing His dependence on Him, before He cried with a voice of almighty power, 'Lazarus, come forth'. What a wondrous blending was here of subjection and authority, of obedience and command, of 'the open ear,' and of the great 'I am'! The dead, hearing the voice of the Son of God, came forth. The corrupt corpse stepped out in life. What a moment of astonishment and delight must that have been to the sisters, as well as to their brother! But here again the Lord alone entered into the minutest details of this astonishing act of power. He saw, or rather felt (for He loved Lazarus), that His friend was still encumbered with the relics of the grave; and he left it not till others awoke from their surprises, to perceive the clothes that bound and troubled the risen one, but gave another command, 'Loose him, and let him go.' " (Mr. G. Soltau.)

4. Its Meaning.

The "hanging for the door" shut off the court of the Tabernacle from the holy place, yet also formed the entrance to it. It was that which gave the priests access to accomplish their service within. It spoke, then, of the Christian's worship and works being acceptable to God through the Lord Jesus Christ. Apart from the Mediator even the saints can offer nothing which the great and holy God will receive. We give thanks unto the Father "in the name of our Lord Jesus Christ" (Eph. 5:20). It is "by Him" we are to continually offer to God a sacrifice of praise (Heb. 13:15). Our spiritual sacrifices are acceptable to God only "by Jesus Christ" (1 Peter 2:12). In our ministry, God is to be glorified in all things, "through Jesus Christ" (1 Peter 4:11). It is striking to note that the "cherubim" are absent from the Door-hanging. They view the Son of man in His judicial character. Whereas, in the "hanging" He is presented in grace to those that were without, as the Way into the privileges of priests.

5. Its Pillars.

"And thou shalt make for the hanging five pillars of shittim wood, and overlay them with gold" (v. 37). The number of the "pillars" confirms what has just been said above respecting the significant omission of the "cherubim" from the "hanging": for five is the number of grace. These pillars served to support the "hanging" and also to display its beautiful colours. Their materials intimate that it is the God-man, in wondrous grace through whom entrance is given into the sphere of priestly privileges. And where is it, in Scripture, that we have these distinctively set forth? Not in the Prophets, nor in the Gospels, but in the N.T. Epistles. And is it not something more than a curious coincidence that the Epistle-writers were just five in number? Just as the Veil was stretched between four pillars, corresponding to the four Gospels; so the Entrance-curtain into the place of worship hung between five pillars, anticipating the ministry of Paul and Peter, James, John and Jude—note how this very term "pillars" is expressly applied to them in Gal. 2:9!

6. Its Chapiters.

"And the five pillars of it with their hooks: and he overlaid their chapiters and their fillets with gold" (36:38). This was in striking contrast from the "pillars" which supported the Veil, for they had none—foreshadowing Christ as the One "cut off" in the midst of His days. But here, as giving access to the antitypical priestly family into the place of worship and service, Christ is pointed to as the One who is "crowned with glory and honour"! And this is the very viewpoint taken in all the Epistles: their writers proceed on the basis of Christ being at the right hand of God!

7. Its Sockets.

"And thou shalt cast five sockets of brass for them" (v. 37). These formed the foundation for the "pillars" and speak therefore, of redemption. "Brass," when used symbolically, always prefigured the capability of the Saviour to "endure the cross." Thus is the worshipper reminded once more, that Christ is the Door by reason of His sufferings in death. May the Spirit of God ever keep before us the tremendous price which was paid to enable the redeeemd to come before God with sacrifices of praise and thanksgiving.

CHAPTER 45

THE BRAZEN ALTAR

EXODUS 27:1-8

In Ex. 25 and 26 we have had before us the vessels that occupied and the materials which composed the Holy of Holies and the Holy Place. Here in chapter 27, we are conducted to the Outer Court. But there is one notable omission: the golden or incense altar, which stood in the Holy Place, has not been mentioned, nor is it referred to till the thirtieth chapter is reached. The reason for this we shall, D.V., endeavor to indicate when we come to that chapter. Suffice it now to say that the golden altar "is not spoken of until there is a priest to burn incense thereon, for Jehovah showed Moses the patterns of things in the heavens according to the order in which these things are apprehended by faith" (C.H.M.).

The Brazen-altar, which we are now to contemplate, was the biggest of the Tabernacle's seven pieces of furniture. It was almost large enough to hold all the other vessels. Its size indicated its importance. It was placed "before the door" (Ex. 40:6), just inside the Outer Court (40:33), and would thus be the first object to meet the eye of the worshipper as he entered the Tent of the congregation. It is designated "the brazen altar" (38:30), to distinguish it from the golden altar. It was also called "the altar of burnt offering" (30:28).

The Brazen-altar was the basis of the Levitical system. To it the sinner came with his Divinely-appointed victim. There was a fire continually burning upon it (Lev. 6:13), and the daily sacrifice was renewed each morning. There it stood: ever smoking, ever blood-stained, ever open to any guilty Hebrew that might wish to approach it. The sinner, having forfeited his life by sin, another life—an innocent one—must be given in his stead. When the Israelite brought his offering, before killing it he laid his hand on the animal's head, thus becoming identified with it, and thereby the acceptableness of the flawless victim passed to him, while his sin is transferred to it. So, too, this Altar stood in

the path of the priests, as they went in to minister within the Holy Place. At this Altar the high priest officiated on the great day of atonement (Lev. 16). Seven things concerning it will now engage our attention:—

1. Its Position.

The Brazen-altar was not placed outside the Gate, but just within the Court (40:33): thus it would be the first object encountered as the Israelite entered the sacred precincts. Herein we may admire the accuracy of the type, and, too, discover in this detail a refutation of much which now passes for sound Gospel-preaching. The New Testament does not teach universal salvation, nor does it represent the sacrifice of Christ as offered for all mankind; rather was it designed for those who believe. The Old Testament types are in perfect accord with this. No lamb was provided for the Egyptians on that night when the angel of death smote the firstborn. On the day of atonement the high priest confessed over the head of the scapegoat only the sins of Israel (Lev. 16:21). So in our present type: the Altar was provided for none save the Chosen People. Had it been designed for the wilderness-tribes also, it had been placed *outside* the Tabernacle's court; but it was not!

Within the Court, the Altar was placed facing the Door into the Tabernacle proper. It was there that Jehovah met with His people (Ex. 29:11; 33:9; Lev. 15:14). As a matter of fact the Laver stood between the Altar and the Door, yet so vital is the connection of that which spoke of Divine judgment with that which gave entrance into the Divine presence, that in several scriptures nothing is said of the Laver coming in between the two (see 40:6, etc.). How forcibly this tells us of the intimate relation between sacrifice and access to God! The Tabernacle could not be entered till one had first passed the Altar. Blood-shedding is the basis of approach to God.

2. Its Materials.

"And thou shalt make an altar of shittim wood . . . and thou shalt overlay it with brass" (vv. 1, 2). Excepting the "taches" for the Curtains (26:11), and the "sockets" for the "pillars" of the Door (26:36), this is the first time we have had "brass" before us. In the former cases the "brass" would be invisible. Those who entered within the inner compartments would see nothing but a dazzling display of gold, and the lovely tints of the inner Curtains, and the Veil. But here in the Outer Court naught but brass met the eye. There is some doubt as to the precise nature of this metal. So far as we can now ascertain, the ancients had no knowledge of "brass" (which is a mixture of copper and zinc), the Romans being the first to use it. Therefore some students prefer to render the Hebrew word "copper," others think it may have been bronze that was used (a mixture of copper and tin). However, we shall continue speaking of it as "brass."

The symbolical import of "brass" in Scripture is as definitely defined as is that of gold and silver. As gold speaks of *glory* and silver of *redemption*, so brass signifies *judgment*. This may be gathered from the connections in which it is found. The serpent (reminder of the one who was responsible for the bringing in of the "curse") which Moses was ordered to make and affix to the pole, was made of *brass* (Num. 21:9). When Jehovah made known the sore judgments which would come upon Israel for their disobedience (see the whole of Deut. 28), among other things He threatened, "and thy heaven that is above thy head shall be *brass* (v. 23). When describing the millennial blessedness of Israel, following their long alienation from God, the promise given is "for brass I will bring gold" (Isaiah 60:17), i.e., judgment shall give place to glory. When Christ appears in judicial character, inspecting His churches, pronouncing sentence upon them, we read that "His feet (were) like unto *fine brass* as if they burned in a furnace" (Rev. 1:15).

Many are the references to "brass" in the Old Testament, but it is invariably found in an evil association. The first time that it is mentioned is in connection with the descendants of *Cain* (Gèn. 4:22)! Samson was *bound* with "fetters of brass" (Judges 16:21); so, too, was Zedekiah (2 Kings 5:27). Goliath's helmet and armour were of "brass" (1 Sam. 17:5, 6). Saul's armour was of the same material, but David disdained it (1 Sam. 17:38). In delivering His people from the prison-house in which sin had placed them, the Lord says, "He hath broken the gates of brass and cut the bars of iron in sunder" (Psalm 107:16). When remonstrating with His wayward and rebellious people, God said, "I know that thou art obstinate, and thy neck is an iron sinew, and thy brow brass" (Isa. 48:4).

"The acacia wood, of which it was made, need occupy us but briefly, as we have already learned its meaning. It speaks of the incorruptible, sinless humanity of our Lord, and therefore not subject to death. How fitting, then, that it should be connected with the constant witness of death —the altar. Our Lord *need not* die, therefore He could 'lay down' His life! On all others, judgment had a claim; none, therefore, could make atonement even for themselves, much less for others. We see then our Lord as 'the Altar that sanctifieth the gift' (Matt. 23:19). But how necessary was this humanity if there was to be an atonement. The very word for altar is connected with 'slaughter'—the shedding of blood. Therefore the one who was to be the true altar must be capable of dying, and at the same time One upon whom death had no claim" (Mr. S. Ridout).

The wooden boards, overlaid with brass, tell us that the Altar points to the capability of the Sin-bearer to endure the judgment of God. The incarnate Son was no feeble Saviour: "I have laid help upon One that is *mighty*" (Psalm 89:19) was Jehovah's witness of old. The shittim wood spoke of the humanity of the Redeemer; the brass of which it was overlaid told of His power to "endure the Cross."

3. Its Meaning.

This is the easiest to interpret of all the holy vessels. Being the place where sacrifice was offered to God, it spoke, unmistakably, of the Cross of Christ. It pointed to the most solemn aspect of Calvary. The Lord Jesus was the Antitype of both the altar and its sacrifice, as also of the priests who there officiated. That which is distinct in our present type is what is set forth by the brass. This is the hardest of all metals, possessing a greater resistance to fire than gold or silver: in Deut. 33:25 and in Jer. 1:18 "brass" is used as the symbol of ability to endure. Our Saviour was the true Brazen-altar, possessed of that power of enduring, in its awful intensity, the fires of God's holiness. He only could *endure* the Cross. He only could stand, unconsumed, under the storm of Divine judgment. As the brass plates on the Altar protected it from the fervent heat and prevented it from being burnt up, so. Christ passed through the fires of God's wrath without being consumed. He is mighty to save, because He was mighty to endure.

As we have shown above, "brass" in Scripture symbolises judgment. Hence we see the solemn propriety of Moses being instructed to make "a serpent of *brass*" to place upon the pole. Many have wondered how it was possible for the Holy One of God to be represented by a "serpent"—surely *that* was the last of all objects suited to portray Him who is fairer than the children of men! . But no mistake was made. As a fact, the "serpent" was the only similitude of all created things which could suitably picture that particular aspect of the Redeemer's death which was there foreshadowed. The "serpent" was the reminder of the "curse" (Gen. 3), and in Gal. 3:13 we are expressly told that Christ was "made a *curse*" for His people. It was because that uplifted object, presented to the eyes of the bitten Israelites, pointed forward to the Lord Jesus as "made a curse," that it was designed in the form of a serpent. For the same reason, that serpent was made not of silver or gold, but of *brass*. As made a curse for us, the *judgment* of God descended upon Christ, and the sword of Divine justice smote Him (Zech. 13:7).

It was at the Brazen-altar that the holiness and righteousness of God were displayed: His hatred of sin, and His justice in punishing it. Have you ever considered the *holiness* of God, dear reader, and how that your *sins* have unfitted you to come before Him? When Isaiah, the best man in all Israel of his day, was brought into God's presence, and saw the unsullied purity of His person, and beheld the seraphim (who had never come into contact with defilement of any kind) veil their faces with their wings and cry, "Holy, holy, holy is the Lord of hosts," there was wrung from his heart that word, "Woe is me! for I am undone; because I am a man of unclean lips, and I dwell in the midst of a people of unclean lips" (Isa. 6:5). When he saw the holiness of God, the righteousness of His throne, the profound reverence of the heavenly intelligences, on the one hand; and on the other, his own sinfulness and the iniquities of the people among whom he lived; he saw also the awful distance there was between his soul and God, and he cried, "Woe is me!"

As another has pointed out, "In the preceding chapter Isaiah had pronounced six woes on six different classes in Israel; but when brought into the Lord's presence, he pronounced the seventh upon *himself*. His neighbour's sin troubled him no more, but his own did. These must be attended to at once; and, thank God, they were, but not by Isaiah. How could *he* put them away by the power of his hand? or wash them away by his tears? or have them removed by any efforts of his own? Ah, no; but thank God, if a sight of God and His throne, and a sight of his own unfitness for the presence of One so holy, led him to pass judgment upon himself and take his place in the dust, it also brought him low enough to see another thing, and that was *the altar*, and the provision of the altar. The live coal had done its work; the sacrifice had been consumed; and nothing remained but 'the live coal'; this was applied to Isaiah's lips, and the sweet and blessed assurance given, 'thine iniquity is taken away, and thy sin is purged" (Isa. 6:7). The look of anguish passes from his face, and there comes instead the light of holy joy as he believes what is said to him" (Gospel Add. on the Tab., by A.H.).

Does the reader understand what is portrayed in Isa. 6? The "altar" is Christ: the sacrifice consumed on it by the live coal speaks of His work on the cross for poor sinners. The "live coal" is a figure of God's holiness consuming that which offends Him. When Christ was "made sin" (2 Cor. 5:21) for all who shall believe on Him, it pleased Jehovah to "bruise" Him, to "put Him to grief," to "make His soul an offering for sin" (Isa. 53). It was then that the "live coal" reached Him, and He exclaimed, "My heart is like wax; it is melted in the midst of My bowels" (Psalm 22:14). Yes, the coal had done its work, its "strange work" (Isa. 28:21); a sacrifice had been presented—all had gone up to God. And that "live coal" (figure of God's holiness) lies now upon the Altar, waiting for the sinner to take the place Isaiah took, and pass judgment on himself, as he did; and the moment he does so his iniquity is taken away and his sin is purged.

The Brazen-altar, inside the Court, faced the door into the Tabernacle proper, and it was at this place Jehovah met with His people: "*There* will I meet with the children of Israel" (Ex. 29:42, 43). So the Cross is now the meeting-place between God and the sinner. "It is on the foundation of what was accomplished there that He can be just and the Justifier of everyone that believeth in Jesus. There is no other ground on which He can bring the sinner into His presence. If the Israelite rejected the brazen altar, he shut himself out for ever from the mercy of God, and, in like manner, whoever rejects the cross of Christ, shuts himself out for ever from the hope of salvation" (E. Dennett). Inexpressibly blessed are the words of Ex. 29:37, "everything that toucheth the altar shall be holy": so every sinner who, by faith, lays hold of Christ is cleansed—cf. Mark 5:27-29.

It is very striking to observe that of the different vessels in the Tabernacle the two "altars" alone are spoken of as being "most holy." The other pieces of furniture are called "holy," but the golden altar (30:10) once, and the brazen altar twice, is termed "most holy" (39:37; 40:10). The reason for this is not far to seek: it was at Calvary, pre-eminently, that the holiness of God was so signally and solemnly manifested. So holy is God that He would not spare His beloved Son (Rom. 8:32) when the sins of His people were laid upon Him.

Though the Altar had no "steps" up to it (Ex. 20:26), yet it is clear from Lev. 9:22 that it stood on elevated ground, for there we read of Aaron ministering at the Altar, and then he "came down." Most probably the ground in the Outer Court was made to slope upwards, and on the top of this ascent stood the Altar. How this reminds us of the "lifted up" Saviour upon that Hill called Golgotha!

4. Its Dimensions.

"Thou shalt make an altar of shittim wood, five cubits long, and five cubits broad; the altar shall be foursquare: and the height thereof shall be three cubits" (v. 1). The measurements here are very striking and blessed. Five, as we have shown before, is the number that tells of *grace,* and this was stamped both on the length and breadth of the Altar. Nowhere was the wondrous grace of God to poor sinners so clearly displayed as it was at the Cross. What could we possibly do which would call for such a costly Sacrifice on our behalf? A ransom so precious was utterly unmerited. It was provided by the pure benignity of God. Nor was it a sudden impulse on the part of the Father to bestow favours on those who had no claims on Him. As we are told in 1 Peter 1:20, the Lamb was "foreordained before the foundation of the world." So in 2 Tim. 1:9 we read, "Who hath saved us, and called us with an holy calling, not according to our works, but

according to His own purpose *and grace,* which was given us in Christ Jesus before the world began." Here then is the *length*: grace appointed the antitypical Altar long ere time began. The *breadth* is also measured by grace. "I will have mercy on whom I will have mercy, and I will have compassion on whom I will have compassion" (Rom. 9:15) expressed this truth. Its height—*three* cubits—speaks of *manifestation.* At the Cross, God, man, sin, Satan, holiness, righteousness, grace and love were exhibited as nowhere else.

"The altar shall be foursquare." Thus it faced each point of the compass, telling of the *world-wide* aspect and application of the Cross. Christ's death was not only for the Israelitish nation, but also for the children of God "scattered abroad" (John 11:51, 52). He is a propitiation for the sins of "the whole world" (1 John 2:2), which does not mean all mankind, but that it was not restricted to Israel, but was also designed for favoured sinners among the Gentiles too.

5. Its Horns.

"And thou shalt make the horns of it upon the four corners thereof, his horns shall be of the same" (v. 2). These horns were for the binding of the sacrifice to the Altar: see Psalm 118:27. In Scripture the "horn" is the symbol of power or strength (see Hab. 3:4). Typically, the "horns" on the Altar pointed to the unfaltering purpose of the Saviour, and the strength of His love. It was not the nails which held Him to the Cross. Christ was bound to the Altar by the constraint of His devotedness to the Father (John 10:19; Phil. 2:9). While on the Cross, His enemies challenged Him to come down; His refusal to do so evidenced the cords which bound Him to its "horns."

6. Its Utensils.

"And thou shalt make his pans to receive his ashes, and his shovels, and his basins, and his fleshhooks, and his firepans: all the vessels thereof thou shalt make of brass" (v. 3). The "pans" were used in receiving the ashes of offering and removing them to their appointed place (Lev. 6:10, 11). The "ashes" testified to the thoroughness of the fire's work in having wholly consumed the offering. They also witnessed to the acceptance of the sacrifice on behalf of the offerer, and so they were to him a token that his sins were gone. The words of Christ from the Cross express the fulfilment of this detail of our type: "It is finished" announced that the Sacrifice had been offered, accepted, and gone up to God as a sweet savor.

The "shovels" were no doubt employed about the fire, collecting the dead embers. The "basins" were receptacles for the blood, in order to convey it to each place of sprinkling. The "fleshhooks" would be for arranging the different parts of the sacrifice on the fire of the Altar. The "firepans" are identical with the "censers," which formed the necessary link between the two Altars (Lev. 16:12, 13). "The utensils speak of all that was necessary in order that the offerings might be presented and dealt with in a suitable manner. We can understand in the case of Christ how perfect it all was: it was 'by the eternal Spirit' that He 'offered Himself without spot to God.' Every detail connected with the offering up of Christ has been provided and arranged and carried out according to God's mind and glory. The Scriptures have been fulfilled in every detail" (C. A. Coates). Each utensil had its own distinctive typical significance, which becomes apparent through prayer, meditation, and comparing scripture with scripture. That all were made of "brass" emphasises, again, the prominent and dominant truth associated with this Altar—the unsparing *judgment* of God upon the believing sinner's Substitute.

"And thou shalt make for it a grate of network of brass; and upon the net thou shalt make four brazen rings in the four corners thereof. And thou shalt put it under the compass of the altar beneath, that the net may be even to the midst of the altar" (vv. 4,5). The Brazen-altar was hollow within, and in its midst was fixed a "grate" on which the fire was built and where the severed parts of the offering were laid. This brings before us the most solemn aspect of all in this type. It tells of the inward sufferings of the Saviour as He endured the wrath of God.

"Our Lord did not bear the fire of Divine judgment in any external, superficial way. It is but a feeble and a partial view of those sufferings which would enlarge upon the persecution of ungodly men, or even the malice of Satan who urged them on. These might explain the bodily anguish to which our holy Lord permitted Himself to be subjected, but the fire of Divine holiness, the heart-searching judgment against sin, went down into the utmost centre of His being. Reverently may we tread upon such holy ground. Sin is not an external thing, though it mars the outward man. Its source is in the heart, the centre of man's being; and therefore in the sinless Substitute the flame searched down into His holy soul. Atoning suffering, like the sin of man, was in the heart. The piercing of the nails, the crown of thorns, the jeers of the people, the spear-thrusts, did not set forth the deep essence of His sufferings. God only, who searcheth the heart, knew what it meant. The Son, who bore the judgment, knows the intensity of that fire which burned down into His soul when made an offering for sin" (Mr. Ridout). In wondrous accord with this fire being *within* the altar, is the fact that its grate was "even in the midst" (v. 5). The Saviour suffered on the Cross for six hours, and they, too, were divided *in the midst*: the first three He suffered at the hands of men; the last three (when darkness overspread the earth) He suffered at the hands of God!

7. *Its Covering.*

The details recorded in Ex. 27:6, 7 show us that provision was made for its carrying about when Israel were on the march. In Num. 4:13, 14 we are told how it was then covered: "And they shall take away the ashes from the altar, and spread a purple cloth thereon . . . and they shall spread upon it a covering of badgers' skins." This was the *only* piece of the Tabernacle's furniture which was wrapped in purple—the royal colour. Was not this to denote how closely connected were Christ's "sufferings" with the "glory which was to follow"? (Luke 21:26; 1 Peter 1:1). Over the purple cloth was spread the badgers' skins; once more telling us of the world's incapacity to discern the preciousness and the value of the Death Divine. The repentant thief discerned the royal purple over the Altar—the Cross—as his words "Lord, remember me, when Thou comest into Thy *kingdom*" clearly denote. His wicked and scoffing companion saw naught but the rough badgers' skins!

Let us summarise. The Brazen-altar was the place where sin was judged and its wages paid. If the Veil told of separation because of sin, the Altar says, *death* is the consequences of sin. But the Altar also speaks of sin remitted. Nature knows nothing of this: break her laws, and you must suffer the consequences; repent, but she knows no mercy and shows no pity. Science is equally powerless: it endeavours to relieve the effects entailed, but has no remedy for the disease itself. Divine revelation alone makes known an adequate provision—the Cross of Christ. There the uncompromising judgment of God dealt with sin; not by punishing the sinner, but by smiting the sinner's Substitute—"Who His own self bear our sins in His own body on the tree, that we (believers), being (legally) dead to sin, should live unto righteousness, by whose stripes we are healed" (I Peter 2:24). Thanks be unto God for His unspeakable Gift.

CHAPTER 46

THE OUTER COURT

EXODUS 27:9-19

The Tabernacle proper, which has already been before us, stood in an open space of ground, an hundred cubits long, by fifty cubits broad, and was enclosed by hangings of fine twined linen. These linen curtains were suspended from sixty pillars, twenty of which stood on the south side, twenty on the north, ten on the west, and ten on the east. The Scriptures do not expressly state of what these pillars were made, but there is good reason to conclude they were of shittim wood. This open space, in which the priestly compartments and the dwelling-place of Jehovah stood, formed the third division of the Tabernacle as a whole, and was designated "the Court." The Court was in form a parallelogram, or double square, being twice the length of its breadth. On its eastern side was a gate or entrance, which was also made of fine linen, but rendered attractive by the same beautiful colours which were wrought into the Veil.

It is striking to note that neither the Court nor the Holy Places were paved. The Tabernacle rested upon the bare sand of the desert. This was in significant contrast from its golden-sheeted sides and beautiful inner ceiling. Thus, more than a hint was given for the priests to *look up*, where all was glorious and gorgeous, and tells us that there is nothing down here to satisfy the heart. In striking contrast from the Tabernacle we read of Solomon's Temple that "the floor of the House he overlaid with gold, without and within" 1 Kings 6:30), foreshadowing the blessed fact that in the Millennium this world will no longer be a wilderness to God's people; for when Christ is present in it again, then shall be fulfilled that word, "As truly as I live, all the earth shall be filled with the *glory* of the Lord" (Num. 14:21).

Immediately around the Court of the Tabernacle were the tents of the Levites; beyond, but encircling them, were grouped the twelve Tribes, three on either side; thus forming a square of vast extent. Consequently, even the Court itself was thoroughly screened from the eyes of the wilderness nomads. The Tabernacle therefore formed the centre of Israel's camp. Outside the Tent, a fire was kept constantly burning, on which the bodies of the sin-offerings were consumed, and where the refuse was destroyed. In contemplating the Court, let us notice:

1. *Its Hangings.*

"And thou shalt make the court of the tabernacle: for the south side southward there shall be hangings for the court of fine twined linen of a hundred cubits long for one side" (v. 9). As we have before pointed out, the "fine linen" is the emblem of *righteousnesses* (Rev. 19:8). The spotless white walls which surrounded the Tabernacle on every side were a standing witness to the holiness of Him whose dwelling it was. This was in striking contrast from the unholiness of those who inhabited the surrounding tents, which were made, most probably, from goats' hair, of a very dark colour. There is a reference to this in Song of Sol., 1:5: "I am black, but comely, O ye daughters of Jerusalem; *as the tents* of Kedar, as the curtains of Solomon": black as the tents of Kedar, comely as the curtains of Solomon. The dark-coloured cloth woven from goats' hair is commonly used for making tents in the East to this day. There would be, then, a most vivid contrast between the white linen surrounding Jehovah's dwelling-place and the dark fabric of the Israelites tents.

The white walls of the Tabernacle's Court served both as a barrier and a protection. To those without, the holiness, of which it spoke, was an exclusion to all who would approach the Divine Courts otherwise than as God Himself had ordered. To those within, it served as a shield, a shelter, an adornment. a glory, a defence. It was the thought of these spotless curtains around the sacred precincts, in which stood the atoning altar and the cleansing laver, which moved David to sing, "How amiable are Thy tabernacles, O Lord of Hosts!

My soul longeth, yea, even fainteth, for the courts of the Lord" (Psa. 84:1, 2).

2. *Its Pillars.*

These were sixty in number, placed at intervals of five cubits all around the Court. The material from which they were made is not expressly stated. The words of v. 10, "and the twenty pillars thereof (i.e., of the south side) and their twenty sockets shall be of brass," have led some to conclude that the pillars themselves were made of brass; but it is to be noted that the words "shall be" are supplied by the translators, there being no verb in the original—the modifying clause "of brass" referring only to the "sockets." That the columns themselves were *not* made of brass seems clear from their omission in Ex. 38:29-31. Nor were they made of silver, for that metal was only used in the foundations and in the upper ornamental parts; whilst gold was employed in covering boards in the Tabernacle and in the construction of certain vessels inside, but was not found at all in the Court.

We believe that these "pillars" were made of shittim wood, and that, for three reasons. First, the other "pillars," i.e., those used for the door and for the support of the Veil (26:32, 37) were of wood, therefore in the absence of any word to the contrary here, we naturally conclude that these also were made of the same material. Second, because from a careful comparison of the twenty-nine talents of gold (Ex. 38:24), the hundred talents of silver (Ex. 38:25, 27), and the seventy talents of brass (Ex. 38:29 with the sizes of the different vessels and the amount of metals required for them, it seems clear that they would not leave sufficient to make sixty pillars for the Court out of the remainder. Third, the typical meaning of the Court requires "wood" rather than one of the metals.

A "pillar" speaks of support and strength. The sixty which were stationed around the sides of the Court sustained the white curtains. There is a word in Song of Sol. 3:6, 7 which seems to borrow its imagery from our present type: "Who is this that cometh out of the wilderness like pillars of smoke, perfumed with myrrh and frankincense, with all powders of the merchants? Behold his bed, which is Solomon's; three score valiant men are about it, of the valiant of Israel." Note first the allusion to "the wilderness!" There a procession is seen: a palanquin or curtained-litter (for this is the literal meaning of the Hebrew word here rendered "bed") is seen, surrounded by all the marks of royalty and majesty; *sixty* mighty ones are about it. The "litter" was the *temporary* resting-place of the king. So the Tabernacle was God's resting-place, in the midst of Israel, during their wilderness wanderings. The "ark" was the symbol of His presence, and as 2 Sam. 7:2 tells us "the ark of God dwelleth *within curtains*," while in Numbers 10:33, 35 a "resting-place" is also mentioned in connection with it. Around the ark in the Holy of Holies, were these sixty pillars of the Court, like the "sixty valiant men" about the wilderness resting-place of Solomon. The typical significance of this will appear in our next division.

3. *Its Meaning.*

Like everything else connected with this first dwelling-place of God on earth, the antitypical significance of the Court is found in the person of the Lord Jesus Christ and in Him alone. It is really pitiful to witness the attempts that have been made to refer the curtains and the pillars to the saints of this New Testament dispensation. Neither individually nor in their corporate capacity are they here in view. The Court is called the "Tent of the Congregation" (Ex. 39:40); it was the appointed place of assembly, where the Israelites came together and worshipped Jehovah, and where He met with them (Ex. 29:42, 43). Now it is in Christ, and in Him alone, that God and His people meet together. The Court, then, spoke of Christ as the Meeting-place between God and His people.

The Court foreshadowed Christ on earth tabernacling among men, accessible to all who sought Him, but His glory beheld only by those who drew near in faith (John 1:14). In the opening paragraphs we have pointed out that the Court was *un*paved, the Tabernacle resting upon the bare earth of the desert. This pointed to Christ as "a Root out of a dry ground"—Israel (Isa. 53:2). But although the floor of the Court was the dust of the wilderness, yet was it a sacred enclosure, so that he who entered it stood on holy ground; from Lev. 16:6, 16 we learn that even the Court itself was termed "the *holy* place." This tells us that Christ, though "a Root out of a dry ground," was none other than "the Holy One of God." We may add, these linen hangings were suspended from pillars seven and a half feet in height, so that all on the outside would be prevented from seeing what was done on the inside; thus making it a truly separated and holy place.

The distinctive spiritual significance of the Court is intimated by its order of mention in Ex. 27. First there is a description of the brazen altar (vv. 1-8), and then follow the details concerning the Court. This is very striking. The natural order would be to have told of the Court first, and then of the altar which stood within it. But here again God's thoughts are different from ours. As we have seen, the altar speaks of the place where sin was dealt with: the consequence of this is, that entrance is afforded into the place where God meets with His people. Thus, that which the altar typified was the *basis* of the privileges foreshadowed by the Court. As soon as the Israelite entered the sacred precincts, the first object to meet his eyes was the standing witness to both the justice and the grace of God. The altar testified that his sins had been put away through the sacrifice offered thereon. It was there God showed, typically, that He is just and the Justifier of the believing sinner (Rom. 3: 26).

It is to be carefully noted that the Court was for an elect and redeemed people. There are several references in the Psalms to this: "Blessed is the man whom Thou choosest, and causest to approach unto Thee, that he may dwell in Thy Courts" (Psalm 65:4); "Enter into His gates with thanksgiving, and into His Court with praise: be thankful unto Him, and bless His name" (Psa. 100:4). But most blessed is it to note that in the Old Testament types of the Court there was a definite hint and foreshadowing of *Gentiles* also entering into and partaking of God's grace (Lev. 17:8, 22:18; Num. 15:14-16). The "stranger" had the same liberty of approach to the altar as had an Israelite. Thus, at that early date, it was intimated "there is no difference between the Jew and the Greek: for the same Lord over all is rich unto all that call upon Him. For whosoever shall call upon the name of the Lord shall be saved" (Rom. 10:12, 13).

The sixty pillars around the Court told of the strength and sufficiency of that Refuge into which the believing sinner has fled: "The name of the Lord is a strong tower: the righteous runneth into it and is safe" (Prov. 18:10). That the pillars were made of "wood" was in harmony with the promise, "And a *Man* shall be as an hiding-place from the wind, and a covert from the tempest" (Isa. 32:2). That these pillars were sixty in number (5 x 12 or grace and perfect *government*), tell us it is the grace which *reigns* in righteousness by Christ Jesus that is our defence. This, like the sixty valiant men about Solomon's litter, is a guard of honour around us, so that none can lay anything to our charge. That there was an interval of five cubits between each pillar, intimates that no matter which aspect of our salvation we contemplate, all is of *grace* alone. The spot-

less white hangings suspended from them, depicted the fitness of the Lord our Righteousness to be the One in whom His God and our God could meet with us.

4. *Its Dimensions.*

In contemplating this we must first consider the measurements of the linen hangings which surrounded the Court, and then the space enclosed by them. From v. 9 we learn that the linen hangings were a hundred cubits long on the south side, ditto on the north side (v. 11), fifty on the west side (v. 12), and thirty on the east side (vv. 14, 15)—the other twenty there being accounted for by the "gate," which differed from the curtains on either side of it, in that it was of "blue and purple and scarlet" (v. 16). Thus there was a total length of these white hangings of two hundred and eighty cubits. The factors of this total would be 7 x 4 x 10, which speak of *perfection on earth,* seen in human *responsibility* fully discharged.

It is striking to note that the length of the white hangings surrounding the Court was identical with the length of the curtains which were spread over the inner Tabernacle. "The curtains of the Tabernacle present Christ, Christ in His nature and character, and Christ in His future glories and judicial authority; but as so presented He was for the eye of God, and for the eye of the priest. As such He could not be seen from without, only within. The fine twined linen hangings (of the Court) present Christ also, but not so much to those within as to those without. *They* could be seen by all in the camp. It is therefore the presentation of Christ to the world, Christ in the purity of His nature. He could thus challenge His adversaries to convict Him of sin. Pilate had to confess again and again that there was no fault in Him; and the Jewish authorities, though they sought with eagle-eyed malice, failed to establish, or even produce, a single proof of failure. Not a single speck could be detected upon the fine twined linen of His holy life, His life of practical righteousness which flowed from the purity of His being" (Mr. E. Dennett). Thus, the linen hangings of the Court being of equal length with the Curtains of the inner tabernacle tell us that Christ manifested on earth *the same* holiness as He had and does before God in heaven!

The linen hangings which formed the walls of the Court were divided by "pillars," which were erected at intervals of five cubits; note in vv. 9, 10 there were "twenty" pillars for the "hundred cubits" of linen on either length. The white linen spoke of righteousness, five is the number of grace; thus, these measurements pronounced that the grace of God to poor sinners is not bestowed at the expense of justice, but, as Rom. 5:21 declares, "As sin hath reigned unto death, even so might grace reign *through righteousness*, unto **eternal** life by Jesus Christ our Lord." Five **is**, again, the dominating number in the measurements of the enclosure: as v. 18 tells us, "the length of the court shall be an hundred cubits, and the breadth fifty everywhere, and the height five cubits." How *small* was the Court in comparison with the camp! Hebrews 13:13, read in the light of that whole Epistle, indicates that the "Camp" refers to the religious world, Christendom—the sphere of nominal Christian profession. The smallness of the Court in contrast from the vastness of the Camp (for how *few* was accommodation provided!) contains more than a hint of the *fewness* of those, from among the crowds of professing Christians, that really enter God's presence! God's "flock" is only a "LITTLE one" (Luke 12:32); only the "few" are in the *Narrow* Way (Matt. 7: 14). Are *you* one of the favoured "few"?

5. *Its Sockets.*

"And their sockets of brass" (v. 18). This detail needs no lengthy comment. The "sockets" formed the foundation for the pillars. The "brass" of which they were composed speaks of endurance, capacity to bear the action of fire: type of Christ suffering, but not being consumed by, the outpoured judgment of God upon the sinner's Substitute. Thus, once more, are the saints reminded of that upon which all their blessings are based.

6. *Its Hooks and Fillets.*

"The hooks of the pillars and their fillets of silver" (v. 11). These "fillets" were connecting-rods from pillar to pillar, and the hooks would link the linen hangings to the fillets. They bring out a most important detail in our present type. As we pointed out in an earlier article, "silver" is the symbol of *redemption*, and it was through the redemption which is in Christ Jesus that Divine righteousness and Divine grace were united. There is an inseparable connection between Christ our Righteousness and Christ our Redeemer: these two must never be separated. Righteousness could never have been imputed to us unless the Lord Jesus had ransomed us by His blood. The worshipping Israelite would see that the boards of the Tabernacle owed their stability to the fact that the **atonement**-money had been paid, for they rested on silver sockets. He would also

perceive that the fine linen curtains of the Court hung securely from silver chapiters and rings, made from the same ransom-money. Beautifully has this been commented upon by one writing of the blessedness of those who had entered the court:—

"While outside, the wall shut *off*, now that he is inside, it shuts him *in*. Instead of being opposed by 'righteousness,' he is now *surrounded* by it. God is just, and as long as the sinner is rejecting Christ He must be against him; but once the latter has come to Him through Christ all is reversed; He is 'just, and the *Justifier* of him which believeth in Jesus (Rom. 3: 26). But how can this be? It can be in the way set forth in this fine linen wall; the linen ("righteousness") was *not* suspended to the brass ("judgment"), but was connected with it by means of silver rods that joined pillar to pillar. Thus, typically we have the truth as it is plainly stated in Rom. 3:24, 'Being justified freely by His grace, *through the redemption* that is in Christ Jesus'" (Mr. C. H. Bright).

Thus, the redeemed Israelite who entered the Court was shut in by walls of righteousness upheld by the tokens of redemption. This is the blessed portion of every sinner who has fled to Christ for refuge. Because Christ was made sin for him, he has been made "the righteousness of God in Him" (2 Cor. 5:21). "For as by one man's disobedience many were made sinners, so by the obedience of One shall many be made righteous" (Rom. 5:19). The Christian is vested with that which meets every requirement of God's holiness. What cause, then, has each believing reader to join with the writer in saying, "I will greatly rejoice in the Lord, my soul shall be joyful in my God; for He hath clothed me with the garments of salvation, He hath covered me with the robe of righteousness" (Isa. 61: 10).

7. *Its Gate.*

"And for the gate of the Court shall be an hanging of twenty cubits, of blue, and purple, and scarlet, and fine twined linen, wrought with needlework: and their pillars shall be four, and their sockets four" (v. 16). This "hanging" which formed the entrance to the Court is closely connected in thought with the Veil and the Gate of the Tabernacle. Each of them served as a door, hiding the interior from one approaching from the outside. All were made of the same materials, and the colours are mentioned in the same order; the dimensions of all were alike, each measuring one hundred square cubits. The same truth was embodied in each of these typical curtains: there could be no access to God of any kind—whether of comparatively distant worship, or of closer intimacy—except by Him who said "I am the Way." The Israelite who came to the brazen altar with his offering must pass through this gate of the Court; the priest who placed incense on the golden altar must enter by the door of the Tabernacle; the high priest who entered the Holy of Holies on the day of atonement must do so through the Veil, thus realising the thrice repeated proof of the only way of access to God.

The antitypical teaching of the Gate is brought before us in John 10:9, where Christ says, "I am the Door, by Me if any man enter in he shall be saved." But as another has observed, "It is not thinking about the Door, or believing that He *is* the Door, but *entering* the Door, that saves. Many need help right on this point. There are (figuratively speaking) crowds of *semi-believers* around the Gate. They believe it *is* the Gate, and the only one, but they *do not take the step.* They are always saying, '*Let* me hide myself in Thee,' instead of hiding in Him once for all. Oh! why not dare to trust Him now, at once and forever? You say that you do not feel that He accepts you. . . . How *can* you, as long as you remain outside? Jesus makes no promise to the one who does not enter, but to the one who does. Enter in, and then, feeling or not, you may know that you are saved, *because He says so.* The Altar was inside the Gate, not outside! How, then, can you know that you are saved until you enter? Come, just as you are, in all your sinfulness, with *no* feeling, with no consciousness of any 'marks of grace,' and *as a sinner* believe in the sinner's Saviour."

CHAPTER 47

THE PRIESTHOOD

EXODUS 27:20—28:2

Once more we would direct the reader's attention to the *order* of Jehovah's instructions to Moses concerning the Tabernacle and all that was connected with it. At first glance the contents of Exodus 28 and 29 seem to depart from the logical sequence and to introduce confusion. Instead of completing the description of the Tabernacle and its furniture, the priesthood is introduced, and then in chapter 30 the last of the holy vessel is described. But fully assured that God is not the Author of confusion, the prayerful student should diligently seek the mind of the Spirit for an explanation of this perplexity. A new subdivision of Exodus begins with the 28th chapter, or more correctly, at 27:20.

Many years ago it was pointed out by Mr. Darby that everything mentioned in Ex. 25:10 to 27:19 foreshadowed God's coming forth unto His people: each article there mentioned was a symbol of *display*, that is, a manifestation of God in Christ. But from 27:20 to the end of chapter 30 the order is reversed, everything there pointing to the provisions of grace which enable us to go in to God: that is to say, the priesthood and the vessels referred to in Ex. 30 have to do with *approach*. But before the laver and the incense altar (the vessels needed for access to God) are brought before us, we are shown the appointment and consecration of the priesthood. Thus we may discern Divine order in the seeming confusion, for there must be designated persons for approach, before the vessels could be used. "God has come out in type and figure to His people; then He indicates those who are to be set apart for His service in the sanctuary—those who are to enjoy the special privilege of access to Himself; and lastly, the vessels, etc., are given, which they would need in their holy employment in the house of God" (Mr. E. Dennett).

The blessed *unity*, amid diversity, of the whole of Jehovah's instructions to Moses in this section of Exodus has been dealt with so helpfully by the late Mr. Soltau that we quote from him at length: "The Tabernacle and its vessels, the Priesthood and the various ministrations connected therewith, form but one subject; although divided for the sake of more distinctly contemplating each portion. The Tabernacle would have been useless without its vessels: and the Tabernacle with its vessels would have been of no service but for a living family of priests, constantly engaged in various active ministrations within the holy places, and about the various holy vessels.

"So closely connected is each part of this subject with the other, that in the directions contained in Exodus, there is no break; but the command for making the holy garments and consecrating the priesthood (Ex. 28 and 29), comes betweeen the enumeration of some of the holy vessels and the various parts of the Tabernacle. Indeed, properly speaking, the 27th chapter should end at v. 19, where 'thou shalt command the children of Israel' begins a new subject, viz.: directions concerning the oil for the light of the sanctuary. The 28th chapter continues with ordering the sacrifices for the day of priestly consecration. The 30th carries on the subject connected with the priesthood, by giving the description of the incense altar; and the whole closes with the Sabbath, at the end of the 31st chapter.

"Again; when all the various parts of the work have been completed, ending with the garments of the priesthood (chapters 36-39:31) the following verse is added: 'Thus was all the work of the tabernacle of the Tent of the Congregation finished; and the children of Israel did according to all that the Lord commanded Moses, so did they'. Here, therefore, the priestly garments were considered part of the work of the Tabernacle! And if we turn to Heb. 8 we find that 'the priests, that offered gifts according to the law, served unto the example and shadow of heavenly things, as Moses was admonished of God, when he was about to make the Tabernacle itself; see, saith He, that thou shalt make all things according to the pattern showed to thee in the mount' (vv. 4, 5).

"The service of the priests in offering gifts and sacrifices was connected with the commandments given to Moses in the mount respecting the making of the Tabernacle. The words 'See, that thou make all things according to the pattern showed thee in the mount', as recorded in Exodus, were spoken to Moses respecting the holy vessels (Ex. 25:40), but are in Heb. 8 quoted to prove that the priests and their ministrations were examples and shadows of heavenly things. The whole subject is therefore much blended."

Still observing the *order* of truth presented to us in our present section, it is most striking to find we have in 27:20, 21 that which is obviously the *connecting link* between the two central lines of thought—God coming out to His people, they going in to Him. "And thou shalt command the children of Israel, that they bring thee pure oil olive beaten for the light, to cause the lamp to burn always. In the tabernacle of the congregation without the vail, which is before the testimony, Aaron and his sons shall order it from evening to morning before the Lord: it shall be a statute forever unto their generations on behalf of the children of Israel." Two things are here brought before us: provision for the maintenance of the light and the ministration of the priesthood. These verses are very rich in their typical teaching and must be carefully weighed as a preparation for what follows. Strictly, they begin the section and are the key to the contents of chapters 28 and 29.

Before a description is given of the garments and consecration of the priests, provision is made for perpetual light in the sanctuary. This takes the precedence. As v. 21 tells us the light was to shine "before the Lord." Priestly ministry was for the benefit of the people; but the claims of God must first be met. This was the order in Gen. 1: the *first* thing there, was "Let there be light." This, before a single creature was brought into existence. So here in Exodus. In figure it tells that Christ had first to meet all the demands of God's holiness, ere He could minister for us as our great High Priest: the Cross first, then His intercession on High.

It was at the Cross that God was fully manifested as the Light (1 John 1:5); that is, in His ineffable holiness—His very nature as eternally antagonistic to sin. And in the typical order of God's revelation of Himself through the vessels of the Tabernacle, beginning with that which was in the Holiest (the ark and the mercy-seat), the movement was ever *outward*, past the table and the lampstand in the holy place, to the brazen altar in the outer Court (27:1), which foreshadowed the Cross: the altar marking the *terminal* of the coming out of God in manifestation. Thus provision having been made through Christ's atonement for "the lamp to burn alway," i.e. for the unsullied holiness of God to act without compromise in His gracious dealing with poor sinners, the way was then clear to make known the provisions which Divine mercy had made for reconciled sinners to draw near to God within the veil.

But as we showed in a previous paper, the Lampstand speaks not only of Christ, but also of the Holy Spirit as His gift to the saints. This explains the fact that in v. 20 it is "the people" who were to supply the "pure oil olive beaten for the light." As was the case in connection with all the other materials (see 25:2, etc.), so that which speaks of the Holy Spirit given us by Christ, was also provided by "the people" themselves. The Tabernacle and its services were not only for Jehovah, but for Israel too: thus their providing the materials for it, witnessed to *their* personal interest in it. In keeping with this we may note that 27:21 mentions, for the first time, "the Tabernacle (Tent) *of the congregation!*"

But further: does not this initial mention of the "Tent of the Congregation," in the present connection, supply more than a hint of the formation of that Church which is the Body of Christ—consequent upon His having satisfied the requirements of God's holiness and the descent of the Holy Spirit? In Matthew 16:18 our Lord employed the future tense, not the present—"I *will* build My Church," *not* "I am building." Ephesians 1:20-23 also plainly teaches that Christ was not given to be the Head over all things to His Church until after His resurrection and ascension. Thus the Church is only seen (typically) *after* the claims of Divine holiness had been met, the throne of God eternally established, and the Holy Spirit sent down as the witness of this: cf. Acts 2:33.

Again; it is in Exodus 27:21 that, for

the *first* time, mention is made of "Aaron and his sons." This also has a double significance. Coming right after mention of "the people" in v. 20, it tells us on whose behalf the Priesthood was instituted. "Aaron and his sons" are mentioned twenty-four times in the book of Exodus, but they are not seen until after instructions were given for the children of Israel to furnish the oil for the light. How plainly this foreshadowed the fact that the priestly ministry of Christ is essential to maintaining the gracious working of the Spirit through His people! Up to this point, nothing whatever had been said of any human agents or ministers appointed to officiate in the tabernacle service and to delight themselves in the dwellingplace of God among men, amidst the heaven-given shadows and emblems of the eternal verities which we have previously contemplated. But in God's light we see light (Psalm 36:9). The light makes manifest—here the divinely-chosen ministers of the sanctuary. This introduces to us the subject of Israel's priesthood—one abounding in precious instruction for us; but to which, alas, the vast majority of the saints are total strangers.

Sixty years ago a servant of God wrote, "To a large portion of those who would be regarded as intelligent Christians, and who are something more than mere routine readers of the Bible, the types of the Tabernacle, with its priesthood, service, and offerings, are barren of comfort and edification. Yet it is generally acknowledged that they are pictures by which God, in His condescension, would teach His children things otherwise all but incomprehensible. It is generally admitted, also, that the key to unlock these treasures of spiritual truth lies ready to the hand of every student in the New Testament. Without inquiring particularly why these treasures have fallen into such general neglect in our day, the following suggestion is worthy of the consideration of the earnest among us: 'The real secret of the neglect of the types,' says one who is entitled to be heard on this point, 'I cannot but think may, in part, be traced to this—that they require more spiritual intelligence than many Christians can bring to them. To apprehend them requires a certain measure of spiritual capacity, and *habitual exercise in the things of God,* which all do not possess, for want of abiding fellowship with Jesus. The mere superficial gaze upon the Word in these parts, brings no corresponding idea to the mind of the reader. The types are, indeed, pictures, but to understand the picture, we should know something of the reality. The most perfect representation of a steam-engine to a South Sea savage would be wholly and hopelessly unintelligible, simply because the reality, the outline of which was presented to him, was something hitherto unknown.'

"Paul arrests himself in speaking of Christ as a priest forever after the order of Melchizedek (Heb. 5:11, etc.), by the reflection that those whom he addressed were incapable of receiving instruction on account of their spiritual childhood. A child of a king is unconscious of the dignity and the inheritance to which he is born; but it is none the less a king's child: and so there are many true children of God who seem to remain babes, content, apparently, that they have life and are children; and so they need milk. This accounts for the spiritual feebleness and inactivity of the Church in our day. Babes, indeed, must be fed on milk, but it is not necessary that Christians should continue babes. May we not, therefore, exhort them, in the words of the apostle, 'To leave the principles of the doctrine of Christ and go on to perfection' (Heb. 6:1)—to manhood—to the condition of those who, 'by reason *of use,* have their senses exercised to discern both good and evil'?" (Waymarks in the Wilderness).

Since then, conditions have not improved. There appear to be as many "babes" among Christians as ever. The greater part of the Bible seems a sealed book to them. "*All* scripture is given by inspiration of God and is profitable," and it is to our irreparable loss if we neglect any portion thereof. "*Whatsoever* things were written beforetime, were written for *our* learning" (Rom. 15:4), and if we fail to give proper attention to the types our souls will be the poorer. Notably is this the case with the subject before us. What hazy and inadequate ideas concerning priesthood are entertained by the average believer. That the Lord Jesus *is* the great High Priest of His people, he knows, but as to the place of Christ's priesthood, the nature of its activities, its relation to other truths, especially to redemption; the design accomplished by it, the blessings secured from it, the portion which the saint enjoys by virtue of it, are most indefinitely defined in the minds of most.

On the Cross the Saviour said, "It *is* finished": all that was needed to satisfy the requirements of God and reconcile to Him His alienated people, was accomplished. Then, wherein lies the necessity for the present ministry of our great High Priest? If His blood fully atoned for all our sins, why should He now be making intercession on our behalf? This is a difficulty which has been felt by many. But the same problem is presented in the book of Exodus. Here we see a (typically) redeemed people, protected from judgment by the sprinkled blood of the lamb, brought out from the house of bondage, separated unto Jehovah, He dwelling in their midst. Yet, a priesthood was appointed to act on their behalf! Why? The same book of Exodus reveals the solution. The priesthood was for the *maintaining*, not securing, their relationship with Jehovah. They were still a people compassed with infirmity, subject to temptation, and alas, frequently failing. The holy God dwelling in their midst could not tolerate that which was unclean. Therefore the same grace which had brought them nigh to Himself, now made provision for the keeping of them nigh.

Priesthood has to do with *fellowship*. Its need arises from the fact that the sinful nature remains in those who have been bought with a price. It is to meet the failures of a people who when they would do good evil is present with them: this evil which causes them to offend in "many things" (James 3:2), makes the priestly ministry of Christ so essential. This was what was foreshadowed in Exodus and Leviticus. The application of these types to Christians to-day calls for a wisdom which only the Holy Spirit can supply, for in the light of the Hebrews' Epistle it is clear that the Levitical shadows present contrasts as well as comparisons, and though containing much which finds its antitypical fulfilment in the spiritual blessings of the Church, there is also not a little which will only be made good to Israel in a coming day. The immediate linking together of the Lampstand and the Priesthood in Ex. 27:21 plainly intimates that only in the light of God can the latter be discerned and understood.

First, let us mark and admire the lovely *grace* of God which is brought out in the type before us. This is seen in the choice that He made. "Take thou unto thee Aaron thy brother, and his sons with him, from among the children of Israel, that he may minister unto Me in the priest's office" (28:1). Not Moses, but Aaron, the inferior brother, was the one selected for this great favour. Moreover, the tribe to which he belonged was one of the least honourable of the twelve; yea, it was under the curse, because of Levi's cruelty—see Gen. 49: 5-7. Not Reuben the firstborn, nor Judah whom his brethren should praise (Gen. 49:8), nor Joseph the fruitful bough,

but Levi, was to be the priestly tribe. How this exhibited the sovereignity of Divine grace! Finally, the matchless and wondrous grace of God in appointing Aaron to be the high priest is seen in the fact that at the very time His choice was made known to Moses, his brother was taking the lead in the idolatrous worship of the golden calf! Nor do these details mar the accuracy of the type; instead, they strikingly illustrate the fact that our great High Priest was the gift of God's marvellous *grace*.

Second, let us now consider the significance of his name. "Aaron" means "very high." He stood supreme as the high priest, exalted not only above his own house, but also above all the people. Thus was he a type of the Lord Jesus, whom God has exalted with His right hand to be a Priest and a Saviour (Acts 5.31). But as if to magnify the high priesthood of Christ above that of all others, the Holy Spirit has added the word "great"—our "great High Priest" (Heb. 4.14), an adjective used of none other, not even Melchizedek.

We may note that in Ex. 28:1 the names of Aaron's sons are also given, and each of them was most appropriate and striking. Nadab means "willing"; Abihu, "my Father is He"; Eleazer, "help of God"; Ithamar, "land of palm." As another has pointed out, "these four words afford a little prophetic intimation of characteristics attaching to the House of which the Son of God is the Head: deriving its life from God the Father, and all its power and help from Him; following in the footsteps also of its blessed Master, in yielding willing and not constrained service to God; and like the palm trees, lofty in righteousness, and ever bringing forth fruit (Psa. 92: 12-14). The palm-tree is one of the ornaments of the future temple described by Ezekiel, and was also one of the embellishments of Solomon's temple. It is peculiarly the tree of the desert, flourishing where no other could exist; ever marking out to the weary traveller the spot. amidst surrounding desolation, where a grateful shade and a spring of living water were to be found; and remarkable for longevity and ceaseless fruitfulness. Thus it was an apt emblem of the heavenly priesthood" (G. Soltau).

Third, let us dwell upon the significance of the singular pronoun in 28:1: "Take unto thee Aaron, and his sons with him, that *he* may minister." This is very striking and most blessed. Aaron and his sons formed together one priesthood, and Aaron's appointment to his office was inseparable from theirs. What a wondrous foreshadowment was this of the *union* between our great High Priest and His House, and what an intimation that His ministry before God concerned His House, and them alone!

And here we must stop. To write at length upon the Priesthood of Christ would necessitate us expounding almost the entire Epistle of the Hebrews, where this blessed theme is developed by the Spirit of God. To that important New Testament book we would refer the interested student. There, the divine Instructor has pointed out both the comparisons and the contrasts between the type and the Antitype. The Aaronic priesthood furnished much that was the *pattern* of Christ's priesthood, but the *order* of it is vastly superior, being that of Melchidezek—the royal priest. God willing, other aspects of the subject will come before us in future papers.

CHAPTER 48

AARON'S GARMENTS

EXODUS 28

In the preceding article we pointed out how that the interpretation and application of the typical teachings found in the Pentateuch concerning Israel's priesthood calls for heavenly wisdom and guidance. In the light of the Epistle to the Hebrews it is clear that there are many points of contrast as well as comparison. But that which it is most important to see is, that when commenting there, on the types of Exodus and Leviticus, the Holy Spirit has expressly declared that the entire ritual of the Tabernacle was "a figure for the time then present" (Heb. 9:9), that it was "a shadow of good things to come, and *not* the very image of the things" (10:1). They were not given to Israel as a model for Christians to imitate, but as a foreshadowing of spiritual things which find their fulfilment in Christ Himself. The holy places made with hands were "figures of the true," that is of "Heaven itself" (Heb. 9: 24). A true apprehension of this is our only safeguard against the sacerdotalism and ritualism which the flesh so much delights in. After the advent, death, resurrection, and ascension of Christ, the shadows must vanish before the substance. As one has well said, "To imitate a revival of that which God Himself has set aside by a fulfilment perfect and glorious, is audacious, and full of peril to the souls of men. It is not even the shadow of a substance; but the unauthorised shadow of a departed shade." It is failure to observe this which has wrought such confusion and havoc in Christendom, resulting in the denial of that which lies at the very foundation of Christianity.

Under the Mosaic economy, the priests were a special class appointed to minister unto God on behalf of the people. They enjoyed privileges which were not shared by others. Theirs was a nearness to Jehovah peculiar to themselves. They were vested with an authority and were permitted to do that which was not given to those whom they represented. But at the

Cross a radical change was brought about. The old order ended, and a new one was inaugurated. Judaism ceased, and Christianity was introduced. Two symbolic actions gave plain intimation of this. First, in Matt. 26:65 we are told, "the high priest rent his clothes," which was expressly forbidden by the law, see Lev. 21:10. God permitted this to show that Israel's priesthood was ended—clothes are only torn to pieces when there is no further use for them. Second, the rending of the vail (Matt. 27:51): the barrier into God's presence no longer existed for His people.

In Heb. 5 and 7 the Holy Spirit has carefully called attention to a number of contrasts between the priesthood of Aaron and that of Christ. One of the things which qualified Israel's high priest to officiate in that office was that he could have compassion on them that were ignorant or out of the way, because he himself was compassed with infirmity (5:2); but the Christian's High Priest is "Holy, harmless, undefiled, separate from sinners" (7:26). Again, in Heb. 5:3 it is pointed out that Israel's high priest needed to offer sacrifice for his own sins: but Christ was "the Holy One of God," and "knew no sin." Again, the priests of the house of Levi were made "without an oath" (7:21), and in consequence, some of them were cut off from the priesthood, as in the case of Nadab and Abihu, and Eli's line; but Christ was made Priest with an oath, "by Him that said unto Him, The Lord swear and will not repent, Thou art a priest forever after the order of Melchizedek" (7:21). Finally, Aaron was made a priest after the law of a carnal commandment (i.e., that which pertained to mortality), but Christ "after the power of an endless life" (7:16).

In view of these differences, and of the exalted superiority of Christ's priesthood over the Aaronic, we are told, "for the priesthood being changed, there is made of necessity a change also of the law" (Heb. 7:12); that is, in its narrower sense, a

258

"change" in the law pertaining to the priesthood; in its wider sense, a "change" concerning the ceremonial law. It is important to note that no part of the ceremonial law was given to Israel till *after* the priesthood was established. Thus, this "change of the law" signified a change of dispensation and everything that pertained to the priesthood.

Now, it is this "change" in the law pertaining to priesthood which the Papacy, and all who are infected by its sacerdotal spirit, sets aside. Romanism is largely a revival of Judaism, plus the corruptions of Paganism. It is a deliberate and pernicious repudiation of what is distinctive in Christianity. It is a wicked denial of the perpetual efficacy of the one offering of the Lord Jesus. Rome perpetuates the Levitical order, claiming that her priests, like Aaron and his sons, are specially authorised and qualified to go to God on behalf of their fellow-men. But 1 Peter 2:5, 9 affirms that *all* believers are now "priests," and that *all* of God's people alike enjoy liberty of access into the Holiest (Heb. 10:19, 22). As another has truly said, "The feeblest member of the household of faith is as much a priest as the apostle Peter himself. He is a spiritual priest—he worships in a spiritual temple, he stands at a spiritual altar, he offers a spiritual sacrifice, he is clad in spiritual vestments." That spiritual temple is Heaven itself, which he enters in spirit through the rent vail; that spiritual altar (Heb. 13:10) is Christ Himself—the altar which "sanctifieth the gift" (Matt. 23:19); that spiritual sacrifice is praise unto God (Heb. 13:15).

Coming now to the robes of Israel's high priest we would call attention once more to the *order* of Jehovah's instructions to Moses. In Ex. 29 we have an account of the *consecration* of Aaron and his sons to their holy office. But before this is given, in Ex. 28, a description is furnished of the various *garments* they were to wear. First, the vestments of the high priest are detailed, and then those of Aaron's sons. The anointed eye may easily discern the propriety of and the reason for this. Typically, the garments foreshadowed the manifold glories of Christ, the great High Priest, which glories and perfections manifested His fitness for that office. The holy garments of Aaron were "for glory and beauty": they gave dignity to his person, being suitable apparel for his position. In figure they pointed to Christ in all His perfections with the Father *before* He was "consecrated" to His work for us.

"And thou shalt make holy garments for Aaron thy brother for glory and for beauty" (v. 2). With this should be compared Lev. 16:4, "He shall put on the holy linen coat, and he shall have the linen breeches upon his flesh, and shall be girded with a linen girdle, and with the linen mitre shall he be attired: these are holy garments." There were two sets of clothing provided for Israel's high priest: the one mentioned in Lev. 16 was what he wore on the annual Day of Atonement. Then he was robed only in spotless white, foreshadowing the personal righteousness and holiness of the Lord Jesus, which fitted Him to undertake the stupendous work of putting away the sins of His people.

It is worthy of note that the garments of Aaron which were "for glory and for beauty" were just *seven* in number. "And these are the garments which they shall make: a breastplate, and an ephod, and a robe, and a broidered coat, a mitre, and a girdle: and they shall make holy garments for Aaron thy brother, and his sons, that he may minister unto Me in the priest's office" (28:4). In addition to the six articles mentioned here, is the "plate of pure gold" on which was engraved the words "Holiness to the Lord" (v. 36). This, as Lev. 8:9 tells us, was "the holy crown." Observe that in the enumeration given in 28:4 the "breastplate" comes before the others, but in the details which follow the order is changed: there it is the ephod, the girdle, the two stones, set upon the shoulders of the ephod, and then the breastplate. The "breastplate" was the chief and most costly of the vestments, the other garments being, as it were, a foundation and background for it—this central article pointing to the very *heart* of Christ Himself.

"And they shall make the ephod of gold, of blue, and of purple, of scarlet, and fine twined linen, with cunning work. It shall have the two shoulder-pieces thereof joined at the two edges thereof; and so it shall be joined together" (vv. 6, 7). The "ephod" is the first garment described in detail. This was the outer robe of the high priest. It was made of two parts, one covering his back and the other his front; these being joined together at the shoulders by golden clasps, which formed the setting for the onyx stones. The ephod served to support the breastplate. The materials of which it was made were "gold," and "fine twined linen"—the blue, purple, and scarlet being emblasoned upon the latter. The mode by which the gold was interlaced with the linen is described in Ex. 39:3: "And they did beat the gold into thin plates, and cut it into wires, to work it in the blue," etc. Thus the strength and sheen of the gold was intimately blended with every part of the ephod, giving firmness as well as brilliancy to the whole fabric.

The spotless linen spoke of the holy humanity of Christ; the gold, of His divine glory; the colours, of the varied perfections of His character. "Christ acts for us as Priest in all that He is as Divine and human, the God-man. The whole value of His person enters into the exercise of His office. . . . The apostle combines these two things in the Epistle to the Hebrews: 'Seeing then that we have a Great High Priest, that is passed into the heavens, Jesus, the Son of God.' He is Jesus, and He is the Son of God. It is this most precious truth that is displayed in type in the materials of the ephod. How it enlarges our conceptions of the value of His work for us as Priest to remember what He is in Himself, and that we are thus upheld in His intercession by all that He is as Jesus, and as the Son of God" (Mr. E. Dennett).

"And the curious girdle of the ephod, which is upon it, shall be of the same, according to the work thereof: gold, blue, and purple, and scarlet, and fine twined linen" (v. 8). In v. 39 we learn that this girdle was made of "needlework." The "girdle" speaks of preparedness for *service*. Beautifully is this brought out in Luke 12:37: "Blessed are those servants, whom the Lord, when He cometh, shall find watching: verily I say unto you, that He shall *gird Himself*, and make them sit down to meat, and will come forth and *serve* them." In the days of His flesh "He took a towel and girded Himself, and then He washed the disciple's feet" (John 13). To-day He stands in the midst of His churches, girt about the breasts with a golden girdle (Rev. 1:13), ready to serve His people on earth. In the millennium it will be said, "And righteousness shall be the girdle of His loins, and faithfulness the girdle of His reins" (Isa. 11:5).

It is most blessed to note that in Jehovah's instructions to Moses He said, "It shall be of the same, according to the work thereof." The girdle of the high priest was of the same materials and beautified with the same lovely colours as the ephod itself. How this tells us that the present gracious activities of Christ's priestly service on our behalf are according to the perfections of His own person and character as the God-man! Though glorified, He is a Servant still, He is gone into heaven to appear in the presence of God for us (Heb.

9:24), and there He "ever liveth to make intercession for us" (Heb. 7:25).

We come next to the two onyx stones—read carefully Ex. 28:9-13. Scholars tell us that the Hebrew word translated "onyx" is derived from an unused root, signifying "to shine with the lustre of fire." They were very different from the "onyx" of modern times, which is neither a costly nor brilliant stone. Job 28:16 speaks of "the *precious* onyx!" Upon these stones were engraved the names of the children of Israel. They were enclosed in "ouches," or, as the Hebrew word denotes, "settings." These, in turn, were secured by "two chains of pure gold" (v. 14), and securely fastened to the shoulders of the ephod. They were borne before the Lord by Aaron "for a memorial." In its typical application to the saints to-day, this tells of their perfect *security*. The "shoulder" (cf. Luke 15:5) is the place of *strength* (Isa. 9:6), and tells us that the omnipotence of Christ is engaged on the behalf of His people. It is not our strength, but His—"Kept by the power of God" (1 Peter 1:5). It is not our perseverance, but His— "*He* is able to keep that which I have committed unto Him" (2 Tim. 1:12). "The shoulder which sustains the universe (Heb. 1:3), upholds the feeblest and most obscure member of the blood-bought congregation" (C.H.M.). The *order* in which the names of Israel's tribes were engraved upon the two shoulder-stones was "according to their *birth*": spiritually this signifies their equality, for as born of God, all the saints have the same nature, the same moral features, the same acceptance to Christ.

Next comes the "breastplate," which we pass by now; as we purpose devoting a separate article to its consideration.

"And thou shalt make the robe of the ephod all of blue. And there shall be an hole in the top of it, in the midst thereof; it shall have a binding of woven work round about the hole of it, as it were the hole of an habergeon, that it be not rent" (vv. 31:32). This robe was worn over the fine linen coat, but underneath the ephod. It was a long loose garment, of woven work, complete in one piece, with openings for head and arms. This is the first time that the word "robe" is found in Scripture. How striking that the "robe" is never seen until the high priest comes before us! The various connections in which this word is found in later passages indicates that this robe of the ephod was a garment of dignity, one of office, one which gave priestly character to Aaron—see 1 Sam. 24:4, 1 Chron. 15:27. Job 29:14, Ezek. 26:16. This robe embodied the colour of the heavens; it was all of blue. It portrayed the heavenly character of our great High Priest, and also pointed to the place where He is now ministering on our behalf. This is most important, for it defines the essential nature of Christianity as contradistinguished from Judaism. The whole system takes its character from the Priest. Because Christ is a *heavenly* Priest, His people are partakers of a heavenly calling (Heb. 3:1), their citizenship is in heaven (Phil. 3:20), their inheritance is there (1 Peter 1). Being worn beneath the ephod itself, this "robe" announces that the official character of Christ is sustained by what He is personally as the Heavenly One (1 Cor. 15:47).

Upon the hem of this "robe of the ephod" were coloured tassels in the form of "pomegranetes," and between each of these was a "golden bell," vv. 33:34. Pomegranate is a fruit, whose seeds float in a crimson liquid; the bell, with its tongue, tells of musical speech. Every step that Aaron took as he went about his sacred duties would cause the golden bells to sound and the variegated pomegranates to be seen. So the activities of our great High Priest cause His voice to be heard in intercession within the heavenly sanctuary, and this results in His fruit being seen through "bringing many sons unto glory" and by the graces which adorn their lives.

The words "his sound shall be heard when he goeth into the holy place before the Lord, and when he cometh out" (v. 35) has a dispensational significance. It was at His ascension that our great High Priest passed into the heavenly sanctuary, and consequent upon this, on the day of Pentecost, His "sound" was heard in the testimony to Himself which was borne by the apostles as the result of the Holy Spirit being poured out from on high. The "fruit" was seen in the multitude that was then saved. Even more glorious will be His sound and fruit when "he cometh out" again, and returns to this earth and redeems His people Israel. The linking of the two together may be seen by a reference to Acts 2:16, 17, where we find Peter quoting from the prophecy of Joel—a prophecy which is to receive its fulfilment in the Millennium: but a sample of which was given on the day of Pentecost.

We next have the "plate of pure gold," upon which was engraved "holiness to the Lord." This was attached to a background of "blue lace" and fastened upon the forefront of the mitre (vv. 36, 37). "The inscription, 'Holiness to the Lord,' signified that the high priest was devoted to, dedi-

cated exclusively to, Jehovah; the golden plate upon which it was engraved sets forth that He who is the One thus truly dedicated to God, 'holy, harmless, undefiled and separate from sinners,' is Divine, the very Son of God: the blue lace upon which it was placed, His heavenliness of character. Thus conspicuous upon Aaron's forehead, it gave its meaning to the whole of his garments and of his office—he was sacred to the Lord, and, as such, interceded for Israel, representing them, and in himself hallowing the gifts of the people" (Mr. C. H. Bright).

"And it shall be upon Aaron's forehead, that Aaron may bear the iniquity of the holy things, which the children of Israel shall hallow in all their holy gifts" (v. 38). "This is the gracious provision which God has made for the imperfections and defilements of our services and worship. He can only accept that which is suited to His own nature. Everything offered to Him, therefore, must be stamped with holiness. This being so, notwithstanding that *we* are cleansed and brought into relation with Him, and have a title to approach, our *offerings* never could be accepted. But He has met our need. Christ, as Priest, bears the iniquity of our holy things; and He is holiness to the Lord, so that our worship, as presented through Him, is acceptable to God. Blessed consolation, for without this provision we were shut out from God's presence! Hence the apostle speaks not only of the blood and the rent veil, but also of the High Priest over the house of God (Heb. 10)." (Mr. E. Dennett)—cf. Rev. 8:3!

Beautiful are the closing words of v. 38: "And it shall be always upon *his* forehead, that *they* may be accepted before the Lord." This golden-plate was the symbol of the essential holiness of the Lord Jesus. The saints are represented by Him and accepted in Him. Because of their legal and vital union with Him, His holiness is theirs. O Christian reader, look away from yourself, with your ten thousand failures, and fix your eye on that golden plate. Behold in the perfections of your great High Priest the measure of thine eternal acceptance with God. Christ is our sanctification as well as our righteousness!

"And thou shalt embroider the coat of fine linen" (v. 39). Apparently the word "embroider" here is explained by what we are told in 39:27: "They made coats of fine linen of *woven* work for Aaron and his sons." This fine linen "coat" was the inner garment, and was supplemented with linen "breeches" or pants (v. 42). These may be called the high priest's *personal* raiment, even as the more beautiful external garments were his *official* vestments. As we have shown previously, "fine linen" was the emblem of purity. There is a verse in the Psalms which confirms this: "Let thy priests be clothed with *righteousness*" (132:9). Typically, these undergarments spoke of the personal righteousness of Christ, over which (so to speak) all His other perfections and glories were displayed. It reminds us of that blessed word in 1 John 2:1, "If any one sin, we have an Advocate with the Father, Jesus Christ *the Righteous*."

"And thou shalt make the mitre of fine linen" (v. 39). This was the head-dress of Aaron, and distinguished him from the ordinary priests, who wore "bonnets" (v. 40). The Hebrew word is derived from a verb which means "to roll, or wind around." This may denote that the high priest's mitre was wound around his head, like a tiara. In 1 Cor. 11:3-10, where we have Divine instruction for the covering of the women's heads in the assembly of the saints, we learn that this symbolises *subjection*. Thus the head-dress of the high priest intimated his subordination to God, his obedience to God's commands and submission to His will. The fine linen of which it was made, tells of the personal righteousness which must be found in the one who stands in the presence of God on behalf of others.

It is most solemn to discover that the only other time "mitznepheth" occurs in Scripture is in Ezek. 21:25, 27, where the Antichrist is in view. There the Hebrew word is translated "diadem," but should have been rendered "mitre" as in Ex. 28. This remarkable prophecy shows that the Man of Sin, who is yet to be revealed, will not only wear the crown of royalty, but will also assume the high priest's mitre. He will not only be the supreme civil head, but the ecclesiastical pontiff as well. This "profane and wicked prince of Israel" will arrogantly and blasphemously wield both regal and priestly power, in Satanic parody of the true Priest and King, the Lord Jesus. This age will close with Satan's son ruling over men, both in the political and religious worlds. Because men have received not the love of the truth that they might be saved, God shall send them strong delusion that they should believe the Lie (2 Thess. 2:3-12).

How profoundly thankful should each Christian reader be for that wondrous grace which has enabled him to flee from the wrath to come and to lay hold of eternal life! What praise is due to God for the great High Priest which His mercy has provided for His feeble and failing people: a Priest who is fully qualified, through His personal perfections, not only to supply our every need, but also to meet every requirement of a holy and righteous God! The last four verses of Ex. 28 will be considered, D.V., when we take up the Consecration of the Priests.

Chapter 49

THE BREASTPLATE

EXODUS 28:15-30

In our last article we pointed out how that the garments of Aaron which were for "glory and for beauty" are seven in number. Six of these, the ephod, girdle, robe, broidered-coat, mitre, and golden-crown, were then briefly considered. Now, we are to meditate upon the remaining one, namely, the Breastplate. This was the chief and most costly of the high priest's vestments, the other garments being as it were a foundation and background for it, this central one pointing to the very *heart* of Christ Himself. Its importance is at once denoted by being mentioned first in Ex. 28:4. A description of it is furnished in 28:15-30. Let us ponder:

1. *Its Workmanship.*

This is described at length in vv. 15, 16, 21, 28, to which we would ask the reader to turn. From these verses it will be seen that the Breastplate itself was made of fine twined linen of cunning work (v. 15). From the remainder of v. 15 we gather that it was richly embroidered with the three colours there mentioned. It was four-square in shape, and thus corresponded with both the brazen and incense altars. Its dimensions were "a handbreadth;" that is, from the tip of the little finger to the end of the outstretched thumb, a distance of about ten and a half inches, or half a cubit. It was "doubled" so as to give it strength and firmness, in order that it might sustain the weight of the precious stones. "Two rings of gold were placed inwards, at the bottom of the breastplate: and two gold rings were attached to the ephod, just above the curious belt (girdle): so that the breastplate was bound to the ephod by a lace of blue, coupling these rings. Two wreathen chains of gold were fastened to the ouches, in which the onyx stones were set; and were also fastened, at their other two ends, to two rings at the top of the breastplate. Thus, the ephod, onyx stones, and breastplate were all linked together in one. It may here be observed that the transla-

tion 'at the ends' (28:14, 22) should, according to Gesenius, be rendered 'twisted work,' like the twisting of a rope, and the passage will then read thus: 'Two chains of pure gold twisted, wreathen work, shalt thou make them'" (G. Soltau).

2. *Its Significance.*

There are at least five things which serve as guides to help us ascertain the distinctive typical meaning of this part of the high priest's dress. First, its name: it is called the "breastplate of judgment" (v. 15). Second, the twelve gems set in it, on which were engraved the names of Israel's twelve tribes (vv. 17-21). Third, its inseparability from the ephod: "that the breastplate be not loosed from the ephod" (v. 28). Fourth, the place where the breastplate was worn: it was upon the high priest's "heart" (v. 20). Fifth, the mysterious "Urim and Thummin" which were placed in it (v. 30). As these will be considered separately, in detail, below, we shall now only generalise.

The purpose or design of the breastplate was to furnish a support to the precious stones which were set in it, as well as to provide a background from which their brilliant beauty might be displayed. Thus there is little or no difficulty in perceiving that which is central in this blessed type. On the jewels were inscribed the names of Israel's twelve tribes. Therefore, what we have foreshadowed here is Christ, as our great High Priest, bearing on His heart, sustaining, and presenting before God, His blood-bought people. There is a slight distinction to be drawn from what we have here and that which is set forth in Ex. 28:9-12. There, too, we have the names of Israel's tribes borne by their high priest before God. But there they are seen resting upon his "shoulders," whereas here (v. 29) they rest upon his heart. In the one it is the *strength* or power of Christ engaged on behalf of His helpless people; in the other, it is His *affections* exercised for them.

It will therefore be seen that it is, primarily, the perfect and lasting *security* of believers which is set forth in our present type. Both the power and the love of Christ are for them, guaranteeing their eternal preservation: "And Aaron shall bear the names of the children of Israel in the breastplate of judgment upon his heart when he goeth in unto the holy place, for a memorial before the Lord *continually*" (v. 29). Their position or standing before God was neither affected nor altered by their changing circumstances, infirmities or sins. Whenever Aaron went into the holy place, there on his heart were the names of all God's people. Emphasising this truth of *security*, note carefully how that their names were not simply written upon (so that their erasure was possible) the precious stones, but "engraved" (v. 21)!

Still emphasising the same thought, notice also how that each jewel was secured to the breastplate by a golden setting: "they shall be set in gold in their inclosings" (v. 20). Thus it was impossible for them to slip out of their places, or for any one of them to be lost! Mark, too, the provision made for firmly fixing in place the breastplate itself. This is brought before us in vv. 21-28. It was fastened by "chains at the ends of wreathen work of pure gold" (v. 22), and these were passed through "two rings of gold on the ends of the breastplate." Thus the people of God (as represented by their names) were *chained* to the high priest!

"The chains were wreathen and twisted like a rope, for both words are used; wreathen, interwoven. The same word is used in Judges 15:13, 14; 16:11, 12; Psa. 12:3; Hosea 1:4—cords of love. 'Twisted work' is Gesenius' translation of the Hebrew word, which our version gives, 'at the ends' (vv. 14, 22). Thus he would translate 'and two chains of pure gold, wreathen shalt thou make them, twisted work.' The object in adding the word 'twisted' to 'wreathen' appears to imply a combination of skill and strength, and that the breastplate might be indissolubly connected with the shoulder-stones. Every movement of the high priest's shoulder would affect the breastplate: and every beat of his heart which agitated the breastplate would be conveyed, by means of the wreathen chains, to the covering of the shoulders.

"There is a beautiful significance in this, reminding us how the mighty power of the arm of the Lord is intimately linked on with the tenderness of His heart of love.

No action of His strength is disconnected from His counsels of mercy and grace towards His saints. He makes all things work together for good to them that love Him. His arm and His heart are combined in sustaining them in their high calling. He is able to keep them from falling, and to present them faultless before the presence of His glory with exceeding joy. They shall never perish, neither shall any pluck them out of the Shepherd's hand: and who shall separate them from His love?" (G. Soltau). How the double "span" or handbreadth in 28:16 confirms this!

3. *Its Jewels.*

These were twelve in number, one for each tribe, set in four rows of three each. They are enumerated in vv, 17-20. With respect to the identity of these precious stones but little is known. There have been many laboured attempts made by learned men to discover the real names of the gems; but, with the exception of four or five, most Biblical students acknowledge the subject to be involved in obscurity. But though we are unable to recognise these stones under their modern names, yet many blessed thoughts are suggested by them.

First, the fact the Jehovah selected gems to represent His people indicates how *precious* they are in His sight. How dear they were, is seen in the fact that He gave up His own beloved Son to die for them. Second, their *excellency* was prefigured. And how accurate the type! The believer's excellency or righteousness is not one of his own, but is imputed. So it is with precious stones. "Whatever beauty each has, the light alone brings it out; in the darkness it has none" (C. H. Bright). Thus it is with the saints: it is only as God sees them in Him who is the "true Light" that they are acceptable unto Him. Third, the perfect *knowledge* of the Lord regarding each disciple is intimated by the individualising of the tribes by name. "The Lord knoweth them that are His." "He calleth His own sheep by name." Such is the omniscience of our High Priest that all our wants are known to Him. Fourth, the *durability* of these stones symbolises the fact that the salvation purchased for sinners is an "eternal" one (Heb. 5:9).

Concerning each stone it has been well said, "Much, very much, of its beauty depends upon its *cutting*. Cut skilfully, so as to refract the rays of light from many sides, it sparkles with a beauty quite unknown to its natural condition. Thus, too, with believers; undoubtedly each one has some inherent characteristic difference, but only as the Divine hand in much patience and skill cuts and polishes the stone to catch and discover the colours of the Divine light which illuminates it doth it appear beautiful. Its beauty is not its own, but it has been endowed with capacity to appreciate and *reflect* the beauty of Him who is light and love; and it is to reflect the beauties of the perfect One that we have been chosen—'that in the ages to come He might *show* the exceeding riches of His grace in His kindness toward us through Christ Jesus' (Eph. 2:7). So when that day of manifestation of the glory of His grace comes, 'the nations shall walk in *her* light,'" Rev. 21:24 (C. H. Bright).

Twelve stones were set in it, all precious stones, but no two of them were alike. They were altogether different in form, hew, character, and also in beauty and value (according to man's estimation); but all of them were *gems* in the sight of God, one as much as another. They were each set in gold, and they rested equally upon the heart of Aaron, when he ministered before the Lord. Doubtless, these precious stones were gathered in lands far sundered. Some from the depths of the ocean it might be, and some from the dark mine. But whatever their variety, or the circumstances of their history, or the distance from which they were quarried, they were *united* upon the high priest's heart: diamond, jasper, and emerald were borne there equally and together for a memorial before the Lord.

What comfort, yea, what joy the realisation of this brings to the Christian. Let not the ruby (sardius) proudly think itself superior to the carbuncle; let not the jasper repine because it is not the diamond. Let us not compare ourselves with others. Each believer is accepted in the Beloved Each believer is clothed with the righteousness of Christ. Each is complete in Him Is it not enough thou art in the Breastplate, set in gold and borne upon His heart!

In conclusion, let us call attention to something which is exceedingly suggestive and significant concerning them as a whole. These jewels which adorned the Breastplate of the high priest of Israel also pointed backward to sinless Eden, and forward to the sinless New Jerusalem. The first precious stone mentioned in Scripture is the "onyx" (Gen. 2:12), and *this* was the gem which bore on each of Aaron's shoulders the "memorial" on which the names of God's people were graven (28:9-12), and to which the Breastplate was united (v.

25). While in Rev. 21:19-20 we learn that the foundations of the Heavenly City will be garnished with twelve precious stones. Thus the "onyx" stones on the high priest's shoulders look back to Gen. 2:10, which contained a hidden *promise* of the re-admission of God's people into the sinless state; while the Breastplate itself looked forward to Rev. 21, where the *fulfilment* of that promise is seen!

4. Its Connections.

The Breastplate was inseparably linked to the ephod. The latter was made for the former, and not the former for the latter. It was never to be separated from it: "that the Breastplate be not loosed from the ephod" (v. 28). The ephod was peculiarly and essentially the high priestly garment. "The names of God's people as borne upon the heart of the priest, shining out in all the sparkling lustre and beauty of the stones on which they are engraven. This symbolises the fact that believers are before God in all the acceptance of Christ. When God looks upon the great High Priest, He beholds His people upon His heart, as well as upon His shoulders, adorned with all the beauty of the One on whom His eye ever rests with perfect delight. Or, looking at it from another aspect, it might be said that Christ presented His people to God, in the exercise of His priesthood, as Himself. He thus establishes in His intercession His own claims upon God on their behalf. And with what joy does He so present them before God! For they are those for whom He has died, and whom He has cleansed with His own most precious blood, those whom He has made the objects of His own love, and whom finally He will bring to be forever with Him; and He pleads for them before God according to all the strength of these ties" (Ed. Dennett).

Thus the truth set forth by the Breastplate is inseparably united to the priestly ministry of Christ. "It is fastened to the ephod by chains of gold, by all that Christ is therefore as Divine. It is also an eternal connection as typified by the rings—the ring being without an end, and hence, an emblem of eternity. As Priest, Christ can never fail us. If He has once undertaken our cause, He will never lay it down. Surely this truth will strengthen our hearts in times of trial or weakness. We may be despondent, but if we look up we may rejoice in the thought that our place upon the heart and shoulders of Christ can never be lost" (Ed. Dennett).

"He preserves us, as that which He has on His heart, to God, He cannot be before Him without doing so, and whatever claim the desire and wish of Christ's heart has to draw out the favour of God, operates in drawing out that favour to us. The light and favour of the sanctuary—God as dwelling there—cannot shine out on him without shining on us, and that as an object presented by Him for it" (Mr. J. N. Darby).

5. Its Name.

It is called "the breastplate of judgment" (v. 15). This term occurs for the first time in Gen. 18:19, where God says to Abraham, concerning his sons, "They shall keep the way of the Lord, to do justice and judgment." Its next occurrence is in Ex. 21:1, where "judgments" signify the decrees or fiats of God—cf. Psalm 19:9. That which is here set forth is that the saints are represented by their High Priest according to God's mind concerning them. Expressing almost the same aspect of truth is that blessed word, "I know the thoughts that I think toward you, saith the Lord, thoughts of peace, and not of evil, to give you an expected end" (Jer. 29:11).

Closely connected with its name is what is said in v. 29: "And Aaron shall bear the names of the children of Israel in the breastplate of judgment upon his heart when he goeth in unto the holy place, *for a memorial* before the Lord continually." A remarkable word is this: A "memorial" is a reminder, for calling to remembrance. But does our Father in heaven need such? To inform His omniscience, no; but to delight His heart and satisfy His love, yes. And this, too, for the strengthening of our faith, that His people might know they have that in heaven for the staying of their hearts.

6. Its Position.

The Breastplate was placed over Aaron's heart. It is striking to observe that three times over we have these words "upon his heart" (vv. 29, 30, 30). As we have seen, the Breastplate was suspended from the shoulders by golden chains connected with the onyx stones, and from golden rings in the lower corners it was fastened to the girdle of the ephod by a lace of blue. Thus it was firmly secured over the heart of Israel's high priest. God's people were thus doubly represented: first, upon his shoulders, the place of strength; and then, upon his heart, the seat of affection. Lovely type was this of our Redeemer in His present heavenly ministry, exercising His power to uphold His poor people; and His deep, tender, unchangeable love embracing them, binding them close to His heart, and presenting them to the Father in the glory

and preciousness of the splendour with which He is invested.

"This is precious, and oftentimes we need to refresh ourselves by 'considering' thus 'the Apostle and High Priest of our confession' (Heb. 3:1). There are times when we forget that we have One on high whom, in grace, cares for and watches over thóse who are treading the path of faith He once trod on earth. And there are times when, though we remember this, we limit either His love or His power. Precious, then, is it to be thus reminded that according to what He *can* do, His love makes us *willing* to do; and according to what His affection is, He hath strength to carry out what it dictates" (C. H. Bright).

It is beautiful to note in the Song of Sol. how the Bride says to her Beloved, "Set me as a seal upon Thine heart, as a seal upon Thine arm" (8:6): let my name be graven deep in Thine heart, where love is strong as death, which many waters cannot quench, which the floods of the Almighty have not drowned. And let my name be also graven in the seat of Thy power, that I may be upheld from sin and folly, that I may not be like the adulterer and adulteress who seek the friendship of the world. If such a prayer suited the desires of an earthy people, how much more may this petition express the devotion and the longings of Christ's heavenly people!

7. Its Lace.

"And they shall bind the breastplate by the rings thereof unto the rings of the ephod with a lace of blue, that it may be above the curious girdle of the ephod, and that the breastplate be not loosed from the ephod" (v. 28). What beautiful completeness this gives to our type! "Blue" is the *heavenly* colour, and "as long as His heavenly priesthood continues, so long is it inseparably connected with bearing us on the breastplate. Not that He will ever cease to love us, but when His church is *with* Him it will no longer need this care which the trials of the way call out. And surely to be *with* one who loves us is better than simply to be *remembered* by him, however faithful that remembrance may be. Christ is made a priest forever after the order of Melkeizedek. His priesthood has for the present an *intercessory* character, as typified in Aaron; but the time will come when—God's judgment upon the nations being executed—He will come forth as the Priest of the Most High God, not to intercede, but to *reward* (Gen. 14:18). At this time His *royal* priesthood will be in exercise, and ours too. 'King of righteousness' He will first be proved to be; then 'King of peace,' Heb. 7:2" (C. H. Bright).

May God be pleased to bless this little meditation to many of His people, and use it to make Christ more precious to them.

CHAPTER 50

THE URIM AND THUMMIM

EXODUS 28:30

"The secret things belong unto the Lord our God: but those things which are revealed belong unto us and to our children forever" (Deut. 29:29). This seems to be a suitable passage with which to introduce our present inquiry. Things which Jehovah has not seen fit to make known unto us, it is presumption and impiety to attempt to pry into; hence the Christian needs constantly to pray, "Keep back Thy servant also from presumptuous sins" (Psa. 19:13). Let us not attempt to be wise above that which is written. Let us seek grace to be kept humble, from invading the prerogatives of the Most High, and from endeavouring to handle things which are "too wonderful" (Psa. 139:6) for us. "Now I know *in part*" (1 Cor. 13:12); let us be thankful for this "part," and leave it with God to grant us a fuller revelation in the Day to come.

On the other hand, let us not forget that the things which *are* revealed "belong" unto us. They are given for our instruction. They are given for us to study prayerfully and carefully. It is only by perseveringly comparing Scripture with Scripture that we learn what God *has* "revealed" in His Word. The Holy Spirit places no premium upon sloth. It is not the dilatory but the "diligent" soul who is "made fat" (Prov. 13:4). A rightly divided Word of Truth calls for a "workman" (2 Tim. 2:15), not a lazy man. It is because they spend, comparatively, so little time over the Scriptures, it is because they cannot truly say "I have esteemed the words of His mouth more than my necessary food" (Job 23:12), that the great majority of professing Christians have little or no conception of how much God has been pleased to reveal to us in His Word.

Now, in connection with the Urim and the Thummim there appear to be some things which God has seen fit to keep "secret," hence the profitless articles which many, who resorted to speculation, have

written on the subject. Concerning the "Urim and the Thummim" no man, Jew or Gentile, knows, or can know, anything, save what God has "revealed" to us in His Word. But as the humble student attentively compares the different passages where they are mentioned, as he notes what is said therein, he discovers that God has been pleased to intimate to us not a little concerning their nature, use, and spiritual significance. Let us now note:—

1. *Their Names.*

Both words are in the plural number, though this (as is often the case in the Hebrew of the O.T.) is probably what is called the "plural of majesty"—used for the purpose of *emphasising* the importance or dignity of a thing. Thus, it is most likely that the "Urim" was but a single object, and the "Thummim" another; but of this we cannot be certain. There is no difficulty in ascertaining the English equivalent of these Hebrew terms. Urim signifies "lights" or "light," being the plural form of the word very frequently used for "light." In Isa. 31:9; 44:16; 47:14; 50:11; Ezek. 5:2 Urim is translated "fire" (its secondary meaning); while in Isa. 24:15 it is rendered "fires." Thummim means "perfections" or "perfection." In the Sept. these two words are translated by "delosis" and "aletheim," meaning "manifestation" and "truth."

It is surely striking that reference is made to these mysterious objects in the Old Testament just *seven* times. In Ex. 28:30, Lev. 8:8, Ezra 2:63, and Neh. 7:65 they are spoken of as the "Urim and Thummim," but in Deut. 33:8 the order is reversed "Thummim and Urim"; while in Num. 27:21 and 1 Sam. 28:6 "Urim" is mentioned alone. It is also to be noted that no command was given to Moses by Jehovah to "make" them; he was simply told to "put" (Heb. nathan "to give") them in the Breastplate. Let us next consider:

2. *Their Place.*

This is made known in Ex. 28:30, "And thou shalt put in the breastplate of judgment the Urim and the Thummim." From v. 16, "Foursquare it shall be doubled," we gather that the linen fabric of which the breastplate was composed was made in the form of a bag, in which (more literally "into which") the Urim and the Thummim were placed. Thus, they also were worn upon the high priest's heart. They would be under the twelve precious stones which bore the names of Israel's tribes, and linked, too, with the onyx stones on Aaron's shoulders.

3. *Their Use.*

This may be gathered from the different passages where they are mentioned. The first is in Num. 27:21, "And he shall stand before Eleazar the priest, who shall ask counsel for him after the judgment of Urim before the Lord: at his word they shall go out, and at his word they shall come in, both he, and all the children of Israel with him, even all the congregation."

From the above quotation it seems clear that, in certain circumstances, the mind of the Lord was conveyed through them. 1 Sam. 28:6 bears this out, for of Saul it is there said, "when he *enquired* of the Lord, the Lord answered him not, neither by dreams nor by Urim, nor by prophets." From these two passages we gather that by means of the Urim, or "light," in the breastplate of the high priest, counsel or prophetic guidance was obtained from God.

Further confirmation of this is found in Ezra 2. In vv. 61, 62 we are told, "And of the children of the priests: the children of Habaiah, the children of Koz, the children of Barzillai; which took a wife of the daughters of Barzillai the Gileadite, and was called after their name: These sought their register among those that were reckoned by genealogy, but they were not found: therefore were they, as polluted, put from the priesthood." Then it is added, "And the governor said unto them, that they should not eat of the most holy things till there stood up a priest with Urim and with Thummim," i.e., till one through whom the mind of the Lord was clearly revealed.

From these Scriptures the late Dr. Bullinger drew the following deductions: "The Urim and Thummim were probably two precious stones, which were drawn out as a lot to give Jehovah's judgment. 'The lot is cast into the lap (Heb. 'bosom'), but the whole judgment thereof is of the Lord' (Prov. 16:33)—bosom is here put for the clothing or covering over it: cf. Ex. 4:6, 7; Ruth 4:10. . . . Thus, these two placed in the 'bag,' and one drawn out, would give the judicial decision, which

would be 'of the Lord.' Hence the breastplate itself was known as 'the breastplate of *judgment'* (v. 15), because, by that, Jehovah's judgment was obtained whenever it was needed. Hence, when the land was divided 'by lot' (Num. 26:55) Eleazar, the high priest, must be present (Num. 34:17 —cf. 27:21—Josh. 17:4). When he would decide it the lot 'came up' (Josh. 18:11), 'came forth' (Josh. 19:1), 'came out' (Josh. 19:17), i.e., 'out' or 'forth' from the bag of the ephod. In Ezra. 2:61-63 no judgment could be given unless the high priest were present with the breastplate, with its bag, with the lots of Urim and Thummim, which gave Jehovah's decision."

4. *Their Connections.*

First, as intimated above, they were deposited in the bag of the breastplate. Not only so, the very name of this important part of the high priest's vestments is taken therefrom, for it was termed "the breastplate of judgment," i.e., of decision, as giving God's mind. In striking accord with this, we may point out how that the word used in the Sept. version (the first translation ever made of the Old Testament into Greek) is "logeion," which means *oracle,* because by it the high priest obtained oracular responses from God.

Second, as pointed out in the preceding article, the breastplate was inseparably connected with, yea, formed an essential part of, the "ephod" itself—see Ex. 28:6, 7, 28 and our notes thereon. Now, the "ephod" was peculiarly the *prophetic* dress of the high priest. By means of it (that is, through the Urim and Thummim) he learned the counsel of God, and was thus able to declare what course the people should take, or what events were about to happen. Upon this, the late Mr. Soltau has most helpfully pointed out:

"Thus we find Saul, accompanied by Ahiah, the Lord's priest in Shiloh, wearing an ephod, commanding the ark to be brought, that he may ascertain the meaning of the tumult among the Philistines. But, instead of waiting to receive any response from God, he binds Israel with a curse and enters into the battle (1 Sam. 14:3, 19, 24). Abiathar, the only surviving priest of the line of Eli, fled to David with the ephod in his hand, having escaped the slaughter at Nob. David ascertained by this means the purpose of the men of Keilah to deliver him up to Saul (1 Sam. 23:6, 10). Again, in the affair at Ziglag, David consulted the Lord through Abiathar and the ephod, and obtained a favourable answer (1 Sam. 30:7, 8). On a subsequent occasion we read of David inquiring of the Lord, and obtaining answers (2 Sam. 2:1), and although in this instance the priest and ephod are not mentioned, yet judging from the previous instances it is probable that the same mode of inquiry was adopted."

5. *Their Significance.*

The twelve gems on which were graven the names of Israel's tribes were worn *upon* the heart of Aaron; the "Urim and the Thummim" were placed *within* the breastplate, beneath the precious stones. Thus they speak, first of all, of that which is found in the heart of the Lord Jesus. As said the apostle who leaned upon His bosom, "The Word became flesh and tabernacled among us, and we beheld His glory, the glory as of the only begotten of the Father, *full* of grace and truth" (John 1:14). "Light" and "Perfection" centre in Him who is our great High Priest.

In Christ Himself we see the antitype of the "Urim." "In Him was life, and the life was the *light* of men . . . . that was the true Light, which lighteth every man that cometh into the world" (John 1:5, 9). Therefore did He say, "I am the light of the world: he that followeth Me shall not walk in darkness, but shall have the light of life" (John 8:12).

"God is light" (1 John 1:5), and Christ could say, "He that hath seen Me hath seen the Father" (John 14:9). Yes, He is the reality of which the Urim was the figure: the light of the knowledge of the glory of God shines "in the face of Jesus Christ" (2 Cor. 4:6).

In Christ we see the antitype of the "Thummim." Every "perfection" is found in Him, for He is *"altogether* lovely" (Song of Sol. 5:16). Concerning His Deity, He is "over all, God blessed forever" (Rom. 9:5). Concerning His humanity, He is "that holy thing" (Luke 1:35). As the God-man, the Father said, "This is My Beloved Son." In His speech He was perfect: "grace is poured into Thy lips" (Psa. 45:2) testified the Spirit of prophecy. "Never man spake like this Man" (John 7:46), confessed His enemies. In His character He was flawless: "a lamb without spot and blemish" (1 Peter 1:19). In His conduct He was perfect: "I do *always* those things that please Him" (John 8:29). Yes, Christ is the reality of which the Thummim was the figure.

But is there not something else here, still more specific? We believe there is. "God is light" (1 John 1:5) and "God is love" (1 John 4:8), make known to us what God *is* in Himself. The *balance* between these, if we may so speak, was per-

fectly maintained and blessedly manifested by the incarnate Son. The love which He exercised was ever an holy love; the light which He displayed was never divorced from this love. In like manner, these two, the Urim and the Thummim—"light" and "perfection"—formed a unit, being *together* within the breastplate upon the high priest's heart. The antitype of this is found in John 1:14, already quoted. "Now, in this expression—'full of grace and truth'— we have, in brief, the two main thoughts of the breastplate. 'Truth' is the effect of the light, and God is light. Light is what manifests, brings out the truth, *is* the truth. Christ, the light of the world, is the truth come into it: everything gets its true character from Him. 'Grace,' while it is what it is in God, is *toward* man" F. W. Grant).

In addition to the names of these two objects (what they were in themselves) foreshadowing that which is in Christ, the purpose for which they were designed, the use to which they were put, also receives its typical fulfilment in Him. As we have seen, they were employed for communicating to the people a knowledge of God's mind and will concerning them. How blessedly this pointed to the Lord Jesus as "the wonderful Counseller" (Isa. 9:6)! In Him "are hid all the treasures of wisdom and knowledge" (Col. 2:3). And therefore could He say, "I am the Truth" (John 14:6). The mind and will of God are perfectly revealed to Him and by Him.

Christ's perfect knowledge of the Father's thoughts are clearly intimated in the following Scriptures: "For the Father loveth the Son and showeth Him *all* things that Himself doeth" (John 5:20)—there is no restraint, no reserve. "No one knoweth the Son save the Father; neither doth any know the Father, save the Son, and he to whosoever the Son willeth to reveal Him" (Matt. 11:27, R.V.). "The Father loveth the Son, and hath given *all* things into His hand" (John 3:35).

Christ's communication to His people of what the Father has given to Him is also without reserve. Speaking to His beloved disciples He says, "Henceforth I call you not servants; for the servant knoweth not what his lord doeth: but I have called you friends; for *all* things that I have heard of My Father I have made known unto you" (John 15:15). This is developed, in a doctrinal way, in the Epistle to the Hebrews: "God hath, in these last days, spoken unto us by *His Son*" (1:1, 2). Perfectly has Christ communicated to His people the mind of God; fully has He revealed the Father's heart. This, we take it, then, is the second great truth foreshadowed by the Urim and Thummim: the counsels of God are only to be learned through the Lord Jesus, our great High Priest; and those counsels (of grace) are inseparably connected with His own dear people—as symbolised by the Urim and Thummim and the twelve precious stones, bearing their names, being *together* in the breastplate.

Another blessed truth was also signified by the Urim and Thummim. When the people of God were doubtful as to what course they should follow, when they desired light upon their path, they could obtain it by coming to and seeking it from the high priest. "And he shall stand before Eleazar the priest, who shall *ask counsel for him*, after the judgment of Urim before the Lord" (Num. 27:21). "Thus we learn that the high priest not only bore the judgment of the congregation before the Lord, but also carried the judgment of the Lord to the congregation. Solemn, weighty, and most precious functions! All this we have, in divine perfectness, in our great High Priest, who has passed into the heavens; He bears the judgment of His people on His heart continually; and He, by the Holy Spirit, communicates to us the counsel of God, in reference to the most minute circumstances of our daily course. We do not want dreams or visions; if only we walk in the Spirit we shall enjoy all the certainty which the perfect 'Urim,' on the breast of our great High Priest, can afford" (C.H.M.)

Yet one other point remains to be considered in this striking type. In the quotation made above from Dr. Bullinger's works it will be seen that the Urim and Thummim played an important part in the allocation of Canaan to the different tribes in the days of Joshua. It was to them that God's mind was made known respecting Israel's portions in the promised land. The antitype of this is most blessed. Christ has purchased for Himself an inheritance (see Psa. 2:8, etc.). His inheritance, both the heavenly and earthly portions of it, He will share with His people, for they are "jointheirs" with Him (Rom. 8:17). In John 17 we find Him saying to the Father, "the glory which Thou gavest Me I have given them" (v. 22). The different positions which His people will occupy during the Millennium will be determined by the Lord Jesus. To one He will say, "have thou authority over ten cities" (Luke 19:17), to another, 'be thou over five cities" (Luke 19:19), and so on. Thus our Joshua (the Hebrew of "Jesus") will apportion the Inheritance according to the mind of God.

To sum up. In Christ, then, we have the reality of all that was foreshadowed by the Urim and Thummim. First, He is the "Light and Perfection" of God—the Brightness of His glory (Heb. 1:3). Second, in Christ the light and life, the righteousness and grace of God, meet together, and their balance is perfectly maintained. Third, Christ is the One in whom all the counsels of God find their Centre. Fourth, the counsels of God which centre in Christ are inseparably connected with His people. Fifth, to Christ and by Christ is made fully known the mind of God, for in Him are hid "*all* the treasures of wisdom and. knowledge" (Col. 2:3). Sixth, from Christ, by His Spirit, directions may be obtained for every step of our pilgrim journey. Seventh, by Christ the promised and purchased inheritance will be administered.

In conclusion, we may note a *dispensational* application which the Urim and Thummim had for the Jews. Ezra 2:63 informs us that there was no one with the Urim and Thummim to communicate the mind of God in the day of Israel's return from their Babylonian captivity. The company seen with Ezra typify the godly Jewish remnant in the Tribulation period. Though sustained by God, the Holy Spirit will not be on earth at that time, and they will be without many of the spiritual privileges which we now enjoy. But at the close of the time of Jacob's trouble, the Lord Jesus shall return to earth: "He shall build the temple of the Lord, and He shall bear the glory, and shall sit and rule upon His throne; and He shall be a priest upon His throne: and the *counsel* of peace shall be between them both" (Zeck. 6:13).

At the beginning of the Millennium, "It shall come to pass that the mountain of the Lord's house shall be established in the top of the mountains, and shall be exalted above the hills; and all nations shall flow unto it. And many people shall go and say, Come ye, and let us go up to the mountain of the Lord, to the house of the God of Jacob; and He will *teach* us of His ways, and we will walk in His paths; for out of Zion shall go forth the law, and the word of the Lord from Jerusalem. And He shall *judge* among the nations. . . . O house of Jacob, come ye, and let us walk in the *light* of the Lord" (Isa. 2:2-5). Then shall Israel enjoy that which, of old, was adumbrated by the Urim and Thummim in their high priest's breastplate.

N.B.—Having completed our own study

of the subject, and after having looked in vain for any help from numerous commentaries ancient and modern, in the good providence of God we found an illuminating article in "Addresses on Hebrews," by P. R. Morford. This led us to follow up his suggestion of linking the "Urim and Thummim" with Hebrews 1 and 2; the results of which we give in a sermon preached thereon. The further and clearer distinction drawn between the spiritual significations of the Urim and Thummim explains the slight variations found in several Old Testament scriptures. In Num. 27:21 and 1 Sam. 28:6 only the "Urim" is mentioned, because that had to do, specifically, with God revealing Himself. In Deut. 33:8 the "Thummim" is mentioned first, in keeping with the thought of the verse as a whole.

CHAPTER 51

THE VESTMENTS OF THE PRIESTS

EXODUS 28:40-43

"Thy testimonies are wonderful" (Psalm 119:129). The one who first penned these words had a much smaller Bible than we now have. Little more than the Pentateuch had been written in the Psalmist's time, yet his study of the first five books of Holy Writ moved David to wonderment as he pondered their contents. All that is said of the tabernacle and its priesthood, down to its minutest detail, is indeed "wonderful": wonderful in its depth, for there is much here which none has yet fathomed; wonderful in its freshness, for the Holy Spirit is ever revealing new beauties therein; wonderful in its preciousness, for the one in communion with its Author must say, "More to be desired are they than gold, yea, than much fine gold: sweeter also than honey or the honeycomb" (Psa. 19:10).

There is another and more comprehensive reason why God's testimonies are "wonderful," and that is, because they are concerned with Him whose name is called "Wonderful" (Isa. 9:6). Said the Lord Jesus, as He came into this world, "Lo I come—in the volume of the Book it is written *of Me*—to do Thy will O God" (Heb. 10:7). Hence, to the unbelieving Pharisees He said, "Search the Scriptures . . . . for they are they which testify of Me." The incarnate Word is the key to the written Word. It is the Person and Work of Christ which gives meaning and blessedness to what is found in the Old Testament types. "And beginning at Moses and all the prophets, He expounded unto them in all the Scriptures the things *concerning Himself*" (Luke 24:27).

But it is just because the Scriptures testify of Christ that He alone can expound them to us. Their Divine Inspirer must also be their Interpreter if we are to discern their spiritual import. As we read in Luke 24:45, "Then opened He their understanding, that they *might* understand the Scriptures." This is our deep need, too, to ask Him to anoint our eyes with

eyesalve that we may see (Rev. 3:18). It is only as He *does* thus anoint our eyes, that we are enabled to discern in many an Old Testament character, ritual, symbol, wondrous and perfect foreshadowments of Himself. Oh that He may, increasingly, instruct both writer and reader.

"Thy testimonies are wonderful," wonderful also in their very *arrangement*. Again and again in the course of these articles upon Exodus we have called attention to this striking feature. In what is now to be before us, we have still another example. The *order* of the contents of Ex. 28 is most suggestive and significant. The whole chapter has to do with the priests and their vestments. First, in v. 1, before details are entered into, Aaron and his sons are seen together. This, as already pointed out, typified Christ and His people in their perfect union. Then, in vv. 2 to 39, we have described the robes and insignia of Aaron himself. Finally, in vv. 40-43, reference is made to the vestments of Aaron's sons. Who can fail to see here the handiwork of God? In all things Christ must have the pre-eminence: first the garments of the high priest are mentioned, then those of the priestly family!

"And for Aaron's sons thou shalt make coats, and thou shalt make for them girdles, and bonnets shalt thou make for them, for glory and for beauty" (v. 40). It is very striking and most blessed to mark that here we have repeated what was said in v. 2. There, we read how that Jehovah said to Moses, "And thou shalt make holy garments for Aaron thy brother, for glory and for beauty." So here in v. 40 the Lord gave instruction that Aaron's sons should also have robes made for them for "glory and for beauty." As pointed out in the previous articles, the various garments worn by Aaron, pointed to the inherent, essential and personal excellencies of our great High Priest. That which was prefigured in those worn by Aaron's sons was the graces with which Christ's people are endowed, by virtue of their association with

273

Him.

All believers are priests. All Christians have been consecrated to and for Divine service; all have access to God, a place within the heavenly sanctuary. They have been made "kings and priests unto God" (Rev. 1:6). They are a "holy priesthood, to offer up spiritual sacrifices, which are acceptable to God by Christ Jesus" (1 Peter 2:5). They are also "a royal priesthood" (1 Peter 2:9), because united to Him who is King of kings. There is no Scriptural warrant at all for a separate priestly class among Christians; all have equal title to draw near to God (Heb. 10: 22). Every Christian is a "priest," for he worships in a spiritual temple (Heb. 10: 19), he stands at a spiritual altar (Heb. 13:10), he offers a spiritual sacrifice (Heb. 13:15). But to be priests to God necessitates holy garments. Those belonging to Aaron's "sons" were four in number, each of which we shall consider separately.

1. *Their Coats.*

"And for Aaron's sons thou shalt make coats" (v. 40). This receives amplification in Ex. 39:27, where we are told, "And they made coats of fine linen of woven work for Aaron and for his sons." As we have seen in earlier articles, the "fine linen" speaks of the spotless purity and holiness of Christ. "The robing of Aaron's sons is really the putting on of Christ; and this, in fact, brings them into association with Him; for the church possesses nothing apart from Christ. If believers, for example, are brought into the position of priests, and the enjoyment of priestly privileges, it is in virtue of their connection with Him. He is the Priest, and He it is that makes them priests (see Rev. 1: 5, 6). Everything flows from Him. Thus, when Aaron is put into company with his sons, it is not so much that he becomes merged into the priestly family, but rather to teach that all the blessings and privileges of the priestly family are derived from Christ. But in order to do this they must first be invested with robes of glory and for beauty—robes which adorn them with the glory and beauty of Christ" (Ed. Dennett).

More specifically, these spotless linen coats of the priests set forth the *righteousness* with which the saints are clothed. Our own righteousnesses are as filthy rags (Isa. 64:6). But these have been removed, and in their place the "best robe" of Christ's righteousness has been placed upon us (Luke 15:22). This is strikingly and blessedly set forth in Zech. 3: "Now Joshua was clothed with filthy garments, and stood before the angel. And he answered and spake unto those that stood before him, saying, Take away the filthy garments from him. And unto him He said, Behold, I have caused thine iniquity to pass from thee, and I will clothe thee with change of raiment" (vv. 3, 4). It is because of this that the believer sings, "I will greatly rejoice in the Lord, my soul shall be joyful in my God, for He hath clothed me with the garments of salvation, He hath covered me with the robe of righteousness, as a bridegroom decketh himself with ornaments, and as a bride adorneth herself with her jewels" (Isa. 61:10).

Of old it was said, "Let thy priests be clothed with righteousness; and let thy saints shout for joy. . . . I will also clothe her priests with salvation" (Psa. 132:9, 16). The answer to this is given in the New Testament, where we are told that God has made Christ to be "unto us wisdom, and righteousness, and sanctification, and redemption" (1 Cor. 1:30); and again, "For He hath made Him to be sin for us, who knew no sin; that we might be made the righteousness of God in Him" (2 Cor. 5:21).

"Aaron, as the high priest, appeared in the presence of the Lord in a representative character, personating, we may say, the whole nation of Israel, and upholding it in the glory and beauty required by God; bearing the names of the tribes on his shoulders and breastplate, graven on precious stones. His sons, the priests, stood in no such official dignity, but had access into the holy place and ministered at the altar on behalf of the people; not as representing them, but rather as leaders of their worship, and instructors of them in the holy things of God. They were types of one aspect of the church of God—the *heavenly* priesthood. In the Revelation, the four and twenty elders have a priestly standing; they form the heavenly council, being 'elders,' and therefore also judges. They are seated on 'thrones' because kings. They are clothed in white raiment as priests, and they have on their heads crowns of gold, that is, victors' crowns as chaplets (Rev. 4:4).

"The countless multitude are also seen clothed with white robes; a priestly company serving day and night in the temple (7:9). The Lamb's wife is seen arrayed in fine linen, clean and white (19:8). We have white raiment also alluded to in Rev. 3:4, 18 and 6:11. Thus the priestly dress of fine linen, and the garments of unsullied whiteness, represent the same thing—spotless righteousness. The standing of the believer in Christ before God not being his own righteousness, but the righteousness of God which is by faith" (H. W. Soltau).

Ere passing from this part of the priests' vestments, we need to be reminded that our desire and aim concerning our state should ever be an approximation unto our standing. The Christian's condition in this world ought to correspond to his position before God. Thus, while in Gal. 3:27 it is said, "For as many of you as have been baptized into Christ *have* put on Christ," in Rom. 13:14 we are exhorted *"put ye on* the Lord Jesus Christ, and make not provision for the flesh, to fulfil the lusts thereof." To do this we need to have the heart constantly engaged with Christ, remembering that He has left us "an example, that ye should follow His steps" (1 Peter 2:21). O to be more engaged with Him who is fairer than the children of men.

2. Their Girdles.

"And thou shalt make for them girdles" (v. 40). With this should be compared what we are told in 39:29, "And a girdle of fine twined linen, and blue, and purple, and scarlet, of needlework; as the Lord commanded Moses." Some have thought that because "girdle" is here found in the singular number that the reference must be to that alone which was worn by the high priest. But this is a mistake, *his* "girdle" is described in 28:8, and it will be seen by a careful comparison with 39: 29 that it differed from those worn by the priests in this respect: his had "gold" in it, theirs did not.

It is only by comparing Scripture with Scripture that we can rightly interpret any figure or symbol. Two thoughts are suggested by the "girdle": it is an equipment for service, it is a means of strength. First, we may note Luke 12:35, 36, "Let your loins be girded about, and your lights burning; and ye yourselves like unto men that wait for their Lord." This is an exhortation from Christ for His people to be ready for His return. Here two things are prefaced: they must be active in service and faithful in testimony. As another has said, "The hope of our Lord's return will not really abide in the heart unless we keep our loins girded, as engaged in the Master's work, and unless our light shines out before men. An inactive believer is sure to become a worldly-minded one. He will have companionship with men of the world, whose intoxicating pursuits of avarice, ambition, and pleasure deaden their hearts and consciences to all the truth of God. 'Occupy till I come' is another precept of the same kind as 'let your loins be girded.'"

Another New Testament exhortation where this figure of the "girdle" is used occurs in 1 Peter 1:13, "Wherefore gird up the loins of your mind, be sober, and hope to the end for the grace that is to be brought unto you at the revelation of Jesus Christ." Here believers are addressed as "strangers and pilgrims," passing through the wilderness on their way to the promised inheritance (vv. 1, 4). Two great motives are presented to them: the sufferings of Christ and the glory that shall follow (v. 11). Thus, in order to be constantly pressing onwards we must stay our minds upon Christ, ever contemplating Him in His two characters as the Victim and as the Victor. A man who fails to use the "girdle," allowing his garments to hang loose, is impeded in his movements and progress. Loose thoughts and wandering imaginations must be gathered in, and our hearts and understandings set upon the death, resurrection, and return of Christ, if we would pursue our journey with less distraction.

Eph. 6 informs us of the *nature* of our "girdle": "Wherefore take unto you the whole armour of God, that ye may be able to withstand in the evil day, and having done all, to stand. Stand, therefore, having your loins girt about *with truth*" (vv. 13, 14). Here the believer is contemplated in still another character. He is not only a priest to serve God, and a pilgrim journeying to another country, he is also a soldier, called on to "fight the good fight of faith" and to "wrestle" (v. 12). But no matter in what relationship he is viewed, the "girdle" is essential. It is striking to note that the "girdle" is mentioned *first* in Eph. 6:14-18, and that here the two separate thoughts suggested in connection therewith are combined. The whole strength of the warrior to stand and wrestle, depends upon the close fitting of his firm girdle. If his outer garments are loose and trailing (carelessness in his ways), or if his loins (the place of strength) be not supported and sustained by God's truth, Satan will soon overcome him, and instead of "standing"—experimentally maintaining his high calling in Christ—he will be cast down, to sink into the darkness of the world's delusions; ensnared either by its vanities and glittering honours, or its learned speculations of "vain philosophy" and "science falsely so called."

Our loins are to be "girt about with truth." The "girdle," then, speaks of the Word of God, particularly, all that centres in Christ and proceeds from Him. *This* is the priest's equipment for service, the pilgrim's source of strength, the warrior's staying power. Additional Scriptures which bring in the thought of *strength* in connection with the "girdle" are found in Rev. 1:13; 15:16. In the former, Christ is seen, "girt about the breasts with a golden girdle," the symbolic significance of this being, the binding of the ephod of blue—the robe of heavenly peace and love —about His heart, so that in the midst of searching words of reproof and warning, mercies might also proceed from "breasts of consolation." In the latter passage, golden girdles are seen about the breasts of the angels—to whom the vials of wrath are entrusted—indicating that their hearts needed strengthening for their terrible work of judgment. Thus, the "girdles" of the priests tell of that equipment and strength for service which is to be found in Christ.

3. Their Bonnets.

"And bonnets shalt thou make for them, for glory and for beauty" (v. 40). "And goodly bonnets of fine linen" (39:28). "The Hebrew word occurs only four times in the Old Testament, and is exclusively used for the head-dress of the priests. It is derived from a verb signifying 'elevation,' often used of a hill. They apparently differed from the mitre of the high priest, in the fact that they were *bound* round the heads of the priests, which is never said of the mitre. In Ex. 29:9 and Lev. 8:13 the margin of the A.V. correctly gives 'bind' for 'put.' They were probably rolls of fine linen, folded like a turban round the head. The word translated 'goodly' (Ex. 39:28) is worthy of notice. It is rendered 'tire' of the heads (Ezek. 24:17, 23); 'beauty' (Isa. 61:3); 'ornaments' (Isa. 61:10), and is derived from a verb signifying 'to beautify or glorify'" (Soltau).

There seems to be two thoughts suggested by these "bonnets," which, though at first glance seem widely dissimilar, are, nevertheless, closely related. From the etymology of the word, they speak of *elevation* or exaltation. On the other hand, from the general tenor of Scripture, the covering of the head betokens *subjection* (1 Cor. 11:4-10, etc). The orthodox Jew, to this day, always keeps his head covered in the synagogue; and even in private, when reading God's Word, he covers his head. How, then, are we to harmonize the two things, so different, suggested by this figure? Thus: the priesthood of believers speaks of the high position to which Divine grace has elevated them—they shall, in Heaven, lead the worship of angels. Yet, are they in subjection to Christ, for *He* will lead their praise (Psa. 22:22). Even now we are in subjection to the revealed

will of God; and *this* is true dignity or elevation. We serve in the liberty of Christ, but as growing "up into Him in all things which is the Head, even Christ" (Eph. 4:15), avoiding the things mentioned in Col. 2:18, which tend unto the "not holding the Head" (Col. 2:19).

"These head-tires of white are said to be 'goodly' or 'ornamental.' There was nothing of display to attract the common gaze, but like the adorning recommended for Christian women (1 Peter 3:4, 5) they were types of the meek and quiet spirit which in the sight of God is of great price. Like the holy women of old who trusted in God, and thus adorned themselves, in subjection to their own husbands" (Soltau). So these "bonnets" of the priests were for glory and beauty. True, complete subjection to God may be little admired by man, but they are lovely in the sight of Heaven.

4. Their Breeches.

"And thou shalt make them linen breeches to cover their nakedness; from the loins even unto the thighs shall they reach. And they shall be upon Aaron and upon his sons, when they come in unto the tabernacle of the congregation, or when they come near unto the altar to minister in the holy place; that they bear not iniquity, and die: it shall be a statute forever unto him and his seed after him" (vv. 42, 43). Before taking up the typical teaching of these verses attention should, perhaps, be called to one point in them which, by a comparison with Lev. 8:13, brings out the strict and high *moral* standard which God set before Israel. A careful reader of Lev. 8:13 will note an omission: Moses was ordered to "put" the coats, girdles, and bonnets upon Aaron's sons, but he was *not* told to "put" the "breeches" or trousers on them, even though they were his own nephews. Those, *they* would put on first, before they came to him to be formally invested with the other garments. They must not appear, even before one of their own sex, in the nude!

Unspeakably blessed is the *spiritual* purport of the present portion of our type, and most helpfully has it been presented by the one from whom we shall now quote. "The first result of the entrance of sin was to discover to man his nakedness (Gen. 3: 7). The feeling of shame, a guilty feeling, crept over his soul; and his attention was immediately directed to some mode of quieting his confidence in this respect, that he might appear unabashed in the presence of his fellow. No thought of his fall as it regarded *God*, or of his inability to stand in His presence, occurred to him. And so it is to this day. The great object which men propose to themselves, is to quieten their own consciences, and to stand well with their neighbours. To this end they invent a religion. But as soon as we have to do with God, the conscience is convicted, and the guilt and shame which before were quieted, spring up within, and nothing can still the restless, uneasiness of the heart. We become aware that all things are naked and opened to the eyes of Him with whom we have to do. The soul in vain attempts concealment. The still, small voice of God sounds within, and drags the culprit out to stand before Him.

"It is here that a righteousness not our own becomes unspeakably precious to the soul. A covering that both blots out all sin, and forever clothes the sinner with spotless purity, which conceals from the searching eye of God all iniquity, and in so doing completely justifies the sinner before Him: Psalm 32:1, 2" (Soltau). Thus these "linen breeches" speak of that perfect provision which God has made for His people in Christ, that which has made an end of the flesh before Him: "Knowing this, that our old man is crucified with Him, that the body of sin might be destroyed, that henceforth we should not serve sin" (Rom. 6:6).

And what is the *practical* lesson to be drawn from the "breeches"? This: all that is of the flesh must be kept out of sight in our priestly activities. As another has said, "That which is of the flesh is bad anywhere, but it is most of all out of place in the holy service of God. What could be more dreadful than for such things as vanity, jealousy, emulation, or desire to make something of oneself, to come into what should be spiritual service? All that would be, indeed, 'the flesh of nakedness': it is not to be seen" (C. A. Coates). Striking are the words of v. 42: "To cover their nakedness from the loins even to the thighs." The whole strength of nature is to be concealed; that power of indwelling evil, which ever opposes God and seeks to mar our walk, must be covered.

Oh, that Divine grace may enable the writer and each Christian reader to put on, experimentally, the linen coat, girdle, bonnet, and breeches; to draw from Christ that strength which will enable us to "deny ungodliness and worldly lusts, and live soberly, righteously and goldly, in this present world" (Titus 2:12).

CHAPTER 52

THE CONTINUAL BURNT OFFERING

EXODUS 29:36-43

Having considered something of the typical teaching connected with the vestments of the priests as described in Ex. 28, we may observe that the next thing which the Holy Spirit brings before us is the consecration of Aaron and his sons, i.e. the ritual belonging to their induction into that sacred office. This is described at length in Ex. 29, a chapter which is rich in spiritual teaching. As, however, almost all of it is found again in Lev. 8, we shall defer a detailed study thereof—if the Lord wills—until we come to that book.

The two accounts given of the consecration of the priests is like unto the twofold description which we have of the tabernacle and its furniture: first, we are told what Moses was commanded *to* make; second, we learn what he actually *did* make. So with the priesthood: in Exodus we learn that this was a blessing which God *proposed* to bestow upon His redeemed, whereas in Leviticus (the tabernacle having been set up) we see the *execution* of His purpose—the activities of the priests there being seen. Moreover, as in the actual making of the tabernacle we read, "According to *all* that the Lord commanded Moses, so the children of Israel made all the work" (Ex. 39:42); in like manner we are told that, in connection with the appointing of the priesthood, "So Aaron and his sons did *all* things which the Lord commanded by the hand of Moses" (Lev. 8:36).

In order to link up our articles on Ex. 28 with the present one, which deals with the closing verses of chapter 29, and those which follow on chapter 30, we will give a brief outline of the ceremonies which were to be observed at the consecration of the priests. It is striking to note that there were exactly seven things done for them. First, they were *taken* "from among the children of Israel" (28:1). How plainly this points to the Father choosing His elect out of Adam's race—the initial step in connection with their salvation—is too obvious to need any en-

larging upon. Second, they were *brought* unto the door of the tabernacle (29:4): the antitype of this is found in 1 Peter 3:18: "For Christ also hath once suffered for sins, the Just for the unjust, that He might bring us to God." Third, they were *washed* (29:4): this foreshadowed the believer's regeneration and sanctification by the Spirit (see John 3:5, Titus 3:5, Eph. 5:26). Fourth, they were *clothed* with their official vestments (29:4-9): this symbolised the putting on of Christ. Fifth, they were *anointed* (29:21): this pointed to the gift of the Spirit to the believer (2 Cor. 1:21; 1 John 2:27). Sixth, their *hands were filled* (29:24)—compare with this 1 John 1:1-3. Seventh, they were *sanctified* (29:44): this contemplates our setting apart unto God, see Rom. 6:13, 22.

It is indeed striking to see that in the above, Aaron and his sons took no active part at all; from first to last they were passive in the hands of another. They did not minister, but were ministered unto. Much was done for them and to them; but they themselves did nothing. Standing in God's stead, Moses did all for them. It was by his word that they were chosen and brought. It was by his hands they were washed, clothed and anointed. It was Moses also who brought the bullock for the sin-offering, as "the ram of consecration." So too the application of the blood to the several parts of their bodies was the work of Moses (v. 20). So with the wave-offering: Moses arranged its several parts (v. 22): he it was who "filled their hands"—he gave, they received (v. 24). Finally, it was Moses who received back from their hands and gave again to God what they had first been given (v. 25).

There were however four exceptions, striking and blessed ones; four things which God required Aaron and his sons to do. First, they were to "put their hands upon the head of the bullock" of the sin-offering (29:10), thus identifying themselves with the victim that was to be slain.

Typically, this is the saints confessing, "But He was wounded for our transgressions, He was bruised for our iniquities: the chastisement of our peace was upon Him; and with His stripes we are healed" (Isa. 53:5). Second, they were to "put their hands on the head of the ram" (v. 15) which was a burnt-offering unto the Lord. This speaks of the believer's assurance of his acceptance in the Beloved. Third, they also placed their hands upon the head of the ram of consecration (v. 19). This foreshadowed the saints as set apart to and for God, in and by Christ—"For by one offering He hath perfected forever them that are set apart" (Heb. 10:14). Fourth, they were to *eat* the flesh of the ram and the shewbread (vv. 32:33). This set forth Christ as the Food of His people: their substance and life. It is as we contemplate and appropriate Christ without, that He is "formed" within us: see Gal. 2:20; 4:19.

A more direct link between the lengthy account furnished in Ex. 29 of the ceremonies connected with the consecration of the priests and the closing verses which form our present portion, is what is said in vv. 35-37: "And thus shalt thou do unto Aaron and to his sons, according to all things which I have commanded thee: seven days shalt thou consecrate them. And thou shalt offer every day a bullock for a sin-offering for atonement: and thou shalt cleanse the altar, when thou shalt make an atonement for it, and thou shalt anoint it, to sanctify it. Seven days thou shalt make an atonement for the altar, and sanctify it; and it shall be an altar most holy; whatsoever toucheth the altar shall be holy."

The fact that these particular ceremonies and the cleansing of the altar were to be repeated and kept up for seven days denotes that Christ's people are completely consecrated in Him (Col. 2:10), and that their altar is a perfect one. Both the consecration of the priests and the sanctification of the altar must alike be according to all the requirements of a holy God. "Approach now must be at a cleansed, anointed, and hallowed altar. It is the first time in Scripture that we read of a cleansed and anointed altar. Previously, the altar was according to the measure of the one who approached, but now approach must be cleansed from every feature of human imperfection—cleansed in all the efficacy of the sin-offering" (C. A. Coates). In other words, all acceptable worship now must be "in spirit and in truth."

This is the force of that word of Christ's, "But the hour cometh, and now is, when the true worshippers shall worship the Father in spirit and in truth: for the Father seeketh such to worship Him. God is spirit: and they that worship Him must worship Him in spirit and in truth" (John 4:23, 24). The Saviour was referring to that great change which would be brought in consequent upon His death. Though such worship shuts out all that is of the flesh, it makes room for all that is of the Spirit and of Christ.

And of what does this cleansed, anointed and sanctified "altar" speak? Clearly of Christ Himself: His blessed person. As we are told in Heb. 13:10, "We have an altar, whereof they have no right to eat which serve the tabernacle." Christ Himself is altar, sacrifice, and priest. *He* is "the Altar that sanctifieth the gift" (Matt. 23:19). Hence believers are now told, "*By Him* therefore let us offer the sacrifice of praise to God continually, that is the fruit of our lips, giving thanks to His name" (Heb. 13:15).

From the parallel Scripture in Lev. 8 we learn that the Lord's word to Aaron and his sons, in this same connection, was, "Therefore shall ye abide at the door of the tabernacle of the congregation day and night seven days, and keep the charge of the Lord, that ye die not." Upon this Mr. Saltau wrote: "They were to be habituated to abide before the Lord; and they were to realise the value of the sin-offering, as thus enabling them so to abide there. The seven days of their week of consecration may, in type, prefigure the whole of our earthly life: our whole week of service. We are to accustom ourselves to be in the presence of our God. Our life is to be spent there; only we have the privilege of abiding, not at the door, but in the very holiest of all. May we rejoice to use this wondrous liberty of access, and not only 'draw near,' but 'abide under the shadow of the Almighty.' And what will be our help and power for this? The sin-offering of atonement, constantly realised by the help of the Holy Spirit."

"Now this is that which thou shalt offer upon the altar; two lambs of the first year day by day continually. The one lamb thou shalt offer in the morning; and the other lamb thou shalt offer at even" (vv. 38, 39). In v. 42 we learn that this offering was called "a *continual* burnt-offering." That which was placed upon the altar was in perfect accord with its now anointed and hallowed character. The "burnt" offering is the highest type of sacrifice in Scripture. The first reference to it in the Word helps us ascertain its distinctive significance. In Gen. 22:2 we read that the Lord said unto Abraham, "Take now thy son, thine only Isaac, whom thou lovest, and get thee into the land of Moriah; and offer him there for a burnt-offering upon one of the mountains which I will tell thee of." That which is to be particularly noted there is the willingness and readiness of Isaac's conforming to his father's will. Thus, the central thought in this offering is *devotedness*. The Hebrew word for burnt-offering literally means, that which "goes up." It might well be designated "the ascending offering." The whole of it, consumed upon the altar, ascended to heaven as a sweet savor.

Lev. 1 furnishes full details concerning the burnt-offering. There we read, in v. 3, that the offerer should "offer it of his own voluntary will." This offering was really the basis of all the other sacrifices, as may be seen not only from the fact that it is given precedence in Lev. 1 to 5, but also because the altar itself took its name from this—"the altar of the burnt offering" (Ex. 40:10). It foreshadowed, therefore, the perfect devotedness of the Son to the Father, which was the basis or spring of the whole of His earthly life, ministry, and sacrificial death. He "glorified not Himself." When He spoke or acted it was ever the Father's honour He sought. He could say, "I came not to do Mine own will, but the will of Him that sent Me." He could say, "I have set the Lord always before Me" (Psalm 16:8). Eph. 5:2 speaks in the language of this particular type: "Christ also hath loved us, and hath given Himself for us, an offering and a sacrifice to God for a sweet-smelling savor."

"Now this is that which thou shalt offer upon the altar; two lambs of the first year, day by day continually. The one lamb thou shalt offer in the morning, and the other lamb thou shalt offer at even." Speaking after the manner of men, it was as though God would keep before Him a constant reminder of the devotedness of His blessed Son. Therefore a "lamb," rather than a bullock or ram (which prefigured Christ more in His strength and sufficiency) was appointed—suitably expressing His gentleness, and yieldedness to the will of God. And, too, that which was ever to be kept before His people also was, that which would set forth the *Godward* aspect of Christ's work. Though the Lord Jesus came here to atone for the sins of His people, it was only because it was the Father's will for Him so to do: cf. Heb. 10:7 with 10:10.

"Inasmuch as the offering before us was perpetual, God laid a foundation thereby on which Israel could stand and be accepted in all its fragrance and savour. It thus becomes no mean type of the position of the believer, revealing the ground of his acceptance in the Beloved; for just as the sweet savour of the continual burnt-offering ever ascended to God on behalf of Israel, so Christ in all His acceptability is ever before His eyes on behalf of His own. We can therefore say, 'As He is, so are we in this world' (1 John 4:17), for we are in the Divine presence in all the savour of His sacrifice, and in all the acceptance of His Person" (Ed. Dennett).

Nor should we lose sight of the *practical* teaching for our own souls in this morning and evening continual burnt-offering. Suitably has this been expressed by another: "God would encourage us to renew in our affections continually the terms on which He is with us. He would have every day to begin and end with a fresh sense of being with God and having God with us, in the sweet odor and acceptance of Christ. He never places His saints on any other ground before Him than that of Christ—the One who has perfectly glorified Him, and done all His will, and in whom He has infinite delight. He never departs from that; He never meets His saints on other or lower ground than that. And He would have the consciousness of it continually renewed on our side."

"And with the one lamb a tenth deal of flour mingled with the fourth part of an hin of beaten oil; and the fourth part of an hin of wine for a drink offering. And the other lamb thou shalt offer at even, and shalt do thereto according to the meat offering of the morning, and according to the drink offering thereof, for a sweet savour, an offering made by fire unto the Lord" (vv. 40:41). This was the accompaniment of the burnt-offering. The meal-offering is often spoken of as an appendix to it, thus, as "the burnt-offering and *its* meal-offering" (Lev. 23:13, 18; Num. 28: 28, 31; 29:3, 6, 9, etc.).

The "meat," or better "meal-offering" is described at length in Lev. 2. It foreshadowed the holy and perfect humanity through which the Son manifested His devotedness to the Father. Mingled with the meal was the fourth part of an hin of beaten oil. This shadowed forth the mystery of the supernatural birth of Christ, under the operation of the Holy Spirit: as said the angel to Mary, "The Holy Spirit shall come upon thee, and the power of the Highest shall overshadow thee: *therefore* also that holy thing which shall be born of thee shall be called the Son of God" (Luke 1:35). So, too, the whole of Christ's earthly life and ministry was permeated by the Holy Spirit. It was by the Spirit He was led into the wilderness to be tempted of the Devil (Matt. 4:1), and from the temptation He "returned in the power of the Spirit into Galilee" (Luke 4:14). It was by the Spirit He cast out demons (Matt. 12:28). It was through the Spirit that He offered Himself without spot to God (Heb. 9:14). And, even after His resurrection, it was "through the Spirit" He gave commandments unto the apostles (Acts 1:2).

Accompanying the burnt-offering there was also a drink-offering, which consisted of "the fourth part of an hin of wine." One of the significations of "wine," when it is employed emblematically, is *joy*—see Judges 9:13; Psalm 104:15. Thus, in our present type, the accompanying drink-offering speaks of the Father's joy in Christ—"This is My Beloved Son, in whom I am well pleased." But more: it was offered here by the Lord's people. Therefore it would also express *their* communion with the joy of God in the perfections and devotion of His Son. God would have us feast on that which delights Him. Beautifully is this brought out in the parable of the prodigal son. When the wanderer had returned in penitence, the Father said, "Bring hither the fatted calf, and kill; and let *us* eat, and *be merry*" (Luke 15:23)—figure of the Father and His child rejoicing together in Christ.

Striking are the words, in this connection, of v. 42: "This shall be a continual burnt-offering throughout your generations." Occupation with the devoted Son and His perfect humanity was to be continual, and every morning and evening the types of these were to be presented by Israel to God, accompanied by the fourth part of an hin of wine. Note again the words of v. 41: "And the other lamb thou shalt offer at even, and shalt do thereto according to the meat-offering of the morning, and according to the drink-offering thereof, for a sweet savour, an offering made by fire unto the Lord." Was not this continuous morning-offering the Lord saying to His people of old, "Rejoice in the Lord alway," and was not the repetition in the evening God's Old Testament *"again* I say, Rejoice" (Phil. 4:4)! Gloominess in the Christian is not glorifying unto God. A long-faced believer is no commendation of Christ to those who know Him not. God does not desire His people to be miserable. Did He not move one of His apostles to say, "These things write we unto you, that your joy may be full" (1 John 1:4)? If the Christian *is* sad and miserable, the fault is entirely his own. The explanation thereof is furnished in the immediate context of the Scripture last quoted: "Our fellowship is with the Father, and with His Son, Jesus

Christ" (1 John 1:3). As this fellowship is experimentally maintained, our joy *will be* "full." Lack of joy, then, is due to lack of fellowship with God.

And how is this to be remedied? Our present type tells us: begin and end each day with a fresh occupation of the heart with Christ, a concentrated meditation upon His excellencies—His devotedness to the Father, His dying love for us. But accompanying this there must be the "oil": it is only by the help and power of the Holy Spirit that we can truly "consider" Christ (Heb. 3:1 cf. John 16:14). And to the extent that we yield to and are filled with the Spirit, and to that extent only, shall we also be filled with joy—note how the "fourth part of an hin of wine" corresponds exactly to the "fourth part of an hin of oil" (v. 40)! To show that this is no mere coincidence, or unimportant detail, let the reader turn to Num. 15:6, 7 where he will find that though the quantities of the oil and wine are different, yet their proportions are the same! O that "the joy of the Lord" may be our strength (Neh. 8:10).

"This shall be a continual burnt-offering throughout your generations at the door of the tabernacle of the congregation before the Lord: where I will meet you, to speak there unto thee. And there I will meet with the children of Israel and they shall be sanctified by My glory" (vv. 42, 43). That which is so unspeakably blessed here is the Lord's repeated promise that He would *meet* with His people. The Hebrew word signifies "to meet as by appointment," and this, in the required manner and place.

"Moses was permitted in grace to meet Jehovah at the mercy-seat (Ex. 25:22); but the people could not pass beyond the door of the tabernacle of the congregation. It was here that the burnt-offering was presented on the brazen altar; and hence this was the meeting-place, on the ground of the sacrifice, between God and Israel. There could be no other possible place; just as now Christ forms the only meeting-place between God and the sinner. It is most important to see this truth—especially for those who are unsaved—that apart from Christ there can be no drawing nigh to God. 'I am the Way, the Truth, and the Life: no man cometh unto the Father, but by Me' (John 14:6). Mark well, moreover, that God cannot be approached except on the ground of the sacrifice of Christ. This is the truth foreshadowed in connection with the burnt-offering. If the cross, Christ crucified, be ignored, no relationships can be had with God, excepting those which may exist between a guilty sinner and a holy Judge. But the moment the sinner is led to take his stand upon 'the sweet savour' of the sacrifice of God, upon the efficacy of what Christ accomplished by His death, God can meet with him, in grace and love" (Ed. Dennett).

There is also a spiritual application of the blessed promise of vv. 42, 43 to the saints of God to-day, considered both singly and collectively. There is such a thing as God "meeting" with us in the *manifestation* of Himself to our hearts—alas, that so many experience this so infrequently. Where there is true soul-occupation with the person and work of Christ, in the power of the Spirit, there is also a making known of Himself (Luke 24:31). So, when the saints assemble for Divine worship, occupied not with their *own* needs, but with Christ's excellency—coming not to obtain a blessing, but to offer to God a sacrifice of praise; there is then such a gracious revelation of Himself that we are made to exclaim: "This is none other than the house of God, and this is the gate of heaven" (Gen. 28:17). O to know more of this blessed experience.

"And I will dwell among the children of Israel, and will be their God. And they shall know that I am the Lord their God, that brought them forth out of the land of Egypt, that I may dwell among them: I am the Lord their God" (vv. 45, 46). As in the previous verses God repeated His promise to "meet" with His worshipping people, so here He says, twice over, "I will dwell among them."

It was for this that Jehovah had delivered His people from Egypt: He could not "dwell" with them *there*. Nor could He dwell with Israel at all until they had been redeemed. This was something entirely new. God never "dwelt" with Adam, nor with Abraham. In the Song of Redemption (see Ex. 15:1, 13), Israel exclaimed, "Thou shalt bring them in, and plant them in the mountain of Thine inheritance, in the place, O Lord, Thou hast made for Thee to *dwell* in, the sanctuary" (15:17). To Moses God said, "Let them make Me a sanctuary; that I may dwell among them" (Ex. 25:8). Now, that promise was to be realised on the ground of the efficacy of the burnt-offering. Most blessed is it to mark God's purpose in thus dwelling in Israel's midst—"They shall know that I am the Lord their God."

Equally precious is the promise which He has given us: "Lo, I am with you alway, unto the end of the age" (Matt. 28:20); and again, "I will never leave thee, nor forsake thee" (Heb. 13:5).

There is no doubt but that, prophetically, our present type looks forward to the second coming of Christ to this earth. Then will it be that "all Israel shall be saved: as it is written, There shall come out of Sion the Deliverer and shall turn away ungodliness from Jacob (Rom. 11:26). And again, "Thus speaketh the Lord of hosts, saying, Behold the man whose name is The Branch; and He shall grow up out of His place, and He shall build the temple of the Lord; even He shall build the temple of the Lord; and He shall bear the glory, and shall sit and rule upon His throne; and He shall be a priest upon His throne: and the counsel of peace shall be between them both" (Zech. 6:12, 13). Then will God say, "Sing and rejoice, O daughter of Zion; for, lo I come, and I will *dwell* in the midst of thee, saith the Lord" (Zech. 2:10). The ultimate fulfilment of our type will be seen on the new earth: "And I heard a great voice out of heaven saying, Behold, the tabernacle of God is with men, and He will *dwell* with them" (Rev. 21:3).

"But there is more than even dwelling with them: there is also relationship—'I will be their God.' It is not, be it remarked, what they shall be to Him, though they were His people by His grace; but what He will be to them. 'Their God'—words fraught with unspeakable blessings, for when God undertakes to become the God of His people, deigns to enter into relationship with them, He assures them that everything they need, whether for guidance, sustenance, defence, succour, yea, everything, is secure for them by what He is to them as their God. It was in view of the blessing of such a wondrous relationship that the Psalmist exclaims, 'Happy is that people whose God is the Lord'—Psalm 144:15" (Ed. Dennett). So, too, on the new earth is it said: "And they shall be His people, and God Himself shall be with them, and be their God" (Rev. 21:3). May the Lord use to His glory these musings upon this blessed type.

CHAPTER 53

THE GOLDEN ALTAR

EXODUS 30:1-10

There were two altars connected with the Tabernacle. Both were made of wood, but covered with a different metal: the one with brass, and so named after it "the brazen altar'" (Ex. 38:30); the other with gold, and so called "the golden altar" (Ex. 39:38). The one was placed outside the building in the court, just before the entrance; the other was inside the holy place, and stood before the vail. These altars were closely connected, but served different uses. Their characteristic names point out their distinctive designs: the former being designated "the altar of burnt offering" (40:6), and was the place of sacrifice; the latter was termed "the altar of incense" (30:27), and was the place of worship. Both altars were needed to set forth our one and only Altar, of whom it is written, "we have an Altar, whereof they have no right to eat which serve the tabernacle" (Heb. 13:10).

Some have wondered why the incense altar was not mentioned in Ex. 25 and 26, where five of the other pieces of the Tabernacle's furniture are referred to, and where the holy place in which it stood is described. Three reasons may be suggested for this. First, the omission of the golden altar from those earlier chapters may have been because of what was typically set forth by the various holy vessels. Those enumerated in Ex. 25 and 26 speak of God in Christ coming out to His people, displaying the riches of His grace; whereas the two which are before us in Ex. 30 tell of the provisions God has made for us to go in to Him, expressing the fullness of His love. Beautifully has this been expounded by another:

"Why, then, does the Lord, when giving directions about the furniture of the 'holy place' omit the altar of incense, and pass out to the brazen altar which stood at the door of the Tabernacle? The reason I believe is simply this: He first described the mode in which He would manifest Himself to man, and then He described

the mode of man's approach to Him. He took His seat upon the throne as 'The Lord of all the earth' (Josh. 3:13). The beams of His glory were hidden behind the vail—type of Christ's flesh (Heb. 10:20); but there was the manifestation of Himself in connection with man, as in the pure table' and by the light and power of the Holy Ghost, as in the candlestick. Then we have the manifested character of Christ as a man down here on this earth, as seen in the curtains and coverings of the tabernacle. And, finally, we have the brazen altar as the grand exhibition of the meeting place between a holy God and a sinner. This conducts us as it were, to the extreme point, from which we return, in company with Aaron and his sons, back to the holy place, the ordinary priestly position, where stood the golden altar of incense. Thus the order is strikingly beautiful" (C.H.M.).

A second reason may be suggested as to why the description of the golden altar and the laver should have been postponed until the 30th chapter of Exodus was reached. This is plainly intimated in Ex. 28 and 29, where we have the appointment, investiture and consecration of the priesthood. Thus, the golden altar was not mentioned until there was a priest to burn incense thereon! It was at the laver the priests washed, and it was at the golden altar they ministered; there, too, it was where Aaron presented himself before Jehovah. Thus the contents of chapters 28 and 29 were needed to bring before us the priestly family before we learn of the two holy vessels with which they were more directly associated. So, too, experimentally, we apprehend that of which the preceding chapters speak, before we value that which chapter 30 sets forth.

A third reason lies in the application of the teaching of the holy vessels to believers. The primary application of each of them is to Christ Himself, but there is a second-

283

ary application to His people. As we shall yet seek to show, one of the fundamental things prefigured by the golden altar is *worship*, and as this is the highest exercise of our priestly privileges, suitably was this the last piece of furniture met with as the sons of Aaron approached unto Jehovah.

"Just as the golden altar was the last object to be reached in the journey from the gate to the vail which hid the mercy-seat from view, just so is *worship* the highest state to be reached on earth and the object for which all other things are preparations. The Father seeks worshippers (John 4:23), and this it was that led the Lord to go through Samaria to meet that sinner, to turn her heart from her sins, by filling it with the satisfying portion of grace, that she might meet the desires of Divine love and give that praise, that worship, that only a sinner (a cleansed sinner) can give. And this it was that led the Lord to take that larger journey from the heaven of light and peace down to the cross of suffering and shame. He sought sinners, He seeketh them still; seeketh them that, having tasted as no angel can possibly taste, the love of God, they might then from a heart overflowing with the consciousness of its indebtedness to the Saviour, and the appreciation of His own excellence, pour forth the fragrant incense of praise" (C. H. Bright).

1. Its Significance.

"And thou shalt make an altar to burn incense upon" (v. 1). It is striking to note that before anything is said about the materials of which the altar was made, its size and shape, or the position it was to occupy, we are first told of the purpose for which it was to be used. It is this which places in our hands a sure key to its spiritual interpretation. Attention is directed straight to the altar and the incense which was burned thereon. The altar speaks of Christ Himself, and the incense was a figure both of His intercession and the praises which He presents to God.

The fact that the golden altar comes before us in Exodus immediately after the investiture and consecration of Aaron and his sons, at once tells us that what is here portrayed is the ministrations of our great High Priest in the heavenly sanctuary. Though He is now seated at the right hand of the Majesty on high, yet He is not inactive. He is constantly engaged before God on behalf of His redeemed, presenting to the Father—in the sweet fragrance of His own perfections—both the pe-

titions and worship of His people. The *position* occupied by the golden altar confirms this. It was not situated in the outer court —all connected with which adumbrated the manifestation of Christ here on earth; but in the holy place, which tells of Christ having gone in to appear before God on behalf of His people. Further confirmation that this is the central thought in our present type is supplied in the words at the close of v. 3: "And thou shalt make unto it a crown of gold round about." Thus, it is Christ in heaven, not on earth, "crowned with glory and honour" (Heb. 2:9).

Unutterably solemn is it to contemplate Christ at the brazen altar there made sin for us, suffering, enduring judgment, bowing His head beneath the awful storm of God's wrath. But unspeakably blessed is it to behold Him at the golden altar, risen from the grave, alive for evermore, maintaining the interests of His people before God's throne, presenting them in all His own excellency and preciousness. "If when we were enemies we were reconciled to God by the death of His Son, much more, being reconciled, we shall be saved by His life" (Rom. 5:10). This is the point which the Spirit of God reserves for the climax in His unanswerable reply to the challenge "Who shall lay anything to the charge of God's elect?" it is God that justifieth. Who is he that condemneth? it is Christ that died, yea rather, that is risen again, who is even at the right hand of God, who also maketh intercession for us" (Rom. 8:33, 34).

"Let my prayer be set forth before Thee as incense; and the lifting up of mine hands as the evening sacrifice" (Psa. 141:2). This gives us the emblematical meaning of "incense." So again in Rev. 5:8 we read, "having every one of them harps, and golden vails full of incense, which are the prayers of saints." The incense burned upon the golden altar, then, foreshadowed Christ in heaven, praying for His people. As we read in Heb. 7:25, "Wherefore He is able also to save them to the uttermost that come unto God by Him, seeing He ever liveth to make intercession for them." Christ's intercession is not for the purpose of completing the believer's justification, for that would show His sacrifice of the cross was insufficient; by that one offering He has perfected us forever (Heb. 10:14); rather does it crown it with glory and honour. The precious incense of our Lord's priestly intercession *maintains* us (through our wilderness journey) in the place of fullest acceptance as a sweet savor unto God.

A striking typical illustration of the wondrous efficacy of our great High Priest's intercession is furnished in Num. 16. There we see, first, how Korah and his company repudiated Aaron as their high priest, claiming equal nearness to God for all Israel, see v. 3. But a sinful people could have no standing before the Holy One save through the priest who offered the sacrifice. This, the rebellious people were made to feel (v. 35). The "gainsaying of Korah" (Jude 11), then, was the practical denial of Christ's person and sacrificial work. Then, in Num. 16, we also behold how the *grace* of God shone forth: Aaron the high priest was told to "take a censer, and put fire therein from off the altar, and put on incense, and go quickly unto the congregation, and make an atonement for them" (v. 46). Blessed was the sequel: "And he stood between the dead and the living; and the plague was stayed" (v. 48). What a foreshadowing of the mediatorial intercession of Christ, interposing on behalf of His erring people, and that, on the ground of His sacrificial death.

It is a mistake, made by most of the commentators, to limit the "incense" as pointing only to the Saviour's intercession; it includes also His offering of praise to God. Did He not say, "In the midst of the church will I sing praise unto Thee" (Heb. 2:12)? So also in Heb. 13:15 we are told, "*By Him*, therefore, let us offer the sacrifice of praise to God continually." He is the One who receives the praises of His people and presents them to God. So again in 1 Peter 2:5 we are told, "Ye also, as living stones, are built up a spiritual house, an holy priesthood, to offer us spiritual sacrifices, acceptable to God by Jesus Christ." Christ is the one who makes our worship acceptable to God. Therefore, the incense has to be burned upon the altar.

2. Its Composition.

"And thou shalt make an altar to burn incense upon it: of shittim wood shalt thou make it" (v. 1). This, as we have seen in earlier types, symbolised the perfect humanity of Christ. "This accacia wood, the emblem of the incorruptible and spotless humanity of the Son of God entered into the composition of the altar of burnt-offering outside in the court, and was covered with brass, enabling it to endure the fire that consumed its victim. The same accacia wood entered into the composition of the table of shewbread; it also entered into the composition of the altar of incense, which was covered and crowned with gold, for no atonement for

sin was ever offered or needed at that altar; all *that* was finished. It also entered into the composition of the ark of the covenant within the vail, identifying all these with the person and salvation-work of our Lord Jesus Christ, teaching us that His perfect humanity—made in all things like His brethren, sin excepted—in all the modifications of His covenant engagements and offices of our behalf, whether at His incarnation, His birth, His walk with God on earth, His death on the cross, or after His resurrection, when He was seen of His disciples for forty days, or after His ascension to the right hand of God, where He ever liveth to make intercession for us—was ever one and the same immortalised humanity in the person of our living and glorified Head, Substitute, and Representative" (Mr Rainsford).

"And thou shalt overlay it with pure gold, the top thereof, and the sides thereof round about, and the horns thereof" (v. 3). This is very lovely, speaking, as it does, of that Divine glory into which the Man Christ Jesus has entered. As the sons of Aaron approached this altar —figures of worshipping believers now drawing near to God—they would see nothing but the gold. So it is not a dead Christ on the cross who is the object of our worship, but a living Christ who has been "received up into glory" (1 Tim. 3:16). Therefore are we bidden "if ye then be risen with Christ, seek those things which are above, where Christ sitteth on the right hand of God: Set your affection on things above, not on things on the earth; for ye are dead, and your life is hid with Christ in God" (Col. 3:1-3). As another has said, "God saw only the gold—that which was suited to Him, suited to His own nature. The remembrance of this gives boldness when bowing in His presence. It is indeed a wondrous mercy that Christ is before the eye of God, and before the eye of the worshipper, Himself the meeting-place between God and His people, as well as the foundation of His people's acceptance" (Ed Dennet).

3. Its Dimensions.

"A cubit shall be the length thereof, and a cubit the breadth thereof; foursquare shall it be; and two cubits shall be the height thereof: the horns thereof shall be of the same" (v. 2). The dimensions of the golden altar differed considerably from those of the brazen altar, the latter being five cubits long, five cubits broad, and three cubits high (27:1). Herein we may see the wonderful accuracy of these types and their perfections down to the minutest detail. The brazen altar was much larger than the golden altar. The former foreshadowed the sacrificial death of Christ; the latter, His present ministry in heaven. But does He not now appear before God on behalf of *all* for whom He died? In one sense, yes; in another sense no. Representatively He does, actively He does not. John 11:51, 52 shows that He died for two distinct companies—"that nation (Israel) and the children of God scattered abroad—God's elect among the Gentiles. But at present Christ *is not* interceding for Israel, nor is He presenting their praises before God! It is only on behalf of the Church that He is now actively engaged: Israel will be taken up in the Day to come, and this will be at His return to the earth, as the brazen altar in the outer court denotes. Thus, there is a wonderful propriety in the golden altar, within the holy place, being smaller than the brazen altar.

May not the fact that it was but one cubit in *length* indicate to us that Christ needs not to repeat His plea on our behalf —once is sufficient, for the Father hears Him always (John 11:42). Though He ever liveth, it is not said, "He ever intercedeth." The tense of the verb (in the Greek) implies that Christ prayed but once for Peter in Luke 22:32. The *breadth* being one cubit would point to the "one body" as the *extent* of those for whom He now intercedes—"I pray not for the world" (John 17:9)! The *two* cubits of its height would perhaps denote that Christ presents to God both the praises of His saints which are now in heaven as those yet on earth. Its being "foursquare" tells us that the objects of His intercession are scattered abroad, reaching to the four corners of the earth. Though we may forget to remember His blood-brought ones in far distant places, He does not!

"Foursquare shall it be" (v. 2). In its application to Christ Himself this tells us that His intercession embraces *all* His people, "scattered abroad." In its application to us we find the New Testament equivalent in 1 Tim. 2:1, "I exhort, therefore, that, first of all, supplication, prayers, intercessions, giving of thanks, be made for all men." In Eph. 6:18 we are bidden to make supplication "for *all* saints." How little of this there is to-day! How self-centered we are, how narrow are our hearts! How little *our* "altar" answers to the foursquareness of the incense altar! May the Lord enlarge our hearts.

4. Its Ornamentation.

"And thou shalt overlay it with pure gold, the top thereof, and the sides there-of round about, and the horns thereof" (v. 3). The "horn" is the symbol of power (Hab. 3:4), so that what we are shown here is Christ's intercessory power with God. A more literal rendering of the Hebrew would be, "Of itself shall be its horns:" all that Christ is in His wondrous person gives Him power with God; blessedly is this seen in John 17.

It will be noted that the number of its "horns" is not given. Many conclude that it had one at each corner, as had the brazen altar (38:2). As there is nothing in Scripture without spiritual significance, even its very omissions manifesting its Divine Authorship, we must enquire, Why has not the Holy Spirit told us there were *four* "horns" here? The answer is not far to seek. Four is the number of the earth, and the golden altar foreshadowed Christ's priestly ministry in Heaven; thus we may see that the *mention* of the "four horns" would have cast a blemish on the perfection of our type.

"And thou shalt make unto it a crown of gold round about" (v. 3). Three of the seven pieces of the tabernacle's furniture had a "crown" upon it. First, the ark of the covenant (25:11), in which were preserved the two tables of stone. This was the crown of the law, which Christ "magnified" and "made honourable" (Isa. 42:21). Second, the table of shewbread (25:24). This was the crown of fellowship: the Christian's highest honour and supremest privilege is to enjoy communion with Him who has been crowned with glory. Or, if we look at it from the dispensational viewpoint, the table with its twelve loaves would speak of Israel in a coming day, restored and in fellowship with Christ—this would be the crown of the kingdom. Here, in connection with the golden altar, it is the crown of the priesthood, and reminds us that Christ, our great High Priest, is seated upon "the *Throne* of Grace!"

5. Its Rings and Staves.

"And two golden rings shalt thou make to it under the crown of it, by the two corners thereof, upon the two sides of it shalt thou make it; and they shall be for places for the staves to bear it withal. And thou shalt make the staves of shittim wood, and overlay them with gold (vv. 4, 5). Thus provision was made for the altar to be carried with them as Israel journeyed from place to place—it was not stationary, so that they had to make pilgrimages to it. Typically, this tells us that God's pilgrims to-day, while they are here below, are enjoying the blessings of

Christ's priestly intercession on high. *Two* "rings" are the number of *witness,* and speak of the Holy Spirit who is here to "testify" of Christ (John 15:26); their being of "gold" announces that He is a Divine person. The "staves" of wood, overlaid with gold, intimate that it is the God-man whom the Spirit is here to glorify.

In its practical application to us, the lesson taught by the rings and staves is both searching and blessed. It is only as we maintain our pilgrim character, in separation from that religious world which rejects Christ, that we can really appropriate and enjoy that which the goldenaltar prefigured. There is a striking passage in Heb. 13 which speaks in the language of our present type: "Let us go forth therefore unto Him without the camp (man's organised Christianity), bearing His reproach. For here have we (in affections and aim) no continuing city, but (as pilgrims journeying) we seek one to come. By Him (the antitype of the altar) therefore let us offer the sacrifice of praise (the burning of incense) to God continually, that is, fruit of our lips giving thanks to His name" (vv. 13, 15).

6. Its Use.

"And Aaron shall burn thereon sweet incense" (v. 7). The altar was used for one thing only. We gather from Lev. 16: 12, 13 and Num. 16: 46 that the fire on which the incense was laid had been taken from off the brazen-altar, where the sin-offering was consumed. There was, therefore, a very intimate connection between the two altars: the activities of the latter being based upon those of the former; in other words, the incense was kindled upon that fire which had first fed upon the sacrifice; thus identifying the priest's service at both altars. This, in figure, tells us that our great High Priest pleads for no blessings which His blood has not purchased, and asks pardon from Divine justice for no sins for which He has not atoned. The measure of the blessings for which He pleads is God's estimate of the life which He gave. Note how in John 17, before He presents a single petition concerning His people, that Christ said, "I have glorified Thee on the earth; I have finished the work which Thou gavest Me to do" (v. 4). *That* was the foundation on which all His pleas were based and urged.

There are other scriptures where the two altars are linked together. As another has said, "Fittingly therefore does the Psalmist in speaking of the house for the lonely sparrow and a nest for the rest-less swallow, refer to these two altars. 'Yea, the sparrow hath found a house, and the swallow a nest for herself, where she may lay her young, even Thine *altars* O Lord of Hosts, my King and my God' (Psa. 84: 3). Both altars are thus connected together and form the solid and abiding rest for the poor and needy soul.

"Thus too. when Isaiah saw the glory of the Lord in the temple, and the adoring seraphim with veiled faces celebrating the majesty of the thrice holy triune God, he was overwhelmed with the sense of his own and Israel's uncleanness, until one of those burning ones (suggesting, perhaps, the fire of God as seen in His executors of judgment) flew with a live coal which he had taken from. off the altar, and touched his lips, saying, 'Lo, this hath touched thy lips; and thine iniquity is taken away, and thy sin purged' (Isa. 6: 7). The coal of Divine holiness had already consumed the sacrifice and was also consuming the sweet incense. Thus symbolically the prophet's lips were cleansed according to God's estimate of the value of the sacrifice and person of our Lord" (Mr. Ridout).

A most solemn contrast from this is presented in the opening verses of Lev. 10. There we are told, "And Nadab and Abihu, the sons of Aaron, took either of them his censer, and put fire therein, and put incense thereon, and offered strange fire before the Lord, which He commanded them not. And there went out fire from the Lord, and devoured them, and they died before the Lord" (vv. 1, 2), These sons of Aaron were consumed by Divine judgment because they "offered *strange* fire before the Lord," that is, the incense in their censers was not burned on fire taken from off the brazen altar, but was of their own kindling. They had departed from the plain word of Jehovah, who had already instructed them as to the mode of their worship. God was very jealous of His types (compare 2 Kings 5: 26, 27). By their actions Nadab and Abihu were signifying that worship may be offered to God on another foundation than acceptance through a crucified Christ; and for this He slew them.

The incense was to be kept sacredly for tabernacle service and he who manufactured any for his personal or family use had to pay the death-penalty for his presumption (30: 28). None but the priests of the seed of Aaron were allowed to handle it. When king Uzziah attempted to usurp the priest's office and daringly challenged the holy God by presuming to burn incense before Him, his impiety was severely punished—see 2 Chron. 26: 16-21. Even royalty must bow in abasement before Jehovah!

The composition and preparation of the sacred incense are specified in Ex. 30: 34, 35. Upon the nature, costliness, and distinctive typical import of the respective spices we cannot here comment. That which we would specially notice is the three things which are said about the incense as a whole. First, it was, "sweet" (v. 7). Exceedingly fragrant must have been its odour, telling of the acceptability and preciousness of Christ's intercessions and praises before God. Second, it was "pure" (v. 35): unlike ours, nothing whatever of the flesh enters into the priestly ministrations of the Redeemer. Third, it was "most holy" (v. 36): Christ's exercises within the heavenly sanctuary are in all the excellences of His peerless person. "Of each shall there be a like weight" (v. 34) should also be observed: no one grace or attribute predominates in the Lord Jesus, there is a perfect balance between all.

It is striking to see how the lighting of the lamps is here linked with the golden altar: "And Aaron shall burn thereon sweet incense every morning: *when* he dresseth the lamps, he shall burn incense upon it. And *when* Aaron lighteth the lamps at even, he shall burn incense upon it" (vv. 7, 8). The maintenance of the light was inseparably associated with the service of the altar. Typically, this tells us that the gift and ministry of the Holy Spirit (as the Spirit of Christ, Rom. 8: 9) is the consequence of the Saviour's intercession—cf. John 14: 16. In its practical application to believers we may see here a setting forth of the fact that, every fresh kindling or exercise of the Spirit in our hearts, results in new outbursts of praise unto God: our worship is ever in proportion to the manifestation of the Spirit's power.

"He shall burn incense upon it, a *perpetual* incense before the Lord throughout your generations" (v. 8). This is very blessed. The fire upon the altar was always burning and the fragrance from the sweet incense was continually rising. So Christ is ever before God, in all the merits of His person and value of His work, on His people's behalf. One third of our lives is spent in sleep; but He never slumbers: "He *ever* liveth to make intercession for us," and because of this He is "able to save unto the uttermost (to the end of their wilderness journey) them that come unto God by Him" (Heb. 7: 25). Thus the golden-altar is a pledge of our eternal security.

"Ye shall offer no strange incense thereon, nor burnt-sacrifice, nor meat-offering; neither shall ye pour drink-offering thereon" (v. 9). For the Levites to offer these upon *this* altar would be to confound it with the brazen-altar. The same sad mistake is made now when Christians gathered together for worship take their place at the cross, instead of within the rent vail. Instead of being occupied with our sins and Christ's sacrifice for them, we should be contemplating the Lord Jesus Himself as He appears in the presence of God for us; nothing short of this will enable us to occupy our true priestly position and exercise our joyous priestly functions.

"And Aaron shall make an atonement upon the horns of it once in a year with the blood of the sin-offering of atonement: once in the year shall he make atonement upon it" (v. 10). This is most blessed. The congregation of Israel could approach unto God only at the brazen-altar; but Aaron and his sons (figure of Christ and His heavenly people) came to the golden-altar, in the holy place. How this tells us that a position has been secured for us within the heavenly sanctuary in all the value of the sin-offering! This interpretation is confirmed by the fact that there is no mention of the golden-altar in Ezekiel's temple, which typifies Israel's millennial relations to God! But we also need to ponder this tenth verse from the practical viewpoint. Looked at thus its teaching is. parallel with that word in Ex. 28: 38, "That Aaron may bear the iniquity of the holy things," cf. Lev. 5: 15. Our prayers are so faulty, our praises so feeble, our worship so far below the level of what it ought to be, that even our "holy things" needed to be cleansed by the blood of atonement. How humbling this is!

7. Its Coverings.

"And upon the golden altar they shall spread a cloth of blue, and cover it with a covering of badgers' skins, and shall put to the staves thereof" (Num. 4: 11). How this confirms what has been said above. The golden-altar being wrapped in a "blue" cloth speaks plainly of the present *heavenly* ministry of Christ. But this was not made known to the earthly people, as the *outer* covering of the badgers' skins indicates. May the Lord add His blessing to this meditation.

CHAPTER 54

THE ATONEMENT MONEY

EXODUS 30:11-15

The above versus present to us that which it is by no means easy to understand at first glance, and up to the point where God grants light upon them the more they are studied the more will the force of their difficulties be felt. That which is central in our present portion is Jehovah commanding His people to give "every man a ransom." This ransom was a *monetary* one, a half shekel of silver, and it was in order "to make an atonement for their souls." But this seems so utterly foreign to the general tone and tenor of Scripture that many have been sorely puzzled by it. How is our present passage to be harmonised with the words of Isa. 55:1, "without money and without price?" How may we interpret it so as not to clash with 1 Peter 1:18 "Forasmuch as ye know that ye were not redeemed with corruptible things as silver and gold?"

Nor is the presenting of money by the Israelites as a "ransom" and for "an atonement" the only difficulty here. The *position* occupied by our present passage seems a strange one. Israel were already a "redeemed" people. Had they not sung at the Red Sea, "Thou in Thy mercy hast led forth the people which Thou hast redeemed" (15:13)! Why, then, was a "ransom" price necessary now? Then, too, why introduce this strange ordinance between descriptions of the golden-altar and the laver; what possible connection was there between the three things? Surely our passage calls for prayer as well as study! May the God of all grace open now our eyes that we may be enabled to behold wondrous things out of His law.

In taking up our passage the first thing we must do is to ponder it in the light of its wider context; that is to say, consider carefully the particular book in which it is found. This is ever essential if we are rightly to ascertain the scope of any passage. Each book of Scripture has a prominent and dominant theme which, as such, is peculiar to itself, around which all its contents are made to centre, and of

which all its details are but the amplification. As stated in our opening article upon Exodus, this book, viewed doctrinally, treats of *redemption*; that is its principal subject, its dominant theme.

This important and blessed truth of redemption is illustrated in Exodus by God's dealings with the children of Israel. First, we are shown their need of redemption —a people in captivity groaning in bitter bondage. Second, we behold the might and holiness of the Redeemer Himself— displayed in His plagues upon Egypt. Third, we see the character of redemption —purchased by blood, emancipated by power. Fourth, we learn the duty of the redeemed—obedience to the Lord. Finally, we have set before us the privileges of the redeemed—worshipping God in His holy habitation. Thus, we are enabled to see at the outset, that our present passage has to do with the people of God entering into the privileges of redemption. Bearing this in mind, let us now attend to the details of our passage.

"*When* thou takest the sum of the children of Israel after their number, *then* shall they give every man a ransom for his soul unto the Lord, when thou numberest them; that there be no plague among them, when thou numberest them" (v. 12). Observe the two words placed in italics. Whenever the Holy Spirit supplies a time-mark like this, it should be carefully pondered: often it supplies a valuable key to a passage— cf. Matt. 13:1; 25:1, etc.; such as the case here. The giving of this ransom-money was connected with the "numbering" of Israel: observe that a reference to this fact is made no less than five times in vv. 12-14. Here, then, is the next thing to be weighed as we seek to ascertain the spiritual meaning of this ordinance. What, then, are the thoughts connected with "numbering" in Scripture?

That this is no unimportant question is at once evidenced by the fact that the fourth book of the Old Testament is designated "Numbers:" its title being taken

from the numberings of the children of
Israel for war, for ministry, and for their
inheritance in Canaan. Thus, a just apprehension of Jehovah's design in these
numberings is essential to a spiritual understanding of the act. Now the most obvious thing suggested by "numbering" is
ownership. Take one or two simple examples which illustrate this. It is natural
for me to number the books in my own
library; but I would never think of doing
so with my neighbour's. A farmer numbers
the sheep of his own flock, but not those
belonging to another. *Property in,* and
consequent *right over* are the thoughts connected with "numbering." So it is in the
Scriptures: when God numbers or orders
anything to be numbered, taking the sum
of them denotes that they belong to Him,
and that He has the sovereign right to do
with them as He pleases. The action itself says of the things numbered, "These
are Mine, and I assign them their place
as I will." If the following passages be
pondered it will be found that they confirm our definition.

"Lift up your eyes on high, and behold
who hath created these things, that bringeth out their hosts by number, He calleth
them all by names by the greatness of His
might, for that He is strong in power; not
one faileth" (Isa. 40:26). The reference
here is to the heavenly bodies. God's
ownership and sovereign disposings of
them. So again in Psalm 147:4 we read,
"He telleth the number of the stars; He
calleth them all by their names."

Let us take now another kind of example: "Therefore will I *number* you to
the sword, and ye shall all bow down to
the slaughter" (Isa. 65:12). This passage
does not, indeed, assert God's property *in*
His enemies, but the expression "number
you to the sword" asserts His power to
dispose of them; and the other is clearly
implied. The Lord "numbers" to the sword
because He has "made all things for Himself: yea, even the wicked for the day
of evil" (Prov. 16:4). A similar instance
is found in the sentence pronounced on
Belshazzar: "MENE, God hath numbered
thy kingdom and finished it" (Dan. 5:26).
This may suffice to show the meaning of
the Divine sum-takings. They assert God's
property rights and His power to do what
He will with His own.

In the numberings of Israel it was God
dealing with the people whom He had
redeemed for Himself, appropriating what
was His, and assigning to each and all
their place before Him. This is what is
made so prominent in the book of Numbers
—Israel were *Jehovah's* soldiers and servants, and He distributed each as He

pleased. As men of war belonging to
the Lord, engaged in a warfare by which
His name was to be glorified, it was for
Him to muster the army for Himself:
"The Lord is a Man of war: the Lord
is His name" (Ex. 15:3). "The Lord
strong and mighty, the Lord mighty in
battle" (Psa. 24:8). All the hosts of
heaven are His, and all the armies of the
earth; therefore it is His prerogative to
number them. How jealously the Lord
guards this prerogative may be seen, with
terrific force, in the history of David.
He had been entrusted with the leading
forth of the armies of the living God,
and so long as he occupied his place before
the hosts it was well; but at length David
forgot God's glory, and sought his own:
"And Satan stood up against Israel and
provoked David to number Israel. And
David said to Joab and to the rulers of
the people, Go, number Israel from Beer-
sheba even to Dan; and bring the number
of them to me, that I may know it. And
Joab answered, The Lord make His people
an hundred times so many more as they
be; but my lord the king, are they not
all my lord's servants? why then doth my
lord require this thing? why will he be
a cause of trespass to Israel? Nevertheless, the king's word prevailed against Joab. . . . and God was displeased with
this thing; wherefore He smote Israel.
And David said unto God, I have sinned
greatly, because I have done this thing:
but now, I beseech Thee, do away the
iniquity of Thy servant; for I have done
very foolishly" (1 Chron. 21:1-4, 7, 8).

It may be asked, What harm was there
in thus numbering the people? Is not a
census valuable? Yes, for men warring
after the flesh and walking according to
worldly principles; but even Joab, a man
of iniquity, knew so well what the numbering of the army of the living God signified, that he protested against the act, as
one flagrantly trenching upon the rights
and glory of the Lord, that judgment was
sure to follow; as it did. God will not
give His glory to another. Alas, David
forgot this, and brought evil upon Israel.
There is only one King, the Captain of
our salvation, who, being entrusted with
the ordering of God's people, never for-
gets the Father's glory. And this is what
is before us in our present type, as God
said to Moses, "When *thou* takest the sum
of the children of Israel:" it was only the
typical mediator who could take the sum
of God's people!

Above, we have pointed out how that
the numberings of Israel recorded in the
fourth book of Scripture set forth God's
appropriation and ordering of a people

whom He had redeemed for and unto Himself. It is this which supplies the key to our present portion. Appropriately is this *first* reference to the "numbering" of Israel found in that book which, doctrinally, treats of *redemption*; and significantly is it said at the beginning of the passage, "when thou takest the sum of the children of Israel after their number, they shall give every man a *ransom* for his soul" (v. 12). Thus, as usual, the key is hung right on the door for us! That which is central in this ordinance of the atonement-money is, that God *appropriates* His elect unto Himself only as a *ransomed* people. A clear proof of this has already been before us in Ex. 12 and 13, where we saw the "firstborn" secured by Him because ransomed to Him.

In Ex. 12 and 13 the "firstborn" were ransomed and secured by blood-shedding; here in Ex. 30 the children of Israel are owned as Jehovah's ("numbered") by "silver." The change of figure should occasion no difficulty. Twice in our passage is the money specifically termed "an *offering* unto the Lord." As was pointed out when commenting upon the silver sockets under the boards of the tabernacle's framework (26:19), the blood of the sacrifices more nearly exhibited the *mode* by which actual atonement was to be made for sin, but the "atonement-money" fitly proclaimed the *preciousness* of that by which sinners should be redeemed. Further confirmation of this is found in Num. 31:49-54, where we learn that the officers of Israel's hosts brought an offering of *gold* "to make an atonement." That our present passage does not stand alone may be seen by a reference to Num. 3:46-51; 18:15, 16, etc.

We learn best the meaning of our type by observing how the Holy Spirit sets it aside once the antitype has come in. Just as we see most clearly the typical meaning of the blood of bulls and goats when, in the presence of the "one sacrifice for sins" God declares it is not possible "that these should take away sins" (Heb. 10:4); so we get hold of the design of the atonement-silver and the atonement-gold (cf. Num. 31:49-54 where the term "gold" is found four times) when, beholding Him in whom is treasured up all redemption's wealth we are told, "Ye were not *redeemed* with corruptible things as silver and gold, from your vain conversation. . . . but with the precious blood of Christ, as of a lamb without blemish and without spot." Thus, the "*precious* blood" (an expression found nowhere else) in *this* connection, tells us that the "ransom" money prefigured the *costliness* of Christ's sacrifice,

as the "blood" did the *character* of it.

Does not this satisfactorily dispose of the first difficulty in our passage to which we called attention at the beginning of this article? True, the Israelite was required to give a monetary ransom for his soul, but this no more signified that salvation might be secured by the sinner's own efforts than did the furnishing of a bullock or lamb imply that the offerer was thereby purchasing God's favour. Instead, it was the Lord teaching His people, in type and figure, of Him who alone could make an atonement for sin, namely Christ: the slaying of the offerer's sacrifice telling of the shedding of His blood, the bringing of the silver or gold speaking of the preciousness of that blood. That each was furnished by the Israelite himself only emphasised the truth that the sinner must, by faith, personally *appropriate* the Lord Jesus, and place Him between his sins and a holy God.

Let us notice next the amount required from each Israelite: "This they shall give, every one that passeth among them that are numbered, half a shekel, after the shekel of the sanctuary: (a shekel is twenty gerahs): an half shekel shall be the offering of the Lord" (v. 13). Thus we learn that the "ransom" stipulated consisted of half a shekel or ten gerahs. This detail in our type is not without its significance, rather does it throw light upon it as a whole.

Ten, as we have shown in previous articles, is the number of human responsibility, and here we see the "ransom" fully meeting this responsibility. Less than ten gerahs would not avail before God—note how the woman in Luke 15:8 was not satisfied with only nine pieces of silver! The sinner imagines that if he discharges his duties toward his fellow-man, that is all which can fairly be required of him; God and His claims are left entirely out of his calculations. But the Ten Commandments begin with man's relations with and responsibility to the Lord God. But where is the one who ever loved the Lord his God with all his heart, or even his neighbour as himself? Ah, there is only one, the Lord Jesus Christ. He it was who presented to God the required ransom: "Christ hath redeemed us from the curse of the law, being made a curse for us" (Gal. 3:13). He was also "made under the law, to redeem them that are under the law" (Gal. 4:4, 5). Though we could not pay the ten gerahs of our responsibility, Christ has paid in full for us: He kept the law perfectly, in thought and word and deed, and also suffered its penalty on our behalf;

thus has He provided the perfect ransom.
"Half a shekel, after the shekel of the sanctuary" (v. 13). This is a most important detail. It was by the *standard* "shekel," which was kept there in the sanctuary that all others were tested: each must be full up to the required weight. So it was with the antitype. The true Atonement has been weighed in the balances of the heavenly sanctuary and found of full value before the throne of God. The Father's acceptance of our Saviour's ransom was convincingly demonstrated when He raised Him from the dead, and afterwards exalted Him to His own right hand. Christ has fully discharged the whole of His people's debt, completely satisfied every demand of Divine holiness, and provided a sure and eternal standing-ground for us before God.

"Every one that passeth among them that are numbered, from twenty years old and above, shall give an offering unto the Lord. The rich shall not give more, and the poor shall not give less than half a shekel, when they give an offering unto the Lord, to make an atonement for your souls" (vv. 14, 15). This is very striking.

"All were to pay alike. In the matter of atonement, all must stand on one common platform. There may be a vast difference in knowledge, in experience, in capacity, in attainment, in zeal, in devotedness, but the ground of atonement is alike to all. The great apostle of the Gentiles and the feeblest lamb in all the flock of Christ stand on the same level as regards atonement. This is a very simple and a very blessed truth. All may not be alike devoted and fruitful, but 'the precious blood of Christ,' and not devotedness or fruitfulness, is the solid and everlasting ground of the believer's rest. The more we enter into the truth and power of this the more fruitful shall we be" (C.H.M.).

"And thou shalt take the atonement money of the children of Israel, and shalt appoint it for the service of the tabernacle of the congregation" (v. 16). The "appointment" of this atonement-money is mentioned in Ex. 38:25-28: *it furnished the foundation* for the Tabernacle! The use to which this ransom money was put supplies additional confirmation of our interpretation of the type. The House of God rested upon the "silver sockets." Thus, the *foundation* of God's people being around Himself is *redemption*. That the silver from which these "sockets" was made was given by Israel at the time of their "numbering," was God, in figure, appropriating His elect unto Himself as a ransomed people.

If we be not ransomed, we are not His. If we are not before Him, in the value of the blood of Christ, we are not numbered to Him as the lot of His inheritance. "The necessity for that is strongly emphasised in that no man could be considered as His at all apart from the redemption money paid for each one. No exemption was made, and no excuse could be pleaded. The rich was not permitted to pay more, nor the poor less than the half shekel. A shekel is said to be equivalent to thirty pence or sixty-two cents. A half shekel each man had to pay alike. God is no respecter of persons and redemption views all men on the same level before God. The rich might think it but a trifle, but it could not be neglected; and none were so poor as to be unable to give it. The prominent thought is the *availability* of the ransom-price, so as to leave each one without excuse: If God is to have a ransomed people among whom He will dwell, it must be according to His, not their, thoughts.

"The price is to be half a shekel, or ten gerahs, according to the shekel of the sanctuary—the Divine estimation. Man might conceive that something else would be more suited for his redemption—his own works, his feelings, his worthiness, or his faithfulness. But God's holiness and righteousness would not permit poor man to be so deceived. The foundation must be according to God's estimation, the shekel must be according to the balances of the sanctuary" (Mr. Ridout).

"And thou shalt take the atonement money of the children of Israel, and shall appoint it for the service of the tabernacle of the congregation; that it may be a memorial unto the children of Israel before the Lord, to make an atonement for your souls" (v. 16). The mention here of the "memorial" is most blessed. A lasting testimony was before God that atonement had been made for the souls of His people. They might but feebly enter into the blessedness of redemption, but the "memorial" of it was ever before Jehovah. The antitype of this is brought before us at length in the Epistle to the Hebrews—Christ now at the right hand of God, there as the Representative of His people.

There is a practical application to be made of our type to Christians to-day. We are under deep and lasting obligations to *own* the redemption-rights of Christ. God ransomed Israel to Himself in Egypt, but after they had been brought on to redemption-ground, they were required to *acknowledge* the responsibility this entailed, by bringing their *ten* gerahs of silver. So often we dwell upon what Christ's ransom has freed us *from*; so little are we occupied with what His ransom has freed us *for*. By ransoming us Christ has acquired rights over us, and He is entitled to our recognition of this in a practical way. Our lives should ever evidence the fact that we are not our own. If they do not, we shall suffer from a "plague" (v. 12)—Divine righteousness will chasten us.

It only remains for us now to point out that the *order* of these types is Divinely perfect. In Ex. 28 and 29 we have seen the establishment of the priesthood, and in consequence, God dwelling in Israel's midst. Then we have had their worship, ascending to Him as a sweet savour (30:1-10). Now we are shown how the people themselves were *identified with* the holy service of the tabernacle *through redemption*. A lasting "memorial" of it remained before Jehovah: a permanent standing-ground was provided before Him in that which, in figure, spoke of the preciousness of the Lamb's atonement. O that we may be increasingly occupied with Him, and our responsibility to glorify Him in our spirits and bodies which are His by purchase right.

CHAPTER 55

THE LAVER

EXODUS 30:17-21

We are now to consider the seventh of the Tabernacle's holy vessels. Though given last in the Divine description of its various pieces of furniture, the Laver was really the second which met the priest in his way into the sacred building. It stood in the outer court, between the brazen-altar and the curtained wall which marked off the holy place. Though closely related to the brazen-altar, everything connected with the Laver was in striking contrast therefrom. The former was made of wood and brass; the latter of brass only. The one was square in shape; the other, most probably, was round. The dimensions of the altar are fully particularised; but no measurements are given in connection with the Laver. The former had rings and staves for carrying it; the latter had not. Instructions were given that the one should be covered when Israel journeyed from camp to camp; but nothing is said of this about the other. The altar was for fire; the Laver for water. The former received the sacrifices of all alike; the latter was for the priests alone. Thus everything about them was sharply distinguished.

That which is most prominent in connection with the Laver was its water for cleansing. "The figure of water is universally familiar, and represents one of the most important and necessary elements in the physical universe. We find it in the vast ocean, comprising by far the largest part of the earth's surface; and in our inland lakes and rivers, which form such exquisite networks both of beauty and convenience and of commercial value. We find it in the vapour of the skies; and the dews that gather about the vegetable creation, and preserve it from withering through the torrid summer. We find it forming the largest proportion of our own bodies. It is a figure of purity and refreshing; of quickening life and power; of vastness and abundance. Without it, life could not be for a single month maintained. And so we find it in the Bible as one of the most important symbols of spiritual things" (Dr. A. B. Simpson).

Even in Eden we find mention of a river "to water the garden" (Gen. 2:10), type of that river "the streams whereof shall make glad the city of God" (Psa. 46:4). This river went out from Eden to water the earth, being parted into four heads: figure of the temporal mercies of God flowing forth to all His creatures. Next, we read of the fearful waters of the Flood, being the instrument of God's unsparing judgment upon sin—compare the destruction of Pharaoh and his hosts by the same element: Ex. 14:1. Then we find it as preserving the life of Hagar and her son (Gen. 16:7, 21:19). Later, we find Jehovah furnishing water from the smitten rock for the refreshment of His people in the wilderness. Water has quite a prominent place in the ministries of Elijah and Elisha. It brought healing to Naaman (2 Kings 5), and saved Jehoshaphat's army from destruction (2 Kings 2).

So in the New Testament "water" is found in widely different connections. It is the element in which the believer is figuratively buried. It is found in connection with Christ's first miracle. From the pierced side of the Saviour there flowed "blood and water." Finally, in the last chapter of Holy Writ, we read of "a pure river of water of life, clear as crystal, proceeding out of the throne of God and of the Lamb" (v. 1). Thus, the contents of the Laver bring before us one of the most far-reaching and many-sided figures of Scripture.

The typical teaching of the Laver is rarely apprehended even among Christians, and their failure at this point has brought in much that is dishonouring to the Lord Jesus. Cleansing by blood and washing with water are sharply distinguished in the Old Testament types, but they are sadly confused in the thoughts of most churchgoers to-day. The sermons they hear, the hymns they sing, the prayers they utter, both express and add to the awful and Christ-dishonouring disorder of these last days. The thorough and prayerful study of the Tabernacle and all connected with it, would correct much which is now regarded as Scriptural, even in orthodox circles. But we will not anticipate. Let us now consider:

1. *Its Signification.*

This we may learn at once from the use to which it was put: "For Aaron and his sons shall wash their hands and their feet thereat" (v. 19). Thus we see at a glance it was designed for priestly purification. At the brazen-altar sins were dealt with and put away. At the golden-altar that which spoke of worship was presented to God. Midway between the two stood the Laver: at it the priests were required to wash their hands and feet, for communion with God necessitates· not only acceptance but purification—a practical answering thereto.

There is therefore no difficulty at all in perceiving the spiritual meaning of the holy vessel which is now before us: happily the commentators are almost unanimous in their interpretation of this type. The Laver tells of the need of cleansing if communion with God is to be maintained: cleansing not from the guilt of sin, but from the defilements of the way. As already said, the question of sin was dealt with at the brazen-altar: *that* must be settled before there can be any approach unto God. Hence the brazen-altar was the *first* holy vessel to be met with in the outer court, being stationed just within the entrance. But having there slain the sacrifice and poured out its blood at the foot of the altar, the sons of Aaron were now able to advance; but ere they were ready to burn incense upon the golden-altar they must wash at the Laver. The need for this will be easily discerned.

Having officiated at the brazen-altar their hands would be unclean, smeared with blood. Moreover, as no shoes were provided for Aaron and his sons, the dust of the desert would soil their feet. These must be removed ere they could pass into the holy place; as it is said concerning the eternal Dwellingplace of God, "And there shall in no wise enter into it anything that defileth" (Rev. 21:27). The spiritual application of this to Christians to-day is obvious. The blood on the hands of Aaron and his sons evidenced that they had come into contact with *death*. So we, in our every-day lives, constantly have dealings with those who are dead in trespasses and sins, and their very influence defiles us. In like manner, our passage through this wilderness world, which lieth in the Wicked one (1 John 5:19), fouls our walk. There is therefore a daily need

for these to be removed.

It is to be carefully noted that it was in their official character as priests, not merely as Israelites, that Aaron and his sons were required to wash their hands and feet at the Laver. Had they failed in this duty, they had still been Israelites, but they were disqualified for entering into the holy place and ministering before God. How clear and blessed is the typical teaching of this. The soiling of our hands and feet through association with the unregenerate, and in consequence sojourning in a world which knows not and loves not Christ, does not in any wise affect our perfect standing before God: "For by one offering He hath perfected *forever* them that are sanctified" (Heb. 10:14). But though the defilements of the way do not affect our standing, they *do* interfere with our communion with God. We cannot enter into our priestly privileges (1 Peter 2:5), nor discharge our priestly duties (Heb. 13:15), till we have been cleansed at the Laver. The Laver, like everything else in the Tabernacle, pointed to the Lord Jesus Christ, and tells of His sufficiency to meet our every need. It shows us that we must have recourse to Him for daily cleansing. This leads us to consider:

2. *Its Contents.*

"And thou shalt put water therein, for Aaron and his sons shall wash their hands and feet thereat: when they go into the tabernacle of the congregation, they shall wash with water" (vv. 18-20). Water and not blood was the element appointed and used for the purification of the priests. As that aspect of God's truth set forth in this detail of our type has largely been lost by the saints, we must examine it with doubly close attention.

In our present type the water within the Laver was plainly a figure of the written Word of God. This same figure is employed in the following passages: "Wherewithal shall a young man cleanse his way? by taking heed thereto according to Thy Word" (Psa. 119:9). "Except a man be born of water and of the Spirit, he cannot enter into the kingdom of God" (John 3:5). "Now ye are clean through the word which I have spoken unto you" (John 15:3). "Christ also loved the church, and gave Himself for it, that He might sanctify and cleanse it with the washing of water by the Word" (Eph. 5:25, 26). "According to His mercy He saved us, by the washing of regeneration, and renewing of the Holy Spirit" (Titus 3:5). "Let us draw near with a true heart in full assurance of faith, having our hearts sprinkled from an evil conscience, and our bodies washed with pure water" (Heb. 10:22). "Seeing ye have purified your souls in obeying the truth through the Spirit" (1 Peter 1:22).

Now, it is of first importance that we should discriminate between two distinct types. In Ex. 29:4 we are told, "And Aaron and his sons thou shalt bring unto the door of the tabernacle of the congregation, and thou shalt wash them with water." While in Ex. 30:19 we read, "Aaron and his sons shall wash their hands and feet thereat." The former was done *for* them; the latter was done *by* them. In the one they were completely washed all over; in the latter, it was only their hands and feet that were concerned. The former was never repeated; the latter was needed every time they would draw near the golden-altar. The one was a figure of regeneration, the other typified the Christian's need of daily cleansing. John 3:5; Titus 3:5; Heb. 10:22 give us the antitype of Ex. 29:4; Psalm 119:9, 1 Peter 1:22 speaks in the language of our present type.

The same distinction noted above is to be observed in the words of Christ to Peter: "He that is washed needeth not save to wash his feet, but is clean every whit" (John 13:10). The R.V. brings out the meaning of the Greek more accurately: "For he that is bathed needeth not save to wash his feet." The washing or bathing received at regeneration needs not to be repeated; the washing of the feet is all that is required to make us "clean every whit." The defilements of the way do not raise any need for me to be regenerated again: the new birth is once and for all. Nothing can affect it; nothing I do can cause me to become unborn; such a thing is impossible, both in the natural and spiritual realms.

But side by side with this blessed truth of a washing once for all, which needs not to be, and which, indeed, cannot be repeated, stands another truth of great practical importance. "He that is bathed needeth not save to *wash his feet.*" This is what is so blessedly brought before us in John 13. The particular point there **which we would now note is the Lord's** words to Peter, when that disciple demurred at the thought of Christ washing his feet. To him the Saviour said, "If I wash thee not, thou hast no part with Me" (v. 8). Observe that Christ did not say *in* Me," but *"with* Me." "In Christ" refers to my spiritual state and standing before God; my acceptance. "With Christ" has to do with fellowship; communion with Him. For this there must be a removal of all that defiles, all that offends His holy eye. For this there must be a coming to Him and a placing of our

feet in His hands—an humbling of ourselves before Him and an asking of Him to cleanse our walk. Thus the Laver points to Christ as the Cleanser of His people; its water to the Word which He uses for this.

3. *Its Position.*

"And thou shalt put it between the tabernacle of the congregation and the altar" (v. 18). As already stated, the Laver stood midway between the two altars. The priest's work at the brazen-altar was completed before he passed on to the Laver. This tells us that the question of our acceptance before God is not raised at the Laver. The interpretation and application of this detail is most important. That which the sons of Aaron needed for the removal of the dust of the desert was not blood, but water. So when the believer contracts defilement by treading the path of life through this world, it is *not* a fresh application of the blood of Christ which he needs, but the water of the Word.

Those Christians who speak and sing of re-applications of the blood of Christ unwittingly degrade His perfect sacrifice to the level of those offered under the Mosaic economy. Every time an Israelite transgressed God's righteous law, a fresh sin-offering was required. Why? Because the blood of bulls and goats could not take away sins (Heb. 10:4). But in contradistinction from those sacrifices, Christ has offered a perfect sacrifice for His people once for all (Heb. 9:26, 28). The blood He shed at Calvary has made full atonement; every claim of God's justice was there met, every demand of His holiness there fully satisfied. There is therefore now no need for any fresh sacrifice. The moment the convicted sinner has "faith in His blood" (Rom. 3:25), i.e., puts his trust in the redemptive-work of Christ as the alone ground of his acceptance before God, that moment is he cleansed "from *all* sin" (1 John 1:7). To him the Spirit saith, "There is therefore now no condemnation to them which are in Christ Jesus" (Rom. 8:1). In simple confidence he may now rest on the Divine declaration that "by one offering He hath perfected forever them that are sanctified" (Heb. 10:14).

True, an evil heart of unbelief still remains within him; true, "in many things we all offend" (James 3:2); but neither the presence of the old nature, nor its evil fruits, can invalidate our perfect standing before God, which rests upon our acceptance in Christ. We are "complete in Him" (Col. 2:10). He has already "made us meet to be partakers of the inheritance of the saints in light" (Col. 1:12). It is the realisation of this which establishes the heart. It is the recognition of this which keeps us in unclouded peace. It is the laying hold of this which fills us with thanksgiving and praise unto God. To ask Him for a re-application of the blood is to repudiate the fact that we stand "unblameable and unreproveable in His sight" (Col. 1:22). Nay, what is worse, it is to deny the efficacy and sufficiency of its once-and-for-all application to us.

What is needed by the exercised believer as he is conscious of the blemishes of his service (the "hands") and the failures of his walk (the "feet"), is to avail himself of that which the Laver and its water prefigured—the provision which God has made for us in His Word. What is needed by us is a practical appropriation of that Word to all the details of our daily lives. It is to seek grace and heed that Word, "He that sayeth he abideth in Him ought himself also so to walk, even as He walked" (1 John 2:6). It is only by obeying the truth, through the Spirit, that we purify our souls (1 Peter 1:22). Christ could say, "By the Word of Thy lips I have kept Me from the paths of the Destroyer" (Psa. 17:4); and such ought to be our experience, too. When we fail, then we must act upon 1 John 1:9.

It is important to note that the Laver stood in the outer court and not within the holy place, which was the chamber of worship. With this should be linked the fact that this vessel was only for the use of Aaron's sons. What is in view here is *priestly* activity, the removing of that which would otherwise disqualify them for service at the golden-altar. What an unspeakable insult unto Jehovah had they passed into the holy place with soiled hands and feet! For them it would have been fatal, as the twice repeated "that they die not" clearly denotes. In like manner, we cannot enter into the worship of God's house if we have not first washed at the Laver; the confessing of our sins and the consequent practical cleansing should take place before—in the outer court. Failure at this point is to, morally, bring in "death." "But let a man examine himself, and *so* let him eat of that bread, and drink of that cup" (1 Cor. 11:28). This involves the taking account of our hands and feet, and washing at the Laver *before* coming to the Lord's table.

4. *Its Composition.*

"Thou shalt also make a Laver of brass" (v. 18). In the outer court everything was made of brass (really "copper"), or covered with brass: altar, laver, pillars, and pins. This was in sharp distinction from the vessels which stood in the inner chamber, which were all of or covered with gold. "It is Divine righteousness testing man in responsibility, and consequently testing man in the place where he is. Brass, on this account, is always found outside of the tabernacle; while gold, which is Divine righteousness as suited to the nature of God, is found within. But testing man, it of necessity condemns him, because he is a sinner; and hence it will be found to have associated with it a constant judicial aspect" (Ed. Dennett).

If the reader will refer back to Article 15 he will there find we have, at some length, entered into the meaning of this symbol. Without again bringing forward the proofs of our definition, we shall here make only the bare statement that "brass" speaks of *judgment*. The Laver, then, typifies Christ in His character of Judge. In John 5:22 we find Him saying, "The Father judgeth no man, but hath committed all judgment unto the Son"; and again, "and hath given Him authority to execute judgment also, because He is the Son of man" (5:27). Hence, in Rev. 1, where One like unto "the Son of man" is seen in the midst of the seven golden lampstands—judging—inspecting, passing sentence—we are told that His feet were "like unto fine *brass*" (v. 19).

Thus the Laver of brass presents the inflexible righteousness of Christ testing, judging His people, condemning that which mars their communion with God. But how blessed to remember that He also supplies that water which *removes* the very things which are condemned! "It is not the execution of judgment upon our Substitute, nor is it the infliction of judgment upon us; but it is the testing and trying of our ways by the Son of God according to the authority given Him to judge among His people, before He judges all the earth in a later day" (Mr. Ridout).

5. *Its Use.*

Strictly speaking, it was not the Laver itself that was used, but the water in it: "Aaron and his sons shall wash their hands and feet thereat," more literally, *"from it."* This, the sons of Aaron were to do for themselves. It speaks, then, of believers, in their priestly character, making practical application to all their ways of the Word of Christ (Col. 3:16). The water in the *brazen* Laver points to the believer *judging* himself, unsparingly, by that Word.

First of all, that Word should be used to *prevent* us falling into evil. God's Word has been given to us for "a lamp unto our feet and a light unto our path"; that is, to expose the snares of Satan and to reveal the path in which we should walk. O that more and more we may be able to say, "Thy Word have I hid in mine heart, that I might not sin against Thee."

Second, that Word is to be used in *cleansing* us from all defilement. We can only heed that exhortation in 2 Cor. 7:1— "Let us cleanse ourselves from all filthiness of the flesh and spirit"—by diligently attending to and daily obeying the precepts of Holy Writ. What a searching word is that in Rev. 22:14, "Blessed are they that wash (by the Word) their robes (emblematic of our external deportment), that they might have the right to the tree of life" (R.V.)!

Third, that Word is to be used for *refreshment.* Though we know of no other commentator who has called attention to this, yet we believe it is definitely taught in our present type. In Ex. 30:20 we are also told that Aaron's sons were required to wash with water "when they come near the altar to minister, to burn offering made by fire unto the Lord." This was upon the brazen altar. It seems to us that the thought here is not so much the removal of defilement, as it is that of coming to the altar in vigour or freshness, as the priests brought with them that which spoke of the highest aspect of Christ's work.

Water is used by us not only for cleansing, but to invigorate—nothing is more refreshing to tired feet than to bathe them. Is not this thought clearly seen in the *first* mention of the washing of feet in Scripture? "Let a little water, I pray you, be fetched, and wash your feet *and rest* yourselves under the tree" (Gen. 18:4). Note how the two angels refused to wash their feet in Lot's house (Gen. 19:2)—there was no refreshment for them in Sodom! The application to us of this detail in our type is plain: in order to minister before God as priests, we must first receive refreshment from His Word. It is by that alone we are "quickened"—revived and refreshed.

6. *Its Manufacture.*

It is striking to note the source from which the material for the Laver was obtained. This we are not told in our present passage, but have it made known in Ex. 38:8: "And he made the laver of brass, and the foot of it of brass, of the looking-glasses of the women assembling, which assembled at the door of the tabernacle of the congregation." These look-ing-glasses or mirrors were not like our modern ones, of glass and quicksilver, but were of highly polished brass or copper. Several lines of thought are pointed to by this important detail.

First, we may admire the lovely product which the grace of God, working in their hearts, brought forth. At the beginning, Jehovah bade Moses, "Speak unto the children of Israel, that they bring Me an offering of every man ("whosoever" 35:5) that giveth it willingly with his heart, ye shall take My offering" (25:8). Here we see the answer of the hearts of the daughters of Israel: they "willingly offered what might gratify vanity, to provide for that vessel of cleansing, that Jehovah's service and worship might not be hindered" (Mr. Ridout). In like manner, God's people to-day delight to give of their substance to the furtherance of His work. But how often the sacrificial giving of the sisters puts the brethren to shame!

Second, have we not here a beautiful foreshadowing of the Lord Jesus setting aside that which ministered to His glory, in order that He might provide cleansing for His people? He left the worship of angels in Heaven, and came here, to the "outer court," in servant form. He came not to be ministered unto, but to minister. It is exceedingly striking to observe that in the Gospels, the only record we have of any ministering to Him of their substance were devoted *women* (Luke 8:2, 3)! So, too, it was women, not the apostles (sad failure on their part!), who washed His feet with tears, and also anointed Him.

Third, the practical application to ourselves is very searching. The very material from which the Laver was made spoke of *surrender,* a willingness to part with what was calculated to make something of self; and this, in order that conditions of holy purity might be maintained in the priests. Thus we, too, must sacrifice what would minister to pride if we are to obtain that cleansing which fits for communion with God!

Fourth, the uselessness of worldly expedients may be seen here—the women had brought their mirrors from Egypt. "We are ever prone to be 'like a man beholding his natural face in a glass; for he beholdeth himself and goeth away, and straightway forgetteth what manner of man he was.' Nature's looking-glass can never furnish a clear and permanent view of our true condition. 'But whoso looketh into the perfect law of liberty, and continueth therein, he being not a forgetful hearer, but a doer of the work, this man shall be blessed in his deed' (James 1:23-25). The man who has constant recourse to the Word of God, and who allows that Word to tell upon his heart and conscience, will be maintained in the holy activities of the Divine life" (C.H.M.).

7. *Its Omissions.*

These were two in number, and very noticeable they are. First, no *dimensions* were prescribed for the Laver, nor are we told the quantity of water which it contained. A similar omission was observed in connection with the lampstand. The measurements of all the other vessels are given. The absence of any here in connection with the Laver and its water plainly denotes that an *unlimited* provision has been made by God for our cleansing. In Christ and His Word is sufficient to minister to our every need.

Second, no directions were given to Israel concerning the *covering* of the Laver while they journeyed from camp to camp. In Num. 4 we find instructions for the protection of the ark, the table, the lampstand, and both the altars; but nothing is said of the Laver. Does not the absence of any covering to this vessel strikingly accord with its typical character? Does it not tell us that the purifying Word is *ever* available, and that we need to use it daily in all our wilderness journeyings! Thus, we see again, that the omissions of Scripture (which the carnal mind would regard as defects) are profoundly significant.

We may also take note of the significant omission of further references to the Laver in the Old Testament. Only once is it referred to after the tabernacle was erected and furnished; and that is when it was anointed (Lev. 8:11). Not until we reach the book of Kings do we find that which took the place of the Laver in Solomon's temple, namely, the "molten sea" (1 Kings 7:23, etc.). Does not *this* omission silently testify to Israel's departure from the Word throughout their history! Probably the "Fountain" of Zech. 13:1 gives us the Millennial Laver.

That which in Heaven corresponds to the Laver is brought before us in Rev. 15: 2, 3—cf. 1 Kings 7:23. Here the saints will no longer need to wash, but they are eternally reminded of the source of their purity. They are seen standing on a "sea" (Laver) of glass, "singing unto the Lamb." Altar and Laver will never be forgotten. The altar says, "without shedding of blood is no remission." The Laver announces "without holiness no man shall see the Lord." Both are witnessed to on High. As another has so beautifully said:

"Here we are permitted to look into the glory. There, in the heavenly sanctuary, is the throne of God and of the Lamb, as the ark was in the tabernacle. The hidden manna is there, answering to the table of shewbread. The seven Spirits of God are before the throne, answering to the candlestick; and the sea of glass, answering to that in Solomon's temple. Notice it is not now the laver filled with water—no need to remove defilement there; it is a sea of transparent glass, reminding us of the laver which has accomplished its work here. When all the redeemed of God are gathered there, the day of cleansing from defilement is over, no more need to wash one another's feet; no more need for the Lord's washing our feet, but there we stand with harps of God in our hands, nothing to hinder praise and worship. But the sea of glass, the witness and perpetual reminder of our cleansing, will flash forth there a continual remembrance of our Lord's gracious and humble service throughout our journey here" (Mr. Ridout).

CHAPTER 56

THE ANOINTING OIL

EXODUS 30:22-33

Having completed His description of the Tabernacle and its furniture, the Holy Spirit now makes mention of the holy anointing oil and the fragrant incense, without which the sanctuary Moses was to erect for Jehovah would have been unacceptable. As the "incense" has already been considered in our study of the golden-altar, we shall dwell here only on the "oil." This was composed of olive oil, into which were compounded four principal spices. It was designed for the anointing of the Tabernacle and its sacred vessels, and was also used at the consecration of Aaron and his sons to their priestly office. Strict instructions were given prohibiting any of the people from making any like unto it, which emphasises its uniqueness.

Like everything else connected with the service of Jehovah's house, the holy anointing oil, with its fragrant ingredients, pointed forward to the person of the Lord Jesus and the excellencies which are to be found in Him, particularly, to those graces which the Holy Spirit manifested through Him. Though there may be some difficulty in determining the precise spiritual import of some of the details, yet the main truth here foreshadowed is too plain to miss. May our eyes now be "anointed" with spiritual "salve" (Rev. 3:18) that we may be enabled to behold and enjoy wondrous things out of God's Law. Let us consider:

I. Its Ingredients.

"Moreover the Lord spake unto Moses, saying, Take thou also unto thee principal spices, of pure myrrh five hundred shekels, and of sweet cinnamon half so much, even two hundred and fifty shekels, and of sweet calamus, two hundred and fifty shekels, and of cassia five hundred shekels, after the shekel of the sanctuary, and of oil olive an hin: And thou shalt make it an oil of holy ointment, an ointment compounded after the art of the apothecary, it shall be an holy anointing oil" (vv. 22-25).

Thus, the ingredients were four in num-
ber, blended together; their fragrance being borne along in the power of the oil. Scholars tell us that the Hebrew word for "spices" is from a root meaning to "smell sweetly." Therefore, the basal thought in the ointment is its sweet scent. *"Principal spices"* signifies those which exceeded others in their rich odor, pre-eminent in their aroma. Surely it is evident that they speak to us of Christ. Our minds at once turn to Psa. 45 where God says to Him, "Thou lovest righteousness, and hatest wickedness; therefore God, Thy God, hath *anointed* Thee with the oil of gladness above Thy fellows. All Thy garments smell of myrrh, and aloes, and cassia, out of the ivory palaces, whereby they have made Thee glad" (vv. 7, 8).

"Myrrh" is the first ingredient mentioned. "This was the gum from a dwarf tree of the terebinth family, growing in Arabia. The gum exudes from the trunk either spontaneously or through incisions made for the purpose. That prescribed for the ointment was 'pure,' literally, free'—the best, what had flowed spontaneously. . . . It is fragrant to the smell, but very bitter to the taste" (Mr. Ridout). To the Scriptures we must turn to learn its typical significance.

It is striking to note that the word itself is found just fourteen times therein, 2 x 7, or a witness unto perfection. Eight of the references are in the Song of Solomon, which at once suggests that the prominent thought emblemised by it is *love.* The keynote is struck in its first occurrence: "A bundle of myrrh is my Well-beloved" (1:13). Further proof that "myrrh" is an emblem of love is found in 5:13, "His cheeks are a bed of spices, as sweet flowers; His *lips* lillies, dropping sweet-smelling myrrh." Significant is the final reference, found in connection with the *death* of Christ (John 19:39)—expressing the *love* of His disciples for Him. Thus, love poured out in a bitter but fragrant death is what was prefigured by the "myrrh." Beautifully is this brought out in the following quotation:

300

"Flowing spontaneously from the tree, as well as through incisions, would suggest on the one hand how willingly He offered all that He was, even unto death, to God, and on the other the 'piercing' to which He was subjected by man, but which only brought out the same fragrance. The bitterness of the myrrh suggests the reality of the *sufferings* through which He went. It was not physical discomfort and pain, nor even death, which gave intensity to His suffering, but the 'contradiction of sinners against Himself' (Heb. 12:3). His very presence in a world where all was against God was bitter to Him. How His perfect soul, enjoying fullest communion with His Father, recognised what an evil and bitter thing it was for men to forsake the Lord! Who could measure sin like the sinless One? He it was who tasted, and drank to the dregs, the bitter cup of God's wrath against sin.

"But all this bitter experience only furnished the occasion for the manifestation not only of a devotedness to God which was perfectly fragrant to Him, but of a love to His own which was as strong as death. And what has been the measure of this love? The myrrh again, from its association with death, may well tell us that it 'passeth knowledge' (Eph. 3:19). 'The Son of God who loved me and gave Himself for Me' (Gal. 2:20)—a measure which cannot be measured, freely flowing from Him whose heart was pierced by and for our sins. Feeble indeed is the estimate we put upon that love at best; but One estimates it at its full value" (Mr. Ridout).

"Cinnamon." Remarkable indeed are the contrasts presented by the four passages in which this word is found. Here in Ex. 30 it pointed to the person of Christ. In Song of Solomon 4:14 it is used in the Bridegroom's description of His bride—referring to that which grace has imputed to her. In the third and fourth references this sweet spice is seen connected with the harlot: Prov. 7:17; Rev. 18:13. There, it is a hypocritical love for souls, used by the usurper of Christ to attract the ungodly. Upon the "cinnamon" Mr. Ridout has said:

"There seems to be no doubt that this spice is the same that is familiar to us under the same name; it is the bark of a small evergreen tree of the laural family. Another tree of the same family is the fragrant camphor. The odor of the cinnamon is sweet and its taste agreeable; it is largely used for flavouring. A valuable essential oil is extracted from the bark, having these properties in an intensified form. It is obtained chiefly from Ceylon, and probably brought from India in the times of the Exodus. The bark is obtained from the young shoots. As a medicine, it is a stimulant and cordial.

"Seeking for light as to its spiritual significance from the etymology of the word, we are met with uncertainty" (Mr. Ridout). But in a footnote he tells us that, one writer has suggested "a possible derivation from two well-known Hebrew words: *Kinna*, 'jealousy' from the root to glow or burn, or be zealous; and *min*, 'form' or 'appearance.' The 'appearance of jealousy.'" To which Mr. Ridout adds, "We need not say, what burning zeal marked our Lord's entire life—'the zeal of Thy house hath eaten Me up' (John 2:17). And this was shown in the holy form of jealousy which would purge that house of all the carnal traffic which had been introduced there. 'Love is strong as death; jealousy is cruel as the grave; the coals thereof are the coals of fire, which hath a most vehement flame' (Song of Sol. 8:6). This gives, at least, a beautiful and significant meaning, and accords with the character of our Lord—a love which was zeal for God's glory and for 'the place where Thine honour dwelleth' (Psa. 26:8). In love for that He would let His own temple, His holy body, be laid low in death. Here was indeed a jealousy of a new form—jealousy for God alone, without one element of selfishness in it. Cruel it was, only in the sense of bearing cruelty rather than suffer one blot to rest upon God's glory—it burned with 'a most vehement flame.'" We believe that this brings out the distinctive thought suggested by the "cinnamon."

"It is well, too, to recall the fact that this tree was an evergreen, passing through no periods of inertness. So our Lord was ever the unchanging devoted One, whose leaf did not wither in time of drought or cold. In the midst of the arid waste of unbelief—as at Chorazin and Bethsaida and Capernaum—there were no marks of feebleness upon Him: 'I thank Thee, O Father,' was His language there as everywhere. Here, too, is medicine, a spiritual tonic and cordial for the faint-hearted. This love and devotedness of our Lord, which knew no change, is not only a most powerful example, but in His grace that which cheers and encourages the fainting of His beloved people" (Mr. Ridout).

"Sweet calamus." The Hebrew word means a "reed" or "cane," being derived from a root-term meaning "to stand upright." Once more we shall take extracts from Mr. Ridout's helpful remarks: "The 'sweet' as in the case of the cinnamon, tells of its fragrance, and this would seem to give us the clue to the article intended. A 'sweet cane' is said to be found in

Lebonan, in India and Arabia. It usually grows in miry soil, from which it sends up the shoots from which its name is derived. The fragrant cane of India is supposed to have been the 'spikenard' of Scripture. The fragrance was obtained by crushing the plant.

"Its growth in the mire may remind us of One who in the mire of this world grew up erect and fragrant for God. Man grows in the mire and gravitates toward it—like the man with the much-rack, who was bowed to earth and saw not the crown of glory offered to him. But our Lord had His eyes and heart only on the heaven above. The mire of earth was but the place where He has come for a special work. Men might grovel in that mire, as, alas, we have! A Job finds that his self-righteousness was covered with the mire of the ditch (Job 9:31). But His surroundings were only the contrast to that erect and perfect life which ever pointed heavenward. His treasure, His all, was with the Father. And wherever He found a 'bruised reed,' to lift it from the mire and establish it erect was the purpose of His heart—'Neither do I condemn thee' (John 8:11).

"This reed was crushed. Wicked men took Him, bound and bruised Him. But what fragrance has filled heaven and earth through that bruising. Again, the aromatic odor of the calamus reminds us that in our Lord there was nothing negative or insipid. That weak word 'amiable' is unsuitable in connection with Him. Thus when the high priest commanded that He be smitten, our Lord neither resents it nor cowers under it; but with what holy dignity did He rebuke that unrighteousness, and bear witness of His kingship before Pilate. A heavenly fragrance pervaded the judgment-hall—the vital fragrance and energy of Holiness, bearing witness to the truth (John 18:33-37)."

"*Cassia.*" Gesenius tells us that the Hebrew name of this spice is derived from a root signifying "to stoop " to "bow down," as in worship. Thus, what was foreshadowed here was the perfect Man's submission to and worship of God. In Luke 4:16 we read that, "As His custom was, He went into the synagogue on the Sabbath day." In the Psalms we find many out-breathings of His worship. In the great Temptation, He refused to fall down before the Devil, reminding him that it was written, "Thou shalt worship the Lord thy God, and Him *only* shalt thou serve."

The only other passage in which "cassia" is mentioned is Ezek. 27:19. There we learn that this was one of the articles in which Tyre—the great merchant nation of the ancients—traded. Like Egypt, Tyre stands for the world. Typically, this tells us that even the world will traffic in the excellencies of Christ in order to further its sordid ends. It is very striking to note that in the very next chapter, Ezek. 28:12-19, Satan is presented as the "king of Tyre." Thus we are there shown that the arch-enemy of God ever seeks to rob Christ, so far as he is permitted, of that worship which is His alone due.

Summarising the emblematic significations of these four principal spices, we learn that, the "myrrh" pointed to the outpouring of Christ's love in a bitter but fragrant death; the "cinnamon" to His holy jealousy for the honour and glory of God; the "calamus" to His uprightness and righteousness in a world of sin and wickedness; the "cassia" to His submission to and worship of God.

2. Its Proportions.

These are given in vv. 23, 24: of the "myrrh" there was five hundred shekels, of the "sweet cinnamon" and the "sweet calamus" two hundred and fifty shekels, and of the "cassia" five hundred shekels. First of all, we must note that there were *four* sweet spices mingled with the oil, and that each of them was taken from *plant* life, which ever speaks of man here on earth. Our minds turn instinctively to the four Gospels, where the Divine record of Christ's earthly life is given. Each of them reveals some special perfection of Christ, yet all are perfectly blended together by the all-pervading "oil," the Holy Spirit.

The *quantities* used of the spices were not of equal weight: of two there were 500 shekels, of two but 250. Thus, we have here a suggestion that there is some truth or aspect of Christ's perfections *common* to the "myrrh" and "cassia," and some truth *common to* the "cinnamon" and "calamus." The *order* in which they are given is 500, 250, 250, and 500 shekels. Comparing them thus with the Gospels, we are hereby bidden to look for some definite link uniting Matthew and John (the First and Fourth) and something shared in common by Mark and Luke, the two middle Gospels. Let us now look, very briefly, first at Matthew's and John's, and then at Mark's and Luke's.

The first and the fourth Gospels present the *highest* glories of Christ, namely, His kingship and His Godhood, agreeing with the *double* quantity of the first and fourth mentioned "spices." Moreover, the *distinctive* character of each Gospel exactly corresponds with the *nature* of the two spices. As already said, the "myrrh" symbolised a bitter death, the death of Christ. It was *this* of which the Israelites were reminded on the Passover-night: the "lamb" must be eaten with "bitter herbs" (Ex. 12:8)! How remarkable then to find that *Matthew,* and he alone, records the wise men presenting to the infant Saviour their gifts of "gold and frankincense and *myrrh*" (Matt. 2:11)! So, it is in this first Gospel that the bitterness of Messiah's experience in being despised and rejected by His brethren according to the flesh, is most fully set out. The etymology of "cassia," the fourth spice, signifies "worship," which at once introduces the *Divine* element. *This* is exactly what we have in the *fourth* Gospel: there Christ is portrayed as the Son of God!

The second and third Gospels both present the *lowliness* of Christ, the one as Servant, the other as Man—the One who had not where to lay His head; and this is in striking accord with the fact that the second and third "spices" were only *half* the quantity of the others! Yet mark how the Holy Spirit here, as ever, guarded the *glory* of Christ, even in His humiliation: the second and third spices alone were termed "sweet"!—telling us that *God* found peculiar delight in His Son's voluntary and obedient condescension. That which is highly esteemed among men is abomination in the sight of God (Luke 16:15); and that which is despised by men is of great price in His sight (1 Peter 3:4). It was when Christ was first "numbered with transgressors," taking His place among those who were "confessing their sins" (Mark 1:5), that the voice of the Father was heard saying, "This is My beloved Son, in whom I am well-pleased" (Matt. 3:17).

The figures 500, 250, 250 and 500 show, at a glance, that the perfections of Christ were all perfectly balanced. In this we behold His uniqueness. Even in His people, in their present state, one grace or other is found predominating. Not so with Christ. Everything was in lovely proportion in Him. The total weight of the spices was fifteen hundred shekels or 5x3x100—the last being 10x10. Five is the number of grace, three is manifestation and also the number of God, ten the measure of responsibility. Thus we have, the grace of God manifested in perfect human responsibility. This is to be found in Christ alone.

Each of the spices was apportioned by weight, "after the shekel of the sanctuary" (v. 24). This was before us in our article on the Atonement-money (30:13). "God is a God of knowledge, and by Him actions are weighed (1 Sam. 2:3). The proud king of Babylon was weighed and found wanting (Dan. 5:27).

And '*all* have sinned and come short of the glory of God.' The Old Testament word for 'glory' is 'weight,' derived from a word 'to be heavy.' So by God's standard, all have come short of the full weight which alone can glorify Him. There is therefore but One in whom, when tested, full and true weight was found, who could say I have glorified Thee upon the earth; I have finished the work which Thou gavest Me to do' (John 17:4)" (Mr. Ridout.)

3. *Its Vehicle.*

This was the "oil olive," a figure of the Holy Spirit; "God *anointed* Jesus of Nazareth with the Holy Spirit and with power" (Acts 10:38). The spices gave fragrance to the oil, and the oil was the element by which their aroma was borne along. So the lovely graces manifested by Christ when He was upon earth were all according to the Spirit (Isa. 11:1, 2), and were all in the power of the Spirit (Luke 4:1, 14, etc.). It was by means of the oil that the sweet spices were blended together; the oil pervaded all and united all. The fragrance of the spices was to be evenly diffused through the whole hin of oil olive, so that no one took precedence over the other; but the oil sent forth the sweetness of each alike. So Christ, ever filled with the Spirit, blended the various fragrances of His character into one holy perfume: His name (that which represents and reveals the person) was, and ever is "as *ointment* poured forth" (Son of Sol. 1:3)!

4. *Its Use.*

It was employed in the anointing of the Tabernacle and all its furniture (Ex. 30:26-29), and at the consecration of the priests (30:30). That which speaks of the sweet savor of Christ was put on all that foreshadowed Him. The vessels of the sanctuary represented various offices and services of our great High Priest, some performed by Him when here on earth, others in which He is now engaged on High. The same eternal Spirit by which He offered Himself as the sacrifice without spot unto God (Heb. 9:14) is still the power of His service in resurrection—cf Acts 1:2:

Very blessed is it to behold the anointing of Aaron's sons with this holy oil, for this, in figure, shows us the people of Christ having communicated to them the selfsame "sweet savour" which gives their

Head acceptance before God. It is the Spirit of God graciously equipping us for priestly ministry. Remarkable is it to note that the instructions concerning the "holy oil" in Ex. 30 follow right after mention of the laver (30:18-21). The "laver" is negative in character, a type of that which *removes* all that would hinder our approach unto God; the "oil" gives us the positive side, *bringing in* that which gives us acceptance before Him. The antitype comes out most preciously in 2 Cor. 2:14, 15, "Thanks be unto God, which always causeth us to triumph *in Christ,* and maketh manifest the savour of His knowledge *by us* in every place. For *we* are unto God a sweet savour of Christ."

5. Its Prohibitions.

"Upon man's flesh it shall not be poured" (v. 32). Only those belonging to the priestly family were anointed. Typically, this means that only the people of God, those in Christ (the "Anointed") are "anointed"—have the Spirit of God. "Because *ye are* sons, God hath sent forth the Spirit of His Son into your hearts" (Gal. 4:6). "Now He which stablisheth us with you *in Christ* and hath anointed us, is God" (2 Cor. 1:22). This is something which man in the flesh has not, and cannot have. "The graces of the Spirit can never be connected with man's flesh, the Holy Spirit cannot own nature. Not one of the fruits of the Spirit has ever yet produced 'in nature's barren soil.' We must be 'born again.' It is only as connected with the new man, as being part of that 'new creation,' that he can know anything of the fruits of the Spirit" (C.H.M.).

"Neither shall ye make any other like it, after the composition of it: it is holy, and it shall be holy unto you" (v. 32). The type must not be imitated or it would not figure that which was *inimitable,* even the perfections of Christ! As no strange altar must be built (Ex. 20:25), as no "strange fire" must be used (Lev. 10:1, 2), so there must be no strange oil. How this word condemns the imitations of Divine worship, the Spirit's operations, the fragrance of Christ, in present-day religious Christendom! Mere head knowledge, ritualism, exquisite music, soulical excitements, are so many human substitutes for the true ministry of Christ in the power of the Spirit.

Unspeakably solemn is the final word: "Whosoever compoundeth any like it, or whosoever putteth any of it upon a stranger, shall even be cut off from his people" (v. 33). "It is thus a heinous sin to imitate the action of the Spirit. Ananias and Sapphira did this when they professed to devote the whole proceeds of the property they had sold to the Lord's service (Acts 5). The same penalty, observe, was attached to putting it upon a stranger, upon those who had no title to it. God is holy, and He jealously guards His sovereign rights, and cannot but visit any infringement of them with punishment. If He seem now to pass by such sins unnoticed, it is owing to the character of the present dispensation being one of grace; but the sins themselves are no less in His sight" (Mr. Ed. Dennett)

CHAPTER 57

THE APPOINTED ARTIFICERS

EXODUS 31:1-11

The 31st of Exodus is an important chapter, both in its typical teachings and its practical lessons. There are three things in it: first, we are shown the Divine provision which was made for the carrying out of Jehovah's instructions concerning the building of the tabernacle and the making of its furniture; second, the Divinely-appointed Sabbath in its special relation to Israel is here defined; third, the actual giving to Moses of the two tables of the testimony, on which were written, by the finger of God, the ten commandments, is here recorded.

Full instructions concerning all the details of the tabernacle had now been given; the provision for the execution of them is next made known. Nothing is left to chance, no place allowed for human scheming. All is of God. Though skilled in all the wisdom of the Egyptians, Moses was not left to draw the plans for Jehovah's dwelling-place; instead, he was bidden to make all things after the pattern shown him in the mount. Now that the "pattern" had been completely set before him, the Lord makes known *who* are to be the principal workmen. The choice of them was His, not Moses'; and their equipment for the work was Divine and not human.

The appointed artificers were Bezaleel and Aholiab, one from the tribe of Judah, the other from the tribe of Dan. We do not have here the actual making of the tabernacle, that is seen in chapters 36 to 39; rather is it the Divine calling and making competent of those who were to engage in that work. That Christ is the One here foreshadowed is evident, for "in the volume of the book it is written of *Me*" is His own express declaration. None but He was capable of building a House for God, and every detail of our present type clearly establishes that fact. May the Spirit of God grant us eyes to see.

"And the Lord spake unto Moses, saying, See, I have called by name Bezaleel, the son of Uri, the son of Hur, of the tribe of Judah: And I have filled him with the Spirit of God, in wisdom, and understanding, and in knowledge, and in all manner of workmanship, to devise cunning (skilful) works, to work in gold, and in silver, and in brass, and in cutting of stones, to set them, and in carving of timber; to work in all manner of workmanship" (vv. 1-5).

In the above verses we have three things: the workman appointed, the workman equipped, the workman's task. Here, as ever in Holy Writ, the proper nouns are pregnant with spiritual significance. The first of the two principal artificers here mentioned is Bezaleel, which means "In the shadow of God" or "the protection of God." He was the son of Uri, which means "light"; the grandson of Hur, which means "free"; from the tribe of Judah, which means "praise." The suitability of these names for one who foreshadowed the person of our Saviour is at once evident.

The similarity of thought between "shadow" and "protection" may be seen by a reference to a number of scriptures in which the former is found. "Hide me under the shadow of Thy wings" (Psa. 17:8); "In the shadow of Thy wings will I make my refuge" (Psa. 57:1); "In the shadow of Thy wings will I rejoice" (Psa. 63:7). The "shadow of Thy wings" speaks of the place of intimacy, of protection, of fellowship. This is the place which the Lord Jesus has ever occupied in His relationship to the Father: "The only begotten Son which is in the *bosom* of the Father" (John 1:18).

Bezaleel was the son of Uri, "light," viz., "the light of Jehovah." The "urim" of the high priests's breastplate is the same word, in the plural number. Now, as the name "Bezaleel" suggests the *place* occupied by the perfect Workman, the Builder of the "true tabernacle," so the "son of Uri" defines His *person*, telling us who He is. The "Son of Light" at once announces that He is the Son of God, for "God is light, and in Him is no darkness

305

at all" (1 John 1:5). Yes, He is "the Brightness of His glory, and the very impress of His substance" (Heb. 1:3). While here on earth, He was "The Light of the world" (John 9:5). When He returns to it, it will be as "the Sun of Righteousness."

Bezaleel was the son of Uri, the son of "Hur," which means "free," or "at liberty." This is very blessed. As the first name speaks of Christ's relation to the Father, and the second tells who He is, so this third one makes known the *manner* in which He entered upon His Divinely-appointed work. That which was here foreshadowed is told out in plain terms in Heb. 10:9, "Then said He, I come to do Thy will, O God." The Lord Jesus *voluntarily* entered upon the great work which He undertook. True it is that the Father "sent" Him (John 9:4, etc.); yet, equally true is it that He "came." Perfectly does this come out in our type: Bezaleel was "called" by God to his work (v. 2), yet was he a son of "liberty."

"Of the tribe of Judah." Beautiful line in the picture is this. Judah was, of course, the royal tribe, as also the one who took the lead when Israel journeyed. But it is the meaning of his name which it is so blessed to note: Judah signifies "praise." Does not this tell us the *spirit* in which the Redeemer entered into His work, that work which involved such humiliation, such suffering, such a death! Listen to His own words in Psalm 40:8, "I *delight* to do Thy will, O God." Behold Him at the very time He was being despised and rejected of men: "In that hour Jesus *rejoiced* in spirit, and said, I thank Thee O Father, Lord of heaven and earth, that Thou hast hid these things from the wise and prudent" (Luke 10:21). Let it be added that while there are not a few of the Psalms which breathe out the sorrows and sufferings of Christ, there are also many of them which express thanksgiving and praise.

Next we have the equipment or qualification of the typical artificer for his work: "And I have filled him with the Spirit of God, in wisdom, and in understanding, and in knowledge, and in all manner of workmanship." This at once makes us think of Isa. 11:1-4, "And there shall come forth a rod out of the stem of Jesse, and a branch shall grow out of his roots: And the Spirit of the Lord shall rest upon Him, the Spirit of wisdom and understanding, the Spirit of counsel and might, the Spirit of knowledge and the fear of the Lord; and shall make Him of quick understanding in the fear of the Lord: and He shall not judge after the sight of His eyes, neither reprove after the hearing of His ears. But with righteousness shall He judge the poor, and reprove with equity for the meek of the earth."

"To work in gold." As it has been pointed out so frequently in previous articles, "gold" speaks of Divine glory, the Divine glory manifested. Ah, only one filled with "the Spirit of God, in wisdom and understanding and in knowledge" was competent to "work in gold." Now, it is in the Gospel of John that the antitype of this is most plainly seen. There, at the close of His public ministry, we find the Son saying to the Father, "I have *glorified* Thee on the earth: I have finished *the work* which Thou gavest Me to do." Details of that "work" are given in the verses that follow: "I have manifested Thy name" (v. 6), "I have given unto them the words which Thou gavest Me" (v. 8), "I have kept them in Thy name" (v. 12), etc.

"And in silver." This symbol has also been before us again and again. It speaks of *redemption*. And who was qualified to "work in silver?" None but He who came from the Father's bosom as the Son of Light. The work of redemption was a more stupendous and wondrous one than the work of creation. It was a work far beyond the power of those who were to be redeemed: "None of them can by any means redeem his brother nor give to God a ransom for him: for the redemption of their soul is precious" (Psa. 49:7, 8). Yes, the redemption of their soul *is* "precious," so precious that naught but the "the precious blood of Christ, as of a lamb without blemish and without spot" (1 Peter 1:19) could avail. The blessed outcome of His "work in silver" is seen in Rev. 5:9, "And they sung a new song, saying, Thou art worthy to take the book, and to open the seals thereof: for Thou was slain, and hast *redeemed* us to God by Thy blood out of *every* kindred, and tongue, and people, and nation."

"And in brass." This is ever the symbol of Divine *judgment*. Here, too, a Divinely-qualified workman was called for, for no mere creature as such was capable of enduring the entire weight of God's judgment upon the sins of His guilty people. Therefore, did God lay help upon One that is "Mighty" (Psa. 89:19). Unspeakably solemn is this aspect of our type. It tells of our blessed Redeemer being "made sin for us" (2 Cor. 5:21), which signifies that He became sacrificially what we were personally. It tells of Him being "made a curse for us" (Gal. 3:13), suffering the inflexible penalty of God's righteous law on our behalf, receiving the wages of sin in our stead. It tells of Him being "lifted up" as Moses lifted up the serpent of brass (John 3:14). The "work in brass" was completed when He cried "It is finished," bowed His head, and breathed forth His spirit (John 19:30).

"And in cutting of stones." The local reference is to the jewels which were to adorn the shoulders and breastplate of Israel's high priest, as he appeared before God on their behalf, jewels on which were engraved the names of all their twelve tribes. Thus, those gems spoke of the people of God, presented before Him in all the merits and excellency of that blessed One whom Aaron foreshadowed. The antitype of this is found in 1 Peter 2:5, "Ye also as living *stones,* are built up a spiritual house." The next words of Ex. 31, "and in carving of timber" look forward, we believe, to the Lord's future dealings with Israel. "To work in all manner of workmanship," which is repeated from v. 3, at once reminds us of that word in Eph. 2:10, "For we are His *workmanship,* created in Christ Jesus unto good works." How blessedly significant to observe that the work of this artificer is given (vv. 4, 5)—in *five* details—all is of Divine grace!

"And I, behold, I have given with him Aholiab, the son of Ahisamach, of the tribe of Dan: and in the hearts of all that are wise-hearted I have put wisdom, that they may make all that I have commanded thee" (v. 6). Many human characters were needed to foreshadow the varied and manifold perfections of the God-man. Creation demonstrates the Creator. Some things in creation manifest His mighty power, some His consummate wisdom, others His abiding faithfulness, still others His abundant mercy. Each and all are required to exhibit the different attributes of their Maker. In like manner, Abel, Noah, Moses, Aaron, David, are all types of Christ, each one pointing to some distinctive aspect of His person, offices, or work. Thus it is in our present type: Aholiab supplements Bezaleel.

"And I, behold, I have given with him Aholiab, the son of Ahisamach, of the tribe of Dan." The meanings of these names are also significant. Aholiab signifies "The Tent of the Father." In the light of John 1:14, "And the Word became flesh and dwelt (Greek, *tented*) among us, and we beheld His glory," the force of this name is clear. Just as of old Jehovah took up His abode in the tabernacle in the wilderness, so did He again find a Dwelling-place on this earth when the Son became incarnate: "God was in Christ reconciling the world unto Himself" (2 Cor. 5:19). The Lord Jesus walking among men was "God manifest in flesh" (1 Tim. 3:16). So perfect and complete was that manifestation He could say, "he that hath seen Me, hath seen the Father" (John 14:9).

Aholiab was the son of Ahisamach, and the latter name signifies "Brother of Support." As another has said, "Probably this name primarily refers to the fact that Aholiab was a fellow-helper to Bezaleel in the work of the tabernacle. But is it not worthy of remark that while we have in Aholiab the name *Father,* we have in the name Ahisamach, the word *Brother;* and may there not be in this a little prophetic hint of that truth contained in Heb. 2:9-11, in which we find the Lord Jesus raised from the suffering of death to a place of exaltation, where everything is put under His feet, and in which also it is declared that 'he (the Lord Jesus) who sanctifieth and they who are sanctified, are all of one, for which cause He is not ashamed to call them brethren.' He is the Dwelling-place of God, and He is the Brother of support to His brethren" (H. W. Soltau).

Aholiab was of the tribe of Dan. As Judah took the lead when Israel was on the march, so Dan brought up the rear. Thus, the spiritual principle here exemplified was that, in the two men appointed to be the chief artificers, all Israel were *represented.* So the Lord Jesus, in the glorious work which He accomplished, represented *all* God's people, the feeblest as well as the strongest. The name Dan signifies "Judge." "The tabernacle of God is a place for worship and *praise,* because therein is revealed God's great act of *judgment* upon sin in the sacrifice of the Lamb of God" (H.W.S.).

"That they may make all that I have commanded thee" (v. 6), words repeated in v. 11. Significant line in the typical picture is this. Every detail of their work was Divinely appointed beforehand. No room was there for the exercise of self-will; all was to be the working out of that which God had willed. Most blessed is it to behold the fulfilment of this in the Antitype. Very explicit are His words: "For I came down from heaven, not to do Mine own will, but the will of Him that sent Me" (John 6:38); "Therefore, doth My Father love Me, because I lay down My life, that I might take it again. No man taketh it from Me, but I lay it down of Myself. I have power to lay it down, and I have power to take it again. This *commandment* have I received from My Father" (John 10:17, 18).

There is no need for us to comment separately on each of the details mentioned in vv. 7-11 as they have all been before us in previous articles. It should be noted, though, that *fourteen* things are specified: (1) "The tabernacle of the congregation (the tent of meeting) ; (2) And the ark of the testimony; (3) and the mercy-seat that is thereupon; (4) and all the furniture of the tabernacle (the pillars, sockets, pins, etc.) ; (5) and the table, and his furniture," etc. In vv. 4, 5 a fivefold work was mentioned; in vv. 7 to 11 the making of fourteen articles is referred to. This tells us that the work of Christ was founded upon Divine grace, and that in the execution of it He displayed a perfect witness to the perfections of God.

Turning now to the *practical* teaching of our passage, it is at once evident that here we have most important instruction upon the subject of Divine *service*: note how the "See !" (v. 2) and "Behold !" (v. 6) direct attention to the weightiness of what follows. The first thing is God's *selection* of His servants. Bezaleel and Aholiab did not presume to intrude into this holy office of themselves, nor were they appointed by Moses, or by a committee made up of the leading Levites; instead, they were "called" by God (v. 2). "This principle runs through all dispensations. The apostle adduces it when speaking of the priesthood of Christ. He says, 'So also Christ glorified not Himself to be made an high priest; but He that said unto Him, Thou art My Son, to-day have I begotten Thee. As He saith also in another place, Thou art a priest forever after the order of Malchizedek' (Heb. 5: 5, 6). In like manner he speaks of himself as an 'apostle by the will of God' (1 Cor. 1:1; 2 Cor. 1:1, etc.)" (Mr. Dennett).

This lies at the foundation of all true service. Those who run without being sent, those who undertake work (though in the name of the Lord) without being called to it by God, are *rebels*, not "servants." Yet how many there are in these days—days which are characterised by self-will and lawlessness—occupying prominent positions in Christendom, yet who have never been called of God. Many, attracted by the prestige and honour of the position, others because it is an easy way of making a living, have thrust themselves into an holy office. Many, influenced by men with more zeal than knowledge, or advised by admiring friends or doting mothers, have been pressed into service for which they had no call from Heaven. Fearful presumption and sin is it for any man to profess to speak in the name of Christ if he has received no call from Him.

The second principle of service which receives both illustration and exemplification in our present passage is God's

equipment of His servants. It is by this that God's people may identify *His* sent servants, and in this way that an exercised heart may ascertain whether or no a call to service has been received from the Lord. God never calls a man to any work without fitting him for it. If God calls one to be an evangelist, He will fill his heart with compassion for the lost, and so burden him with a sense of the doom awaiting the wicked, that he will cry "Woe is me, if I preach not the Gospel." If God calls a man to be a pastor, He will bestow upon him the necessary gifts; if to be a missionary, He will endow him with a special aptitude for learning a foreign language; and so on.

What is still more to the point, and so essential for us to note is that, when God calls a man to be His servant, He fills him with "the Spirit of God, in wisdom, and in understanding, and in knowledge" (v. 3). For other examples of this, see 1 Kings 7:13, 14; Luke 1:5; Acts 10:38; 2:4; 6:3. Vastly different is this from the expedients and substitutes of men. Colleges, universities, theological seminaries, Bible-training schools do not and cannot impart these spiritual gifts. God alone can bestow them. And where He *has* done so, then all the schools of men are needless. The servant who has been endowed with power and wisdom from on High is entirely independent of men. Human wisdom is of no avail in the service of God. This is all very humbling to the flesh, but it is God's way, for He is a jealous God, and will not share His glory with another.

The third important principle in connection with service to be noted in our passage is God's *appointment* of the servant's work: "that they may make all that I have commanded them" (vv. 6, 11). The very essence of all real service lies in obedience, obedience to the will of our master. So it is in connection with Divine service. Listen again to the words of the perfect Servant, "I came down from Heaven, not to do Mine own will, but the will of Him that sent Me" (John 6:38). Bezaleel and Aholiab were not left free to pick and choose what they should do or not do; all was ordered for them. Thus it is with the Lord's servants to-day: the Word sets forth his marching-orders— what he should preach, what he should do, how he should do it.

A very simple but searching principle is this. As another has said, "The Word is both the guide of the servant and the test of his service—the proof of its being done with divine wisdom and according to the divine mind." God's work must be done in God's way, or we cannot count upon *His* blessing thereon. He has promised, "them that honour Me, I will honour," and the only way to honour God is to keep His precepts diligently, to preach nothing but His Word, to employ no methods save those expressly sanctioned by Holy Writ. Anything other than this is self-will, and that is *sin*. O what need is there for pondering the basic principles of service as made known in Exodus 31!

Finally, we may observe here the Divine *sovereignty* exercised in the selection of the servants called. One was from the tribe of Judah, the other from the tribe of Dan. This is the more striking in the light of the history of those tribes. The former was the one from which Christ, according to the flesh, came; the other is the tribe from which, most probably, the Antichrist shall arise (Gen. 49:17). At any rate, Dan was the tribe that took the lead in apostasy. "Such a selection speaks of divine sovereignty. God has taken pains to show by many examples that He acts for Himself, and that He does not find His motive in the character, conduct, or genealogy of those whom He blesses. It is a comfort to see that a man from Dan comes in as well as from Judah. It shows the principle on which *all* really comes in; that is, as 'vessels of mercy'" (C. A. Coates).

Dan was the very last tribe from which the natural understanding would expect to find a man selected to be one of the principal artificers of the tabernacle. Yes, and fishermen and publicans are the last classes among whom one would look for the apostles of the Lamb! Ah, God's thoughts and ways are ever different from man's. The one chosen to deliver Egypt from an unparalleled famine-crisis, was called from the dungeon. He who was to lead Israel's hosts across the desert was called from the back-side of the wilderness. The man after God's own heart who was to sit on Israel's throne, was taken from the sheepcote.

It is not without reason that Christians are enjoined to "condescend of men of low estate," for *that* is God's way. It is still His way. "That which is highly esteemed among men is abomination in the sight of God" (Luke 16:15). And, conversely, those who are rated lowest by the world are often the ones through whom God performs His greatest wonders. "For God hath chosen the foolish things of the world to confound the wise; and God hath chosen the weak things of the world to confound the things which are mighty; And base things of the world, and things which are despised, hath God chosen, and things which are not, to bring to naught things that are" (1 Cor. 1:27, 28). Why? "That no flesh should glory in His presence." May the Lord bless His own truth to His poor and needy people.

CHAPTER 58

THE SABBATH AND ISRAEL

EXODUS 31:13-18

As was pointed out at the commencement of our last article, the contents of Ex. 31 fall under three clearly-defined divisions. First, the provision made by Jehovah for the carrying out of the instructions which He had given to Moses concerning the making of the tabernacle. This, as we have seen, was His calling and equipping of the principal artificers and the appointing of their work. Second, the mention, once more, of God's holy Sabbath, and the defining of its special relation to Israel. Third, a brief word in v. 18 of the actual giving to Moses of the tables of testimony, on which were inscribed the ten commandments. It is the last two divisions we are about to consider; may the Spirit of God graciously preserve us from all error and guide us into all truth.

"And the Lord spake unto Moses, saying, Speak thou also unto the children of Israel, saying, Verily My sabbaths ye shall keep: for it is a sign between Me and you throughout your generations; that ye may know that I am the Lord that doth sanctify you. Ye shall keep the sabbath therefore for it is holy unto you: every one that defileth it shall surely be put to death: for whosoever doeth any work therein, that soul shall be cut off from among his people. Six days may work be done; but in the seventh is the sabbath of rest, holy to the Lord: whosoever doeth any work in the sabbath day, he shall surely be put to death. Wherefore the children of Israel shall keep the sabbath, to observe the sabbath throughout their generations, for a perpetual covenant. It is a sign between Me and the children of Israel forever: for in six days the Lord made heaven and earth, and on the seventh day He rested, and was refreshed" (vv. 12-17). In pondering what is here said concerning the Sabbath we propose to look first at its typical significance, then at its dispensational bearings, and lastly at the judicial aspects of our passage.

It may strike the thoughtful reader as strange that any reference should be made here to the Sabbath: coming right after the description of the tabernacle, its furniture, its priesthood and its artificers; the more so, as full mention of it had already been made in Ex. 20:8-11. There are no mere repetitions in Holy Writ, and though a thing may be mentioned more than once, or the same command or ordinance be given again and again, yet it is always with another end in view, or for the purpose of enforcing a different design, or with the object of bringing in fuller details. Generally the Spirit's purpose may be discerned by taking note of the *connection* in which each statement occurs.

The first time the Sabbath is mentioned in Exodus is in 16:23-29, from which it should be quite apparent that this holy day unto the Lord was no new appointment at that time: the words of v. 28 (occasioned by Israel's desecration of the Sabbath, see v. 27) are too plain to be misunderstood: "And the Lord said unto Moses, How long refuse ye to keep My commandments and My laws?" Thus, the initial reference to the Sabbath in Exodus contains the Lord's expostulation with His people for having disregarded His commandments—referring no doubt to the evil way in which they had, for centuries, conducted themselves in Egypt: see Ezek. 20:5-9.

The second time the Sabbath is found in Exodus is in chapter 20, where we have the ten commandments given to Israel orally. They were given to Israel as a redeemed people, which the Lord had brought "out of the house of bondage." They expressed the rights of God, His claims upon His people, that which He righteously required from them. Those commandments were not a yoke grievous to be borne, but the making known of a path in which love was to walk. In them God promised to show mercy unto thousands (*not* "millions") of them that love Me and keep My commandments" (v. 6). God's commandments are just as truly the expressions of His love as are His pro-

310

mises, and a heart that loves Him in return should rejoice in the one as much as in the other. God's commandments express both His authority over and His solicitude for His people. It is in that light this second mention of the Sabbath in Exodus is to be viewed.

The third reference in Exodus to the Sabbath is found in chapter 31, a section of the book where everything speaks loudly of Christ. Unless this be carefully noted the meaning of our present passage will be missed. It should be evident at once that the *typical* significance of the Sabbath is the first thing to be looked at here. True, that by no means exhausts the scope and value of these verses, yet it does supply the key which unlocks for us their primary meaning. Here, again, we have another example of a principle which holds good of every part of the Word, namely, if we ignore the *context* we are sure to err in our interpretation.

Now in seeking to discover the typical meaning of the Sabbath we cannot do better than turn back to the first mention of it in Scripture: "And on the seventh day God ended His work which He had made; and He rested on the seventh day from all His work which He had made. And God blessed the seventh day, and sanctified it: because that in it He had rested from all His work which God created and made" (Gen. 2:2, 3). It will be observed that three actions of God in connection with the Sabbath are here mentioned: He ended His work which He had made and "rested on the seventh day," He "blessed the seventh day," He "sanctified" it. We believe the order in which these three things are mentioned is the order of spiritual importance—confirmed by the first thing mentioned being repeated.

In order to apprehend aright the spiritual import of the Sabbath, it is most necessary to observe that the first thing of all connected with it is *the rest of God*. The fact that God rested on the seventh day is undoubtedly recorded for the purpose of teaching that the Creator graciously condescended to set an example before His creatures of how to spend and enjoy the Sabbath; yet that there is also a deeper meaning to this statement will scarcely be denied. Nor do we think that the reference is solely to the Creator's delight and satisfaction in the works which He had made during the six days preceding; rather would it appear (from subsequent scriptures) that this "rest" was *anticipatory*—spiritually, of that rest which the Christian enjoys now; dispensationally, of the millennial Sabbath; typically, of the eternal Sabbath.

Now in the light of what is before us in the first eleven verses of Ex. 31, is there any difficulty in discovering the perfect propriety of a reference to *the Sabbath* in what immediately follows? What else *could* have been more appropriate? In the first part of the chapter we have a most lovely foreshadowing of Him who had ever dwelt in the bosom of the Father, the Son of Light, voluntarily undertaking to "work in gold, silver, brass, and of precious stones." The stupendous work therein typified having been gloriously completed, we have at once mentioned that which speaks of the rest of God. How suitable, how blessed the connection! As cause stands to effect, so is the relation between the labours of the tabernacle-artificers and the mention here of the Sabbath. The rest of God is the consequence of the finished Work of Christ: first, that in which God Himself finds complacency; second, that into which His redeemed are brought.

The wicked are like the troubled sea which cannot rest (Isa. 57:20). And why? Because they are away from God. Away from God, they are seeking satisfaction in that which cannot provide it. Theirs is a ceaseless quest after that which will give peace and joy. But over all the varied cisterns to which they have recourse, is written these words, "Whosoever drinketh of this water shall thirst again" (John 4:13). "There is *no* peace, saith my God, unto the wicked" (Isa. 57:21), for they are strangers to the Prince of peace. It is not until the Spirit of God has shown us that all under the sun is but "vanity and vexation of spirit," has convicted us of our sinful and lost condition, has shown us our desperate need of the Saviour, and drawn us to Him, that we hear the Lord Jesus saying, "Come unto Me, all ye that labour and are heavy laden, and I will give you rest." Then it becomes true that, "we which have believed *do* enter into rest" (Heb. 4:3).

"Verily My sabbaths ye shall keep: for it is a sign between Me and you throughout your generations; that ye may know that I am the Lord that doth *sanctify* you. Ye shall keep My Sabbaths *therefore,* for it is holy unto you" (vv. 13, 14). Surely the meaning of this is too plain for us to miss. The Sabbath was now, for the first time, appointed as a "sign" between Jehovah and Israel that they were His "sanctified" people—a people set apart unto Himself. So, also, that of which the Sabbath spoke—the rest of God—was also the portion of a sanctified people, a people "chosen in Christ before the foundation of the world" (Eph. 1:4). This people was sanctified by God the Father before they were called (Jude 1), even from all eternity. They were sanctified by God the Son "with His own blood" (Heb. 13: 12). They are sanctified by God the Spirit (2 Thess. 2:13) when they are quickened into newness of life, and thus separated from those who are dead in sins. And the "sign" between God and His sanctified people is still the "Sabbath," i.e., the fact that they have entered into *rest*.

Turning back from the antitype to the type, we can see at once why the Sabbath should be the appointed "sign" between Jehovah and Israel. At the time He entered into covenant relation with them, all other nations had been given up by God (Rom. 1:19-26). Not liking to retain Him in their knowledge, they gave themselves unto idolatry. For this cause God gave them up to a reprobate mind. The heathen nations, therefore, kept no Sabbath, and, in all probability, by that time knew not that the Creator required them to. But to Israel God made known His laws, and the appointed sign or token that they were His peculiar people was their observance of the Sabbath. So that of which, spiritually, the Sabbath speaks, is still the portion of none but God's chosen people.

Dispensationally, the *rest* to which the Sabbath pointed, was the Millennial era, the seventh of earth's great "days." In view of the inspired declaration, "But, beloved, be not ignorant of this one thing, that one day is with the Lord as a thousand years, and a thousand years as one day" (2 Peter 3:8) we believe, with many others, that the "six days" of Gen. 1 give us a prophetic forecast of the world's history, and that the "seventh day" of Gen. 2:2, 3 points to the final dispensation. This is confirmed by Rev. 20 where, again and again, the reign of Christ and His saints over this earth is said to be of a "thousand years" duration. The Millennium will be the earth's great Sabbath. Then shall this scene which has witnessed six thousand years of strife, turmoil, bloodshed, enjoy an unprecedented era of rest. The Prince of peace shall be here; Satan shall be in the bottomless pit; war shall be made to cease to "the end of the earth" (Psa. 4:6:9); the curse which now rests upon the lower orders of creation shall be lifted (Isa. 11: 6-9).

But not only did the original Sabbath of Gen. 2:2, 3 anticipate the spiritual rest which is, even now, the portion of God's people; not only did it forecast the millennial peace which this earth will yet enjoy; but it also typified an eternal Sabbath, into which nothing shall ever enter to disturb and mar its perfect tranquility and bliss. *This* is what the Work of Christ (adumbrated in Ex. 31:1-11) has secured, and toward which all things are moving. When the present heaven and earth shall have passed away, and a new heaven and earth shall have come into existence, then shall be fulfilled that precious word of Rev. 21: 3-5, "And I heard a great voice out of heaven saying, Behold, the tabernacle of God is with men, and He will dwell with them, and they shall be His people, and God Himself shall be with them, and be their God. And God shall wipe away all tears from their eyes; and there shall be no more death, neither sorrow nor crying, neither shall there be any more pain, for the former things are passed away. And He that sat upon the throne said, Behold, I make all things new."

A beautiful foreshadowing of this is to be found in Zeph. 3:17, "The Lord thy God in the midst of thee is mighty; He will save, He will rejoice over thee with joy; He will rest in His love, He will joy over thee with singing." The immediate reference is to the restoration of Israel to God's favour, to their land, and to the fulfilment of His purpose and promises concerning them. But the ultimate reference, we believe, is to that which shall characterise the Eternal State. Then, in the midst of His redeemed, and as the fruit of His Son's perfect work, God Himself shall rejoice over His people with joy and *"rest* in His love."

Once more we pause to admire the striking and lovely *order* in which God's truth is presented before us. In the first part of Ex. 31 we behold the Divine provision made for giving effect to all that was in the will of God; therefore, in the very next section, that which speaks of Divine rest, is brought before us. In keeping with this it is most blessed to take note of one word which is found here, and nowhere else: "In six days the Lord made heaven and earth, and on the seventh day He rested, *and was refreshed"* (Ex. 31:17). The fact that these words are found not in Gen. 2: 2, 3, or Ex. 20:8-11, but here, right after what is typically in view in 31:1-11, tells, unmistakably, of that refreshment, that joy, that resting in His love, which shall be the eternal portion of God—Father, Son, and Holy Spirit. What is here in view is that rest of God which is the consequence of the bringing into effect, the actual realisation, of the whole will of God as set forth in the tabernacle. When "the tabernacle *of God* is with men" (Rev. 21:3), then shall there be an holy, unbreakable, eternal rest. God will rest in His love, and His sanctified people will rest with Him.

"I think it is in the light of the tabernacle system, and of its taking form for the pleasure of God, that He adds the words, 'And was refreshed.' God was refreshed because even in the material creation He was forming a sphere where all His own blessed thoughts of grace and glory in Christ could be worked out. Those thoughts first came to light in a definite, though figurative, form in the tabernacle, and in the light of them all being brought into effect God could, as it were, carry back into Gen. 2 a secret not revealed. When God made the heavens and the earth He had 'the holy universal order' of the tabernacle in His mind. He was making a material universe, and this in itself could not afford Him refreshment. But He was making it so that it might be the scene for the introduction of 'the holy order of the tabernacle,' which represented the vast scene in which God's glory is displayed in Christ, and in view of the introduction of this He was 'refreshed'! The Sabbath speaks of things being brought to completion, so that there is no more work to be done; all is finished, and there is holy rest for God and His people" (C. A. Coates).

Having pondered the typical significance of the Sabbath's being mentioned in Ex. 31, having sought to point out its dispensational application, it now remains for us to consider the judicial aspect of our passage. This is brought before us in vv. 14, 15, "Ye shall keep the Sabbath therefore; for it holy unto you: every one that defileth it shall surely be put to death: for whosoever doeth any work therein, that soul shall be cut off from among his people. Six days may work be done; but in the seventh is the Sabbath of rest, holy to the Lord: whosoever doeth any work in the Sabbath day, he shall surely be put to death." A solemn example of this threat is recorded in Num. 15:32-36, "And while the children of Israel were in the wilderness they found a man that gathered sticks upon the Sabbath day. And they that found him gathering sticks brought him unto Moses and Aaron, and unto all the congregation. And they put him in ward, because it was not declared what should be done to him. And the Lord said unto Moses, "The man shall surely be put to death: all the congregation shall stone him with stones without the camp. And all the congregation brought him without the camp, and stoned him with stones, and he died."

It seems strange that so many have experienced a difficulty with the above passages. The key to them is surely found in noting the character and design of the Mosaic economy. *That* Dispensation was a legal and a probationary one. It was preparatory to the fuller and final revelation which God made of Himself in and through Christ. It is a mistake to look upon it as a stern regime of unmixed law. True, it was marked at the beginning by the proclamation of the Ten Commandments, but it should not be forgotten that this was immediately followed by the revelation concerning the Tabernacle and the institution of the priesthood, and (see the book of Leviticus) by the Divine appointment of a series of offerings and sacrifices, wherein provision was made for God's people to approach unto Him through their representatives. Though all of this was a typical foreshadowing of that which was to be made good and secured by and through the person and work of Christ, yet it should not be forgotten that it was also a most gracious provision of God for His people at that time.

On the other hand, there was not, and, in the nature of the case, could not be, a full and perfect revelation of the *grace* of God during the Mosaic economy. Law is law, and righteousness requires the strict enforcing of its terms and penalties. Mercy might, and did, make provision for "sins of ignorance" (Lev. 4:2-4; Num. 15:27, 28), and for the unavoidable contact with that which defiled (Num. 19:11-19); but for pre-meditated or deliberate transgressions no sacrifice was available—"he that *despised* Moses' law died without mercy" (Heb. 10:28). A notable case in point which illustrates this distinction is to be found in connection with the requirement of the Mosaic law when a man had been slain. We refer to the "cities of refuge": let the reader carefully consult Num. 35:9-24. If any person had been killed "unawares" (vv. 11, 15)—that is, without "malice aforethought"—then he might find an asylum in one of those cities; but if that person had been deliberately slain, then the word was, "the murderer shall surely be put to death" (vv. 16:17).

What has just been said explains a reference in Psalm 51, which, though very familiar, is understood by but few. That Psalm records the deep penitence of David. He was guilty of murder, the murder of Uriah. In v. 16 he says, "For Thou desirest not sacrifice; else would I give it: Thou delightest not in burnt offering." No "sacrifice" was *available* for murder! What, then, could poor David do? This: cast himself on the "mercy" of God (v. 1), acknowledge his transgression (v. 3), and cry for deliverance from "blood-guiltiness" (v. 14). That his cry was heard, we all know, and the very hearing of it testified to the blessed truth that "mercy rejoiceth against judgment" (James 2:13).

What has just been pointed out should

greatly modify the prevailing conception of the harshness of the Mosaic dispensation. True, the Law, as such, showed no mercy; but side by side with the Law was the Levitical sacrifices, and over and above these was the mercy of God, available for those who sought it out of a broken heart. Thus, unless we keep both of these facts in mind, and learn to distinguish between things that differ, confusion of thought and conception must necessarily ensue.

"Whosoever doeth any work on the Sabbath day, he shall surely be put to death." This was the exaction of Law as such, the righteous enforcement of its penalty. Nor was this peculiar to the fourth commandment; it obtained equally with the other nine. The following passages may serve as illustrations and proofs, "And he that smiteth his father, or his mother, shall surely be put to death" (Ex. 21:15) ; "And the man that committeth adultery with another man's wife, even he that committeth adultery with his neighbour's wife, the adulterer and the adulteress shall surely be put to death" (Lev. 20:10) ; "And he that blasphemeth the name of the Lord, he shall

surely be put to death" (Lev. 24:16) ; see also Deut. 13:6-10, etc.

Our chapter closes with the mention of God's giving the tables of testimony unto Moses: "And He gave unto Moses, when He had made an end of communing with him upon Mount Sinai, two tables of testimony, tables of stone, written with the finger of God" (v. 18). This completes the section of the book of Exodus begun at 24:18. For forty days Moses had been in the mount receiving instructions from Jehovah. That those instructions closed with the giving of these two tables of stone is most significant. Coming here after the appointing of the tabernacle-artificers and the mention of the Sabbath it announces, typically, that the rights and claims of God have been made good and eternally secured by and through the person and work of the Lord Jesus. Grace now "reigns," but "through righteousness" (Rom. 5:21). That there is also a close connection between Ex. 31:18 and what follows will, D.V., be shown in our next article.

CHAPTER 59

THE GOLDEN CALF

EXODUS 32:1-10

Our present portion, which runs on to the end of chapter 34, commences a new and distinct section of Exodus, a section which, in one sense, is parenthetical in its character and contents. This will at once appear if Ex. 32 to 34 be omitted and chapter 35 be read right after chapter 31. In Ex. 24 to 31 inclusive we have recorded the communications which Moses received from Jehovah while he was with Him in the mount, instructions which concerned the making of the tabernacle and the institution of the priesthood. In chapter 35 Moses makes known to the people the revelations which he had received from the Lord, and forthwith the making of the holy vessels and the house for them is proceeded with. But in chapters 32 to 34 the flow of the tabernacle theme is interrupted, and a very different subject is brought before us. Here we are given to see what transpired among the Congregation while Moses was in the mount. Here we behold the awful sin of Aaron and the people during the interval of their leader's absence, with the fearful consequences which it entailed.

A more frightful contrast than that which is presented in these two sections in the book of Exodus is scarcely possible to imagine. In the former we are permitted to witness the condescending grace of Jehovah as He spoke with Moses; in the latter we are called upon to gaze at that which exhibited the awful depravity of fallen man. In the one we are occupied with that which unveils to us the manifold glories of Christ; in the other we have exposed the awful abominations which Satan produces. First we are shown the provisions which God made for His people to worship Him, according to His own holy appointments; then we witness the idolatrous manufacture of a golden calf, and the children of Israel bowing down before it in worship. Verily, truth *is* stranger than fiction. "God hath made man upright," *but* they have sought out many inventions (Eccl. 7 : 29), inventions which only serve to make manifest the exceeding sinfulness of sin and the fearful depths of depravity into which fallen man has descended.

Above, we have stated that Ex. 32 to 34

forms a parenthetical section of the book, inasmuch as the contents of these chapters break in upon the narrative concerning the tabernacle. But looked at from another standpoint they contain the historical sequel to what is recorded in Ex. 19. There we see the children of Israel, in the third month after their going forth out of Egypt, encamped before Sinai. They were bidden to sanctify themselves, wash their clothes, and come not at their wives, and then on the third day, the Lord came down "in the sight of all the people upon Mount Sinai." Most awe-inspiring was the Divine manifestation: "There were thunders and lightnings, and a thick cloud upon the mount, and the voice of the trumpet exceeding loud; so that all the people in the camp trembled. . . And Mount Sinai was altogether on a smoke, because the Lord descended upon it in fire: and the smoke thereof ascended as the smoke of a furnace, and the whole mount quaked greatly " (19 : 16, 18).

Moses was then called up into the mount, where he received the laws enumerated in Ex. 20-23. Then, in 24 : 3 we read, " And Moses came and told the people all the words of the Lord, and all the judgments: and all the people answered with one voice, and said, All the words which the Lord hath said will we do." This vow of the people was most solemnly ratified: Moses wrote all the words of the Lord in a book, " And he took the book of the covenant and read it in the audience of the people: and they said, All that the Lord hath said will we do, and be obedient. And Moses took the blood and sprinkled it on the people, and said, Behold the blood of the covenant, which the Lord hath made with you concerning all these words (24 : 7, 8).

Following this, we are told, " And the Lord said unto Moses, Come up to Me into the mount, and be there. . . . And Moses rose up, and his minister Joshua: and Moses went up into the mount of God. And he said unto the elders, Tarry ye here for us, until we come again unto you : and, behold Aaron and Hur are with you : if any man have any matters to do, let him come unto them. . . . And Moses went into the midst of the cloud, and gat him up into the mount : and Moses was in the mount forty days and forty nights " (24 : 12-14, 18). It was while Moses was on the mount on this occasion that he received the Divine communications recorded in chapters 25 to 31. And what of the people during the interval ? How were they conducting themselves during this most solemn period ? Our present portion contains the answer ; to it we are now ready to turn.

"And when the people saw that Moses delayed to come down out of the mount, the people gathered themselves together unto Aaron, and said unto him, Up, make us gods, which shall go before us ; for this Moses, the man that brought us up out of the land of Egypt, we wot not what is become of him " (v. 1). The key to this incident is found in part of Stephen's address, recorded in Acts 7 : " This is He that was in the church in the wilderness . . . to whom our fathers would not obey, but *thrust from them,* and in their hearts turned back again into Egypt, saying unto Aaron, Make us gods to go before us " (vv. 38-40). It was not that they were peeved at the lengthy absence of Moses, but that they had cast off their allegiance to Jehovah, their hearts had departed from Him.

What we have said above is confirmed by Israel's reference to Moses on this occasion as " the man that brought us up out of the land of Egypt." Instead of owning their Divine Deliverer, their vision was narrowed to the human instrument which had been employed. It is ever thus with a people whose hearts are divorced from God. Compare the words of apostate Israel at a later date : " Then the men of Israel said unto Gideon, Rule thou over us, both thou, and thy son, and thy son's son also : for *thou* hast delivered us from the hand of Midian " (Judges 8 : 22). Here in Ex. 32 the human instrument was contemptuously referred to as " this Moses," so little did they appreciate his unwearied service and prayers on their behalf.

It is not without reason that our present portion is immediately preceded by these words : " And He gave unto Moses, when He had made an end of communing with him upon Mount Sinai, two tables of testimony, tables of stone, written with the finger of God " (31 : 18). On those tables of stone were written the ten commandments, the first of which was, " Thou shalt have no other gods before Me." And the second, ,, Thou shalt not make unto thee any graven image " (20 : 3, 4,). It is the deliberate, public and united disobedience of these commandments which our lesson records. Man must have an object, and when he turns from the true God, he at once craves a false one.

What we have here has been perpetuated in every generation ; nor has Christendom proved any exception to the rule. As another has said, " Alas ! alas ! it has ever been thus in man's history. The human heart lusts after something that can be seen ; it loves that which meets and gratifies the senses. It is only faith that can 'endure as seeing Him who is invisible.' Hence, in every age, men have been forward to set up and lean upon human imitations of Divine realities. Thus it is we see the counterfeits of corrupt religion multiplied before our eyes. Those things which we know, upon the authority of God's Word, to be Divine and heavenly realities, the professing Church has transformed into human and earthly inventions. Having become weary of hanging upon an invisible arm, of trusting in an invisible sacrifice, of having recourse to an invisible Priest, of committing herself to an invisible Head, she has set about 'making' these things ; and thus from age to age, she has been busily at work, with ' graving tool ' in hand, graving and fashioning one thing after another, until we can at length recognize as little similarity between much that we *see* around us, and what we *read* in the Word, as between a ' molten calf ' and the God of Israel " (C.H.M.)

Israel had served false gods in Egypt (Joshua 24 : 14), and the flesh in them was still unchanged. It is true that Israel as a nation were only typically redeemed—the vast majority of them being children in whom was *no* faith (Deut. 32 : 20)—yet we must never forget when reading their history that, " These things were our examples, to the intent we should not lust after evil things, as they also lusted " (1 Cor. 10 : 6). Yea, does not the apostle at once follow this with, " Neither be ye idolators as were some of them " (v. 7). And again he says, " Wherefore, my dearly beloved, flee from idolatry " (v. 14). So, too, John, whose Epistle is addressed to those to whom he could say, " truly our fellowship is with the Father, and with His Son Jesus Christ," closes with the exhortation, " Little children, keep yourselves from idols." May God grant us hearts to heed these solemn and needed warnings. There is but one safeguard and preventative, and that is, being constantly occupied with Christ.

What has just been before us is of such immense practical importance that ere passing on we feel we must add a further word. The typical picture is unmistakably plain in its present-day application to God's people. Moses was away from Israel, up in the mount ; so Christ is away from the earth, on High before God. But before He went away, He said to His disciples, " Ye believe in God, believe also in Me " (John 14 : 1). *He* is the Object of faith, and it is only as our affections are set upon Him, as we are in daily communion with Him, that our hearts are kept from idols. But just as surely as Israel's turning away from Jehovah was at once followed by the making of the golden calf, just as surely as (in the history of the corporate Christian profession) the leaving of first love (Rev. 2 : 4) was followed by the setting up of the " synagogue of Satan " (Rev. 2 : 9), so now, the estranging of the heart from Christ opens the door for all sorts of abominable idolatries.

" And Aaron said unto them, Break off the golden earrings, which are in the ears of your wives, of your sons, and of your daughters, and bring unto me " (v. 2). As Ex. 24 : 18 informs us, Moses was absent from Israel for forty days, a number which, in Scripture, is almost always connected with *probation*. It hardly needs to be said that such a length of time was not needed by God : had He so pleased He could within the space of a few hours (or even in a moment) have told Moses all that is recorded in Ex. 25 to 31 and made him understand it. Why, then, those forty days ? For the testing of Israel—to make manifest whether or no they would patiently wait for the ordinances they had promised to observe. But so far from keeping their solemn vows, they would not even wait to hear what God said.

Aaron, with Hur, was left to adjudicate upon any question that might arise while Moses and his minister, Joshua, was away (24 : 14). Aaron is now put to the test. It was the first time he had been left in charge of the Congregation, and wretchedly did he acquit himself. Instead of putting his trust in the Lord, the fear of man brought him a snare. Instead of boldly withstanding the people, he, apparently without any struggle, yielded to their evil designs. Alas, it but supplies another tragic illustration of the fact that when responsibility is committed to man, he betrays his trust. Thus it has been in the history of Christendom : instead of the leaders refusing to follow the worldly wishes of their people, they have heeded, and oftentimes encouraged them.

" And all the people brake off the golden earrings which were in their ears, and brought them unto Aaron. And he received them at their hand, and fashioned it with a graving tool, after he had made it a molten calf : and they said, These be thy gods, O Israel which brought thee up out of the land of Egypt " (vv. 3, 4). Another has pointed out an analogy between what we have here and that which is recorded in Matt. 17 : 1-18. " There is a striking resemblance, in one aspect, between this scene and that witnessed at the foot of the mount of transfiguration. In both alike Satan holds full sway. In the one before us, it is the nation who have fallen under his power, in the other it is the child whom he has possessed ; but the child again is a type of the Jewish nation of a later day. The absence of Christ on high (shown in figure also by Moses on Sinai) is the oppor-

tunity seized by Satan—under God's commission—for the display of his wicked power, and man (Israel) in the evil of his heart becomes his wretched slave." (Ed. Dennett.)

The calf, or ox, was the principal Egyptian god—" Apis "—with which they had been familiar in the land of bondage. " These be thy gods " is expounded in Neh. 9 : 18 as meaning, " This is thy god." The inspired comment of the Psalmist is very solemn, " They made a calf in Horeb, and worshipped the molten image. They changed their Glory into the similitude of an ox that eateth grass. They forgat God their Saviour, which had done great things in Egypt " (106 : 19-21). The making of that idol and the rendering worship to it was an act of open apostasy, the bitter harvest from which continued to be reaped until they were carried into Babylon (Acts 7 : 43). Such is the flesh : ever ready to forget God's deliverances, despise the light He has given us, disobey His commands, act in self-will, and bring in that which effectually shuts Him out.

" And when Aaron saw it, he built an altar before it " (v. 5). Still darker become the clouds which hang over this awful scene. Not content with substituting a false god for the true One, they must, perforce, cover up their wickedness under the cloak of religion. An " altar " is now erected. Thus it has always been, and still is : man ever seeks to hide the shame of his idolatry by putting over it the name of Deity. Therefore the next thing that we read here is that, " Aaron made proclamation, and said, To-morrow is a feast to the Lord " (v. 5). As a fact, this was a pretence, for there were no " feasts " in either the third or fourth months. (See Lev. 23.)

What is before us in this 5th verse but gives the prototype of what is now going on almost everywhere in Christendom. Men have set up their idols and then sought to dignify and sanctify their inventions by worshipping them in the name of Christ. Romanism and Ritualism give us one form of it. Wordliness and fleshly indulgencies another. Just as Aaron proclaimed the honours paid to the calf and the carnal merriment that followed as " a feast unto the Lord," so many a " church supper," bazaar, religious carnival, whist drive, &c., is officially carried out under the name of Christianity. What a mockery it all is ! Aaron had no Scripture to justify his proclamation, nor have the present-day leaders any word from God to warrant their doings.

" And they rose up early on the morrow, and offered burnt offerings and brought peace offerings " (v. 6). Terrible travesty was this. Those offerings which spoke of the devotedness of Christ unto the Father, and the fellowship which He has made possible between a holy God and His people, were now presented to this fetish of their own corrupt imaginations. It is significant to mark the absence of any *sin* offering ! But that had no place in their thoughts. How could it ? When there is departure from God, the conscience becomes calloused : " The way of the wicked is as darkness, they know not at what they stumble " (Prov. 4: 19). That is why the unscriptural and Christ-dishonouring performances in the churches occasion no uneasiness to those engaged in them.

" And the people set down to eat and to drink, and rose up to play " (v. 6). Having formally presented their offerings, they now felt free to indulge the lusts of the flesh. And, be it remembered, what we have here is something more than the inspired record of an incident which happened long ago. God's Word is a *living* Word, describing things as they actually are. It was in the " early " hours that the burnt and peace offerings were presented. So the early morning mass or " communion " remains popular, and is still followed by the offerers spending the remainder of the day eating, drinking, and playing : " As in water face answereth to face, so the heart of man to man " (Prov. 27 : 19) !

" And the Lord said unto Moses, Go, get thee down ; for thy people which thou broughtest out of the land of Egypt have corrupted themselves " (v. 7). These words of the Lord must be read in the light of what is recorded in Ex. 24 : 6-8. There we read of a " covenant " which the Lord made with Israel on the ground of His law and their avowal to keep it. It was a purely legal compact between the two contracting parties. Israel had now broken their agreement : they had disowned their Deliverer (32 : 1), they had broken His law (32 : 6) Therefore the Lord now, in view of the broken covenant, disowns them : He speaks of them to Moses as " *thy* people."

" They have turned aside quickly out of the way which I commanded them : they have made them a molten calf, and have worshipped it, and have sacrificed thereunto, and said, These be thy gods, O Israel, which have brought thee up out of the land of Egypt " (v. 8). Alas *how* " quickly " had they departed from the path of obedience and loyalty ! Less than five months before they had declared, " The Lord is my strength and song, and He is become my salvation : He is my God, and I will prepare Him an habitation : my father's God, and I will exalt Him " (15 : 2). Instead of so doing, they had raised up that which effectively shut Him out, and instead of exalting Him they had debased themselves. It is solemn to note the Lord here quotes to Moses the identical language the people had used with Aaron : though engaged in " communing " with His servant, He had heard the very

words of His wayward people down below. And He still hears and records all our words !

" They have turned aside quickly out of the way which I commanded them." It has been thus all through the piece. How " quickly " Adam " turned aside " from the way of his Creator's command ! How " quickly " Noah failed after he came out from the Ark ! How " quickly " Nadab and Abihu did that which the Lord " commanded them not " (Lev. 10 : 1) after the priesthood was instituted ! How " quickly " sin entered Israel's camp after Canaan was entered (Josh. 7). And so we might go on. Alas, how " quickly " the young Christian leaves his " first love " and loses his early joy ! Failure is written large across every page of human history. And what is the chief cause of all such failure ? Do not the next words of Jehovah to Moses make known the answer ?

" And the Lord said unto Moses, I have seen this people, and, behold, it is a stiff-necked people " (v. 9). What is signified by this oft-used figure ? It signifies a state of insubordination : note the order in Deut. 31 : 27, " I know thy rebellion, and thy stiff neck." It is the opposite of submission to the will of God : " Be ye not stiff-necked, as your fathers were, but *yield yourselves unto* the Lord " (2 Chron. 30 : 8). It is a state into which we may bring ourselves : " They obeyed not, neither inclined their ear, but *made* their necks stiff, that they might not hear, nor receive instruction " (Jer. 17 : 23). It is brought about by not yielding ourselves to God : " Ye stiff-necked and uncircumcised in hearts and ears, ye do always resist the Holy Spirit " (Acts 7 : 51). A stiff-necked person is one who bows not to God : **he is one in whom self-will is at work.** This was the state of Israel, therefore did God go on to say :

" Now therefore let Me alone, that My wrath may wax hot against them, and that I may consume them : and I will make of thee a great nation " (v. 10). Having by their sins forfeited all the blessings engaged to them on the terms of their own covenant, the Lord at once stands against them, disclaims them, and threatens to execute consuming judgment upon them. "Thus Israel, if dealt with according to the righteous requirements of the law which they had accepted, and to which they had promised obedience as the condition of blessing, were lost beyond recovery, and would perish through their own wilful sin and apostasy " (Ed. Dennett). The reason why God did not totally destroy His stiff-necked people on this occasion we must leave for consideration, D.V., to our next article. In the meantime let us seek grace to heed this solemn warning. By nature none of us are a whit better than Aaron and the Israelites. Were God to withdraw His grace from us, we, too, would surely and speedily fall into as great and gross sin as they did. Then let us cry with the Psalmist, " Hold Thou me up, and I shall be safe, and I will have respect unto Thy statutes continually " (119 : 117).

CHAPTER 60

THE TYPICAL MEDIATOR

EXODUS 32:11-14

· In our last article we were occupied with the inspired account of Israel's idolatrous worship of the golden calf. It was the first time that they were guilty of this awful sin since their leaving of Egypt as a nation. The subject of idolatry is both solemn and important, and as the nature and cause of it are so little understood we propose to offer here a few general remarks on the subject.

Man is the only creature who lives on the earth that was originally created with faculties capable of apprehending God, and with a sentiment of veneration for Him. True, all creation is to the praise of the Creator, but man's praise is the homage of an intelligent heart and of a conscious choice or preference. But this capacity to offer intelligent praise is necessarily accompanied by responsibility. This was made evident in connection with Adam. The tree of the knowledge of good and evil was the visible means of the first man's paying homage to God: abstention from its fruit was the witness of his subjection to the authority of his Maker. Obedience to God's command concerning that tree would not only secure to him all the blessings of Eden, but was also the link which bound him to the Creator. Thus, that which united man to God at the beginning was the obedience of the will, subjection of heart. Whilst this was maintained God was honoured and man was blest.

But that link was broken. Through disobedience man became " alienated *from* the life of God " (Eph. 4 : 18), and thus he lost his happiness and was turned out of the Garden. The original link being broken, it could never be reformed. If man was ever again to be in relationship with God, it must be on entirely new ground, namely, redemption-ground, resurrection-ground, the ground of new creation. Into Eden fallen man could never re-enter. It was a garden of delights for innocence alone ; and guilt once incurred made a return to it impossible. But for His own people God has provided a new garden, the " paradise of God " (Rev. 2 : 7), where the guilty are restored to more than the pleasures of Eden. That new garden is anticipated by faith, and there is found forgiveness of sins and eternal life.

Now when man fell, though he became alienated from God (which is what spiritual " death " is) he lost none of his original faculties, nor was his responsibility destroyed. In his essential nature man remained after the Fall all that he was before it. True, his nature became vitiated by sin, and, in consequence, his whole being was corrupted ; nevertheless, the " breath of life " which God had breathed into him at the beginning, remained his portion after his expulsion from Eden. True, all the faculties of his being now became the " instrument of unrighteousness unto sin " (Rom. 6 : 13), yet none of them had ceased to exist or to function.

It is the very character of man's nature (that which distinguishes him from and elevates him above the beasts) which has made his fall his ruin. It has been rather vulgarly said that " Man is a religious animal," by which is meant that man, by nature, is essentially a religious creature, *i.e.*, made, originally, to pay homage to his Creator. It is this religious nature of man's which, strange as it may sound, lies at the root of all idolatry. Being alienated from God, and therefore ignorant of Him, he falls the ready dupe of Satan. It was to this fact of fallen man's essential nature that Christ had reference when He said, " If therefore the light that is in thee be darkness, how great is that darkness " (Matt. 6 : 23). The " light " in man is that which distinguishes him from the beasts, and that which is (potentially) capable of communing with God. But, as we have said, that faculty in man which is capable of communion with God, is, as the result of sin, put to a wrong use, and thus the " light " in him has become " darkness." Instead of worshipping God, he now serves his own lusts, and honours idols which are patterned after his lusts.

Man must have his god, otherwise he would not be man, and because the " natural man "—what he now is as a fallen creature—has lost his knowledge of the true God, he turns to the resources of his own mind to fill the void. And, as another has said (from whom part of the above has been condensed),

320

" From the mental image formed in a corrupt mind, it is but a short step to the golden or wooden idol in the temple. Every shape and form had its prototype in the imagination, which to the philosopher was supplemented by the material things of nature ; but to the vulgar, surrounding objects were the basis upon which the superstructure of idolatry rested. Through the senses their imagination was fed by the things seen and felt ; and though these be not the sole source of idolatry, they greatly modified its form and multiplied its gods. For the mountain and the valley, the river, the grove, the heavens above and the waters beneath had their divinities, and everywhere that which in nature most impressed man soon took rank as a god.

" Nor let us forget the greatest factor which produced this confused mass of superstition and credulity. Not only did man not like to retain the knowledge of God and thus became the dupe of his senses, but over all was the delusive power of Satan, who held man in captivity through his fears and lusts. The loss of the knowledge of the true God, to a creature endowed with religious faculties, must result in subjective idolizing. Satan, the god of this world, presented himself in a tangible form and made it objective.

" The religious element in man's nature was not eradicated by sin, but while every faculty of his mind and every instinct of his nature is debased and perverted, man's complete ruin and his greatest guilt are seen in the degradation of those same faculties, originally given as the means of worshipping God. The endowments which placed him above all other creatures, now sink him beneath them " (" The Bible Tresury, 1882).

What has been said above not only serves to explain the universality of idolatry, but supplies the key to what is recorded in Exodus 32. There we behold the favoured Israelites making and worshipping a golden calf. It was inexcusable, open, blatant, united idolatry. For a very good reason, the first command which God had written, with His own finger, upon the tables of stone, was " Thou shalt have no other gods before Me "; and here was the deliberate and concerted violation of it. What, then, must be the sequel ? Jehovah turns to Moses, acquainted him with the awful sin of the people down below, and says, " Now therefore let me alone, that My wrath may wax hot against them, and that I may consume them : and I will make of thee a great nation."

Solemn and fearsome as those words sound, yet a closer examination reveals a door of hope opened by them. When the Lord said to Moses, " Let Me alone . . . I will make of thee a great nation," it was as though He placed Himself in the hands of the typical mediator. " Let Me alone " plainly suggests that Moses stood between Jehovah and His sinful people. This was indeed the case.

But for Moses they were surely lost : he only stood between the holy wrath of God and their thoroughly merited doom. What would he do ? When menaced by the Egyptians at the Red Sea, Moses had cried unto the Lord on their behalf (14 : 15). So, too, at the bitter waters of Marah he had supplicated Jehovah for them (15 : 25). When at Rephidim they had no water, yet again Moses had cried unto the Lord and obtained answer on their behalf (17 : 4). When Amelek came against Israel, it was the holding up of Moses' hands which gained them the victory (17 : 11). But now a far graver crisis was at hand. Would Moses fail them now ? or would he again intervene on their behalf ?

" And Moses besought the Lord his God, and said, Lord, why doth Thy wrath wax hot against Thy people, which Thou hast brought forth out of the land of Egypt with great power, and with a mighty hand ? " (v. 11). Moses did not fail his people in this hour of their urgent need. Most blessed is it to behold how he conducted himself on this occasion : God had said to him, " Let me alone, that My wrath may wax hot against them . . . and I will make *of thee* a great nation," but Moses uses his place of nearness to God not on his own behalf, but for the good of the people.

At an earlier date he had " refused to be called the son of Pharaoh's daughter, choosing rather to suffer affliction with the people of God than to enjoy the pleasures of sin for a season ; esteeming the reproach of Christ greater riches than the treasures in Egypt : for he had respect unto the recompense of the reward " (Heb. 11 : 24-26). So now he declines to be made the head of another nation, choosing rather to be identified with this stiff-necked and disobedient people. Is there not here a blessed foreshadowing of Him who " made Himself of no reputation " (Phil. 2 : 7), and who became one with His sinful people ? Yes, indeed ; and, as we shall see, in more respects than one.

" And Moses besought the Lord his God, and said, Lord, why doth Thy wrath wax hot against Thy people, which Thou hast brought forth out of the land of Egypt with great power, and with a mighty hand ? " This was the typical mediator's response to what Jehovah had said to him in v. 7, " Go, get thee down ; for *thy* people, which *thou* broughtest out of the land of Egypt have corrupted themselves." We believe there is a double force to these words. In their local significance they furnish God's answer to the wicked declaration of Israel recorded in v. 1. There the people had disowned their Divine Deliverer ; here He righteously disclaims them. But there is a *typical* meaning, too, and most precious is it to contemplate this.

In v. 7 the Lord practically turns the Nation over to Moses, calling them " thy people "; here in v. 11 the typical mediator, as it were, gives them back again unto God, saying " Thy people." Was not this a plain adumbration of what we find in John 17 ? First, in v. 2, the antitypical Mediator speaks of a people whom God had given to Him : " As Thou hast given Him power over all flesh, that He should give eternal life to as many as Thou hast *given Him."* Then, in v. 9, we behold Him giving back that people to God, " I pray for them : I pray not for the world, but for them which Thou hast given Me ; for they *are Thine."*

Let us notice now the various *grounds* upon which Moses pleaded before " the Lord *his* God." They are three in number : he appealed to the grace of God, the glory of God, and the faithfulness of God. His appeal to God's grace is found in v. 11, " Lord, why doth Thy wrath wax hot against Thy people, which Thou hast brought forth out of the land of Egypt ? " It was grace, pure and simple, which had actuated Jehovah when He delivered the Hebrews from the House of Bondage. There was absolutely nothing in them to merit His esteem ; rather was there everything in them to call forth His wrath. It was sovereign benignity, unadulterated grace, the Divine favour shown to them, unasked and unmerited.

But let it not be overlooked that the Divine grace which was shown to unworthy Israel was not exercised at the expense of the claims of justice, for it is ever true that grace reigns " through righteousness " (Rom. 5 : 21). So it was in Egypt : the passover-lamb had been slain, its blood shed and applied. Thus, it is on the ground of *redemption* that grace flowed forth. And it is still the same, " Being justified freely by His grace *through* the redemption that is in Christ Jesus " (Rom. 3 : 24).

Now it was to *this* that Moses made his first appeal. Israel had sinned, sinned grievously, and Moses made no effort to deny or excuse it. Later, we find him acknowledging the Lord's charge against His people, owning " it *is* a stiff necked people " (34 : 9). Nevertheless, they were *God's* people—His by redemption. They were His purchased property. Unworthy, unthankful, unholy ; but yet, the Lord's redeemed. Blessed, glorious, heart-melting fact : O may the realisation of it create within us a greater hatred of sin and a deeper appreciation of the precious blood of the Lamb. Is it not written, " If any man (Greek " any one "—of those spoken of in 1 John 1 : 3) sin, we have an Advocate with the Father, Jesus Christ the righteous " (1 John 2 : 1) ? And what is the ground of His advocacy ? What but His blood shed once for all !

" Wherefore should the Egyptians speak, and say, For mischief did He bring them out, to slay them in the mountain, and to consume them from the face of the earth ?

Turn from Thy fierce wrath, and repent of this evil against Thy people " (v. 12). Here is the second ground on which Moses pleaded with God : he appealed to His glory. Where would be His honour in the sight of the heathen were He to consume the children of Israel here at Sinai ? Would not reproach be cast upon His name by the Egyptians ? The thought of this was more than Moses could endure ; therefore did he beseech Jehovah to relent against His erring people. " Spite of their shameful apostasy, the plea of Moses was that they were still Gods' people, and that His glory was concerned in sparing them—lest the enemy should boast over their destruction, and thereby over the Lord Himself. In itself it was a plea of irresistible force. Joshua uses one of like character when the Israelites were smitten before Ai. He says " the Canaanites and all the inhabitants of the land shall hear of it, and shall environ us round, and cut off our name from the earth : *and what wilt Thou do unto Thy great name ?* ' (Joshua 7 : 9. In both cases it was faith taking hold of God, identifying itself with His own glory, and claiming on that ground the response to its desires—a plea that God can never refuse " (Ed. Dennett).

This ground of appeal to God is not made by any of us to-day nearly as much as it should be. The prayer of Moses here in Ex. 32 is also recorded for our learning. It brings before us the essential elements of those " effectual fervent prayers of a righteous man " which " availeth much." This was not the only occasion on which Moses appealed to the glory of the Lord's name : let the reader consult carefully Numbers 14 : 13-16, and Deut. 9 : 28, 29 ; for others who used this plea, see Psa. 25 : 11 ; Joel 2 : 17, &c. It is the glory of His own name which God ever has before Him in all that He does.

It was for the honour of His name that He had, originally, brought Israel out of Egypt : " I wrought for My name's sake, that it should not be polluted before the heathen, among whom they were, in whose sight I made Myself known unto them, in bringing them forth out of the land of Egypt " (Ezek. 20 : 9). So, at a later date in Israel's sinful history He declared, " For My name's sake will I defer Mine anger, and for My praise will I refrain from thee, that I cut thee not off. . . . For Mine own sake, even for Mine own sake, will I do it : for how should My name be polluted ? " (Isa. 48 : 9, 11). It is " for *His* name's sake " " that He leads His people in the paths of righteousness " (Psa. 23 : 3).

Blessed is it to behold the Lord Jesus in His high priestly prayer, recorded in John 17, using this same plea before God. In that prayer He is heard presenting many petitions, and varied are the grounds upon which He presents them. But underlying all, first and foremost He asked, " glorify Thy Son, *that* Thy Son also may glorify Thee" (v. 1) ! Here is one of the prime secrets in prevailing prayer. Just as bowing of the heart to God's sovereign will is the first requirement in a praying soul, so the having before us the glory of God and the honour of His name is that which, chiefly, ensures an answer to our petitions. " Whatsoever ye do, do all to the glory of God " (1 Cor. 10 : 31) applies as strictly to our praying as to any other exercise. Let us take to heart, then, this important lesson taught us in this successful prayer of Moses.

" Remember Abraham, Isaac, and Israel, Thy servants, to whom Thou swearest by Thine own self, and saidst unto them, I will multiply your seed as the stars of heaven, and all this land that I have spoken of will I give unto your seed, and they shall inherit it forever " (v. 13). Here is the third ground which Moses took in his intercession before Jehovah. He appealed to His faithfulness ; he pleaded His promises ; he reminded Him of His oath. There was no ground to go on and no plea which he could make from anything that was to be found in Israel, so he fell back upon that which God is in Himself.

" In the energy of his intercession—fruit surely of the action of the Spirit of God— he goes back to the absolute and unconditional promises made to Abraham, Isaac and Jacob, reminding the Lord of the two immutable things in which it was impossible for Him to lie (Heb. 6 : 18). A more beautiful example of prevailing intercession is not to be found in the Scriptures. Indeed, in the emergency which had arisen, everything depended on the mediator, and in His grace God had provided one who could stand in the breach, and plead His people's cause—not on the ground of what they were, for by their sin they were exposed to the righteous indignation of a holy God—but on the ground of what God was, and on that of His counsels revealed and confirmed to the patriarchs, both by oath and promise " (Ed. Dennett).

But let us look a little more closely at this third feature of Moses' prayer. In the above quotation there are two slight inaccuracies : it was not God's promises to " Abraham, Isaac and *Jacob*," but " and Israel "—the difference intimating the height to which Moses' faith had risen ; nor were God's revealed counsels confirmed to the patriarchs " both by oath and by promise," but, instead, by promise and oath—note the order in Heb. 6 : 13-18, which is the same as in Gen. 12 : 3, and then Gen. 22 : 15, 16. But that which we would here dwell upon is that Moses made these the final grounds of his pleading before God.

The *Word* of God is " quick and powerful " (Heb. 4 : 12), not only in its effects upon us, but also in its moving power with God

Himself. If this were more realized by Christians, the very language of Holy Writ would have a larger place in their supplications, and more answers from above would be obtained. God has magnified His Word above all His name (Psa. 138 : 2), and so should we. He has expressly declared, " Them that honour Me, I will honour," and how can we more honour Him in our prayers than by employing the very words of Scripture, *His* words, rather than our own ? Ah, here too, our speech betrays us. If the Word of Christ dwelt in us more richly, it would find fuller expression in our intercessions, for " out of the abundance of the heart the mouth speaketh." Christ has left us a perfect example : His prayers were the outbreathing of the Psalms, and a close examination of the one which He taught His disciples reveals the fact that every clause of it was a quotation from the O.T. ! And He explicitly enjoined His disciples, " after *this* manner therefore pray ye " (Matt. 6 : 9). But we do not ; hence so many unanswered prayers.

Now that which Moses pleaded before God from His Word were the *promises* which He had made to the patriarchs. This, too, is recorded for our learning. It is the humble, simple, trustful spreading of the Divine promises before the throne of grace which secures the ear of God. *That* is what real prayer is : a presenting of our need before the Lord, and then reverently reminding Him of His own declaration that He will supply it. It is a confident asking with David, " Do as Thou hast said " (2 Sam. 7 : 25). This is what the " exercise of faith " signifies : a laying hold of God's promises, an " embracing " (Heb. 11 : 13) of them, a counting upon them. " Hath He said, and shall He not do it ? or hath He spoken, and shall He not make it good ? " (Num. 23 : 19).

Men like a written agreement in " black and white," and the great God has condescended to give us such. How strange, then, that we do not treat His promises as *realities*. Jehovah never trifles with His words : His engagements are always kept· Joshua reminded Israel, " This day I am going the way of all the earth : and ye know in all your hearts and in all your souls, that not one thing hath failed of all the good things which the Lord your God spake concerning you ; *all* are come to pass unto you, not one thing hath failed thereof " (Joshua 23 : 14). Then let us seek grace to emulate Abraham, the father of all them that believe, of whom it is recorded, " He staggered not at the promise of God through unbelief ; but was strong in faith, giving glory to God ; and being fully persuaded that, what He had promised, He was able also to perform " (Rom. 4 : 20, 21).

" And the Lord repented of the evil which He thought to do unto His people " (v. 14).

These words do not mean that God changed His mind or altered His purpose, for He is "*without* variableness or shadow of turning" (James 1 : 17). There never has been and never will be the smallest occasion for the Almighty to affect the slightest deviation from His eternal purpose, for everything was foreknown to Him from the beginning, and all His counsels were ordered by infinite wisdom. When Scripture speaks of God's repenting it employs a figure of speech, in which the Most High condescends to speak in our language. What is intended by the above expression is that Jehovah answered the prayer of the typical mediator.

" And the Lord repented of the evil which He thought to do unto His people " (v. 14). Blessed is it to note how Israel is still spoken of as " *His* people." " What encouragement to faith ! If ever there was an occasion when it seemed impossible that prayer should be heard, it was this ; but the faith of Moses rose above all difficulties, and grasping the hand of Jehovah claimed His help ; and, inasmuch as He could not deny Himself, the prayer of Moses was granted " (Ed. Dennett). May this little meditation be blest of God to many to the enriching of thier spiritual lives.

CHAPTER 61

THE RIGHTEOUS JUDGE

EXODUS 32:15-29

Our present section presents to us a vastly different scene than the one upon which we gazed in the preceding verses. There we beheld the typical mediator pleading so graciously and effectually before the Lord, turning away His wrath from His stiffnecked people. Here we see Moses coming down from the mount, where he had been in such wondrous and blessed communion with God, angered at the sin of idolatrous Israel, breaking the tables of stone, grinding the golden calf to powder, strewing it upon the water and making the people to drink. Here we see this man of prayer arraigning Aaron, the responsible and guilty leader, and then calling upon the Levites to put on their swords and "slay every man his brother." The contrast is so radical, so strange, that many have been perplexed, so grotesque have been some of the explanations attempted.

It is therefore pertinent to ask at once, Does our type now fail us? Is Moses in our present passage no longer a foreshadowing of Christ? Surely after all that has been before us in the previous chapters of Exodus we should be slow to answer these questions in the affirmative. If we are unable to perceive the spiritual meaning and application of this picture, certainly that is no reason why we should say or even imagine that there is a defect in the holy Word of God. Far better and becoming for us to confess the dimness of our vision and betake ourselves to the great Physician, that He may anoint our eyes with eyesalve that we may see (Rev. 3 : 18). It is only in His light that we ever "see light" (Psa. 36 : 9). If we who take up our pens to write upon the Oracles of God did this more faithfully and frequently, there would be far less of darkening "counsel by words without knowledge" (Job 38 : 2). Not that we dare to imply, though, that other writers have done this less than ourselves.

In his "Notes on Exodus," which are for the most part very spiritual and helpful, and from which, under God, the writer himself has received not a little help, C.H.M. says on the opening verses of our present passage, "How different is this from what we see in Christ! He came down from the bosom of the Father, not with the tables in His hands, but with the law in His heart. He came down, not to be made acquainted with the condition of the people but with a perfect knowledge of what that condition was. Moreover, instead of destroying the memorials of the covenant and executing judgment, He magnified the Law and made it honourable and bore the judgment of His people in His own blessed Person, on the cross" (page 316). Here is a case in point which shows the need for all of us to heed the Divine admonition, "*Prove* all things; hold fast that which is good" (1 Thess. 5 : 21)—which applies to our own writings equally as much as any others—for only thus shall we be able to "take forth the precious from the vile" (Jer. 15 : 19).

In the first place, what we have here is *not* a type, either by comparison or contrast, of the first advent of God's Son coming here to seek and to save that which was lost. How could it be, when the section immediately preceding gives us a picture of His intercession on High? In the second place, when Christ was here, He *did* come with the ten commandments in His hands, came to enforce their righteous demands, though not to execute their inexorable penalty. He came here, full not only of "grace," but of "truth" as well (John 1 : 14), saying, "Think not that I am come to destroy the law or the prophets : I am not come to destroy, but to fulfill" (Matt. 5 : 17). In the four Gospels we see the tables of stone in the hands of Christ again and again : see Matt. 5 : 27-32; 15 : 3-6; 19 : 16-19; 23 : 2-3. In the third place, Moses did *not* come down from the mount " to *be* made acquainted with the condition of the people," instead, he already had full knowledge of their awful state and sin before he descended, as vv. 7-9 clearly enough show.

That what is before us in the second half of Ex. 32 possesses a deep and wondrous typical significance we are fully assured, though nought but Divine guidance will enable us to rightly divide this portion of the Word of Truth. We believe that this type has a twofold application, first to Israel, second to Christendom. Its application to Israel has already been pointed out at the close of our comments upon Ex. 24 (Article 32), but as many of our present readers have not seen them, we shall here repeat briefly

325

what was then said.

First, in Ex. 24 : 18 we behold Moses entering the glory (the "cloud") consequent upon his having erected the altar and sprinkled the blood (vv. 4-8). If the reader will consult 24 : 16, 18 he will find that it was after "six days"—which speaks of work and toil, on the seventh day, which tells of *rest,* that the typical mediator was called by God to enter the glory. Beautiful foreshadowment was this of Christ, as it is said of Him in Heb. 4 : 10, "He that is entered into His rest, He also hath ceased from His works, as God from His." And what was the "rest" into which He entered? Does not His own request in John 17 : 4, 5 tell us! Thus, Moses going up into the mount and entering the cloud to commune with Jehovah is a type of the *ascension* of Christ, following the triumphant completion of the work which had been given Him to do. That which formed the subject of communion between the Lord and Moses in the mount was the revelation concerning the Tabernacle and its priesthood, which, coming in at *this* place in the book, tells of the provision of God's grace for His people, secured to them by and in Christ during His absence.

Now the next event, chronologically, was Moses' *descent,* recorded in Ex. 32. He did not end his days on the mount, but, in due time, returned unto the people. In like manner, the One whom Moses foreshadowed, is not to remain on High forever, but will come back again as truly and as literally as He went away. It is indeed striking to observe that Moses came down from Sinai *twice* after he had entered the glory. First, as recorded in 32 :: 15; second, in 34 : 29, having of course returned thither in the interval. So also will there be *two* stages in the second advent of Christ: the first when He descends into the air, to catch up His saints away from this scene (1 Thess. 4 : 16, 17); the second when He returns to the earth itself (Zech. 14 : 4). These two stages in the Redeemer's return will affect Israel very differently: the first will be followed by terrible judgment, the second will usher in an era of unparalleled blessing, even the Millennium.

That which we have in our present passage is what immediately followed the *first* descent of Moses. During his absence in the mount, the people had gathered themselves unto Aaron, saying "Up, make us gods which shall go before us out of the land of Egypt, we wot not what is become of him" (32:1). Is not that an accurate description of the spiritual state of the Jews all through this Day of Grace? They are all at sea over the long absence of their Messiah, not knowing what to think. While Moses was away, they made and worshipped a golden calf. And has not history again repeated itself? That which has characterised the Jews has not been the love of conquest or the lure of pleasure, as it has been with the Gentiles, but the lust for *gold.*

Now just as at his first descent Moses found Israel worshipping the golden calf, so at the first stage in the second advent of our Saviour, Israel will still be pursuing their mad quest after material riches; and just as Moses' response was to act in judgment, making them drink the dust of their idol and calling for the sword to smite them, so shall the Jews be made to drink the outpoured vials of God's wrath and suffer beneath the sword. But just as the Nation was not completely exterminated under the anger of Moses, neither shall it be under the far sorer afflictions of the Tribulation period. In Ex. 33 and 34 that which followed the *second* descent of Moses anticipates millennial conditions.

Having dwelt on the application of our present type to Israel, let us view it now as it bears on Christendom. The action of Moses in the passage before us foreshadowed Christ in another character than that which was before us in our last article. There we viewed Him as the Mediator, making intercession for His people; here we behold Him as Judge, not consuming, but inspecting and executing *corrective* judgment. "Moses coming down from the mountain to expose and judge what was going on in the camp is very much like the Lord's attitude in Rev. 2, 3. He takes His place in the midst of the seven lamps to pass judgment upon what is evil and idolatrous, and also to take account of such faithfulness as might answer to what was found in the sons of Levi" (C. A. Coates). We believe it is the first three chapters of the Revelation which supply the key to the meaning of our present type.

"And Moses turned, and went down from the mount, and the two tables of the testimony were in his hand: the tables were written on both their sides; on the one side and on the other were they written. And the tables were the work of God, and the writing was the writing of God, graven upon the tables" (vv. 15, 16). This is not contradictory, but complementary, to that which precedes. First we have that which speaks of the *grace* of God, now that which brings out His *government.* The tables of stone in the hands of Moses announced that the righteous requirements of the law cannot be set aside. "Whatsoever a man soweth, that shall he also reap" was addressed not to worldlings, but to Christians. Let the reader note attentively the inspired description of Christ in Rev. 1 : 12-18. There we behold One "like unto the Son of *man*" (cf. John 5 : 27) in the midst of the seven lampstands, and "out of His mouth goeth a sharp two-edged sword, and His countenance was as the sun shineth in his strength" (v. 16)!

"And when Joshua heard the noise of the people as they shouted, he said unto Moses, There is a noise of war in the camp. And he said, It is not the voice of them that shout for mastery, neither is it the voice of them that cry for being overcome; but the noise of them that sing do I hear" (vv. 17, 18). An important spiritual principle here receives exemplification. If the reader will turn back to Ex. 24 : 13-18 it will be found that though both Moses and Joshua went up into the mount, leaving the congregation below at its base, yet Moses alone went into the midst of the cloud, to talk to Jehovah. For forty days Joshau had, apparently, been left alone, while Moses "communed" with the Lord (31 : 18). The *effect* of this we see in the verses before us: Moses, and not Joshua, is the one who discerns the true state of affairs in the camp. His ear was able to interpret aright the noise and din which came up to them. Ah, it is not only true that in God's light we alone see light, but only by much communion with Him do we acquire the *hearing* "ear."

"And it came to pass, as soon as he came nigh unto the camp, that he saw the calf, and the dancing: and Moses' anger waxed hot, and he cast the tables out of his hands, and brake them beneath the mount" (v. 19). A most appalling spectacle was spread before these servants of God. The very people who had only recently bowed before the manifested majesty of Jehovah, were now obscenely sporting around the golden image of a calf. In holy indignation Moses dashes the tables of stone to the ground, just as in the days of His flesh the Lord Jesus "made a scourge of small cords" and drove out of the Temple those who had desecrated His Father's house; and just as in Rev. 1 He is seen with "His eyes as a flame of fire" (v.14).

"And Moses' anger waxed hot, and he cast the tables out of his hands, and brake them beneath the mount." This affords a most striking illustration of what is said in James 2 : 10, "For whosoever shall keep the whole law, and yet offend in one point, he is guilty of all." Israel *had* offended "in one point." God had said to them. "Thou shalt not make unto thee any graven image, or any likeness of anything that is in heaven above or that is in the earth beneath, or that is in the water under the earth: thou shalt not bow down thyself to them, nor serve them (Ex. 20 :4, 5). This they had disobeyed, and the law being a unit, they are guilty of all"—hence the breaking of the two tables to show that the ten commandments, as a whole, had been violated.

"And he took the calf which they had made, and burnt it in the fire, and ground it to powder, and strawed it upon the water, and made the children of Israel drink of it" (v. 20). Some of the so-called "higher critics" with their customary scepticism have called into question the reference to Moses strawing the powder upon "the water;" but if these men would but take the trouble to "search the Scriptures," they would find that the Holy Spirit has granted light upon this point, though not in this chapter (for the Bible does not yield its meaning to lazy people),but in another book altogether. In Deut. 9 : 21 we read, "I took your sin, the calf which ye had made, and burnt it with fire,

and stamped it, and ground it very small, even until it was as small as dust: and I cast the dust thereof into the *brook* that descended out of the mount." What that "brook" was that "descended out of the mount" Ex. 17 : 6 tells us.

Moses' actions here in grinding the idol to powder, strawing it upon the water, and making the children of Israel drink thereof, are very solemn. The Christian is bidden to keep himself from idols (1 John 5 : 21), which, we need scarcely add, covers very much more than bowing down to graven images. An "idol" is anything which displaces God in my heart. It may be something which is quite harmless in itself, yet if it absorbs me, if it be given the first place in my affections and thoughts, it becomes an "idol." It may be my business, a loved one, or my service for Christ. Any one or any thing which comes into competition with the Lord's ruling me in a practical way, is an "idol." And if I have set up an idol, then God, in His faithfulness and love, will break it down; not If I sow to the flesh, then of the flesh I must reap corruption (Gal. 6 : 8).

"And Moses said unto Aaron, What did this people unto thee, that thou hast brought so great a sin upon them?" Moses now arraigns the one who had been left in charge of the people, just as in Rev. 2, 3, Christ addresses, in each case, the responsible "angel" or "messenger" of the local church. Sad it is to hear the reply of the one who should have maintained the honor and glory of Jehovah.

"And Aaron said, Let not the anger of my Lord wax hot: thou knowest the people, that they are set on mischief . For they said unto me, Make us gods, which shall go before us: for this Moses, the man that brought us up out of the land of Egypt, we wot not what is become of him" (vv. 22, 23). Very sad indeed is this. There was no sense of the terribleness of the sin committed, no sign of repentance; instead, there was a throwing of the blame upon others. Thus it was at the beginning: when the Lord arraigned Adam, he blamed his wife (Gen. 3 : 12); and when Eve was questioned, she blamed the Serpent. How often we hear the leaders in Christendom saying, "We have to make these concessions because the people demand it."

"What a contrast there is here between Aaron and Moses! Aaron afraid of the people, instead of protesting against their idolatrous wishes, actually making the calf; and then excusing himself in a way which is just a sample of the kind of excuses people make for doing evil (v 24). Moses comes down in an energy that could take a stand single-handed against six-hundred-thousand men, that could execute judgment on their sin, and maintain what was due to God. It is just the contrast between the servant who is *with men* and the servant who is *with God*. If a man acts with God he always acts in power. He may have plenty of exercise as to his own weakness in secret, but in public he acts in power and with no uncertainty or hesitation" (C.A.C.).

"And I said unto them, Whosoever hath any gold, let them break it off. So they gave it me: then I cast it into the fire, and there came out this calf" (v. 24). The breaking off of their "golden" ornaments was a figure of their being stript of their *glory*. This is ever what precedes all idolatry. What is man's "glory?" To be in subjection to his Maker and to be grateful for His mercies. Man is only in honor when God is given His true place. Just as we read of the Gentiles, in Rom. 1 : 21, "When they knew God, they glorified Him not as God, neither were thankful." What followed? This: they "changed the glory of the uncorruptible God into an image made like to corruptible man" etc. Nothing will preserve from idolatry but a will bowed to God's authority and a heart lifted up in thanksgiving for His bounties. If I do not bow to God, I shall quickly bow to something else that is of the creature, and thus be stript of my "gold," my glory.

"So they gave it me: then I cast it into the fire, and there came out this calf." In this purile manner did Aaron seek to deny all personal responsibility in the matter. Really, he told a downright lie, as a reference to v. 4 will show. Great indeed was his sin: marvellous the mercy which pardoned it. It is blessed to learn from Deut. 9 : 20 that the life of Aaron was spared in answer to the supplications of Moses. Thus we see in type, again, the efficacy of the Mediator's intercession for His people.

"And when Moses saw that the people were naked; (for Aaron had make them naked unto their shame among their enemies): Then Moses stood in the gate of the camp, and said, Who is on the Lord's side? let him come unto me" (vv. 25, 26). The situation called for drastic action. Having arraigned Aaron, Moses now considers the condition of the people, and beheld them naked and demoralised, having indulged in the idolatrous sensualism which they had so often witnessed in Egpyt, and whose mad merriment they had, no doubt, remembered with many a sigh. They had been disturbed in their abominable orgies, and had yielded only to the terror of Moses' presence. A swift and summary vengeance must therefore be visited upon them, in order that the survivors might be brought to soberness and repentance, and that the Divine wrath, which had only been suspended by his intreaties, might be averted from utterly consuming the Nation.

"Who is on the Lord's side?" That was now the issue, clearly defined. "It was no time for concealment of the evil or for compromise. When there is open apostasy there can be no neutrality. Neutrality when the question is between God and Satan is itself apostasy. He

that is not with the Lord, at such a time, is against Him. And mark, moreover, that this cry is raised in the midst of those who were the Lord's professing people. They were all Israelites. But now there must be a separation, and the challenge of Moses, 'Who is on the Lord's side?' makes all manifest. He becomes the Lord's centre; and hence to gather to Him was to be *for*, to refuse his call was to be *against* the Lord" (Ed. Dennett).

"And all the sons of Levi gathered themselves together unto him" (v. 26). The Levites were the "overcomers" (cf. Rev. 2, 3) of that day. They had, apparently, been preserved from the awful sin of their nation, and now promptly responded to the call of God's servant. A most searching and severe test was presented to them: "And he said unto them, Thus saith the Lord God of Israel, put every man his sword by his side, and go in and out from gate to gate through the camp, and slay every man his brother, and every man his companion, and every man his neighbour" (v. 27).

Natural inclinations might well shrink from compliance with such a command. Sentiment would say, Not so, let us be gentle and gracious, we shall accomplish more by kindness than severity. Reason would argue, We can do no good by slaying people: there is far more power in love than in the sword; let us seek to woo and win them back to God. Such arguments sound very plausible, but the call was distinct and decisive, "Put every man his sword by his side." There was nothing else for it in view of that calf. So in preaching to idolators today it is the *wrath* of a holy God, and not His love (which is a truth for His own people only), which needs pressing upon them.

As another has said in his application of this verse, to the saints to-day, "It was obedience at all costs to the divine call, and hence complete separation from the evil into which Israel had fallen. God often tests His people in the same way; and whenever confusion and declension have begun, the only path for the godly is that which is marked out by the course of Levi—that of full-hearted, unquestioning obedience. Such a path must be painful, involving for those who take it the surrender of some of the most intimate associations of their lives, and breaking many a tie of nature—of kindred and relationship; but it is only the path of blessing. Well may all challenge their hearts and inquire, if in this evil day they are apart from all that dishonours the Lord's name, in subjection to His Word."

The terrible sequel we must leave for our next article. May the Lord sanctify to our souls the solemn yet salutary lessons contained in the verses which have been before us.

CHAPTER 62

ISRAEL PLAGUED

EXODUS 32:28—33:2

Our last article closed with the descent of Moses from the mount and, upon his beholding the idolatries of Israel, his giving a stern commission to the Levites: "Put every man his sword by his side, go in and out from gate to gate throughout the camp, and slay every man his brother, and every man his companion, and every man his neighbour." In their response we behold the spirit triumphing over the flesh, the claims of Jehovah's holiness over-riding all natural and sentimental considerations: "And the children of Levi did according to the word of Moses: and there fell of the people that day about three thousand men. For Moses had said, Consecrate yourselves to-day to the Lord, even every man upon his son, and upon his brother; that He may bestow upon you a blessing this day" (vv. 28, 29).

The above verses present several most striking contrasts. First, from what is recorded in Gen. 34 : 25, 26, where, too, the "sword" is seen in the hand of Levi, not for Jehovah's glory, but in fleshly anger—cf. Gen. 49 : 5-7. Second, from what is said in Ex. 28 : 41, where we read of the sons of Aaron being consecrated that they might minister unto the Lord in the priest's office. The word "consecrate" means to "fill the hand," the reference being to the sweet-savour offerings and fragrant incense with which they were to appear before Jehovah. But here in our present portion their hands were filled with swords, to slay those who had apostatised. Third, from what is recorded in Acts 2 : 41: on the day of Israel's idolatry there fell of the people "about three thousand men," on the day of Penticost "about three thousand souls" were saved!

Fearful was the ensuing carnage. Stupefied with terror and awed by the irresistable power with which Moses was known to be invested, and by the sight of the threatening Cloud upon the mount above them, the people offered no resistance, and three thousand of them were put to death. "And so they were left for the night: the day of sin had ended in lamentation and woe. The camp, which in the morning had resounded with unholy merriment and licentious song, was full of groans and sighs: the dead awaited burial, and the wounded cried for

pain. And every soul was weighed down, if not with remorse for the sin, at least with dread, lest wrath should go forth from the Lord, and the destroying angel appear with sword outstretched to smite the wicked people, who, after hearing the law uttered by the awful voice of God Himself, and promising to do all that He had spoken, and then, even before the signs of His presence were removed, lightly passed over to idolatry and fornication" (G. H. Pember).

"Now all these things happened unto them for types" (1 Cor. 10 : 11), that is, types *for us;* "types" mark, not precedents, not examples for us to imitate. The weapons of our warfare "are not carnal," (2 Cor. 10 : 4), but "spiritual." No place for the literal sword is provided in the Christian's equipment. It is a perversion of the Scriptures, a failure to rightly divide the Word of Truth, to appeal to Israel's history as warrant for us to use physical force. No, No; the material things connected with them, were but figures of the spiritual things which belong to us. What, then, is the lesson for us in this solemn work committed to the Levites? Is not the answer obvious? Uncompromising and unsparing dealing with all that is dishonouring to God, with everything that savours of idolatry.

The Christian possesses a sword, but it is "the sword of the Spirit, which is the Word of God" (Eph. 6 : 17). With that sword we are called on to smite every enemy which lifts up its head against Christ. "The sword must be drawn against every influence that corrupts the people of God, even though it may have a place in those nearest us. It might seem very severe to treat brethren, friends, neighbours, in this way, but it was the only way to be consecrated to Jehovah, and to secure His blesing. When what is due to the Lord is in question, it is with those nearest to you that you have to be most decided. There is no particular consceration in drawing the sword against people you care little about. But to take a definite stand for the Lord against influences which are not of Him, even in those that you regard and truly love, secures great blessing. . . If I am going on with something that does not recognise the rights of Christ, or maintain what is due to God, the kindest thing we can do is to take a definite stand against it. I may, *now* call you narrow, uncharitable, bigoted! But when I meet you in the light of the judgment-seat of Christ I shall thank you for it?'' (C. A. Coates).

As we said in the preceding article, these Levites were the ''overcomers'' of that day, and if the reader will consult Rev. 2 and 3 he will find that all the promises contained in those chapters were made to the overcomers. How blessed then to find that these Levites were richly rewarded for their faithfulness. In Deut. 33 : 8-11 we read, ''And of Levi he said, Let thy Thummin and Urim be with thy holy one, whom Thou didst prove at Massah and with whom Thou didst strive at the water of Meribah; Who said unto his father and to his mother, I have not seen him; neither did he acknowledge his brethren, nor knew his own children : for they have observed Thy word and kept Thy covenant. *They* shall teach Jacob Thy judgments, and Israel Thy law : they shall put incense before Thee, and whole burnt sacrifice upon Thine altar.'' It was because they crucified the flesh ''with its *affections* and lusts,'' (Gal. 5 : 24) ignoring natural ties, knowing no man according to nature, not even acknowledging their own brethren when it came to maintaining the claims of God's holiness; it was because they observed His word and kept His covenant, that unto this Tribe were committed the ''Thummin and Urim,'' the gift of teaching, and the privilege of burning incense on the altar. Truly God *does* honour those who honour Him, but they who despise Him are lightly esteemed.

''And it came to pass on the morrow, that Moses said unto the people ye have sinned a great sin'' (v. 30). It is solemn to note the absence of any recorded word of Israel's repentance. Nothing is said of their contrition and horror at having so grievously offended against the Lord. Ominous sign was that. The rod of chastisement had fallen heavily upon them, yet, so far as we can gather, they had not bowed in heart beneath it. But God will not be mocked : if His chastening be ''despised'' (Heb. 12 : 5) it will return in a more acute form. It did so here, as we shall see in the immediate sequel. May the Lord grant each of us the hearing ear

Moses did not wink at their wickedness, nor did he attempt to minimise the enormity of it. Just as when he first came down from the mount he charged Aaron with having brought ''so great a sin'' upon Israel (v. 21), so now, on the morrow, he says unto the people, ''Ye have sinned a great sin.'' That he truly and clearly loved his people, the verses that follow plainly testify; yet, this did not deter him from dealing faithfully with them. As the Holy Spirit declares in Heb. 3 : 5, ''Moses verily was faithful in all his house, as a servant, for a testimony of those things which were to be spoken after.'' In this too was he a type of Christ, the Holy One of God, who ever stressed the heinousness of sin.

''And now I will go up unto the Lord; peradventure I shall make an atonement for your sin'' (v. 30). Care needs to be exercised lest we read into these words what they do not really contain. It was not the penal sentence upon their sin, but, we believe, the remitting of the *governmental consequences* to which Moses referred. It must not be forgotten that we have already been told in v. 14 that ''The Lord repented of the evil which He thought to do unto His people.'' In answer to the earnest supplications of the typical mediator, the wrath of God in utterly ''consuming'' the people (v. 10) had been averted, and this, we say, should be carefully borne in mind as we endeavour to understand that which follows—admittedly a most difficult passage.

''Peradventure I shall make an atonement for your sin.'' The ''peradventure' here ought not to occasion any difficulty, though more than one commentator has tripped over it. The uncertainty was due to the character and circumstances of his mission. Moses was about to appear before God on behalf of a people who had evidenced no sorrow for their great sin; therefore it was doubtful whether or not the governmental consequences of it might be remitted. There are quite a number of similar cases recorded in Scripture. In 2 Sam. 16 : 12, following Shimei's cursing of him, we find David saying, ''It *may be* that the Lord will look on mine affliction and that the Lord will requite me good for his cursing this day.'' When wayward Israel was threatened by the Assyrians, Hezekiah sent to Isaiah saying, ''It *may be* the Lord thy God will hear all the words of Rabshakeh, whom the king of Assyia his master hath sent to reproach the living God.''

Nor are such cases restricted to the O.T. In N.T. times we read of Peter saying to Simon the sorcerer, ''Repent therefore of this thy wickedness, and pray God, *if perhaps* the thought of thine heart may be forgiven thee'' (Act 8 : 22). While in 2 Tim. 2 : 25 we read, ''In meekness instructing those that oppose themselves; *if* God *peradventure* will give them repentance to the acknowledging of the truth.'' The careful reader will observe two things common to all these instances: first, each had in view the governmental consequences of sin; hence, second, each emphasises the note of uncertainty —because forgiveness was dependent upon their repentance.

''And Moses returned unto the Lord'' (v. 31). Very blessed is this. Moses was, preeminently a man of prayer. In every crisis we find him turning unto the Lord : see Ex. 5 : 22; 8 : 30; 9 : 33; 14 : 15; 17 : 4. Beautiful foreshadowing was this of the Apostle and High Priest of our profession, who, in the days of His flesh, ever maintained and manifested a perfect spirit of dependency upon the One who had sent Him.

"And Moses returned unto the Lord, and said, Oh, this people have sinned a great sin, and have made them gods of gold. Yet now, if Thou wilt forgive their sin;—and if not, blot me, I pray thee, out of Thy book which Thou hast written" (vv. 31 : 32). Let us consider first the practical lesson which this incident contains for our hearts. Most helpfully has this been brought out by another.

"But if we speak of drawing the sword in this way, let us remember that the same man who said in the camp, 'Slay every man his brother' went up to Jehovah and said, 'And now,' if Thou will forgive their sin . . .but if not, blot me, I pray Thee, out of Thy book that Thou hast written.' It was the same spirit of Christ which led him to take a decided stand in public against those who had allowed what was contrary to God, that led him to go up and pray for them in secret with such intense yearning for their good. He went as far as it was possible for man to go in the way of self-sacrifice. He could not be made a curse for them; only the Blessed One could go to that depth; but he was truly in the Spirit of Christ. It might be thought that slaying the people and interceding for them were not consistent. But the same spirit of Christ that would stand for Jehovah even against the nearest and dearest, was the spirit that would plead with God to be blotted out rather than that they should not be forgiven. The man who takes the strongest ground against me when I am wrong, and when I have set aside what is due to the Lord, is probably the one who prays most for me" (C. A. Coates).

"And Moses returned unto the Lord, and said, Oh, this people have sinned a great sin, and have made them gods of gold. Yet now, if Thou wilt forgive their sin;—and if not, blot me I pray Thee, out of Thy book which Thou hast written." Unspeakably precious is the typical picture presented here. How it brings out the intense devotion of Moses both to Jehovah and to His people. No sin on their part could alienate his affections from them. "Many waters cannot quench love, neither can the floods drown it" (Song of Sol. 8 : 7). Superlatively was this manifested by the One whom Moses here foreshadowed: Having loved His own which were in the world, He loved them unto the end" (John 13 : 1). Yes, notwithstanding the fact that all would be offended because of Him that night, yea, that all would forsake Him and flee, yet, He "loved them unto the end."

Moses gave proof that his affections were bound up with Israel, though they were a sinful people. So much were their interests his, he was willing to be blotted out of God's book, if He would not forgive them. Here again we must be careful not to read into his words what is not there. Moses said, "Thy book," not "the book of life." In Psalm 69 : 28 we read, "Let them be blotted out of the book of *the*

living, and not be written with the righteous." In Isa. 4 : 3 it is said, "And it shall come to pass, that he that is left in Zion, and he that remaineth in Jerusalem, shall be called holy, even every one that is written among *the living* in Jerusalem." Thus it seems clear from these references that the "book" mentioned by Moses was *not* "the Lamb's book of life" (Rev. 21 : 27), which was written "from the foundation of the world" (Rev. 17 : 8), but the Divine register in which are recorded the names of those living on the earth. whose names are "blotted out" at the death of each one. God has various "books :" see Mal. 3 : 16, Rev. 20 : 12.

"And the Lord said unto Moses, Whosoever hath sinned against Me, him will I blot out of My book" (v. 33). God was speaking here from the viewpoint of the unchanging principles of His righteous government. Is not Gal. 6 : 7, 8 a parallel passage? "Be not deceived; God is not mocked : for whatsoever a man soweth, that shall he also reap. For he that soweth to the flesh shall of the flesh reap corruption." Does not Rom. 8 : 13 sound-forth the same warning note? "For if we live after the flesh, we shall die?"

"Therefore now go, lead the people unto the place of which I have spoken unto thee : behold, Mine angel shall go before thee : nevertheless in the day when I visit I will visit their sin upon them" (v. 34). Here is further proof that their penal deserts were cancelled. Equally clear is it that the governmental consequences of their sin were not remitted. They were not consumed, yet in due time God would deal with them. Does then our type fail us at this point? Certainly not; it only serves to exhibit the perfect accuracy of it. In connection with the mediation of Christ, we find the same two things: His intercession averts the penal wrath of God, but does not remove the governmental consequences of His people's sins. The latter is conditioned upon our true repentance and confession, and the laying hold of God's restoring grace.

"And the Lord plagued the people, because they made the calf which Aaron made" (v. 35). In view of what we said in our last article, namely, that what is found here in Ex. 32 has a prophetic application not only to Israel in the Tribulation period, but also to Christendom in this present era, probably the reader is ready to ask, But how could this terrible sequel to Israel's sin ever have its counterpart in God's dealings with His own in this Dispensation of Grace? Surely Christ has never called for the "sword", to smite His own; surely He does not "plague" His redeemed! Ah, dear friend, the picture that is now before us was not drawn by man, and the heavenly Artist makes no flaws. If it be recalled that Rev. 1 to 3 supplies the key to the present application of our type, it will not be difficult to discover the antitype.

In the second of the seven epistles found there, we read, "Fear none of those things which thou shalt suffer: behold, the Devil shall cast some of you into prison, that ye may be tried." This epistle to Smyrna contemplates the second stage in the history of the Christian profession. It was a period marked by opposition and persecution, suffering and death. It was the martyr age, covering the last half of the first century A.D. and most of the second and third centuries. It was the time when the early Christians suffered so sorely under Nero and the other Roman emperors that succeeded him. It is unnecessary to enter into detail, most of our readers being doubtless aware of the fearful conditions that then prevailed, and of the fiery trials through which the people of God were called to pass. But what is not so well known, what in fact has been quite lost sight of by most Christian historians, is the *cause* of that era of suffering, as to *why* God permitted the Enemy to rage against His people—for, of course, neither the Roman emperors, or Satan who stirred them up, could move at all without *His* direct permission.

God does not afflict willingly (Lam. 3 : 33), nor are the sufferings of His people arbitary. The Scriptures expressly declare, "When a man's ways please the Lord, He maketh even his enemies to be at peace with him" Prov. 16 : 7). The reason *why* God sent such tribulation upon His people in the second era of Christendom's history was because of their evil conduct in the first period. The epistle which precedes the Smyrean in Rev. 2, namely, the Ephesian, makes known what that evil conduct was: "Thou hast left thy first love" (Rev. 2 : 4). Affection for Christ had waned: *He* was no longer "all and in all" to them. And, inward decline was swiftly followed by outward corruption, as is evidenced by the fearful fact that by the time the Smyean era had dawned the "synagogue of Satan" (Rev. 2 : 9) had already become established in their midst. Thus, as cause stands to effect, the leaving of "first love" at the beginning, occasioned the sufferings of the second and third centuries. It was God *chastening* His backslidden people!

Had the people of God remained true to Christ, had not the love of the world crept into their hearts, how vastly different history would have been! Nor is this a mere conjecture of ours. After Israel had suffered so severely from their enemies (see the book of Judges) God said through the Psalmist, "Oh that My people had hearkened unto Me, and Israel had walked in My ways! I *should soon* have subdued their enemies, and turned My hand against their adversaries" (81 : 13, 14)! But they did *not* "hearken" unto Him, nor did they walk in His ways. Sadly did history repeat itself. Just as God chastened Israel with the sword and "plague" then, so did He chasten and plague the early Church, using the Roman emperors as His scourge. Thus, what is seen in our type in Ex. 32 finds its counterpart in the history of Christendom. When there was departure from the Lord, when the spirit of idolatry came in, He called for the sword to smite them.

"And the Lord said unto Moses, Depart; and go hence, thou and the people which thou hast brought up out of the land of Egypt, unto the land which I sware unto Abraham, to Isaac, and to Jacob, saying, Unto thy seed will I give it: And I will send an angel before thee: and I will drive out the Canaanite, the Amorite, and the Hittie, and the Perizzite, the Hivite, and the Jebusite: Unto a land flowing with milk and honey: for I will not go up in the midst of thee; for thou art a stiffnecked people: lest I consume thee in the way" (33 : 1-3). Thus Moses by his supplication secured the immediate safety of the people, and the promise of an angelic guide and protector to go before them; but the further chastisement of their sin must yet be visited upon them. Nor were they restored to their covenant relations with Jehovah.

Moses was next directed to return to the camp with a message from the Lord. The details of that message, its effect upon the people, with the sequel, we must leave for consideration till our next article. May what has been before us bring to each of our hearts a greater horror and hatred of sin, and a more earnest crying unto God to be delivered from it.

CHAPTER 63

OUTSIDE THE CAMP

EXODUS 33:4-10

In order to enter into the significance of of what is to be before us on this present occasion, and especially to discern its typical application to Christendom to-day, careful attention must be paid to the context. Moses' pitching of the tent "outside the camp," and the seeking unto it of "every one which sought the Lord" can only be interpreted aright by noting carefully the imperative necessity for such a drastic action, and that, in the light of all which occasioned it. The section of Exodus in which our present portion is found begins with 32 : 1. In that chapter, as we have already seen, Israel is shown committing the awful sin of making and worshipping the golden calf. That, in turn, was the consequence of their throwing off allegiance to Jehovah. Having, in their hearts, cast off the God they loved. not, they now set up an idol patterned after their own evil lusts—a beast, graven in gold.

That the Lord did not there and then let loose the thunderbolts of His wrath and completely exterminate Israel is something which should bow our hearts before Him in wonder and worship, the more so when we observe what it was and who it was that averted His righteous anger against them, namely, the earnest and effectual supplications of the typical mediator. Blessed foreshadowment was this of Him who has entered into heaven itself, "now to appear in the presence of God for us" (Heb. 9 : 24), and who is "able also to save them unto the uttermost (to the last extremity) that come unto God by Him, seeing that He ever liveth to make intercession for them" (Heb. 7 : 25). Had there been no Moses to plead their cause, Israel had perished. And had we no High Priest to plead before God the merits of His atoning sacrifice on our behalf, we too would perish in this wilderness scene. It is the ministry of Christ on High which succors and sustains us while we journey to the promised inheritance.

How Moses must have *loved* his people! Do we not have more than a hint of this in the words of the Spirit in Heb. 11 : 24,

25, "By faith Moses, when he was come to years, refused to be called the son of Pharaoh's daughter: Choosing rather to suffer affliction *with* the people of God, than to enjoy the pleasures of sin for a season." His love for them is brought out again in Acts 7 : 23, "And when he was full forty years old, it came into his *heart* to visit his brethren the children of Israel." Blessed adumbrations were these of a greater than Moses, who refused not to lay aside His heavenly glory and come down to this sin-curst earth, where His "brethren" (Heb. 2 : 11) were in cruel bondage to sin and Satan. More blessed still is it to follow out the love of Moses for his people under the severest trials and testings. Though they appreciated him not, though they repeatedly murmured and rebelled against him, though they manifested their utter unworthiness of his unselfish devotion to them, yet nothing quenched his love for them. So too we read of Him to whom Moses pointed, "having loved His own which were in the world, He loved them *unto the end*" John 13 : 1). Nor could the awful sin of His people kill the affections of Moses: when unsparing judgment at the hands of a holy God was their only due, he stepped into the breech, and stood between them and His wrath.

But, as we saw in our last article, though the intercession of Moses averted the consuming wrath of God, yet it did not preclude the manifestations of His displeasure in a governmental way. The nation was not "consumed" (32 : 10), but it *was* "plagued" (32 : 35). This was due to no failure in the prayer of Moses, but to the lack of repentance on the part of the people. Most solemnly does this speak to us, and timely is its warning. How sadly neglected is this truth to day! If there be little or no preaching of "repentance" to the unsaved, there is still less to those who are saved. Yet, concerning the one we read "But, except ye *repent*, ye shall all likewise perish" (Luke 13 : 3); and of the other, it is to be noted, that the very first admonitory word of Christ to the seven churches in Rev. 2, 3 is, "Remember therefore from

333

whence thou are fallen, and *repent*" (2 : 5)! It is because there is so little repentance among God's people to-day that His chastening hand is laid so heavily on many of them.

"And the Lord said unto Moses, Depart, go up hence, thou and the people which thou hast brought up out of the land of Egypt, unto the land which I sware unto Abraham, to Isaac, and to Jacob, saying, Unto thy seed will I give it" (33 : 1). In these words Jehovah presses upon Moses the solemn position which Israel occupied. Having broken the covenant which they had made only a few weeks before (Ex. 19 : 5, 8; 24 : 7), they had thus forfeited their relationship to God as *His* people. Having rejected Him, He speaks to them according to their transgression, saying to Moses, "The people which *thou* hast brought up out of the land of Egypt." Nevertheless, He promised them the land, according to His absolute and unconditional promises to the patriarchs—to which Moses had appealed in his intercession (32 : 13). "And I will send an angel before thee: and I will drive out the Canaanite, the Amorite, and the Hittite, and the Perizzite, the Hivite, and the Jebusite : unto a land flowing with milk and honey" (vv. 2, 3).

Next, the Lord added, "For I will not go up in the midst of thee; for thou art a stiffnecked people : lest I consume thee in the way (v. 3). Solemn word was this; a real test of Israel's heart. "At the beginning of this book, when the people were in the furnace of Egypt, the Lord could say, 'I have surely seen the affliction of My people which are in Egypt, and have heard their cry by reason of their taskmasters; for I know their sorrows.' But now he has to say, 'I have seen this people, and, behold, it is a stiffnecked people', An afflicted people is an object of grace; but a stiffnecked people must be humbled. The cry of the oppressed Israel had been answered by the exhibition of grace; but the song of idolatrous Israel must be answered by the voice of stern rebuke" (C.H.M.).

Then we read, "And when the people heard these evil tidings, they mourned" (v. 4). Here was the first hopeful sign that the people gave. The Hebrew word for "mourn" in this passage means to sorrow or lament. The threat that Jehovah Himself would not accompany them moved Israel to deep contrition. How sad is the contrast presented in Rev. 3! There too the Lord is viewed as *not* being "in the midst" of His people, but outside (v. 20). Yet Laodicea is indifferent, content without Him (v. 17). When the Lord is no longer "in the midst" of His people, it is high time for them to "mourn."

"And no man did put on his ornaments. For the Lord had said unto Moses, Say unto the children of Israel, ye are a stiffnecked people : I will come up in the midst of thee in a moment, and consume thee : therefore now put off thy ornaments from thee, that I may know what to do unto thee" (vv. 4, 5). The removal of their ornaments was for the purpose of evidencing the genuineness of their contrition. Outward adornment was out of keeping with the taking of a low place before God. Contrariwise, external attractions and displays show up the absence of that lowliness of spirit and brokenness of heart which are of great price in the sight of God. The more true spirituality declines, the more an elaborate ritual comes to the fore. All around us Christendom is *putting on* as many "ornaments" as possible.

"And the children of Israel stripped themselves of their ornaments by the mount Horeb" (v. 6). This was a still more hopeful sign. Here we see Israel obeying God's command to humble themselves. This is ever the ground of further blessing. The promise is, "he that humbleth himself shall be exalted." A New Testament parallel to what we have before us here, is found in the case of the Corinthians. To them the apostle wrote, "Now ye are full, now ye are rich, ye have reigned as kings" (1 Cor. 4 : 8). There we see them with all their "ornaments" on. Later he was able to write, "For though I made you sorry with a letter, I do not repent, though I did repent : for I perceive that the same epistle hath made you sorry, though but for a season. Now I rejoice, not that ye were made sorry, but that ye sorrowed *to repentance; for ye were made sorry after a godly manner*" (2 Cor. 7 : 8, 9). They had "stripped themselves" of their "ornaments"!

"And Moses took the tabernacle, and pitched it without the camp, afar off from the camp, and called it the tabernacle of the congregation" (v. 7). This movement of Moses denoted three things : it was an act of *submission*, it was an act of *faith*, it was an act of *grace*. Let us enlarge a little upon these things. The going forth of Moses outside the camp was an act of submission, it was a bowing to God's righteous verdict. While Israel was a stiffnecked people, Jehovah could not remain in their "midst" (v. 3). While they continued in a state of impenitency He could not own them as His people (v. 1). Accordingly, Moses is here seen acquiescing in the Lord's holy judgment, and therefore leaves the place where He no longer was. Well would it be—both for God's glory and for their own good—if His people would act on this same principle to-day.

But more : the going forth of Moses outside the camp was an act of *faith*. This comes out plainly and most blessedly in what Israel's leader did on this occasion: he "*took*" the tabernacle and "pitched it without the camp." It should be pointed out that this was not the Tabernacle proper, with its three apartments, for this had not yet been erected. If the reader will refer back to Ex. 24 : 18 and 32 : 1 it will be found that Israel committed their great sin of worshipping the golden calf while Moses was up in the mount, during which time Jehovah had said to him, "Let them make Me a sanctuary: that I may dwell among them" (25 : 8)—details concerning which are found in the chapters that follow to the end of 31.

In the opening paragraphs of article 41 of this series (May 1927) on "The Coverings," we called attention to the distinction which is to be drawn between "the Tabernacle" (Heb. "mishkan") and "the Tent" (Heb. "Ohel"): the former signifies "dwelling-place"; the latter, simply "tent." The one refers to the abode of Jehovah, the other to the meeting-place for His people. The two are clearly distinguished in several scriptures, for example in Num. 3 : 25 we read of "the tabernacle *and* the tent." In the majority of passages where the A.V. has "tabernacle of the congregation," the Heb. reads "tent of the congregation." This holy building was Jehovah's place of abode, but Israel's place of assembly; they visited it, He remained there.

Now it was the "tent" and not the "tabernacle" which Moses here "took" and "pitched it outside the camp," for, as we have said, the tabernacle proper had not yet been built. In this action of Israel's leader we may discern the exercise of real faith. "Faith cometh by hearing, and hearing by the word of God" (Rom. 10 : 17). Moses had been hearing the word of God yonder in the mount, and now that he is down in the camp again his heart lays hold of, and anticipates, the actual erection of Jehovah's dwelling place. It was a temporary provision to meet a pressing emergency. "It does not appear that Moses, in pitching the tabernacle outside the camp, was acting under any direct commandment from the Lord. It was rather spiritual discernment, entering into both the character of God and the state of the people. Taught of God, he feels that Jehovah could no longer dwell in the midst of a camp which had been defiled by the presence of the golden calf. He therefore made a place outside, afar off from the camp, and called it the 'tabernacle of the congregation' " (Ed. Dennett).

Again; the pitching of the tent outside the camp was an act of *grace*. This will be seen the more clearly if we revert once more to the context; "The Lord had said unto Moses, Say unto the children of Israel, Ye are a stiffnecked people: I will come up in the midst of thee in a moment, and consume thee: therefore now put off thy ornaments from thee, that I may know what to do unto thee." God was here speaking after the manner of men—just as He does when He is said to "repent." It was as though He were weighing the condition of His wicked people, waiting to see whether or not their "mourning" was genuine. Before He smote, He would furnish opportunity for repentance. The people availed themselves of His forbearance: humbled by their sin, awed by the solemn tidings of iminent destruction, they stripped themselves of their ornaments. Then, as another has said, "He who pronounced judgment upon the people for their sins, provided a way for their escape." Those who "sought the Lord" were not only spared, but permitted to go forth unto the tent. Thus, "where sin abounded, grace did much more abound."

"And it came to pass, that every one which sought the Lord went unto the tent of the congregation, which was without the camp" (v. 7). Once more we have a striking illustration of the word "even so might grace reign through righteousness" (Rom. 5 : 21). God is "the God of all grace," yet it ever needs to be remembered that He never exercises grace at the expense of righteousness. God forgives sins, but it is because they were atoned for by Christ. Israel was delivered from the avenging angel in Egypt, but only because they were sheltered beneath the blood. So here: God maintained His righteousness. Holiness forbade Him entering the defiled camp, but grace made it possible for the people to meet Him outside.

"And it came to pass, that every one which sought the Lord went out unto the tent of the congregation, which was without the camp" (v. 7). Let us now consider the typical significance of this. We think at once of Heb. 13 : 13, "Let us go forth therefore unto Him, without the camp, bearing His reproach." Obviously, the Holy Spirit here had Ex. 33 : 7 before Him, and it is in the light of what is there recorded that we must interpret this New Testament exhortation. What we have there is a call to separation, but unless we pay close attention to the type we shall err in our application of the antitype. The all-important thing is to bear steadily in mind the *circumstances* under which Moses pitched the Tent "outside the camp." It was not when Israel murmured (Ex. 16 : 2), when they desecrated the sabbath (16 27, 28), when the Amalekites fought against them (17 : 8); it was after Israel had disowned Jehovah and set up the golden calf. General and *open idolatry* in the camp constitutes the call to "go forth" outside it!

The same principle holds good in the interpretation of Heb. 13 : 13. This exhortation was not given to the Corinthians, where a sectarian spirit prevailed, where immorality had been condoned, and where the Lord's supper had been turned into a carnal feast. Nor was the call given to the Galatians, among whom false doctrine, of a serious character, had come in. Instead, it was addressed to "Hebrews." The believing Jews were enjoined to forsake the unbelieving Nation who had despised and rejected Christ. The "camp" was guilty of the murder of God's Son, hence the call to forsake it. What we would here press upon the Christian reader is that neither Ex. 33 : 7 nor Heb. 13 : 13 supplies any warrant for Christians forsaking "churches" or companies of God's professing people where Christ *is* owned, honoured, worshipped. There are those claiming to "gather unto the Lord," who insist they are the *only* people that are on true scriptural ground. They have separated themselves not only from false systems, but from the great majority of God's own people. Little wonder that to-day *they* are more sectarian than any of the denominations, and that God has blown upon their proud and pharisaical claims. To "go forth unto Him without *the camp*" is a vastly different thing than separating from *God's own people*. All who are dear to Christ should be dear to the Christian.

It was corporate idolatry which made Jehovah refuse to continue in Israel's midst. It was when the Lord Himself had been rejected, and not till then, that Moses pitched the Tent outside the camp. Nothing short of this ever warrants a Christian from breaking away from those who profess the name of Christ. Perfection will be found no where on this earth, and the loftier the pretentions of those claiming to come nearest to perfection, the least grounds for such a profession they will evidence. A drum makes a big noise, but it is very hollow inside! No, ideal conditions, a faithful carrying out of all the revealed will of God, are not to be met with among *any* company of Christians. Failure is stamped upon everything which. God has committed to man. But that does not justify me in holding aloof from my erring brethren and sisters, and assuming an attitude of "I am holier than thou"; for in the sight of God I am probably a greater failure than they are. We are all of us quick to discover the mote in another's eye, while complacently impervious to the *beam* in our own eye.

"Strengthen the things which remain (not "pull down"), that are ready to die," is God's word to us (Rev. 3 : 2). "Lift up the hands which hang down, and the feeble knees" (Heb. 12 : 12): obedience to this will accomplish far more than criticising and condemning every body and every thing. "Forbearing one another in love" (Eph. 4 : 2), implies there is that in each of us which is a trial to the other. There will be much to test patience and love in any "church" or gathering, but if the Lord is there, that is the place for me too. He is "long-suffering," so must I be. But when He is disowned, when a *false* god is set up in His place, when "another Jesus" (2 Cor. 11 : 4) is preached (a "Jesus" who is not the God man, born of a virgin, died for the sins of His people, rose again in bodily triumph over death), it is high time for me to get out. To remain in a place where He is denied would be for me to dishonour my Lord. It was on *this* principle that Moses here acted; and not Moses only, but "every one who sought the Lord."

Thus, the principle which is to guide us to-day in our application of Heb. 13 : 13 to any local situation, is simple and plain. If I am worshipping with a company of Christians where the Lord Jesus is owned as the Christ of God, as the alone Saviour for sinners, as the Exemplar of His people, though the preaching there may not be as edifying as I could desire, though my fellow disciples may come far short of what I wish, that is no reason why I should desert them; rather it is an occasion for me to be much in prayer on their behalf, and by my own walk seek to show them the way of the Lord more perfectly. But, on the other hand, if I am in a place where the Christ of God is denied, the inspiration of the Scriptures repudiated, the Holy Spirit quenched through a false god having been set up, then no matter what my friends may do, no matter what may be the decision of my brethren, I am responsible before God to separate myself from what is so grossly dishonouring to Him.

"And it came to pass, when Moses went out unto the tabernacle, that all the people rose up, and stood every man at his tent door, and looked after Moses, until he was gone into the tabernacle" (v. 8). From this it appears that not many responded to the call of separation. "The majority stood at their tent doors, interested in Moses, and looking after him, and seeing the pillar of cloud stand at the entrance of the tent, but not going out! They seem to represent those who have reverence for divine things, and are interested in the truth, but who remain in the camp. God-fearing persons, but not knowing the presence of the Lord in its attractive and satisfying power" (C. A. Coates).

"And it came to pass, as Moses entered into the tabernacle, the cloudy pillar descended, and stood at the door of the tabernacle, and the Lord talked with Moses" (v. 9). The "cloudy pillar" was the visible symbol of Jehovah's presence. This is the third time in Exodus we find mention of it. First, in 13 : 21 we read, "And the Lord went before them by day in a pillar of a cloud, to lead them the way; and by night in a pillar of fire, to give them light." Second, in 14 : 19, 20 we are told, "And the pillar of the cloud went from before their face, and stood behind them: and it came between the camp of the Egyptians and the camp of Israel; and it was a cloud and darkness to them, but it gave light by night to these: so that the one came not near the other all the night." Third, "the cloudy pillar descended, and stood at the door of the tabernacle, and the Lord talked with Moses." Thus it was connected first with *guidance*, then with *protection*, now with *communion*.

"The cloudy pillar descended, and stood at the door of the tabernacle, and the Lord talked with Moses." Blessed answer of God was this to the confidence of His servant.

How true are His words "them that honour Me I will honour." Moses was not put in confusion : his submission and faith were amply rewarded. God never disappoints those who seek His glory and count upon His grace. It is the compromisers, the fearers of men, and the unbelieving who are the losers. O for more single-eyed devotion to the Lord, then we shall have Him "talk with" (not "to") us.

"And all the people saw the cloudy pillar stand at the tabernacle door : and all the people rose up and worshipped, every man in his tent door" (v. 10). Nothing but a gracious manifestation of the Lord will produce real worship, and the more we are conscious of His *unmerited* favour, the more fervent will our worship be. Nor must we ignore the Spirit's notice of the *position* occupied by these prostrate Israelites : they "worshipped every man in his *tent* door." This has a voice for us if we have hearts to receive it. The "tent" is the symbol of the pilgrim, and it is only as *this* character is maintained that worship will be sustained. The blessed sequel we must leave for consideration till our next article. May the Lord exercise each of us by what has been before us.

CHAPTER 64

GRACE ABOUNDING

EXODUS 33:11-17

Our present passage brings before us one of the most wondrous and blessed scenes described anywhere on the pages of the Old Testament Scriptures. Apart from the circumstances and occasion which gave rise to it, the character of this incident itself should move our hearts to profoundest wonderment and praise. Here we behold the typical mediator prevailing in his intercession for a sinful people, not only in averting the wrath of God, but in securing His continued presence in their midst. Here we are given to see not only the external symbol of His presence drawing near unto men, but the Lord Himself speaking to Moses "as a man speaketh unto his friend." Here we listen to the Lord not only promising to conduct Israel across the howling wilderness, but saying, "I will give thee rest." Verily, "Where sin abounded, grace did much more abound."

Let it be pointed out though, that this precious revelation of the abounding grace of God is recorded not only for our admiration, but also for our learning. Most valuable instruction is to be found here if we take to heart the *order* of events in this portion of the Divinely inspired account of the history of Israel. First, we have in Ex. 32 : 1-6 the narrative of their awful sin. Second, we have the intercession of Moses averting the "consuming" wrath of God (32 : 11-14). Third, we have the sore chastening of the people for it (32 : 25-28, 35). Fourth, we have the repentance of Israel (33 : 4-6). Fifth, we have Moses pitching the Tent "outside the camp," and every one "which sought the Lord," going forth unto it (33 : 7-10). Now we have Jehovah's response to this action of His servant: He speaks "face to face" with Moses. Such amazing condescension, such wondrous grace, was only manifested after sin had been owned and separation from it had been evidenced. The important practical lessons to be drawn from this will be pointed out in our exposition below.

At the beginning of Ex. 33 we hear Jehovah saying, "I will not go up in the midst of thee ; for thou art a stiffnecked

people ; lest I consume thee in the way" (v. 3). Israel's terrible sin had necessitated the retirement of a holy God from them. To have remained among them would have required their total destruction. The mediation of Moses had averted the threatened storm of God's wrath, but until Israel repented the Lord could not come in among them again. The same principle holds good to-day in connection with any company who profess to be the people of God. While gross sin is allowed, the Lord will not manifest Himself among them, and to such a people His word is "Draw nigh to God, and He will draw nigh to you. Cleanse your hands, ye sinners ; and purify your hearts, ye double minded" James 4 : 8.

The next thing we read in our chapter is, "When the people heard these evil tidings, they mourned" (v. 4). The greatness of their sin began to be realized, and so their "drinking and playing" (32 : 6) was turned into sorrow. Then we are told "and the children of Israel stripped themselves of their ornaments" (v. 6). This evidenced the genuineness of their contrition ; this was a bringing forth of "fruits meet for repentance" (Matt. 3 : 8) ; it was the outward expression of their having taken a lowly place before God. Finally, "It came to pass that every one which sought the Lord went out into the Tent of the congregation, which was without the camp" (v. 7). This corresponds with, "He that covereth his sins shall not prosper : but whoso confesseth and *forsaketh* them, shall have mercy" (Prov. 28 : 13).

Following Moses' going forth from the camp and his entrance into the Tent, which, by faith he had pitched, "the cloudy pillar descended, and stood at the door of the Tent, and the Lord talked with Moses." The effect of this upon the penitent and ornament-stripped people is blessed to behold : "And all the people rose up and worshipped, every man in his tent 'door" (v. 10). Jehovah was once more given His true place. The false god (the golden calf) was repudiated ; the true God was now worshipped. Thus were they, in infinite grace, brought back from their wanderings and made to bow in wondering adoration before the manifested symbol of Jehovah's presence. The blessed sequel we are now to contemplate.

" And the Lord spake unto Moses face to face, as a man speaketh unto his friend " (v. 11). This was the most glorious moment in all the life of Moses, and the most blessed revelation he every received from God. This even surpassed his experience in the Mount, when he received such wondrous communications from Jehovah. There was an intimacy of approach and a closeness of communion such as he had not been permitted to enjoy before. In the 12th of Numbers, where we read of Miriam and Aaron challenging the authority of Moses, Jehovah vindicated him by saying, " My servant Moses is not so, who is faithful in all Mine house " (v. 7) ; and then He added, " With him will I speak mouth to mouth, even apparently, and not in dark speeches."

" And the Lord spake unto Moses face to face, as a man speaketh unto his friend." These words must not be interpreted in such a way as to clash with the last verse of our chapter : " And thou shalt see My back parts, but My face shall not be seen." That which is before us here is free and intimate fellowship between the Lord and His servant. And this, be it noted, was the immediate sequel to his separation from what was dishonouring to Jehovah. Ah, dear reader, going forth unto Him without the camp may, yea, must, involve " bearing His reproach " (Heb. 13 : 13) ; but O the *compensation* — He rewards such faithfulness by manifestations of Himself, by the intimacies of His love, as are never enjoyed while we remain in associations which are derogatory to His honour.

" And the Lord spake unto Moses face to face, as a man speaketh unto his friend." That Moses, the mediator, is here also a blessed type of Christ, hardly needs saying. What we have here is a precious adumbration of the relations existing between the Father and the Son. Before the incarnation He could say, " That I was by Him, as one brought up with Him : and I was daily His delight, rejoicing always before Him " (Prov. 8 : 30). After the incarnation, we read of " the Only-begotten Son which is in *the bosom* of the Father " (John 1 : 18). And again, " For the Father loveth the Son, and showeth Him all things that Himself doeth " (John 5 : 20). And again, " I am not alone, because the Father is with Me " (John 16 : 32). So now, He is seated upon *the Father's* throne (Rev. 3 : 21)—the place of affection and intimacy.

" And he turned again into the camp : but his servant Joshua, the son of Nun, a young man, departed not out of the tent " (v. 11). Let us seek to ponder first the practical lesson exemplified for us in this statement, before we point out its typical signification. That which here receives illustration is most important to lay hold of, particularly for those who are called by God to occupy positions of leadership. Before a servant of God is qualified to minister unto His people he must himself seek unto the Lord; before he has any message for them, the Lord must speak " face to face " unto him. In other words, power for service is obtained only by maintaining intimate fellowship with God. But more : though he returns and ministers unto the people, yet in spirit he remains still inside the Tent. Here, as always in the book of Exodus, Moses and Joshua have to be considered *together*, as mutually complementing each other.

" This section closes with a double type— Moses returning to the camp, and Joshua departing not from within the Tent. Moses represents the energy of love that would serve the people of God. It is a man with whom Jehovah has spoken ' face to face, as a man speaketh with his friend ' who can return to serve the people of God in all the holy separation of the spot where he has been, and of the communications which have been made to him. Such a man would not compromise the truth, nor would he allow himself to be entangled with what compromised the truth, but he would be in readiness to serve all in grace and faithfulness in relation to the will of God. But such service ever has as its attendant the spirit of Joshua. Whatever activities of service there may be, *in spirit* the servant does not leave his sweet retreat ; he is always in spirit ' outside the camp.' His affections have their abiding place there ; his satisfaction and rest is in the Lord " (C. A. Coates).

" And he turned again into the camp : but his servant Joshua, the son of Nun, a young man, departed not out of the camp." It is by no means an easy matter to work out the details of this type—due, no doubt, to the dimness of our spiritual vision. There are several passages in which Moses and Joshua are linked together in Exodus — the book which speaks of redemption. This is the more noticeable as Joshua is not mentioned at all in Leviticus. First, in Ex. 17, we find Moses and Joshua supplementing each other in connection with resisting the onslaught of Amalek. As we sought to show in article 25 of this series (Jan., 1926), Joshua there is a type of the Holy Spirit subjugating, but not exterminating, the " flesh " in the Christian. Then, in Ex. 24 : 13, we read, " And Moses rose up, and his *minister* Joshua : and *Moses* went up into the Mount of God." Here we have in figure the Holy Spirit as the Minister of an ascended Christ : during the present dispensation the Holy Spirit is maintaining the interests and glorifying Christ. Then, in 32 : 17, 18, we have, in type, the Holy Spirit taking note of the sins of God's people. Here in 33 : 11 it seems to be the Spirit's indwelling the true

Church, compare 1 Cor. 3 : 16, Eph. 2 : 22.

" And Moses said unto the Lord, See, thou sayest unto me, Bring up this people; and thou hast not let me know whom Thou wilt send with me. Yet Thou hast said, I know thee by name, and thou hast also found grace in My sight" (v. 12). Here, and in the verses which immediately follow, we have another blessed foreshadowment of Christ as our Mediator, interceding before God, maintaining us in His *favour*. What is of first importance to take note of is, that it is as a man who has " found grace " in the sight of God, Moses here pleads. Mark how strikingly this particular feature is emphasised by its repeated mention: in vv. 12, 13, 16, 17 the words " found grace in Thy sight " or " found grace in My sight " are found. How plainly this points to the Lord Jesus as the One who, on behalf of His poor people, has obtained favour before God. It is on the ground of His own acceptableness that Christ now pleads for us. It is the apprehension of this which gives peace to the heart. God's favour to His people is based upon nothing that He finds in them ; it is solely the consequence of what He has obtained through Christ.

" And Moses said unto the Lord, See, Thou sayest unto me, Bring up this people: and Thou hast not let me know whom Thou wilt send with me." At first sight this may seem to clash with what the Lord had said to Moses in 32 : 34, " Therefore now go, lead the people unto the place of which I have spoken unto thee: behold, Mine Angel shall go before thee." But a closer reading will observe a notable distinction. In 32 : 34 Jehovah had spoken of His Angel going " *before* thee " for, while Israel remained impenitent the Lord Himself could not remain " in the midst of thee " (33 : 3). But now that the people had repudiated their sin, and had evidenced their separation from it, Moses says, " Thou hast not let me know whom Thou wilt send *with* me." Blessed distinction: may our hearts lay hold of it. Moses knew full well who *would go* with them, but, in view of Israel's sin, he here takes the place of a supplicant.

" Yet Thou hast said, I know thee by name, and thou hast also found grace in My sight." This carries us back to Ex 3. At the burning bush, where God first called Moses, He had addressed him by name: " God called unto him out of the midst of the bush, and said, Moses, Moses " (3 : 4). And *why is it* that Moses now refers to that memorable experience at the backside of the desert? Because it was there that Jehovah had made Himself known as " the God of Abraham, the God of Isaac, and the God of Jacob " ; as the One who declared, " And I am come down to deliver them out of the hand of the Egyptians, and to bring them out

of that land *unto a good land* and a large, unto a land flowing with milk and honey " (3 : 8). God having pledged Himself to this, His word must be fulfilled, His purpose accomplished, no matter what the contrariety of the people might be. Thus we behold the boldness of Moses' faith. Here, too, we should look from the type to the anti-type. It is on the ground of God's everlasting *covenant* with Christ that He now exercises mercy to His unworthy people.

" Now therefore, I pray Thee, if I have found grace in Thy sight, show me now Thy way, that I way know Thee, that I may find grace in Thy sight " (v. 13). Very blessed is this. The sad failure of Israel presented itself now to Moses only as an occasion for the unfolding of God's way, and of the knowledge of Him. God had made promises, He had sworn by Himself, and His promises ensured the actual entrance of Israel into Canaan, not their extermination in the wilderness. Moses therefore seeks unto Him now to learn His way. God's " way " is the course He takes in faithfulness in order to make good that which He has pledged.

A number of valuable practical thoughts are suggested by this verse. First, we are unable to discover God's " ways " for ourselves. This was recognized by the Psalmist when he prayed, " Show me Thy ways, O Lord ; teach me Thy paths " (25 : 4). And again, " Teach me Thy way, O Lord, and lead me in a plain path " (27 : 11). Second, only God Himself can " show " us His way. Even the incarnate Son (having taken the place of perfect subjection) said, " Thou wilt *show* Me the path of life " (Psa. 16 : 11). Ah, it ever needs to be remembered that " the meek will He guide in judgment, and the meek will He teach His way " (Psa. 25 : 9). Third, it is as God condescends to show us His way that we get to know Him better: " Show me Thy way *that* I may· *know* Thee."

" And consider that this nation is Thy people " (v. 14). This was Moses' answer to the word of Jehovah before the Tent had been pitched outside the camp. Then the Lord had said, " Depart, and go up hence, thou and the people which *thou* hast brought up out of the land of Egypt." Here was the response of faith: " Consider that this nation is Thy people." It was Moses casting himself back upon the word, the oath, the covenant of Jehovah to Abraham, Isaac and Jacob, renewed to himself at the burning bush. It is to be noted that Moses made the same plea at a later stage in Israel's history, when, in consequence of their unbelief at Kadesh-barnea, they again provoked the Lord to anger: see Deut. 9 : 26 and context. In a coming day, the godly Jewish remnant will repeat this argument: Joel 2 : 17. Finally, it is to be noted that our great High Priest makes this the ground of His plea too: "I pray not for the world, but for them which Thou has given Me; for they are *Thine*" (John 17 : 9).

"And He said, My presence shall go with thee, and I will give thee rest" (v. 14). We believe that the translators of our English Version have quite missed the point here. As it reads, the response of Moses in v. 15 wou'd be the language of doubt and unbelief. If Jehovah had positively affirmed that His presence *would* go with Moses, to answer, "If Thy presence go *not* with us" would be excuseless. So too his question in v. 16. is meaningless if God had already given him assurance. Finally, in such a case, the Lord's words in v. 17 would be a needless repetition. All difficulty is at once removed if, with the "Companion Bible" we punctuate v. 14 as a question: "Shall My presence go with thee? and shall I give thee rest?" It was as much as to say, How can My presence go with thee after this rejection of Me? The Lord was emphasising the enormity of Israel's sin, and pressing the claims of His holiness.

"And he said unto Him, If Thy presence go not with me, carry us not up hence" (v. 15). The issue was still in the balance. The Lord had bidden Moses say to Israel, "put off thy ornaments from thee, that I may know what to do unto thee" (v. 5). Israel had obeyed this command, and Moses had gone forth without the camp to seek unto the Lord (v. 7). His faith is now put to the test; not so much his faith in God personally, but in the superabounding of His grace. "Shall My presence go with thee? and shall I give thee rest?" was a challenge to his heart. The Lord frequently tests His people thus that He may the better discover to themselves the real ground of their confidence. When many of His disciples were forsaking Him, Christ asked the twelve, "Will ye also go away?" (John 6 : 66, 67). He knew, and they knew, that they would not; but He was drawing out their hearts unto Himself.

"And he said unto Him, If Thy presence go not with me, carry us not up hence." Nobly did Moses rise to the occasion; or, shall we say, Blessedly did his heart respond to Jehovah's challenge. He felt that without the Lord's own presence with them, all was in vain. No confidence did he have in himself; nor was he satisfied with the prospect of the Angel going "before" them. It was the Lord's own presence, *communion* with Him, his soul craved. And is not this still the longing of every renewed heart? Very touching is it to behold Moses now identifying Himself with Israel: "Carry *us* not up hence." How blessedly did he again foreshadow Him who has said, "Behold I *and* the children which God hath given Me" (Heb. 2 : 13)

"For wherein shall it be known here that I and Thy people have found grace in Thy sight? Is it not in that *Thou* goest with us? So shall we be separated, I and Thy people, from all the people that are upon the face of the earth" (v. 16). It is to God's sovereign and illimitable grace (limited only by the bounds which our lack of faith puts upon it) that Moses now appeals. It was all he could appeal to, but, as the next verse shows, it was enough; his appeal was not in vain. Again we see him identifying himself with the sinful and penitent nation: twice over in this verse he says, "I and Thy people." "This is no mean adumbration of the heart of Christ—this intense love of Moses for Israel, linking them with himself in *his* place of favour before God. And not only so, but rising higher, he now links them with God. We have remarked that God took Israel on their own ground, and since they had rejected Him, He had said to Moses, 'thy' people. But now—now that Moses acts as mediator, has gained the ear of God, he says again, 'Thy people'" (Ed. Dennett).

"So shall we be separated, I and Thy people, from all the people that are upon the face of the earth." This is very important. The Lord's presence in the midst of His people is for the purpose of *separating* them from all others who are not His people. How little this is apprehended to-day. But let us return again to the blessed typical picture here: "he thus claims, as it were, as proof of Divine favour—restoration of favour—God's own presence with His people. It could not be otherwise known, and the fact of His presence would separate them off from all other people. It is the same in principle during this dispensation. The presence of the Holy Ghost on earth, building His people into an habitation for God, separates from all else, and so completely, that there are but two spheres — sphere of the presence and action of the Holy Ghost, and sphere of the action and power of Satan" (Ed. Dennett).

"And the Lord said unto Moses, I *will do* this thing also that thou hast spoken: for thou *hast* found grace in My sight, and I know thee by name" (v. 17). The mediation of Moses completely prevailed. This word of Jehovah's was His own answer to the questions He had asked in v. 14: "My presence shall go with thee, and I will give thee rest." This was the Lord's own response to the pleas of His servant, and it was all that was needed for the assurance of his heart and as the guaranty of Israel's safe conduct across the wilderness. It was grace pure and simple, sovereign and long-suffering grace. Grace vouchsafed to a people who had forfeited every claim upon God. Grace granted in response to the prevailing intercession of the mediator. Reference to this was made long after by Jehovah through one of the prophets, "Thus saith the Lord, The people which were left of the sword found grace in the wilderness; even Israel, when I went to cause him to rest" (Jer. 31 : 2).

How blessed to know that Israel's God is the Christian's God. "My presence shall go with thee": this same precious assurance is given to us while we journey through this world. No matter what the roughness of the path may be, no matter what the trials and disappointments of the way, the Lord Himself is with us. Has He not said, "Lo I am *with you* alway, even unto the end of the age" (Matt. 28 : 20)! With us to guard and protect, to lead and guide, to counsel and cheer. Ever with us, "a very *present* help in trouble" (Psa. 46 : 1). O for faith to realize this. O for a faith to *act* upon it— an ever-present, all sufficient Christ, by our side.

How differently should we conduct ourselves did we but live in the enjoyment and power of this! "Fear thou not, for I am *with* thee: be not dismayed, for I am thy God" (Isa. 41 : 10). "When thou passest through the waters, I will be *with* thee; and through the rivers, they shall not overflow thee: when thou walkest through the fire, thou shalt not be burned; neither shall the flame kindle upon thee" (Isa. 43 : 2). Was He not with the three Hebrews in Babylon's furnace! Then let us exclaim, "Yea, though I walk through the valley of the shadow of death, I will fear no evil: for Thou art *with* me" (Psa. 23 : 4). Yes, His own promise is, "I will *never* leave thee nor forsake thee" (Heb. 13 : 5). Praise and glory be to His name.

"My presence shall go with thee, and I will give thee rest." There are two things here: the Lord's "presence" for the present, "rest" assured for the future. What more can we ask? Blessed promise! Glorious prospect! "Rest," the rest of God (Heb. 4 : 1). Rest from sin, rest from toil, rest from sorrow. O for faith to anticipate it. O for hope to enjoy it even now, for "faith is the substance of things hoped for, the evidence of things not seen" (Heb. 11 : 1). Gird up thy loins, fellow-pilgrims. This wilderness journey is not to last for ever. A few more years at most, perhaps only moments, and thou shalt be where the wicked cease from troubling and where the weary are at rest. In the meantime, He will deal with us as He dealt with Israel of old: "He redeemed them, and He bare them, and *carried* them all the days of old" (Isa. 63 : 9). This was grace, grace abounding over all their sin. And this God is our God, "the God of all *grace*" (1 Peter 5 : 10). May our hearts adore Him and our lives show forth His praise.

CHAPTER 65

SOVEREIGN MERCY

EXODUS 33:18-23

In studying the varied contents of Ex. 33 we need to remind ourselves of the particular book in which these events are recorded. They are found not in Leviticus, but in Exodus. Everything has been placed by the Holy Spirit in each book of Scripture according to a principle of selection: only that which was in perfect accord with the special design of that book, only that which contributed directly to its theme, is given a place; every thing irrelevant, every thing which did not illustrate or amplify the purpose and character of it, being excluded. This is true not only of the Gospels (see our book "Why Four Gospels?"), where each evangelist was guided by the Inspirer of Scripture to include only that which was in full accord with the particular character in which he was setting forth the Lord Jesus, but it holds good just as truly and strikingly of the four books dealing with the early history of the nation of Israel. It is only by recognising this that we can appreciate the perfections of the Spirit's handiwork, and as we do so, often the key is found which opens the deeper meaning of many a passage.

Genesis is the book wherein we have illustrated the foundation-truth of Divine *election*. This is seen in God's singling out of Abram, and making him the progenitor of His chosen people. Exodus sets forth the blessed truth of Divine *redemption*, God ransoming and emancipating an enslaved people from the house of bondage, and bringing them into a place of nearness to Himself. Leviticus is the book of Divine *worship*, of priestly privileges and exercises, revealing to us the provisions which God has made for His people to approach unto Him. Thus, in these first three books of Holy Writ we have wrought before us that which relates, peculiarly, to each of the Persons in the Godhead. The Father's predestination, the Son's propitiation," the Spirit's inspiration to worship.

As we have just said, the great subject which is unfolded in the book of Exodus is that of *redemption*. This was pointed out by us several times in the earlier articles of this series, but we mention it again because it throws light on the chapter now before us. What we would here call attention to is, that redemption not only procures deliverance from surfdom and slavery, not only brings its favoured objects into a place of nearness to God, but, through the mediation of the Redeemer, it secures a *continuance* of God's grace and mercy while His redeemed are still journeying to the purchased inheritance; and it ensures the *continued* presence of the Lord in the midst of His feeble and failing people. In 33 : 13-16 Moses is found pleading for God's continued presence with them. In v. 17 the Lord answers, "I will do this thing also that thou hast spoken." At the close of our book, we behold the fullfilment of this. After Moses had erected the tabernacle, the visible symbol of Jehovah's presence, descended and filled it, and we read, "The cloud of the Lord was upon the tabernacle by day, and fire was on it by night, in the sight of all the house of Israel, throughout *all* their journeys" (40 : 38).

In our last few articles we have been occupied with the love of Moses for his people, and his prevailing intercession on their behalf before God. In this present one we find him a beautiful type of the Lord Jesus. But what we would here emphasise is the fact that the record of this is found in the book of *Exodus,* teaching us that the intercession of Christ on our behalf, with all the blessings which it secures, is the fruit of that *redemption* which He has wrought out for His people. Now as we have seen, the first great blessing which the prayer of Moses obtained for his people was the averting of God's consuming wrath (32 : 10, 14). The second grand privilege his supplications won for them—on the ground of having *himself* found favour in the eyes of God—was the securing of Jehovah's continued presence with them (32 : 12-17). Keeping these things in mind, let us now turn to the seventh and last recorded thing in Ex. 32 and 33—compare the second paragraph in the preceding article.

" And he said, I beseech Thee, show me Thy glory " (v. 18). Our pen falters as we take up such a verse as this, for what sinful creature is competent to write upon such an exalted theme as the glory of God? Nevertheless, some blessed thoughts are suggested by this request of Moses. First of all, contemplating it in the light of the book in which it is found, are we not taught thereby that this is both the longing of the redeemed and the goal of their redemption—to behold the glory of God! That this longing is yet to be fully realised, that this wondrous goal will be reached, we know from the last chapter but one of Holy Writ, for of the Eternal City we read, " And I saw no temple therein, for the Lord God Almighty and the Lamb are the temple of it. And the city had no need of the sun, neither of the moon, to shine in it: for the *glory* of God did lighten it, and the Lamb is the light thereof " (Rev. 21 : 22, 23).

"And he said, I beseech Thee, show me Thy glory." Pondering this verse next in the light of its immediate context, we are shown what is the sure product of intimate fellowship with God. The great Jehovah had condescended to draw very near to the one who had separated himself from evil, for we are told, " the Lord spake unto Moses face to face, as a man speaketh unto his friend " (v. 11). And what was the consequence of this upon Moses? Not only did he have freedom in supplicating His grace, but there was a holy longing to know more of Himself. Such is ever the outflow of real and close communion with God: the more we know of Him, the more we desire to know. The closer God deigns to draw near to His people, the more constrained are they to cry, "Lord, lift Thou up the light of Thy countenance upon us " (Psa. 4 : 6).

" And he said, I beseech Thee, show me Thy glory." If the connection between this and the previous verse be noted, we are taught here another valuable lesson on prayer, one which we do well to take to heart. In the previous verse we read, " And the Lord said unto Moses, I will do this also that thou hast spoken: for thou hast found grace in My sight, and I know thee by name." Twice Moses had petitioned Jehovah; first not to consume His people; then, to beg His continuance in their midst. Each of these supplications had been graciously granted. Emboldened by his success, instead of being content therewith, Moses presents (we may well say) a still greater petition. And, as the Lord's response denotes, He was not displeased at his servant's importunity. Oh to remember in prayer that "We are coming to a *King*," then let us *"large* petitions with us bring." It is thus that we *honour* Him.

" And He said, I will make all My goodness pass before thee " (v. 19). How striking to learn here that God's "glory" is His "goodness," His "goodness" His "glory." And what is the goodness of the Lord? Ah, who is capable of returning answer: human definitions are worthless. Shall we say that His "Goodness" is what He *is* in Himself, the sum of His personal excellencies? But has not the Lord Himself answered our question, and fulfilled His promise to Moses when He declared, "The Lord, The Lord God, merciful and gracious, long-suffering, and abundant in goodness and truth, Keeping mercy for thousands, forgiving iniquity and transgression and sin, and that will by no means clear the guilty; visiting the iniquity of the fathers upon the children" (34: 6, 7).

"And I will proclaim the name of the Lord before thee" (v. 19). Was not this the renewal and confirmation of what He had announced at the beginning, when, at the burning bush, He first called Moses? Moses had asked, "When I come unto the children of Israel, and shall say unto them, The God of your fathers hath sent me unto you; and they shall say unto me, *what is His name?* What shall I say unto them?" He made answer, "I am that I am: and He said, Thus shalt thou say unto the children of Israel, I AM hath sent me unto you;" and then He added, "Thus shalt thou say unto the children of Israel, The Lord God of your fathers, the God of Abraham, the God of Isaac, and the God of Jacob, hath sent me unto you; *this* is My name *forever,* and this is My memorial unto all generations" (Ex. 3 : 13-15).

"And will be gracious to whom I will be gracious, and will show mercy on whom I will show mercy" (v. 19). These words bring before us one of the most precious truths found in Scripture for the comfort of God's people, yet is it one that is little understood to-day. In 2 Tim. 2 : 15 the servant of God is bidden, "Study to show thyself approved unto God, a workman that needeth not to be ashamed, *rightly dividing* the word of truth." But how few "rightly divide" between the *grace* of God and the *mercy* of God! How many regard them as being virtually synonymous. How much we lose by failing to distinguish between things that differ, by confusing in our thoughts things which are perfectly distinct. Scripture never confuses the grace and mercy of God, and it is to our deep loss if we do so.

The *order* in which these two attributes of God are here mentioned supplies the key to the distinction between them:

"mercy" comes in after the "grace" of God. Why is this? Because mercy is the wondrous provision of God to meet the desperate needs of a people who have failed to respond to His grace. And *this* is what is so blessedly brought out here in Ex. 33. From Egypt to Sinai God had dealt with Israel on the ground of pure *grace*. In themselves they were no better than the Egyptians, yet had God, in His sovereign benignity, brought them out of the house of bondage, conducted them through the Red Sea, separated them unto Himself, supplied their every need in the wilderness. But how had the people requited such favours and blessings? They had revolted against Him, they had repudiated Him, they had set up an idol in His place. Was, then, their case hopeless? True they had "mourned," stripped themselves of their ornaments, and bowed in worship before the symbol of His manifested presence by the Tent. But could a God whose favours had been so lightly esteemed go on with them any further?

As we have seen, the typical mediator had interceded on behalf of the people who had sinned so heinously. And now it was that the Lord made one of the most blessed revelations of His character to be found anywhere in Holy Writ. Something was here made known of God's nature which had never before been revealed in its real depths, namely, His *mercy*. It is true we have mention of that precious word in the book of Genesis, but the full interpretation of its meaning is not there discovered. It was here in Ex. 33 that this deep and blessed spring in God's Being was made manifest—so rich, so full, so blessed. Man's extremity was God's opportunity. The Divine outflow of *grace* had been abused, His righteous law had been broken, the relation entered into by the Sinitaic covenant (Ex. 24) had been disrupted by the rebellion of Israel. Now, "mercy" sovereign and absolute, was the resource of Him who retires into Himself and acts from Himself; only by the exercise of *mercy* could sinning Israel be extricated from their merited doom.

As we have said above, from the time when Jehovah first took up His enslaved people in the land of Pharoah, till the waters gushed out of the smitten rock at Rephidim, all was a stream of pure grace, that is, free gifts, Divine favours to a people who had no worthiness or merits of their own. But here in Ex. 33 Israel were given cause to praise God on an altogether different ground, and from this time onwards we find that ground the great theme of Israel's songs—"O give thanks unto the Lord, for He is good: for His *mercy* endureth forever" (Psa 106 : 1). In proof of this contrast, note the contents of Psa.

105 and 106. Let the reader turn to them and mark carefully how that in Psa. 105, which also opens with "O give thanks unto the Lord," that the *grace*-history of Israel is taken up, beginning with Jehovah's dealings with the patriarchs (v. 9), and recounting what God had done for their descendants, till Rephidim was reached. In v. 41 we read, "He opened the rock, and the waters gushed out," and there the Psalmist stops. It will be observed that the word "mercy" does not occur in it a single time.

Now let the reader turn to Psalm 106, where we have the *mercy*-history of Israel's journeyings. Observe how frequently this Psalm makes mention of Israel's sins:— their unbelief (v. 7), their impatience (v. 13), their lusting (v. 14), their envy of Moses (v. 16), their idolatry (v. 19), their murmuring (v. 25), their unfaithfulness (v. 28), their provoking the Lord (v. 33), their disobedience (v. 34), their wickedness (vv. 35, 37). As v. 43 summarises it, "Many times did He deliver them; *but* they provoked Him with their counsel." Thus did Israel evilly requite the wondrous grace of God. What then? Did He annihilate them? Well He might have done so. But instead, we are told, "And He remembered for them His covenant, and repented according to the multitude of His *mercies*" (v. 45)!

From Sinai and onwards Israel's songs never recounted God's *grace*. No, it was too late for that after the golden calf had been set up. His grace had been abused, flung back, as it were, into His face. His law had been violated, His covenant broken. But His *mercy* "endureth forever." Hallelujah! Mercy, then, is that blessed quality of God's nature which meets the deep and dire needs of those who have sinned against His grace. The background of God's grace is our emptiness, poverty, worthlessness. The foil for His mercy is our sinfulness, wickedness, vileness. That is why we are bidden to come to the Throne of *Grace* that we may "obtain *mercy* and find grace to help in time of need" (Heb. 4: 16).

The distinction just drawn above serves to explain what is found in the opening salutation of the N.T. epistles. We would urge the reader to consult for himself each passage now to be referred to. In Rom. 1: 7, 1 Cor. 1: 1, 2, 2 Cor. 1: 1, 2, Gal. 1:3, Eph. 1: 2, Phil. 1:2, Col. 1: 2, 1 Thess. 1: 1, 2, 2 Thess. 1: 2, each Christian company is saluted with "*grace* be unto you." But when we turn to 1 Tim. 1: 2, 2 Tim. 1: 4, Titus 1: 4 we find "mercy" is added: "grace, *mercy* and peace." Why is this? We know of no writer that has ever advanced what we believe is the true answer. But does not the history of Israel supply the key? Alas, has not history repeated itself? has not the course of Christendom corresponded to that of Israel? Has not Christendom, too, *abused* the wondrous "grace" of God? And has He not, most blessedly, fallen back upon His *mercy* in His dealings with us?

It should be carefully observed that when we come to the epistles of Timothy (see 1 Tim. 4: 1, 2 Tim. 3: 1) we are brought down to the *closing* days of this dispensation. Ah, were it not for that mercy which "endureth forever" where would God's unfaithful, backslidden, and lukewarm people be! Still more significant is it to note that the salutation of Jude's epistle, the *last* one (treating of conditions in the end-time) *opens* with "mercy unto you." Verily, "mercy" *is* our last hope. Nor does it fail us. Yea, we are "looking for the *mercy* of our Lord Jesus Christ unto eternal life" (Jude 21)—the reference being to His second advent: compare 2 Tim. 1: 18.

Oh Christian readers, have our *own* souls understood and apprehended this glorious attribute of mercy in which our God is so "rich" (Eph. 2: 4)? Have we not often confused it with His grace, and thereby failed to perceive its distinctive glory and blessedness? Have not *we* not only broken His holy law again and again, but despised His very grace? What then is left but to fall back upon His *mercy*, which very attribute supposes this is our last resource! Well aware are we that this very truth may be misappropriated and misused, but for those whose hearts *desire* to please and glorify God, it is unspeakably precious. The mercy of God can only be truly apprehended by those who have been made to feel how grievously they have sinned against His grace. It is such who will welcome the invitation to come boldly ("freely") to the Throne of Grace, that there they may "obtain mercy" for the unrequited grace of yesterday, and there also find fresh supplies of grace for the needs of today.

In perfect accord with all that has been said above, is the *first* mention of God's "mercy" in Holy Writ: "And while he lingered, the men laid hold upon his hand, and upon the hand of his wife, and upon the hand of his two daughters; the Lord being *merciful* unto him: and they brought him forth and set him without the city" (Gen. 19: 16). This regarded Lot, and it is blessed to note his own acknowledgment of it, "Behold now, Thy servant hath found grace in Thy sight, and Thou hast magnified Thy mercy, which Thou hast showed unto me in saving my life" (v. 19). Yes,

he had "found grace" in God's sight, for he was one of the Lord's people (2 Peter 2 : 7). But O how basely had he treated that grace! He had not only forsaken Abraham, but had settled down in wicked Sodom. The *only* hope for such an one was *mercy*, and this God had "magnified."

It only remains for us now to point out how that in Ex. 33: 19 the Lord emphasises His *sovereignty* in the exercise of this attribute, saying, "I will show mercy on whom *I will* show mercy." Necessarily it must be so. Mercy is that which none can claim as a right: might they justly do so, it would cease to be *mercy*. Hence God reserves to Himself the right to extend it to whom He pleases, and to withold it from whom He pleases. To this principle the apostle, when treating at length of the sovereignty of God, called attention in Rom. 9: 18. Nor is God unrighteous in this. None is wronged if "mercy" be witheld. God is therefore free to act as He pleases: "Is it not lawful for Me to do what I will with Mine own?" (Matt. 20: 15).

"And He said, thou canst not see My face: for there shall no man see Me, and live (v. 20). We must ever distinguish between God's absolute character and His relative making known of Himself. In His absolute character and essence no man hath seen nor can see God, for He is "Spirit" (John 4: 24), and therefore unseeable. But relatively He has made Himself known to us by His many names and titles, by the manifestation of His many and varied attributes, and more fully and blessedly still, by and in the person of Christ. Yet it remains true that, absolutely, God is the invisible God, "dwelling in the light which no man can approach unto: whom no man hath seen, nor can see" (1 Tim. 6: 16). In O.T. times, when God made Himself known to Abraham, Moses, Joshua, Gideon it was the second Person of the Trinity, yet not in His essential Deity, but in human or angelic form. No human creature is capable of perceiving the infinite and eternal Spirit in all His majesty and ineffable glory.

"And the Lord said, Behold there is a place by Me, and thou shalt stand upon a rock: And it shall come to pass while My glory passeth by, that I will put thee in a clift of the rock, and will cover thee with My hand while I pass by: And I will take away Mine hand, and thou shalt see My back parts: but My face shall not be seen" (vv. 21-23). This is most blessed. In order for sinful man to be able clearly to contemplate the Divine perfections of an infinitely righteous, holy God, it is necessary that he should be put into a place of security and peace. This God *has*, in His infinite condescension and grace, provided for us. To faith that "rock" is Christ. Augustus Toplady beautifully represented this in his well-known hymn,

"Rock of Ages cleft for me,
Let me hide myself in Thee."

Or, as we prefer to sing it,

"Rock of Ages cleft for me,
Grace hath hid me safe in Thee."

God graciously permitted Moses to have an impression and perception of His presence such as he was capable of. A beautiful illustration of what we have in view here, we borrow from Dr. Cuyler's work on the Holy Spirit:—

"I was talking about Christ to an impenitent neighbour the other day. He said 'Why can't I feel about Him as you do? I have read the Bible a good deal—I have heard a good deal of preaching, yet I can't get up any enthusiasm in regard to this Saviour that you talk so much about.' I said to him, 'You make me think of my visit to the White Mountains some years ago. We were told that there was a wonderful piece of natural statuary there—a man's face chiselled out of a granite cliff. When we went to see it, we found what we supposed was the cliff, but there was no appearance of human features—no form or comeliness such as we had been told of. We were about to turn away disappointed when a guide came along and said. 'You are not looking from the right point.' He led us up the road a few rods, and then said, 'Turn and look!' We did so, and there was the face as distinct as any of ours, though of gigantic size. Until we reached the right spot we could see only a jagged rock, and not a symmetrical face. The vision of the form and comeliness *depended upon the angle of observation*. And it is so with you, my friend. Come with me under the shadow of the Cross. Come there as a penitent sinner. Look there upon that visage so marred more than any man.

Realize that the mangled, thorn-crowned Sufferer is dying for you, and you will see in Him a beauty that will ravish your soul."

By linking together a clause out of v. 21 with what is stated in v. 22 we get a beautifully-complete type of the believer's absolute security. First. "thou shalt stand upon a rock." This at once reminds us of, "By faith we have peace with God through our Lord Jesus Christ; by whom also we have access by faith into this grace wherein we *stand*" (Rom. 5: 1, 2). Second, mark well the words, "*I will put thee* in a clift of a rock," for no sinner of himself can do this. Blessed figure was it of an elect soul being "*created in* Christ Jesus" (Eph. 2 : 10). Third, "and will cover thee with My hand." "He that dwelleth in the secret place of the most High shall abide *under the shadow* of the Almighty" (Psa. 91 : 1). Not only is the believer in Christ. but he is also protected by the Father's hand (John 10 : 29). Finally, observe it is only as we are in the "clift of the rock" that God's "goodness" passes before us (v. 22). His "glory" can only come into view as the flesh is altogether *hidden*; that is, as we are made "new creatures in Christ."

"And I will take away Mine hand, and thou shalt see My back parts: but My face shall not be seen" (v. 23). This was in keeping with the Legal economy: the law had only "a shadow of good things to come, and not the very image of the things" (Heb. 10 : 1). But how blessed the contrast now: "For God who commanded the light to shine out of darkness, hath shined in our hearts, to give the light of the knowledge of the glory of God in *the face* of Jesus Christ" (2 Cor. 4 : 6)! O may Divine grace enable both writer and reader to walk worthy of such a God, and such a revelation of Himself (1 Tim. 3 : 16) as He has now made to us in and through Christ (John 14 : 9).

CHAPTER 66

GOD'S GOVERNMENTAL PRINCIPLES

EXODUS 34:1-7

Our present passage gives the sequel to what was before us in Ex. 19 and Ex. 24. Up to Ex. 19 God had dealt with Israel on the ground of His unconditional covenant with Abraham: see Gen. 15 : 18; Ex. 2 : 24; 6 : 3, 4. The last thing recorded before Israel reached Sinai was the miraculous giving of the water at Rephidim, and concerning that the Psalmist tells us, "He opened the rock, and the waters gushed out; they ran in the dry places like a river. For He remembered His holy promise, Abraham His servant" (105 : 41, 42). But at Sinai, God's relationship to Israel was placed upon a different basis.

In Ex. 19 : 5 we find God, from the mount, bidding Moses say unto the people, "Now therefore, if ye will obey My voice indeed, and keep My covenant, then ye shall be a peculiar treasure unto Me above all people: for the earth is Mine." In connection with the covenant that He had made with Abraham there was nothing which Israel *could* "keep;" there were no conditions attached to it, no stipulations, no proviso's. It was unconditional so far as Abraham and his descendants were concerned. It was a covenant of pure grace, and it was on the ground of *that* covenant God will again take up Israel after this dispensation is over. But at Sinai God proposed another covenant, to which there should be two parties—Himself and Israel: It was a *conditional* covenant, a covenant which Israel must "keep" if they were to enjoy the blessings attached thereto; note carefully the "if" in 19 : 5.

The *charter* of the Siniatic covenant was the two tables of stone, upon which were engraved the ten commandments, see Ex. 34 : 27, 28, Deut. 4 : 13. The terms of this covenant Israel freely accepted (19 : 8, 24 : 3), and accordingly, it was solemnly ratified by blood (24 : 4-8). In proposing this covenant, God had two things before Him: the maintaining of His own rights, and the good of His people. Grace ever reigns "through righteousness" (Rom. 5 : 21), and in His sovereign benignity to Abraham's seed, God must uphold the claims of His throne. But this was also for their good: God's commands "are not grievous" (1 John 5 : 3), and in keeping of them there is great reward. In article 28 of this series we sought to show that, so far from redemption setting aside the rights of God over His creatures, it supplies an additional motive for recognising and meeting them.

Now at the close of Ex. 24 we hear Jehovah saying to Moses, "Come up to Me into the mount, and be there: and I will give thee tables of stone, and a law, and commandments which I have written; that thou mayest teach them (v. 12). Accordingly Moses, accompanied by his minister Joshua, goes up into the mount, and as v. 18 tells us, he was "in the mount forty days and forty nights." The next seven chapters are occupied with a description of the Tabernacle, details of which God also gave to Moses on that occasion. Then, in Ex. 32, we learn how the people below had been conducting themselves during the absence of their leader: the great sin of the golden calf, with its idolatrous worship, had been committed. Nothing but the intercession of the typical mediator had saved them from utter extermination by the wrath of God. As we have seen, they were severely chastised for their wickedness, the Tent of meeting was removed outside the camp, and following Israel's repentance and Moses' repeated supplication, they were restored again to communion with God.

Therefore the next thing we read is, "And the Lord said unto Moses, Hew thee two tables of stone like unto the first: and I will write upon these tables the words that were on the first tables, which thou breakest. And be ready in the morning, and come up in the morning unto mount Sinai, and present thyself there to Me in the top of the mount. And no man shall come up with thee, neither let any man be seen throughout all the mount; neither let the flocks nor herds feed before that mount" (34 : 1-3). Thus, as we have said in the opening sentence of this article, our present passage gives the sequel to what was before us in Ex. 19 and 24. Though Israel had, during the interval, sinned so grievously, Moses *must* return to Jehovah and receive from Him the inscribed tables of stone. No purpose of the Most High can fail. To the outward eye it may appear that the wickedness of the creature *is* thwarting, or at least hindering, the execution of His counsels. But it is only *seeming*; in reality it is not so: "My counsel shall stand, and I will do all My pleasure" (Isa. 46 : 10), in His sure and unchanging declaration.

The ground we have sought to review above is especially rich in its typical teaching. The first tables of stone were broken (32 : 19) in view of Israel's sin—a figure of man's inability to keep God's Law. The first tables of stone were provided by Jehovah Himself "I will give thee" (24 : 12), but the second were to be supplied by Moses himself: "hew *thee*" (34 : 1)—type of Christ the Mediator who declared. "Think not that I am come to destroy the law, or the prophets: I am not come to destroy, but to fullfill" Matt. 5 : 17). Accordingly, the second set of tables were securely deposited in the ark (Deut. 10 : 5)—type, again, of Him who said, "I delight to do Thy will, O My God: Yea, Thy law is *within* My heart" (Psa. 40 : 8).

Again; the covenant which God made with Abraham at the beginning (Gen. 15), and on the ground of which He had delivered Israel from Egypt and brought them unto Himself, foreshadowed that eternal covenant which God made with Christ (2 Tim. 1 : 9; Titus 1 : 2; Heb. 13 : 20), on the basis of which God's people are saved and blest (Eph. 1 : 3, 4). The covenant God made with Israel at Sinai, which brought in the establishing of His rights and the good of His people on earth, foreshadowed the present *government* of God over His people, pressing upon us our responsibilities and obligations, making known to us the terms on which we receive blessings from Him in this life, and revealing the principles which regulate God Himself in His dealings with us. As these will receive amplification in what follows, we pass on now to notice one other typical feature of importance and preciousness.

In the interval between the two ascents of Moses into the mount to receive from Jehovah the engraved tables of stone, we have the solemn account of Israel's wickedness; but, where sin abounded "grace did much more abound." Very blessed is it to see illustrated there that word in Psa. 76 : 10, "Surely the wrath of man shall praise thee." Israel's sin, so far from defeating the purpose of God, only provided occasion for

Him to reveal the wondrous provisions which He has made for His failing people : seen in the unfailing love and prevailing intercession of the typical mediator. It is this which has been before us in the last few articles, finding its glorious climax in the making known of the *mercy* of God—that wondrous spring in the Divine character which ministers to those who have failed to respond to His grace—and the making of His "goodness" to pass before Moses (33 : 19). That "goodness" was inseparably connected with the proclamation of " the name of the Lord," and what *that* signified we shall learn from our present passage.

"One other remark should be made. Satan had come in, and for the moment seemed as if he had succeeded in frustrating the purposes of God with respect to His people. But Satan is never so completely defeated as in his apparent victories. This is nowhere so fully illustrated as in the cross, but the same thing is perceived in connection with the golden calf. This was Satan's work; but the failure of Israel becomes the occasion through the mediation of Moses, which God in His grace had provided, of the fuller revelation of God, and of His mingling grace with law. The activity of Satan does but work out the purposes of God, and his wrath is made to praise Him against whom all his malice and enmity are directed" (Ed. Dennett).

"And he hewed two tables of stone like unto the first; and Moses rose up early in the morning, and went up unto mount Sinai, as the Lord had commanded him, and took in his hand the two tables of stone" (v. 4). The typical teaching of this verse brings out an important truth which is now very frequently denied, namely, that God's redeemed are still under law : not as a condition of salvation, but as the Divine rule for their walk. Let it be remembered that what we have here in Ex. 34 follows right after what is recorded in chapter 33, where we have a most manifest and lovely foreshadowing of the intercession of our great High Priest on high.

Many are the New Testatment passages which give us the antitype of this. Said the Lord Jesus to His disciples, "If ye *love Me*, keep My commandments " (John 14 : 15), which is, obviously, paralell with, " Showing mercy unto thousands of them that *love Me*, and keep My commandments " (Ex. 20 : 6). In perfect accord with this, is that word in Rom. 13: 10, " Love is the fulfilling of the law." The law has not been abrogated, nor is love lawless. Equally plain is that word in 1 Cor. 9: 21, where the apostle affirms that New Testament saints are "under the law to Christ." Nor does Rom. 6: 14 set this aside, for God's Word does not contradict itself. When the apostle there says, "Ye are not under the law, but under grace," he is referring to our justification, not to our walk as believers.

" And the Lord descended in the cloud, and stood with him there, and proclaimed the name of the Lord " (v. 5). This at once introduces to us a subject of much importance, but, alas, like many another, sadly neglected today: the teaching of Holy Writ concerning *the Name* of the Lord. God is very jealous of His name as the third commandment in the decalogue shows: the Lord will not hold guiltless that one who taketh His name in vain. In the prayer which Christ taught His disciples, the *first* petition is "Hallowed be Thy name." In Prov. 18: 10 we read, " The name of the Lord is a strong tower: the righteous runneth into it and is safe." From Mal. 3: 16 we learn that God has written a book of remembrance " for them that feared the Lord and that *thought upon His name.*" While the last chapter of Scripture tells us that God's name shall be in the foreheads of His people (22: 4).

" And the Lord descended in the cloud, and stood with him there, and proclaimed the name of the Lord." This was the fulfillment of the promise which He had made to Moses in 33: 19. There He had said, " I will make all My goodness pass before thee, and *I will* proclaim the name of the Lord before thee." To proclaim His "name" signified to *reveal* Himself, to make Himself known. Just as the angel said to Joseph concerning the Child Mary was to bear, " Thou shalt call His name Jesus, *for* He shall save His people from their sins " (Matt. 1: 21): the " name " Jesus revealed what He was—the Divine Saviour. Or, just as Christ commanded His disciples to baptize " in the name of the Father, and of the Son, and of the Holy Spirit" (Matt. 28 : 19), because it is thus that the Triune God now stands revealed.

The *particular character* in which Jehovah was about to reveal Himself to Moses is best perceived by noting the place and circumstances of this gracious manifestation of Himself. It was upon Sinai, in connection with the giving of the Law. It was, as we have said above, at the time when the Lord was enforcing His own rights on the people, following upon the exercise of His grace toward them. It was when Jehovah took His place in Israel's midst as their king. It was there, upon *the Mount* that He made known that " righteousness and judgment are the habitation of His throne " (Psa. 97: 2). Many are the scriptures which connect the " mount " with Divine government. For example, it was upon the mount (Matt. 5: 1) that the Lord

Jesus proclaimed the principles which are to regulate those who are the subjects of "the kingdom of heaven." It was on the "holy mount " that He was transfigured (Matt. 17), which set forth in vivid tableau the features which shall attend the establishment of His Messianic kingdom here on earth. While in Zech. 14: 4 we are told, that when He returns with the "government upon His shoulder " (Isa. 9: 6), " His feet shall stand in that day upon the mount of Olives."

At the burning bush Jehovah proclaimed His name, but there it was not a making known of the principles which regulate Him in the government of His people, rather was it a revelation of what He *is* in Himself—the great " I AM," the all-sufficient, self-subsisting One, " with whom is no variableness neither shadow of turning " (James 1: 17). How appropriate was such a revelation of Himself on that occasion! Moses was about to appear, first, to his oppressed brethren, who would, at the onset, welcome him, but subsequently blame him because of their increased burdens; later before Pharaoh, who would first display an haughty and defiant spirit, and then a vacillating and temporising one. Well was it for Moses to lay firm hold of the glorious fact that he was an ambassador of the great " I AM."

" And the Lord descended in the cloud, and stood with him there, and proclaimed the name of the Lord." With this should be compared, or rather contrasted what we read of in John 17. There we find our Saviour rendering an account of His work to the One who had sent Him here; and, as He entered into detail, the first thing that He says is, " I have *manifested Thy name.*" But how different was this from what we have in Ex. 34 : There it was God making Himself known *in government;* here it was God made manifest by the Son *in grace.* This is at once evidenced by the words immediately following, " I have manifested Thy name unto the men which *Thou gavest Me* out of the world: Thine they were, and Thou gavest them Me"; it was grace, pure and simple, eternal and sovereign, which gave us to Christ. So again in the 26th verse we hear our great High Priest saying to the Father, "I have declared unto them Thy name, and will declare it: *that* the love wherewith Thou hast loved Me may be *in them.*" Ah, that was grace, the " riches of His grace" (Eph. 1: 7), yea, " the *glory* of His grace " (Eph. 1: 6).

" And the Lord passed by before him, and proclaimed, The Lord, The Lord God, merciful and gracious, longsuffering, and abundant in goodness and truth, Keeping mercy for thousands, forgiving iniquity and transgression and sin, and that will by no means clear the guilty; visiting the iniquity of the fathers upon the children, and upon the children's children, unto the third and fourth generation" (vv. 6, 7). These are the most important as well as the most blessed verses in our passage. In them the Lord makes known the principles or attributes which are exercised in the government of His people. The *perfections* of that government appear in that *seven* principles are here enumerated. A careful study of them supplies the key to and explains all the subsequent dealings of God with Israel.

It is a most profitable exercise to go through the remainder of the Old Testament in view of these verses: by them much light is thrown upon the later history of Israel. Many are the passages in the prophets which have their roots in Ex. 34: 6, 7; many are the prayers whose appeals were based upon their contents. But that which is the most important for us to heed is that, here we have proclaimed what marked the "ways" of Jehovah with Israel. As we trace His dealings with them from Sinai onwards, it will be found that each one of these seven attributes were in constant exercise. Let us now consider, though briefly, each one separately.

"The Lord God merciful." How unspeakably precious is it to mark that *this* is mentioned first. It is, we might say, the fount from which all the others flow: because God is *merciful*, He is "gracious, longsuffering, abundant in goodness" etc. Mercy was the hope of David when he had sinned so grievously: "Let us fall now into the hand of the Lord, for His *mercies* are great" (2 Sam. 24: 14. Solomon owned God's "mercy" to Israel (1 Kings 3 : 6: 8 : 23). So Jehosaphat (2 Chron. 20 : 21). So too Nehemiah at a later date: mark how he recalled the constant mercy of God to Israel: 9: 19, 27, 28, 31. So too did Daniel encourage himself in the mercy of God: 9: 9, 18. To Jeremiah God said, "Go and proclaim these words toward the north, and say, return, thou backsliding Israel, saith the Lord; and I will not cause Mine anger to fall upon you: *for I am merciful,* saith the Lord" (3: 12).

It is on the ground of "mercy" that God will take up Israel again in a coming day. He shall say, "For a small moment have I forsaken thee; but with *great mercies* will I gather thee" (Isa. 54: 7). "And I will show mercies unto you, that he may have mercy upon you, and cause you to return to your own land" (Jer. 42: 12). So the Lord Jesus shall yet say "And I will strengthen the house of Judah, and I will save the house of Joseph, and I will bring

them again to place them; for I have *mercy* upon them: and they shall be as though I had not cast them off" (Zech. 10: 6).

"And gracious." This tells us the *ground* on which God bestows His mercies: it is not for anything in man or from him, but solely because of His own benignity. All of God's mercies are gifts, free favours to a people entirely devoid of any worthiness. Many are the appeals to the grace of God recorded in the Old Testament. David cried, "O God, the proud are risen against me, and the assemblies of violent men have sought after my soul; and have not set Thee before them. But Thou O Lord, art a God full of compassion, and *gracious*" (Psa. 86: 14, 15). Hezekiah appealed to the Divine clemency (2 Chron. 30: 9). So did Jonah (4:2). Isaiah assured the people in his day, "And therefore will the Lord wait, that He may be *gracious* unto you" (Isa. 30: 18). Through Joel God said to Israel, "Rend your heart, and not your garments, and turn unto the Lord your God: for He is *gracious*" (2: 13). While in the last book of the Old Testament the prophet exhorted, "And now, I pray you, beseech God that He will be *gracious* unto us" (1: 9).

"Longsuffering." How strikingly did the whole history of Israel bear witness to the wondrous patience of God! The word longsuffering signifies "slow to anger." It was to the "longsuffering" of Jehovah that Moses first appealed when Israel had sinned so grievously at Kadesh-barnea (Num. 14: 18). It was the realisation of God's great patience which stayed David's heart (Psa. 145: 8). To it Nehemiah referred when reviewing Israel's history and God's long forebearance with them (9 : 18). In Nahum's brief but powerful message we read, "The Lord is slow to anger and great in power" (1 : 3). The Lord Jesus pointed to the same perfection when He said to the Jews. "O Jerusalem, Jerusalem, thou that killest the prophets, and stonest them which are sent unto thee, *how often* would I have gathered thy children together" (Matt. 23: 37).

"Abundant in goodness." The Hebrew word for goodness is more frequently translated "kindness." David acknowledged it when he said, "Blessed be the Lord; for He hath showed me His marvellous *kindness* in a strong city" (Psa. 41: 21). So too Nehemiah (9: 17). In a coming day the Lord will say to Israel, "In a little wrath I hid My face from thee for a moment; but with everlasting *kindness* will I have mercy on thee" (Isa. 54 : 8). The Hebrew word is also rendered "loving-kindness." Frequent mention of it is made in the Psalms: "For Thy lovingkindness is before mine eyes " (26 : 3); " How excellent is Thy lovingkindness, O God!'" (36 : 7); "We have thought of Thy lovingkindness, O God, in the midst of Thy temple " (48 : 9). Isaiah said, " I will mention the lovingkindnesses of the Lord" (63 : 7). Through Jeremiah God said, " But let him that glorieth glory in this, that he understandeth and knoweth Me, that I am the Lord which exercise *lovingkindness,* judgment, and righteousness, in the earth : for in these things I delight " (9 : 24).

" And truth." The Hebrew word signifies " stedfastness." It is rendered " verity" in Psalm 111 : 7 : "The works of His hands are verity and judgment." It is translated "faithful" in Nehemiah 7 : 2. To the men of Jabesh-gilead David said, "The Lord show kindness and truth unto you " (2 Sam. 2 : 6). Unto Jehovah the Psalmist sang, " For Thy mercy is great above the heavens : and Thy *truth* reacheth unto the clouds " (Psa. 108 : 4). God is faithful to His covenant-engagements, true to both His promisings and His threatenings.

" Keeping mercy for thousands—*forgiving* iniquity and transgressions and sin." How often God pardoned Israel for her sins! " And they remembered that God was their rock, and the high God their redeemer. Nevertheless they did flatter Him with their mouth, and they lied unto Him with their tongues. For their heart was not right with Him, neither were they stedfast in His covenant. *But He,* being full of compassion, *forgave* their iniquity, and destroyed them not : yea, many a time turned He His anger away " (Psa. 78 : 35-38). So in a coming day the Lord will say, " I will *forgive* their iniquity, and I will remember their sin no more " (Jer. 31 : 34).

" And that will by no means clear the guilty : visiting the iniquity of the fathers upon the children, and upon the children's children, unto the third and fourth generation." Though God pardons, often He does not remit the consequences of sin : " Thou wast a God that forgavest them, *though* Thou tookest vengeance of their inventions" (Psa. 99 : 8). To this day the Jews are suffering because of the sins of their forefathers.

It only remains for us to add that, inasmuch as God changes not, the seven principles contemplated above *now* regulate His government of Christendom corporately and the Christian individually. How merciful, how gracious, how longsuffering, has God been to those who profess His name! How good, how faithful, how forgiving, all through these nineteen centuries! Yet the sins of the fathers have also been visited upon their children. Today we are suffering from the compromisings, unfaithfulness, sectarianism, pride, and wickedness, of those who went before us. May the Lord bless to the reader what has been according to His own Word.

CHAPTER 67

A JEALOUS GOD

EXODUS 34:8-17

We turn now to contemplate a portion of the further communication which Jehovah made to Moses in the Mount. It is not easy to break up this chapter into sections of suitable length for these comparatively brief articles, and therefore we are obliged to spend a little time in reviewing the ground covered in the previous one, that the continuity of thought may be preserved. In our last, we beheld God asserting His rights over those whom He had redeemed unto Himself: Moses being called to receive the Law at His hands. There we heard Him enunciating the principles of His government. These are seven in number, and close attention to them is called for if we would appreciate His "ways" with Israel of old, and enter intelligently into that which regulates Him in His dealings with us now.

God is "light" (1 John 1:5), as well as "love" (1 John 4:8), and therefore we are exhorted, "Behold therefore the goodness **and** the severity of God" (Rom. 11: 22). The two sides to the Divine character shine forth in all His dealings with man. In Eden we behold His "goodness" in making promise of the coming of the woman's Seed to bruise the Serpent's head (Gen. 3:15), but we also see His "severity" in that "He drove out the man" (3:24) God as Love provided a shelter for Noah and his house; God as Light sent the flood and destroyed those who had corrupted their way on earth. The "goodness" of God commissioned two angels to deliver Lot, but His "severity" rained-down fire and brimstone and consumed wicked Sodom. God as Love preserved His people under blood in Egypt, God as Light slew all the firstborn of the Egyptians. The "goodness" of God, in response to the intercession of Moses, spared the idolatrous Nation from utter extermination, but His "severity" called for the sword to do its work (Ex. 32:27).

We may observe the clear display of these two sides of the Divine character in the ministry of the incarnate Son. The Lord Jesus came here "full" not only of grace, but "of grace **and truth**" (John 1: 14). He was the Friend of publicans and sinners, but He was the Enemy of self-righteous hypocrits. The same One who was "moved with compassion" as He beheld the multitude (Matt. 14:14), "looked round upon them with anger" (Mark 3:5) as He beheld the hard-hearted critics of the synagogue. He who wept over Jerusalem, "made a scourge of small cords" and drove out of the temple the defilers of the Father's house (John 2:15). He who "blessed His disciples" (Luke 24:51) cursed the fig tree (Matt. 21:19). His "beatitudes" in Matt. 5 are balanced by His denunciatory "woe's" in Matt. 23. If we read of the "love of Christ" (Eph. 3:19), we read also of "the wrath of the Lamb" (Rev. 6:16).

The same conjunction of these Divine perfections is to be discerned in the proclamation of the name of the Lord, which He gave to Moses on the Mount in connection with the enunciation of His governmental principles. He is both "abundant in goodness **and truth**" (v. 6). If He "keeps mercy for thousands," yet He declares that He will "by no means clear the guilty." Though He **forgives** "iniquity, transgression, and sin," yet He also **visits** "the iniquity of the fathers upon the children." The sin of Ham was visited upon his descendants (Gen. 9:25); the sin of Korah and his company resulted in the earth opening its mouth and swallowing them up **and** their houses (Num. 16:32). When Achan was punished for his sin, there were stoned with him "his sons and his daughters" (Josh. 7:24, 25). When the Jews crucified Christ, they cried, "His blood be upon us, and upon our children" (Matt. 27:25), and God took them at their word.

And what is the practical application to us of these things? This: God is a God to be loved, but He is also a God to be feared, for "**our** God is a consuming fire"

(Heb. 12:29). Did we perceive that God is Light as well as Love, we should stand more in holy awe of Him. Did we behold His "severity" as readily as we do His "goodness," we should be more fearful of displeasing Him. Did we bear in mind that He not only pardons, but also visits the iniquities of the fathers upon the children, we should be more careful about our walk than we are. "God is greatly to be feared in the assembly of the saints, and to be had in reverence of all them that are about Him" (Psa. 89:7). In Heaven itself the saints not only sing the praises of God, but they "fall down before Him" (Rev. 4:10). Then let us seek grace to heed that word, "work out your own salvation with fear and trembling" (Phil. 2:12).

"And Moses made haste, and bowed his head toward the earth, and worshipped" (v. 8). It is blessed to note the effect upon Moses of the wondrous and glorious communication which he had just received from the mouth of Jehovah: filled with adoration and awe he takes his place in the dust before Him. No formal or perfunctory homage was it that Moses now rendered. The words "made haste" seem to point to the spontaneity of his worship; the bowing of his head toward the earth shows how deeply his spirit was stirred. And if our hearts really lay hold of the perfections of God's administration, we too will be bowed before Him as worshippers.

"And Moses made haste, and bowed his head toward the earth, and worshipped." This is ever the result when the Lord condescends to reveal Himself to one of His own. When He appeared before Abram and said, "I am the Almighty God; walk before Me, and be thou upright," we are told that "Abram fell on his face" (Gen. 17:3). When He appeared before Joshua as "Captain of the host of the Lord," we are told that "Joshua fell on his face to the earth, and did worship" (Josh. 5:14). When His glory filled the temple which Solomon had built, all the children of Israel "bowed themselves with their faces to the ground upon the pavement, and worshipped and praised the Lord" (2 Chron. 7:3).

"And Moses made haste, and bowed his head toward the earth, and worshipped." Let us not lose sight of the immediate link between this and the close of the preceding verse. The last things mentioned there are that God will by no means clear the guilty, and that He visits the sins of the fathers upon the children. Instead of showing resentment, Moses acquiesced; instead of challenging the righteousness of these things, he worshipped.

Well for us if we follow his example.

"And he said, If now I have found grace in Thy sight, O Lord, let my Lord, I pray Thee, go among us; for it is a stiffnecked people; and pardon our iniquity and our sin, and take us for Thine inheritance" (v. 9). Very beautiful is this. Moses continues to use the favour which he had personally found before God for the good of others. His affections were bound up with His people. Blessedly does he identify himself with them: "Let my Lord, I pray Thee, go among us." How this brings to mind that wondrous word of our Redeemer's when, presenting Himself for baptism, He said to His amazed forerunner, "Thus it becometh us to fulfil all righteousness" (Matt. 3:16). Verily, "He that sanctifieth and they who are sanctified are all of one" (Heb. 2:11).

Let us note carefully the reason now presented by Moses for the Lord's accompanying His people: "Let my Lord, I pray Thee, go among us, for it is a stiffnecked people." This is very striking, though to some of the commentators it has presented a difficulty. It was their need which Moses spread before Jehovah; it was His grace to which he appealed. Seeing that God was "merciful, gracious, longsuffering," He was just the One suited to a "stiffnecked" people. None but He could bear with them. At the very time that Israel were worshipping the golden calf the Lord Himself had said to Moses, "I have seen this people, and, behold, it is a stiffnecked people: Now, therefore, let Me alone, that My wrath may wax hot against them" (32:9, 10). Now, Moses not only acknowledged the truth of God's charge, but, in wondrous faith, turns it into a plea for Him to continue in Israel's midst! Beautifully has another commented on this:

"The relationship between Moses personally and God, was fully established, so that he could present the people such as they were, because of his (Moses' own) position, and, consequently, make of the difficulty and sin of the people a reason for the presence of God, according to the character He had revealed. It is the proper effect of mediation; but it is exceedingly beautiful to see, grace having thus come in, the reason God had given for the destruction of the people, or at the very least of His absence, becoming the motive for His presence. We know this ourselves; my sinfulness in itself would be the reason for God's giving me up. But now I am in grace, I can plead it with God as a reason, blessed be His name, for His going with me. never should I overcome and get safe across the wilderness. if He was not with me. Surely the flesh is there, but it is wondrous grace" (Mr.

J N. Darby).

Verily, it is all of grace from first to last. Christ came here not to call the righteous, but sinners to repentance (Matt. 9:13). The proud Pharisees resented it, murmured, and said, "This man receiveth sinners and eateth with them" (Luke 15: 2). Thank God He still does so, and the more the Holy Spirit reveals to us the "plague" of our heart (1 Kings 8:38), the more we are enabled to apprehend the wondrous grace of God, the more shall we crave His presence with us, and that because we are, by nature, a "stiffnecked" people. The more we discover the true character of the "flesh"—its unimprovableness, and our own powerlessness to contend against it, the more shall we long for an Almighty arm to lean on. So, too, the more we realize that this world is a "wilderness," affording nothing for our souls, the more shall we perceive the need of the presence of Him who—all praise to His name—is the Friend that "sticketh closer than a brother" (Prov. 18:24).

"And pardon our iniquity and our sin, and take us for Thine inheritance." Here again we perceive the boldness of Moses' faith. This was the climax of his petitions on Israel's behalf. First, he had besought the Lord that His wrath should not wax hot against them (32:11). Then, he had pleaded for the Lord's continued presence in their midst (33:15, 16). Now he asks that the Lord will pardon their iniquity (note how graciously he identifies himself with his sinning people: "**our** iniquity and **our** sin"), and "take us from Thine inheritance." When Sinia had first been reached, God had said, "Now therefore, if ye will obey My voice indeed, and keep My covenant, then ye shall be a peculiar treasure unto Me above all people" (19:5). But the sin of the golden calf had severed every relationship. But here Moses as their mediator and intercessor pleads that **everything** should be restored.

That his prayer was answered we know from other scriptures. In Deut. 32:9 we find him saying, "For the Lord's portion is His people; Jacob **is** the lot of His inheritance." So also we find David declared, "Blessed is the nation whose God is the Lord; and the people whom He hath chosen for His own **inheritance**" (Psa 33:12). Blessed is it to know that Israel, though temporarily cast aside for our sakes, is God's "inheritance" forever: "For the Lord will not cast off His people, neither will He forsake His **inheritance**" (Psa. 94:14). In a coming day the word shall go forth, "Sing and rejoice, O daughter of Zion: for, lo, I come, and I will dwell in the midst of thee saith the Lord, and many nations shall be joined to the Lord in that day and shall be My people: and I will dwell in the midst of thee, and thou shalt know that the Lord of hosts hath sent Me unto thee. And the Lord shall **inherit** Judah His portion in the holy land, and shall choose Jerusalem again" (Zech. 2:10-12).

"And take us for Thine inheritance." Again we would remind the reader that we are dealing with the contents of that book whose theme is **redemption.** How blessed then to learn that, through redemption, God has obtained for Himself an "inheritance!" Eph. 1:18 speaks of the "riches of the glory of **His** inheritance in the saints." A truly marvelous concept is that, one to which our poor minds are quite incapable of rising—that the great and selfsufficient God should deem Himself **enriched** by worms of the earth whom He hath saved by His grace. This "inheritance," like all others, has come in **through death**, the death of God's own Son. That death not only vindicated Divine justice by putting away the sins of His people, but it has brought in that which shall **glorify** God through the endless ages of eternity. God will **occupy** His "inheritance" forever. "Behold, the tabernacle of God is with men, and He will **dwell with them**, and they shall be His people, and God Himself shall be with them, and be their God." (Rev. 21:3).

"And He said, Behold, I make a covenant, before all thy people, I will do marvels, such as have not been done in all the earth, nor in any nation: and all the people among which thou art shall see the work of the Lord: for it is a terrible thing that I will do with thee." (v. 10). This verse presents a difficulty, which is by no means easy of solution. God here promised that He would do unprecedented miracles on Israel's behalf, "marvels such as have not been done in all the earth" Had these words been spoken at the burning bush, before Moses first interviewed Pharaoh, their application had been obvious: but here, at Sinai, their meaning is not easy to fix. God had already wrought great "**marvels**" on Israel's behalf: the plagues upon Egypt, when water was turned into blood, dust into lice, frogs entering the homes of the Egyptians, but avoiding those of the Israelites, a supernatural darkness lasting for three days, though "all the children of Israel had light in their dwellings." (Ex. 10:22, 23); the dividing asunder the Red Sea; **the** raining of manna from heaven, and **in** such quantities as to supply the needs **of** two million souls; the bringing of **water** out of the rock—these were, one and all, prodigies of power. But here God announces still greater wonders!

We believe that the last book of the Bible describes the fulfillment of this word of Jehovah's to Moses. There we read of plagues more dreadful and wondrous than those which came upon Pharaoh and his people. Upon Egypt God sent natural "locusts," but in a soon-coming day the bottomless pit shall be opened, and from it shall issue **infernal** "locusts," who instead of consuming vegetation, shall torment men, so that "in those days shall men seek death, and shall not find it." (Rev. 9:6.) In Rev. 15:1 we read, "And I saw another sign in heaven, great and marvelous, seven angels having the seven last plagues; for in them is filled up the wrath of God." How little the world dreams of what is shortly coming upon it!

In the past God put forth His power and delivered Israel from Egypt, but in a coming day He will, with still greater displays of His might and by means of judgments of far sorer intensity, deliver the scattered Jews from **all** countries among which they are now dispersed: "And it shall come to pass in that day, that the Lord shall set His hand again the second time to recover the remnant of His people, which shall be left, from Assyria, and from Egypt, and from Pathros, and from Cush, and from Elam, and from Shinar, and from Hamath, and from the Islands of the sea. And He shall set up an ensign for the nations, and shall assemble the outcasts of Israel, and gather together the dispersed of Judah from the four quarters of the earth." (Isa. 11:11-12). "And I will gather the remnant of My flock out of all countries whither I have driven them, and will bring them again to their folds; and they shall be fruitful and increase . . . Therefore they shall no more say, The Lord liveth, which brought up and which led the seed of the house of Israel out of the north country, and from all countries whither I had driven them: and they shall dwell in their own land." (Jer. 23:3, 7, 8)

Of old, God divided the Red Sea for His people to pass through; but in a coming day He shall completely **dry it up** for them. "And the Lord shall utterly destroy the tongue of the Egyptian sea; and with His mighty wind shall He shake His hand over the river, and shall smite it in the seven streams, and make men go over dry shod. And there shall be an highway for the remnant of His people, which shall be left from Assyria, like as it was to Israel in the day that he came up out of the land of Egypt." (Isa. 11:15, 16, compare also Zech. 10:11). So too we read, "And the sixth angel poured out his vial upon the great river Euphrates; and the water thereof was **dried up**, that the way of the kings of the east might be prepared." (Rev. 16:12).

But not only will God perform mighty miracles on Israel's behalf, but as Ex. 34:10 adds, "It is a terrible thing that I will do **with** thee." Clearly this refers to the Great Tribulation, when God will deal with Israel for their sins. As Jeremiah predicted, "Alas! for that day is great so that none is like it: it is even the time of Jacob's trouble." (30:7). Of that dreadful period Christ declared, "For in those days shall be affliction, such as was not from the beginning of the creation which God created unto this time, neither shall be. And except that the Lord had shortened those days, no flesh should be saved." (Mark 13:19, 20.)

At Sinai God appeared before Israel with the most awe-inspiring manifestations: "And mount Sinai was altogether on a smoke, because the Lord descended upon it in fire: and the smoke thereof ascended as the smoke of a furnace, and the whole mount quaked greatly." (Ex. 19:18) But when the incarnate Son returns to this world, we are told that He "Shall be revealed from heaven with His mighty angels, in flaming fire taking vengeance on them that know not God, and that obey not the Gospel of our Lord Jesus Christ." (2 Thess. 1:7, 8). To this grand event the Apostle Paul referred when quoting from Haggai: "Whose voice then shook the earth: but now He hath promised, saying, Yet once more I shake not the earth only, but also heaven." (Heb. 12:26.)

Should it be asked, What is **the connection** between the awful contents of this 10th verse of Ex. 34 and its context? The answer is not far to seek. At the close of v. 9 we find Moses beseeching Jehovah, "Take us for thine inheritance." The next thing we read is, "**And** He said, Behold I make a covenant," etc. With His omniscient eye, God looked down the centuries, and then made known to His servant what must, ultimately, take place before Israel became His "inheritance" in fact. When this Covenant of Marvels has been fulfilled, the prayer of Moses will receive its final answer. It is in the Millennium, following the awful judgment of the Great Tribulation, that the Lord will enter upon His heritage. Then shall it be said, "Sing, O daughter of Zion; shout, O Israel, be glad and rejoice with all the heart, O daughter of Jerusalem. The Lord hath taken away thy judgments, He hath cast out thine enemy; the King of Israel, even the Lord is in the midst of thee: thou shalt not see evil any more. In that day it shall be said to Jerusalem, Fear thou not: and to Zion, Let not thine hands be slack. The Lord thy God in the midst of thee is mighty; He will save, **He will rejoice** over thee with joy; **He will rest** in His love, He will joy over thee with singing." Zeph. 3:14-17.)

"Observe thou that which I command thee this day: behold, I drive out before thee the Amorite, and the Canaanite, and the Hittite, and the Perizzite, and the Hivite, and the Jebusite." (v. 11). Here the Lord returns to the more immediate present. Note the **"this** day," and the change from the "I **will** do marvels" and "it is a terrible thing that I **will** do with thee" of the previous verse, to "I drive out." It should also be observed that the extermination of the Canaanites is attributed not to the military prowess of Israel, but to the alone power of Jehovah.

"Take heed to thyself, lest thou make a covenant with the inhabitants of the land whither thou goest, lest it be for a snare in the midst of thee." (v. 12.) This was a call to separation. There must be no unequal yoke uniting the people of God with the children of the Devil. The Lord was taking Moses at his word: in 33:16 he had said, "Is it not in that Thou goest with us? so shall we be **separated**, I and Thy people, from all the people that are upon the face of the earth." It is solemn to discover how Joshua, at a later date, disobeyed this very exhortation, see Joshua 9:14, 15. Centuries after, serious trouble issued from Joshua's sin, see 2 Sam. 21:1-9.

"But ye shall destroy their altars, break their images, and cut down their groves." (v. 13.) This also has its **spiritual** application to us. Not that Christians are called upon to reform society and improve the world, by engaging in crusades against vice and drunkenness. The counterpart in our experience to what we have here in v. 13 is that we should wage an unsparing war upon that which prevents us from enjoying our inheritance in Christ. Everything that would displace God in our lives

and in our affections must be demolished. Every idol—that which comes between the Lord and my heart—must be ruthlessly hewn down.

"For thou shalt worship no other God: for the Lord, whose name is Jealous, is a jealous God." (v. 14). Very searching, but very blessed is this. First, God is "jealous' of **His own glory.** Through Isaiah He has declared, "I am the Lord: that is My name; and My glory will I not give to another" (42:8). That is why God has chosen the foolish things of this world, weak things, things which are despised, yea, non-entities **"that** no flesh should glory in His presence." (1 Cor. 1:27-29).

Second, God is "jealous' of the **affections of His peop'e.** He is grieved when our love is given to another. "My son, **give Me** thine heart." (Prov. 23:26) is His appeal. "Set **Me** as a seal upon thine heart." (Song of Sol. 8:6) is His call to each of us.

Third, God is "jealous" of **His people:** "He that toucheth you toucheth the apple of His eye." (Zech. 2:8) is His own avowal.

As we have practically reached the limits of our space, we refrain from commenting in any detail upon v. 15, 16. The more so because what is there said has been before us in Ex. 13 and 23. That which is therein enjoined is separation from the Canaanites themselves, from their ways, and from their worship. In view of what had so recently taken place, the closing words of our passage are very solemn: "Thou shalt make thee no molten gods." (v. 17.) May the Lord grant both writer and reader that purpose of heart to cleave fully unto Himself, and that singleness of eye that has in view nought but His own glory, ever remembering that our God is a jealous God.

CHAPTER 68

GOD'S CLAIMS

EXODUS 34:18-21

The verses which are now to be before us seem, at first sight, very disconnected, presenting, apparently, a series of miscellaneous duties which the Lord enjoined upon Israel. First, mention is made of "The feast of unleavened bread" (v. 18). Next, we have the redemption of the firstborn, both of beasts and Israel's sons (vv. 19, 20). Then reference is made to the sabbath (v. 21). This is followed by instruction concerning the observance of the feast of weeks and the feast of ingathering (vv. 22-24). Next we have prohibitions concerning the offering of leaven with God's sacrifices, and the leaving over of the passover feast till the next morning (v. 25). Finally, God's claims upon all the first-fruits of the land is made, and command is given that a kid is not to be seethed in its mother's milk (v. 26). Thus, no less than seven different things are brought before us in these few verses. What, then is the link which binds them together? Wherein lies the unity of our passage?

We believe the answer to our question is to be found in• the promise which the Lord gave when He first appeared to Moses at the burning bush: "And He said, certainly I will be with thee; and this shall be a token unto thee, that I have sent thee: When thou hast brought forth the people out of Egypt, ye shall **serve God** upon this mountain" (Ex. 3:12). The sequel to this is found in 19:3,4: "And Moses went up unto God, and the Lord called unto him out of the mountain, saying, Thus shalt thou say to the house of Jacob, and tell the children of Israel: Ye have seen what I did unto the Egyptians, and how I bear you on eagles' wings, and brought you **unto Myself**." Here in Ex. 34 Jehovah makes known the **character** of that "service" which He required from Israel.

First of all, we have the two tables of stone, on which were inscribed the ten words of the Law. Submission to Himself, obedience to His revealed will is what God requires from His people. Second, Jehovah made known the principles which regulate the government of His people (vv. 6, 7). Third, the call to absolute separation from the heathen (v. 12), from their religion (v. 15), and from intermarriage with them (v. 16) is next given. No unequal loke must be formed between the children of God and the children of the Devil: compare 2 Cor. 6:14-18. God had brought them unto Himself (see 1 Peter 3:18), and this wondrous and glorious fact must now be witnessed to in all their ways. In the verses that follow, comprising our present portion, we have the **positive** side brought out.

"The feast of unleavened bread shalt thou keep. Seven days shalt thou eat unleavened bread, as I commanded thee, in the time of the month Abib: for in the month Abib thou camest out from Egypt" (v. 18). How blessedly this tells forth God's grand design in redemption: it is not only for the purpose of emancipating His people and bringing them unto Himself, but also that they may be happily gathered around Himself. That is what the "feast" speaks of, communion and joy. God gathered His redeemed around Himself in holy convocation, Himself the centre of peace and blessing.

The feast of unleavened bread was inseparably connected with the Passover. The passover provided that sacrifice upon which the feast itself was based. The antitype of it is found in 1 Cor. 5:7, 8: "For even Christ our passover is sacrificed for us: therefore let us keep the feast, not with old leaven, neither with the leaven of malice and wickedness; but with the unleavened bread of sincerity and truth." The two together tell us that **holiness is the consequence of redemption.** The two cannot be separated. It is because our sins have been put away, that God can now take us into communion with Himself. First, **God** counts us to have "died with Christ" (Rom. 6:4-8). Second, **we** are to "reckon" upon this fact

(Rom. 6:11; 2 Cor. 5: 14): faith is to appropriate it. Third, there is to be the **practical expression** of this in our daily lives: "Always bearing about in the body the **dying** of the Lord Jesus, that the life also of Jesus might be made manifest in our body" (2 Cor. 4:10).

We must distinguish between what the "unleavened bread" itself emblemized, and what Israel's actual feasting thereon typified. The bread was the Divinely-appointed symbol of Him who declared, "I am the living bread which came down from heaven: if any man eat of this bread, he shall live forever: and the bread that I will give is My flesh, which I will give for the life of the world" (John 6:51). Hence, because His person is holy, **un**leavened bread was appointed: "Seven days shall ye eat unleavened bread; even the first day ye shall put away leaven out of your houses: for whosoever eateth leavened bread from the first day until the seventh day, that soul shall be cut off from Israel" (Ex. 12:15). If then God gave such explicit instructions to His people of old, to use only that kind of bread which suitably and accurately represented the immaculate body of His blessed Son, by what right may we today be less particular in the loaf selected for "the Lord's supper?"

The Lord Jesus Himself instituted that "Supper" as a memorial of Himself, given in death for His pepole. Concerning the emblems which **He** appointed, if we are subject to the Scriptures, there cannot be the slightest room for question. They were, first, bread, **unleavened**, as is clear from the fact that this "Supper" was instituted right after the paschal one (Matt. 26:29)—therefore, when **all** leaven was rigidly excluded from their houses. The second was the "cup," containing "the fruit of the vine" (Matt. 26:29). Therefore when reminding the Corinthians of these, the apostle Paul wrote, "As often as ye eat (not simply "bread," any bread, but) **this** bread, and drink **this** cup, ye do show the Lord's death till He come" (1 Cor. 11:26). Alas, in this day of laxity, compromise and departure from the written Word, man's substitutes for God's appointments are received in most places without a murmur.

In Central Africa, where flour is difficult to obtain, one company of professing native-Christians, with their white missionaries, use cocoanut in lieu of bread, and its milk for the cup. Another company known to us in Australia, use raspberry-juice. And why not? If we are justified in changing unleavened bread into leavened bread, prepared pieces of bread cut into cubes instead of a loaf

broken—to remind us of the body of Christ broken for us; and an evening feast, a "supper," into a morning ordinance; then who has the right to say **where** the line of departure shall be drawn? Personally, the writer had far rather never partake of the Lord's supper again, than be a party to the sin of setting forth the blessed person of Christ by means of bread which has in it that which, in Scripture, is always the symbol of **evil**. If the loaf on the table has any symbolic significance at all, then a **leavened** one portrays a Christ with a corrupt humanity, and such is **not** the Christ of Holy Writ.

We are well aware of the objection which is likely to be made, namely, We must not be occupied too closely with the symbols themselves, lest the heart be taken off Christ. Such language may sound very pious, but it ill-becomes those who use it. Precisely the same objection is made by many pedo-baptists against immersion. They say, It is not the mere outward form, but the **spirit** behind the act that matters. But our Lord has said, "**This** do in remembrance of Me:" then how dare we "do" something else? If the outward symbols are of little or no moment, then why not be consistent and follow the "Quakers," and abandon the external ordinances altogether? We can and do "remember" Christ at other times than when we are gathered around His table. But we can only "**show** the **Lord's** death" (1 Cor. 11:26), when we adhere strictly to His own appointments. And is our obedience in this, a small matter to Him who commanded Moses to "make **all** things" (even the pins and cords) for the Tabernacle "after the pattern shown him in the mount?" It still stands written, "Behold, to obey is better than sacrifice, to hearken than the fat of rams" (1 Sam. 15:22).

Others object, If you are going to be such a stickler for the particular kind of bread used at the Lord's table, you might just as well insist that we select an "upper room," and partake of it sitting on the ground as the first disciples did. Our reply is, These details contributed nothing to the **showing forth** of "the Lord's death," which is the central design of the Supper. For that reason nothing whatever is said about **these** details in 1 Cor. 11, where the bread and the cup **are** particularized. Had the apostle mentioned them **there**, then we should have been under obligation to heed and emulate them. But he has not. Really, such an objection is nothing more than an idle quibble. Let those who are responsible for making the arrangements at the Lord's table, weigh in **His** presence what we have written. Let them ask, What kind of bread, leavened or unleavened, is the more scriptural? is the more appropriate as an emblem of the holy person of Christ? And which is least calculated to distress and stumble those of His people who, by grace, desire to be subject the Word in **all** things?

Returning now to our type. That which was prefigured by the "unleavened bread" was the person of Him who is "without blemish and without spot" (1 Peter 1:19). Israel's **participation** in the feast itself typified that holiness which is the believer's in Christ. Note how Paul could say, to the failing Corinthians, "ye **are unleavened**" (1 Cor. 5:7). But we must daily seek grace from on high to make this good in our lives, by walking in separation from all that defiles and corrupts: "Be ye holy, for I am holy" (1 Peter 1:16), is the unchanging demand of God upon us. And that upon which His demand is based is, "Ye are not your own, ye are bought with a price." If we are, by His wondrous grace, washed in the precious blood of Christ, He surely looks that we should keep our garments undefiled. If then we delight to contemplate the Passover, let us also keep, in a practical way, "the feast of unleavened bread," and that for "seven days"—a complete period, the whole of our life on earth.

"The feast of unleavened bread must be kept; God has provided us with it in Christ. He has brought in a new character of Manhood that we might feed upon it, and purge out all that is contrary to it. We see every where in the world an inflating principle, giving importance to that which has no true value before God. But in Christ we see One marked by purity, holiness, sincerity and truth: all that is delightful to God; and nothing inflated—nothing appearing to be greater than it really was. When they said to Him, Who art thou? He answered, 'Altogether that which I also say to you.' That is unleavened bread, and as we appreciate it and feed upon it, we shall become unleavened; we shall hate and purge out every kind of leaven" (C. A. Coates).

"All that openeth the matrix is Mine" (v. 19). God is the universal Proprietor. As the Creator of all, His rights are beyond question. But how little are they recognized and owned in a practical way! Our present verse is one which ought to be much before those who are parents. Listen fond mother, doting father, that little one in the cradle is not **yours** absolutely; in reality, it belongs to God. "Lo, children are an heritage of the Lord" (Psa. 127:3). Have you acknowledged this? Have you dedicated your litlte one to God? "Thou shalt **set apart unto the Lord** all that openeth the matrix" (Ex. 13:12) was God's word to His people of old, and it has never been repealed. O that you may be able to say with the mother of Samuel, "For this child I prayed; and the Lord hath given me my petition which I asked of Him: Therefore also I have **returned him to the Lord**" (1 Sam. 1:27, 28).

This is a subject of great practical importance, and there is much need to press it upon parents today. Scripture does not teach infant "christening," or infant baptism, but it **does** infant dedication. Even the parents of Christ, when He was a child, "brought Him to Jerusalem **to present Him to** the Lord" (Luke 2:22). And note that both here and in Samuel's case, it was the parents personally, and not a priest, who performed the solemn act. The act of dedication is the formal acknowledgment that the child belongs to God: it is saying, as David said, "For all things come of Thee; and **of Thine own** have we given Thee" (1 Chron. 29:14). The whole subsequent training of the child should be in the remembrance of this fact. Hold your children in trust from God, and "bring them up in the nurture **and** admonition (mark the 'balance of Truth') of the Lord" (Eph. 6:4).

"All that openeth the matrix is Mine; and every firstling among thy cattle, or sheep" (v. 19). Clearly it is God here pressing His claims upon His people. The cattle upon a thousand hills are **His**. So too He declares, "The silver is Mine, and the gold is Mine. saith the Lord of hosts" (Haggai 2:8). How often we forget this! Ah, it is one thing to sing. 'Naught that I have I call mine own, I hold it for the Giver; For I am His, and He is mine. Forever and forever," but it is quite another matter to recognize that we are but **stewards,** holding everything in trust from Him and for Him: "Moreover it is required in stewards, that a man be found **faithful**" (1 Cor. 4:2). If we shall be called to account for "every idle word" that we have uttered (Matt. 12:36), how much more shall we for every pound or dollar that we have wasted!

It is very striking and solemn to observe that in the three parables which our Lord gave on the subject of service and its reward, that, in each instance, He selected a **coin** to illustrate His theme. First, in the parable of the labourers in the vineyard, a "penny" (Matt. 20). Second, in the parable of the Nobleman, "He called His ten servants and delivered them ten pounds, and said unto them, Occupy till I come" (Luke 19:13). Third, in the parable of the Man travelling into a far country He called His own servants, and delivered unto them His goods: and unto one He gave five talents, to another two, and to another one; to every man according to his several ability" (Matt. 25:14, 15). The word talent signifies "a sum of money." With it His disciples were to trade during the time of His absence. If the teaching of these parables were more before our hearts, Christians would be more diligent and faithful in laying up for themselves "treasure in heaven" (Matt. 6:20).

"But the firstling of an ass thou shalt redeem with a lamb: and if thou redeem him not, then shalt thou break his neck. All the firstborn of thy sons thou shalt redeem" (v. 20). This is a repetition of what was before us in Ex. 13:13. As so many of our present readers have not seen what we wrote thereon, almost four years ago, we deem it advisable to go over the same ground again, or at least to review what we then said.

The words "the firstling of an ass thou shalt redeem **with a lamb**," at once carry our minds back to the Passover night, when the firstborn of the Hebrews was "redeemed with a lamb." Thus the Lord has linked together the redemption of His own people with the redeeming of asses. Again, it is to be noted that, "if thou redeem not (the "ass"), thou shalt b́reak his neck," just as the Israelites would most certainly have been smitten by the avenging Angel unless they had slain the lamb and sprinkled its blood. Thus God here compares the natural man with the ass! Deeply humbling is this! As we read in Job 11:12 "For vain man would be wise, though man be born like a wild ass's colt."

Under the Mosaic law, the "ass" was an **unclean** animal, neither chewing the cud nor dividing the hoof. So too the natural man is unclean: "But we all as an unclean thing" (Isa. 64:4). Though a man may be most particular about his habits, yet within is he full "of uncleanness" (Matt. 23:27). The "divided hoof" symbolizes a separated walk, a life that is lived with God and for God. The "chewing of the cud" speaks of rumination, meditation,—meditating in God's Law day and night (Psa. 1:2). But to these two things the natural man is a total stranger. Thus, the "ass" accurately represents him. He is unclean. But thank God there is a fountain opened "for sin and for uncleanness" (Zech. 13:1).

Again, the "ass" is a **stupid and senseless** creature. It has less of what we call

"instinct" than has almost any other beast. In this too it resembles the natural man. Proudly as he may boast of his powers of reason, conceited as he may be over his intellectual attainments, the truth is, that he is utterly devoid of any spiritual intelligence: "But the natural man receiveth not the things of the Spirit of God: for they are foolishness unto him; neither can he know them, because they are spiritually discerned" (1. Cor. 2:14). And again, "Walk not as other Gentiles walk, in the vanity of their mind, having the understanding **darkened**, being alienated from the life of God through the ignorance that is in them, because of the blindness of their heart" (Eph. 4:17, 18). How thankful Christians should be that, "We know that the son of God is come, and hath **given us an understanding,** that we may know Him that is true" (1 John 5:20).

Once more; the "ass" is a **stubborn and intractable** animal. Often he is as hard to move as a mule. Such also is fallen man. He is a rebel against God. The history of every descendant of Adam is summed up in those terrible words, "we have turned every one to his **own** way" (Isa. 53:6). "There is none that seeketh after God" (Rom. 3:11). When God became incarnate and tabernacled among men, He had to say, "Ye will not come to Me, that ye might have life" (John 5:40). When a sinner does come to Christ, it is because Divine power has "drawn" him (John 6:44). And after we become Christians, the Holy Spirit has to take us in hand and "lead" us in "the paths of righteousness" (Psa. 23:3. Rom. 8:14).

Most unpalatable to our proud hearts is such a line of truth as the above. Yet is it blessed if we bow to it and take our true place before God—in the dust. Only the illumination of the Holy Spirit can bring any of us to realize **how** ass-like we are. For this reason Solomon wrote, "I said in mine heart concerning the estate of the sons of men, that God might manifest them, and **that they might see** that they themselves are beasts" (Eccl. 3:18). Has God opened your eyes, my reader? Do you **own** that the "ass" accurately portrays all that you are in yourself—unclean, senseless, intractable, fit only to have your neck broken? If so, you can appropriate and appreciate those blessed words, "Christ died for the ungodly" (Rom. 5:6). How marvelous the grace that has provided salvation for such: "The firstling of an ass thou shalt redeem with a lamb!"

"And none shall appear before Me empty" (v. 20). How can they! Once a poor sinner has had his eyes opened to see the ruin which sin has wrought in him, once he learns that he was "redeemed by the Lamb," his heart is filled to overflowing, filled with gratitude and praise. The language which best expresses his thankfulness is, "Bless the Lord, O my soul: and all that is within me, bless His holy name" (Psa. 103:1). No, the redeemed cannot appear before the Redeemer "empty." Spontaneously must they heed that word, "By Him therefore, let us offer the sacrifice of praise to God continually, that is, the fruit of our lips giving thanks to His name' (Heb. 13:15).

"And. none shall appear before Me empty." If this were expressed in its positive form, it would read, "They shall come before Me as worshippers," for worship is the presenting of something to God. As we have recently had three articles upon this subject in our magazine, there is the less need for us now to enlarge upon it. The first mention of "worship" in the O. T. gives us the basic and central thought in connection with the subject. In Gen. 22:5 we read that Abraham said, "I and the lad will go yonder and worship." Abraham was about to offer his son unto the Lord! So the first time we read of worship in the N. T. we find the wise men presenting gifts to the infant Saviour (Matt 2). Our hearts should be filled with love and our mouths with praise as we appear before our gracious God.

"Six days thou shalt work, but on the seventh day thou shalt rest: in earing time and in harvest thou shalt rest" (v. 21). The order of Truth presented in our passage is very beautiful. First, we have had that which speaks of absolute separation unto God (v. 18). Next, dedication unto God (vv. 19:20). Then, worship before, or the adoration of, God (v. 20). Now we get mention of the sabbath, the Lord's provision of mercy for our soul's occupation with Himself. It is to be observed that here a word is added to the previous references to the Sabbath which were before us in Ex. 16, 20, 31. Upon this Mr. Coates has said:

"The rest of the sabbath must be observed, and the distinctive feature of it in this case is that 'in ploughing-time and in harvest thou shalt rest.' It intimates the necessity for recurring periods in which we cease from activity to contemplate in rest what God has done. The sabbaths must be kept, no matter what the needs of the Lord's work may be; for I suppose that ploughing-time and harvest might typify the most exacting and strenuous times in His work. The soul must know what it is to lay aside its activities, and have its rest with God. I am afraid we do not always keep our sabbaths. We are either doing something, or occupied with what we are going to do. There is not enough restfulness with God."

CHAPTER 69

THE SINAIATIC COVENANT

EXODUS 34:22-27

The key verse to the whole of Ex. 34 is the 27th: "And the Lord said unto Moses, Write thou these words: for after the tenor of **these** words I have made a **covenant** with thee and with Israel." Hence the title to our present article. In the verse following the one just quoted, we read, "And he was there with the Lord forty days and forty nights; he did neither eat bread, nor drink water. And he wrote upon the tables those words of **the covenant**, the ten commandments." Thus, the Sinaiatic covenant was a **legal** one, but as vv. 6, 7 have shown us, it was Law administered in mercy and patience, as well as righteousness and holiness.

We have already considered the Law as expressing God's government over His redeemed people; let us now look at it in its **dispensational** bearings. In Rom. 5:20 we read, "the law entered, that the offence might abound;" that is, that sin might appear "exceeding sinful" (Rom. 7:13); that the wickedness of the human heart might be manifested; that it should be the more fully demonstrated that men **are** sinners; and this in order that, "Every mouth might be stopped, and all the world may become guilty before God" (Rom. 3:19).

In the light of what has just been before us, we should carefully bear in mind that God gave the Law to Moses **twice**: Ex. 31:18; 34:1, 28. The first giving of the Law demonstrated that man is **ungodly**. As we have seen, before the Law was written upon tables of stone, it was first given to Moses orally (Ex. 20), and Moses then repeated it to Israel (24:3), and they affirmed, "all the words which the Lord hath said will we do." The first word He **had** said was, "Thou shalt have no other gods before Me." But at the very time He was engraving those words on the stones, Israel was saying to Aaron, "Up, make us gods which shall go before us" (32:1). And the next thing was that the golden calf was made and worshipped. The immediate sequel was the visitation of God's anger upon them (32:27, 28).

Thus, the first trial of man—not of Israel only, for "As in water face answereth to face, so the heart of man to man" (Prov. 27:19)—ended in judgment.

As the first giving of the Law demonstrated that man was "ungodly," so the second giving of it was to be followed by a manifestation that he is "without strength" to keep it. These are the two things which characterize fallen man (Rom. 5:6), and these were what the double giving of the law was designed to show. The first was demonstrated speedily; the second was made evident more slowly, yet none the less surely. God gave man fair and full opportunity to show whether he had power to keep the law. In the nation of Israel he was represented and tested under the most favourable circumstances. Israel was separated from the heathen; Jehovah Himself dwelt in their midst. They were given a land flowing with milk and honey; and, as the apostle says, unto them pertained "the adoption, and the glory, and the covenants, and the giving of the law, and the service of God, and the promises" (Rom. 9:4). Well might Jehovah say to them at a later date, "What could have been done more to My vineyard, that I have not done in it? wherefore when I looked that it should bring forth grapes, brought it forth wild grapes?" (Isa. 5:4).

Yes, the vineyard of the Lord's planting brought forth only "wild grapes." Graciously and longsufferingly did He bear with them, sending one prophet after another to exhort, admonish, rebuke, and warn. But all to no purpose (see Mark 12:1-5). One generation after another was tested, but always with the same result, in that the Law was "weak through the flesh" (Rom. 8:3). Man had no ability to meet the righteous requirements of God. He was "without strength." Therefore, as was inevitable, this second testing of man under the Law also ended with Divine judgment. And most impressive was the longsuffering mercy of God seen in that too. The full and final stroke of His wrath did not fall upon guilty Israel all at once, but was meted out slowly and in stages.

First, God delivered up His people into the hands of the Chaldeans. As He said through Isaiah, "O Assyrian, the rod of Mine anger, and the staff in their hand is Mine indignation. I will send him against an hypocritical nation, and against the people of My wrath will I give him a charge, to take the spoil, and to take the prey, and to treat them down like the mire of the streets" (10:5,6). Israel's second testing under the Law had come to an end. The "glory of the Lord" (the Shekinah) had departed from the holy city (Ezek. 11:23, 24), and Israel's sons were carried down captive into Babylon; and through the prophet Hosea the Nation was disowned of God: "Then said God, Call his name Lo-ammi: for ye are not My people" (1:9).

Later, a remnant was permitted to leave Babylon and return to the land of their fathers, unto the city which had been ruined through their folly and rebellion, to raise it up again and to build the temple. But they came back not as God's people, but as "Lo-ammi." And though a temple was erected, yet no Shekinah glory abode in it. **It was empty!** God no longer dwelt in their midst. The prophets which He sent unto them at that period emphasized the ruin which had come in, and pointed forward to the advent of the Saviour. The great test then was no longer obedience to the Law (though that was not repealed), but an humble acceptance of the Divine judgment which was upon them, and a waiting in contrition of spirit for the Deliverer. But instead of humbling themselves before God, instead of repenting for their sins, instead of owning that they **were** "without strength," they were more self-righteous than ever. Ably has this been set forth by another:

"But now, alas! you find again what the power of Satan is, and how subtly he can blind, through man's folly, the heart of man. It is very striking, and people generally notice it as favorable to Israel, that after their return, they were no more idolators. It had been their special sin. The prophet asks, you remember, 'Hath a nation changed their gods, which are yet no gods? but My people have changed their glory for that which doth not profit.' Even from the wilderness they had. There was first the golden calf, and all through the wilderness they had taken up 'the tabernacle of Moloch, and the star of their god Remphan, figures which they made to worship them.' God had declared that he was the one God, but they were idolators to the core of the heart.

"But as soon as there was no god in their midst—as soon as the temple was empty and the glory had departed—as soon as they were in the ruin which their sin had brought about, then immediately Satan came forward, not in the garb of idolatry any more, but now to resist the sentence which God had pronounced upon them—now to persuade them that after all they were **not** as Lo-ammi—that they **were** God's people, and to say, 'The temple of the Lord, the temple of the Lord are we.' In fact, pharisaism was the growth of that period, and pharisaism was the self-righteousness which resisted God's sentence upon them, pretending to have a righteousness when God had emphatically declared that man had none. So it was when that Deliverer prophesied of came, and when the glory, in a deeper and more wonderful way than ever was once more in their midst,—aye, the 'glory of the only begotten Son, in the bosom of the Father'—the Antitype of the glory of that tabernacle of old,—when He who was to come did come, and was amongst them in love and grace, ready to meet them with all mercy and tenderness,—not coming to be ministered to, but to minister,—not requiring, but to give with both hands—to give without limit—to give as God,—alas! these phasisees could turn comfortably to one another and say, 'which of the pharisees have believed on Him?' Pharisees they were who slew the Lord of glory" (Mr. F. W. Grant).

Then it was, as a matter of course, that Judaism ended. The high priest's rending of his garments (Matt. 26:65), though unknown to himself (cf. John 11:51), intimated that the priesthood had served its day. Man's second trial under Law was over. Nothing now remained but judgment, yet even that lingered for a further forty years, till, in A.D. 70, Jerusalem was captured, the temple destroyed, and the Jews dispersed abroad. Even before that judgment fell, God's call to His own people was, "Save yourselves **from** this untoward generation' (Acts 2:40). And again, "Let us go forth therefore unto Him, **without the camp**" (Heb. 13:13). But we must now retrace our steps, and return to the point from which we started. The central thing in Ex. 34 is the "covenant" which Jehovah made with Israel at Sinai.

As we pointed out in the opening paragraphs of our last article, that covenant was based upon the ten words engraved upon the tables of stone. It was a covenant of law, but law administered in mercy, grace, patience, as well as holiness and righteousness. In that covenant God pressed His **claims** upon man. First, He demanded absolute separation, unto Him-self (v. 18). Second, entire consecration for Himself (vv. 19, 20). Third, complete submission to His appointed sabbath, no exception being permitted even in harvest-time (v. 21). Here follows our present passage.

"And thou shalt observe the feast of weeks, of the first fruits of wheat harvest" (v. 22). The central thought in connec-tion with each of Israel's "feasts" was the gathering together the people around Jehovah Himself, on the ground of re-demption accomplished. Thus, it was cor-porate responsibility which is here in view, and, we may add, corporate privilege, for there is no greater privilege enjoyed on earth than for God's saints to be gathered together, in festive assembly, around Him-self.

The "feast of weeks," better known as "Pentecost," is described at greatest length in Lev. 23:15-21. Here it is con-nected with "the first fruits of wheat harv-est." This at once makes us think of James 1:18: "Of His own will begat He us with the Word of truth, that we should be a kind of **firstfruits** of His creatures." Dis-pensationally, the feast received a partial fulfillment at the descent of the Spirit in Acts 2. We say "partial fulfillment," for Peter's words in Acts 2:16, "But this **is that** which was spoken by the prophet Joel," rather than "this is the **fulfillment** of that which was spoken by Joel," tell us that the complete realization is yet fu-ture; as indeed it is. The "two loaves" of Lev. 23:17 pointed, first, to Jew and Gen-tile now gathered together and made fel-low-members of the Body of Christ; but, ultimately they foreshadowed the re-unit-ing of the two houses of Israel (cf. Ezek. 37:16) when, after this dispensation has run its course, the Jews will be restored once more to Divine favour.

"And the feast of ingathering at the year's end" (v. 22). This is better known as "the feast of tabernacles." It was the final one on Israel's religious calendar. Its dispensational fulfillment is therefore yet future. "The feast of tabernacles is the joy of the millennium, when Israel hath come out of the wilderness, where their sins have placed them: but to which will be added this first day (the "eighth day" of Lev. 23:36" A. W. P.) of another week —the resurrection joy of those who are raised with the Lord Jesus, to which the presence of the Holy Spirit answers mean-while. Consequently, we find that the feast of tabernacles took place after the increase of the earth had been gathered in, and, as we learn elsewhere, not only after the harvest, but after the vintage

also; that is, after separation by judg-ment, and the final execution of judgment on the earth, when heavenly and earthly saints shall all be gathered in" (Mr. J. N. Darby).

"Thrice in the year shall all your men children appear before the Lord God, the God of Israel" (v. 23). The particular oc-casions specified were, "in the feast of unleavened bread, and in the feast of weeks, and in the feast of tabernacles" (Deut. 16:16). Really, those feasts con-templated three distinct dispensations: the first, the O. T., when Israel was separated unto the Lord. The second, this present interval, when in addition to the "rem-nant according to the election of grace" (Rom. 11:5) from the stock of Abraham, God is also visiting "the Gentiles, to take out of them a people for His name" (Acts 15:14). The third, to the millennium, when the Lord "will return, and will build again the tabernacle of David, which is fallen down; and will build again the ruins thereof, and will set it up: That the resi-due of men might seek after the Lord, and all the Gentiles, upon whom My name is called" (Acts 15:16, 17). We may add that each of the three persons in the God-head are, distinctively, contemplated in these feasts. The feast of unleavened bread, which is inseparably connected with the Passover, speaks to us of God the Son. The feast of weeks or Pentecost is marked by the descent of the Spirit (Acts 2:2; Joel 2:28). The feast of tabernacles will witness the answer to that oft-prayed pe-tition, "Our Father which art in heaven . . . **Thy** kingdom come" (compare Matt. 13:43; 16:27). The **order** is the same as in the three-one parable of Luke 15: the work of the Shepherd, the work of the Spirit, bringing into the Father's house. Thus it is experimentally.

As we have said, the "feasts" had to do with corporate responsibility, and corpor-ate privilege too, for, "Behold, how good and how pleasant it is for brethren to dwell together in unity" (Psa. 133:1). But alas, history has repeated itself. At the beginning of Israel's national history, they were a united "congregation." So it was at the beginning of this dispensation: "And all that believed were together" (Acts 2:44). For a time all went well; then failure and sin came, followed by Divine chastisement and judgment; true alike of Israel and Christendom. Ulti-mately Israel was carried captive into Babylon, so too, all through the 'dark ages' the "mystery Babylon" of Rev. 17 domi-nated Europe. A remnant of Israel re-turned from Babylon and the true wor-ship of God was restored in Israel, though not after its primitive glory. So there was a Reformation, a remnant was delivered from the papacy, and God again was magnified, though the streams of truth was not as pure as it was at the beginning.

But at the end of the Old Testament period the corporate testimony of Israel was a complete wreck and ruin: the priesthood had "corrupted the covenant of Levi" (Mal. 2:7, 8); polluted bread was offered upon God's altar (Mal. 1:7). Judah had "profaned the holiness of the Lord" (Mal. 2:11), and Jehovah had to say, "I have no pleasure in you . . . neither will I accept an offering at your hand" (Mal. 1:10). In like manner, the corporate testimony of Christendom has long since fallen into ruins. The last of the Epistles to the churches depicts Christ as being on the **outside** (Rev. 3:20), and His voice is addressed to the individual only, "If any man hear My voice."

"For I will cast out the nations before thee and enlarge thy borders: neither shall any man desire thy land, when thou shalt go up to appear before the Lord thy God thrice in the year" (v. 24). How remarkably does this verse illustrate Prov. 16:7: "When a man's ways please the Lord, He maketh even his enemies to be at peace with him." God will not allow any man to be His debtor: He has promised, "Them that honour Me, I will honour" (1 Sam. 2:30). So it was here. These Israelites were going up to the temple to worship the Lord; in their absence He would guard their homes.

"Neither shall any man desire thy land, when thou shalt go up to appear before the Lord thy God thrice in the year." How strikingly does this demonstrate the absoluteness of God's control of His creatures! And man, though fallen and rebellious, is no exception. As Dan. 4:35 tells us, "He doeth according to His will in the army of heaven, **and** among the inhabitants of the earth: and none can stay His hand." So it was here. The male Hebrews were to leave their farms and go up to the temple in Jerusalm (Deut. 16:16)—for many of them, a long journey. They were surrounded by hostile heathen but so complete is God's control of man, every man, that none shall be allowed to molest their families or flocks while they were away. Thus, we see that God not only restrains the activities of the wicked, but even regulates the desires of their evil hearts: "The king's heart is in the hand of the Lord, as the rivers of water: He turneth it whithersoever He will" (Prov. 21:1).

"Thou shalt not offer the blood of My sacrifice with leaven" (v. 25). God was very jealous of the types. Why? Because they pointed forward to the person and work of Christ. Thus, His jealousy of the types was His guarding of the glory of His beloved Son. Therefore, inasmuch as the sacrifices pointed forward to the Lord Jesus, leaven (which is an emblem of evil) must be excluded, for He is "holy, harmless, undefiled, separate from sinners" (Heb. 7:26).

"Thou shalt not offer the blood of My sacrifice with leaven." Very wonderful and blessed is it to observe how the Lord here refers to the sacrifice: He does not say "the blood of **thy** sacrifice," but "**My** sacrifice." This is also the language of the antitype: The Sacrifice "offered once for all," was of God's appointing, was of God's providing, was for God's satisfaction. Man had no part or lot in it whatsoever. "Salvation is of the Lord." Frequently is this same truth brought out in the types. In Gen. 22:8 we hear Abraham saying to his son's query of "Where is the lamb for the burnt offering?—God will provide **Himself** a lamb." In Ex. 12:27 we are told, "It is **the Lord's** passover." In connection with the two goats on the day of atonement, lots were cast, "one lot **for the Lord**" (Lev. 16:8); and so on.

"Neither shall the sacrifice of the feast of the passover be left unto the morning" (v. 25). The paschal lamb was to be eaten on the same night it had been slain and roasted in fire, not left over to be partaken of on the morrow (see 12:10). The application of this detail of the type is very solemn and searching. To have eaten the lamb on the morrow, would have been to dissociate it from the import of its death. The eating of the lamb speaks to us of the believer (already sheltered by His blood) feeding on Christ: eating the lamb the same night it was killed, tells us that we are ever to feed upon Christ with a deep sense in our souls of what His death and bearing judgment for us ("**roast** with fire") really involved for Him. Note how Christ Himself emphasized this in John 6: first vv. 50, 51, then vv. 53-56!

"The first of the firstfruits of thy land thou shalt bring unto the house of the Lord thy God" (v. 26). This Divine ordinance receives amplification in Deut. 26:1-11. The interested reader would find it profitable to prayerfully study in detail the whole of that passage for himself; we can but summarise its teaching here. First, it had to do with Israel's possession of their inheritance (v. 1). Second, this "first of the firstfruits of thy land" was the Divine pledge or earnest of the coming harvest (v. 2). Third, Israel acknowledged this by their presentation unto the priest (v. 3). Fourth, the Israelite was then required to look back and acknowledge his previous state of shame and bondage (v. 5-7). Fifth, he then owned the Lord's goodness in deliverance (v. 8). Sixth, he expressed his gratitude for the goodly portion the Lord had given him (v. 9). Seventh, he presented the "firstfruits" in worship before Him (vv. 10: 11).

All of the above is rich in its typical teaching, much of which has already been before us in other connections. That which is here distinctive, is the contrast presented between what we find in Ex. 34:22 and here in v. 26. The "firstfruits of wheat harvest" refers to Christ (cf. John 12:24 with 1 Cor. 15:23). But the "first of the fruits of thy land" or "inheritance" speaks, we believe, of the Holy Spirit, who is "the earnest of our inheritance until the redemption of the purchased possession" (Eph. 1:13, 14). Do we not get the antitype of Ex. 34:26 in Rom. 8:22, "Ourselves also, which have the **firstfruits of the Spirit!**" And in the light of Deut. 26:10, 11 are we not taught that we should thank God as heartily for the gift of the Spirit as for the gift of His Son? Do we realize that we are as much indebted to, and therefore have as much cause of praise for, the work of the Spirit in us, as the work of Christ **for** us!

"Thou shalt not seethe a kid in his mother's milk" (v. 26). Upon this we have nothing better to offer than the brief comment of Mr. Dennett: "This remarkable prohibition is found three times in the Scriptures (Ex. 23:19; 34:26; Deut. 14:21). God will have His people tenderly careful, guarding them from the violation of any instinct of nature. The milk of the mother was the food, the sustenance of the kid, and hence this must not be used to seethe it as food for others."

"And the Lord said unto Moses, Write thou these words: for after the tenor of these words have I made a covenant with thee and with Israel" (v. 27). This verse summarises all that has been before us in the previous verses of the chapter. An imperishable record was to be made of all that Jehovah had said unto His servant. The words, "I have made a covenant **with thee** (the typical mediator) and with Israel," gives assurance that all will yet be made good through the person and millennial administration of Christ. Israel failed in the past, but there will be no failure with Him who shall yet effectuate God's counsels and glorify Him in this very scene where His people have so grievously dishonoured Him. May the Lord hasten that glad day.

CHAPTER 70

THE GLORIFIED MEDIATOR

EXODUS 34:28-35

The Law had "a shadow of good things to come" (Heb. 10:1). A beautiful illustration and exemplification of this is found in the closing verses of Ex. 34, in which we behold Moses descending from the mount with radiant face. The key to our present portion is found in noting the exact position that it occupies in this book of redemption. It comes after the legal covenant which Jehovah had made with Israel; it comes before the actual setting up of the tabernacle and the Shekinah-glory filling it. As we shall see, our passage is interpreted for us in 2 Cor. 3. What we have here in Ex. 34 supplies both a comparison and a contrast with the new dispensation, the dispensation of the Spirit, of grace, of life more abundant. But before that dispensation was inaugerated, God saw fit that man should be fully tested under Law, and that, for the purpose of demonstrating what he is as a fallen and sinful creature.

As was shown in our last article, man's trial under the Mosaic economy demonstrated two things: first, that he is "ungodly;" second, that he is, "without strength" (Rom. 5:6). But these are negative things: in Rom. 8:7 a third feature of man's terrible state is mentioned, namely, that he is "enmity against God." This was made manifest when God's Son became incarnate and tabernacled for thirty-three years on this earth. "He came unto His own, and His own received Him not" (John. 1:11). Not only so, but He was "despised and rejected of men." Nay, more, they hated Him, hated Him "without a cause" (John 15:25). Nor would their hatred be appeased till they had condemned Him to a malefactor's death and nailed Him to the accursed cross. And, let it be remembered, that it was not merely the Jews that put to death the Lord of glory, but the Gentiles also; therefore did thte Lord say, when looking forward to His death, "Now is the judgment of this wor'd" (John 12:31)—not of Israel only. There the probation or testing of man ended.

Man is not now under probation. He is under condemnation: "As it is written, There is none righteous, no, not one: There is none that understandeth, there is none that seeketh after God. They are all gone out of the way, they are together become unprofitable; there is none that doeth good, no not one" (Rom. 3: 10-12). Man is not on trial: he is a culprit, under sentence. No pleading will avail; no excuses will be accepted. The present issue between God and the sinner is, will man bow to God's righteous verdict.

This is where the Gospel meets us. It comes to us as to those who are already "lost," as to those who are "ungodly, without strength, enmity against God." It announces to us the amazing **grace** of God— the only hope for poor sinners. But that grace will not be welcomed until the sinner bows to the sentence of God against him. That is why both repentance and faith are demanded from the sinner. These two must not be separated. Paul preached, "repentance toward God, and faith toward our Lord Jesus Christ" (Acts 20:21). Repentance is the sinner's acknowledgement of that sentence of condemnation under which he lies. Faith is the acceptance of the grace and mercy which are extended to him through Christ. Repentance is not the turning over of a new leaf and the vowing that I will mend my ways; rather is it a setting of my seal that God is true when He tells me that I am "**without** strength," that in myself my case is hopeless, that I am no more able to "do better next time" than I am of creating a world. Not until this is really believed (not as the result of my experience, but on the authority of God's holy Word), shall I really turn to Christ and welcome Him—not as a Helper, but as a **Saviour.**

As it was dispensationally so it is experimentally: there must be "a ministration of death" (2 Cor. 3:7), before there is a "ministration of spirit" or life (2 Cor. 3:

8); there must be "the ministration of condemnation," before "the ministration of righteousness" (2 Cor. 3:9). Ah, a "**ministration** of condemnation and death" falls strangely upon our ears, does it not? A "ministration of **grace**" we can understand, but a "ministration of condemnation" is not so easy to grasp. But this latter was man's first **need**: it must be shown what he is in himself: a hopeless wreck, utterly incapable of meeting the righteous requirements of a holy God—before he is ready to be a debtor to mercy alone. We repeat: as it was dispensationally, so it is experimentally: it was to this (his own experience) that the apostle Paul referred when he said, "For I was alive without the law once: but when the commandemnt came, sin revived, and I died" (Rom. 7:9). In his unregenerate days he was, in his own estimation "alive," yet it was "**without** the Law," i. e., apart from meeting its demands. "But when the commandment came," when the Holy Spirit wrought within him, when the Word of God came in power to his heart, then "sin revived," that is, he was made aware of his awful condition; and then he "died" to his self-righteous complacency—he saw that, in himself, his case was hopeless. Yes, the appearing of the glorified mediator comes not before, but after, the legal covenant.

"And he was there with the Lord forty days and forty nights; he did neither eat bread, nor drink water." And he wrote upon the tables the words of the covenant, the ten commandments" (v. 28). Our passage abounds in comparisons and contrasts. The "forty days" here at once recalls to mind the "forty days" mentioned in Matt. 4. Here it was Moses; there it is Christ. Here it was Moses on the mount; there it was Christ in the wilderness. Here it was Moses favoured with a glorious revelation from God; there it was Christ being tempted of the Devil. Here it was Moses receiving the Law, at the mouth of Jehovah; there it was Christ being assailed by the Devil to repudiate that Law. We scarcely know which is the greater wonder of the two: that a sinful worm of the earth was raised to such a height of honour as to be permitted to spend a season in the presence of the great Jehovah, or that of the Lord of glory should stoop so low as to be for six weeks with the foul Fiend.

"And it came to pass, when Moses came down from mount Sinai with the two tables of testimony in Moses' hand, when he came down from the mount, that Moses wist not that the skin of his face shone while he talked with Him." Very blessed is it to compare and contrast this second

descent of Moses from the mount with that which was before us in the 32nd chapter. There we see the face of Moses diffused with anger (v. 19); here he comes down with countenance radiant. There he beheld a people engaged in idolatry, here he returns to a people abashed. There we behold him dashing the tables of stone to the ground (v. 19); here he deposits them in the ark (Deut. 10:5).

"And it came to pass, when Moses came down from mount Sinai with the two tables of testimony in Moses' hand, when he came down from the mount, that Moses wist not that the skin of his face shone while he talked with Him." This also reminds us of a N. T. episode, which is very similar, yet vastly dissimilar. It was on the mount that the face of Moses was made radiant, and it was on the mount that our Lord was transfigured. But the glory of Moses was only a reflected one, whereas that of Christ was inherent. The shining of Moses' face was the consequence of his being brought into the immediate presence of the glory of Jehovah; the transfiguration of Christ was the outshining of His own personal glory. The radiance of Moses was confined to his face, but of Christ we read, "His raiment was white as the light" (Matt. 17:3). Moses **knew not** that the skin of his face shone; Christ did, as is evident from His words, "Tell the vision to no man" (Matt. 17:9).

This 29th verse brings out, most blessedly, what is the certain consequence of intimate communion with the Lord, and that in a twofold way. First no soul can enjoy real fellowship with the all-glorious God without being affected thereby, and that to a marked degree. Moses had been absorbed in the communications received and in contemplating the glory of Him who spake with him; and his own person caught and retained some of the beams of that glory. So it is still: as we read in Psa. 34:5, "They looked unto Him, and their faces were radiant" (R. V.). It is communion with the Lord that conforms us to His image. We shall not be more Christlike till we walk more frequently and more closely with Him. "But we all, with open face, beholding as in a glass the glory of the Lord, are **changed** into the same image from glory to glory, by the Spirit of the Lord" (2 Cor. 3:18).

The second consequence of real communion with God is that we shall be less occupied with our wretched selves. Though the face of Moses shone with 'a light not seen on land or sea,' he wist it not. This illustrates a vital difference between self-righteous phariseeism and true godliness:

the former produces complacency and pride, the latter leads to self-abnegation and humility. The pharisee (and there are many of his tribe still on earth) boasts of his attainments, advertises his imaginary spirituality, and thanks God that he is not as other men are. But the one who, by grace, enjoys much fellowship with the Lord, learns of Him who was "meek and lowly in heart," and says "Not unto us, O Lord, not unto us, but unto Thy name give glory" (Psa. 115:1). Being engaged with the beauty of the Lord, he is delivered from self-occupation, and therefore is unconscious of the very fruit of the Spirit which is being brought forth in him. But though **he** is not aware of his increasing conformity to Christ, **others** are.

"And when Aaron and all the children of Israel saw, Moses, behold the skin of his face shone; and they were afraid to come nigh him" (v. 30). This shows us the third effect of communion with God: though the individual himself is unconscious of the glory manifested through him, others are cognizant of it. Thus it was when two of Christ's apostles stood before the Jewish sanhedrin: "Now when they saw the boldness of Peter and John and perceived that they were unlearned and ignorant men, they marvelled; and they took knowledge of them, **that they had been with Jesus**" (Acts 4:13). Ah, we cannot keep company very long with the Holy One, without His impress being left upon us. The man who is thoroughly devoted to the Lord needeth not to wear some badge or button in his coat-lapel, nor proclaim with his lips that he is "living a life of victory." It is still true that actions speak louder than words.

"And when Aaron and all the children of Israel saw Moses, behold, the skin of His face shone; and they were **afraid** to come nigh him." The typical meaning of this is given in 2 Cor. 3:7, "But if the ministration of death, written and engraven in stones was glorious, so that the children of Israel **could not** steadfastly behold the face of Moses for the glory of his countenance." Concerning this another has said: "Why then, were they afraid to come near him? Because the very glory that shone upon his face searched their hearts and consciences—being what they were, sinners, and unable of themselves to meet even the smallest requirements of the covenant which had now been inaugurated. It was of necessity a ministration of condemnation and death, for it required a righteousness from them which they could not render, and, inasmuch as they must fail in the rendering it, would pronounce their condemnation, and

bring them under the penalty of transgression, which was death. The glory which they thus beheld upon the face of Moses was the expression to them of the holiness of God—that holiness which sought from them conformity to its own standards—and which would vindicate the breaches of that covenant which had now been established. They were therefore afraid, because they knew in their inmost souls that they could not stand before Him from whose presence Moses had come" (Mr. Ed. Dennett).

Typically (not dispensationally) the covenant which Jehovah made with Moses and Israel at Sinai, and the tables of stone on which were engraved the ten commandments, foreshadowed that new covenant which He will yet make with Israel in a coming day: "For I will take you from among the heathen, and gather you out of all countries, and will bring you into your own land. Then will I sprinkle clean water upon you, and ye shall be clean from all your filthiness, and from all your idols, will I cleanse you. A new heart also will I give you, and a new spirit will I put within you: and I will take away the stony heart out of your flesh, and I will give you an heart of flesh. And I will put My Spirit within you, and cause you to walk in My statutes, and ye shall keep My judgments and do them. And ye shall dwell in the land that I gave to your fathers; and ye shall be My people, and I will be your God" (Ezek. 36:24-28). "Behold, the days come, saith the Lord, that I will make a new covenant with the house of Israel, and with the house of Judah . . . After those days, saith the Lord, I will put My law in their inward parts, and write it **in their hearts;** . . . and they shall teach no more every man his neighbour, and every man his brother, saying, Know the Lord: for they shall all know Me, from the least of them unto the greatest of them, saith the Lord" (Jer. 31:31-34).

Spiritually, this is made good for Christians even now. Under the gracious operations of the Spirit of God **our hearts** have been made plastic and receptive. It is to this fact that Paul referred at the beginning of 2 Cor. 3. "The saints at Corinth had been 'manifested to be Christ's epistle ministered by us, written not with ink, but the Spirit of the living God; not on stone tables, but on fleshly tables of the heart.' Their hearts being made impressionable by Divine working, Christ could write upon them, using Paul as a pen, and making every mark in the power of the Spirit of God. But what is written is the knowledge of God as revealed through the Mediator in the grace of the new covenant, so that it might be true in the hearts of the saints—'They shall all know Me.' Then Paul goes on to speak of himself as made competent by God to be a new covenant ministry, 'not of letter, but of spirit'" (C. A. Coates).

"And Moses called unto them; and Aaron and all the rulers of the congregation returned unto him: and Moses talked with them. And afterward all the children of Israel came nigh: and he gave them in commandment all that the Lord had spoken with them in Mount Sinai. And till Moses had done speaking with them, he put a veil on his face" (vv. 31-33). Ah, does not this explain their fear as they beheld the shining of Moses' face? Note **what** was in his hands! He carried the two tables of stone on which were written the ten words of the law, the "ministration of condemnation." The nearer the light of the glory came, while it was connected with the righteous claims of God upon them, the more cause had they to fear. That holy Law condemned them, for man in the flesh could not meet its claims. "However blessed it was **typically,** it was **literally** a ministry of death, for Moses was not a quickening Spirit, nor could he give his spirit to the people, nor could the glory of his face bring them into conformity with himself as the mediator. Hence the veil had to be on his face" (C. A. Coates).

The dispensational interpretation of this is given in 2 Cor. 3:13: "And not as Moses, which put a veil over his face, that the children of Israel could not steadfastly look **to the end** of that which is abolished." Here the apostle is treating of Judaism as an economy. Owing to their blindness spiritually, Israel was unable to discern the deep significance of the ministry of Moses, the purpose of God behind it, that which all the types and shadows pointed forward to. The **"end"** of 2 Cor. 3:13: is parallel with Rom. 10:4. "For Christ is **the end** of the law for righteousness to every one that believeth." "The veil on Israel's heart is self-sufficiency, which makes them still refuse to submit to God's righteousness. But when Israel's heart turns to the Lord the veil will be taken away. What a wonderful chapter Exodus 34 will be to them then! For they will see that **Christ** is the spirit of it all. What they will see, we are privileged to see now. All this had an 'end' on which **we** can, through infinite grace, fix our eyes. The 'end' was the glory of the Lord as the Mediator of the new covenant. He has come out of death and gone up on high, and the glory of all that God is in

grace is shining in His face" (C. A. Coates).

"But when Moses went in before the Lord to speak with Him, he took the veil off, until he came out. And he came out, and spake unto the children of Israel that which he was commanded. And the children of Israel saw the face of Moses, that the skin of Moses' face shone; and Moses put the veil upon his face again, until he went in to speak with Him" (vv. 34, 35). Moses unveiled in the presence of the Lord is a beautiful type of the believer of this dispensation. The Christian beholds the glory of God shining in the face of Jesus Christ (2 Cor. 4:6). therefore, instead of being stricken with fear, he approaches with boldness. God's law **cannot** condemn him, for its every demand has been fully met and satisfied by his Substitute. Hence, instead of trembling before the glory of God, we "**rejoice** in hope of the glory of God" (Rom. 5:2).

"There is no veil now either on **His** face or **our** hearts. He makes those who believe on Him to **live** in the knowledge of God, and in response to God, for He is the quickening Spirit. And He gives His Spirit to those who believe. We have the Spirit of the glorified Man in whose face the glory of God shines. Is it not surpassingly wonderful? One has to ask sometimes, Do we really believe it? 'But we all, looking on the glory of the Lord with unveiled face, are transformed according to the same image from glory to glory even as by the Lord the Spirit' (2 Cor. 3:18). If we had not His Spirit we should have no liberty to look on the glory of the Lord, or to see Him as the spirit of these marvelous types. But we have liberty to look on it all, and there is transforming power in it. Saints under newcovenant-ministry are transfigured.

"This is the 'surpassing glory' which could not be seen or known until it shone in the face of Him of whom Moses in Exodus 34 is so distinctly a type. The whole typical system was temporary, but its 'spirit' abides, for **Christ** was the Spirit of it all. Now we have to do with the ministry of the Spirit and of righteousness, and all is abiding. The ministry of the new covenant subsists and abounds in glory" (C. A. Coates).

As a sort of appendix to this article we shall proffer, for the sake of those who may value it, an outline of the apostle's argument in 2 Cor. 3. The authority of Paul's apostleship had been called into question by certain Judaisers. In the first verses of this chapter he appeals to the Corinthians themselves as the proof of his God-commissioned and God-blessed ministry. In v. 6 he defines the **character** of his ministry, and this for the purpose of showing its superiority over that of his enemies. He and his fellow-gospellers were "ministers of the **new** testament" or covenant. A series of contrasts is then drawn between the two covenants, that is, between Judaism and Christianity. That which pertained to the former is called "the letter" that relating to the new, "the spirit," i. e., the one was mainly concerned with that which was external, the other was largely internal: the one slew, the other gave life—this was one of the leading differences between the Law, and the Gospel.

In what follows the apostle, while allowing that the Law was glorious, shows that the Gospel is still more glorious. The old covenant was a "ministration of death," for the Law could only condemn; therefore, though a glory was connected with it, yet was it such that man in the flesh could not behold (v. 7). Then how much more excellent would be, must be, the glory of the new covenant, seeing that it was "a ministration of the Spirit" (v. 8)—compare v. 3 for proof of this. If there was a glory connected with that which "concluded all men under sin" (Gal. 3:23), much more glorious must be that ministration which announces a righteousness which is "unto all and upon them that believe" (Rom. 3:22). It is more glorious to pardon than to condemn; to give life, than to destroy (v. 9). The glory of the former covenant therefore pales into nothingness before the latter (v. 10). This is further seen from the fact that Judaism is "done away," whereas Christianity "remaineth" (v. 11)—compare Heb. 8:7, 8.

At v. 12 the apostle draws still another contrast between the two economies, namely, the plainness or perspicuity over against the obscurity and ambiguity of their respective ministries (vv. 12-15). The apostles used "great plainness of speech," whereas the teaching of the ceremonial law was by means of shadows and symbols. Moreover, the minds of the Israelites were blinded, so that there was a veil over their hearers, and therefore when the writings of Moses were read, they

were incapable of looking beyond the type to the Antitype. This veil remains upon them unto this day, and will continue until they turn unto the Lord (vv. 15, 16). **Literally** the covenant of Sinai was a ministration of condemnation and death, and the glory of it had to be veiled. But it had an "end" (v. 13), upon which Israel could not fix their eyes. They will see that "end" in a coming day; but in the meantime, **we** are permitted to read the old covenant without a veil, and to see that **Christ** is the "spirit" of it all, and that it had in view that which could only have its fulfillment under new covenant conditions, namely, God's glory secured in and by the Mediator.

The language of v. 17 is involved in some obscurity: "Now the Lord is that Spirit." This does not mean that Christ is the Holy Spirit. The "spirit" here is the same as in v. 6—"not of the letter, but of the spirit:" cf. Rom. 7:6. The Mosaic system is called "the letter" because it was purely objective. It possessed no inward principle or power. But the Gospel deals with the heart, and supplies the spiritual power (Rom. 1:16). Moreover, **Christ** is the spirit, the life, the heart and center of all the ritual and ceremonialism of Judaism. **He** is the key to the O. T. for, "In the volume of the Book" it is written of Him. So also Christ is the spirit and life of Christianity; He is "a quickening Spirit" (1 Cor. 15:45). And, "Where the Spirit of the Lord is, there is liberty." Apart from Christ, the sinner, be he Jew or Gentile, is in a state of bondage: he is the slave of sin and the captive of the Devil. But where the Son makes free, He frees indeed (John 8:32).

Finally the apostle contrasts the two **glories,** the glory connected with the old covenant—the shining on Moses' face at the giving of the Law (when the covenant was made)—with the glory of the new covenant, in the person of Christ. "But we all, with open (unveiled) face beholding as in a glass the glory of the Lord, are changed into the same image from glory to glory, even as by the Spirit of the Lord." Note here: first, "we **all.**" Moses alone beheld the glory of the Lord in the mount: every Christian now beholds it. Second, we with "open face," with freedom and with confidence; whereas Israel were afraid to gaze on the radiant and majestical face of Moses. Third, we are "changed into the same image." The law had no power to convert or purify; but the ministry of the Gospel, under the operation of the Spirit, **has** a transforming power. Those who are saved by it, those who are occupied with Christ as set forth in the Word (the "mirror") are, little by little, conformed to His image. Ultimately, when we "see Him as He is" (1 John 3:2), we shall be "Like Him"—fully perfectly, eternally.

CHAPTER 71

THE LORD'S DWELLING PLACE

EXODUS 35-40

In the last six chapters of Exodus four things are brought before us. First, mention is made once more of the Sabbath (35:1-3). Second, the people of Israel bring unto Moses all the materials required for the Tabernacle (35:4-29). Third, the setting to work of the appointed artificers with their assistants, and the actual making of the Tabernacle and its furniture (35:30—39:43). Fourth, the setting up of the Tabernacle and the glory of the Lord filling His house in Israel's midst (40). Nearly all that we have mentioned in 35-39 is a recapitulation of what has been before us in 25-31. As we pointed out in artcile 33 of this series, what we find in Ex. 25-31 is a description of the Tabernacle as it was given by Jehovah Himself directly to Moses in the mount; whereas 35-39 records what was actually made according to the pattern shown to Moses. Typically, this double account of that which, in every part, prefigured Christ, tells us that all which was originally planned in Heaven shall yet be accomplished on earth.

That which is central and distinctive about our present lengthy passage is the actual setting up of Jehovah's dwelling-place in the midst of His redeemed people. Before we attempt to bring out something of the deep and rich spiritual significance of this, a few remarks need to be made upon the opening sections of Ex. 35. In vv. 21-29 we behold the children of Israel bringing an offering unto the Lord, giving to Him of their substance. At the beginning of 36 we see the appointed artificers actively engaged in their work, the work of the Lord. But before these, at the very beginning of 35, mention is made of the sabbath as "a rest unto the Lord," in which no work was to be done. The **doctrinal** significance of this is: before we are fitted to work for Him, we must rest in Him; before we can bring to Him, we must receive from Him. Most important for our hearts is this seventh and last mention of the sabbath in Exodus. It was Solomon, "a man **of rest**" (1 Chron.

22), who alone could build a house to Jehovah's name.

It is to be noted that an additional feature is here added to the Sabbath restriction: "Ye shall kindle no fire throughout your habitations upon the Sabbath day." As another has said, "That speaks of the absence of consideration for one's own comfort in a natural way. In keeping a true sabbath one is neither occupied with one's own activity nor with one's natural consideration." That needs to be borne in mind in this day of fleshly ease and gratification. God's word to us on this point is: Thou shalt "call the sabbath a delight, the holy of the Lord, honourable; and shalt honour Him, not doing thine own ways, **nor finding thine own pleasure,** nor speaking thine own words: Then shalt thou delight thyself in the Lord; and I will cause thee to ride upon the high places of the earth, and feed thee with the heritage of Jacob thy father" (Isa. 58:13, 14).

In its deeper spiritual significance, this mention of the sabbath and the non-kindling of the fire in our dwelling, coming right after what is recorded at the end of Ex. 34, signifies that the privileges of the new covenant and our enjoyment of the glory of God as it shines in the face of Jesus Christ, calls for the **setting aside** of the desires of the flesh. Only as we rest in God, and only as we give heed to that word, "**Mortify** therefore your members which are upon the earth" (Col. 3:5), shall we be free to enter into the enjoyments and employments of the new-creation realm. On the other hand, the words "six days shall work be done" announce very distinctly that nought connected with our natural responsibility is to be neglected.

The second thing we have in Ex. 35 is the people's response to Jehovah's invitation in 25:1, 2. There we read, "Speak unto the children of Israel, that they bring Me an offering: of every man that giveth it willingly with his heart, ye shall take My offering." The materials out of which

374

the Tabernacle was made were to be provided by the voluntary offerings of devoted hearts. Most blessed is it to read what is said in 35:21, 22, "And they came, every one **whose heart** stirred him up, and every one whom his spirit **made willing**, they brought the Lord's offering to the work of the Tabernacle of the congregation, and for all His service, and for the holy garments. And they came, both men and women, as many as were **willing hearted**, and brought bracelets, and earrings, and rings, and tablets, all jewels of gold: and every man offered an offering of gold unto the Lord." No unwilling donors were these, who had to be begged and urged to give. Spontaneously, freely, joyfully, did they avail themselves of their privilege.

Commenting on what has just been before us, Mr. Dennett has well said: "It is therefore of the first importance to remember that everything offered to God must proceed from hearts made willing by His Spirit, that it must be spontaneous, not the result of persuasion or of external pressure, but from the heart. The church of God would have been in a very different state today if this had been remembered. What has wrought more ruin than the many worldly schemes of raising money? and what more humbling than the fact that solicitations of all kinds are used to induce the Lord's people to offer their gifts? Moses was content with announcing that the Lord was willing to receive, and he left this gracious communication to produce its suited effect upon the hearts of the children of Israel. He needed not to do more; and if saints now were in the current of God's thoughts they would imitate the example of Moses, and would shun the very thought of obtaining even the smallest gift, except it were presented willingly, and from the heart, as the effect of the working of the Spirit of God. And let it be remarked, that there was no lack; for in the next chapter we find that the wise men who wrought came to Moses and said, 'The people bring much more than enough' (36:5-7).

"If the first Pentecostal days be excepted, there has probably never been seen anything answering to this even in the history of the church. The chronic complaint now is concerning the insufficiency of means to carry on the Lord's work. But it cannot be too often recalled—first, that the church of God is never held responsible to obtain means; secondly, that if the Lord gives work to do, He Himself will lay it upon the hearts of His people to contribute what is necessary; thirdly, that we are travelling off the

ground of dependence, and acting according to our own thoughts, if we undertake anything for which the needful provision has not **already** been made; and lastly, that gifts procured by human means can seldom be used for blessing."

It is very beautiful to note the relation between the two things which have now been before us: first, the keeping of the sabbath; second, the bringing of an offering unto the Lord, an offering which was the outflow of a **heart** "stirred up." First the resting in, delighting itself in the Lord, then the affections drawn out towards Him. This too finds its accomplishment on new-covenant-ground. It is a redeemed people, a people who behold the glory of the Lord, that are devoted to His cause. The giving of their substance is not a legal thing, a mere matter of duty, but a privilege and a joy. Here too it is the love of Christ which "constraineth." We love Him because He first loved us, and we delight to give because **He** first gave to us. Nothing so moves the heart as the contemplation of the love and grace of God as now revealed to us in the glorified Mediator. In article 34 we have already pointed out the typical significance of each part of Israel's offerings; so we pass on now to notice, briefly, the work of the artificers.

Upon the two principal workmen, Bezaleel and Aholiab, we have already commented in article 57. There we dwelt upon the significance of the workmen's names, the equipping of them for their appointed tasks, and the particular service allotted them. Here we read, "**Then** wrought Bezaleel and Aholiab, and every wise hearted man, in whom the Lord put wisdom and understanding to know how to work all manner of work for the service of the sanctuary, according to all that the Lord had commanded" (36:1). Note carefully the opening word, and also the expression "every one whose heart **stirred him up** to come unto the work" in v. 2. Ah, wherever there is a spirit of devotion, manifested by a free and liberal offering unto the cause of God, He will not be backward in raising up qualified workers, whose hearts have been stirred by His Spirit, to make a wise and God-glorying use of His peoples' gifts.

But let us now seek to take note of **the connection** between this third item and what has gone before. First we have had the sabbath, the soul resting in God; second, we have had the free will offering of the people, the heart's affections drawn out to the Lord. Now we get active work. This puts **service** in its true position. Occupying as it does the **third** place, it shows us that acceptable service to God can only proceed from those who have passed from death unto life. Following, as it does, the other two, it intimates that the vital **prerequisites** for service are, delighting ourselves in the Lord and the affections flowing forth unto Him. Only then can we truly "abound in the work of the Lord." Anything else is either the outcome of the restless energy of the flesh, or is merely "bricks" produced under the whip of taskmasters.

There is one detail given us here that has not come before us in the previous chapters. "And all the women that were wise hearted did spin with their hands, and brought that which they had spun, of blue, and of purple, of scarlet, and of fine linen. And all the women whose hearts stirred them up in wisdom spun goats' hair" (35:25, 26). This brings in the thought of **co-operation** in the Lord's work: the sisters have their place and part too. Yet note it is a subordinate place: they "spun," not provided the material. The character of their work also shows us the legitimate **sphere** of their labours—in the home.

"And the rulers brought onyx stones, and stones to be set for the ephod, and for the breastplate" (35:27). The **leaders** set the people a godly example. This is as it should be. But, alas, how often is it otherwise. The preacher who sets before his people the teaching of Scripture on the subject of stewardship and the privilege of giving to the cause of God, but who is miserly himself, is not an honest man: he says one thing, but does another. God's word to pastors is, "Be thou an **example** of the believers, in word, in faith, in purity" (1 Tim. 4:12). "In all things showing thyself a **pattern** of good works" (Titus 2:7).

Before turning to the 39th chapter, there is one detail in the 38th which should be noted. In v. 21 we read, "This is the sum of the Tabernacle, even of the tabernacle of testimony, **as it was counted**, according to the commandment of Moses." Then we are told, "All the gold that was occupied for the work . . . was twenty and nine talents . . . and the silver of them **that were numbered** of the congregation was an hundred talents," etc. (vv. 24, 25). This conveys to us a most important practical lesson in connection with the work of the Lord. Everything was counted, weighed, numbered. What attention to detail was this! "People talk of essentials and nonessentials, but when they do, you may be sure they are only thinking of man's side. Every detail of the divine mind is essential to the glory of God in Christ. A missing peg would mean a slack cord, and

a slack cord would mean a curtain out of place, and so the disorder would spread. Indeed the whole tabernacle would suffer if one detail were out of place" (C. A. Coates).

In the 39th chapter of Exodus the work of the Tabernacle is finished. Blessed is it to note that all was done "**as the Lord commanded Moses**." Mark how this expression occurs eight times in that chapter: vv. 1, 5, 7, 21, 26, 29, 31, 43; while in vv. 32, 42 it is added, "and the children of Israel did according to **all** that the Lord commanded Moses, so did they . . . According to all that the Lord commanded Moses, so the children of Israel made **all** the work." "The Lord had given the most minute instruction concerning the entire work of the tabernacle. Every pin, every socket, every loop, every tach, was accurately set forth. There was no room left for man's expediency, his reason, or his common sense. Jehovah did not give a great outline and leave man to fill it up. He left no margin whatever in which man might enter his regulations. By no means. 'See that thou make **all things** according to the pattern showed to thee in the mount' (Ex. 25:40). This left no room for human device. If man had been allowed to make a single pin, that pin would most assuredly have been out of place in the judgment of God. We can see what man's 'graving tool' produces in chapter 32. Thank God, it has no place in the tabernacle. They did, in this matter, just what they were told—nothing more, nothing less. Salutary lesson this for the professing church! There are many things in the history of Israel which we should earnestly seek to avoid,—their impatient murmurings, their legal vows, and their idolatry; but in two things we may imitate them: may our devotedness be more whole-hearted, and our obedience more implicit" (C. H. M.).

Yes, the obedience of Israel is recorded for our learning. We too have received commandment from the Lord concerning the work which He has given **us** to do. His complete Word is now in our hands. It is to be our guide and regulator in all things. It is given that "the man of God may be complete, thoroughly furnished unto all good works" (2 Tim. 3:17). If we desire God's blessing, then His work must be done according to **His** appointments. Human expediency, convenience, originality, are to have no place. The approval of God, not that of his fellows, is what every servant of the Lord must continually aim at. **Faithfulness,** not success, is what our Master requires. The quality of service is to be tested not by visible results, but by its conformity to

God's Word.

There is one other detail in Ex. 39 which, in its spiritual application to ourselves, is very searching: "And they brought the tabernacle unto Moses, the tent, and all his furniture, etc. . . . And Moses did **look upon** all the work" (vv. 35, 43). Every thing was brought before the typical mediator for his inspection. All had to pass under the scrutiny of his eye. The typical significance of this is obvious. In 2 Cor. 5:10 we read, "For we must all appear before the judgment seat of Christ; that every one may receive the things done in his body, according to that he hath done whether it be good or bad." This does not refer to a **general** Judgment-day at the end of the world, but to that which follows the Lord's return for His people, and precedes His coming back to the earth to set up His millennial kingdom.

A further word on this same subject is found in 1 Cor. 3, "For other foundation can no man lay than that is laid, which is Jesus Christ. Now if any man **build upon** this foundation—gold, silver, precious stones; wood, hay, stubble. Every man's **work** shall be made manifest: for the day shall declare it, because it shall be revealed by fire; and the fire shall try every man's work of what sort it is. If any man's work abide which he hath built thereon, he shall receive a reward. If any man's work shall be burned, he shall suffer loss: but he himself shall be saved, yet so as by fire" (vv. 11-15). The reference here is to the Christian's **service**: 2 Cor. 5:10 treats more of his **walk**. Discrimination is made between two classes of service. On the one hand, "gold," the emblem of divine glory; "silver" which speaks of redemption; "precious stones" which are imperishable. Only that which has been done for God's glory, on the ground redemption, and which will stand the test of fire, shall abide and be rewarded. On the other hand, "wood, hay, stubble," which, though much greater in bulk, **will not** endure the coming fiery trial. The difference is between quality and quantity; that which is of the Spirit, and that which is of the flesh.

"And Moses did look upon all the work, and behold, they had done it as the Lord had commanded, even so had they done it: and Moses **blessed** them" (39:43). So will Christ in the coming Day. That which has been done in full accord with God's Word, though despised by man, shall be owned and rewarded of Him. His own words, in the final chapter of Holy Writ, are "And, behold, I come quickly; and My reward is with Me, to give every man according as his work shall be" (Rev. 22:12). In view of this, how earnestly and prayerfully should we heed that exhortation, "And now, little children, **abide in Him**; that, when He shall appear, we may have confidence, **and not be ashamed** before Him at His coming" (1 John 2:28).

In the last chapter of Exodus we have the actual setting up of the Tabernacle. Let us take note, first, of the **time** when it was erected: "And the Lord spake unto Moses saying, On the first day of the first month shalt thou set up the tabernacle" (vv. 1, 2). It was on the anniversary of Israel's departure from Egypt (12:2). This is very striking. As their deliverance from the house of bondage constituted the commencement of their spiritual history, so the dwelling of Jehovah in their midst marked an altogether new and most blessed stage in their experiences. That which was foreshadowed by this we shall point out later. Its spiritual application to Christians is given in Matt. 18:20, "For where two or three are gathered together in My name, there am I **in the midst** of them."

Next we would observe that Moses is the sole actor in this chapter: "And Moses reared up the tabernacle, and fastened his sockets, and set up the boards thereof, and put in the pillars thereof, and reared up his pillars" (v. 18). All subordinates disappear from view and only Moses is seen: read vv. 19-33, at the end of which we are told, "so Moses finished the work." The present application of this is given us in Heb. 3:3-6, "For this Man was counted worthy of more glory than Moses, inasmuch as He who hath builded the house hath more honour than the house. For every house is builded by some man; but He that built all things is God. And Moses verily was faithful in all His house, as a servant, for a testimony of those things which were to be spoken after; But Christ as a Son over His own house; whose house are we, if we hold fast the confidence and the rejoicing of the hope firm unto the end."

Finally, we read, "**Then** a cloud covered the tent of the congregation, and the glory of the Lord filled the tabernacle" (v. 34). The "then" points back to the "so Moses finished the work" of v. 33. The N. T. equivalent was what took place on the day of Pentecost: "And when the day of Pentecost was fully come, they were all with one accord in one place. And suddenly there came a sound from heaven as of a rushing mighty wind, and **it filled all the house** where they were sitting. And there appeared unto them cloven tongues like as **of fire**, and it sat upon each of them. And they were all filled with the Holy Spirit."

As an appendix to this glorious incident we are told in the closing verse of our book, "For the cloud of the Lord was upon the tabernacle by day, and fire was on it by night, in the sight of all the house of Israel throughout all their journeys." They needed only to keep their eyes on the Cloud. "The Lord thus undertook for His people. He had visited them in their affliction in Egypt; He had brought them out with a high hand and an outstretched arm; and had led them forth through the Red Sea into the wilderness. Now He Himself would lead them 'by the right way that they might go to a city of habitation.' Happy,' we might well exclaim, 'is that people that is in such a case; yea, happy is that people whose God is the Lord.' For surely there was nothing more wanted to the blessing of Israel. Jehovah was in their midst. The cloud of His presence rested upon, and His glory filled the tabernacle" (Mr. Dennett).

It only remains for us now to point out the most striking and lovely dispensational picture which is presented before the anointed eye in the last six chapters of Exodus. What is recorded there is that which followed the **second** descent of Moses from the Mount. In the opening paragraphs of article 61 we called attention to the fact that when Moses was called up unto Sinai to receive from Jehovah the tables of stone (the words of which formed the basis of His **new** covenant with Israel—the old one being the Abrahamic) Moses descended twice(having, of course, returned thither in the interval): see 32:15; 34:29. What immediately followed these two descents foreshadowed that which shall follow the two stages of the second coming of Christ, as these bear upon the Jews. Just as the first descent of Moses was succeeded by sore judgments on Israel, so the descent of Christ into the air to catch up His saints unto Himself (1 Thess. 4) will be succeeded by the great Tribulation, the Time of Jacob's trouble.

But let us now review that which attended the **second** descent of Moses. First, he appeared before them with radiant face: type of the glorified Mediator as He will come back to Israel (Col. 3:4). Second, the tables of stone were not broken this time, but deposited and preserved in the ark (Deut. 10:4): so when the Lord Jesus makes the new covenant with Israel,

He declares, "I will put My law in their **inward** parts and write it in their hearts" (Jer. 31:33). Third, this last section of the book of Exodus opens with a reference to the sabbath (35:1-3), telling us that it is in **the Millennium** when all of this shall be made good. Fourth, the next line in the picture is the hearts of Israel flowing forth unto the Lord in free-will offerings (35:23, 24): the antitype of this is seen in Zeph. 3:9, 10, "Then will I turn to the people a pure language, that they may all call upon the name of the Lord, to serve Him with one consent. From beyond the rivers of Ethiopia My suppliants, even the daughter of My dispersed, shall bring Mine **offering**." Fifth, next we see Israel engaged in the work of Jehovah, doing all "as He had commanded:" so in Ezek. 36:27, we read, "And I will put My Spirit within you, and cause you to walk in My statutes, and ye shall keep My judgments and **do them**." Sixth, the tabernacle was now set up: compare with this, "Behold the Man whose name is the Branch; and He shall grow up out of His place, and He shall build the temple of the Lord . . . and He shall bear the Glory" (Zech. 6:13). Seventh, the Lord then dwelt in Israel's midst: "Sing and rejoice, O daughter of Zion: for, lo, I come, and I will dwell in the midst of thee, saith the Lord" (Zech. 2:10). Eighth, the glory of the Lord was visibly displayed: "And the Lord will create upon every dwelling place of mount Zion, and upon her assemblies, a cloud and smoke by day, and the shining of a flaming fire by night: and above all **the glory** shall be a covering" (Isa. 4:5). May the Lord hasten that glad time.

Thus, in the closing chapter of this book of redemption we behold the full and perfect accomplishment of God's purpose of grace. Notwithstanding man's failure, notwithstanding Israel's sin of the golden calf, notwithstanding the broken tables of stone; in the end, grace superabounded over sin, and all the counsels of God were made good by the typical mediator. In its ultimate application what has been before us points forward to the new earth: "Behold, the tabernacle of God is with men, and He will dwell with them and they shall be His people and God Himself shall be with them, and be their God. And God shall wipe away all tears from their eyes; and there shall be no more death, neither sorrow nor crying, neither shall there be any more plague: for the former things are passed away" (Rev. 21:3, 4).

CHAPTER 72

MOSES—A TYPE OF CHRIST

"The life of Moses presents a series of striking antitheses. He was the child of a slave, and the son of a king. He was born in a hut, and lived in a palace. He inherited poverty, and enjoyed unlimited wealth. He was the leader of armies, and the keeper of flocks. He was the mightiest of warriors, and the meekest of men. He was educated in the court, and dwelt in the desert. He had the wisdom of Egypt, and the faith of a child. He was fitted for the city, and wandered in the wilderness. He was tempted with the pleasures of sin, and endured the hardships of virtue. He was backward in speech, and talked with God. He had the rod of a shepherd, and the power of the Infinite. He was a fugitive from Pharaoh, and an ambassador from Heaven. He was the giver of the Law, and the forerunner of Grace. He died alone on mount Moab, and appeared with Christ in Judea. No man assisted at his funeral, yet God buried him. The fire has gone out of mount Sinai, but the lightning is still in his Law. His lips are silent, but his voice yet speaks" (Dr. I. M. Haldeman).

But the most striking thing of all in connection with this most remarkable man, is the wonderful way and the many respects in which he was a type of the Lord Jesus In the Introductory article of this series (Jan. 1924) we stated: "In many respects there is a remarkable correspondency between Moses and Christ, and if the Lord permits us to complete this series of articles, we shall, at the close, summarise those correspondencies, and show them to be as numerous and striking as those which engaged our attention when Joseph was before us"—see the last seven chapters in Vol. 2 of our work "Gleanings in Genesis". We shall now seek to fulfil that promise.

Ere we attempt to set forth some (for we do not profess to exhaust the subject) of these correspondencies, let us first appeal to the Word itself in proof that Moses **was** a type of Christ. In Deut. 18:

15 we find Moses saying, "The Lord thy God will raise up unto thee a Prophet from the midst of thee, of thy brethren, **like unto me**; unto Him ye shall hearken". Thus it will be seen from these words that we are not trafficking in human imagination when we contemplate Moses as a type of Christ. Such is the plain teaching of Holy Writ.

As we desire to bring to a close these "Gleanings in Exodus" in the current issue, and therefore can devote but one article to our present theme, and as the points to be considered are so numerous, we cannot take up each one separately and comment upon it at length. Rather shall we, with a few exceptions, simply give the references, and ask the reader to look them up for himself.

1. **His nationality.**

Moses was an Israelite (Ex. 2:1, 2). So, according to the flesh, was Christ.

2. **His Birth.**

This occurred when his nation was under the dominion of a hostile power, when they were groaning under the rule of a Gentile king (Ex. 1). So the Jews were in bondage to the Romans when Christ was born (Matt. 2:1 cf. Luke 24: 21).

3. **His Person.**

"In which time Moses was born, and was exceeding fair to God" (Acts 7:20). How blessedly did he, in this, foreshadow the Beloved of the Father! **His** estimate of the "fairness" of that Child which lay in Bethlehem's manger, was evidenced by the sending of the angels to say unto the shepherds, "Unto you is born this day in the city of David a Saviour, which is Christ the Lord" (Luke 2:11).

4. **His Infancy.**

In infancy his life was endangered, imperilled by the reigning king, for Pharaoh had given orders that, "Every son that is born ye shall cast into the river" (Ex.

1:22). How this reminds us of Matt. 2:16: "Then Herod . . . sent forth and slew all the children that were in Bethlehem, and in all the coasts thereof"!

5. His Adoption.

Though, previously, he was the child of another, he yet was made the son of Pharaoh's daughter: "And became her **son**" (Ex. 2:10). Thus he had a mother, but **no father**! What anointed eye can fail to see prefigured here the mystery of the Virgin-birth! Christ was the Son of Another, even the Son of God. But, born into this world, He had a mother, but no human father. Yet was He, as it were, adopted by Joseph: see Matt. 1:19-21.

6. His Childhood.

This was spent in Egypt. So also was Christ's: "Behold the angel of the Lord appeareth to Joseph in a dream, saying, "Arise, and take the young Child and His mother, and flee into Egypt, and be thou there until I bring thee word" (Matt. 2:13). Thus was fulfilled God's ancient oracle, "And called My Son out of Egypt" (Hos. 11:1).

7. His Sympathy for Israel.

He was filled with a deep compassion for his suffering kinsmen according to the flesh, and he yearned for their deliverance. Beautifully does this come out in Acts 7:23, 24, "And when he was full forty years old, it came into **his heart** to visit his brethren of the children of Israel. And seeing one of them suffer wrong, he defended him." So too Christ was filled with pity toward His enslaved people, and love brought Him here to deliver them.

8. His early knowledge of his Mission.

Long years before he actually entered upon his great work, Moses discerned, "how that God by **his** hand **would** deliver them" (Acts 7:25). So as a Boy of twelve, Christ said to His perplexed mother, "Wist ye not that I must be about My Father's business?" (Luke 2:49).

9. His condescending Grace.

Though legally the "son of Pharaoh's daughter", yet he regarded the Hebrew slaves as his **brethren**: "And it came to pass in those days, when Moses **was** grown, that he went out unto his brethren" (Ex. 2:11). So it is with Christ: "He is not ashamed to call them **brethren**" (Heb. 2:11).

10. His great Renunciation.

"By faith Moses, when he was come to years, refused to be called the son of Pharaoh's daughter■; Choosing rather to suffer affliction with the people of God, than to enjoy the pleasures of sin for a season; Esteeming the reproach of Christ greater riches than the treasures in Egypt" (Heb. 11:24-26). What a foreshadowing was this of Him "Who, being in the form of God, thought it not robbery to be equal with God; But made Himself of no reputation, and took upon Him the form of a servant" (Phil. 2:6, 7)! Like Moses, Christ too voluntarily relinquished riches, glory, and a kingly palace.

11. His Rejection by his brethren.

"And the next day he showed himself unto them as they strove, and would have set them at one again, saying, Sirs, ye are brethren; why do ye wrong one to another? But he that did his neighbour wrong **thrust him away**, saying, Who made thee a ruler and a judge over us?" (Acts 7:26, 27). This is very sad; sadder still is it to read of Christ, "He came unto His own, and His own received Him not" (John 1:11). This same line in the typical picture was before us when we considered Joseph. But mark this difference: In the case of Joseph, it was his brethren's enmity against his **person** (Gen. 37:4); here with Moses, it was his brethren's enmity against his **mission**. Joseph was personally hated; Moses officially refused—"who made thee a **ruler** and a judge over us"? So it was with Christ. Israel said, "We will not have this Man to **reign over us**" (Luke 19:14).

12. His Sojourning among the Gentiles.

"But Moses fled from the face of Pharaoh, and dwelt in the land of Midian" (Ex. 2:15). Following Christ's rejection by the Jews, we read, "God at the first did visit the **Gentiles,** to take out of them a people for His name" (Acts 15:14).

13. His Seat on the well.

Away from his own land, we read of Moses, "And he sat down by a well" (Ex. 2:15). So the only time we read of the Lord Jesus seated by the well, was when He was outside Israel's borders, in Samaria (John 4:4, 6).

14. His Shepherdhood.

"Now Moses kept the flock of Jethro his father-in-law" (Ex. 3:1). This is the character which Christ sustains to His elect among the Gentiles: "And other sheep I have, which are not of this fold, them also I must bring, and they shall hear My voice; and there shall be one flock, one Shepherd" (John 10:16).

15. His Season of Seclusion.

Before he entered upon his real mission, Moses spent many years in obscurity. Who had supposed that this one, there "at the backside of the desert", was destined to such an honourable future? So it was with the incarnate Son of God. Before He began His public ministry, He was hidden away in despised Nazareth. Who that saw Him there in the carpenter's shop, dreamed that He was ordained of God to the work of redemption!

16. His Commission from God.

He was called of God to emancipate His people from the house of bondage: "Come now therefore, and I will send thee unto Pharaoh, that thou mayest bring forth My people the children of Israel out of Egypt" (Ex. 3:10). So Christ was sent forth into this world to "seek and to save that which was lost" (Luke 19:10).

17. His Apostleship.

Thus he was God's apostle unto Israel, for "apostle" signifies one "sent forth": "Now therefore go" (Ex. 4:12). So Christ was the Sent One of God (John 9:4 etc); yea, in Heb. 3:1 He is designated "the Apostle".

18. His Credentials.

His commission from God was confirmed by power to work miracles. So also Christ's mission was authenticated by wondrous signs (Matt. 11:4, 5). It should be noted that Moses is the first one mentioned in the O. T. that performed miracles; so is Christ in the N. T.—John the Baptist performed none (John 10:41).

19. His first Miracles.

Moses wrought many wonders, but it is most striking to observe that his first two miraculous-signs were power over the serpent, and power over leprosy (Ex. 4:6-9). So after Christ began His public ministry, we read first of His power over Satan (Matt. 4:10, 11), and then His power over leprosy (Matt. 8:3).

20. His Return to his own land.

In Ex. 4:19 we read, "And the Lord said unto Moses in Midian, Go, return into Egypt: for all the men are dead which sought thy life". The antitype of this is found in Matt. 2:19, "An angel of the Lord appeareth in a dream to Joseph in Egypt, saying, Arise, and take the young Child and His mother, and go into the land of Israel: for they are dead which sought the young Child's life"!

21. His Acceptance by his brethren.

This is recorded in Exodus 4:29-31. How different was this from his first appearing before and rejection by the Hebrews (Ex.

2)! How beautifully it prefigured Israel's acceptance of their Messiah at His second appearing!

22. His powerful Rod.

Moses now wielded a rod of mighty power: see Ex. 9:23; 10:13; 14:16. So also is it written of Christ, "Thou shalt break them with a rod of iron" (Psa. 2:9).

23. His Announcing solemn Judgments.

Again and again he warned Pharaoh and his people of the sore punishment of God if they continued to defy him. So also Christ declared, "Except ye repent, ye shall all likewise perish" (Luke 13:3).

24. His deliverance of Israel.

Moses perfectly fulfilled his God-given commission and led Israel out of the house of bondage: "The same did God send to be a ruler and a **deliverer**" (Acts 7:35). So Christ affirmed, "If the Son therefore shall make you free, ye shall be free indeed" (John 8:36).

25. His Headship.

Remarkably is this brought out in 1 Cor. 10:1, 2, "All our fathers were under the cloud, and all passed through the sea; and were all baptized **unto Moses**". So obedient Christians are "baptized **unto Jesus Christ**" (Rom. 6:3).

26. His Leadership of Israel's Praise.

"Then sang Moses and the children of Israel" (Ex. 15:1). Of Christ too it is written, "In the midst of the congregation will I praise Thee" (Psa. 22:22).

27. His Authority challenged.

This is recorded in Numbers 16:3; the antitype in Matt. 21:23.

28. His person Envied.

See Psa. 106:16, and compare Mark 15:10.

29. His person opposed.

Though Israel were so deeply indebted to Moses, yet again and again we find them "murmuring" against him: Ex. 15:24, 16:2, etc. For the N. T. parallel see Luke 15:2, John 6:41.

30. His life Threatened.

So fiercely did the ungrateful Hebrews oppose Moses that, on one occasion, they were ready to "stone" him (Ex. 17:4). How this brings to mind what we read of in John 8:59, 10:31!

31. His Sorrows.

Moses felt keenly the base ingratitude of the people. Mark his plaintive plea as recorded in Num. 11:11, 14. So too the Lord Jesus suffered from the reproaches of the people: He was "the Man of sorrows and acquainted with grief".

32. His unwearied Love.

Though misunderstood, envied, and opposed, nothing could alienate the affections of Moses from his people. "Many waters cannot quench love, neither can the floods drown it" (Song of Sol. 8:7). Beautifully is this seen in Ex. 32. After Israel repudiated Jehovah and had worshipped the golden calf, after the Lord has disowned them as His people (Ex. 32: 7), Moses supplicates God on their behalf, saying "Oh, this people have sinned a great sin, and have made them gods of gold. Yet now, if Thou wilt forgive their sin—; and if not, blot me, I pray Thee, out of Thy book which Thou hast written" (vv. 31:32). How this reminds us of Him who "having loved His own which were in the world, He loved them unto the end" (John 13:1)!

33. His Forgiving spirit.

"And Miriam and Aaron spake against Moses . . . Hath the Lord indeed spoken only by Moses? Hath He not spoken also by us"? (Num. 12:1, 2). But he answered not a word. How this pointed to Him who, 'when He was reviled, reviled not again" (1 Peter 2:23). When Miriam was stricken with leprosy because of her revolt against her brother, we are told, "Moses cried unto the Lord, saying, Heal her now, O God, I beseech Thee" (Num. 12:13).

34. His Prayerfulness.

An example of this has just been before us, but many other instances are recorded. Moses was, pre-eminently, a man of prayer. At every crisis he sought unto the Lord: see Ex. 5:22, 8:12, 9:33, 14:15, 15:25, 17:4, etc. Note how often in Luke's Gospel Christ is also presented as a Man of prayer.

35. His Meekness.

"Moses was very meek, above all the men which were upon the face of the earth" (Num. 12:3) cf. Matt. 11:29.

36. His Faithfulness.

"Moses verily was faithful in all his house" (Heb. 3:5). So Christ is "The faithful and true Witness" (Rev. 3:14).

37. His providing Israel with water.

See Num. 20:11 and compare John 4:14, 7:37.

38. His Prophetic office.

Deut. 18:18 and compare John 7:16, 8:28.

39. His Priestly activities.

"Moses and Aaron among His priests" (Psa. 99:6). Illustrations are found in Lev. 8: "And Moses took the blood, and put it upon the horns of the altar . . . and he took all the fat . . . and burned it upon the altar" (vv. 15, 16 and see 19:23). So Christ, as Priest, "offered Himself without spot to God" (Heb. 9:14).

40. His Kingly rule.

"Moses commanded us a law, even the inheritance of the congregation of Jacob. And he was king in Jeshurun" (Deut. 33: 4, 5). So Christ is King in Zion, and will yet be over the Jews (Luke 1:32, 33).

41. His Judgeship.

"Moses sat to judge the people: and they stood by Moses from the morning until the evening" (Ex. 18:13). Compare 2 Cor. 5:10.

42. His Leadership.

Moses was the head and director of God's people, as He said to him, "Lead the people unto the place of which I have spoken" (Ex. 32:34). So Christ is called, "The Captain of their salvation" (Heb. 2:10).

43. His Mediation.

What a remarkable word was that of Moses to Israel, "I stood between the Lord and you" (Deut. 5:5): "There is one God, and one Mediator between God and men, the Man Christ Jesus" (1 Tim. 2:5).

44. His Election.

In Psa. 106:23 he is called, "Moses His chosen". So God says of Christ, "Behold My Servant, whom I uphold, Mine elect" (Isa. 42:1).

45. His Covenant-engagement.

"And the Lord said unto Moses, Write thou these words: for after the tenor of these words I have made a covenant with thee and with Israel" (Ex. 34:27): so Christ is denominated, "The Mediator of a better covenant" (Heb. 8:6).

46. His sending forth of the Twelve.

"These are the names of the men which Moses sent to spy out the land" (Num. 13: 16 see previous verses). So Christ sent forth twelve apostles (Matt. 10:5).

47. His Appointing of the Seventy.

"And Moses went out and told the people the words of the Lord, and gathered the seventy men of the elders of the people" (Num. 11:24). So Christ selected seventy (Luke 10:1).

48. His Wisdom.

"Moses was learned in all the wisdom of the Egyptians" (Acts 7:22). Compare Col. 2:3.

49. His Might.

"And was mighty in words and in deeds" (Acts 7:22). Behold the antitype of this in Matt. 13:34: "They were astonished, and said, Whence hath this Man this wisdom, and these mighty works"?

50. His Intercession.

"And Moses brought their cause before the Lord" (Num. 27:5). Compare Heb. 7:25.

51. His Intimate Communion with God.

"And there arose not a prophet since in Israel like unto Moses, whom the Lord knew face to face" (Ex. 34:10). So, on earth, Christ was "The only-begotten Son, which is in the bosom of the Father" (John 1:18). It is striking to behold in Ex. 31 to 34 how Moses passed and repassed between Jehovah in the mount and the camp of the congregation: expressive of his equal access to heaven and earth—compare John 3:13.

52. His Knowledge of God.

See Psa. 103:7 and cf. John 5:20.

53. His holy Anger.

See Ex. 32:19 and cf. Mark 3:5, etc.

54. His Message.

He was the mouthpiece of God: "And Moses came and told the people all the words of the Lord" (Ex. 24:3). Compare Heb. 1:2.

55. His Commandments.

See Deut. 4:2 and cf. Matt. 28:20.

56. His Written Revelation.

See Ex. 31:13 and cf. Rev. 1:1.

57. His Fasting.

See Ex. 34:28 and cf. Matt. 4:2.

58. His Transfiguration on the mount.

See Ex. 34:29, 35 and cf. Matt. 17:2.

59. His Place Outside the Camp.

See Ex. 33:7 and cf. Heb. 13:13.

60. His Arraigning of the responsible head.

See Ex. 32:21 and cf. Rev. 2:12, 13.

61. His Praying for Israel's Forgiveness.

See Num. 14:19 and cf. Luke 23:34.

62. His Washing his Brethren with Water.

"And Moses brought Aaron and his sons, and washed them with water" (Lev. 8:6). Who can fail to see in that a foreshad-

owing of what is recorded in John 13:5: "After that He poureth water into a basin and began to wash the disciples' feet"!

63. His Prophecies.

See Deut. 28 and 33 and cf. Matt. 24 and Luke 21.

64. His Rewarding God's servants.

See Num. 7:6, 32:33, 40 and cf. Rev. 22:12.

65. His perfect Obedience.

"Thus did Moses according to all that the Lord commanded, so did he" (Ex. 40:16). What a lovely foreshadowing was this of Him who could say, "I have kept My Father's commandments" (John 16:10)!

66. His erecting the Tabernacle.

See Ex. 40:2, and cf. Zech. 6:12.

67. His Completing of his Work.

"So Moses finished the work" (Ex. 40:33). What a blessed prefiguration was this of Him who declared, "I have finished the work which Thou gavest Me to do" (John 17:4).

68. His Blessing of the People.

"And Moses blessed them" (Ex. 39:43). So too we read in Luke 24:50, "And He led them out as far as to Bethany, and He lifted up His hands, and blessed them".

69. His Anointing of God's House.

"And Moses took the anointing oil (the O. T. emblem of the Holy Spirit), and anointed the tabernacle and all that was therein" (Lev. 8:10). Carefully compare Acts 2:1-3, 33.

70. His Unabated Strength.

"His eye was not dim, nor his natural force abated" (Deut. 34:7): compare Matt. 27:50, and note the "loud voice".

71. His Death was for the benefit of God's people.

"It went ill with Moses **for their sakes**" (Psa. 106:32; "But the Lord was wroth with me **for your sakes**" (Deut. 3:26). What marvelous foreshadowings of the Cross were these!

72. His Appointing of another Comforter.

Moses did not leave his people comfortless, but gave them a successor: see Deut. 31:23 and cf. John 14:16, 18.

73. His giving an Inheritance.

"The land which Moses gave you on this side of Jordan" (Josh. 1:14): in Christ believers "have obtained an inheritance" (Eph. 1:11).

74. His Death necessary before Israel

could enter Canaan.

"Moses My servant is dead; **now there-fore** arise, go over this Jordan, thou, and all this people, unto the land which I do give to thee" (Josh. 1:2). "**Except** a corn of wheat fall into the ground **and die,** it abideth alone: but if it die, it bringeth forth much fruit" (John 12:24).

75. His Second Appearing.

Moses was one of the two Old Testament characters which **returned** to this earth in New Testament times (Matt. 17:3)—type of Christ's second coming to the earth.

Our space is already exhausted so we shall leave it with our readers to search the Scriptures for at least twenty-five other points in which Moses foreshadowed our Lord. The subject is well-nigh exhaustless. And a most blessed subject it is, demonstrating anew the Divine authorship of the Bible. May the Lord bless to many this very imperfect attempt to show that "in the volume of the Book" it **is** written of Christ.